I0881775

The Reparation System of the International Criminal Court

The Reparation System of the International Criminal Court

Its Implementation, Possibilities and Limitations

by

Eva Dwertmann

MARTINUS NIJHOFF PUBLISHERS

LEIDEN • BOSTON
2010

This book is printed on acid-free paper.

Library of Congress Cataloging-in-Publication Data

Dwertmann, Eva.
The reparation system of the International Criminal Court : its implementation, possibilities and limitations / by Eva Dwertmann.
p. cm.
Includes bibliographical references and index.
ISBN 978-90-04-17810-6 (hardback : alk. paper) 1. International Criminal Court--Rules and practice. 2. International criminal courts--Rules and practice. 3. Reparation (Criminal justice) 4. Rome Statute of the International Criminal Court (1998) I. Title.
KZ6324.D88 2010
344.03'288--dc22
2010000712

ISBN: 978 90 04 17810 6

Copyright 2010 by Koninklijke Brill NV, Leiden, The Netherlands.
Koninklijke Brill NV incorporates the imprints Brill, Hotei Publishing, IDC Publishers, Martinus Nijhoff Publishers and VSP.

http://www.brill.nl

All rights reserved. No part of this publication may be reproduced, stored in a retrieval system, or transmitted in any form or by any means, electronic, mechanical, photocopying, microfilming, recording or otherwise, without written permission from the Publisher.

Authorization to photocopy items for internal or personal use is granted by Brill provided that the appropriate fees are paid directly to The Copyright Clearance Center, 222 Rosewood Drive, Suite 910, Danvers MA 01923, USA.
Fees are subject to change.

PRINTED IN THE NETHERLANDS.

Table of Contents

Acknowledgments xi

Table of Abbreviations xiii

Chapter 1 Introduction 1
A. Aims of the Study 1
B. Structure and Methodology of the Study 5
C. The Term "Reparations" 10

Chapter 2 Historical and Legal Context of Reparations for Victims of Crimes under International Law (Overview) 13
A. National Law 13
B. International Law 15
I. Reparations in the Context of State Responsibility 15
II. State Reparations to Individuals and Groups 17
III. Reparations from Individual Perpetrators of International Crimes to Individual or Collective Victims 22
C. International Criminal Law 23

Chapter 3 Purpose of Reparations in International Criminal Law 29
A. Victims and the Purposes of International Criminal Justice 29
B. Interests Protected by International Criminal Law 32
C. Purposes of Reparations 37
D. Assessment 43

Chapter 4 Reparation Principles and Determination of the Scope and Extent of any Damage, Loss and Injury to, or in Respect of, Victims (Art. 75 (1) ICC Statute) 45
A. Establishing Principles Pursuant to Art. 75 (1) s. 1 ICC Statute 45
I. Purpose of Reparation Principles 45
II. Organ Responsible for Establishing Reparation Principles and their Legal Nature 46
III. Scope and Content of Principles 48

IV. Who Can the Reparation Principles Be Addressed to? 51
1. States 51
2. Corporations and other Judicial Persons 56
3. International Community 59
V. Assessment 61
B. Determination of Damage, Loss, Injury (Art. 75 (1) s. 2 ICC Statute) 62

Chapter 5 The ICC Reparation Order (Art. 75 (2) ICC Statute) 67
A. Liability for Reparations 68
I. The Conviction as a Pre-Condition for an ICC Reparation Order 68
II. Determination of Liability 71
B. Eligibility for Reparations Ordered by the ICC 75
I. Qualification as a Victim under Rule 85 76
1. Individual Victims (Rule 85 (a)) 78
a) Natural person 78
b) Harm 78
1) Forms of Harm 79
i) Emotional Suffering 80
ii) Physical and Mental Injury 82
iii) Economic Loss/Material Harm 82
iv) Other Damage 83
v) Assessment 84
2) Direct and Indirect Harm 84
i) Determination of Indirectly Harmed Persons Eligible for Reparations 87
ii) Assessment 89
c) Crime within the Jurisdiction of the Court 90
d) Causation 92
2. Organizations and Institutions 96
II. Collective Beneficiaries of Reparations 98
III. Other Eligibility Criteria 102
1. Neediness 102
2. Exclusion of Eligibility 104
3. Time Limits 107
IV. Reparations "in Respect of, Victims" 111
1. International and National Law and Human Rights 113
2. Assessment 114
V. Discretionary Decision of the Court to Order Reparations to Victims 114
VI. Assessment 116
C. Content of ICC Reparation Orders 118
I. Type of Reparations: Individual and Collective Awards 119
1. Individual Reparations 120
2. Collective Reparations 121
a) Appropriateness of Collective Awards 121
b) Content of Collective Awards 124

3. Assessment 127

II. Form of Reparations 129

1. Restitution 129

a) International and National Law and Human Rights 130

b) Assessment 132

2. Compensation 133

a) Types of Compensable Harm 134

1) Pecuniary or Material Damage 135

i) ICC Reparation System 135

ii) International and National Law and Human Rights 136

2) Non-Pecuniary or Moral Damage 137

i) ICC Reparation System 137

ii) International and National Law and Human Rights 138

3) Assessment 141

b) Compensation and Causation 141

1) International and National Law and Human Rights 142

2) Assessment 145

3. Rehabilitation 146

a) ICC Reparation System 146

b) International and National Law and Human Rights 146

c) Assessment 148

4. Other Forms of Reparations 149

a) Symbolic and Non-Monetary Forms of Reparations 150

1) ICC Reparation System 150

2) International and National Law and Human Rights 151

i) Cessation of Violations, Exposition of Truth, Punishment of Perpetrators 152

ii) Guarantees of Non-Repetition 153

iii) Acknowledgment of Responsibility 153

iv) Apology 154

v) Commemoration 155

vi) Monetary Measures to Benefit the Harmed Community 156

3) Assessment 157

b) Punitive Damages 159

5. Assessment 161

III. Standard of Reparations 162

IV. Scope of the Compensation Order 166

1. Valuation and Calculation of Damages 167

a) ICC Reparation System 167

b) International and National Law and Human Rights 168

1) Calculating Non-Pecuniary and Pecuniary Harm 168

i) Pecuniary Harm (Material Damage) 168

ii) Non-Pecuniary Damage (Moral Damage) 169

2) Standardization and Estimation of Damage 172

c) Assessment 178

2. Other Factors Potentially Impacting the Compensation Order 181
   a) Degree of Fault of the Convicted Person 181
   b) Financial Capacity of the Convicted Person 183
      1) ICC Reparation System 184
      2) International and National Law and Human Rights 185
      3) Assessment 186
   c) Impact on the Scope of the Reparation Order When Several Persons Caused the Harm 187
3. Assessment 192

Chapter 6 ICC Reparations Proceedings **195**

A. Procedural Requirements for a Reparation Order (Art. 75 (1), (2) ICC Statute) 196
   I. Initiation of the Reparations Proceedings by, or on Behalf of, Victims 196
      1. Victims' Requests for Reparations 196
         a) Claim to be a Victim 196
         b) Who can Claim to be a Victim? 197
         c) Do Collectives Have the Right to Claim Reparations? 198
      2. Form of the Request for Reparations 202
      3. Content of the Request for Reparations 203
         a) Information about the Claimant, the Damage and Kind of Reparations Requested 203
         b) Identification of the Person Believed to be Responsible for the Damage 203
      4. Documentation of the Data Contained in the Request 204
      5. Other Procedural Requirements 205
         a) Unavailability of Reparations in Other Fora (Complementarity) 205
         b) Participation in the Court Proceedings 207
   II. Court-Initiated Reparations Proceedings 208
   III. Assessment 210
B. Communications of the Court in the Reparations Proceedings (Art. 75 (3), Art. 76 (3) ICC Statute) 211
   I. Notification and Publication of Reparations Proceedings 211
      1. Notification 211
      2. Publication 214
   II. Expert Consultation 216
   III. Participation in the Reparations Proceedings 217
      1. Victims 217
      2. Parties other than Victims 222
   IV. Assessment 224
C. Standard and Burden of Proof 226
   I. ICC Reparation System 227
      1. Standard of Proof 227
      2. Burden of Proof and Demonstration of Facts 231
   II. International and National Law and Human Rights 233
   III. Assessment 242
D. Reparations and Penalties (77 (2), 78 (1) ICC Statute) 245

I. Reparations and the Determination of Sentence 247
1. Impact of the Offender's Behavior towards Victims on the Sentence 247
2. Reparations and the Imposition of Fines and Forfeiture Orders 251
a) Fines 251
b) Forfeiture Orders 255
3. Review Concerning the Reduction of Sentence and the Impact of the Offender's Post-Conviction Behavior Towards Victims 257
II. Use of Money or Property Collected through Orders of Reparations, Fines and Forfeiture and the Role of the Victims Trust Fund 258
III. Assessment 260
E. Appeal against a Reparation Order (Art. 82 (4) ICC Statute) 261
F. Implementation of ICC Reparation Awards (Art. 75 (2), Art. 79 ICC Statute) 265
I. ICC Reparation System 265
1. Role of the ICC and the Trust Fund for Victims 265
2. Reparations 266
a) Direct Awards (Art. 75 (2) 1. Alt., Rule 98 (1)) 267
b) Awards through the Trust Fund (Art. 75 (2) 2. Alt., Rule 98 (2) and (3)) 267
1) Individual Awards 268
2) Collective Awards 270
c) Distribution through Organizations (Rule 98 (4)) 271
3. Complementing Reparation Awards with "Other Resources of the Trust Fund" 272
G. Protective Measures and Enforcement of Reparation Orders (Art. 75 (4) and (5) ICC Statute) 277
I. Protective Measures 277
II. Enforcement 279
III. Assessment 281

Chapter 7 Assistance to Victims and Their Families by the Trust Fund (Art. 79 ICC Statute, Rule 98 (5)) 285
A. Funding 286
B. Measures for the Benefit of Victims and their Families other than Reparations 287
C. Relation between the Court and the Trust Fund for Victims 289
D. Assessment 291

Chapter 8 Summary and Conclusion 295
A. Towards the Implementation of the ICC Reparation System (Summary) 295
B. Potential of the ICC Reparation System 299
C. Conclusion 302

Appendix 303
A. Bibliography 303
B. Table of Cases 321
D. Materials 331

Index 357

Acknowledgments

This book is a revised version of my doctoral thesis which I completed at the Law Faculty of Humboldt University of Berlin, Germany. First of all I wish to thank my PhD supervisor Prof. Dr. Gerhard Werle, who inspired this study and provided great support in every phase up to completion. Many thanks to the second reporting professor as well, Prof. Dr. Martin Heger, for his valuable advice and for the swift compilation of his report. I also greatly appreciate the assistance of Prof. Dr. José Brunner, who enabled me to work at Tel Aviv University, Dr. Boris Burghardt for his helpful comments and Anja Schepke for her reliable organisational support.

I would like to acknowledge the Hamburger Stiftung zur Förderung von Wissenschaft und Kultur for providing me with generous funding.

I am also deeply indebted to Carla Ferstman, Dr. Robert Heinsch and all the other practitioners at the International Criminal Court and elsewhere who took time to discuss the challenges of reparations before the ICC and to answer other questions that came up during my research. These exchanges were indispensable to my work.

I am grateful to my colleague Maren Burkhardt for her valuable and critical input on the related topics of our research and for reading my thesis. I would also like to thank Dr. Miriam Saage-Maaß for her inspiration, Rebecca Wachsberg for proofreading, Susanne Buscher for editing, Kolja Thierfelder for his technical support, and all the other friends who helped me in completing this book.

Finally, I would like to sincerely thank my family for their emotional support, in particular Yiftach and Noam for their love, patience and cheerfulness, and Hanna as well as my parents.

Table of Abbreviations

ASP	Assembly of States Parties
American Convention	American Convention on Human Rights
Court Regulations	Regulations of the International Criminal Court
2001 EU Framework Decision	Council of the European Union Framework Decision on the Standing of Victims in Criminal Proceedings
ECHR	European Convention for the Protection of Human Rights and Fundamental Freedoms
2005 Guidelines on Child Victims	Guidelines on Justice in Matters involving Child Victims and Witnesses of Crime
ICC	International Criminal Court
ICC Statute	Rome Statute of the International Criminal Court
ICCPR	International Covenant on Civil and Political Rights
ICTR	International Criminal Tribunal for the Prosecution of Persons Responsible for Genocide and Other Serious Violations of International Humanitarian Law Committed in the Territory of Rwanda and Rwandan Citizens Responsible for Genocide and Other Such Violations Committed in the Territory of Neighbouring States between 1 January and 31 December 1994
ICTR Rules	Rules of Procedure and Evidence of the International Criminal Tribunal for Rwanda
ICTR Statute	Statute for the International Criminal Tribunal for Rwanda
ICTY	International Tribunal for the Prosecution of Persons Responsible for Serious Violations of International Humanitarian Law Committed in the Territory of the Former Yugoslavia since 1991
ICTY Rules	International Criminal Tribunal for the Former Yugoslavia, Rules of Procedure and Evidence
ICTY Statute	Statute for the International Criminal Tribunal for the Former Yugoslavia
ILC Draft Articles	International Law Commission Draft Articles on the Responsibility of States for International Wrongful Acts

Nuremberg Charter	Charter of the International Military Tribunal, Nuremberg
Preparatory Commission	Preparatory Commission for an International Criminal Court
Registry Regulations	Regulations of the Registry of the International Criminal Court
Rules	Rules of Procedure and Evidence of the International Criminal Court
Standard Application Form for Individuals	Standard Application Form for Reparations before the International Criminal Court for Individuals and Persons Acting on their behalf
Standard Application Form for Organizations	Standard Application Form for Reparations before the International Criminal Court for Victims which are Organizations or Institutions
Tokyo Charter	Charter of the International Military Tribunal for the Far East
Trust Fund	Trust Fund for Victims of the International Criminal Court
Trust Fund Regulations	Regulations of the Trust Fund for Victims of the International Criminal Court
UNCC	United Nations Compensation Commission
UN Handbook	United Nations Handbook on Justice for Victims on the Use and Application of the United Nations Declaration of Basic Principles of Justice for Victims of Crime and Abuse of Power
2005 Victims Principles	Basic Principles and Guidelines on the Right to a Remedy and Reparation for Victims of Gross Violations of International Human Rights Law and Serious Violations of International Humanitarian Law
1985 Victims Declaration	Declaration of Basic Principles of Justice for Victims of Crime and Abuse of Power
Victims Participation Booklet	Booklet – Victims Before the International Criminal Court – A Guide for the Participation of Victims in the Proceedings of the Court

Chapter 1 Introduction

A. Aims of the Study

Before the International Criminal Court ("ICC" or "the Court"), victims of crimes which fall within its jurisdiction have the right to file applications for reparations. Victims are accorded rights and a "double status" before the ICC in that they can both seek reparations from the Court and participate in the proceedings.[1] This stands in contrast to other international criminal tribunals established before the ICC which did not recognize victims as rights-holders.

In the view of one of the ICC's Chambers, "the reparation scheme provided for in the Statute is not only one of the Statute's unique features. It is also a key feature. In the Chamber's opinion, the success of the Court is, to some extent, linked to the success to its reparation system".[2]

Also from the outside, high expectations have developed specifically of the ICC reparation system. Commentators have regarded to it as "one of the most important aspects" of the ICC Statute[3], and an appropriate means to repair grave violations of international humanitarian law.[4] Others have said that the ICC reparations scheme is "[f]rom many points of view [...] the ideal solution for victims of crimes under

---

1 Art. 68 (3), Art. 75 (2) ICC Statute. Furthermore, victims may transmit information to the Prosecutor requesting the initiation of an investigation, Art. 15 (3), and make observations on the decision on admissibility or jurisdiction, Art. 19 (3). Victims and witnesses are to be protected by appropriate measures by the Court, Art. 43 (6), Art. 57 (3), Art. 68 (1), (4).

2 Situation in the Democratic Republic of the Congo in the Case of *The Prosecutor v. Thomas Lubanga Dyilo*, Decision on the Prosecutor's Application for a Warrant of Arrest, Article 58, Pre-Trial Chamber I, 10 February 2006, ICC-01/04-01/06 (annexed to ICC-01/04-01/06-8-Corr, 24 February 2006), para. 136.

3 P. Lewis; H. Friman: "Reparations to Victims". In: The International Criminal Court – Elements of Crimes and Rules of Procedure and Evidence. Ed. R. S. Lee. Ardsley, New York, 2001, pp. 474 et seq.

4 W. Heintschel von Heinegg: "Entschädigung für Verletzungen des Humanitären Völkerrechts". In: Entschädigung nach bewaffneten Konflikten – Die Konstitutionalisierung der Welthandelsordnung. Eds. W. Heintschel von Heinegg; S. Kadelbach; B. Heß (et al.). Heidelberg, 2003, pp. 1 et seq. at p. 55 with further references.

international law"[5] and a "historic possibility to the world community to recognise and enforce the right of victims to reparations".[6] Moreover, the ICC's Trust Fund for Victims ("Trust Fund") has been termed a "very promising reparations mechanism"[7], which has "the potential to be one of the most significant international human rights organs in the world."[8]

Generally, the ICC Statute has been defined as "victim-centered"[9], the position of victims in the ICC system has been described as "one of the most distinctive features of the [ICC] Statute"[10] and "one of the great innovations" of the ICC.[11]

Thus, the ICC's reparation system in particular, has already received much praise, although it is yet untested. The concept that individual criminal responsibility in international law requires the perpetrator to make reparations to the victims of his or her crime has not been tried in practice and in fact faces multiple challenges. This study will examine this concept, as embodied in the ICC reparation system, with four main aims. In view of the novelty of reparations to victims in international criminal law, first the historical and legal background of the concept is to be examined. The second aim is to analyze the reparations mechanism as provided in the ICC's constituting legal instruments. Third, this study attempts to outline a draft for a potential effective functioning of the ICC reparation system by developing criteria for its possible implementation. Finally, the potential of the ICC reparations mechanism to repair the harm of victims of crimes under its jurisdiction is to be critically assessed.

5 I. Bottigliero: Redress for Victims of Crimes under International Law. Leiden, 2004, p. 242 with further references.

6 D. Donat-Cattin: "Article 75 – Reparations to Victims". In: Commentary on the Rome Statute of the International Criminal Court – Observers' Notes, Article by Article. Ed. O. Triffterer. Baden-Baden, 1999, pp. 965 et seq. at p. 966.

7 C. Lasco: "Repairing the Irreparable – Current and Future Approaches to Reparations". In: Human Rights Brief 10 (2003), pp. 18 et seq. at p. 21. See Resolution on the Establishment of a Fund for the Benefit of Victims of Crimes Within the Jurisdiction of the Court, and the Families of such Victims, adopted 9 September 2002, ICC-ASP/1/Res.6 (2002).

8 P. G. Fischer: "The Victim's Trust Fund of the International Criminal Court – Formation of a Functional Reparations Scheme". In: Emory International Law Review 17 (2003), pp. 187 et seq. at p. 239.

9 C. M. Bassiouni: Introduction to International Criminal Law. Ardsley, New York, 2003, p. 528.

10 S. A. Fernandez de Gurmendi; H. Friman: "The Rules of Procedure and Evidence of the International Criminal Court". In: Yearbook of International Humanitarian Law. Ed. A. McDonald. Vol. 3. The Hague, 2000, pp. 289 et seq. at p. 312.

11 G. Bitti; G. González Rivas: "The Reparations Provisions for Victims under the Rome Statute of the International Criminal Court". In: Redressing Injustices through Mass Claims Processes – Innovative Responses to Unique Challenges. Ed. The International Bureau of the Permanent Court of Arbitration. Oxford, 2006, pp. 299 et seq. Similarly F. Terrier: "The Procedure before the Trial Chamber". In: The Rome Statute of the International Criminal Court – A Commentary. Eds. A. Cassese; P. Gaeta; J. R. W. D. Jones. Vol. 2. Oxford, 2002, pp. 1277 et seq. at p. 1317.

This study intends to comprehensively analyze the ICC reparation system. This is being undertaken because while multiple references can be found in academic literature, studies offering in-depth and comprehensive analysis on ICC reparations are insufficient.[12] Thus, all aspects of the ICC's legal framework that are linked with reparations shall be examined. This covers the Court's obligation to establish reparation principles (Art. 75 (1)), it's competence to order convicted persons to make reparations to victims (Art. 75 (2)), the reparations procedure (Art. 75 (3), Art. 76 (3)), and protective measures and the enforcement of the reparation order (Art. 75 (4), (5)). Further aspects of the ICC reparations mechanism that will be evaluated are the interdependence between penalties and reparations (Art. 76, 77 (2)) and the role of the Trust Fund for Victims (Art. 79).

The focus of this study is the ICC's power to order the convicted person to make reparations to victims (Art. 75 (2)). In this context, the following issues will be examined in depth: The first issue covers the question as to when the Court can make use of its competence to order the convicted person to make reparations to victims, as well as the pre-conditions for the exercise of this power. Further key questions are who can be considered a victim or other person eligible for reparations, what forms of reparations can be ordered, and what kinds of damages be compensated. Another issue concerns the factors that can or need to be considered when determining the scope of a compensation award. The question as to how reparation orders are to be implemented will be dealt with, and, in particular, how the tasks between the Court and Trust Fund, experts, and national, intergovernmental and non-governmental organizations can be distributed, and how applications for reparations can be verified. Other relevant questions that concern protection measures and the enforcement of ICC reparation orders and Trust Fund assistance will be touched on.

The ICC reparations regime faces challenges unique to reparations awarded in the context of international criminal justice. The ICC has the mandate to hold individuals accountable for international crimes and to find them responsible for reparations to the victims of such crimes. The ICC's legal instruments also grant individual victims

12 See for recent publications covering certain aspects of the ICC reparation system A.-M. de Brouwer: "Reparation to Victims of Sexual Violence – Possibilities at the International Criminal Court and at the Trust Fund for Victims and Their Families". In: Leiden Journal of International Law 20 (2007), pp. 207 et seq.; M. Henzelin; V. Heiskanen; G. Mettraux: "Reparations to Victims before the International Criminal Court – Lessons from International Mass Claims Processes". In: Criminal Law Forum 17 (2006), pp. 317 et seq.; G. Bitti; G. González Rivas: "The Reparations Provisions for Victims under the Rome Statute of the International Criminal Court". In: Redressing Injustices through Mass Claims Processes – Innovative Responses to Unique Challenges. Ed. The International Bureau of the Permanent Court of Arbitration. Oxford, 2006, pp. 299 et seq.; C. Ferstman: "The International Criminal Court's Trust Fund for Victims – Challenges and Opportunities". In: Yearbook of International Humanitarian Law 2003. Ed. A. McDonald. Vol. 6. The Hague, 2006, pp. 424 et seq.; D. Shelton: Remedies in International Human Rights Law. 2nd ed. Oxford, 2005, p. 233; I. Bottigliero: Redress for Victims of Crimes under International Law. Leiden, 2004; M. Heikkilä: International Criminal Tribunals and Victims of Crime. Turku, 2004.

of crimes under its jurisdiction the right to claim reparations.[13] In this way, the ICC reparation system creates an international legal relationship between private persons.[14]

At the same time, all crimes under international law require that the deed be committed in the context of gross or systematic violations, and it is regularly a collective that is responsible for the violations, typically a state.[15] International criminal law, in contrast to international law, does not establish the responsibility of a state, and the ICC is not authorized to order states to make reparations.[16] Rather, by criminalizing the deed and punishing the perpetrator, and ordering him or her to make reparations for the harm caused, the responsibility for the crime is individualized.[17] However, its consequences, the victimization, remain collective in nature.

---

13 Art. 75, Rule 94. Thus, an individual right to claim reparations has been established as a part of international (treaty) law, this study does not need to discuss the question as to whether there exists an individual right to reparation based on customary international law. Much academic discussion is related to this issue, see e.g. R. Hofmann: "Victims of Violations of International Humanitarian Law – Do They Have an Individual Right to Reparation against States under International Law?". In: Völkerrecht als Wertordnung – Common Values in International Law – Festschrift für Christian Tomuschat – Essays in Honour of Christian Tomuschat. Eds. P.-M. Dupuy; B. Fassbender; M. N. Shaw; K.-P. Sommermann. Kehl am Rhein (et al.), 2006, pp. 341 et seq.; M. Nowak: "The Right to Reparation of Victims of Gross Human Rights Violations". In: Reparations – Redressing Past Wrongs. Eds. G. Ulrich; L. Krabbe Boserup. (Human Rights in Development – Yearbook 2001). The Hague, 2003, pp. 275 et seq.; E.-C. Gillard: "Reparation for Violations of International Humanitarian Law". In: International Review of the Red Cross 851 (2003), pp. 529 et seq.; C. Tomuschat: "Reparation for Victims of Grave Human Rights Violations". In: Tulane Journal of International and Comparative Law 10 (2002), pp. 157 et seq. See also below Chapter 2 B. II ("Historical and Legal Context of Reparations for Victims of Crimes under International Law").

14 C. Tomuschat: "Reparation for Victims of Grave Human Rights Violations". In: Tulane Journal of International and Comparative Law 10 (2002), pp. 157 et seq. at p. 182.

15 G. Werle: Principles of International Criminal Law. The Hague, 2005, p. 34. The contextual requirements for the crimes under the jurisdiction of the ICC (Art. 5 ICC Statute) are that an act is "committed with the intent to destroy, in whole or in part, a national, ethnical, racial, religious group" (Art. 6, Genocide), "committed as part of a widespread or systematic attack directed against any civilian population" (Art. 7, Crimes Against Humanity), committed in the context of armed conflict, "in particular when committed as part of a plan or policy or as part of a large-scale commission of such crimes" (Art. 8, War Crimes).

16 Under Art. 75 (2) "[t]he Court may make an order directly against a convicted person specifying appropriate reparations [...]".

17 Furthermore, the Office of the Prosecutor has declared its intention to focus on those who bear the greatest responsibility of the crime: "The global nature of the ICC, its statutory provisions and logical constrains support a preliminary recommendation that, as a general rule, the Office of the Prosecutor should focus its investigative and prosecutorial efforts and resources on those who bear the greatest responsibility, such as the leaders of the State or organisation allegedly responsible for those crimes", see Paper on Some Policy Issues before the Office of the Prosecutor, ICC-OTP, September 2003. Available

Thus, a distinct asymmetry exists between the individualized responsibility to provide reparations, and the collective nature of the crimes that commonly leads to massive qualitative and quantitative harm is inherent to the ICC reparation system. It creates a tension that impacts virtually all aspects of reparations ordered by the ICC.

Furthermore, in the implementation of the reparations provisions in its proceedings the Court is likely to face serious challenges in ensuring the expeditious conduct of proceedings.[18]

This work attempts to offer some clarification as to how the concept of reparations in the context of international criminal justice could function, within the parameters set in the ICC's legal foundations. Due to the wide spectrum of issues discussed, some of the relevant aspects can only be shortly addressed.[19]

Finally, the potential of the ICC reparations mechanism to repair the harm suffered by victims of crimes under its jurisdiction shall be critically assessed. Are praise and high expectations towards the ICC reparations regime justified, or must it be expected that its practical effects are likely to be rather modest?[20] Is there even a chance that the reparations mechanisms incorporated into the ICC Statute will in fact have a negative impact on victims of crimes under international law who are receiving reparations? It is to be assessed whether reparations awarded in the context of international criminal justice are an appropriate approach to redress the harm caused to victims of crimes under international law.

B. Structure and Methodology of the Study

This study is structured in eight Chapters. In Chapters 1 to 3 of this study, the foundations of reparations in international criminal law are briefly examined. This includes an overview of their historical and legal context, the interests protected by international criminal law, and the purpose of reparations, particularly in the context of international criminal law. Chapters 4 to 7 contain the main part of this study. Their structure is guided by the order in which the ICC Statute presents the different issues regarding reparations in the key Articles 75, 76, 77 and 79. In Chapter 8, conclusions

at http://ww.icc-cpi.int/library/organs/otp/03/09/05_Policy_Paper.pdf, last accessed 21 April 2009, p. 7.

18 Art. 64 (2). According to G. Bitti; G. González Rivas: "The Reparations Provisions for Victims under the Rome Statute of the International Criminal Court". In: Redressing Injustices through Mass Claims Processes – Innovative Responses to Unique Challenges. Ed. The International Bureau of the Permanent Court of Arbitration. Oxford, 2006, pp. 299 et seq. at p. 321: "it may, arguably, be much more difficult for the Court to determine thousands of claims than to decide on several criminal cases for each situation".

19 Furthermore, generalization will often be necessary as in different jurisdictions and legal traditions the same legal issues are discussed under different headings or terms, particularly regarding causation, liability and proof. This examination attempts to abstract from national variations and to concentrate on the discussion of essential principles.

20 As assumed by C. Tomuschat: "Reparation for Victims of Grave Human Rights Violations". In: Tulane Journal of International and Comparative Law 10 (2002), pp. 157 et seq. at p. 181.

will be summarized and the potential of the reparations mechanism to restore the lives of victims of the crimes under the ICC's jurisdiction will be critically assessed. As the main aim of this study is to analyze the provisions in the ICC's legal instruments and to examine how they could be implemented, the Statute's Art. 21 is crucial to evaluate as it provides the guidelines for the method to be applied. The article specifies the law applicable to the Court in its decisions. It states that the application of the ICC Statute and its Rules of Procedure and Evidence ("ICC Rules" or the "Rules") has priority.[21] Then, "applicable treaties and the rules and principles of international law" are to be applied, and, failing that, "general principles of law derived by the Court from national laws of legal systems of the world".[22]

The Statute and Rules provide only rough guidance for a number of issues that concern the functioning of the ICC reparation system.[23] Their drafters opted not to clearly determine the substantive and procedural aspects of reparations to victims and the Trust Fund.[24] With regard to reparations, the ICC Statute consciously leaves lacunae, and obliges the Court to establish principles on reparations (Art. 75 (1)).[25] However, the wording of Art. 21 clarifies that the Court in its decision-making is also and especially bound to proceed in accordance with the determinations made by Art. 21 when the ICC Statute does not provide for a proximate solution to a particular question. In addition, due to its principal character the relevance of Art. 21 goes beyond the ICC Statute. Thus, it is necessary to consult the sources of law listed in Art. 21 when implementing the ICC reparations mechanism.[26] In particular, under Art. 21 (3) the application and interpretation of law "must be consistent with interna-

21 Rules of Procedure and Evidence, ICC-ASP /1/3 (2002).

22 Art. 21 (1) ICC Statute.

23 See M. Henzelin; V. Heiskanen; G. Mettraux: "Reparations to Victims before the International Criminal Court – Lessons from International Mass Claims Processes". In: Criminal Law Forum 17 (2006), pp. 317 et seq. at p. 320.

24 C. M. Bassiouni: The Legislative History of the International Criminal Court. Vol. 3. Ardsley, New York, 2005, p. 97 suggests that this is because international law is not settled in the question of victims' rights.

25 C. Jorda; J. de Hemptinne: "The Status and Role of the Victim". In: The Rome Statute of the International Criminal Court – A Commentary. Eds. A. Cassese; P. Gaeta; J. R. W. D. Jones. Vol. 2. Oxford, 2002, pp. 1387 et seq. at p. 1409 point out that while certain decisive issues expressly are to be resolved by the Court, other major problems seem to have been swept under the carpet. C. M. Bassiouni: The Legislative History of the International Criminal Court. Vol. 3. Ardsley, New York, 2005, p. 97 observes that Art. 75 and 79 would not satisfy most legal codifications.

26 See also D. Donat-Cattin: "Article 75 – Reparations to Victims". In: Commentary on the Rome Statute of the International Criminal Court – Observers' Notes, Article by Article. Ed. O. Triffterer. Baden-Baden, 1999, pp. 965 et seq. at p. 972 pointing out that the Court will make use of the sources of law listed in Art. 21. Similarly G. Bitti; G. González Rivas: "The Reparations Provisions for Victims under the Rome Statute of the International Criminal Court". In: Redressing Injustices through Mass Claims Processes – Innovative Responses to Unique Challenges. Ed. The International Bureau of the Permanent Court of Arbitration. Oxford, 2006, pp. 299 et seq. at p. 312.

tionally recognized human rights." This approach has been confirmed by the Court in its first decisions.[27] Furthermore, since the ICC Statute is an international treaty, the general principles of interpretation set forth in Articles 31 and 32 of the Vienna Convention on the Law of Treaties (1969) are applicable.[28]

In the current study, sources of law listed in Art. 21 are drawn upon in order to examine the reparations mechanism provided in the ICC Statute and Rules, and its possible implementation. Thus, where the ICC's legal foundations do not clarify an aspect of the reparations regime, international and national legal sources are examined for principles and solutions possibly applicable in the context of the ICC. Consequently, the methodology used throughout the different chapters varies depending on the degree that a certain aspect of the reparations regime has been clarified in the ICC's legal instruments.

Provisions relevant in the context of reparations before the ICC are contained in its Statute and Rules of Procedure and Evidence, in the Court Regulations, Registry Regulations and Trust Fund Regulations. On the unresolved issues, relevant international and national legal sources are drawn upon for solutions possibly applicable in the ICC system. Thus, the aim is not to examine these international and national sources comprehensively or comparatively, but only as far as useful for the clarification of the questions left open in the ICC Statute and Rules.

Relevant documents and practice that will be examined, where appropriate, include international documents and mechanisms and national procedures which deal with reparations to victims. In the international context, and in order to secure consistency with "internationally recognized human rights", reference will be made mainly to the UN Declaration of Basic Principles of Justice for Victims of Crime and Abuse of Power ("1985 Victim Declaration")[29], the Basic Principles and Guidelines on the Right to a Remedy and Reparation for Victims of Gross Violations of International Human Rights Law and International Humanitarian Law ("2005 Victims Principles")[30] and to the ILC Draft Articles on State Responsibility ("ILC Draft Arti-

27 In applying the definition of "victim" in the context of victim participation in the proceedings, ICC's Pre-Trial Chamber I decided that in the absence of a definition, the term "harm" must be interpreted in the light of Art. 21 (3) of the Statute, according to which "[t]he application and interpretation of law pursuant to this article must be consistent with internationally recognized human rights", see *Situation in the Democratic Republic of The Congo*, Decision on the Applications for Participation in the Proceedings of VPRS 1, VPRS 2, VPRS 3, VPRS 4, VPRS 5 and VPRS 6, ICC Pre-Trial Chamber I, 17 January 2006, ICC-01/04-101, paras. 81 et seq.

28 See also method of interpretation applied e.g. by Pre-Trial Chamber I, ibid., paras. 80 et seq.

29 UN Declaration of Basic Principles of Justice for Victims of Crime and Abuse of Power, G.A. Res. 40/34 of 29 of November 1985.

30 Basic Principles and Guidelines on the Right to a Remedy and Reparation for Victims of Gross Violations of International Human Rights Law and Serious Violations of International Humanitarian Law, G.A. Res. 60/147 of 16 December 2005.

cles"),[31] the Council of the European Union Framework Decision of 15 March 2001 on the Standing of Victims in Criminal Proceedings ("2001 EU Framework Decision")[32] and international human rights jurisprudence.[33] The 2005 Victims Principles present the most modern approach to reparations and deal not only with state, but also individual responsibility and address the issue of reparations in the context of mass crimes.[34] Its predecessor documents particularly influenced the drafting of Art. 75 ICC Statute.[35] Therefore, the 2005 Victims Principles are particularly relevant for the interpretation of the ICC reparations provisions.

Regarding national laws, reference will be made to options existing in various countries to obtain reparations in criminal and civil proceedings and to the experi-

---

31 International Law Commission: Draft Articles on Responsibility of States for Internationally Wrongful Acts, Report on the Work of its Fifty-third Session, Official Records of the General Assembly, Fifty-sixth Session, Supp. No. 10, UN Doc. A/56/10 (2001), chp. VI/E/1.

32 Council of the European Union: Framework Decision of 15 March 2001 on the Standing of Victims in Criminal Proceedings, Official Journal of the European Communities, 22 March 2001, L.82/1. See also Guidelines on Justice in Matters involving Child Victims and Witnesses of Crime, ECOSOC Res. 2005/20 of 22 July 2005 ("2005 Guidelines on Child Victims").

33 Particularly that of the Inter-American Court of Human Rights and the European Court of Human Rights, but also of the Bosnian Chamber of Human Rights and Human Rights Committee. As to their relevance in the context of reparations for victims of crimes under international law, I. Bottigliero: Redress for Victims of Crimes under International Law. Leiden, 2004, p. 139 states that "[t]he activities of Inter-American Institutions remain particularly relevant to the determination of victims' redress standards for crimes under international law. The Inter-American human rights system has dealt frequently with human rights violations of a serious and systematic character that often amount to crimes under international law [...]. In contrast, the European human rights system has been confronted mainly with individual violations of a lesser magnitude, although its jurisprudence on serious human rights violations continues to develop rapidly, while the African system is still at an early stage and has yet to make a significant contribution to the development of redress standards."

34 According to G. Bitti; G. González Rivas: "The Reparations Provisions for Victims under the Rome Statute of the International Criminal Court". In: Redressing Injustices through Mass Claims Processes – Innovative Responses to Unique Challenges. Ed. The International Bureau of the Permanent Court of Arbitration. Oxford, 2006, pp. 299 et seq. at p. 312, the term "internationally recognized human rights" refers to the jurisprudence of the European and Inter-American Court of Human Rights, while the 2005 Victims Principles and the 1985 Victims Declaration are part of the "principles and rules of international law".

35 For the drafting history of the provision see P. Lewis; H. Friman: "Reparations to Victims". In: The International Criminal Court – Elements of Crimes and Rules of Procedure and Evidence. Ed. R. S. Lee. Ardsley, New York, 2001, pp. 474 et seq. The predecessor documents were reports by Prof. van Boven to the UN Commission on Human Rights. See also reference to Art. 75 ICC Statute in the preamble of the 2005 Victims Principles.

ences made in mass claims proceedings on the basis of human rights violations.[36] Where appropriate, reference will be made to national and international reparations mechanisms specifically set up to provide victims of a particular case of genocide, war crimes and other large scale crimes with reparation, in particular compensation.[37]

However, none of the mentioned legal sources or documents explicitly deals with the scenario that exists with the ICC reparations mechanism. There is no precedent for reparations awarded to individual and collectives of victims from individual offenders in the course of international criminal procedure.[38] In international law "[t]here is no general body [...] governing individual reparation claims. In particular,"[a] vacuum exists [...] with regard to most of the substantive aspects".[39] Established theory and practice regarding reparation for international crimes exist in the context of state responsibility only. While national criminal laws have been regarded as the closest examples and role models for the possibility to award reparations before the ICC[40], their direct applicability to the context of the ICC is questionable. Legal concepts applicable in national legal systems regularly deal with crimes or violations in the context of a conflict between individuals. Yet, it is in particular the nature of the crimes under the jurisdiction of the ICC, typically leading to dozens, hundreds or thousands of victims, that demands to modify both substance and procedure. It seems that it

36 Here, to a far extent, secondary sources are used, e.g. M. E. I. Brienen; E. H. Hoegen: Victims of Crimes in 22 European Criminal Justice Systems – The Implementation of Recommendation (85) 11 of the Council of Europe on the Position of the Victims in the Framework of Criminal Law and Procedure. Nijmegen, 2000; M. Delmas-Marty; J. R. Spencer (eds.): European Criminal Procedures. Cambridge, 2002; A. Eser; S. Walther (eds.): Wiedergutmachung im Kriminalrecht – Internationale Perspektiven – Reparation in Criminal Law – International Perspectives. Vol. 1-3. Freiburg i. Br., 1996-2001; M. Joutsen: The Role of the Victim of Crime in European Criminal Justice Systems – A Crossnational Study of the Role of the Victim. Helsinki, 1987.

37 Reference will be e.g. be made to German compensation payments to victims of the Nazi Regime, reparations made in South Africa to victims of Apartheid, compensation programs of the United Nations Compensation Commission (UNCC) and in Rwanda.

38 See also C. Jorda; J. de Hemptinne: "The Status and Role of the Victim". In: The Rome Statute of the International Criminal Court – A Commentary. Eds. A. Cassese; P. Gaeta; J. R. W. D. Jones. Vol. 2. Oxford, 2002, pp. 1387 et seq. at p. 1388. Similarly C. Tomuschat: "Reparation for Victims of Grave Human Rights Violations". In: Tulane Journal of International and Comparative Law 10 (2002), pp. 157 et seq. at p. 181, stating that "the relevant provisions tread on new ground".

39 C. Tomuschat: "Darfur – Compensation for the Victims". In: Journal of International Criminal Justice 3 (2005), pp. 579 et seq. at p. 584.

40 C. Ferstman: "The Reparation Regime of the ICC – Practical Considerations". In: Leiden Journal of International Law 15 (2002), pp. 667 et seq. at p. 670. Similarly F. Terrier: "The Procedure before the Trial Chamber". In: The Rome Statute of the International Criminal Court – A Commentary. Eds. A. Cassese; P. Gaeta; J. R. W. D. Jones. Vol. 2. Oxford, 2002, pp. 1277 et seq., stating that in the system of the ICC, through manifest borrowing from the procedural system in the Latin tradition, civil reparations are associated with penal sanction.

will not be sufficient for the ICC to directly adopt characteristics of either a common law or a civil law system.[41] Thus, before applying principles taken from international or national law to the ICC reparations mechanisms, their applicability to the specific context of the ICC reparations function is to be examined.

The method chosen to achieve the aims of this study is based on the presumption that the ICC reparation system is legally unique and not a reproduction of any system in national or international law and that its implementation shall be guided by and be consistent with international human rights law.

C. The Term "Reparations"

For the purposes of the current study, the use and meaning of the term "reparations" will be guided by the ICC Statute. The ICC Statute provides that the Court can order a person it convicted to make "appropriate reparations to, or in respect of, victims, including restitution, compensation and rehabilitation".[42]
Further guidance will be taken from the "2005 Victims Principles".[43] The 2005 Victims Principles define that "reparation is intended to promote justice by redressing gross violations of international human rights law or serious violations of international humanitarian law"[44] and that "[i]n accordance with domestic law and international law, and taking account of individual circumstances, victims of gross violations of international human rights law and serious violations of international humanitarian law should, as appropriate and proportional to the gravity of the violation and the circumstances of each case, be provided with full and effective reparation [...] which

41 See also G. Bitti; G. González Rivas: "The Reparations Provisions for Victims under the Rome Statute of the International Criminal Court". In: Redressing Injustices through Mass Claims Processes – Innovative Responses to Unique Challenges. Ed. The International Bureau of the Permanent Court of Arbitration. Oxford, 2006, pp. 299 et seq. at p. 308, referring to victim participation.

42 Art. 75 (2).

43 An interpretation of the term "reparations" as used in the ICC Statute in accordance with the 2005 Victims Principles and the 1985 Victims Declaration is in line with the intention of the drafters of the Statute. A footnote contained in Art. 73 of the ICC Draft Statute that for the purposes of defining "victims" and "reparation", reference should be made to the definitions contained in Art. 44 (4) and Art. 68 (1) and its accompanying footnote and the 1985 Victims Declaration and the Draft Basic Principles and Guidelines on the Right to a Remedy and Reparation for Victims of Violations of Human Rights and International Humanitarian Law. See D. Donat-Cattin: "Article 75 – Reparations to Victims". In: Commentary on the Rome Statute of the International Criminal Court – Observers' Notes, Article by Article. Ed. O. Triffterer. Baden-Baden, 1999, pp. 965 et seq. at p. 969, Fn.23. The former "Draft Basic Principles and Guidelines on the Right to a Remedy and Reparation for Victims of Violations of Human Rights and International Humanitarian Law", have now been adopted by the UN General Assembly (2005 Victims Principles).

44 Art. 15.

include the following forms: restitution, compensation, rehabilitation, satisfaction and guarantees of non-repetition".[45]

While neither the ICC Statute nor the 2005 Victims Principles provide for a precise definition, in compliance with other modern approaches[46] both use "reparations" as a generic legal term for various concepts and measures provided by the responsible party to redress crimes or other violations of international and human rights law, including restitution, compensation and rehabilitation. It is in this sense that the term "reparations" is used for the purposes of the present study.

45 Art. 18.

46 Also the ILC Draft Articles and international human rights jurisprudence use "reparations" as a generic legal term: while the American Convention's key article on reparation, Art. 63, speaks of "fair compensation", the Court's judgments have broadly interpreted "reparation" as a generic term covering the various means a state can redress the international responsibility it has incurred. These include restitution, compensation, satisfaction and guarantees of non-repetition. In contrast, the 1985 Victims Declaration does not use the term "reparation" but instead uses "compensation", and in particular "restitution" as generic terms.

Chapter 2 Historical and Legal Context of Reparations for Victims of Crimes under International Law (Overview)

In this chapter an overview will be provided of the historical and legal context of the ICC reparation system. Generally, the incorporation of the Court's mandate to order the offender to make reparations to victims is in line with a growing trend both in the national and international law context. The focus of this trend is the right of victims of crimes, including crimes under international law, gross violations of international human rights law and grave violations of international humanitarian law, to reparations.[47]

A. National Law

Providing reparations to the victim of a crime has a long history in the domestic sphere. In many ancient communities, reparations awarded by the offender to the victim or his or her tribe was the central element of sanctioning a crime.[48]Also, at the origins of criminal law, victims were responsible for the initiation of proceedings against the offender.[49] With the transfer of criminal justice from the private to the public sphere, the role of victims in criminal proceedings progressively faded.[50] While in more traditional societies the victim continued to play a more active role in

47 See for a general overview e.g. E. Barkan: The Guilt of Nations – Restitution and Negotiating Historical Injustices. New York, 2001, pp. 329 et seq.; W. Hassemer; J. P. Reemtsma: Verbrechensopfer – Gesetz und Gerechtigkeit. München, 2002; M. Joutsen: The Role of the Victim of Crime in European Criminal Justice Systems – A Crossnational Study of the Role of the Victim. Helsinki, 1987, pp. 33 et seq.

48 Regarding pre-colonial African and Aboriginal societies e.g. N. Nsereko: "Uganda". In: Wiedergutmachung im Kriminalrecht – Internationale Perspektiven – Reparation in Criminal Law – International Perspectives. Eds. A. Eser; S. Walther. Vol. 2. Freiburg i. Br., 1997, pp. 321 et seq. at pp. 325 et seq. On Western legal history e.g. A. Ashworth: "Some Doubts About Restorative Justice". In: Criminal Law Forum 4 (1993), pp. 277 et seq.; C. Roxin: "Strafe und Wiedergutmachung". In: Festschrift für Werner Lorenz zum 80. Geburtstag. Eds. T. Rauscher; H.-P. Mansel. München, 2001, pp. 51 et seq. For an overview see I. Bottigliero: Redress for Victims of Crimes under International Law. Leiden, 2004, pp. 13 et seq.

49 S. Zappalà: Human Rights in International Criminal Proceedings. Oxford, 2003, p. 219.

50 Ibid.

criminal justice, in most societies of the North, the focus of criminal justice was on the perpetrator of the crime only.[51] Bassiouni assesses that "[f]or reasons of social order or because of a social implied "social contract", organized society has substituted the individual's right of unilateral vengeance or redress with a social system represented in the twin aspects of legal redress embodied in criminal and civil branches of the law and judicial organizations. In other words, organized society [...] separated the right to exact punishment, which devolved from the individual to the state, from the right to civil redress, which remained the individual's prerogative."[52] Particularly in jurisdictions with a common law background a tradition was established of a strict separation between criminal prosecution, left in the hand of the state authorities, and civil litigation, being the only context in which victims could present their claims.[53] In traditionally civil law countries, an effort was made to preserve a role for victims in the criminal process in the form of a right to participation in the proceedings (as a *partie civile*), with the central purpose of obtaining reparation.[54]

Starting in the late 1960s, in systems following both legal traditions, greater attention has been paid to the role of victims in criminal trials, and their role and rights have been strengthened.[55] A shift of paradigms can be observed, a move away from

51 M. Nowak: "The Right to Reparation of Victims of Gross Human Rights Violations". In: Reparations – Redressing Past Wrongs. Eds. G. Ulrich; L. Krabbe Boserup. (Human Rights in Development – Yearbook 2001). The Hague, 2003, pp. 275 et seq. at p. 278.

52 C. M. Bassiouni: "The Philosophy and Policy of International Criminal Justice". In: Man's Inhumanity to Man – Essays on International Law in Honour of Antonio Cassese. Eds. L. C. Vorah; F. Pocar; Y. Featherstone (et al.). The Hague, 2003, pp. 65 et seq. at pp. 97 et seq.; S. Schafer: Victimology – The Victim and His Criminal. Reston, Virginia, 1977, p. 179: "As the state monopolized the institution of punishment, the rights of the injured were slowly separated from the penal law: composition, as the obligation to pay damages, became separated from criminal law and became a specific field of civil law".

53 See e.g. S. Zappalà: Human Rights in International Criminal Proceedings. Oxford, 2003, p. 219; M. Heikkilä: International Criminal Tribunals and Victims of Crime. Turku, 2004, pp. 46 et seq.

54 S. Zappalà: Human Rights in International Criminal Proceedings. Oxford, 2003, p. 219.

55 E.g. numerous victim compensation schemes were established with included methods such as victim-offender mediation, family conferencing, the ability of crime victims to present victim impact statements in the sentencing phase has become widespread, in particular in common law jurisdictions, and other reparative measures. The culmination of many of these initiatives was the unanimous agreement by the UN General Assembly of the 1985 Victims Declaration. For further discussion see e.g. M. Joutsen: The Role of the Victim of Crime in European Criminal Justice Systems – A Crossnational Study of the Role of the Victim. Helsinki, 1987, pp. 50 et seq.; S. Garkawe: "Victims and the International Criminal Court – Three Major Issues". In: International Criminal Law Review 3 (2003), pp. 345 et seq. at pp. 347 et seq.; M. Heikkilä: International Criminal Tribunals and Victims of Crime. Turku, 2004, p. 166; P. R. Dubinsky: "Human Rights Law Meets Private Law Harmonization – The Coming Conflict". In: Yale Journal of International Law 30 (2005), pp. 211 et seq. at p. 314; C. Jorda; J. de Hemptinne: "The Status and Role of the Victim". In: The Rome Statute of the International Criminal Court – A Commentary. Eds. A. Cassese; P. Gaeta; J. R. W. D. Jones. Vol. 2. Oxford, 2002, pp. 1387 et seq. at p.

the focus on the perpetrator towards the victim of crime, a trend towards 'restorative justice'.[56] Recent international documents also encourage combined criminal and reparations proceedings.[57] Furthermore, particularly from the 1990s a number of national administrative reparation schemes have been established with the purpose of awarding reparations to victims of large-scale and systematic crimes.[58]

B. International Law

I. Reparations in the Context of State Responsibility

Reparations for war damages have long historical roots.[59] From the Peace at Westphalia in 1648, states have been the primary subject of international law, and war was understood as an inter-relationship between states, and so were reparations for the consequences of war.[60] In 1928, the Permanent Court of International Justice determined in the Factory at Chorzow case that a violation of international obligations gives automatic rise to the duty to provide reparation.[61] Since then this is a fundamen-

1401. For the strengthening of the status of victims in the criminal procedure of England and Wales see M. E. I. Brienen; E. H. Hoegen: Victims of Crimes in 22 European Criminal Justice Systems – The Implementation of Recommendation (85) 11 of the Council of Europe on the Position of the Victims in the Framework of Criminal Law and Procedure. Nijmegen, 2000, pp. 278 et seq.

56 E.g. W. Hassemer; J. P. Reemtsma: Verbrechensopfer – Gesetz und Gerechtigkeit. München, 2002, p. 14; W. A. Schabas: An Introduction to the International Criminal Court. 2nd ed. Cambridge, 2004, pp. 146 et seq.; C. Möller: Völkerstrafrecht und Internationaler Strafgerichtshof – kriminologische, straftheoretische und rechtspolitische Aspekte. Münster, 2003, pp. 536 et seq.

57 See Art. 9 2001 EU Framework Decision; Art. 36 2005 Guidelines on Child Victims.

58 E. Barkan: The Guilt of Nations – Restitution and Negotiating Historical Injustices. New York, 2001, p. 317 states that "new reconciliation committees and public apologies are continuously reported in locations around the world. The moral economy of restitution enjoys a growing popularity in the private and public sectors alike".

59 See D. J. Bederman: "The United Nations Compensation Commission and the Tradition of International Claims Settlement". In: New York Journal of International Law and Politics 27 (1994), pp. 1 et seq. at p. 1.

60 See C. M. Bassiouni: "International Recognition of Victims' Rights". In: Human Rights Law Review 6 (2006), pp. 203 et seq. at p. 212; W. Heintschel von Heinegg: "Kriegsentschädigung, Reparation oder Schadensersatz". In: Zeitschrift für vergleichende Rechtswissenschaft 90 (1991), pp. 113 et seq. at pp. 115 et seq.

61 *Factory at Chorzow Case* (F.R.G. v. Pol), Permanent Court of International Justice, 12 September 1928, Ser. A, No. 17, Indemnity, p 29: "[I]t is a principle of international law, and even a general conception of law, that any breach of an engagement involves an obligation to make reparation". The Chorzow Factory Judgment "remains the cornerstone of international claims for reparations" not only when presented by states, but also by other litigants, see D. Shelton: "Righting Wrongs – Reparations in the Articles on State Responsibility". In: American Journal of International Law 96 (2002), pp. 833 et seq. at p. 836.

tal principle of public international law and international humanitarian law. Between states, the principle remains undisputed and functions reasonably well in practice.[62] According to the traditional law of state responsibility, a state can seek redress for damage inflicted upon one of its nationals from the injuring state.[63] Individuals are merely beneficiaries and must claim their rights via their state of nationality.[64]
This concept of reparations in international law is predominant until today, yet it is slowly adjusting to the changing order of states, individuals and other actors.

62 See for example *LaGrand Case* (Germany v. United States of America), 27 June 2001, International Court of Justice 466, § 28; *Avena and Other Mexican Nationals* (Mexico v. United States of America), 31 March 2004, International Court of Justice 128, § 119; *Legal Consequences of the Construction of a Wall in the Occupied Palestinian Territory*, Advisory Opinion, 9 July 2004, International Court of Justice 131, § 152. See also Art. 1 ILC Draft Articles: "Every internationally wrongful act of a State entails the international responsibility of that State", and Art. 42 (1): "The injured State is entitled to obtain from the State which has committed an internationally wrongful act full reparation in the from of restitution in kind, compensation, satisfaction and assurances and guarantees of non-repetition, either singly or in combination". For international humanitarian law see Art. 3 Convention Respecting the Laws and Customs of War on Land (Hague Convention IV), 18 October 1907: "[a] belligerent Party which violates the provisions of the [...] Regulations [respecting the Laws and Customs of War on Land] shall, if the case demands, be liable to pay compensation". Art. 41 of this Convention establishes an inter-State duty of compensation for losses caused by individuals who violate the terms of armistice acting on their own initiative. Art. 51 of Geneva Convention I, Art. 52 of Geneva Convention II, Art. 131 of Geneva Convention III, and Art. 148 of Geneva Convention IV refer to the liability of states for grave breaches of the Convention, see also Art. 68 Geneva Convention III. Art. 91 Protocol Additional to the Geneva Conventions of 12 August 1949, and Relating to the Protection of Victims of International Armed Conflicts (Protocol I), 8 June 1977 establishes that if a Party to the conflict violates the provisions of the Conventions or of the Protocol, it "shall, if the case demands, be liable to pay compensation. It shall be responsible for all acts committed by persons forming part of its armed forces".

63 This approach is traditionally adopted by peace treaties, which often include, for individuals who have suffered losses, lump-sum payments that the recipient state is responsible for distributing, C. M. Bassiouni: "International Recognition of Victims' Rights". In: Human Rights Law Review 6 (2006), pp. 203 et seq. at p. 212; E.-C. Gillard: "Reparation for Violations of International Humanitarian Law". In: International Review of the Red Cross 851 (2003), pp. 529 et seq. at p. 535. Where large numbers of victims were involved, such as after a war, victims' reparation claims have often been settled by mixed claims commissions or arbitral tribunals usually established through bilateral agreements in which the responsible state agrees to pay an amount to the injured state, which in turn can distribute funds to individual victims according to criteria generally agreed on, see e.g. D. J. Bederman: "Eligible Claimants before the Iran-United States Claims Tribunal". In: The Iran-United States Claims Tribunal – Its Contribution to the Law of State Responsibility. Eds. R. Lillich; D. B. Magraw. New York, 1998, pp. 47 et seq. See generally M. N. Shaw: International Law. 5th ed. Cambridge, 2003, pp. 232 et seq.

64 E.g. E.-C. Gillard: "Reparation for Violations of International Humanitarian Law". In: International Review of the Red Cross 851 (2003), pp. 529 et seq. at pp. 536 et seq.

II. State Reparations to Individuals and Groups

In the early 20th century, the concept of direct access of individuals to some international courts and tribunals was introduced, enabling them to file claims against states.[65] However, it was only in the second half of the 20th century that major development and codification of international legal standards for the rights of individuals, including their right to reparations, took place.[66] After World War II, there was an increasing concern with the individuals involved in the atrocities, which included both the individual criminal responsibility of perpetrators, and the rights of victims to reparations.[67] A parallel and related development was the rise of the human rights paradigm that has been seen as a response to the atrocities of World War II.[68] Since then, individuals and groups as well have been equipped with a "standing" in international law, as reflected in a number of UN documents and international conventions and practice.

---

65 F. Orrego Vicuna: International Dispute Settlement in an Evolving Global Society. Cambridge, 2004, pp. 48 et seq. referring to Art. 4 and 5 Hague Convention XII of 1907 which granted individuals the right to appeal against decisions of national prize courts before the international prize Court, however this Convention never entered into force. The possibility was created for individuals before the Central American Court of Justice, which existed between 1907 and 1918, to file a claim against States; however none of the claims filed by individuals were successful. The Art. 304 b) of Section VI Treaty of Versailles, 28 June 1919 allowed nationals of the Allied and associated powers to bring claims against Germany before a Mixed Arbitral Tribunal. Similar rights of individuals were granted in other peace treaties, e.g. the Arbitral Tribunal established between Germany and Poland under the Convention for the Protection of Minorities, 15 May 1922. See also B. Heß: "Kriegsentschädigungen aus kollisionsrechtlicher und rechtsvergleichender Sicht". In: Entschädigung nach bewaffneten Konflikten – Die Konstitutionalisierung der Welthandelsordnung. Eds. W. Heintschel von Heinegg; S. Kadelbach; B. Heß (et al.). Heidelberg, 2003, pp. 107 et seq. at pp. 132 et seq.

66 See C. M. Bassiouni: "International Recognition of Victims' Rights". In: Human Rights Law Review 6 (2006), pp. 203 et seq. at pp. 213 et seq.; E.-C. Gillard: "Reparation for Violations of International Humanitarian Law". In: International Review of the Red Cross 851 (2003), pp. 529 et seq. at p. 529. For an overview of the development of reparation as a broader "cultural, political and legal concept" see E. Barkan: The Guilt of Nations – Restitution and Negotiating Historical Injustices. New York, 2001, pp. XXII et seq., pp. 314 et seq., pp. 317 et seq.; J. Torpey: "Introduction – Politics and the Past". In: Politics and the Past – On Repairing Historical Injustices. Ed. J. Torpey. Lanham, Maryland, 2003, pp. 1 et seq. at pp. 4 et seq.

67 E.g. G. Echeverria: "Codifying the Rights of Victims in International Law – Remedies and Reparation". In: Redressing Injustices through Mass Claims Processes – Innovative Responses to Unique Challenges. Ed. The International Bureau of the Permanent Court of Arbitration. Oxford, 2006, pp. 279 et seq. at p. 283.

68 J. Torpey: "Introduction – Politics and the Past". In: Politics and the Past – On Repairing Historical Injustices. Ed. J. Torpey. Lanham, Maryland, 2003, pp. 1 et seq. at p. 4 citing further references.

There are numerous other universal and regional human rights instruments that protect the individual, such as the Charter of the United Nations, 1949 Geneva Conventions and their Additional Protocols of 1977, the Human Rights Committee and the various instruments of refugee law.[69] Some instruments specifically protect the right of individuals to an effective remedy,[70] i.e. more general than reparations "[t]he means of enforcing a right or preventing or redressing a wrong",[71] and the right to compensation,[72] i.e. a specific form of reparations, which are to be ensured by domestic authorities.[73] The right of victims to reparations has been recognized in regional human rights mechanisms,[74] and the regional human rights courts have the power to afford reparations to the injured party, which are to be awarded by the state.[75] Furthermore,

69 See for further details e.g. F. Orrego Vicuna: International Dispute Settlement in an Evolving Global Society. Cambridge, 2004, pp. 51 et seq.; E.-C. Gillard: "Reparation for Violations of International Humanitarian Law". In: International Review of the Red Cross 851 (2003), pp. 529 et seq. at p. 530; C. Tomuschat: "Reparation for Victims of Grave Human Rights Violations". In: Tulane Journal of International and Comparative Law 10 (2002), pp. 157 et seq. at pp. 167 et seq. Regarding the "[r]ecent trend towards the individualization of the human rights discourse" see M. Nowak: "The Right of Victims of Gross Human Rights Violations to Reparation". In: Rendering Justice to the Vulnerable – Liber Amicorum in Honour of Theo van Boven. Eds. F. Coomans; F. Grünfeld; I. Westendorf; J. Willems. The Hague, 2000, pp. 203 et seq. at p. 218; R. Pisillo Mazzeschi: "Reparation Claims by Individuals for State Breaches of Humanitarian Law and Human Rights – An Overview". In: Journal of International Criminal Justice 1 (2003), pp. 339 et seq.

70 See e.g. Art. 8 Universal Declaration of Human Rights, G.A. Res. 217 A(III) of 10 December 1948; Art. 2(3) ICCPR; Art. 13 ECHR; Art. 4 and Art. 18-21 1985 Victims Declaration. Generally, an "effective remedy" includes the right to bring claims before a judicial system capable of resolving allegations of human right abuses, issuing judgments, and granting enforceable awards of compensation, Principle 11 2005 Victims Principles.

71 B. A. Garner (ed.): Black's Law Dictionary. 8th ed. St. Paul, Minnesota, 2004, p. 1320.

72 Art. 14 Convention against Torture and Other Cruel, Inhuman or Degrading Treatment or Punishment, 10 December 1984; Art. 9 (5), 14 (6) ICCPR; Art. 8-21 1985 Victims Declaration; Art. 19 Declaration for the Protection of All Persons from Enforced Disappearances, G.A. Res. 47/133 of 18 December 1992; Art. 39 of the Convention on the Rights of the Child, 20 November 1989; Art. 6 of the International Convention on the Elimination of All Forms of Racial Discrimination, 7 March 1966; Art. 35-37 2005 Guidelines on Child Victims.

73 However, most of the existing international instruments do not provide individuals with a directly enforceable right and some of the instruments are not legally binding; see for further discussion e.g. C. Tomuschat: "Darfur – Compensation for the Victims". In: Journal of International Criminal Justice 3 (2005), pp. 579 et seq. at pp. 582 et seq.

74 See Art. 21 African (Banjul) Charter on Human Rights and Peoples' Rights, 27 June 1981, O.A.U. Doc. CAB/LEG/3 rev.5. Reprinted in: International Legal Materials 21 (1982), pp. 58 et seq.; Art. 10 American Convention; Art. 5 (5) ECHR; Art. 19 Cairo Declaration on Human Rights in Islam, adopted and issued 5 August 1990 ("Right to resort to justice").

75 Art. 41 ECHR; Art. 63 American Convention. Before the African Court on Human and Peoples' Rights, the rights of individuals before it depend on the relevant State's acceptance, see Art. 5 (3), Art. 34 (6), Art. 27 (1) Protocol to the African Charter on Human and

in the past decades, individuals have filed claims against states or their agents for compensation for violations of international law before national fora that have occasionally been successful.[76] Recently, international quasi-judicial bodies have been set up that grant individuals and corporations victimized by international crimes the right to claim compensation from governments.[77]

It is now accepted that individuals have rights under international law. Yet, the traditional view that only states are subjects of international law with full rights and obligations, and individuals are merely beneficiaries and must claim their rights via their state of nationality, is still at the base of many of the hurdles faced by individuals when attempting to directly enforce their rights under international law.[78]

Although views regarding the recognition of an individual victim's right to reparation for violations of international humanitarian law and gross and systematic violations of human rights in customary international law differ, an increasingly broad acknowledgement of the existence of such a right can be observed.[79]

People's Rights on the Establishment of an African Court on Human and Peoples' Rights, 9 June 1998, O.A.U. Doc. OAU/LEG/EXP/AFCHPR/PROT (III), entered into force 25 January 2004. See for a detailed discussion D. Shelton: Remedies in International Human Rights Law. 2nd ed. Oxford, 2005, pp. 189 et seq.; H. Rombouts; P. Sardaro; S. Vandeginste: "The Right to Reparation for Victims of Gross and Systematic Violations of Human Rights". In: Out of the Ashes – Reparation for Victims of Gross and Systematic Human Rights Violations. Eds. K. de Feyter; S. Parmentier; M. Bossuyt (et al.). Antwerp, 2005, pp. 345 et seq. at pp. 371 et seq.

76 An example for a successful claim before national courts is *Prefecture of Voiotia v. Federal Republic of Germany*, Case No. 137/1997, Court of First Instance of Leivdia, Case No.11/2000, Hellenic Supreme Court, 4 May 2000. However, the judgment could not be enforced as the German Supreme Court refused to recognize the Greek Judgment due to sovereign immunity, *Distomo Massacre case*, BGH (German Supreme Court) III ZR 245/98, Decision of 26 June 2003. In: International Legal Materials 42 (2003), pp. 1030 et seq. Regarding international fora, individuals have long had the opportunity to file claims against the state responsible for the violation of international law before "mixed claims commissions" (special arbitral tribunals established by (usually bilateral) treaty.

77 E.g. United Nations Compensation Commission; Foundation "Remembrance, Responsibility and Future" (also contributions by companies). For property claims see Commission for Real Property Claims of Displaced Persons and Refugees in Bosnia and Herzegovina; Housing and Property Directorate and Housing Property Claims Commission in Kosovo; Claims Tribunal for Dormant Bank Accounts in Switzerland.

78 Most claims fail on one or more of the following grounds: 1. individual claims were precluded by a peace settlement; 2. sovereign immunity; or 3. the non-self-executing nature of the right to reparations under international law. Other legal challenges to direct enforcement of reparations via individual claims are, e.g. expiry of time limitations to file claims, see E.-C. Gillard: "Reparation for Violations of International Humanitarian Law". In: International Review of the Red Cross 851 (2003), pp. 529 et seq. at pp. 536 et seq.

79 See Principle 15 2005 Victims Principles; UN Commission of Inquiry on Darfur: UN Report of the International Commission of Inquiry on Darfur, 11 February 2005, UN Doc. S/2005/60 suggests regarding the individual's legal position under international law that under the influence of the UN Charter, a new legal system has merged which accepts

In the ILC Draft Articles, an open position on the question as to who should be the beneficiary of the state obligation to make reparation for an internationally wrongful act is adopted: Art. 33 (2) indicates that the ILC's approach to the question of state responsibility does not prejudice "any rights, arising from the international responsibility of a State, which may accrue directly to any person or entity other than a State". Principle 14 of the 2005 Victims Principles recognizes both the responsibility of the states and "a person, legal person, or other entity [which] is found liable for

the individual human being as a beneficiary not only of the primary rules, but also of the secondary rights that can be exercised by the legal subject damaged by an internationally wrongful act (§§ 595-598); H. Rombouts; P. Sardaro; S. Vandeginste: "The Right to Reparation for Victims of Gross and Systematic Violations of Human Rights". In: Out of the Ashes – Reparation for Victims of Gross and Systematic Human Rights Violations. Eds. K. de Feyter; S. Parmentier; M. Bossuyt (et al.). Antwerp, 2005, pp. 345 et seq. at p. 501 point out that "[e]very human rights violation [...] entails a duty for the responsible State to provide reparation and a corresponding right of victims to obtain reparation". M. Nowak: "The Right of Victims of Gross Human Rights Violations to Reparation". In: Rendering Justice to the Vulnerable – Liber Amicorum in Honour of Theo van Boven. Eds. F. Coomans; F. Grünfeld; I. Westendorf; J. Willems. The Hague, 2000, pp. 203 et seq. at p. 218: "[t]he right of victims of (gross) human rights violations to adequate reparation [...] is already fairly well established under international law". UN Commision on Human Rights, Sub-Commission on Prevention of Discrimination and Protection of Minorities: Study Concerning the Right to Restitution, Compensation and Rehabilitation for Victims of Gross Violations of Human Rights and Fundamental Freedoms, Final Report Submitted by Mr. Theo van Boven, Special Rapporteur, 2 Juli 1993, E/CN.4/Sub.2/1993/8, p. 19: "the obligations resulting from State responsibility for breaches of international human rights law entail corresponding rights on the part of the individual persons who are under the jurisdiction of the effecting State and who are victims of those breaches. The principal right these victims are entitled to under international law is the right to effective remedies and just reparations". More cautious C. Tomuschat: "Reparation for Victims of Grave Human Rights Violations". In: Tulane Journal of International and Comparative Law 10 (2002), pp. 157 et seq.: "At the present time there exists no general rule of customary international law to the effect that any grave violation of human rights creates an individual reparations claim under international law". R. Hofmann: "Victims of Violations of International Humanitarian Law – Do They Have an Individual Right to Reparation against States under International Law?". In: Völkerrecht als Wertordnung – Common Values in International Law – Festschrift für Christian Tomuschat – Essays in Honour of Christian Tomuschat. Eds. P.-M. Dupuy; B. Fassbender; M. N. Shaw; K.-P. Sommermann. Kehl am Rhein (et al.), 2006, pp. 341 et seq. at p. 357; F. Orrego Vicuna: International Dispute Settlement in an Evolving Global Society. Cambridge, 2004, p. 48. See also *Distomo Massacre case*, BGH (German Supreme Court) III ZR 245/98, Decision of 26 June 2003. In: International Legal Materials 42 (2003), pp. 1030 et seq. at p. 1037; *Bridge of Varvarin case*, Oberlandesgericht Köln, Decision of 28 July 2005, Case No. 7 U 8/04. See generally on this question A. Randelzhofer; C. Tomuschat (eds.): State Responsibility and the Individual – Reparation in Instance of Grave Violations of Human Rights. The Hague, 1999; W. Heintschel von Heinegg; S. Kadelbach; B. Heß (et al.) (eds.): Entschädigung nach Bewaffneten Konflikten – Die Konstitutionalisierung der Welthandelsordnung. Heidelberg, 2003.

reparation" to provide reparations to the victim.[80] At the same time it upholds that reparations can also be awarded to a state, but only where it has already compensated the victim.[81] The right to claim reparations under Art. 75 ICC Statute is conceived as an example of the significant trend in international law in regard to the legal personality of the individual.[82]

The shift to the standing of groups in international law can be explained to be a result of the characteristics of the Nazi crimes to target specific groups of individuals, which impacted whom reparations were to be made to by Germany after the war.[83] In particular the great numbers of stateless among the Jewish survivors of the Nazi regime made clear that the traditional concept, that states would receive reparations for violations committed against their nationals could no longer be upheld.[84] Thus, among others, payments were made to the Conference on Jewish Material Claims against Germany ("Jewish Claims Conference"), which was recognized as a representative organ of Jews worldwide.[85]

The 2005 Victims Principles also recognize that a collective can be victimized by gross violations of human rights law and serious violations of international humanitarian law and thus be entitled to reparation.[86]

---

80 Principle 15 s. 3 provides that "[i]n accordance with its domestic laws and international legal obligations, a State shall provide reparation to victims for acts or omissions which can be attributed to the State and constitute gross violations of international human rights law or serious violations of international humanitarian law. In cases where a person, a legal person, or other entity is found liable for reparation to a victim, such party should provide reparation to the victim or compensate the State if the State has already provided reparation to the victim."

81 Ibid.

82 R. Hofmann: "Victims of Violations of International Humanitarian Law – Do They Have an Individual Right to Reparation against States under International Law?" In: Völkerrecht als Wertordnung – Common Values in International Law – Festschrift für Christian Tomuschat – Essays in Honour of Christian Tomuschat. Eds. P.-M. Dupuy; B. Fassbender; M. N. Shaw; K.-P. Sommermann. Kehl am Rhein (et al.), 2006, pp. 341 et seq. at p. 356.

83 J. Torpey: "Introduction – Politics and the Past". In: Politics and the Past – On Repairing Historical Injustices. Ed. J. Torpey. Lanham, Maryland, 2003, pp. 1 et seq. at p. 5. On the history of the crime of genocide, which is closely related to the recognition of groups, G. Werle: Principles of International Criminal Law. The Hague, 2005, pp. 190 et seq.

84 E.g. B. Heß: "Kriegsentschädigungen aus kollisionsrechtlicher und rechtsvergleichender Sicht". In: Entschädigung nach bewaffneten Konflikten – Die Konstitutionalisierung der Welthandelsordnung. Eds. W. Heintschel von Heinegg; S. Kadelbach; B. Heß (et al.). Heidelberg, 2003, pp. 107 et seq. at p. 233.

85 The legal basis of the payments is the Luxemburg Agreement of 1952, see for detailed discussion e.g. N. Goldmann: "Über die Bedeutung der Wiedergutmachung des Nationalsozialistischen Unrechts". In: Die Freiheit des Anderen – Festschrift für Martin Hirsch. Eds. H. J. Vogel; H. Simon; A. Podlech. Vol. 5. München, 1981, pp. 215 et seq.

86 Principle 8. The preamble of the 2005 Victims Principles stresses that this documents does "not entail new international or domestic legal obligations but identify mechanisms,

III. Reparations from Individual Perpetrators of International Crimes to Individual or Collective Victims

In public international law, a sharp distinction is made between the responsibility of states and the responsibility of individuals.[87] While the principle of individual criminal responsibility for violations of international crimes has been accepted since World War II, solely states have had the obligation to make reparations.[88] Only in recent years, with the increasing recognition of the individual as subject under international law, have there been instances in which individual violators were obliged to make reparations.[89]

Claims of individual victims of international crimes have been successfully filed against individual perpetrators in US courts, pursuant to the Alien Tort Claims Act.[90] While in these cases courts do exercise extraterritorial jurisdiction as they concern violations committed outside the US, they are based on domestic, not international law.

---

modalities, procedures and methods for the implementation of existing legal obligations under international human rights law and international humanitarian law". However, this has been disputed, see e.g. reasoning of German government to abstain from supporting the adoption of these and C. Tomuschat: "Darfur – Compensation for the Victims". In: Journal of International Criminal Justice 3 (2005), pp. 579 et seq.

87 See e.g. Art. 58 ILC Draft Articles; C. Tomuschat: "Reparation for Victims of Grave Human Rights Violations". In: Tulane Journal of International and Comparative Law 10 (2002), pp. 157 et seq. at p. 181.

88 See G. Werle: Principles of International Criminal Law. The Hague, 2005, pp. 2 et seq. for a description of the history of the concept of individual criminal responsibility. D. Donat-Cattin: "Article 75 – Reparations to Victims". In: Commentary on the Rome Statute of the International Criminal Court – Observers' Notes, Article by Article. Ed. O. Triffterer. Baden-Baden, 1999, pp. 965 et seq. at p. 967 describes that "[t]he ILC decided to delete from its Draft Statute an article on reparation, article 47, which was part of its 1993 preliminary draft, with the argument that a criminal court was not the appropriate forum in which to order the return of stolen property, a remedy which [some of the members of the commission] considered to be more appropriate in a civil than in a criminal case[...]. On balance the Commission considered that these issues were best left to national jurisdictions and to international judicial co-operation agreements". In its current version, the ILC Draft Articles on State Responsibility stress the penal responsibility of individuals violating international law (Art. 2 (1)).

89 Yet, the idea that individuals are liable for violations of international law is not new. In 1872 Gustave Moynier, one of the founders of Red Cross and Red Crescent Movement, insisted on the importance of having compensation paid directly from the perpetrator, and suggested that the state should only hold a subsidiary obligation to pay damages in case the perpetrator was unable to do so, see C. K. Hall: "The First Proposal for a Permanent International Criminal Court". In: International Review of the Red Cross 322 (1998), pp. 57 et seq.

90 28 USC § 1350. See also US Torture Victims Protection Act, Foreign Sovereign Immunities Act. While the ATCA is an important tool for establishing the responsibility of violators to compensate their victims, in practice very few awards have been enforced.

Principle 15 of the 2005 Victims Principles expressly incorporates the possibility that reparations may not only be made by states, but also by "a person, a legal person, or other entity found liable for reparation to a victim."[91] However, Art. 75 ICC Statute for the first time enables an international court to actually order the individual perpetrator to make direct reparations to the victims of crimes, an order that is based on international law.

C. International Criminal Law

Thus, the negotiations leading to the Rome Statute of the International Criminal Court were conducted in the "context of a growing emphasis on the importance of victims in international human rights law and international humanitarian law [...] [and] an important trend in criminal justice towards 'restorative justice', an approach that it victim-oriented."[92]

Neither victims nor reparations were mentioned in the Nuremberg and Tokyo Charters.[93] The Statutes of the ICTY and ICTR provide that, in addition to imprison-

91 See also Principle 17: "States shall, with respect to claims by victims, enforce domestic judgements for reparation against individuals or entities liable for the harm suffered and endeavour to enforce valid foreign legal judgements for reparation in accordance with domestic law and international legal obligations". However, whether the 2005 Victims Principles reflect existing international law is disputed.

92 W. A. Schabas: An Introduction to the International Criminal Court. 2nd ed. Cambridge, 2004, pp. 146 et seq. M. Nowak: "The Right to Reparation of Victims of Gross Human Rights Violations". In: Reparations – Redressing Past Wrongs. Eds. G. Ulrich; L. Krabbe Boserup. (Human Rights in Development – Yearbook 2001). The Hague, 2003, pp. 275 et seq. at p. 278 has defined "restorative justice" as "concept [that] aims to involve the offender, the victim and the community on a more or less equal basis in their search for repair, reconciliation and justice. Rather than punishing only the perpetrator for the crimes committed, this concept includes measures of mediation, community service, restitution and other forms of diversion aimed at providing redress to the victim and reconciliation between victim and offender". S. Garkawe: "Victims and the International Criminal Court – Three Major Issues". In: International Criminal Law Review 3 (2003), pp. 345 et seq. at pp. 348 et seq. describes as causes for the greater awareness for the victims of crime the realization as to what psychological effects war and other gross crimes as well as a criminal trial can have on victims, and that treating victims appropriately will deter victims from taking justice into their own hands.

93 However, both enabled the Tribunals to order the deprivation of stolen property and granted an extremely wide degree of discretion to the Tribunal in that it was allowed to order any "punishment as shall be determined by [the Tribunal] to be just". Thus, theoretically, reparatory measures, e.g. restitution to victims, could have been ordered, see Art. 27 Nuremberg Charter: "The Tribunal shall have the right to impose upon a defendant on conviction, death or such other punishment as shall be determined by it to be just". Art. 28 states: "In addition to any punishment imposed by it, the Tribunal shall have the right to deprive the convicted person of any stolen property and order its delivery to the Control Council for Germany". Similar provisions were contained in the Tokyo Charter, see R. E. Fife: "Article 77 – Applicable Penalties". In: Commentary on the Rome Statute of

ment, a Trial Chamber may order the return of any property and proceeds acquired by criminal conduct to their rightful owners.[94] Thus, restitution is the only form of reparation that can be ordered.[95] The Rules of the ICTY and ICTR set forth that the Trial Chamber can determine the matter of restitution of property only after a judgment of conviction of the accused and where the judgment contains a specific finding that the unlawful taking of property by the accused was associated with the crime.[96] However, there is no case in the jurisprudence of either Tribunal where a Chamber has ordered an individual that it convicted to return stolen property or criminal proceeds.[97] Regarding compensation to victims, while the Rules of both Tribunals provide for a definition of "victim", they set forth that compensation proceedings can only be initiated before a national court that is then bound by the findings of the tribunal on the criminal responsibility of the convicted person.[98] Judges of both Tribunals concluded in reports on compensation to victims that the Statutes of the Tribunals did not give them the mandate to decide on the issue.[99] However, assistance

the International Criminal Court – Observers' Notes, Article by Article. Ed. O. Triffterer. Baden-Baden, 1999, pp. 985 et seq. at p. 988.

94 Art. 23 (3) ICTR Statute; Art. 24 (3) ICTY Statute. Victims do not have the right to initiate an action for restitution. See generally P. Chifflet: "The Role and Status of the Victim". In: International Criminal Law – Developments in the Case Law of the ICTY. Eds. W. A. Schabas; G. Boas. Leiden, 2003, pp. 75 et seq. at pp. 98 et seq.

95 According to J. Sarkin: "Reparations for Gross Human Rights Violations as an Outcome of Criminal versus Civil Proceedings". In: Out of the Ashes – Reparation for Victims of Gross and Systematic Human Rights Violations. Eds. K. de Feyter; S. Parmentier; M. Bossuyt (et al.). Antwerp, 2005, pp. 151 et seq. at p. 177 these provisions do not deal with reparations, but rather allow for a process to return to victims goods that were taken from them.

96 Rule 105 ICTY Rules and ICTR Rules. See also Rule 98 ICTY Rules, Rule 88 ICTR Rules.

97 G. Mettraux: International Crimes and the Ad Hoc Tribunals. Oxford, 2005, p. 58 points out that there were several opportunities to do so, referring e.g. to the Kunarac case before the ICTY. This seems hardly surprising in view that these provisions "were included in the Rules as a symbolic afterthought rather than being expected to produce concrete results", as pointed out by T. van Boven: "The Position of the Victims in the Statute of the International Criminal Court". In: Reflections on the International Criminal Court – Essays in Honour of Adriaan Bos. Eds. H. von Hebel; J. G. Lammers; J. Schukking. The Hague, 1999, pp. 77 et seq. at pp. 81-82.

98 Rule 2 ICTY Rules and ICTR Rules on the victims definition, Rule 106 ICTY Rules and ICTR Rules on compensation. For further discussion regarding the ICTR's compensation provisions, see V. Morris; M. P. Scharf: The International Criminal Tribunal for Rwanda. Vol. 1. Irvington-on-Hudson, New York, 1998, pp. 595 et seq.

99 However, they recommended the Security Council to consider a possible mechanism to deal with reparation to victims, see ICTY: Victims' Compensation and Participation – Report prepared by the ICTY Rules Committee. Appendix to a Letter dated 12 October 2000 from the President of the ICTY addressed to the UN Secretary-General, Annex to UN Doc. S/2001/1063 of 3 November 2000; ICTR: Letter of the President of the ICTR to the UN Secretary General. Annex to a Letter from the UN Secretary General to the Secu-

is provided to victims of sexual violence who appear as witnesses before the ICTR in the form of general medical services by a medical unit set up in Rwanda.[100]

In the concept of international criminal justice that existed until the establishment of the International Criminal Court, participation in the proceedings was left to the Prosecutor, who was supposed to represent the international community, including victims. Obtaining reparations fell mainly within the jurisdiction of domestic courts. This concept fails to do justice to victims when the Prosecutor does not represent the interests of victims and when national courts that lack the power or will to award reparations.[101] Thus, until the adoption of the ICC Statute, reparations for victims were not part of international criminal justice. Concern for victims was labeled the "missing link" of this area of law.[102]

In the formation of the Rome Statute there were widely varying views about the role of victims in the international criminal process, rooted in the different approaches varying national systems take to victims in criminal procedure.[103]

Eventually, the incorporation of an option for the Court to order the offender to make reparations to victims, as well as the possibility to allow victims to participate in the proceedings, was agreed upon.[104] Thus, the statutory scheme of the ICC reflects the most advanced position on victims that exists in established international

rity Council, UN Doc. S/2000/1198 of 14 December 2000. Eighth ICTY Annual Report, UN Doc. A/56/352 of 17 September 2001, para. 49: the report confirms the gradual formation of a right of victims to compensation under international law and recommends the creation of an international commission for compensation. The ICTR, through the Office of the Registrar, attempted at one point not only to provide assistance to witnesses, but also contributed to projects in Taba township, the locality where the mayor was convicted of genocide and where hundreds of survivors lived. But the tribunal soon found that the needs exceeded its capacity and scaled back its efforts, see ICTR: Letter of the President of the ICTR to the UN Secretary General. Annex to a Letter from the UN Secretary General to the Security Council, UN Doc. S/2000/1198 of 14 December 2000.

100 A.-M. de Brouwer: "Reparation to Victims of Sexual Violence – Possibilities at the International Criminal Court and at the Trust Fund for Victims and Their Families". In: Leiden Journal of International Law 20 (2007), pp. 207 et seq. at p. 217, pointing out that the ICTR thereby accepted a duty on the basis of Rule 34 of its Rules. The medical unit is financed by the Voluntary Trust Fund and that this is in contrast to the ICTY which only supports witnesses with basis support during their testimony before the Tribunal.

101 See C. Jorda; J. de Hemptinne: "The Status and Role of the Victim". In: The Rome Statute of the International Criminal Court – A Commentary. Eds. A. Cassese; P. Gaeta; J. R. W. D. Jones. Vol. 2. Oxford, 2002, pp. 1387 et seq. at p. 1388.

102 See e.g. B. Ferencz: "The Experience of Nuremberg". In: International Crimes, Peace and Human Rights – The Role of the International Criminal Court. Ed. D. Shelton. Ardsley, New York, 2000, pp. 1 et seq. at p. 3.

103 See e.g. W. A. Schabas: An Introduction to the International Criminal Court. 2nd ed. Cambridge, 2004, p. 171; C. Muttukumaru: "Reparation to Victims". In: The International Criminal Court – The Making of the Rome Statute – Issues, Negotiations, Results. Ed. R. S. Lee. The Hague, 1999, pp. 262 et seq.

104 As international law is not settled in the question of victims' rights, the drafters opted not clearly determine the substantive and procedural aspects of those rights in Art. 75 and

criminal justice.[105] The ICC reparation system is also innovative in international law in general. It marks the departure from the traditional inter-state approaches to the right granted to individuals to claim reparations for crimes under international law, towards a more comprehensive scheme in which individuals and collectives of victims have a right to apply for reparations directly from the individual perpetrator.[106] It has been described as a "concrete manifestation of the perhaps no longer merely 'emergent' right to reparations for victims of grave human rights abuses,"[107] and at the same time as a "further step towards the consolidation of an international civil liability of individuals".[108]

None of the hybrid or internationalized criminal tribunals established in recent years in Sierra Leone, East Timor, Kosovo, and Cambodia have carried on with the standard set forth by the ICC Statute, for lack of power to order direct reparations to victims.

Yet, according to some of the legal foundations, the possibility of reparations to victims is envisioned. Regarding the Special Court for Sierra Leone, it is stated that a victim of a crime within its jurisdiction "may claim compensation in accordance with the Criminal Procedure Act, 1965 if the Special Court has found a person guilty of that crime."[109] Furthermore, the Special Court may order as a penalty the forfeiture of property, proceeds and assets acquired unlawfully and order their return to their rightful owner.[110] The trials before the Extraordinary Chambers in the Courts

79, see C. M. Bassiouni: The Legislative History of the International Criminal Court. Vol. 3. Ardsley, New York, 2005, p. 97.

105 C. M. Bassiouni: The Legislative History of the International Criminal Court. Vol. 3. Ardsley, New York, 2005, p. 177.

106 See I. Bottigliero: Redress for Victims of Crimes under International Law. Leiden, 2004, p. 214.

107 P. de Greiff; M. Wierda: "The Trust Fund for Victims of the International Criminal Court – Between Possibilities and Constraints". In: Out of the Ashes – Reparation for Victims of Gross and Systematic Human Rights Violations. Eds. K. de Feyter; S. Parmentier; M. Bossuyt (et al.). Antwerp, 2005, pp. 225 et seq. at p. 225 also referring to the Trust Fund.

108 H. Rombouts; P. Sardaro; S. Vandeginste: "The Right to Reparation for Victims of Gross and Systematic Violations of Human Rights". In: Out of the Ashes – Reparation for Victims of Gross and Systematic Human Rights Violations. Eds. K. de Feyter; S. Parmentier; M. Bossuyt (et al.). Antwerp, 2005, pp. 345 et seq. at p. 419.

109 Art. 45 Special Court Agreement (Ratification) Act, 2002.

110 Art. 41 Statute of the Special Court for Sierra Leone, Annexed to the Agreement between the United Nations and the Government of Sierra Leone on the Establishment of a Special Court for Sierra Leone, signed on 16 January 2002. The property may also be returned to the State of Sierra Leone. Furthermore, the Lomé Peace Accords envisage the establishment of a special fund for victims in Sierra Leone, and the Truth and Reconciliation Commission for Sierra Leone recommended the establishment of a reparation program, see Art. XXIX of the Lomé Peace Accords: the "Government, which the support of the International Community, shall design and implement a program for the rehabilitation of war victims. For this purpose, a special fund shall be set up"; also a Truth Commission is to be set up under Art. XXVI, Art. XXVIII. Neither has been established

of Cambodia are to be conducted in accordance with Cambodian law, which grants victims the right to claim reparation in the course of criminal proceedings.[111] The Serious Crimes Panels in East Timor were to have a Trust Fund for Victims, funded by forfeited assets collected from the convicted persons.[112]

The Statute of the Iraqi High Criminal Court grants victims' families and "Iraqi persons harmed" the right to directly file a civil suit "for the harm they suffered from the actions that constitute crimes according to the provisions of this Statute".[113]

see W. A. Schabas: "Reparation Practices in Sierra Leone and the Truth and Reconciliation Commission". In: Out of the Ashes – Reparation for Victims of Gross and Systematic Human Rights Violations. Eds. S. Parmentier; K. de Feyer; M. Bossuyt; P. Lemmens. Antwerp, 2005, pp. 289 et seq. at pp. 295 et seq.

111 See D. Boyle: "The Rights of Victims – Participation, Representation, Protection, Reparation". In: Journal of International Criminal Justice 4 (2006), pp. 307 et seq.

112 See UN Transitional Administration in East Timor (UNTAET): Reg. 2000/15, On the Establishment of Panels with Exclusive Jurisdiction over Serious Criminal Offences, 6 June 2000, p. 25. However, the Trust Fund has not been established, see C. P. R. Romano; A. Nollkaemper; J. K. Kleffner: International Criminal Courts and Tribunals – Sierra Leone, East Timor, Kosovo and Cambodia. Oxford, 2004, p. 288.

113 Art. 22. The Iraqi Court is empowered to "adjudicate such claims in accordance with the Iraqi Criminal Code No. 23 of 1971 and other relevant laws." The Iraqi Criminal Code stipulates that "A person who has suffered direct material or ethical damage from any offence has the right to bring a civil case against the accused and the person responsible under civil law for the actions of the accused" (Art. 10). It also provides that "a civil case against those responsible under civil law may be brought either collectively or individually in accordance with criminal procedures" (para. 13). The Iraqi Criminal Code affords legal rights to the plaintiff, such as the "right to object to the intervention in the criminal proceedings of the person under civil law" (Statute of the Iraqi High Criminal Court, Law No. 10/2005, Official Gazette of the Government of Iraq No. 4006, 18 October 2005, para. 15 (a)). Iraqi victims have reportedly not filed a civil suit under Art. 22 of the Statute, either individually or collectively, see International Commission of Jurists: Iraq – The Trial of Saddam Hussein and the Rights of Victims, October 2005. Available at www.icj.org/IMGpdf/IQTrial_Saddam_R.victims_pdf, last accessed 22 April 2009, p. 7.

Chapter 3 Purpose of Reparations in International Criminal Law

In this chapter the purpose of reparations ordered by the ICC shall be examined. The ICC Statute does not set forth the purpose of reparation awards to victims. Being aware of the purpose of reparations is essential both for the interpretation of the ICC reparations provisions and for their effective implementation.[114] Furthermore, it provides guidance as to what can potentially be expected from the ICC reparation system. A brief look at the general purposes and protected interests of international criminal law is necessary in order to elaborate on the purpose of reparations in the ICC context and their relation to the general purposes of international criminal justice.

A. Victims and the Purposes of International Criminal Justice

The ICC Statute does not expressly define the purposes which the Court and the trials before it shall serve. The only reference is made in the preamble where it is said that putting an end to impunity of serious international crimes will "contribute to the prevention of such crimes" (para. 5).[115]

114 W. A. Schabas: "Interpreting the Statutes of the Ad Hoc Tribunals". In: Man's Inhumanity to Man – Essays on International Law in Honour of Antonio Cassese. Eds. L. C. Vorah; F. Pocar; Y. Featherstone (et al.). The Hague, 2003, pp. 846 et seq. at p. 861, referring primarily to the Vienna Convention on the Law of Treaties and the jurisprudence of the ICTY; confirmed by the method of interpretation applied by the Court e.g. in *Situation in the Democratic Republic of The Congo*, Decision on the Applications for Participation in the Proceedings of VPRS 1, VPRS 2, VPRS 3, VPRS 4, VPRS 5 and VPRS 6, Pre-Trial Chamber I, 17 January 2006, ICC-01/04-101, 17 January 2006, para.50.

115 W. A. Schabas: An Introduction to the International Criminal Court. 2nd ed. Cambridge, 2004, p. 164 points out that to recognize that the Court has a deterrent effect is not exactly the same as suggesting that sentencing as such has a deterrent effect. In contrast, O. Triffterer: "The Preventive and the Repressive Function of the International Criminal Court". In: The Rome Statute of the International Criminal Court – A Challenge to Impunity. Eds. M. Politi; G. Nesi. Aldershot, 2001, pp. 137 et seq. states that both the function to prevent and to repress crimes are expressly mentioned in the ICC Statute in Art. 28 in the context of military commanders or other superiors, next to a reference in the preamble.

Recently, the purpose of international criminal law in general and the ICC in particular has been moving toward an inclusion of the rights and interests of the crimes' victims.[116] Previously, international criminal justice did not adapt current trends in contemporary domestic criminal law and in the international human rights context, where there has been increasing consensus that the aim to restore social harmony cannot be achieved merely by convicting and sentencing the guilty.[117] The ICC's mandate goes beyond the determination of the criminal responsibility of perpetrators of crimes under international law. It is expected to 'contribute to efforts to restore and maintain peace and security and guarantee lasting respect for and enforcement of international justice'.[118] Also, that victims have been granted attention and potential rights in the ICC Statute may have broadened the perspective on the purposes of international criminal law so as to include the victims' perspective.

Donat-Cattin states that the punitive and preventive role of the Court vis-à-vis the most serious crimes of concern to the international community as a whole "must not be confined to the prosecution and punishment of the perpetrators [...]. The content of article 75, combined with article 68 and several other Statutory provisions, makes justice of this approach and renders the ICC an institution in which victims will be a central element of the penal proceedings."[119] Bassiouni takes a similarly broad perspective by assessing that international criminal justice has "three essential value-oriented goals", reflecting certain values embodied in the historical experiences of national criminal justice systems: 1. prevention through deterrence and the strengthening of social values; 2. enhancement of peace by providing retribution and corrective justice which makes violators accountable and punishable, which in turn reduces victims' needs for revenge, 3. provide victims with redress, which in some ways compensates them for the harm they have suffered and the losses incurred.[120]

116 Critical as to whether international criminal prosecutions serve the interests of victims P. Stolle; T. Singelnstein: "On the Aims and Actual Consequences of International Prosecution". In: International Prosecution of Human Rights Crimes. Eds. W. Kaleck; M. Ratner; T. Singelnstein; P. Weiss. Berlin, 2007, pp. 37 et seq. at pp. 44-45; for discussion on victims and the purposes of criminal trials in the German national context T. Hörnle: "Die Rolle des Opfers in der Straftheorie und im materiellen Strafrecht". In: Juristenzeitung 61 (2006), pp. 950 et seq.

117 C. Jorda; J. de Hemptinne: "The Status and Role of the Victim". In: The Rome Statute of the International Criminal Court – A Commentary. Eds. A. Cassese; P. Gaeta; J. R. W. D. Jones. Vol. 2. Oxford, 2002, pp. 1387 et seq. at p. 1388; see also F. McKay: "Are Reparations Appropriately Addressed in the ICC Statute?". In: International Crimes, Peace and Human Rights – The Role of the International Criminal Court. Ed. D. Shelton. Ardsley, New York, 2000, pp. 163 et seq. at p. 164.

118 Report of the International Criminal Court, UN Doc. A/60/177 (2005), p. 4.

119 D. Donat-Cattin: "Article 75 – Reparations to Victims". In: Commentary on the Rome Statute of the International Criminal Court – Observers' Notes, Article by Article. Ed. O. Triffterer. Baden-Baden, 1999, pp. 965 et seq. at pp. 977 et seq.

120 C. M. Bassiouni: "The Philosophy and Policy of International Criminal Justice". In: Man's Inhumanity to Man – Essays on International Law in Honour of Antonio Cassese. Eds. L. C. Vorah; F. Pocar; Y. Featherstone (et al.). The Hague, 2003, pp. 65 et seq. at p. 125.

According to Werle, international trials serve the two specific functions of truth-finding and, through the conviction of the perpetrators of crime, official acknowledgment of past injustices and the suffering of victims.[121]

Lagodny sees the justification for international criminal law in a "victim-oriented retributive concept embedded in human rights."[122] Similarly, Bottigliero describes the ICC Statute as "based on a compromise approach bringing tighter focus of victims of genocide, crimes against humanity and war crimes, while preserving the essential retributive function of international criminal justice."[123] According to Bachrach, international criminal law exists for two purposes: to prosecute the perpetrators of the "world's most horrendous crimes" and to end impunity; and "to bring some form of justice and solace to their victims".[124]

Also the purposes of punishment in international criminal law are often justified with reference to the interests of victims. Fife mentions "collective reconciliation and reparations to victims" as purpose of penalties in international criminal law, next to the more traditional purposes.[125] Among others, Schabas stresses that punishment is also expected to fulfill an objective of rehabilitation, aiming to serve the paramount aims of reconstruction and reconciliation in a society where human rights violations have been taking place.[126] Möller advocates that the restoration of the dignity of victims is paramount, and thus an appropriate purpose of the punishment of a perpetrator pursuant to international law. Accordingly, the restoration of the individual victim is at the same time precondition for the "healing" of the entire society.[127] In her

121 G. Werle: Principles of International Criminal Law. The Hague, 2005, p. 31 citing further authorities; see also W. A. Schabas: An Introduction to the International Criminal Court. 2nd ed. Cambridge, 2004, p. 164 with reference to the jurisprudence of ICTY and ICTR. According to F. N. M. Mumba: "Topics within the Sphere of Sentencing in International Criminal Law". In: Man's Inhumanity to Man – Essays in Honour of Antonio Cassese. Eds. L. C. Vorah; F. Pocar; Y. Featherstone (et al.). The Hague, 2003, pp. 567 et seq. at p. 571, "what is desired [by victims] is a judgment, a declaration by society, the identification and stigmatization of the perpetrator. This alone is often sufficient redress".

122 O. Lagodny: "Legitimität und Bedeutung des Ständigen Internationalen Strafgerichtshofs". In: Zeitschrift für die gesamte Strafrechtswissenschaft 113 (2001), pp. 800 et seq. at p. 806.

123 I. Bottigliero: Redress for Victims of Crimes under International Law. Leiden, 2004, p. 37.

124 M. Bachrach: "The Protection and Rights of Victims under International Criminal Law". In: The International Lawyer 34 (2000), pp. 7 et seq. at p. 7.

125 Retribution, general prevention or deterrence, individual prevention, reformation of criminals, protection of society, see R. E. Fife: "Article 77 – Applicable Penalties". In: Commentary on the Rome Statute of the International Criminal Court – Observers' Notes, Article by Article. Ed. O. Triffterer. Baden-Baden, 1999, pp. 985 et seq. at p. 986 quoting further references.

126 W. A. Schabas: "Sentencing by International Tribunals – A Human Rights Approach". In: Duke Journal of Comparative and International Law 7 (1997), pp. 461 et seq. at p. 502.

127 C. Möller: Völkerstrafrecht und Internationaler Strafgerichtshof – kriminologische, straftheoretische und rechtspolitische Aspekte. Münster, 2003, p. 604 (translation by the author).

view, the restoration of the belief in the exercise of rights without becoming victims of repression is an "additional purpose of punishment".[128] She concludes that triggering this individual and collective healing process is thus an independent and justified purpose of punishment.[129] In contrast, Glickman favors a retributive sentencing for international criminal trials which "mandates a clear and direct relationship between the severeness of punishment and the seriousness of the crime, as defined in terms of harm to the victim" while arguing that reconciliatory and restorative measures, such as victim compensation, should be achieved by measures beyond sentencing.[130]

Thus, almost all current approaches to the purposes of international criminal justice refer to the acknowledgment and restoration of victims' harm to justify their position, even though conclusions as to the most appropriate purpose vary. As the ICC system contains restorative elements, restoration and acknowledgment of victims' harm is a purpose of international criminal law as incorporated in the ICC Statute. However, while the ICC Statute recognizes that measures beneficial to victims and punishment are interrelated,[131] viewing restoration of victims as an additional purpose of punishment could lead to the assumption that by punishing the perpetrator, restoration of victims is sufficiently served. The ICC Statute recognizes that in order to provide acknowledgment and restoration to victims, measures that reach beyond punishment are necessary. The approach of current international criminal law, as embodied in the ICC Statute, also serves the purpose of victim restoration and acknowledgement. Therefore, an expansion of the purposes of international criminal law that goes beyond the purposes of punishment of the perpetrators to include the acknowledgement and restoration of victims can be assessed.

B. Interests Protected by International Criminal Law

Victims have been granted rights under the ICC Statute, and the purpose of international criminal law and punishment is legitimized with reference to the interests of victims. However, whether the rights and interests of individuals are protected by international criminal law is controversial. The interests protected by international criminal law are important to the potential shape of a reparations mechanism that functions in the context of international criminal justice.

International criminal law protects "peace, security and well-being of the world", the fundamental values of the international community.[132] All crimes under international

128 Ibid., p. 605.

129 Ibid., p. 606 quoting further authorities, adding that it is also a precondition for reconciliation.

130 Describing and promoting the latter approach S. Glickman: "Victims' Justice – Legitimizing the Sentencing Regime of the International Criminal Court". In: Columbia Journal of Transnational Law 43 (2005), pp. 229 et seq. at pp. 242 et seq.

131 See Chapter 6 D. ("Reparations and Penalties").

132 See Preamble of the Rome Statute for an International Criminal Court, para. 3; M. Bergsmo; O. Triffterer: "Preamble". In: Commentary on the Rome Statute of the International Criminal Court – Observers' Notes, Article by Article. Ed. O. Triffterer. Baden-

law presume an international element, i.e. a context of systematic or large-scale use of force.[133] International criminal law individualizes accountability for these crimes for which, as a rule, a collective is responsible, typically a state.[134]

Some legal scholars therefore generally reject the idea that interests of individuals are protected by international criminal law.[135] According to this view, "it is inappropriate to utilize international criminal procedure for the purpose of rehabilitation of individual victims".[136] Individualizing victims would push aside the predominantly collective character of the crime and would mean a selection of individual victims from the collective of victims that is necessarily arbitrary.[137] It is argued that the aim of international criminal justice is to restore solely the values of the international community[138] and that the reconciliation among the people or nations that were involved in the conflict is merely a positive side effect.[139] Thus, victims might feel acknowledged through international criminal law that confirms that their victimization contradicted the values of the international community and is being sanctioned as such.[140]

Others affirm the inclusion of the individual's interests in the sphere of international criminal law. Bassiouni takes a clear position, stating that "[i]nternational criminal law protects categories of victims, be they individuals or part of a group

Baden, 1999, pp. 1 et seq. at p. 9 citing further authorities; G. Werle: Principles of International Criminal Law. The Hague, 2005, pp. 27 et seq.

133 G. Werle: Principles of International Criminal Law. The Hague, 2005, p. 29.

134 Ibid., pp. 29 and 31.

135 O. Lagodny: "Legitimität und Bedeutung des Ständigen Internationalen Strafgerichtshofs". In: Zeitschrift für die gesamte Strafrechtswissenschaft 113 (2001), pp. 800 et seq. at p. 803; C. J. M. Safferling: "Das Opfer völkerrechtlicher Verbrechen – Die Stellung der Verbrechensopfer vor dem Internationalen Strafgerichtshof". In: Zeitschrift für die gesamte Strafrechtswissenschaft 115 (2003), pp. 352 et seq.

136 C. J. M. Safferling: "Das Opfer völkerrechtlicher Verbrechen – Die Stellung der Verbrechensopfer vor dem Internationalen Strafgerichtshof". In: Zeitschrift für die gesamte Strafrechtswissenschaft 115 (2003), pp. 352 et seq. at p. 383, further stating at p. 370 that this is the case in spite of acknowledging that the definition in Rule 85 refers to individual victims (i.e. natural persons). It seems that disregarding the role of individual victims before the ICC *per se* contradicts the wording of Rule 85 and other Rules, their context and legislative history.

137 C. J. M. Safferling: "Das Opfer völkerrechtlicher Verbrechen – Die Stellung der Verbrechensopfer vor dem Internationalen Strafgerichtshof". In: Zeitschrift für die gesamte Strafrechtswissenschaft 115 (2003), pp. 352 et seq. at p. 370.

138 Ibid., p. 383. In a similar direction H. Küpper: Kollektive Rechte in der Wiedergutmachung von Systemunrecht. Vol. 1. Frankfurt a. Main, 2004, p. 1096.

139 C. J. M. Safferling: "Das Opfer völkerrechtlicher Verbrechen – Die Stellung der Verbrechensopfer vor dem Internationalen Strafgerichtshof". In: Zeitschrift für die gesamte Strafrechtswissenschaft 115 (2003), pp. 352 et seq. at p. 384.

140 Ibid.

[…]".[141] Triffterer maintains that the interests of individuals are protected by international criminal law, next to the legal values of the community of nations.[142] In his opinion, "peace and security of mankind [...] [represent] the basic, inherent values of the community of nations which had to be protected in the interest of all, individuals and States alike".[143] He argues that the phrase "well-being of the world" in the Statute's preamble mirrors the war crimes definitions of Art. 8, where one of the alternatives is defined as "outrages upon personal dignity",[144] and thus includes the protection of the individual. According to Triffterer "all crimes within the Court's jurisdiction may, even if attacking individual persons only, threaten the peace and security of mankind and thus be of concern to the whole international community (and directly punishable under the laws of the community of nations)".[145] He further argues that the interests of individual persons are included in the protection of international criminal law not only as direct victims of international crimes, in particular war crimes, but also as a part of "security and peace of mankind", whose protection includes both states and individuals as part of the community of nations.[146] Tomuschat expresses that "[g]enocide is certainly the worst of all offences against both human dignity and

141 C. M. Bassiouni: "The Protection of 'Collective Victims' in International Law". In: International Protection of Victims. Ed. C. M. Bassiouni. Eres, 1988, pp. 181 et seq. at p. 186. See also C. Möller: Völkerstrafrecht und Internationaler Strafgerichtshof – kriminologische, straftheoretische und rechtspolitische Aspekte. Münster, 2003, p. 547.

142 O. Triffterer: "Preliminary Remarks – The Permanent International Criminal Court – Ideal and Reality". In: Commentary on the Rome Statute of the International Criminal Court – Observers' Notes, Article by Article. Ed. O. Triffterer. Baden-Baden, 1999, pp. 17 et seq. at p. 26.

143 M. Bergsmo; O. Triffterer: "Preamble". In: Commentary on the Rome Statute of the International Criminal Court – Observers' Notes, Article by Article. Ed. O. Triffterer. Baden-Baden, 1999, pp. 1 et seq. at p. 10.

144 Ibid., referring to Prosecutor v. Anto Furundzija, Case No. IT-95-17/1-T, 10. Dec.1998, p. 72, para. 183: "The essence of the whole corpus of humanitarian law as well as human rights law lies in the protection of the human dignity of every person, whatever his or her gender".

145 M. Bergsmo; O. Triffterer: "Preamble". In: Commentary on the Rome Statute of the International Criminal Court – Observers' Notes, Article by Article. Ed. O. Triffterer. Baden-Baden, 1999, pp. 1 et seq. at p. 14. Even C. J. M. Safferling: "Das Opfer völkerrechtlicher Verbrechen – Die Stellung der Verbrechensopfer vor dem Internationalen Strafgerichtshof". In: Zeitschrift für die gesamte Strafrechtswissenschaft 115 (2003), pp. 352 et seq. at p. 355 states with regard to international crimes: "not only the individual person was the target of the violation, but the perpetrator aimed at harming or destroying the family, the village, the ethnic group the victim belongs to. The entire social environment is victimized," thus making clear that causing harm to the collective often also implies individual victims.

146 See above, M. Bergsmo; O. Triffterer: "Preamble". In: Commentary on the Rome Statute of the International Criminal Court – Observers' Notes, Article by Article. Ed. O. Triffterer. Baden-Baden, 1999, pp. 1 et seq. at p. 10.

international peace and security".[147] Human dignity is the essence of an individuals' rights and interests.

Others advocate a distinction between the different international crimes: While crimes against humanity also protect individual and concrete legal interests, the crime of genocide supposedly only protects values transcending the individual.[148] With regard to war crimes, reference can be made to the statement of Sassoli, that "[t]he term "International Humanitarian Law" applies to those rules of international law which aim to protect the victims of armed conflict".[149] "International Humanitarian Law [...] belongs to the increasingly important branch of international law meant to protect the interests of individuals against States and not only the mutual interest of States [...]".[150]

The ICC Statute, by granting attention and rights to victims, takes a position on the issue. The preamble of the ICC Statute provides context for this position, emphasizing to be "[m]indful that during this century millions of children, women and men have been victims of unimaginable atrocities that deeply shock the conscience of humanity [...]". The wording "children, women and men" draws attention to the fate of victims also as individual human beings, even before referring to "peace, security and the well-being of the world".[151] Triffterer points out that after the atrocities of World War II, the "concept of justice was revisited so that it could be meted out not only in the name of individuals or groups of victims, but also on behalf of humanity as such".[152] The wording of the preamble of the ICC Statute can be understood as an indication that the concept of international criminal law is neither only concerned with the interests of individual human beings, nor exclusively that of "humanity as such". Rather, individual and collective interests are inclusive.

147 C. Tomuschat: "The Duty to Prosecute International Crimes Committed by Individuals". In: Tradition und Weltoffenheit des Rechts – Festschrift für Helmut Steinberger. Eds. H.-J. Cremer; T. Giegerich; D. Richter (et al.). Berlin, 2002, pp. 315 et seq. at p. 329.

148 G. Werle: Principles of International Criminal Law. The Hague, 2005, p. 28; H. Vest: "Humanitätsverbrechen – Herausforderung für das Individualstrafrecht?". In: Zeitschrift für die gesamte Strafrechtswissenschaft 113 (2001), pp. 457 et seq. at pp. 463 et seq.

149 M. Sassoli: "The Victim-Oriented Approach of International Humanitarian Law and of the International Committee of the Red Cross (ICRC)". In: International Protection of Victims. Ed. C. M. Bassiouni. Eres, 1988, pp. 147 et seq. at p. 154 pointing out that the documents in which international humanitarian law is basically codified, i.e. the four Geneva Conventions of 1949, the two 1977 Protocols additional to the Geneva Conventions and to some degree in the Hague Convention IV of 1907 and its Annexed Regulations protect all kinds of persons afflicted by armed conflicts and not only those suffering as a result of a violation of the law of armed conflict.

150 Ibid., also referring to international human rights law, further stating that historically, international humanitarian law was the first part of international law to be concerned with the fate of individuals as such

151 See para. 3, 4 Preamble to the ICC Statute.

152 M. Bergsmo; O. Triffterer: "Preamble". In: Commentary on the Rome Statute of the International Criminal Court – Observers' Notes, Article by Article. Ed. O. Triffterer. Baden-Baden, 1999, pp. 1 et seq. at p. 8.

The individual appears in the ICC Statute not only as a suspect, an accused and a convicted person, but also as an individual witness and victim. Both the established right for victims to apply for participation in the proceedings and for reparations refer, primarily, to individual victims.[153] In the ICC system, the rights of collectives or groups of victims derive from individual rights. The Statute, in Art. 75 on reparations, leaves open whether "harm, damage and loss" for which reparations can be awarded only refers to the goods and rights of a collective, rather than individuals. However, the wording of Art. 79 (1) on the Trust Fund clarifies that "victims" does not only refer to collectives of victims, as it speaks of "victims and their families". The Rules are explicit on the issue: Reparation awards can be addressed to the harm caused to individual victims and collectives, whereas individual awards are designed as the regular scenario.[154] Regarding participation of victims, the Rules envision that "victims or groups of victims" can participate in the proceedings. Group representation shall take place only when "appropriate".[155]

The rights granted to victims in the ICC Statute concern both the interests of individual victims and interests transcending the individual. As Jorda and de Hemptinne point out "participation of victims in the proceedings and the award to them of compensation are matters which are in the direct interests of the international community in that they enable victims to regain a certain equanimity and thereby helping to restore peace".[156]

International criminal law as contained in the ICC Statute recognizes that the interests protected by international criminal law are not restricted to encompass abstract collective values of the "international community", "mankind", or "humanity as such", but also those of individuals that are part of these. The interests current international criminal law protects both with regard to the international community and collectives as well as individuals are not exclusive, but interdependent and of reciprocal effect.

153 Art. 68, Art. 75. L. Mekhemar: "The Status of the Individual in the Statute of the International Criminal Court". In: The Rome Statute of the International Criminal Court – A Challenge to Impunity. Eds. M. Politi; G. Nesi. Aldershot, 2001, pp. 123 et seq. at p. 128 points out that the right to claim reparation falls close to granting the individual a status close to a implicit locus standi in judicio, also referring to Art. 15 (2).

154 Rule 98 (1), (2). Regarding the victims definition in Rule 85, see below Chapter 5 C. on eligibility. M. Henzelin; V. Heiskanen; G. Mettraux: "Reparations to Victims before the International Criminal Court – Lessons from International Mass Claims Processes". In: Criminal Law Forum 17 (2006), pp. 317 et seq. at p. 328 note that "the purpose of victim reparation is in principle to dispense individual justice".

155 Rule 90.

156 C. Jorda; J. de Hemptinne: "The Status and Role of the Victim". In: The Rome Statute of the International Criminal Court – A Commentary. Eds. A. Cassese; P. Gaeta; J. R. W. D. Jones. Vol. 2. Oxford, 2002, pp. 1387 et seq. at p. 1401 with further reference.

C. Purposes of Reparations

The ICC's legal instruments do not postulate which purpose ICC reparation orders serve.

Clarification will be sought by taking a brief look at the existing approaches and discussing their appropriateness in the ICC context.

Reparations can be based on different rationales and theories. The basic purpose recognized in international and national justice systems is "to rectify the wrong done to a victim, that is, to correct injustice".[157] International jurisprudence sets forth that "reparation must, as far as possible, wipe-out all the consequences of the illegal act and reestablish the situation which would, in all probability have existed if that act had not been committed."[158] The 2005 Victims Principles state that "reparation is intended to promote justice [...]".[159]

Thus, both in the national and in the international legal context, the general principle applies that justice is achieved by awarding reparations that are intended to return the victim to the position he or she would have been if the violation had not occurred (*status quo ante*). However, already in the context of "regular" wrongdoing, often this aim is paradoxical as it is impossible to achieve.[160] Many consequences of crimes under international law are by their very nature irreparable.[161] In addition, the quality and quantity of these crimes characteristically create large numbers of victims that regularly overwhelm the financial resources available for reparations. In particular, as "full reparation" is hardly realistic, financial reparation awards can only be a partial remedy. Also, the overall social context in which the remedies for gross and systematic violations are afforded differs from the individual case. Where there have been widespread crimes, the entire society is affected, often traumatized.[162]

---

157 D. Shelton: Remedies in International Human Rights Law. 2nd ed. Oxford, 2005, pp. 10, 51 referring to "corrective or remedial justice".

158 Ibid, p. 52, reproducing *Factory at Chorzow Case* (F.R.G. v. Pol), Permanent Court of International Justice, 12 September 1928, Ser. A, No. 17 at 47. See also *Lusitania* (United States of America v. Germany), Reports of International Arbitral Awards, 21 February 1924, Vol. VII, pp. 256-257.

159 Principle 15.

160 See for further discussion e.g. N. Roht-Arriaza: "Reparations, Decisions and Dilemmas". In: Hastings International and Comparative Law Review 27 (2004), pp. 157 et seq. at p. 158; E.-C. Gillard: "Reparation for Violations of International Humanitarian Law". In: International Review of the Red Cross 851 (2003), pp. 529 et seq. at p. 530; S. Zappalà: Human Rights in International Criminal Proceedings. Oxford, 2003, p. 228.

161 UN Commision on Human Rights, Sub-Commission on Prevention of Discrimination and Protection of Minorities: Study Concerning the Right to Restitution, Compensation and Rehabilitation for Victims of Gross Violations of Human Rights and Fundamental Freedoms, Final Report Submitted by Mr. Theo van Boven, Special Rapporteur, 2 Juli 1993, E/CN.4/Sub.2/1993/8, para. 131 referring to gross violations of international human rights law and serious violations of international humanitarian law.

162 See S. Bock: "Das Opfer vor dem Internationalen Strafgerichtshof". In: Zeitschrift für die gesamte Strafrechtswissenschaft 119 (2007), pp. 664 et seq. at pp. 669 with further references.

Therefore, most contemporary approaches conclude that reparations for harm suffered by crimes under international law should reach beyond individual financial compensation. It is argued that the aim of reparations is "the restoration of dignity and the acknowledgement of the harm suffered".[163] Both by material and moral means, reparations might serve to provide recognition of and a show of remorse and atonement for the harms inflicted and aim to repair the damage caused, to the extent possible, in order to enable victims to try to rebuild their lives.[164] Furthermore, reconciliation in affected societies is viewed as one of the core purposes of reparations in the context of gross and systematic crimes.[165] Reparations could serve the aim of restoring the social harmony between the communities that have been at war with each other.[166] The objective of generating reconciliation could work both at the level of victims and society, as well as that of groups and individuals.[167] Reparations to victims might create conditions that can achieve the goal of preventing the recurrence of further violations and thus to secure peace and security.[168] Thus, a number of the

163 C. Ferstman: "The Reparation Regime of the ICC – Practical Considerations". In: Leiden Journal of International Law 15 (2002), pp. 667 et seq. at p. 668. See also G. Ulrich: "The Moral Case for Reparations – Three Theses about Reparations for Past Wrongs". In: Reparations – Redressing Past Wrongs. Eds. G. Ulrich; L. Krabbe Boserup. (Human Rights in Development – Yearbook 2001). The Hague, 2003, pp. 369 et seq. at p. 372; and similar on the experience with compensation for victims of Nazi crimes e.g. G. Saathoff: "Entschädigung für Zwangsarbeiter? Entstehung und Leistungen der Bundesstiftung 'Erinnerung, Verantwortung und Zukunft' im Kontext der Debatte um die 'Vergessenen Opfer'". In: Nach der Verfolgung – Wiedergutmachung Nationalsozialistischen Unrechts in Deutschland?. Eds. H. G. Hockerts; C. Kuller. Göttingen, 2003, pp. 241 et seq. at p. 259.

164 See e.g. N. Roht-Arriaza: "Reparations, Decisions and Dilemmas". In: Hastings International and Comparative Law Review 27 (2004), pp. 157 et seq. at p. 159; P. Lewis; H. Friman: "Reparations to Victims". In: The International Criminal Court – Elements of Crimes and Rules of Procedure and Evidence. Ed. R. S. Lee. Ardsley, New York, 2001, pp. 474 et seq.

165 E.g. P. Lewis; H. Friman: "Reparations to Victims". In: The International Criminal Court – Elements of Crimes and Rules of Procedure and Evidence. Ed. R. S. Lee. Ardsley, New York, 2001, pp. 474 et seq. For a broad approach to reparation, see E. Barkan: The Guilt of Nations – Restitution and Negotiating Historical Injustices. New York, 2001, p. 348. G. Ulrich: "The Moral Case for Reparations – Three Theses about Reparations for Past Wrongs". In: Reparations – Redressing Past Wrongs. Eds. G. Ulrich; L. Krabbe Boserup. (Human Rights in Development – Yearbook 2001). The Hague, 2003, pp. 369 et seq. at p. 372 states that "reparations serve as a means of coming to terms with difficult events in the past, facilitating a positive orientation towards the future, facilitating reconciliation". D. Shelton: Remedies in International Human Rights Law. 2nd ed. Oxford, 2005, p. 390.

166 C. Jorda; J. de Hemptinne: "The Status and Role of the Victim". In: The Rome Statute of the International Criminal Court – A Commentary. Eds. A. Cassese; P. Gaeta; J. R. W. D. Jones. Vol. 2. Oxford, 2002, pp. 1387 et seq. at p. 1398.

167 D. Shelton: Remedies in International Human Rights Law. 2nd ed. Oxford, 2005, p. 390.

168 C. M. Bassiouni: Introduction to International Criminal Law. Ardsley, New York, 2003, p. 721 quoting further authorities; C. Muttukumaru: "Reparations to Victims". In: Collec-

purposes of reparations mentioned are congruent with the considered purposes of international criminal justice.

Contemporary penal policy, often discussed under the heading 'restorative justice', aims at developing alternatives to punishment and lack of attention to victims in criminal proceedings. While the concept of restorative justice originated in national legal systems which regularly deal with crimes committed between individuals, it might be applicable in the context of grave and systematic crimes as well.[169] Restorative justice has been defined as "an evolving response to crime that respects the dignity and equality of each person, builds understanding, and promotes social harmony through the healing of victims, offenders and communities".[170] Restorative justice can be divided into a procedural and a substantive aspect. The procedural aspect aims at bringing together perpetrators and those affected by the wrongdoing. In regard to substance, restorative justice emphasizes redress to or restoration of victims and the wider community, and often the reintegration of the offender, and rather than punishment.[171] In particular, making symbolic or financial reparations may provide an opportunity for reintegration into society for the perpetrator.[172]

---

tion of Essays on the Rome Statute of the International Criminal Court. Eds. F. Lattanzi; W. A. Schabas. Ripa di Fagnano Alto, 1999, pp. 301 et seq. at p. 304. D. Shelton: Remedies in International Human Rights Law. 2nd ed. Oxford, 2005, pp. 390 et seq. points out the goal of preventing the recurrence of violence.

169 D. Shelton: Remedies in International Human Rights Law. 2nd ed. Oxford, 2005, pp. 14 et seq.; P. Roberts: "Restoration and Retribution in International Criminal Justice – An Exploratory Analysis". In: Restorative Justice and Criminal Justice – Competing or Reconcilable Paradigms. Eds. A. v. Hirsch; J. v. Roberts; A. Bottoms (et al.). Oxford, 2003, pp. 117 et seq.

170 Para. 3 Preamble of the Basic Principles on the Use of Restorative Justice Programmes in Criminal Matters, ECOSOC Res. 2002/12 of 12 August 2003. P. Rock: Constructing Victims' Rights – The Home Office, New Labour, and Victims. Oxford, 2004, p. 288 remarks that "[t]he motives and meanings of restorative justice have been as diverse as its forms".

171 D. Shelton: Remedies in International Human Rights Law. 2nd ed. Oxford, 2005, p. 15; A. v. Hirsch; A. Ashworth; C. Shearing: "Specifying Aims and Limits for Restorative Justice – A 'Making Amends' Model?". In: Restorative Justice and Criminal Justice -Competing or Reconcilable Paradigms. Eds. A. v. Hirsch; J. v. Roberts; A. Bottoms (et al.). Oxford, 2003, pp. 21 et seq. at pp. 22 et seq.; A. Ashworth: "Victims' Rights, Defendants' Rights and Criminal Procedure". In: Integrating a Victim Perspective within Criminal Justice – International Debates. Eds. A. Crawford; J. Goodey. Aldershot, 2000, pp. 185 et seq. at pp. 193 et seq.

172 C. Jorda; J. de Hemptinne: "The Status and Role of the Victim". In: The Rome Statute of the International Criminal Court – A Commentary. Eds. A. Cassese; P. Gaeta; J. R. W. D. Jones. Vol. 2. Oxford, 2002, pp. 1387 et seq. at p. 1401: "the duty to provide reparation responds to the demands of contemporary penal policy, by affording a means of reintegration into society for the criminal, by helping him to come to terms with the cruelty of his actions and by reinstalling in him a sense of his human and social responsibilities". See also D. Shelton: Remedies in International Human Rights Law. 2nd ed. Oxford, 2005, p. 14.

It is furthermore discussed that reparations serve the aims of deterrence and punishment. In national and international legal systems, deterrence is widely accepted as an additional aim to compensation or reparations.[173] In the context of state responsibility, the goal to restore the rule of law in the interest of the international community, and to thus deter future violations, is one of the conceptual premises of reparations.[174] There is a less unified view as to whether reparations should serve the purpose of punishment.[175] Arguments in favor of viewing punishment as a purpose of reparations are that this could constitute an important acknowledgement of the rights of victims on the criminal process. Furthermore, some forms of reparations, such as obliging the perpetrator to leave public office, are by their nature a form of penalty.[176] It could thus be considered that reparations ordered by the ICC might complement the ICC's function to hold individuals criminally responsible and contribute to the implementation of international humanitarian law and international human rights by punishing and deterring potential perpetrators from committing their crimes.

The applicability of these named purposes of reparations in the context of ICC is to be examined. As to the purpose of compensation, i.e. materially repairing the harm caused, it is indicative that the ICC Statute and Rules require that before the nature

173 See e.g. D. Shelton: Remedies in International Human Rights Law. 2nd ed. Oxford, 2005, pp. 12 et seq., p. 54, p. 390. For the national context see e.g. U. Magnus: "Comparative Report on the Law of Damages". In: Unification of Tort Law – Damages. Ed. U. Magnus. The Hague (et al.), 2001, pp. 185 et seq. at p. 187.

174 D. Shelton: "Righting Wrongs – Reparations in the Articles on State Responsibility". In: American Journal of International Law 96 (2002), pp. 833 et seq. at p. 838.

175 In some national jurisdictions, punishment is not recognized as a goal of reparation, while in others a compensation order against the offender serves as an additional sanction, e.g. the English compensation order, see M. E. I. Brienen; E. H. Hoegen: Victims of Crimes in 22 European Criminal Justice Systems – The Implementation of Recommendation (85) 11 of the Council of Europe on the Position of the Victims in the Framework of Criminal Law and Procedure. Nijmegen, 2000, pp. 267-268. In some national systems, punitive damages or other measures can be awarded that aim at punishing the perpetrator, see e.g. B. Stephens: "Translating Filártiga – A Comparative and International Law Analysis of Domestic Remedies for International Human Rights Violations". In: Yale Journal of International Law 27 (2002), pp. 1 et seq. at p. 39. For examples, see the cases cited in J. J. Paust: "On Human Rights – The Use of Human Right Precepts in US History and the Right to an Effective Remedy in Domestic Courts". In: Michigan Journal of International Law 10 (1989), pp. 618 et seq. at pp. 623-624: "Civil or criminal sanctions for private violations of international law were often interchangeable depending on who was seeking enforcement, an individual, the government or both."

176 F. McKay: "Are Reparations Appropriately Addressed in the ICC Statute?". In: International Crimes, Peace and Human Rights – The Role of the International Criminal Court. Ed. D. Shelton. Ardsley, New York, 2000, pp. 163 et seq. at p. 173. For more on goals of reparation, in particular psychological and social functions see D. Shelton: Remedies in International Human Rights Law. 2nd ed. Oxford, 2005, pp. 10 et seq.; and D. Shelton: "Reparations for Victims of International Crimes". In: International Crimes, Peace, and Human Rights – The Role of the International Court. Ed. D. Shelton. Ardsley, New York, 2000, pp. 137 et seq. at p. 140.

of the reparations award is determined, the Court shall assess and "take into account any damage, loss or injury".[177] Thus, the key reference point the ICC's legal instruments provide for the determination of appropriate reparations is the harm caused.

While the competence of the Court to act *ex proprio motu* with regard to reparations claims could be interpreted as an indication against a predominately civil nature of the reparation order, the fact that victims have the right to refuse an individual reparation award to be made to him or her speaks in favor of predominately compensatory purposes of the ICC reparation order.[178] However, with regard to the first argument, in some national jurisdictions where reparations can be initiated not only by the victim, but also the prosecutor or criminal court, or even triggered automatically by the public prosecutor, the nature of the order is considered as civil, aiming primarily at compensation.[179] Thus, that the Court is equipped with the power to initiate reparations proceedings does not seem to be a valid argument against a predominantly compensatory purpose of reparations.

The potential of the ICC reparation system to fulfill deterrent purposes can be generally questioned. It seems doubtful that the obligation to make reparations would prevent potential perpetrators from committing a crime, and almost certainly it will not have an effect on the acts of states in whose framework the crimes under the Court's jurisdiction are often committed.[180]

It thus appears that before the ICC, and in international criminal law in general, the goal of upholding the rule of law, of deterrence and punishment, is in any case

177 Art. 75 (1), (2), Rule 97 (1), (2).

178 Rule 95; however individual victims cannot hinder a collective award.

179 See e.g. M. E. I. Brienen; E. H. Hoegen: Victims of Crimes in 22 European Criminal Justice Systems – The Implementation of Recommendation (85) 11 of the Council of Europe on the Position of the Victims in the Framework of Criminal Law and Procedure. Nijmegen, 2000, pp. 316-317 on compensation in criminal proceedings in Spain; generally B. Timm: "The Legal Position of Victims in the Rule of Procedure and Evidence". In: International and National Prosecution of Crimes under International Law. Eds. H. Fischer, C. Kreß; S. R. Lüder. (Bochumer Schriften zur Friedenssicherung und zum Humanitären Völkerrecht). Berlin, 2001, pp. 289 et seq. at pp. 306 et seq. describing that claims for reparations in most national jurisdictions that allow for adhesion procedure are considered as essentially civil claims, which are to be pursued in an essentially civil procedure. The nature of the reparations and their enforcement remains strictly civil; C. Muttukumaru: "Reparations to Victims". In: Collection of Essays on the Rome Statute of the International Criminal Court. Eds. F. Lattanzi; W. A. Schabas. Ripa di Fagnano Alto, 1999, pp. 301 et seq. at p. 309. In other national legal systems, there is no uniform view on the legal nature of the reparation order in the criminal trial, or it is of expressly mixed criminal and civil nature, see e.g. L. Zedner: "England". In: Wiedergutmachung im Kriminalrecht – Internationale Perspektiven – Reparation in Criminal Law – International Perspectives. Eds. A. Eser; S. Walther. Vol. 1. Freiburg i. Br., 1996, pp. 109 et seq. at pp. 169-180.

180 See also W. Heintschel von Heinegg: "Entschädigung für Verletzungen des Humanitären Völkerrechts". In: Entschädigung nach Bewaffneten Konflikten – Die Konstitutionalisierung der Welthandelsordnung. Eds. W. Heintschel von Heinegg; S. Kadelbach; B. Heß (et al.). Heidelberg, 2003, pp. 1 et seq. at p. 43.

primarily served by the core function to hold the perpetrators criminally responsible. The drafting debates of the Statute also do not support the view that the purpose of the ICC reparation order is punitive, as the option discussed to categorize reparations as a penalty was rejected.[181] Thus, reparations ordered by the ICC should focus on the victims, rather than the perpetrator of the crimes under the ICC's jurisdiction. This means that it is appropriate that ICC-ordered reparations be utilized for compensatory or restorative purposes.[182]

However, before the ICC, full compensation to individual victims, just as in the context of gross and systematic crimes in general, is, for expected lack of resources and the often irreparable nature of the harm caused, to a large extent unrealistic. Thus, due to necessity on the one hand and the broader, societal nature of the harm often caused by crimes under the ICC jurisdiction, it seems appropriate that ICC reparations serve purposes that focus on the restoration of victims' dignity, improvement of living conditions, as well as broader reconciliation. This is also supported by the strong part that is granted to the Victims Trust Fund which emphasizes the restorative and rehabilitative character of the ICC reparations scheme.

It seems that the applicability of the purposes of restorative justice in the ICC-context is restricted, in particular with regard to the side of the perpetrator. In view of the gravity of the crimes under the ICC's jurisdiction, the aspect of reintegration of offenders is inapplicable. Also regarding the purpose of reconciliation between victims and perpetrators by bringing them together, the options before the ICC seem limited.

However, victims' participation in the proceedings and reparation awards ordered by the ICC could potentially achieve effects both on the individual and collective level: to compensate or reduce harm, to restore the dignity of individual victims and to reintegrate them into society, as well as to trigger or support a broader process of societal reconciliation.[183]

181 See R. E. Fife: "Penalties". In: The International Criminal Court – The Making of the Rome Statute – Issues, Negotiations, Results. Ed. R. S. Lee. The Hague, 1999, pp. 319 et seq. at p. 330; F. McKay: "Are Reparations Appropriately Addressed in the ICC Statute?". In: International Crimes, Peace and Human Rights – The Role of the International Criminal Court. Ed. D. Shelton. Ardsley, New York, 2000, pp. 163 et seq. at pp. 169, 173; D. Donat-Cattin: "Article 75 – Reparations to Victims". In: Commentary on the Rome Statute of the International Criminal Court – Observers' Notes, Article by Article. Ed. O. Triffterer. Baden-Baden, 1999, pp. 965 et seq. at p. 973.

182 For a further discussion of the meaning of reparations for victims of gross and systematic crimes see M. Minow: Between Vengeance and Forgiveness – Facing History after Genocide and Mass Violence. Boston, 1998, p. 93 (focussing on psychological support); T. Winstel: "Über die Bedeutung der Wiedergutmachung im Leben der Jüdischen NS-Verfolgten – Erfahrungsgeschichtliche Annährungen". In: Nach der Verfolgung – Wiedergutmachung Nationalsozialistischen Unrechts in Deutschland?. Eds. H. G. Hockerts; C. Kuller. Göttingen, 2003, pp. 199 et seq. at p. 215 focussing on the relevance of material support.

183 Similar C. M. Bassiouni: Introduction to International Criminal Law. Ardsley, New York, 2003, p. 721 citing further authorities; D. Shelton: "Reparations for Victims of Interna-

Various forms of reparations may emphasize different purposes, While monetary forms of reparations emphasize the purpose of compensating harm, symbolic forms, such as an apology, predominately serve broader aims of reconciliation and restoration of individuals and collectives. It is also possible that reparations serve different purposes at the same time, e.g. ordering the convicted person to contribute to build a memorial might serve both punishment and reconciliation. However, if there is a conflict between the various purposes of reparations, then the primary focus should be on restoration and compensation, leaving punishment and deterrence to be achieved by the criminal conviction.

D. Assessment

The purpose of ICC-ordered reparations can be summarized as two-fold: firstly, it is in line with contemporary concepts of justice, that those found responsible for a crime are not only punished, but also obliged to repair, as far as possible, the harm caused to the victims of crime.

Secondly, reparations awarded by the ICC serve to complement its role to hold accountable individuals responsible for the commission of crimes under its jurisdiction. The underlying principle is that "true justice" can only be achieved when the crimes' victims are considered and their suffering is addressed.[184] Most victims will hardly be satisfied by a criminal conviction unless their harm is repaired in addition to the penalties applied. As the criminal proceedings and the conviction focus on the perpetrator, the reparation order made against the person convicted by the ICC shall primarily serve the needs and interests of victims. In the context of international criminal justice, these are determined by the harm suffered as a result of the crimes under international law.

International criminal law also protects the interests of individuals harmed by crimes under international law. However, due to the nature and scope of crimes under the ICC's jurisdiction, for which the ICC can only hold individuals responsible, individual compensation may remain partial. Thus, reparations should also aim at contributing to the broader restoration of, and reconciliation between victimized individuals, groups and societies.

The purpose of reparations awarded by the ICC cannot be to satisfy all needs of victims of crimes under its jurisdiction. The objectives of reparations are restricted to redress the harm caused to victims by a particular wrongdoing. Before the ICC that particular wrongdoing is the crime for which a person was convicted. However, the establishment of the ICC, and in particular the rights victims are granted before it,

tional Crimes". In: International Crimes, Peace, and Human Rights – The Role of the International Court. Ed. D. Shelton. Ardsley, New York, 2000, pp. 137 et seq. at p. 140.

184 G. Bitti; G. González Rivas: "The Reparations Provisions for Victims under the Rome Statute of the International Criminal Court". In: Redressing Injustices through Mass Claims Processes – Innovative Responses to Unique Challenges. Ed. The International Bureau of the Permanent Court of Arbitration. Oxford, 2006, pp. 299 et seq. at pp. 300-301.

can provide recognition, respect and compensation to victims of the crimes under the ICC's jurisdiction.

It has been demonstrated in this chapter that the ICC reparation system complements, rather than contradicts, the purposes of international criminal justice.

Chapter 4 Reparation Principles and Determination of the Scope and Extent of any Damage, Loss and Injury to, or in Respect of, Victims (Art. 75 (1) ICC Statute)

In the first Chapter of the main part of this study, the first provision of the reparation system mentioned in the ICC Statute will be examined. Art. 75 (1) contains two different competences: it establishes that the Court is legally required to establish principles relating to reparations and that it is within the discretion of the Court to determine the scope and extent of victims' damage, loss or injury.

A. Establishing Principles Pursuant to Art. 75 (1) s. 1 ICC Statute

The establishment of principles is the primary entitlement of the Court regarding reparations, as any other decision of the Court concerning reparations is discretionary.[185] There are several unresolved aspects regarding this competence, namely the question as to which purpose the principles serve, which Court organ shall establish them, and their possible legal nature and content.

I. Purpose of Reparation Principles

The Statute does not determine for which purpose the Court is to establish principles on reparations. They could set forth internal Court guidelines on all kinds of issues regarding reparations, in particular determination of damage, loss and injury (Art. 75 (1) s. 2) and reparations orders (Art. 75 (2)). These guidelines could be binding or declaratory. The reparations principles could also aim at an external effect, e.g. by referring to the available national procedures under which individual victims may have effective access to an appropriate civil remedy.[186] Or they could be addressed directly

185 Art. 75 (1) s. 1 states that "[t]he Court shall establish principles relating to reparations to, or in respect of, victims, including restitution, compensation and rehabilitation". In contrast, Art. 75 (1) s. 2 states that "the Court may [determine] the scope and extent of any damage, loss and injury [...]"; and Art. 75 (2) "The Court may make an order [...] specifying [...] reparations" (emphasis added).

186 See D. Donat-Cattin: "Article 75 – Reparations to Victims". In: Commentary on the Rome Statute of the International Criminal Court – Observers' Notes, Article by Article. Ed. O. Triffterer. Baden-Baden, 1999, pp. 965 et seq. at pp. 969, 972. This was proposed in Art. 45 bis A/51/22, S. 224 (G), while the possibility for the Court to itself make repara-

to neutral institutions, to states, and possibly to non-state actors or the international community.

The Statute indicates that in its decisions on the harm caused, the Court shall "state the principles upon which it is acting" (Art. 75 (1) s. 2). From this, and also from the fragmentary character of the reparations provisions, it can be concluded that the reparations principles are needed to set forth guidelines for, and limitations to, the activities of the Court and the implementing organs regarding reparations.

The principles seem important in order to secure conformity, fairness and a sufficient degree of legal certainty in the Court's decision-making on reparations, and in handling victims' claims. Legal certainty has been defined as one of modern jurisprudence's central concerns.[187] In accordance with the rule of law, justice is administered by enabling victims to be aware of fixing standards prior to the controversy and guarantees the same treatment for all individuals. While some flexibility is necessary, reparations principles are essential in order to prevent uncertainty and arbitrariness in the decision-making on reparations.[188] In order to achieve this aim, any internal guidelines on reparations should be binding upon the Court.

However, the establishment of principles that are not restricted to function as internal Court guidelines on reparations might increase the Court's potential to help achieve the purposes of reparations, namely to redress victims' harm and to contribute to reconciliation. Reparations principles aiming at an external effect may contribute to the clarification and strengthening of victims' rights to reparation for harm caused by gross and systematic crimes in general. This could help the effective implementation of this right in the national and international context. However, it seems preferable if they were not of merely general and declaratory character, as the 2005 Victims Principles exist for that purpose. The Court furthermore has the power to utilize the reparation principles to, if necessary, impose pressure on other responsible organs and institutions in order for them to join the efforts to redress the harm caused to victims under the ICC jurisdiction.

II. Organ Responsible for Establishing Reparation Principles and their Legal Nature

Art. 75 (1) generally states that "the Court" is to establish principles and thus does not specify which organ or organs is to do so. The Court is composed of the Registry, the Office of the Prosecutor, the Presidency, and the Chambers (consisting of the Pre-Trial, Trial and Appeals Divisions, Art. 34 ICC Statute). Thus, from the wording

tion order was only proposed later in the drafting phase, see proposal 2, 3 Draft ICC Statute "Zutphen-Draft", UN Doc. A/AC.249/1998/L.13, p. 124, see C. Möller: Völkerstrafrecht und Internationaler Strafgerichtshof – kriminologische, straftheoretische und rechtspolitische Aspekte. Münster, 2003, pp. 585-589.

187 See D. Shelton: "Reparations for Victims of International Crimes". In: International Crimes, Peace, and Human Rights – The Role of the International Court. Ed. D. Shelton. Ardsley, New York, 2000, pp. 137 et seq. at pp. 140-141.

188 Ibid.

of Art. 75 (1), it might be the duty of the Chambers in their judicial capacity, or the Court as an administrative organ, to adopt a sort of practice directions for reparations.[189]

Art. 75 is part of Part 6 of the Statute, termed "The Trial". The article refers to the "Court" and not the "Trial Chamber" and therefore permits the Court's other chambers to be involved in the establishment of the principles. The other paragraphs of Art. 75 and the congruent Rules mostly refer to the powers and tasks of "the Court" in contrast to the "Registry" or "Presidency".[190] The location of the article, and the tasks and competences assigned to "the Court", as e.g. set forth in Art. 75 (2) containing the competence of the Court to order the convicted person to make reparations, suggests that "the Court" shall be interpreted as the "Trial Chamber". Earlier drafts of Art. 75 included the statement that it would be for the "Trial Chamber" to establish principles regarding reparations.[191] In the relevant literature, it is assumed that it is the duty of the judges to establish principles.[192] From the context and history of Art. 75 (1), as well as the demand for a uniform interpretation of the term "the Court" in the entire reparations provisions, it is suggested that "the Court" is to be interpreted as the Trial Chambers, or Chambers in general.

As to the possible legal nature of the reparations principles, the Statute also leaves open whether they should be established as an abstract document, or developed on a case-by-case basis.[193] It could be argued that the placement of Art. 75 suggests a reference to the judicial function of the Court and thus the principles should be established jurisprudentially on a case-by-case basis.[194] If the principles are developed in the course of the Court's jurisprudence, the question remains whether they should be

189 See also S. Zappalà: Human Rights in International Criminal Proceedings. Oxford, 2003, p. 228.

190 E.g. Rules 94-96.

191 See text of Art. 45 bis ICC Statute (the forerunner of Art. 73/75) which intended to enable the Trial Chamber to "determine the scope and extent of the victimization and establish principles relating to compensation for damage caused to victims and to restitution of property unlawfully acquired by the person convicted [...]" referred to e.g. in C. Muttukumaru: "Reparations to Victims". In: Collection of Essays on the Rome Statute of the International Criminal Court. Eds. F. Lattanzi; W. A. Schabas. Ripa di Fagnano Alto, 1999, pp. 301 et seq. at pp. 304-305.

192 D. Donat-Cattin: "Article 75 – Reparations to Victims". In: Commentary on the Rome Statute of the International Criminal Court – Observers' Notes, Article by Article. Ed. O. Triffterer. Baden-Baden, 1999, pp. 965 et seq. at pp. 966, 977.

193 *Argumentum e contrario* of the wording of Art. 75 (1) s. 2 seems to suggest that the principles shall be rather general than being part of a decision referring a particular case: The Court shall establish principles and "[o]n this basis, in its decision, the Court may [...] determine the scope and extent of any damage [...]". The provisions on reparations in the Rules of Procedure and Evidence do not mention the principles of Art. 75 (1).

194 G. Bitti; G. González Rivas: "The Reparations Provisions for Victims under the Rome Statute of the International Criminal Court". In: Redressing Injustices through Mass Claims Processes – Innovative Responses to Unique Challenges. Ed. The International Bureau of the Permanent Court of Arbitration. Oxford, 2006, pp. 299 et seq. at p. 311.

of general character and thus applicable to all cases, or rather relate to specific cases before the Court. The Court´s verdicts could either include general statements on the right to restitution, compensation and rehabilitation. Verdicts could also include determinations on specific means of restitution or the quantum of compensation or the modalities that are aimed to contribute to rehabilitation.[195]

When the principles are established on a case-by-case basis, the risk is that different trial chambers could establish divergent principles, despite the same factual situations. However, in this case the Court's Appeals Chamber could harmonize the principles.[196]

A document containing abstract and binding reparations principles that are applicable in all cases would ensure legal certainty, prevent the impression of arbitrary decisions-making, and could manage victims' expectations towards reparations.[197] Yet, it seems difficult for the Court to determine a list of abstract reparations principles, as this would demand that all possible scenarios and cases must be considered and decided beforehand. Therefore, the danger with abstract principles is that they remain too general and thus do not substantially contribute to legal certainty.

As the Court has refrained from establishing abstract reparations principles so far, it seems that they will be established jurisprudentially by the Court's chambers on a case-by-case basis.

III. Scope and Content of Principles

The scope and content of the reparation principles is also left open by the Statute, providing the Court with almost unrestricted discretion. The term "principles" is broad and grants flexibility. Basic restrictions to the Court's discretion are provided by Art. 75 (1) where is stated that the principles shall relate to reparations to, or in respect of, victims, and shall include restitution, compensation and rehabilitation.[198]

195 D. Donat-Cattin: "Article 75 – Reparations to Victims". In: Commentary on the Rome Statute of the International Criminal Court – Observers' Notes, Article by Article. Ed. O. Triffterer. Baden-Baden, 1999, pp. 965 et seq. at pp. 969 et seq. furthermore suggests that in cases with large numbers of victims, specific determinations on reparations could be left to ad hoc arrangements with national authorities or the co-operation of states could be called upon to assist in reclaiming the assets taken by the perpetrators in accordance with Art. 109.

196 G. Bitti; G. González Rivas: "The Reparations Provisions for Victims under the Rome Statute of the International Criminal Court". In: Redressing Injustices through Mass Claims Processes – Innovative Responses to Unique Challenges. Ed. The International Bureau of the Permanent Court of Arbitration. Oxford, 2006, pp. 299 et seq. at p. 311.

197 In favor of a scope of principles that "extends to a generalized application" also M. Henzelin; V. Heiskanen; G. Mettraux: "Reparations to Victims before the International Criminal Court – Lessons from International Mass Claims Processes". In: Criminal Law Forum 17 (2006), pp. 317 et seq. at pp. 330-331.

198 I. Bottigliero: Redress for Victims of Crimes under International Law. Leiden, 2004, p. 223 points out that this non-exhaustive language resolved the lengthy debate at the Rome conference over redress terminology.

In addition, the general provisions on the scope of the Court's jurisdiction apply to its competence to establish reparation principles. Thus, the Court is only authorized to establish reparation principles that refer to crimes within the jurisdiction of the Court pursuant to Art. 5. In "accordance with this Statute" the principles must concern crimes committed after the entry into force of the Statute (Art. 11), committed on a territory or by a national over which the Court has jurisdiction or when a non-member state that has accepted jurisdiction (Art. 12).

The Court is also required to adhere to the principle of complementarity when establishing reparation principles.[199] That the ICC is complementary to national criminal jurisdictions "is an essential quality of the Court's jurisdictional system".[200] It determines that the Court shall be complementary to domestic criminal jurisdictions and shall have jurisdiction only where domestic courts are unwilling or unable to prosecute and punish individuals responsible for genocide, crimes against humanity, war crimes and eventually the crime of aggression.[201] The Statute does not expressly state what the complementarity principle means regarding reparations for victims. It could be considered advantageous for victims if the complementarity principle would not apply, so that in cases such as those where there is unwillingness to provide reparations on a national level, the reparation principles according to Art. 75 (1) might contribute to the legitimacy of victims' claims for reparations.[202]

However, as the ICC reparation system complements the Court's key task as a criminal court, it seems that the complementarity principle applies to reparations as well, including the power to establish reparation principles. Thus the Court's jurisdiction is complementary when domestic courts choose to investigate or prosecute cases that concern crimes under the Court's jurisdiction, even though the state in question is unable or unwilling to provide reparations to the victims of such crimes. While reference to a particular set of crimes that are being prosecuted by domestic courts would thus seem critical, reparation principles of general and declaratory character would not violate the complementarity principle.

199 Regarding issues of reparations and complementarity, see T. Ingadottir: "The Trust Fund for Victims (Art. 79 of the Rome Statute)". In: The International Criminal Court – Recommendations on Policy and Practice – Financing, Victims, Judges, and Immunities. Ed. T. Ingadottir. Ardsley, New York, 2003, pp. 111 et seq. at p. 119 and further discussion below Chapter III. 4.2).

200 M. Bergsmo; O. Triffterer: "Preamble". In: Commentary on the Rome Statute of the International Criminal Court – Observers' Notes, Article by Article. Ed. O. Triffterer. Baden-Baden, 1999, pp. 1 et seq. at 15.

201 Preamble, Art. 1, see also Art. 17 ICC Statute.

202 I. Bottigliero: Redress for Victims of Crimes under International Law. Leiden, 2004, pp. 235 et seq. suggests that in case domestic courts or institutions continue to be unwilling or unable to provide reparations the Court could then consider a serious and structural lack of adequate and effective domestic redress mechanisms among the criteria to determine the liability of a state to administer justice in a situation falling within the jurisdiction of the ICC in order to then exercise jurisdiction directly or allow victims' access to the ICC Trust Fund.

In Art. 75 (1) the drafters of the Statute have equipped the Court with an almost legislative function. However, in establishing reparation principles the Court is to act in accordance with the requirements set forth by Art. 21.[203] Thus, the principles must be consistent with the ICC Statute and Rules, and, if appropriate, in line with applicable treaties and the principles and rules of international law, and comply with general principles of law derived by the Court from national laws of legal systems of the world.[204]

Except for the restrictions deriving from the Statute and Rules, the Court is free to decide on the content of the reparation principles. At the Rome Conference, the key issues debated in this context were the concept of "reparations" and the scope of "victims", while the main controversy centered on the extent to which the Court should engage in individual cases of damage, loss and injury in relation to a crime.[205] Principles could also be of mainly procedural content, clarifying issues such as burden and standard of proof, and causation. While a definition of "victim" was included in the Rules, the other issues were left open, leaving them for the Court to determine in its principles.[206]

Art. 21 on applicable law provides guidelines according to which the reparation principles are to be established. In particular, it is crucial to ensure that that their content conforms with "internationally recognized human rights".[207] The drafting history of Art. 75 suggests that the concept and content of reparations shall be determined with reference to the 1985 Victims Declaration and the draft Basic Principles, which have since been adopted in form of the 2005 Victims Principles.[208]

---

203 On Art. 21 and its relevance for the ICC reparations mechanism, see Chapter 1 B. above.

204 According to Art. 21 (1) c) general principles of national laws include the national laws of States that would normally exercise jurisdiction over the crime, provided that those principles are not inconsistent with this Statute and with international law and internationally recognized norms and standards.

205 P. Lewis; H. Friman: "Reparations to Victims". In: The International Criminal Court – Elements of Crimes and Rules of Procedure and Evidence. Ed. R. S. Lee. Ardsley, New York, 2001, pp. 474 et seq. at p. 477.

206 A footnote in the Report of the Working Group on Procedural Matters of the Rome Conference reflected the view of some delegations regarding Art. 75 (1) that "This provision intends that where there are only a few victims the Trial Chamber may make findings about their damage, loss or injury. Where there are more than a few victims, however, the Trial Chamber will not attempt to take evidence from or enter orders identifying separate victims or concerning their individual claims for reparations. Instead, the Trial Chamber may make findings as to whether reparations are due because of the crimes and will not undertake to consider and decide claims of individual victims." footnote 6 to Art. 73 on reparations to victims in Report of the Working Group on Procedural Matters of the Rome Conference, A/CONF.183/C.1/WGPM/L.2/Add.7 (1998).

207 See discussion on the relevance of Art. 21 for the implementation of the ICC reparation system above Chapter 1 B.

208 The footnote contained in Art. 73 of the ICC Draft Statute that for the purposes of defining "victims" and "reparation", reference should be made to the definitions contained in

IV. *Who Can the Reparation Principles Be Addressed to?*

If it is decided that the reparation principles shall go beyond establishing internal guidelines, the question arises as to whom the Court is competent to address the principles to. While the Court can only order a convicted individual person to make reparation[209], it might also be competent to address reparation principles to other entities that carry responsibility, such as states, corporations and the international community.

1. States

An individual may be convicted by the Court for a crime under its jurisdiction that at the same time gives rise to state responsibility.[210] At the Rome Conference the issue of state responsibility for reparations was the most difficult to resolve during the negotiations on Art. 75.[211] As the majority of states clearly rejected the possibility of the Court imposing liability onto states, the proposal that contained the Court's

Art. 44 (4) and Art. 68 (1) and its accompanying footnote and the 1985 Victims Declaration and the Draft Basic Principles and Guidelines on the Right to a Remedy and Reparation for Victims of Violations of Human Rights and International Humanitarian Law, see D. Donat-Cattin: "Article 75 – Reparations to Victims". In: Commentary on the Rome Statute of the International Criminal Court – Observers' Notes, Article by Article. Ed. O. Triffterer. Baden-Baden, 1999, pp. 965 et seq. at p. 969 (footnote 23). The former "Draft Basic Principles and Guidelines on the Right to a Remedy and Reparation for Victims of Violations of Human Rights and International Humanitarian Law", have now been adopted by the UN General Assembly ("2005 Victims Principles").

209 Art. 75 (2). The lack of competence to make reparations orders against states may also be seen as the consequence of the core purpose of the ICC Statute to prosecute and convict individual persons responsible for committing grave crimes, as opposed to states (or other entities). See C. Muttukumaru: "Reparations to Victims". In: Collection of Essays on the Rome Statute of the International Criminal Court. Eds. F. Lattanzi; W. A. Schabas. Ripa di Fagnano Alto, 1999, pp. 301 et seq. at p. 308: "If awards of reparations could be made against States, the principle of individual responsibility would have become meaningless."

210 See G. Werle: Principles of International Criminal Law. The Hague, 2005, pp. 35 et seq.; M. Frulli: "Jurisdiction Ratione Personae". In: The Rome Statute of the International Criminal Court – A Commentary. Eds. A. Cassese, P. Gaeta; J. R. W. D. Jones. Vol. 1. Oxford, 2002, pp. 527 et seq. at p. 533: "It may happen-and it is very likely in some situations-that individuals brought to trial before the ICC are organs of a State, or de facto agents of State or acted 'in the name of the State', even if not endowed with any legal power". See for the context of the different crimes under the ICC jurisdiction and state responsibility P.-M. Dupuy: "International Criminal Responsibility of the Individual and International Responsibility of the State". In: The Rome Statute of the International Criminal Court – A Commentary. Eds. A. Cassese; P. Gaeta; J. R. W. D. Jones. Vol. 2. Oxford, 2002, pp. 1085 et seq. at p. 1088 et seq.

211 C. Muttukumaru: "Reparations to Victims". In: Collection of Essays on the Rome Statute of the International Criminal Court. Eds. F. Lattanzi; W. A. Schabas. Ripa di Fagnano Alto, 1999, pp. 301 et seq. at p. 307.

competence to order or recommend states to award reparations to victims was not incorporated into the ICC Statute.[212] However, the drafting history is a "supplementary means of interpretation" of a norm in an international treaty.[213]
For a number of reasons, active cooperation and support by states involved in the cases before it is essential to the functioning of the ICC reparation system. In view of the large numbers of victims that genocide, crimes against humanity and war crimes regularly cause, collective entities like states are often in a more appropriate position to provide effective reparations to victims than individual perpetrators. Furthermore, certain forms of reparations can by their nature only be imposed by states, e.g. the release of prisoners, enacting appropriate remedial legislation or granting access to public services. For other types of measures, consultations with governments may be necessary and desirable to implement certain forms of reparations. This is particularly true in regard to collective reparations.[214] Furthermore, without state cooperation to enforce protective measures and to implement reparation orders, as well as conducting their own national reparation measures, it could prove difficult to effectively provide reparations and justice to victims.[215] It is therefore worth examining whether the ICC Statute would allow the Court to address reparation principles to states.

The wording of Art. 75 (2) is unambiguous in stating that only the convicted person can be ordered to make reparations. The Court's power to exercise judicial func-

212 The Preparatory Committee Draft Statute had a provision containing that " [t]he Court may also [make an order] [recommend] that an appropriate form of reparations to, or in respect of, victims, including restitution, compensation, rehabilitation, be made by a State]: [if the convicted person is unable to do so himself/herself; [and – if the convicted person was, when committing the offense, acting on behalf of that State in an official capacity, and within the course and scope of his/her authority]]; c) [in any case other than those referred to in subparagraph b), the Court may also recommend that States grant an appropriate form of reparations to, or in respect of, victims, including restitution, compensation and rehabilitation] ", see Report on the Establishment of an International Criminal Court, Draft Statute and Final Act, UN Doc. A/Conf.183/2/Add.1 (1998), supra note 12, Art. 73. Another proposal set forth that "[t]he Court may also determine that an appropriate form of reparation to, or in respect of, a victim or victims, including restitution, compensation a rehabilitation shall be granted by national courts or Governments in accordance with the terms of any order the Court may make pursuant to the provisions of paragraph of this article", Art. 66 [45 bis] Compensation to victims; A/AC.29/1998WG.4/DP.19/10 February, see C. Möller: Völkerstrafrecht und Internationaler Strafgerichtshof – kriminologische, straftheoretische und rechtspolitische Aspekte. Münster, 2003, p. 590.

213 Art. 32 Vienna Convention on the Law of Treaties (1979).

214 See Chapter 5 C. 4 ("Other Forms of Reparations") below.

215 C. Jorda; J. de Hemptinne: "The Status and Role of the Victim". In: The Rome Statute of the International Criminal Court – A Commentary. Eds. A. Cassese; P. Gaeta; J. R. W. D. Jones. Vol. 2. Oxford, 2002, pp. 1387 et seq. at p. 1410 quoting further authorities, noting that it will be difficult to avoid directly implicating the state concerned in responsibility for these mass crimes while at the same time imposing measures which are of a nature that the whole community or nation will be touched.

tions relates to natural persons only.[216] However, it is questionable whether establishing reparation principles is an exercise of a judicial function. Art. 25 (4) sets forth that "[n]o provision in this Statute relating to individual criminal responsibility shall affect the responsibility of States under international law". One of the ICC's fundamental principles is that of complementarity. Accordingly, the Statute emphasizes that despite the existence of the ICC and its reparation system, the obligation of states under international and national law not only to prosecute, but also to make reparations to victims remains.[217]

Due to the collective nature of the crimes under the jurisdiction of the Court, often the persons prosecuted and convicted by the Court are organs of a state, de facto agents of state or acting 'in the name of the state', even when not endowed with any legal power.[218] Under these circumstances, state responsibility to make reparations arises. The Statute emphasizes that an ICC reparation order against the convicted person does not diminish any responsibility to make reparations to victims that rests upon states under other treaties.[219] The 2005 Victims Principles state that "[i]n accordance with its domestic laws and international legal obligations, a State shall provide reparation to victims for acts or omissions which can be attributed to the State and constitute gross violations of international human rights law or serious violations of international humanitarian law" and that "States should endeavour to establish

216 Art. 1 attributes to the Court jurisdiction over persons for the most serious crimes of international concern. In a similar way Art. 25 (1) determines that the "Court shall have jurisdiction over natural persons" only. See M. Frulli: "Jurisdiction Ratione Personae". In: The Rome Statute of the International Criminal Court – A Commentary. Eds. A. Cassese, P. Gaeta; J. R. W. D. Jones. Vol. 1. Oxford, 2002, pp. 527 et seq. at p. 537 referring to *The Prosecutor v. Blaskić*, Judgement on the Request of the Republic of Croatia for Review of the Decision of Trial Chamber II, ICTY Appeals Chamber, 18 July 1997, Case No. IT-95-14, para.28.

217 See Preamble, Art. 75 (6). For the relation of state responsibility and individual reparations claims, see R. R. Hofmann: "Victims of Violations of International Humanitarian Law – Do They Have an Individual Right to Reparation against States under International Law?". In: Völkerrecht als Wertordnung – Common Values in International Law – Festschrift für Christian Tomuschat – Essays in Honour of Christian Tomuschat. Eds. P.-M. Dupuy; B. Fassbender; M. N. Shaw; K.-P. Sommermann. Kehl am Rhein (et al.), 2006, pp. 341 et seq.

218 In fact, the Charters of the Nuremberg and Tokyo International Military Tribunals authorized them to consider only cases of individuals who acted 'on behalf of' the Axis countries. Art. 6 of the Nuremberg Charter determines that this covers both individual state agents and those who de facto acted for the Nazi state, see further P.-M. Dupuy: "International Criminal Responsibility of the Individual and International Responsibility of the State". In: The Rome Statute of the International Criminal Court – A Commentary. Eds. A. Cassese; P. Gaeta; J. R. W. D. Jones. Vol. 2. Oxford, 2002, pp. 1085 et seq. at pp. 1087 et seq.

219 Art. 75 (6) reads "Nothing in this article shall be interpreted as prejudicing the rights of victims under national or international law". Art. 25 (4) states that "[n]o provision in this Statute relating to individual criminal responsibility shall affect the responsibility of States under international law].

national programmes for reparation and other assistance to victims in the event that the party liable for the harm suffered is unable or unwilling to meet their obligations."[220] Under the 1985 Victims Declaration, when crimes are committed by public officials or those acting in quasi-official authority, victims should receive restitution from the government whose officials or agents are responsible for the harm inflicted; if this state or government no longer exists, the successor government shall instead be responsible for compensating victims.[221] Thus, there may be a sufficient legal basis for the Court to remind states to comply with their legal obligations to award reparations to victims as a primary or secondary responsibility as a part of the reparation principles established pursuant to Art. 75 (1).

There is no consensus among commentators as to whether the Court is competent to express its opinion regarding a state's duty to make reparations to victims.

It has been argued that the Court will not be prevented from expressing its opinion regarding the State's complicity in the crime "through its judgments".[222] Others have noted that "the possibility of vicarious liability remains open where the individual in question was a State actor".[223] Others advocate that the Court, even though it only deals with individual criminal responsibility, may consult with governments in order to achieve similar forms of reparations as are available under state responsibility.[224]

In contrast, a number of commentators assert that the Court lacks competence both to order states to award reparations and to articulate recommendations to states, mainly referring to the rejection of this competence in the making of the Statute.[225]

220 Principles 15, 16.

221 Art. 11.

222 C. Muttukumaru: "Reparations to Victims". In: Collection of Essays on the Rome Statute of the International Criminal Court. Eds. F. Lattanzi; W. A. Schabas. Ripa di Fagnano Alto, 1999, pp. 301 et seq. at pp. 307 et seq.

223 I. Bottigliero: Redress for Victims of Crimes under International Law. Leiden, 2004, p. 223; see also B. Timm: "The Legal Position of Victims in the Rule of Procedure and Evidence". In: International and National Prosecution of Crimes under International Law. Eds. H. Fischer, C. Kreß; S. R. Lüder. (Bochumer Schriften zur Friedenssicherung und zum Humanitären Völkerrecht). Berlin, 2001, pp. 289 et seq. at p. 308 notes that it is typically for a criminal sanction that the offender has to pay reparations from its own pocket while with civil compensation, any other person or entity, could fulfill this obligation as it is only relevant that the damage is compensated. Thus, e.g. the state responsible, could substitute the payment of the convicted person.

224 G. Bitti; G. González Rivas: "The Reparations Provisions for Victims under the Rome Statute of the International Criminal Court". In: Redressing Injustices through Mass Claims Processes – Innovative Responses to Unique Challenges. Ed. The International Bureau of the Permanent Court of Arbitration. Oxford, 2006, pp. 299 et seq. at p. 310.

225 W. Heintschel von Heinegg: "Entschädigung für Verletzungen des Humanitären Völkerrechts". In: Entschädigung nach Bewaffneten Konflikten – Die Konstitutionalisierung der Welthandelsordnung. Eds. W. Heintschel von Heinegg; S. Kadelbach; B. Heß (et al.). Heidelberg, 2003, pp. 1 et seq. at p. 43; D. Donat-Cattin: "Article 75 – Reparations to Victims". In: Commentary on the Rome Statute of the International Criminal Court – Observers' Notes, Article by Article. Ed. O. Triffterer. Baden-Baden, 1999, pp. 965 et seq. at pp. 966

A need to unilaterally address principles on reparations to states might be avoided when the Court seeks the involvement of interested states in the reparations proceedings.[226] States might themselves have an interest to implement reparations. Thus, possibly even countries that have been "unwilling or unable" to prosecute the crimes which fall within the jurisdiction of the ICC may be willing to assist in the implementation of reparation awards, whose aims to reconcile and to reconstruct might be acknowledged. A state might be especially willing to cooperate with the Court and to implement reparations when the ICC's investigations have been triggered by a referral by a state party that would regularly have jurisdiction over the crimes to the ICC.[227]

Clearly, the ICC does not have the power establish principles that are binding on states, as this would come close to ordering them to make reparations, a power that is not covered by the Statute.[228] The wording and context of Art. 75 (1) neither expressly exclude nor allow for the possibility of establishing principles that may also contain recommendations to states to implement certain reparation measures to victims.

However, as a criminal court it is particularly obliged to construe strictly the powers it derives from its legal instruments.[229] Furthermore, allegations that the Court acts *ultra vires* – whether justified or not – could seriously impair the willingness of member states and non-member states to cooperate with the Court. As the Court has thus much to lose, it seems necessary for the Court to be cautious in addressing even non-binding reparations principles to states. Clearly, this power should only be exercised in cases in which the Court orders reparations pursuant to Art. 75 (2) or

et seq.: "It is [...] necessary to clarify from the outset that article 75 does not deal with any issue relating to States' responsibility, either in the sense of sanctioning the State for the benefit of the individual victim, or in respect of issuing orders against the State"; F. McKay: "Are Reparations Appropriately Addressed in the ICC Statute?". In: International Crimes, Peace and Human Rights – The Role of the International Criminal Court. Ed. D. Shelton. Ardsley, New York, 2000, pp. 163 et seq. at p. 173: "Some were disappointed that the Court will not have power to order states to provide reparation, or even to recommend them to do so"; C. Jorda; J. de Hemptinne: "The Status and Role of the Victim". In: The Rome Statute of the International Criminal Court – A Commentary. Eds. A. Cassese; P. Gaeta; J. R. W. D. Jones. Vol. 2. Oxford, 2002, pp. 1387 et seq. at 1410 stating that "the main difficulty facing the judges will be to avoid directly implicating the State concerned in responsibility for such mass crimes".

226 See Rules 94-98 and discussion in Chapter 6 B. 3 b).

227 Art. 14 ICC Statute reads: "A State Party may refer to the Prosecutor a situation in which one or more crimes within the jurisdiction of the Court appear to have been committed requesting the Prosecutor to investigate the situation for the purpose of determining whether one or more specific persons should be charged with the commission of such crimes."

228 Art. 25 (1); Art. 75 (2).

229 The rule of strict construction of criminal law is codified in Art. 22, see W. A. Schabas: "Interpreting the Statutes of the Ad Hoc Tribunals". In: Man's Inhumanity to Man – Essays on International Law in Honour of Antonio Cassese. Eds. L. C. Vorah; F. Pocar; Y. Featherstone (et al.). The Hague, 2003, pp. 846 et seq. at p. 848.

would be able to do so. Generally, it seems more promising for the Court to enter into a voluntary mutual dialogue with interested states on implementing reparations to victims.

In this context it can be noted that with regard to states parties the ICC is equipped with mandatory powers to oblige states to carry out certain measures, encompassing international cooperation and judicial assistance which do not have to be stated in the reparation principles.[230]

2. Corporations and other Judicial Persons

Corporations, such as multinational companies, might be accomplices in the commission of crimes under the jurisdiction of the ICC.[231] Military regimes can be contracted to provide security for the business enterprises of corporations, and multinational corporations have been among the primary beneficiaries of situations in which gross and systematic crimes are committed.

While legal persons can be recipients of reparations ordered by the ICC, the ICC lacks the authority to impose legal responsibility onto corporations. [232] Art. 25 (1), (2) and (3) leave no doubt that "by limiting criminal responsibility to individual natural persons, the Rome Statute implicitly negates – at least for its own jurisdiction – the punishability of corporations and other legal entities".[233] As stated, Art. 75 (2) only allows for reparation orders against the convicted person.

The Draft Statute of 1998 contained a proposal which allowed subjecting legal entities – with the exception of states – to the jurisdiction of the ICC if 'the crimes were committed on behalf of such legal persons or by their agencies or representatives'.[234] The primary intention of the inclusion of legal persons was to make it easier

230 Part 9 ICC Statute, in particular Art. 93 and Art. 109. M. Frulli: "Jurisdiction Ratione Personae". In: The Rome Statute of the International Criminal Court – A Commentary. Eds. A. Cassese, P. Gaeta; J. R. W. D. Jones. Vol. 1. Oxford, 2002, pp. 527 et seq. at p. 537, terming the Court's competence regarding States "ancillary (or incidental) mandatory powers vis-à-vis States" with reference to ICTY jurisprudence.

231 See e.g. A. Clapham: "The Question of Jurisdiction under International Criminal Law over Legal Persons – Lessons from the Rome Conference on an International Criminal Court". In: Liability of Multinational Corporations under International Law. Eds. M. T. Kamminga; S. Zia-Zarifi. The Hague, 2000, pp. 139 et seq.; D. Shelton: Remedies in International Human Rights Law. 2nd ed. Oxford, 2005, pp. 155 et seq.; H. Rombouts; P. Sardaro; S. Vandeginste: "The Right to Reparation for Victims of Gross and Systematic Violations of Human Rights". In: Out of the Ashes – Reparation for Victims of Gross and Systematic Human Rights Violations. Eds. K. de Feyter; S. Parmentier; M. Bossuyt (et al.). Antwerp, 2005, pp. 345 et seq. at pp. 485-486.

232 Pursuant to Art. 75 (2) read in conjunction with Rule 85 (b), also legal persons can qualify as victims eligible for reparations.

233 A. Eser: "Individual Criminal Responsibility". In: The Rome Statute of the International Criminal Court – A Commentary. Eds. A. Cassese; P. Gaeta; J. R. W. D. Jones. Vol. 2. Oxford, 2002, pp. 767 et seq. at p. 778.

234 For a summary of the discussion on the punishment for corporate entities also R. E. Fife: "Article 77 – Applicable Penalties". In: Commentary on the Rome Statute of the Interna-

for victims to obtain restitution and compensation.[235] As with state liability, during the negotiations leading to the ICC Statute, the proposal to include corporate liability was dropped.[236]

However, individuals that are part of or represent a corporation or other collective entity can be held responsible by the Court. The current ICC Chief Prosecutor, Luis Moreno-Ocampo, announced an investigation into the activities of corporations in a number of states who are suspected of helping to finance ethnic violence in the Congo, expressing the intention that corporate executives who knowingly trade with the perpetrators of war crimes shall be prosecuted as "participants in crimes".[237]

Particularly when the activity of a corporation or other legal entity can be traced back and attributed to a person convicted before the Court recommendations, for these entities to make reparations to victims could be part of the reparation principles. As with recommendations that the ICC can possibly address to states, it is clear that recommendations concerning corporations or other legal entities can only be of non-binding nature.

However, reference to the responsibility of corporations or other legal persons to make reparations as a part of the ICC reparation principles is more complex than addressing such a responsibility for states. Firstly, the ICC Statute only refers to state responsibility.[238] Secondly, the international law of state responsibility is well established. In contrast, while corporations possess rights and duties under international law, which implies that corporations are legally responsible for complying with international standards, the obligations of corporations are self-imposed or declaratory, rather than legally binding.[239]

---

tional Criminal Court – Observers' Notes, Article by Article. Ed. O. Triffterer. Baden-Baden, 1999, pp. 985 et seq. at pp. 993-994 referring to Report on the Establishment of an International Criminal Court, Draft Statute and Final Act, UN Doc. A/Conf.183/2/Add.1 (1998), at pp. 121-122; W.A. Schabas, Penalties, in A. Cassese [et al.] (eds.), The Rome Statute of the International Criminal Court, p. 1497 at pp. 1503-1304.

235 A. Eser: "Individual Criminal Responsibility". In: The Rome Statute of the International Criminal Court – A Commentary. Eds. A. Cassese; P. Gaeta; J. R. W. D. Jones. Vol. 2. Oxford, 2002, pp. 767 et seq. at p. 779 quoting further authorities.

236 Ibid.; I. Bottigliero: Redress for Victims of Crimes under International Law. Leiden, 2004, p. 214. The arguments raised against this proposal were, among others, that the ICC would face great evidentiary problems when prosecuting legal entities, that criminal liability of corporations is still rejected in many national legal orders, and that it was felt "morally obtuse for States to insist on the criminal responsibility of all entities other than themselves", and that enforcement would be difficult.

237 S. Glickman: "Victims' Justice – Legitimizing the Sentencing Regime of the International Criminal Court". In: Columbia Journal of Transnational Law 43 (2005), pp. 229 et seq. at p. 266 quotes A. Deutsch: "Prosecutors will Investigate Businesses for Links to Congo War Crimes". Associated Press Newswires. 23 September 2003. Available at www.encyclopedia.com/doc/1P1-81326245.html, last accessed 14 May 2008.

238 Art. 25 (4).

239 T. A. Bridgeford: "Imputing Human Rights Obligations on Multinational Corporations – The Ninth Circuit Strikes Again in Judicial Activism". In: American University Interna-

The 2005 Victims Principles determine that "[i]n cases where [...] a legal person, or other entity is found liable for reparation to a victim, such party should provide reparation to the victim or compensate the State if the State has already provided reparation to the victim."[240] Furthermore, the United Nations Economic and Social Council recently drafted the "Human Rights Principles and Responsibilities for Transnational Corporations and Other Business Enterprises", which reaffirm the responsibility of multinational corporations, thereby contributing to the development of international law that speaks directly to their responsibilities and obligations.[241] The Charter of the International Military Tribunal for Nuremberg did contain provisions on criminal organizations, although it did not provide for penalties against such organizations.[242] In national legal systems major differences exist as to the individual legal responsibility of legal persons.[243] In particular in courts of the US, victims have effectively filed claims against multinational companies and banks as perpetrators of international

tional Law Review 18 (2003), pp. 1009 et seq. at p. 1015 refers to N. Jumagers: "The Legal Status of the Multinational Corporation under International Law". In: Human Rights Standards and the Responsibility of Transnational Corporations. Ed. M. K. Addo. The Hague, 1999, pp. 259 et seq.; see generally M. T. Kamminga; S. Zia-Zarifi (eds.): Liability of Multinational Corporations under International Law. The Hague, 2000.

240 Principle 15. The 1985 Victims Declaration leaves open the option of reparations for victims of crime for which third parties are responsible, see Principle 8: "Offenders or third parties responsible for their behaviour should, where appropriate, make fair restitution to victims, their families of dependants."

241 See UN Commission on Human Rights: Norms on the Responsibility of Transnational Corporations and Other Business Enterprises with regard to Human Rights, 13 August 2003, E/CN.4/Sub.2/2003/12/Rev.2, particularly Art. 11.

242 Art. 9.

243 See R. E. Fife: "Article 77 – Applicable Penalties". In: Commentary on the Rome Statute of the International Criminal Court – Observers' Notes, Article by Article. Ed. O. Triffterer. Baden-Baden, 1999, pp. 985 et seq. at pp. 993-994.

crimes.[244] Their responsibility was constructed by applying the international criminal standard for aiding and abetting.[245]

The ICC could address non-binding reparation principles to legal persons with reference to Art. 75 (6) and to precedents set in national courts and international documents which support victims' rights to reparations vis-à-vis corporations. While the legal basis for a corporation' responsibility to make reparations is weak, from a strategic point of view it could be less critical to take a pro-active approach towards corporations. In contrast to states, the functioning of the ICC does not depend on the support and cooperation of corporations. Non-binding recommendations to corporations and other legal entities might trigger their voluntary contributions to the Trust Fund or their involvement in affording reparations to victims in national reparations programs. [246]

3. International Community

On the basis of two grounds, reparation principles could call upon the international community to join efforts to repair the harm caused to victims of crimes under the ICC jurisdiction.[247]

---

244 E.g. Doe I v. Unocal Corp., Nos. 00-56603, 00-57197, 00-56628, 00-57195, 2002 WL 31063976, at 24 (9th Cir. Sept. 18, 2002: Decision obliging the multi-national corporation Unocal Corporation, Unocal Oil Company of California, and two Unocal executives to make reparation to 15 Myanmar villagers mostly in the US under the ATCA. See generally T. A. Bridgeford: "Imputing Human Rights Obligations on Multinational Corporations – The Ninth Circuit Strikes Again in Judicial Activism". In: American University International Law Review 18 (2003), pp. 1009 et seq. At times these lead to settlements and subsequent establishment of compensation funds for victims, see e.g. Swiss Bank Settlement; claims against German industry leading to the establishment of the Foundation "Remembrance, Responsibility, Future"; Riggs Bank and two members of the bank's controlling family agreed to pay $ 9 million to a foundation established for victims of the Pinochet Regime before a Spanish Court, see T. O'Hara: "Allbrittons, Riggs to Pay Victims of Pinochet". In: Washington Post (Saturday, 26 February 2005, p. A01). Available at www.washingtonpost.com/wp-dyn/articles/A53805-2005Feb25.html, last accessed 21 April 2009.

245 Doe I v. Unocal Corp., Nos. 00-56603, 00-57197, 00-56628, 00-57195, 2002 WL 31063976, at 24 (9th Cir. Sept. 18, 2002), p. 12 stating that liability under the ATCA is the aiding and abetting theory developed by the ICTY and ICTR.

246 T. Ingadottir: "The Trust Fund for Victims (Art. 79 of the Rome Statute)". In: The International Criminal Court – Recommendations on Policy and Practice – Financing, Victims, Judges, and Immunities. Ed. T. Ingadottir. Ardsley, New York, 2003, pp. 111 et seq. at pp. 128-129, observes that corporations might have interest in contributing to victims redress themselves and suggests the possibility of contributions to the Trust Fund with reference of agreement of German companies and the State of Germany with the US on slave labor compensation.

247 The "International Community" can be defined as "[t]he sum total of all states, international intergovernmental organizations, and all of civil society acting collectively […]", H. V. Condé: A Handbook of International Human Rights Terminology. 2nd ed. Lincoln (et al.), 2004, p. 131.

First, there might be cases where the view is justified that the international community did not live up to their "responsibility to protect" and did not prevent the commission of crimes under the ICC jurisdiction.[248] The international community might therefore bear moral, rather than legal responsibility to repair the consequences of the crime.[249] This argument could be drawn upon either when organizations representing the international community refrained from intervening in the commission of the crimes or when UN or other troops representing sections of the "international community" did intervene, but did not succeed in preventing the commission of genocide, crimes against humanity and war crimes.[250]

Secondly, the principle of collective solidarity could justify addressing reparation principles to the international community. Particularly when the ICC cannot establish the liability of an individual because the accused is not arrested or the convicted person does not have sufficient assets to compensate the harm caused, the international community could consider itself responsible to ensure the functioning of the ICC reparation system.[251]

Securing reparation awards to victims from means provided for by the international community would strengthen the principle of collective solidarity on an international level, a principle which is familiar in the national and international law context. [252]

248 As pronounced e.g. in World Summit Outcome 2005, G.A. Res. 60/1 of 24 October 2005.

249 See also S. Zappalà: Human Rights in International Criminal Proceedings. Oxford, 2003, p. 231, stating that by doing so, the international community could show its concern and support for the victims of a crime that it failed to prevent. On the concepts of moral and legal responsibility E. van Sliedregt: The Criminal Responsibility of Individuals for Violations of International Humanitarian Law. The Hague, 2003, pp. 347 et seq.

250 E.g. see critical role of UN and NATO troops in conflict situations are the scenarios of the massive atrocities committed in Rwanda and the former Yugoslavia.

251 See also C. Jorda; J. de Hemptinne: "The Status and Role of the Victim". In: The Rome Statute of the International Criminal Court – A Commentary. Eds. A. Cassese; P. Gaeta; J. R. W. D. Jones. Vol. 2. Oxford, 2002, pp. 1387 et seq. at p. 1415 suggesting that where the accused is not arrested, or where a convicted person does not have sufficient assets, victims should be awarded compensation through the Trust Fund. The cost for this shall be borne directly by the International Community. This would also enshrine on the international level the principle of collective solidarity which is familiar in the field of domestic law. Once the perpetrator is arrested and convicted, he shall be required to reimburse the sums due to the Trust Fund; similar A. Strand: "Bombs and Butter – Compensation Issues in Protracted Conflicts and the Case of Afghanistan". In: Reparations – Redressing Past Wrongs. Eds. G. Ulrich; L. Krabbe Boserup. (Human Rights in Development – Yearbook 2001). The Hague, 2003, pp. 109 et seq. at pp. 113-114.

252 See Art. 12 1985 Victims Declaration; Principle 16 2005 Victims Principles; Art. 13 2001 EU Framework Decision; regarding the international context Art. 41 ILC Draft Articles provides that "States shall cooperate to bring to an end through lawful means any serious breach within the meaning of Article 40". Examples of peremptory norms of international law which Art. 40 refers to are the prohibition of aggression, genocide, apartheid, racial discrimination, slavery, slave trade, referred to in D. Shelton: "Righting Wrongs – Repara-

The international community cannot be addressed in reparation principles with reference to provisions in the ICC Statute. A failure of the international community to prevent the commission of international crimes does not give rise to a duty beyond a moral obligation. However, the Court could consider establishing principles that appeal to organizations and other entities representing the international community to make voluntary payments to the Trust Fund, or support victims of crimes under the ICC's jurisdiction in other ways.

V. *Assessment*

The reparation principles are necessary in order to establish internal guidelines that the Court shall regard as binding in order to reach some degree of legal certainty and consistency, and also would assist to manage victim expectations. Furthermore, the establishment of reparation principles is necessary in order to safeguard an efficient functioning of the Court. For example, setting forth criteria for eligibility to reparations might reduce the number of clearly ineligible reparation claims.[253]

The principles may be formulated by the Chambers of the Court.

The term "principles" grants the Court broad authority to formulate reparations policy. While the content of the ICC reparation principles shall be in line with international standards, it is not restricted to reproduce the principles established in international and national documents and practice only. Reparations in international criminal law are legally unique. Thus, while international and national documents and practice must be drawn upon to justify and support the establishment of certain concepts, the principles pursuant to Art. 75 (1) may deviate from established law and practice, where appropriate.

Especially in cases where the convicted person acted on behalf of states, corporations or other legal entities, principles that are established in a case-by-case basis could also address the corresponding entity, in the form of non-binding recommendations.[254] On a case-by-case basis, certain states, the international community or

tions in the Articles on State Responsibility". In: American Journal of International Law 96 (2002), pp. 833 et seq. at p. 839. See also preamble of the 2005 Victims Principles that state the international community's "human solidarity with victims of violations of international law [...]".

253 In this context M. Henzelin; V. Heiskanen; G. Mettraux: "Reparations to Victims before the International Criminal Court – Lessons from International Mass Claims Processes". In: Criminal Law Forum 17 (2006), pp. 317 et seq. at pp. 326-27, point out that "[f]ailure on the part of the Court to give due consideration to these matters may lead to a flood of ineligible claims, wasting Court time and resources".

254 See also G. Bitti; G. González Rivas: "The Reparations Provisions for Victims under the Rome Statute of the International Criminal Court". In: Redressing Injustices through Mass Claims Processes – Innovative Responses to Unique Challenges. Ed. The International Bureau of the Permanent Court of Arbitration. Oxford, 2006, pp. 299 et seq. at p. 311: "The effective implementation of the reparations principles may therefore rely solely on the moral authority of the Court and the duty of states to apply treaties in good faith".

private legal persons could be called to make direct reparations to victims. Alternatively, abstract and generally applicable principles of a declaratory nature could be formulated, or victims could be referred to available national procedures through which they can claim reparations. Also, the principles could recommend that the mentioned entities make voluntary contributions to the Trust Fund pursuant to Rule 98 (5). The more clear, concrete and precise the principles are formulated, the more likely it is that they will have practical effects.

For the purposes of safeguarding the expedient conduct of proceedings, it is in the interest of the Court that victims of crimes under its jurisdiction also receive reparations and support from other sources than the individual perpetrators it has convicted. In cases where neither national or international programs nor Trust Fund assistance is available, victims might utilize their rights under the Statute to pressure both the Pre-Trial Chamber and the Office of the Prosecutor to prosecute more cases so as to have a better chance of receiving reparations from the Court.[255] In order to contribute to avoiding this situation, the Court can establish reparation principles with external effect that might increase voluntary contributions to the Trust Fund and strengthen victims' rights in other fora.

B. Determination of Damage, Loss, Injury (Art. 75 (1) s. 2 ICC Statute)

In addition to the duty to establish principles on reparations, Art. 75 (1) also allows the Court to determine the "scope and extent of any damage, loss and injury". The determination procedure may be initiated on request of victims or, exceptionally, on the Court's own motion.[256] Art. 75 (1) s. 1 states that the Court is to determine damage, loss and injury in accordance with the reparation principles established under Art. 75 (1) s. 1 and "will state the principles on which it is acting". Thus, damage, loss and injury can only be determined once the reparation principles have been established. The Rules equip the Court with the power to appoint experts to assist in the assessment and determination of the scope, extent of any damage, loss or injury to, or in respect of, victims (Rule 97 (2)).

The Statute, just as with regard to the duty to establish reparation principles, speaks unspecifically of "the Court" that may determine damage, loss or injury. Considering what has been discussed above, from the given context it can be concluded that the trial judges are meant to make the determinations, since it is for them to make judicial decisions.[257]

The determinations the Court may make under Art. 75 (1) s. 2 concerns the consequences of the crime to, and in respect of, its victims. The concepts of "damage, loss

255 Ibid., p. 321 only referring to the Trust Fund.

256 Art. 75 (1) s. 2; Rule 94 (procedure upon request) and Rule 95 (procedure on the motion of the Court). See for details on the initiation of the reparations proceedings Chapter 6 A. I.-II. below.

257 See also C. Jorda; J. de Hemptinne: "The Status and Role of the Victim". In: The Rome Statute of the International Criminal Court – A Commentary. Eds. A. Cassese; P. Gaeta; J. R. W. D. Jones. Vol. 2. Oxford, 2002, pp. 1387 et seq. at p. 1399.

and injury" are to be determined by the Court as a part of its principles or decisions pursuant to Art. 75 (1). The terms included in the phrase "damage, loss and injury" seem to be largely exchangeable. E.g. Rule 94 on the "Procedure upon Request" of victims uses the slightly differing terms "injury, loss or harm".[258] The term "injury" is used several times in the Statute to define acts constituting war crimes and crimes against humanity, primarily referring to personal injury.[259] The Statute seems to use the term "damage" in the context of violations to objects and the environment.[260] The term "loss" is only used in the context of loss of life.[261] The 2005 Victims Principles and the 1985 Victims Declaration use similar, albeit not identical terms: Under these documents, the recognized consequences of crimes or gross violations of international human rights law or serious violations of international humanitarian law are "harm, including physical or mental injury, emotional suffering, economic loss or substantial impairment of their fundamental rights".[262] It has been suggested that the use of the terms "damage, loss and injury" suggest that not only various types of physical damage but also personal injury and financial or other losses are intended to be covered.[263]

---

258 Rule 94 (1) (b). See also Part E No.1 Standard Application Form for Individuals that picks up these terms.

259 E.g. Art. 7 (1) k), 8 (2) a) (iii), 8 (2) b) (iv), (vi) ICC Statute. According to the International Law Commission: Draft Articles on the Responsibility of States for Internationally Wrongful Acts – With Commentaries, 2001. Available at http://untreaty.un.org/ilc/texts/instruments/english/commentaries/ 9_6_2001.pdf, last accessed 16 April 2009, p. 25 "[t]he notion of 'injury' [...] is to be understood as including any damage caused by that [wrongful] act."

260 Art. 8 (2) b) (iv) ICC Statute.

261 Art. 8 (2) b) (iv) ICC Statute .

262 Principle 8 2005 Victims Principles; Art. 1 1985 Victims Declaration. Black's Law Dictionary defines damage as "[l]oss or injury to person or property" or "[o]f or relating to monetary compensation for loss or injury to a person or property", B. A. Garner (ed.): Black's Law Dictionary. 8th ed. St. Paul, Minnesota, 2004, p. 417. The Oxford Dictionary defines "damage" as sum of money claimed or awarded in compensation for a loss or and injury; harm or injury impairing the value or usefulness of something, or the health or normal function of a person, J. M. Hawkins, J. M.; R. Allen (eds.): Oxford Encyclopedic English Dictionary. Oxford, 1991. Injury is defined as "[a]ny harm or damage" or "[t]he violation of another's legal right, for which the law provides a remedy" B. A. Garner (ed.): Black's Law Dictionary. 8th ed. St. Paul, Minnesota, 2004, p. 801. J. M. Hawkins, J. M.; R. Allen (eds.): Oxford Encyclopedic English Dictionary. Oxford, 1991, p. 731 defines injury as physical harm or damage; damage to one's good name etc. B. A. Garner (ed.): Black's Law Dictionary. 8th ed. St. Paul, Minnesota, 2004, p. 963: Loss is ordinarily defined as "[a]n undesirable outcome of a risk; the disappearance or diminution of value, usu. in an unexpected or relatively unpredictable way" or "[t]he failure to maintain possession of a thing". J. M. Hawkins, J. M.; R. Allen (eds.): Oxford Encyclopedic English Dictionary. Oxford, 1991, p. 731 defines loss: "a person, thing or amount lost".

263 M. Henzelin; V. Heiskanen; G. Mettraux: "Reparations to Victims before the International Criminal Court – Lessons from International Mass Claims Processes". In: Criminal Law Forum 17 (2006), pp. 317 et seq. at p. 324, noting that the same terms, damage, loss or

Under the wording of Art. 75 (1), the Court can determine the damage, loss and injury of victims unconnected to a reparation order pursuant to Art. 75 (2). Accordingly, the purpose of the determination of damage, loss and injury could be to enable the enforcement of rights of victims in national jurisdictions.[264] This is in line with earlier drafts of Art. 75, which provided for the determination of "the scope and extent of victimization [...] in order to allow victims to rely on that judgment for the pursuit of appropriate forms of reparation [...] either in national courts or through their governments in accordance with national law."[265] Furthermore, the determination and official recognition of the damage caused to the victims as a result of the crime, expressed in a declaratory judgment, could be seen as a part of reparations to victims.[266]

However, the Rules seem to anticipate that, under normal circumstances, the Court will determine the damage, loss and injury only in the context of reparation orders under Art. 75 (2). Rule 97 (1) provides that, with regard to the Court's reparation orders the "scope and extent of damage, loss and injury shall be taken into account" when determining whether individual or collective awards shall be made. Rule 97 (2) states that expert assistance can be drawn upon not only to assess the extent of damage, loss and injury occurred, but also to determine the "appropriate types and modalities of reparations".

Rule 94 does not create the possibility for victims to request the determination of damage, loss and injury, but the possibility to request reparations. The connection between Art. 75 (1) and the Court's reparation orders is supported by Rule 95, which refers to the Court's power to order reparations *ex propio motu*. Furthermore, since the Court has discretion to delegate the implementation of awards to the Trust Fund, the possibility exists that the Court restricts itself to order reparations to be made through the Trust Fund to victims, and leaves it for the Trust Fund to determine the damage, injury or loss caused.[267]

It can be concluded that the determination of damage, loss or injury could either serve an acknowledgement of the harm suffered by victims, the enforcement of

---

injury, were employed in Security Council Resolution 687 (1991) establishing Iraq's liability for the consequences of the invasion and occupation of Kuwait and that the UNCC took the view that these terms covered a wide range of various types of damage, loss and injury.

264 W. A. Schabas: An Introduction to the International Criminal Court. 2nd ed. Cambridge, 2004, p. 174.

265 Art. 45, A/AC.249/1997/WG.4DP.3 (proposal submitted by France to the August 1997 session of the PrepCom). The Article furthermore contained the option that in case national authorities are unable or otherwise unavailable, the Court shall proceed with the reparations judgment directly.

266 See e.g. Art. 22 d) 2005 Victims Principles ("satisfaction").

267 Art. 75 (2), Rules 97 (2), (3). Reg. 55 Trust Fund Regulations provides that "[s]ubject to the order of the Court, the Trust Fund shall take into account the following factors in determining the nature and/or size of awards, inter alia: the nature of the crimes, the particular injuries to the victims and the nature of the evidence to support such injuries, as well as the size and location of the beneficiary group."

reparations in national jurisdictions, or provide the foundation of the Court's own reparation orders.[268]

However, it seems questionable that it would be purposeful for the Court to engage in complicated and time-consuming procedures of damage assessment if not for the objective of directly ordering reparations. Rather, it can be assumed that the intention of placing the determination in Art. 75 (1) s. 2 was to ensure that procedurally the harm is assessed before reparations are ordered.

It might have been clearer to formulate in the Statute both the right of victims to request the determination of damage, loss and injury, and the power of the Court to initiate reparations proceedings on behalf of victims with reference to the reparation order pursuant to Art. 75 (2).

268 See also Art. 44 Trust Fund Regulations: "Where no further stipulations or instructions accompany the orders, the Board of Directors may determine the uses of such resources in accordance with rule 98 of the Rules of Procedure and Evidence, taking into account any relevant decisions issued by the Court on the case at issue and, in particular, decisions issued pursuant to article 75, paragraph 1, of the Statute and rule 97 of the Rules of Procedure and Evidence."

Chapter 5 The ICC Reparation Order (Art. 75 (2) ICC Statute)

The reparation order is the key function of the ICC reparation system. Under Art. 75 (2), the Court has the power to order the convicted person to make reparations to, and in respect of, victims.
The application of the provision to order reparation awards is discretionary. This is underlined by the permissive nature of the statutory language used in Art. 75 (2): "[T]he Court may make an order [...] specifying appropriate reparations".[269] Thus, the ICC Statute and Rules do not provide victims with a right to, under certain legally defined conditions, obtain reparations from the Court.[270] The fact that the application of the Court's power to award reparations is discretionary was a conscious decision of the drafters of the Statute and Rules to ensure that the expediency in adjudication will not be jeopardized by complex decision-making in the area of reparations.[271] However, its discretionary nature does not diminish the relevance of the Court's power to order reparations.[272]

Whereas in the ICC's legal framework many of the procedural requirements for a reparation order have been determined, major substantive issues of the reparation order have, to a great extent, remained unresolved. These include the question as to under which conditions the Court shall order reparations, who may benefit from reparation orders and the content of such orders. In this chapter, the ICC's legal instruments are analyzed and the attempt is made to clarify unresolved issues with reference to relevant international and national legal documents and practice. Procedural requirements for an reparation order are examined in detail in Chapter 6. However, the separation is not strict, which is also the result of the intention to follow

269 Also Rule 97 (1) states that "the Court may award reparations".

270 B. Timm: "The Legal Position of Victims in the Rules of Procedure and Evidence". In: International and National Prosecution of Crimes under International Law. Eds. H. Fischer, C. Kreß; S. R. Lüder. (Bochumer Schriften zur Friedenssicherung und zum Humanitären Völkerrecht). Berlin, 2001, pp. 289 et seq. at p. 303 stating that victims are not provided with a "classic 'claim' for reparations with legally defined conditions for the award."

271 D. Donat-Cattin: "Article 75 – Reparations to Victims". In: Commentary on the Rome Statute of the International Criminal Court – Observers' Notes, Article by Article. Ed. O. Triffterer. Baden-Baden, 1999, pp. 965 et seq. at p. 972.

272 See for further discussion below Chapter 5 C. IV.

the relevant provisions of the ICC Statute and Rules, which do not strictly distinguish between the procedural and substantial aspects of a reparation order.

A. Liability for Reparations

In this chapter it is to be examined under which conditions the Court can make a reparation order, i.e. what are the requirements in order for a the convicted person to be liable to make reparations.

The issue of liability to make reparations is connected to the question of eligibility to receive reparations. In cases of wrongdoing between two individuals, when the wrongdoer is obligated to make reparations to the person affected by the wrongdoing, his or her liability to repair the harm is equivalent to the victim's eligibility to reparations for the harm he or she suffered.

This is not the case in the context of the ICC reparations mechanism. First, due to the collective nature of the wrongdoing under the pursue of the ICC, there is regularly not one, but a number of persons that harm was caused to, and to whom the convicted person is to make reparations. Second, those who suffered harm do not necessarily receive reparations directly from the wrongdoer. Different methods by which the victim can benefit from a reparation order have been provided for. Besides directly awarding reparations from the convicted person to the victim (Art. 75 (2) s. 1, Rule 98 (1)), it is possible for the Court to order the money which is to be paid by the convicted person to victims through the Trust Fund, or possibly through an intergovernmental, international or national organization (Art. 75 (2) s. 2, Rules 98 (2) – (4)). Furthermore, due to the collective nature of the crimes, there might be several persons responsible for a victim's harm. Also, victims can benefit from a convicted person's assets outside of reparation orders. Victims could benefit from fines and forfeited assets obtained from the convicted person as a part of the sentence, and distributed by the Trust Fund (Art. 77 (2), Art. 79 (2)).[273] Thus, in the context of the ICC the perpetrator' liability and the eligibility of victims to receive reparations are two different, though linked matters, which will be discussed in the two following chapters.

I. The Conviction as a Pre-Condition for an ICC Reparation Order

Art. 75 (2) ICC Statute sets forth that only a person convicted by the Court can be held liable to make reparations to victims.[274] It might be argued the restriction of

---

273 For further analysis see Chapter 6 D. II. ("Use of Money and Property Collected Through Orders of Reparations, Fines and Forfeiture") below.

274 For further discussion e.g. S. A. Fernandez de Gurmendi; H. Friman: "The Rules of Procedure and Evidence of the International Criminal Court". In: Yearbook of International Humanitarian Law. Ed. A. McDonald. Vol. 3. The Hague, 2000, pp. 289 et seq. at p. 314; M. Heikkilä: International Criminal Tribunals and Victims of Crime. Turku, 2004, p. 182; C. M. Bassiouni: Introduction to International Criminal Law. Ardsley, New York, 2003, p. 528; P. G. Fischer: "The Victim's Trust Fund of the International Criminal Court – Forma-

the Court's competence to order reparations only against individuals after their conviction can already be concluded from the ICC's nature as a criminal court.[275] Yet, discussions at the Rome Conference and broader powers of national criminal courts show that this was not the only possible solution.[276] In fact, considering the standard of equality and fairness, to require a conviction can be problematic, as those victims whose offenders are not prosecuted by the Court are not eligible for reparations from the ICC.

The first consequence of the requirement that ICC reparation orders can only be made against a conviction of the perpetrator is that reparations cannot be awarded prior to a conviction. In the drafting process of the Rules, delegations argued that the Court should be in the position to provide interim relief pending the outcome of what might be a long trial.[277] However, the view prevailed that any reparation payments ordered by the Court must be a part of the sanction ordered against the convicted person, as ordering reparations prior to conviction could be construed as an indication that the Court had already determined the guilt of the accused.[278]

Second, reparations cannot be awarded in cases where the accused is acquitted. In contrast, in some national jurisdictions criminal courts are permitted to order the person that has caused harm to the victim to order compensation despite an

tion of a Functional Reparations Scheme". In: Emory International Law Review 17 (2003), pp. 187 et seq. at p. 205.

275 For further discussion see Chapter 4 A. IV. ("Who Can the Reparation Principles be Addressed to?").

276 See D. Donat-Cattin: "Article 75 – Reparations to Victims". In: Commentary on the Rome Statute of the International Criminal Court – Observers' Notes, Article by Article. Ed. O. Triffterer. Baden-Baden, 1999, pp. 965 et seq.; C. Muttukumaru: "Reparation to Victims". In: The International Criminal Court – The Making of the Rome Statute – Issues, Negotiations, Results. Ed. R. S. Lee. The Hague, 1999, pp. 262 et seq.; H. Rombouts; S. Vandeginste: "Reparation for Victims in Rwanda – Caught between Theory and Practice". In: Out of the Ashes – Reparation for Victims of Gross and Systematic Human Rights Violations. Eds. K. de Feyter; S. Parmentier; M. Bossuyt (et al.). Antwerp, 2005, pp. 309 et seq. at pp. 317 et seq. describe that Rwandan criminal courts can e.g. determine the liability of the state to make compensation.

277 E.g. Report of the Preparatory Commission's third session, Rule E (C), PCNICC/1999/L.5/Rev.1/Add.1 (1999), at p. 67, quoted in P. Lewis; H. Friman: "Reparations to Victims". In: The International Criminal Court – Elements of Crimes and Rules of Procedure and Evidence. Ed. R. S. Lee. Ardsley, New York, 2001, pp. 474 et seq. at p. 488.

278 P. Lewis; H. Friman: "Reparations to Victims". In: The International Criminal Court – Elements of Crimes and Rules of Procedure and Evidence. Ed. R. S. Lee. Ardsley, New York, 2001, pp. 474 et seq. at p. 488.

acquittal[279], or allow for claims not only against the person that was found criminally responsible, but also against persons civilly responsible for the accused's offense.[280]

Thirdly, the ICC can neither hold a convicted person liable for harm he or she did not cause, nor for harm the convicted person caused, but not through a crime that he or she was convicted for. An example for the first situation would be that a person who is a victim of a crime a person was convicted for by the Court suffered a trauma as a result of a particular conflict, but it cannot be established that the trauma is caused by the specific crime that a person was convicted for by the ICC. An example for the second situation is that a person can demonstrate his or her bodily harm was inflicted by the convicted person, but the relevant assault does not constitute a crime that the person was convicted for. This might be the case when the wrongdoing does not qualify as a crime under the jurisdiction of the ICC, or when the Office of the Prosecutor decides to not charge him or her with a certain wrongdoing which might constitute a crime under the ICC's jurisdiction. One of the consequences is, e.g., the concern that the ICC's limited charges against Thomas Lubanga exclude victims of his crimes and victim populations and creates rivalries between the victims.[281]

---

279 See possibilities in national jurisdictions, J. A. Jolowicz: "Procedural Questions". In: International Encyclopedia of Comparative Law. Ed. A. Tunc. Vol. 11. Tübingen, 1986, pp. 13-4 et seq. at pp. 13-13 and 13-18; C. Roxin: "Strafe und Wiedergutmachung". In: Festschrift für Werner Lorenz zum 80. Geburtstag. Eds. T. Rauscher; H.-P. Mansel. München, 2001, pp. 51 et seq. explains that this is a key element of Wiedergutmachung in national laws: A person can be acquitted as a consequence of his or her efforts to "repair" the damage his or her deed caused or when there was not sufficient evidence to convict the accused, yet it is sufficient to make against him an award for reparation (compensation). However, this concept is not applicable to grave crimes such as those under the ICC's jurisdiction. In France, ordering compensation despite an acquittal is only allowed under exceptional circumstances, see V. Dervieux; M. Benillouche; O. Bachelet: "The French System". In: European Criminal Procedures. Eds. M. Delmas-Marty; J. R. Spencer. Cambridge, 2002, pp. 218 et seq. at pp. 227; M. E. I. Brienen; E. H. Hoegen: Victims of Crimes in 22 European Criminal Justice Systems – The Implementation of Recommendation (85) 11 of the Council of Europe on the Position of the Victims in the Framework of Criminal Law and Procedure. Nijmegen, 2000, p. 320.

280 See J. A. Jolowicz: "Procedural Questions". In: International Encyclopedia of Comparative Law. Ed. A. Tunc. Vol. 11. Tübingen, 1986, pp. 13-4 et seq. at pp. 13-16 et seq.; see e.g. T. Lappi-Seppälä: "Finland". In: Wiedergutmachung im Kriminalrecht – Internationale Perspektiven – Reparation in Criminal Law – International Perspectives. Eds. A. Eser; S. Walter. Vol. 1. Freiburg i. Br., 1996, pp. 317 et seq. at p. 366 who points out that most third party cases concern insurance companies, i.e. cases of vicarious liability; and not for the a fault which is attributable to someone personally.

281 See e.g. The Redress Trust: Limited ICC Charges May Trigger Recriminations in Eastern Congo – Press Statement, The Hague, 28 November 2006. Available at http://www.redress.org/news/Limited %20ICC%20charges%2028-11-2006.pdf, last accessed 29 April 2008. See also Observations of the Legal Representative of victims VPRS 1 to 6 further to observations of the Prosecutor and the Defence Council on the subject of the status of applicants VPRS 1 to VPRS 6 as victims in the case *The Prosecutor v. Thomas Lubanga Dyilo*, reproduced in Decision on the Application for Participation in the Proceedings

The Trust Fund may allow victims to receive assistance prior to conviction, or in cases where no conviction is obtained.[282] Victims who appear before the Court might also receive assistance from the Victims and Witnesses Unit (Art. 43 (6)). However, in view of the unambiguous wording of Art. 75 (2), these measures do not constitute reparations in the sense of the ICC's legal framework.

II. Determination of Liability

Difficulties establishing the liability of individuals for harm derive mainly from the fact that the commission of crimes under international law is typically the result of the cooperation of a large number of persons.[283] Most crimes under international law "do not result from a single propensity of a single individual, but constitute manifestations of collective criminality: the crimes are often carried out by groups of individuals acting in pursuance of a common criminal design."[284] The challenge international criminal law faces is both to establish individual contributions to crimes within the network of collective action, and to weigh the individual contribution to the crime.[285]

While the perpetrator's contribution to the crime is relevant to his or her conviction, reparations focus on the perpetrator's contribution to the consequences for the crime's victims.[286] The modalities of international criminal responsibility and modes of criminal participation have been established in the jurisprudence of the international criminal tribunals and are clarified in the ICC Statute.[287] However, the ICC's

---

Submitted by VPRS 1 to VPRS 6 in the Case the Prosecutor v. Thomas Lubanga Dyilo, International Criminal Court, Pre-Trial Chamber I, 29 June 2006, ICC-01/04-01/06.

282 The Board of Directors can decide to provide "physical or psychological rehabilitation or material support for the benefit of victims and their families" when it has notified the Court on its intention to do so and the Court has not objected, see Reg. 50 (a) Trust Fund Regulations. See for further discussion below Chapter 7 ("Assistance to Victims and Their Families by the Trust Fund").

283 G. Werle: Principles of International Criminal Law. The Hague, 2005, p. 116.

284 *The Prosecutor v. Tadić*, Judgement, ICTY Appeals Chamber, 15 July 1999, Case No. IT-94-1-A, para. 191.

285 G. Werle: Principles of International Criminal Law. The Hague, 2005, p. 117.

286 B. Stephens: "Conceptualizing Violence – Present and Future Developments in International Law – Panel I – Human Rights and Civil Wrongs at Home and Abroad – Old Problems and New Paradigms – Conceptualizing Violence under International Law – Do Tort Remedies Fit the Crime?" In: Alabama Law Review 60 (1997), pp. 579 et seq. at p. 582, points out the formal differences of criminal responsibility and civil liability: in order to establish criminal responsibility, the mental side of the perpetrator is crucial, while in determining civil liability, the consequences of the crime (damage) are decisive. See also Rule 97 (3): "In all cases, the Court shall respect the rights of victims and the convicted person."

287 Art. 25-33 ICC Statute, see for further discussion e.g. G. Werle: Principles of International Criminal Law. The Hague, 2005, pp. 116 et seq.

legal instruments do not specify which standard or concepts of liability to reparations should apply.

In the legal systems that apply the concept of partie civile or adhesion procedure, there are two basic approaches to the liability of a convicted person to pay compensation. In some of them, as a general rule, civil and criminal liability is equated, while in others it is not.[288] In some jurisdictions, civil liability automatically follows the finding of criminal responsibility of a person.[289] The success of the compensation claim principally depends on the conviction of the defendant as the determination of criminal responsibility also implicates the offender's civil liability.[290] For example, in Rwandan criminal courts, the criminal responsibility of persons in positions of authority and persons leading and supervising the killings in the context of the Rwandan genocide "goes hand in hand with a joint civil liability for all the damages caused all over the country as a result of their participation in criminal acts".[291] In other legal systems, as

288 J. A. Jolowicz: "Procedural Questions". In: International Encyclopedia of Comparative Law. Ed. A. Tunc. Vol. 11. Tübingen, 1986, pp. 13-4 et seq. at p. 13-26 (*argumentum e contrario*); see e.g. T. Lappi-Seppälä: "Finland". In: Wiedergutmachung im Kriminalrecht – Internationale Perspektiven – Reparation in Criminal Law – International Perspectives. Eds. A. Eser; S. Walter. Vol. 1. Freiburg i. Br., 1996, pp. 317 et seq. at p. 368. In traditional civil law jurisdictions, the impact of the finding of criminal responsibility on the perpetrator's civil liability varies. In some jurisdictions that allow for civil claims in criminal procedure, the success of the claims depends on the criminal conviction of the perpetrator, in others the success of the civil claim does not depend on the offender's conviction, or despite the criminal conviction, and additional assessment of the civil liability is needed.

289 J. A. Jolowicz: "Procedural Questions". In: International Encyclopedia of Comparative Law. Ed. A. Tunc. Vol. 11. Tübingen, 1986, pp. 13-4 et seq. at p. 13-11 listing France as a paradigm jurisdiction, Venezuela, Sweden, Mexico, "developing countries influenced by French jurisprudence".

290 See K. Madlener: "Spanien". In: Wiedergutmachung im Kriminalrecht – Internationale Perspektiven – Reparation in Criminal Law – International Perspectives. Eds. A. Eser; S. Walther. Vol. 3. Freiburg i. Br., 2001, pp. 273 et seq. at pp. 314-315. The scope and extent of the reparation order as well as the kind of liability where there are several persons civilly liable is determined in Art. 110-115 Codigo Penal 1995/96; B. Stephens: "Translating Filártiga – A Comparative and International Law Analysis of Domestic Remedies for International Human Rights Violations". In: Yale Journal of International Law 27 (2002), pp. 1 et seq. at p. 19; S. Grassi: "Italien". In: Wiedergutmachung im Kriminalrecht – Internationale Perspektiven – Reparation in Criminal Law – International Perspectives. Eds. A. Eser; S. Walther. Vol. 3. Freiburg i. Br., 2001, pp. 130 et seq. at p. 204 describing that the success of a civil claim filed in criminal procedure depends on the perpetrator's conviction. Ground of liability is the crime a person is convicted for.

291 H. Rombouts; S. Vandeginste: "Reparation for Victims in Rwanda – Caught between Theory and Practice". In: Out of the Ashes – Reparation for Victims of Gross and Systematic Human Rights Violations. Eds. K. de Feyter; S. Parmentier; M. Bossuyt (et al.). Antwerp, 2005, pp. 309 et seq. at p. 320.

a general rule, criminal courts do not recognize equating civil and criminal liability.[292] Even where a civil claim is filed in criminal proceedings, the claimant must, in theory, establish the specific preconditions of civil liability. However, in practice, proof of a criminal offense and of a causal connection between the offense and the damage suffices to establish civil liability in the majority of cases.[293] Under both approaches, when the offender has been found guilty of a criminal offense, this normally also solves the question of liability to provide compensation.[294]

As in national systems in which the possibility exists to file compensation claims in criminal procedure, it can be concluded from Art. 75 (2) that the liability to make reparations to those who have suffered harm as a result of the crime is the immediate consequence of the conviction of a person by the ICC.[295] The mode of criminal participation under Art. 25 or superior responsibility pursuant to Art. 28 the convicted person was found guilty for determines the applicable standard for liability for reparations.[296]

For example, when the Court held a person criminally responsible as a superior, the harm suffered by a "victim of the case" would only have to be linked to a specific policy of a state or non-state actor, or military action that the convicted person has been found responsible for.[297]

---

292 J. A. Jolowicz: "Procedural Questions". In: International Encyclopedia of Comparative Law. Ed. A. Tunc. Vol. 11. Tübingen, 1986, pp. 13-4 et seq. at p. 13-26 names Germany, the Netherlands and Switzerland as examples for this approach.

293 Ibid., at 13-26.

294 Ibid., at 13-7 points out that in contrast, traditionally common law countries, the fact that a particular course of conduct offends against the criminal law is in general regarded as irrelevant for the civil liability of the offender, to be determined in civil procedure this is also true for Israel, South Africa, Japan.

295 When entering the reparations stage, a person's criminal responsibility for a crime or crimes under the ICC's jurisdiction has already been established. In order to convict the accused, the Court must have been convinced of his guilt beyond reasonable doubt, Art. 66 (3).

296 This approach is supported by the relevant explanations in the adopted ICC Victims Participation Booklet, p. 36. M. Henzelin; V. Heiskanen; G. Mettraux: "Reparations to Victims before the International Criminal Court – Lessons from International Mass Claims Processes". In: Criminal Law Forum 17 (2006), pp. 317 et seq. at p. 329 suggest that the Court must establish in a detailed manner the degree to which the relevant crimes impacted on victims, or categories of victims. In case there are several perpetrators of the same crime tried before the Court, it is a related question what impact does the extent and quality of the convicted person's contribution to the crime have on the scope and form of the reparation order, if any. See for further discussion of this question Chapter 5 D. IV. ("Scope of the Compensation Order") below.

297 For a detailed examination of national jurisprudence on superiors' liability for reparations in cases of gross human rights violations, see in particular the Marcos case: Hilao v. Marcos, No. 86-2449 (reported in table at 878 F.2d 1438), at 10 (Sept. 1992); Clementine v. Marcos; Ortigas v. Marcos; Sison v. Marcos; Hilao v. Marcos; Trajano v. Marcos. For a discussion see D. Shelton: Remedies in International Human Rights Law. 2nd ed. Oxford, 2005, pp. 159 et seq.; and various contribution in C. Scott (ed.): Torture as a Tort – Com-

As the convicted person's liability to make reparations follows already from Art. 75 (2), possibly read in conjunction with Art. 25 or Art. 28, depending on the form of commission of the crime, it seems to be irrelevant whether or nor this finding will be expressly stated in the guilty verdict.[298]

The combination of the large scale and systematic nature of the crimes under the jurisdiction of the Court might lead to a situation where a victim's harm can be attributed to several persons, acting in concert or separately.[299] In many national jurisdictions, legal concepts such as joint and several liability, or "alternative liability" are applied to overcome uncertainties regarding causation.[300] Similar approaches have been applied by reparations mechanisms dealing with mass crimes in the context of state responsibility.[301] Thus, it is indicated that also before the ICC, when several persons committed a crime or wrongdoing together, all of them may be held liable

parative Perspectives on the Development of Transnational Human Rights Litigation. Oxford, 2001.

298 Therefore, it would not be necessary for the Court to add to the guilty verdict a finding as to the scope of the convicted person's 'civil liability', as has been suggested by M. Henzelin; V. Heiskanen; G. Mettraux: "Reparations to Victims before the International Criminal Court – Lessons from International Mass Claims Processes". In: Criminal Law Forum 17 (2006), pp. 317 et seq. at p. 325.

299 B. A. Koch; H. Koziol: "Comparative Analysis". In: Compensation for Personal Injury in a Comparative Perspective. Eds. B. A. Koch; H. Koziol. Wien, 2003, pp. 407 et seq. at p. 417 provide that all Western European Jurisdictions allow for the mentioned "classical" instruments to overcome uncertainties, depending on the cause of the relevant damage.

300 Joint and several liability, see below Chapter 5 C. IV. ("Scope of Compensation Order"). For uncertain liability see A. Porat; A. Stein: Tort Liability under Uncertainty. Oxford, 2001, pp. 61 et seq. for further discussion. For the liability of several perpetrators in the context of forced labor, see R. Schröder: "Zwangsarbeit – Rechtsgeschichte und Zivilrechtliche Ansprüche". In: Jura 3 (1994), pp. 118 et seq. at pp. 121-122.

301 Regarding the UNCC, according to para. 6 of Governing Council Decision No. 6 "where the full extent of the loss, damage or injury arose as a direct result of Iraq's unlawful invasion and occupation of Kuwait, it should be compensated notwithstanding the fact that it may also be attributable to the trade embargo and related measures." The Federal German Compensation Law of 1953 for victims of Nazi crimes contained, in accordance with civil law principles, that principally, damage that would have also occurred without the persecution cannot be compensated. In these cases, compensation will only be awarded until the point of time the harm would have been probably caused with by another cause ("Reserveursache", § 9 (5) BEG); see for details H. Giessler: "Grundsatzbestimmungen des Entschädigungsrechts". In: Die Wiedergutmachung Nationalsozialistischen Unrechts in der Bundesrepublik Deutschland – Das Bundesentschädigungsgesetz. Eds. Bundesminister der Finanzen; W. Schwarz. Vol. 4. München, 1981, pp. 1 et seq. at p. 94; K. Weiss: "Schaden an Körper oder Gesundheit aus rechtlicher Sicht". In: Die Wiedergutmachung Nationalsozialistischen Unrechts in der Bundesrepublik Deutschland – Das Bundesentschädigungsgesetz. Eds. Bundesminister der Finanzen; W. Schwarz. Vol. 4. München, 1981, pp. 185 et seq. at p. 246.

when their participation in the crime or wrongdoing is certain and only the causality of the concrete act of a person for the harm is uncertain.[302]

Therefore, because the criminal responsibility of the person has already been established when entering the reparations stage, the convicted person can and should always be held liable by the ICC to make reparations. The convicted person is liable for the harm caused by the crime he or she was convicted for, even if it is uncertain whether his or her concrete act caused the harm.

B. Eligibility for Reparations Ordered by the ICC

The ICC's legal instruments do not set forth precise conditions under which a person is eligible for reparations. Yet, the Statute and Rules indicate that certain requirements have to be met, which are to be clarified in this chapter. As many questions remain unanswered, reference is also made to relevant international and national legal and human rights standards for possible solutions.

When reparations are to be awarded for crimes under international law, the identification of its beneficiaries is one of the key difficulties. The selection of the beneficiaries of reparations is often an issue with fundamental societal impact, as it determines who should be acknowledged as a victim of injustices in the context of the particular conflict.[303] This may often be critical, in particular as in an increasing number of internal conflicts, distinctions between combatants and civilians, i.e. perpetrators and victims, are blurred.[304]

Defining the criteria for eligibility to reparations is crucial, because they decide who will be recognized as a victim deserving reparations. Before the ICC, the Court's

302 § 830 (1) s. 2 German Civil Law Code (BGB).

303 H.-J. Brodesser; B. J. Fehn; T. Franosch (et al.): Wiedergutmachung und Kriegsfolgenliquidation – Geschichte, Regelungen, Zahlungen. München, 2000, p. 96 in regard to reparations for victims of the Nazi-regime; generally D. Shelton: "Reparations for Victims of International Crimes". In: International Crimes, Peace, and Human Rights – The Role of the International Court. Ed. D. Shelton. Ardsley, New York, 2000, pp. 137 et seq. at p. 141; H. Rombouts; P. Sardaro; S. Vandeginste: "The Right to Reparation for Victims of Gross and Systematic Violations of Human Rights". In: Out of the Ashes – Reparation for Victims of Gross and Systematic Human Rights Violations. Eds. K. de Feyter; S. Parmentier; M. Bossuyt (et al.). Antwerp, 2005, pp. 345 et seq. at pp. 466 et seq.; G. Ulrich: "The Moral Case for Reparations – Three Theses about Reparations for Past Wrongs". In: Reparations – Redressing Past Wrongs. Eds. G. Ulrich; L. Krabbe Boserup. (Human Rights in Development – Yearbook 2001). The Hague, 2003, pp. 369 et seq. at p. 375.

304 See e.g. *Situation in the Democratic Republic of The Congo*, Prosecution's Application for Leave to Appeal Pre-Trial Chamber I's Decision on the Application for Participation in the Proceedings of VPRS 1, VPRS 2, VPRS 3, VPRS 4, VPRS 5 and VPRS 6, ICC, Office of the Prosecutor, 23 January 2006, ICC-01/04-103, p. 9 stating in the context of the decision of the Court to allow victims' participation in the investigative stage of the situation in the Democratic Republic of Congo: "given the complexity of the situation in the DRC, persons who may be potential accuseds in one case may well be accepted as victims in the broader context of the situation".

jurisdiction and the decision of the Prosecutor whom to prosecute against, and the success in doing so, are decisive for the decision as to who can be determined to benefit from ICC reparation orders. This implicates the necessity to select those specifically connected to the cases tried before the ICC from others victimized by genocide, war crimes and crimes against humanity and other crimes and injustices that occur during large scale conflicts.

Even when states award reparations it is a common problem that there are a great number of claimants on the one side and few resources available for reparations on the other side. As the ICC can only hold individuals liable to make reparations, the problem is even more severe in this context.

A number of issues relevant to the question as to who may benefit from ICC reparations are linked to questions discussed in other chapters. As discussed in the previous subchapter, whether and to what extent persons and entities harmed can benefit from reparations depends on whether, and to what extent, the convicted person can be held liable to make reparations. The question as to who might benefit from reparations also depends on the content of the reparation order. E.g. the content of a collective reparations award impacts who is selected as a recipient, and vice versa.

Art. 75 (2) ICC Statute sets forth that reparations can be ordered "to, or in respect of, victims", and thus provides for a potentially wide range of beneficiaries. In order to clarify the issue, it is essential to be aware that the ICC reparations mechanism allows for several paths through which persons can benefit from reparations. Victimized individuals, collectives and legal persons might benefit through reparations made directly to them by the person convicted by the Court (Art. 75 (2) s. 1, Rule 98 (1)). They might also indirectly benefit from reparations awarded through the Trust Fund (Art. 75 (2) s. 2, Rule 98 (2)-(3)), or organizations (Rule 98 (4)). Additionally, they might benefit from reparations in their status as individuals, or as a part of a collective, or both (Rule 97 (1)).

Furthermore, decisions on eligibility to obtain reparations do not have to be made by the Court alone. When the Court orders reparations to be made through the Trust Fund it is within its discretion to decide how detailed it wants to determine the scope of beneficiaries.[305] If the Court has left open certain issues, it is for the Trust Fund to decide on them.[306]

I. Qualification as a Victim under Rule 85

Even though victims are mentioned numerous times in the Statute, it does not provide for a definition of "victims". As stated, only the Rules contain a victims' definition: Rule 85 is "applicable for the purposes of the Statute and the Rules of Procedure and Evidence".

305 The same is true regarding the determination of the nature and amount of reparation awards to victims.

306 See Reg. 43-46 Trust Fund Regulations; Reg. 60-61 Determination of beneficiaries; Reg. 69, 70 Determination of nature and scope of reparation awards, see Reg. 55.

Since reparations are the focus of this work, the victim definition in Rule 85 will be examined with special attention dedicated to the victim definition as far as it is relevant in the context of reparations.[307] While generally, the Court's decision that a person qualifies as a victim shall apply throughout the proceedings, such a decision can also be modified.[308]

As victims may participate in the Court's proceedings, it can be assumed that the normal procedure is to recognize individuals or collectives as victims of the case for the purposes of participation in the trial proceedings. However, it is not automatically clear whether, or to what extent they will also benefit as victims from a reparation order made against the convicted person. The Court's trial proceedings might not result in a conviction in all charges of the indictment, so that persons recognized as victims for the purpose of the trial proceedings might not be recognized as victims eligible to reparations. Since participation is not a precondition for eligibility to reparations, there might be a number of applicants for reparations whose victim status according to Rule 85 has not been determined when the proceedings enter the reparations stage.

As Art. 75 (2) states that reparation orders may be made "to, or in respect of, victims", it is clear that the qualification as a victim is not a necessary precondition in order to be to able to benefit from reparations. However, in view of Art. 75 (2) the first step in determining whether a person is entitled to reparations under the ICC reparations regime is to assess whether he or she qualifies as a victim under the definition provided in Rule 85.

Due to the various contexts and stages of proceedings in which rights and measures are conditioned upon the qualification as a victim, the definition cannot be plainly applied, but requires interpretation in order to be usable. It seems almost inevitable to flexibly interpret the definition according to the relevant context or stage of proceedings.[309] Thus, for the purposes of the current study an interpretation for the purposes of the reparations proceedings will be undertaken.

307 See on the drafting history of the victim definition e.g. B. Timm: "The Legal Position of Victims in the Rule of Procedure and Evidence". In: International and National Prosecution of Crimes under International Law. Eds. H. Fischer, C. Kreß; S. R. Lüder. (Bochumer Schriften zur Friedenssicherung und zum Humanitären Völkerrecht). Berlin, 2001, pp. 289 et seq.; P. Lewis; H. Friman: "Reparations to Victims". In: The International Criminal Court – Elements of Crimes and Rules of Procedure and Evidence. Ed. R. S. Lee. Ardsley, New York, 2001, pp. 474 et seq.

308 See Rule 91 (1); Reg. 89 (8) Court Regulations; while both provisions are located in sections referring to the participation of victims in the proceedings, this seems to be of general relevance.

309 This approach has been practiced in decisions on victim participation rendered by the Court. Pre-Trial Chamber I assumed that "victims" under Rule 85 could be "victims of a situation" or "victims of a case", according to the relevant stage of the proceedings, see *Situation in the Democratic Republic of The Congo*, Decision on the Applications for Participation in the Proceedings of VPRS 1, VPRS 2, VPRS 3, VPRS 4, VPRS 5 and VPRS 6, ICC Pre-Trial Chamber I, 17 January 2006, ICC-01/04-101, pp. 22 et seq.; Decision on the Application for Victims' participation of 21 July 2005; Prosecution's Application for

1. Individual Victims (Rule 85 (a))

The definition included in Rule 85 (a) defines who shall qualify as a "victim" in a very general manner.

To be recognized as a victim, the individual must
(1) be a natural person
(2) have suffered harm
(3) a crime within the jurisdiction of the Court must have been committed, and
(4) the harm must be a result of the crime (causal link).

a) Natural person

The ordinary meaning of the term "natural person" is "a human being".[310]

b) Harm

No definition of what constitutes "harm" has been provided for in the ICC Statute or Rules.[311] The ordinary meaning of the term "harm" has been defined as "injury, loss,

---

Leave to Appeal Pre-Trial Chamber I's Decision on the Application for Participation in the Proceedings of VPRS 1, VPRS 2, VPRS 3, VPRS 4, VPRS 5 and VPRS 6, ICC, Office of the Prosecutor, 23 January 2006, ICC-01/04-103 and Victims Participation Booklet, p. 19: "What is the difference between a victim of the situation and a victim of the case?". In the decision on victim participation in the investigative stage of the DRC situation of 17 January 2006, the Chamber introduced, inter alia, a possible method of adjusting the requirements for the qualification as a "victim" to the particular stage of proceedings by applying varying degree of burden of proof for meeting the requirements set forth by the victim definition, pp. 24 et seq. For further discussion see below Chapter 5 C. 1. d) ("Causation").

310 *Situation in the Democratic Republic of The Congo*, Decision on the Applications for Participation in the Proceedings of VPRS 1, VPRS 2, VPRS 3, VPRS 4, VPRS 5 and VPRS 6, ICC Pre-Trial Chamber I, 17 January 2006, ICC-01/04-101, p. 21 with reference to the definition provided in B. A. Garner (ed.): Black's Law Dictionary. 8th ed. St. Paul, Minnesota, 2004, p. 1178: "So far as legal theory is concerned, a person is any being whom the law regards as capable of rights and duties. Any being that is capable is a person, whether a human being or not being that is not so capable is a person, even though he be a man. Persons are the substances of which rights and duties are the attributes. It is only in this respect that persons possess juridical significance, and as this is the exclusive point of view from which personality receives the legal recognition." Pre-Trial Chamber I further refers to the definition provided in G. Cornu: Vocabulaire Juridique. Paris, 2003, p. 653: "[un] etre humain tel qu'il est consideréré par le droit; la personne humaine prise comme sujet de droit, par opposition à la personne morale."

311 The definitions of "victim" discussed in the Preparatory Commission defined harm as physical or mental, including emotional suffering, economic loss or substantial impairment of fundamental rights, see UN Doc. PCNICC/1999/INF/2 and PCNICC/1999/L.5/Add.1n.8. However, no consensus could be achieved regarding certain kinds of harm, see B. Timm: "The Legal Position of Victims in the Rule of Procedure and Evidence". In: International and National Prosecution of Crimes under International Law. Eds. H. Fischer, C. Kreß; S. R. Lüder. (Bochumer Schriften zur Friedenssicherung und zum Humanitären Völkerrecht). Berlin, 2001, pp. 289 et seq. at p. 290.

damage".[312] "Harm" as provided in the definition of "victim" pursuant to Rule 85 can – in the context of Art. 75 (1) and Rule 97 (1) – be constructed as consisting of the sub-categories "damage, loss, injury". This would also be in line with the 1985 Victims Declaration, which was intended by the drafters of the ICC Statute to provide guidelines for the determination of the concept of "victim": the 1985 Victims Declaration indicates that "harm" is an umbrella term.[313] Yet, the reparations application requires "[a] description of injury, loss or harm".[314] Thus, it is not clear whether "harm" is an umbrella term for the purpose of the ICC Statute and Rules, and if it is, what the content of the subcategories "damage, loss, injury" is.[315]
It is to be examined which forms of harm might qualify as "harm" under the victims definition in Rule 85 (a), and whether indirect harm should be recognized along with harm directly suffered. The latter question is linked to the requirements for causation between the crime and harm suffered. Furthermore, the notion of harm is particularly relevant to the question of which harm is recognized for the purposes of compensation, which will be discussed below.[316]

The approach of Pre-Trial Chamber I in its decision on victim participation in the pre-trial stage presumes that the forms of harm recognized for the purpose of the victim definition of Rule 85 are the same in all stages of the proceedings.[317] In the absence of a definition, the term "harm" must be interpreted in particular in the light of Art. 21 (3) of the Statute, according to which "[t]he application and interpretation of law pursuant to this article must be consistent with internationally recognized human rights".[318]

1) Forms of Harm

The ICC Statute mentions the term "harm" only in the context of genocide: This crime can be committed by causing serious mental or bodily harm to members of the group.[319] However, when presuming that "harm" is an umbrella term that includes "damage, loss and injury", further forms of harm can be found in the ICC Statute.[320]

312 B. A. Garner (ed.): Black's Law Dictionary. 8th ed. St. Paul, Minnesota, 2004, p. 734. further defining harm as "material or tangible detriment".

313 Art. 1. See also H. Rombouts; S. Vandeginste: "Reparation for Victims of Gross and Systematic Human Rights Violations – The Notion of Victim". In: Third World Legal Studies (2000-2003), pp. 89 et seq. at p. 96.

314 Rule 94 (1) (b).

315 See Chapter 4 B. ("Determination of Damage, Loss and Injury") above.

316 See Chapter 5. C. IV. ("Scope of the Compensation Order).

317 *Situation in the Democratic Republic of The Congo*, Decision on the Applications for Participation in the Proceedings of VPRS 1, VPRS 2, VPRS 3, VPRS 4, VPRS 5 and VPRS 6, ICC Pre-Trial Chamber I, 17 January 2006, ICC-01/04-101, pp. 29 et seq.

318 Ibid., p. 21, referring only to Art. 21 (3).

319 Given that the perpetrator meets the specific intent requirements, see Art. 6 b) ICC Statute.

320 See also above Chapter 4 B. ("Determination of Damage, Loss and Injury").

The ICC recognizes different forms of harm that a victim might suffer as a result of crimes under its jurisdiction.[321] The Standard Application Form for Individuals suggests various categories of harm the crime may have caused. While it remains for the judges to decide whether they recognize those forms of harm, their listing in the Standard Application Form, which was approved by the Presidency, strongly indicates that they will be recognized as harm under Rule 85.[322]

In the international human rights context, as well as in national laws, recognized forms of harm are often divided into non-pecuniary or immaterial harm on the one hand, and pecuniary or material harm on the other.[323] Non-pecuniary harm can be roughly divided into "moral damage" and "physical damage". In contrast to the human dimensions of physical and moral harm, material harm refers to the value of the thing to which an injured person was entitled to and any resulting special or consequential harms or losses.[324] Moral damages are an almost necessary consequence of the crimes under the ICC's jurisdiction, since these crimes typically involve a violation of human dignity.[325]

i) Emotional Suffering

The ICC has recognized that emotional suffering constitutes "harm" within the meaning of Rule 85.[326] The Standard Application Form for Individuals lists "mental pain and anguish" as a possible form of injury, loss or harm suffered as a result of the crime.[327] The section termed "reparations" describes four types of "mental harm and anguish" in a detailed manner: emotional problems, mental problems, physical reactions and behavioral changes and pain, complaints and/or concerns related to experiences of sexual violence.[328] The Victims Participation Booklet published by the

321 See *Situation in the Democratic Republic of The Congo*, Decision on the Applications for Participation in the Proceedings of VPRS 1, VPRS 2, VPRS 3, VPRS 4, VPRS 5 and VPRS 6, ICC Pre-Trial Chamber I, 17 January 2006, ICC-01/04-101, pp. 21, 26 et seq.; Victims Participation Booklet, p. 36.

322 Reg. 23 Court Regulations.

323 Non-pecuniary losses are often also termed "moral damages". Terminology and classifications in the relevant documents and fora vary. Classifications are sometimes also made according to the kind of damage, namely whether the damage is made to a person's physical and mental condition (personal damage), property damage, or whether it is purely economic (pure financial loss).

324 See D. Shelton: Remedies in International Human Rights Law. 2nd ed. Oxford, 2005, pp. 301 et seq.

325 E.g. B. Saul: "Compensation for Unlawful Death in International Law – A Focus on the Inter-American Court of Human Rights". In: American University International Law Review 19 (2004), pp. 523 et seq. at p. 549.

326 *Situation in the Democratic Republic of The Congo*, Decision on the Applications for Participation in the Proceedings of VPRS 1, VPRS 2, VPRS 3, VPRS 4, VPRS 5 and VPRS 6, ICC Pre-Trial Chamber I, 17 January 2006, ICC-01/04-101, paras. 116, 147.

327 Part E question 1 Standard Application Form for Individuals.

328 Part F question 3 Standard Application Form for Individuals. Further descriptions of the three first types are provided.

ICC describes that crimes under the ICC's jurisdiction can cause emotional suffering "by which a person's mind is affected because of what she or he has experienced or witnessed".[329]

Pain and suffering as consequences of certain acts constitutes an element of crimes against humanity and war crimes under the ICC Statute.[330] Primarily, the Statute requires that the suffering caused satisfies a certain qualification, i.e. that it is "unnecessary", "great" or "severe".

Emotional suffering has also been recognized as a form of "harm" in the 1985 Victims Declaration[331], the 2005 Victim Principles[332], the 2001 EU Framework Decision[333] and the jurisprudence of the Inter-American Court of Human Rights[334], the European Court of Human Rights[335] and the Bosnian Chamber of Human Rights.[336]

---

329 Victims Participation Booklet, p. 36

330 Art. 7 (1) f) read in conjunction with Art. 7 (2) e), Art. 7 (1) k), Art. 8 (2) a) (iii), Art. 8 (2) b) (xx).

331 Para. 1, para. 18.

332 Principle 8.

333 Art. 1 a).

334 E.g. *Aloeboetoe et al. v. Suriname*, Reparations, Inter-American Court of Human Rights, § 20, 10 September 1993, Ser. C, No. 15, para. 52; *Neira Alegria et al. v. Peru*, Reparations, Inter-American Court of Human Rights, 19 September 1996, 29 Ser. C, paras. 56, 57; *Garrido and Baigorria v. Argentina*, Reparations, Inter-American Court of Human Rights, 27 August 1998, Series C No.39, para. 49, *Plan de Sanchez Massacre*, Reparations, Inter-American Court for Human Rights, December 2004, No.116 (2004), paras. 80-89, 117 and 25.

335 E.g. *Selmouni v. France*, Judgment, European Court of Human Rights, 28 July 1999, Application No. 25803/94, para. 123 (torture is an assault on a person's physical and moral integrity and hence constitutes harm); *Aksoy v. Turkey*, Judgment, European Court of Human Rights, 18 December 1996, Application No. 21987/93, para. 113; *Olsson v. Sweden*, Judgment, European Court of Human Rights, 24 March 1988, Application No. 10465/83, para. 102; *Kenaan v. United Kingdom*, Judgment, European Court of Human Rights, 3 April 2001, Application No. 27229/25, para. 138 (non-pecuniary damage for the anguish and distress the victim suffered on account of the conditions in which her son had been detained).

336 *Damjanovic v. Federation*, Decision on the Claim for Compensation, Human Rights Chamber for Bosnia and Herzegovina, 16 March 1998, Case No.CH/96/30 (fear of execution); *Hermas v. Federation*, Decision on Admissibility and Merits, Human Rights Chamber for Bosnia and Herzegovina, 18 February 1998, Case No. CH/97/45 (moral damages for arbitrary detention, discrimination, ill-treatment and forced labor). J. Torpey: "Introduction – Politics and the Past". In: Politics and the Past – On Repairing Historical Injustices. Ed. J. Torpey. Lanham, Maryland, 2003, pp. 1 et seq. at p. 4 refers to M. Minow: Between Vengeance and Forgiveness – Facing History after Genocide and Mass Violence. Boston, 1998, pp. 61 et seq. who points out that the recognition of moral damages reflects "[a]n important feature of contemporary reparation politics [...] to give much greater weight to psychic harm and 'trauma' than was the case up to and immediately following World War II."

ii) *Physical and Mental Injury*

Pre-Trial Chamber I has recognized that physical suffering constitutes "harm" within the meaning of Rule 85.[337] In the Standard Application Form for Individuals "physical injury" is listed as a recognized form of harm suffered as a result of the crime.[338] In the context of reparations, it is described to encompass "dismemberment, disfigurement, loss or limitation of use of a body organ, member, function or system, including sexual/reproductive health problems".[339] The Victims Participation Booklet describes that crimes under the ICC jurisdiction can cause "psychological or mental harm by which a person's mind is affected because of what she or he has experienced or witnessed".[340]

Causing physical or mental injury as a consequence of certain acts constitutes an element of crimes against humanity and war crimes under the ICC Statute.[341] The Statute primarily requires that the injury caused can be characterized as "serious" or "superfluous".

Physical and mental injury are recognized forms of harm under the 1985 Victims Declaration[342], the 2005 Victims Principles[343], the Council of the European Union Framework Decision[344] and the jurisprudence of the Inter-American Court of Human Rights,[345] the European Court of Human Rights[346] and the Bosnian Human Rights Chamber.[347]

iii) *Economic Loss/Material Harm*

The ICC Statute recognizes that "[e]xtensive destruction and appropriation of property", committed under certain conditions, constitutes a war crime.[348] The ICC has

337 *Situation in the Democratic Republic of The Congo*, Decision on the Applications for Participation in the Proceedings of VPRS 1, VPRS 2, VPRS 3, VPRS 4, VPRS 5 and VPRS 6, ICC Pre-Trial Chamber I, 17 January 2006, ICC-01/04-101, paras. 116, 147.

338 Part E question 1, Part F question 2 Standard Application Form for Individuals.

339 Part F question 2 Standard Application Form for Individuals.

340 Victims Participation Booklet, p. 36.

341 See Art. 7 (1) k), Art. 8 (2) a) (iii), Art. 8 (2) b) (vii), Art. 8 (2) b) (xx).

342 Para. 1.

343 Principle 8.

344 Art. 1 a).

345 E.g. *Velásquez-Rodríguez v. Honduras*, Judgment, Inter-American Court of Human Rights, 29 July 1988, Series C No.4, paras. 156, 175, 187 (prolonged detention in specific circumstances is detrimental to physical and moral integrity).

346 Concerning "Physical suffering" *X and Y v. the Netherlands*, Judgment, European Court of Human Rights, 26 March 1985, Application No. 8978/80, para. 22; *Y.F. v. Turkey*, Judgment, European Court of Human Rights, 22 July 2003, Application No. 24209/94, para. 33.

347 E.g. *Odobasic v. R.S.*, Decision on the Admissibility and Merits, Human Rights Chamber for Bosnia and Herzegovina, 5 November 1999, CH/98/1786.

348 Art. 8 (2) b) (iv).

decided that economic loss constitutes harm within the meaning of Rule 85.[349] The Standard Application Form for Individuals lists "loss of or damage to property" as possible types of harm.[350] Examples set forth in the part titled "reparations" are loss or damage to home(s), land, personal property, including household goods, animal(s) or other losses.[351] Furthermore, in the same part the Standard Application Form for Individuals lists "loss of income, unpaid salaries, loss of support and other losses connected to the employment", "loss of savings at banks, stocks or other securities" under the heading "other damage".[352] The Victims Participation Booklet sets forth that "there could be material harm, such as when property is damaged or lost as a result of the crime, including your home or other property".[353]

Economic loss is a recognized form of harm under, inter alia, the 1985 Victims Declaration,[354] in the jurisprudence of the Inter-American Court of Human Rights[355] and the European Court of Human Rights,[356] and the Bosnian Human Rights Chamber.[357]

iv) Other Damage

The standard application form for individuals, in the section on reparations, lists under the heading "other damage", among others, "social status" and "legal rights".[358] This might indicate that these are also recognized as "harm", even though they are not expressly listed in the section on "injury, loss or harm suffered" of the application form.[359]

The ICC Statute recognizes that certain acts, combined with a particular mental element or respective contextual requirements, constitute genocide, war crimes or crimes against humanity without causing a visible material, physical or mental injury.

349 *Situation in the Democratic Republic of The Congo*, Decision on the Applications for Participation in the Proceedings of VPRS 1, VPRS 2, VPRS 3, VPRS 4, VPRS 5 and VPRS 6, ICC Pre-Trial Chamber I, 17 January 2006, ICC-01/04-101, para. 116.

350 Part E question 1.

351 Part F question 4.

352 See Part F question 5.

353 Victims Participation Booklet, p. 36.

354 Para. 1.

355 E.g. *El Amparo v. Venezuela*, Reparations, Inter-American Court of Human Rights, 14 September 1996, 28 Ser. C., No. 28, paras. 28 to 63.

356 E.g. *Ayder and Others v. Turkey*, European Court of Human Rights, 8 January 2004, Application No. 23656/94, paras. 10, 141 et seq. (pecuniary damages in respect of the destruction of housing).

357 E.g. *Hermas v. Federation*, Decision on Admissibility and Merits, Human Rights Chamber for Bosnia and Herzegovina, 18 February 1998, Case No. CH/97/45 (loss of income); *Medan, Bastijanovic and Marcovic v. BH and the Federation*, Decision on the Merits, 7 November 1997, Cases No. CH/96/3, 8, and 9 (loss of property); *O.K.K. v. R.S.*, Decision on the Admissibility and Merits, 9 March 2001, Case No. CH/98/834.

358 See Part F question 5.

359 Also the ICC's Victims Participation Booklet does not mention this as a type of harm.

It recognizes that persons or groups of persons have certain fundamental rights, and their violation constitutes a crime under the ICC Statute.[360]

The 1985 Victims Declaration and the 2005 Victims Principle both regard substantial impairment of fundamental rights as "harm".[361] Before the European Court of Human Rights, in order for a victim to be awarded with "just satisfaction", he or she must demonstrate to have suffered "prejudice" or "detriment".[362]

v) *Assessment*

The ICC Statute explicitly recognizes that certain forms of harm caused by particular acts constitute crimes under the ICC's jurisdiction. Certain restrictions may have to be made in order to comply with the requirements of the ICC Statute. For example, it is justified to consider that a certain degree of severity or seriousness of physical or mental injuries or suffering must be required in order to qualify as "harm" under Rule 85.[363]

However, the commission of crimes under the ICC Statute causes forms of harm not explicitly mentioned in the elements of the crimes listed in the ICC Statute. An interpretation of the term "harm" in accordance with internationally recognized human rights demands a broad recognition of all forms of material and immaterial harm resulting from the crime as sufficient in order to meet the requirement of "harm" for the purpose of the victim definition pursuant to Rule 85.

It would also be consistent with international human rights documents and practice to recognize substantial violations of fundamental rights as form of harm for the purposes of the ICC victim definition. While this seems to be indicated in the standard applications form for individuals, the Court's decision-making on this issue so far seems to indicate that this cannot be anticipated offhand.

2) Direct and Indirect Harm

Regarding the notion of "victim", the ICC's legal instruments do not expressly set forth whether indirect harm is also included in the term "harm" under the definition of Rule 85 (a). This is relevant to the question of whether persons who have suffered indirect harm shall be considered victims. Whereas direct victims are those who have suffered directly from the crime, indirect victims might be those persons

360 See e.g. Art. 6 c), d), e), Art. 7 (1) b), c), d), e), g), h), i), j), Art. 8 (2) a) (iii), Art. 8 (2) b) (vii), Art. 8 (2) b) (xx).

361 See para. 1 1985 Victims Declaration and Principle 8 2005 Victims Principles.

362 See P. Leach: Taking a Case to the European Court of Human Rights. 2nd ed. Oxford, 2005, p. 129 (*argumentum e contrario*).

363 E.g. with regard to damage caused to the "natural environment" the ICC Statute seems to demand that an additional requirement, namely that it be "widespread, long term and severe", shall be fulfilled, see Art. 8 (2) b) (iv) ICC Statute. M. Henzelin; V. Heiskanen; G. Mettraux: "Reparations to Victims before the International Criminal Court – Lessons from International Mass Claims Processes". In: Criminal Law Forum 17 (2006), pp. 317 et seq. at p. 325 discuss whether a minimum level of harm must be required in order to be able to claim reparations before the ICC.

linked to the direct victims.[364] Indirectly harmed persons may include family members and dependants of the direct victim, e.g. the mother or child of a person who has disappeared, neighbors and acquaintances who suffered emotional or financial consequences.[365] Other persons indirectly harmed may be those who were harmed when helping direct victims.

The wording of Rule 85 (a) only requires a person to have generally "suffered harm as a result of [...] any crime" and thus does not explicitly require that the individual was the direct target of the crime.

In the immediate context of Rule 85 (a), the comparison with the wording of Rule 85 (b) strongly suggests the inclusion of indirect harm. Individuals are required to have suffered "harm", whereas organizations and institutions can only be victims if they have sustained "direct harm".

Art. 75 (1) provides for reparation orders "to, or in respect of, victims" and therefore seems to clarify that not only direct victims of the crime, but also other, possibly indirectly harmed persons can benefit from reparation awards. If they were considered "victims" themselves, the addition "or in respect of, victims" would be unnecessary.[366] However, this interpretation could be questioned. Other interpretations of the wording "in respect of, victims" are possible: it might refer to collective reparations or the succession of awards.[367]

The preparatory works concerning Art. 75 reveal that in interpreting the term "victims", its drafters intended that reference be made to the 1985 Victims Declaration and the draft Basic Principles and Guidelines on the Right to Reparations for victims of violations of human rights and international humanitarian law, which correspond with the adopted 2005 Victims Principles.[368] These documents extend the "victim's

364 See H. Rombouts; P. Sardaro; S. Vandeginste: "The Right to Reparation for Victims of Gross and Systematic Violations of Human Rights". In: Out of the Ashes – Reparation for Victims of Gross and Systematic Human Rights Violations. Eds. K. de Feyter; S. Parmentier; M. Bossuyt (et al.). Antwerp, 2005, pp. 345 et seq. at p. 467.

365 UN Office for Drug Control and Crime Prevention: Guide for Policymakers on the Implementation of the United Nations Declaration of Basic Principles of Justice for Victims of Crime and Abuse of Power. New York, 1999. Available at http://www.uncjin.org/Standards/9857854.pdf, last accessed 16 April 2009, p. 15.

366 D. Donat-Cattin: "Article 75 – Reparations to Victims". In: Commentary on the Rome Statute of the International Criminal Court – Observers' Notes, Article by Article. Ed. O. Triffterer. Baden-Baden, 1999, pp. 965 et seq. at p. 969 quoting further authorities; C. J. M. Safferling: "Das Opfer Völkerrechtlicher Verbrechen – Die Stellung der Verbrechensopfer vor dem Internationalen Strafgerichtshof". In: Zeitschrift für die Gesamte Strafrechtswissenschaft 115 (2003), pp. 352 et seq. at p. 379.

367 See Chapter 5 B. IV. ("Reparations "in Respect of, Victims"").

368 The compromise reached among states on the text of Art. 75 and the footnote inserted in the report, designed at orienting the interpretation of the language "in respect of victims", support the inclusion of indirectly harmed persons into the definition of "victims", see D. Donat-Cattin: "Article 75 – Reparations to Victims". In: Commentary on the Rome Statute of the International Criminal Court – Observers' Notes, Article by Article. Ed. O. Triffterer. Baden-Baden, 1999, pp. 965 et seq. at p. 969.

right to reparation" to indirectly harmed individuals, such as the families of victims and their successors.[369] The drafters deliberately chose not to adopt the narrow definition in the ICTY and ICTR systems, which only includes direct victims.[370] Thus, the drafters chose the wording of Art. 75 (1) to secure the inclusion of persons who suffered indirect harm as a result of the crime as victims.[371]

The drafting history of Rule 85 shows that no agreement could be reached to expressly include family members of direct victims and persons who suffered harm when intervening to help in the definition of "victim" contained in Rule 85.[372] The idea to explicitly include "family members" in the definition of victims was rejected for two reasons: Firstly, it was felt that the inclusion of the term would lead to the need of a complex and long definition of its own. The second reason was that harm suffered by the victims may already include harm to their family members as a result of a possible causal connection between the harm suffered by the victims' families and the harm suffered by the victims themselves.[373] Thus, the drafting history of the Rules suggests that the decision not to explicitly mention family members in the definition of "victims" is not to be interpreted as a decision against their inclusion as victims.

In an important decision on victims' participation, the Court's Appeal Chamber has now unambiguously decided that indirect victims can also be victims of a crime within the jurisdiction of the Court pursuant to Rule 85 (a). Regarding natural persons, it found that "[t]he issue for determination is whether the harm suffered is personal to the individual. If it is, it can attach to both direct and indirect victims. Whether or not a person has suffered harm as the result of a crime within the jurisdiction of the Court and is therefore a victim before the Court would have to be determined in light of the particular circumstances".[374] Thus, the Appeals Chamber determined that the existence of personal harm is decisive in order for a person to qualify as a victim pursuant to Rule 85 (a). Trial Chamber I summarized that, as a result of the decision of the Appeals Chamber, "two categories of victims can participate. First, "direct" victims: those whose harm is the "result of the commission of a crime within the ju-

369 See next subchapter below.

370 See e.g. S. A. Fernandez de Gurmendi: "Definition of Victims and General Principle". In: The International Criminal Court – Elements of Crimes and Rules of Procedure and Evidence. Ed. R. S. Lee. Ardsley, New York, 2001, pp. 427 et seq. at p. 428.

371 C. J. M. Safferling: "Das Opfer Völkerrechtlicher Verbrechen – Die Stellung der Verbrechensopfer vor dem Internationalen Strafgerichtshof". In: Zeitschrift für die Gesamte Strafrechtswissenschaft 115 (2003), pp. 352 et seq. at p. 369.

372 B. Timm: "The Legal Position of Victims in the Rule of Procedure and Evidence". In: International and National Prosecution of Crimes under International Law. Eds. H. Fischer, C. Kreß; S. R. Lüder. (Bochumer Schriften zur Friedenssicherung und zum Humanitären Völkerrecht). Berlin, 2001, pp. 289 et seq. at p. 290 listing further references.

373 K. Kittichaisaree: International Criminal Law. Oxford, 2001, p. 324.

374 Situation of the Democratic Republic of The Congo in the Case of *The Prosecutor v. Thomas Lubanga Dyilo,* Judgment on the appeals of the Prosecutor and the Defence against Trial Chamber I's Decision on Victims' Participation of 18 January 2008, Appeals Chamber, 11 July 2008, ICC-01/04-01/06-1432, para. 32.

risdiction of the Court". Second, "indirect victims": those who suffer harm as a result of the harm suffered by direct victims".[375] Applied in the context of reparations, this means that also indirect victims can claim reparations in their own capacity.

i) *Determination of Indirectly Harmed Persons Eligible for Reparations*

The next question is who should be recognized as an "indirect victim". Trial Chamber I has clarified that "indirect victims must establish that, as a result of their relationship with the direct victims, the loss, injury, or damage suffered by the latter gives rise to harm to them. It follows that the harm suffered by indirect victims must arise out of the harm suffered by direct victims, brought about by the commission of the crimes charged."[376] According to the Appeals Chamber, "this is evident for instance, when there is a close relationship between the victims, such as the relationship between a child soldier and the parents of that child."[377] The harm suffered by these indirect victims may include psychological suffering experienced as a result of the sudden loss of a family member or the material deprivation that accompanies the loss of the direct victim's contributions.[378]

A person being harmed when intervening to prevent one of the crimes alleged against the accused may also qualify as an indirect victim.[379]

However, delimiting the group of indirect victims may in practice be delicate.[380] As mentioned previously, the issue of who should be considered as an "indirectly harmed person", in particular concerning family members of a direct victim, was already discussed during the drafting of the Statute at the Rome Conference.[381] Its relevance was confirmed in the first statements and decisions of the Court's organs

375 Situation of the Democratic Republic of The Congo in the Case of *The Prosecutor v. Thomas Lubanga Dyilo,* Redacted version of "Decision on 'indirect victims'", Trial Chamber I, 8 April 2009, ICC-01/04-01/06-1813, para. 44.

376 Ibid, para. 49.

377 Situation of the Democratic Republic of The Congo in the Case of *The Prosecutor v. Thomas Lubanga Dyilo,* Judgment on the appeals of the Prosecutor and the Defence against Trial Chamber I's Decision on Victims' Participation of 18 January 2008, Appeals Chamber, 11 July 2008, ICC-01/04-01/06-1432, para. 32.

378 Situation of the Democratic Republic of The Congo in the Case of *The Prosecutor v. Thomas Lubanga Dyilo,* Redacted version of "Decision on 'indirect victims'", Trial Chamber I, 8 April 2009, ICC-01/04-01/06-1813, para. 50.

379 Ibid, para. 51.

380 See for examples H. Rombouts; P. Sardaro; S. Vandeginste: "The Right to Reparation for Victims of Gross and Systematic Violations of Human Rights". In: Out of the Ashes – Reparation for Victims of Gross and Systematic Human Rights Violations. Eds. K. de Feyter; S. Parmentier; M. Bossuyt (et al.). Antwerp, 2005, pp. 345 at p. 468.

381 E.g. C. Muttukumaru: "Reparation to Victims". In: The International Criminal Court – The Making of the Rome Statute – Issues, Negotiations, Results. Ed. R. S. Lee. The Hague, 1999, pp. 262 et seq. at pp. 269-270.

regarding the assessment of victims' applications to participate in the investigative stage of the proceedings in the situation of the DRC.[382]

It has been suggested that recognition of persons indirectly affected as victims may vary culturally, in particular regarding the recognition of family members: whereas in Western societies family members are primarily limited to the nuclear family, a broader notion of family may be applied in other cultural contexts.[383]

A similar approach has been practiced by the Inter-American Court for Human Rights in order to determine who should be recognized as indirectly harmed family members and who are the heirs and successors of the direct victim, which are eligible for reparation. While successors of deceased victims inherit the victims' right to compensation on the one hand, on the other they are also presumed to have suffered their own actual and moral damages due to the loss of life to the direct victim. The Inter-American Court applies "rules, generally accepted by the community of nations", that designate spouses and children as successors, instead of applying national legislation.[384] Successors "need only to show their family relationship."[385] It has determined that "injured party" in Art. 63 also includes the direct victim's family members, and that the term family members shall be understood in a broad sense to include all those persons linked by a close relationship, including the children, parents and siblings.[386] In another case, the Inter-American Court determined that local law should

382 "With regard to the harm suffered, VPRS 2 stated he lost [...] family members [...]. Ad hoc Defense Counsel argues that the statement by VPRS 2 is vague and fails to indicate his degree of relationship with the deceased person, although the terms 'son' and 'sister' are used. He points out that in Africa one may call a person 'father', 'mother', 'brother' or 'sister' without having any biological tie with the person concerned, and that the Chamber should demand to know exactly what the term 'family member' means in this context", see *Situation in the Democratic Republic of The Congo*, Decision on the Applications for Participation in the Proceedings of VPRS 1, VPRS 2, VPRS 3, VPRS 4, VPRS 5 and VPRS 6, ICC Pre-Trial Chamber I, 17 January 2006, ICC-01/04-101, para. 129.

383 H. Rombouts; P. Sardaro; S. Vandeginste: "The Right to Reparation for Victims of Gross and Systematic Violations of Human Rights". In: Out of the Ashes – Reparation for Victims of Gross and Systematic Human Rights Violations. Eds. K. de Feyter; S. Parmentier; M. Bossuyt (et al.). Antwerp, 2005, pp. 345 et seq. at p. 468.

384 *Aloeboetoe et al. v. Suriname*, Reparations, 10 September 1993, Ser. C, No. 15, para. 62. According to H. Rombouts; S. Vandeginste: "Reparation for Victims of Gross and Systematic Human Rights Violations – The Notion of Victim". In: Third World Legal Studies (2000-2003), pp. 89 et seq. at p. 107, the Inter-American Court "has tended to develop its own law" to determine who can rightfully claim to be a heir or successor.

385 *Velásquez Rodríguez v. Honduras*, Compensatory Damages, Inter-American Court of Human Rights, 21 July 1989, Ser. C, No. 7, paras. 13 (4), (5), 54: "family members [...] are not required to follow the procedure of Honduran inheritance law"; *Gangaram Panday Case*, 21 January 1994, Ser. C, No. 16, para. 69, where the Court declared the spouse and children of the deceased victim as his heirs.

386 *Loayza Tamayo v. Peru*, Reparations, Inter-American Court of Human Rights, 27 November 1998, Ser. C, No. 42, paras. 140 et seq.

apply to determine next of kin and beneficiaries of the victim.[387] In this case, that dealt with victims from a tribal community in Suriname which had maintained matriarchal social structure and polygamy, the Inter-American Court found that Surinamese family law was not effective in the region and therefore was not the local law for the purposes of the case. As a result, multiple wives and children of the direct victims were recognized by the Court.[388] However, in the same case the Inter-American Court rejected the inclusion of the tribe itself as a beneficiary of reparation.[389]

The 2005 Victims Principles suggest that the term "victim" may include the immediate family or dependants of the direct victim and persons who have suffered harm in intervening to assist victims in distress or to prevent victimization "in accordance with domestic law" and "where appropriate".[390]

Thus, there is some agreement that, when determining who should be recognized as indirect victim, reference is to be made to the relevant cultural and legal setting and the criterion of "appropriateness". However, it does seem entirely unproblematic if the ICC were to apply different standards to in different cases to determine whether a person qualifies as a victim, depending on the person's cultural background.

ii) Assessment

The ICC Statute clearly allows for family members and other persons who are not direct victims of the crime to be entitled to reparations. As a result of an *e contrario* interpretation of Rule 85 (b), which expressly requires that institutions and organizations have suffered direct harm in order to qualify as victims, and the clear inclusion of indirectly harmed persons in the victim definition pursuant to Rule 85 (a) in the Court's recent jurisprudence on victim participation, indirect victims are also entitled to claim reparations on their own behalf.

As examined in this chapter, the 2005 Victims Principles allow for the inclusion of indirectly harmed persons with the condition that it is considered appropriate. It might also be useful for the ICC to adopt the criterion of appropriateness with regard to the eligibility of indirect victims to reparations. In cases where the ICC grants victims rights as individuals (as opposed to members of a group), delimitation of the victim group will often be inevitable in view of the limited capacities of the ICC with regard to reparations. Under certain circumstances, it might be appropriate to require a close and direct link of the harm to the crime under the ICC's jurisdiction, which serves as an objective criterion to delimit those victims eligible for reparation. When a large number of directly harmed individuals claim reparations and the resources available are insufficient, it might not be appropriate to compensate indirect victims.

---

387 *Aloeboetoe et al. v. Suriname*, Reparations, Inter-American Court of Human Rights, 10 September 1993, Ser. C, No. 15, para. 19.

388 Ibid., para. 62.

389 As claimed by the victims' lawyer and the Commission on the grounds that under the tribal customs, "a person is not only a member of his or her own family group, but also of his or her own village community or tribal group", ibid., para. 19.

390 Principle 8.

Under certain circumstances, indirect victims, e.g. close family members of the deceased direct victims, can file two applications for reparations: one for emotional suffering as the result of loss of life on their own behalf as indirect victims, and on behalf of their deceased relative who was directly harmed by the crime.

c) Crime within the Jurisdiction of the Court

Only individuals who have suffered harm as a result of "a crime within the jurisdiction of the Court" (Rule 85 (a)) can be recognized as "victims" under the ICC Statute and Rules. The crimes under the jurisdiction of the Court are listed in Art. 5 and include war crimes (Art. 8); crimes against humanity (Art. 7) and genocide (Art. 6).[391] Pursuant to Art. 13, the Court may exercise jurisdiction with respect to one of these crimes under the following conditions:

> "(a) A situation in which one or more of such crimes appears to have been committed is referred to the Prosecutor by a State Party in accordance with article 14; (b) A situation in which one or more of such crimes appears to have been committed is referred to the Prosecutor by the Security Council acting under Chapter VII of the Charter of the United Nations; or (c) The Prosecutor has initiated an investigation in respect of such a crime in accordance with article 15."

The Court has the mandate to exercise jurisdiction over the crimes listed in Art. 5 when the crime was committed within the time period set forth in Art. 11, thus after entry into force of the Statute, which occurred on 1 July 2002. If a state becomes a party after the Statute entered into force, the Court may exercise its jurisdiction only with respect to crimes committed after the entry into force of this Statute for that state, unless that state has accepted the exercise of jurisdiction of the Court under Art. 12 (3).

Lastly, in order for the Court to exercise jurisdiction, one of the two alternative conditions described in Art.12 (2) have to be fulfilled:

> "In the case of article 13, paragraph (a) or (c), the Court may exercise its jurisdiction if one or more of the following States are Parties to this Statute or have accepted the jurisdiction of the Court in accordance with paragraph 3: (a) The State on the territory of which the conduct in question occurred [...]; (b) The State of which the person accused of the crime is a national."[392]

391 See also Art. 5 (2) ICC Statute: "The Court shall exercise jurisdiction over the crime of aggression once a provision is adopted in accordance with articles 121 and 123 defining the crime and setting out conditions under which the Court shall exercise jurisdiction with respect to this crime."

392 See generally for the requirements of this pre-condition *Situation in the Democratic Republic of The Congo*, Decision on the Applications for Participation in the Proceedings of VPRS 1, VPRS 2, VPRS 3, VPRS 4, VPRS 5 and VPRS 6, ICC Pre-Trial Chamber I, 17 January 2006, ICC-01/04-101, p. 23.

This limitation is a logical consequence of the principle of complementarity that governs the ICC.[393] Extending the scope of victims to include persons who suffered harm from crimes other than those under its jurisdiction would mean to act *ultra vires.*

The determination of fulfilling the criterion "crime within the jurisdiction of the Court" is critical before a conviction has been made. It may prove problematic for the presumption of innocence, as it appears to presuppose that a crime has been committed, whereas that remains to be proved at trial.[394]Accordingly, the Office of the Prosecutor has expressed concerns that any finding might be exposed to the "criticism that at the time it makes a determination for the purposes of Rule 85, it is simultaneously prejudging, at a minimum, whether the crimes in question have been committed."[395]

Thus, the required element that each case it based on a "crime within the jurisdiction of the Court" needs to be adjusted to the relevant stage of proceedings. In its decision on victim participation in the investigative stage, the Court applied the standard that there must be "grounds to believe" that the alleged harm was caused by crimes under the jurisdiction of the Court.[396] In the assessment of whether there are "grounds to believe" that the alleged harm was caused by a "crime within the jurisdiction of the Court", reference was made to the situation under investigation. While participation as a victim in the trial proceedings requires reference to the case pending before the Court, in the investigative stage, for the purpose of determination of who might be a victim, reference to the jurisdiction *ratione temporis, ratione loci* (and *ratione personae*) of the relevant situation that is being investigated was made.[397]

For the purpose of reparations, the person must be a victim of a crime that was under prosecution before the Court, and that has resulted in a conviction. Thus, the

393 Art. 17 ICC Statute. On complementarity see e.g. C. Cárdenas: Die Zulässigkeitsprüfung vor dem Internationalen Strafgerichtshof – Zur Auslegung des Art. 17 IStGH-Statut unter besonderer Berücksichtigung von Amnestien und Wahrheitskommissionen. Berlin, 2005, pp. 33.; J. T. Holmes: "The Principle of Complementarity". In: The International Criminal Court – The Making of the Rome Statute – Issues, Negotiations, Results. Ed. R. S. Lee. The Hague, 1999, pp. 41 et seq.

394 C. Jorda; J. de Hemptinne: "The Status and Role of the Victim". In: The Rome Statute of the International Criminal Court – A Commentary. Eds. A. Cassese; P. Gaeta; J. R. W. D. Jones. Vol. 2. Oxford, 2002, pp. 1387 et seq. at p. 1403.

395 *Situation in the Democratic Republic of The Congo*, Prosecution's Application for Leave to Appeal Pre-Trial Chamber I's Decision on the Application for Participation in the Proceedings of VPRS 1, VPRS 2, VPRS 3, VPRS 4, VPRS 5 and VPRS 6, ICC, Office of the Prosecutor, 23 January 2006, ICC -01/04-103, para. 26.

396 *Situation in the Democratic Republic of The Congo*, Decision on the Applications for Participation in the Proceedings of VPRS 1, VPRS 2, VPRS 3, VPRS 4, VPRS 5 and VPRS 6, ICC Pre-Trial Chamber I, 17 January 2006, ICC-01/04-101, paras. 95 et seq. and Chapter 6 C. ("Standard and Burden of Proof") below.

397 *Situation in the Democratic Republic of The Congo*, Decision on the Applications for Participation in the Proceedings of VPRS 1, VPRS 2, VPRS 3, VPRS 4, VPRS 5 and VPRS 6, ICC Pre-Trial Chamber I, 17 January 2006, ICC-01/04-101, paras. 86 et seq.

requirement is not only that the harm was caused by a crime under the jurisdiction of the Court, but also that it was committed by a person convicted by the Court for that crime.[398]

The application of the victim definition by the Trust Fund might again require adjusting this criterion of the victim definition of Rule 85. The Trust Fund Regulations provide that "the resources of the Trust Fund shall be for the benefit of victims of crimes within the jurisdiction of the Court, as defined in Rule 85 of the Rules of Procedure and Evidence, and, where natural persons are concerned, their families."[399] The term "crime under the jurisdiction of the Court", will have to be interpreted with consideration given to which of its two functions the Trust Fund is fulfilling. When the Trust Fund implements reparation orders, "crime within the jurisdiction of the Court" can only mean a crime that a person has been convicted for by the Court. However, if it provides assistance from its resources received under Rule 98 (5), neither the Rules nor the Trust Fund Regulations require a link to the Court's proceedings or other limiting criteria.[400] Thus, for the purposes of Trust Fund assistance, "crime under the ICC jurisdiction" for the purpose of the victims definition can include genocide, war crimes and crimes against humanity under the territorial or personal and temporary jurisdiction of the Court that it does not deal with.[401] However, it might be that usually, in interpreting the criterion "crimes under the ICC jurisdiction" reference will be made to a situation the Court deals with, e.g. measures of assistance to victims in the investigative stage or during the trial proceedings.[402]

d) Causation

The last criterion to be fulfilled in order to qualify as a victim pursuant to Rule 85 (a), reflected in the words "as a result of", is that of a causal link between the crime within the jurisdiction of the Court which a person has been convicted for, and the harm suffered by the natural person.[403] Causation concerns the question as to how closely

398 See Art. 75 (2) read in conjunction with Rule 85.

399 Reg. 42 Trust Fund Regulations titled "Beneficiaries" provides: "The resources of the Trust Fund shall be for the benefit of victims of crimes within the jurisdiction of the Court, as defined in Rule 85 of the Rules of Procedure and Evidence, and, where natural persons are concerned, their families."

400 See Reg. 42, 47 Trust Fund Regulations.

401 This might be the case when the Court has decided not to investigate or prosecute the crimes because the state is dealing with the situation or because it will not serve the interests of justice, and where no national or international programs for the benefit of victims and their families exist. See I. Bottigliero: Redress for Victims of Crimes under International Law. Leiden, 2004, pp. 230 et seq.

402 Reg. 50 Trust Fund Regulations that speaks of "relevant Chamber of the Court", and thus seems to refer to a Chamber that is dealing with the situation in which the Trust Fund has decided to impose measures of assistance. For a discussion of the different options discussed as to the scope of Trust Fund beneficiaries before the adoption of the Trust Fund Regulations.

403 See *Situation in the Democratic Republic of The Congo*, Decision on the Applications for Participation in the Proceedings of VPRS 1, VPRS 2, VPRS 3, VPRS 4, VPRS 5 and VPRS

a person's harm needs to be linked to the crime for which a person was convicted by the Court in order for that person to be able to claim and receive reparations as a "victim".

Neither the Statute nor the Rules provide for indications as to the precise requirements for the causal link between the crime and the harm for the purpose of obtaining reparations.[404]

A controversial question regarding the required standard of causation between the crime a person was convicted for and the harm suffered as a result of the crime is whether persons that only indirectly suffered harm due to the crime can be recognized as victims under Rule 85 (a), particularly family members of the direct victim. This question was already discussed in the context of "harm" as a requirement of the victims' definition.[405]

The experience of reparations claims in the context of mass crimes or violations has shown that the establishment of causation is often controversial and practically difficult.[406] In its few years of existence, the Court has already received a significant number of applications for participation as victims from persons whose suffered harm is unconnected to the investigations and trials before the Court. It can be expected that, for example, a number of persons whose houses were destroyed in the course of a conflict over which the Court exercises jurisdiction file applications for reparations with the Court. It will then be the task of the Court to establish that the destruction of each house was or was not the consequence of a crime a person was convicted for.

Thus, in practice the finding that the crime a person was convicted for by the ICC caused the harm a person claims to have suffered is, to a large extent, connected to questions of proof. This is demonstrated in early decisions of the ICC relating to the question of causality. According to the decision of Pre-Trial Chamber 1, the requirements for establishing a causal link between the crime and the harm suffered for the purpose of qualifying as a "victim" may vary according to the stage of proceedings in which the qualification of a "victim is determined".[407] According to the Chamber,

6, ICC Pre-Trial Chamber I, 17 January 2006, ICC-01/04-101, p. 24.

404 For a summary of the discussions on issues regarding evidence and causation during the sessions of the Preparatory Commission, see P. Lewis; H. Friman: "Reparations to Victims". In: The International Criminal Court – Elements of Crimes and Rules of Procedure and Evidence. Ed. R. S. Lee. Ardsley, New York, 2001, pp. 474 et seq. at p. 485 et seq.

405 Chapter 5 C. II. 2) above.

406 P. D. Rheingold: Mass Tort Litigation. Deerfield, Illinois, 1996, § 11:10, and furthermore states that "proving and establishing that the plaintiffs' injuries were factually and legally due to his fault is often the central issue in the case".

407 *Situation in the Democratic Republic of The Congo*, Decision on the Applications for Participation in the Proceedings of VPRS 1, VPRS 2, VPRS 3, VPRS 4, VPRS 5 and VPRS 6, ICC Pre-Trial Chamber I, 17 January 2006, ICC-01/04-101, para. 98: regarding the determination of a causal link for the purpose of victim participation in the investigative stage, the Chamber "considers it necessary to establish that there are grounds to believe that the harm suffered is the result of the commission of crimes falling within the jurisdiction of the Court".

in the investigative stage "it is not necessary to determine in any great detail [...] the precise nature of the causal link [...]".[408] Following this approach, for the purposes of qualifying as a victim eligible for reparations, there must be no reasonable doubt that the harm suffered by a person is a result of a crime that a person was convicted for by the ICC.[409]

While the Court has thus so far declined to specify an applicable standard for causation, the Office of the Prosecutor, in observations on applications for participation in the Lubanga case, took the view that qualification as a victim under Rule 85 (a) required a direct connection between the harm suffered and the crime the accused is charged with.[410]

An overview of the relevant human rights jurisprudence and standards in national law on the question of causation between the violation or crime for the purposes of establishing who is eligible for reparations has already been provided.[411]

For the purpose of obtaining compensation in the course of national criminal proceedings, the crime's victims are regularly required to establish a direct link between their harm suffered and the crime an accused was held criminally responsible for.[412] The Model Code of Criminal Procedure for Ibero-America sets forth the requirement that a direct link between the harm suffered and the crime exist in order for a person to qualify as a victim.[413] In addition to the criteria of directness, foreseeability and remoteness of harm, other concepts exist that impact whether there is a

408 Ibid., para. 94.

409 See for further discussion on the requirements for proof Chapter 6 C. ("Standard and Burden of Proof").

410 Situation in the Democratic Republic of The Congo in the Case of *The Prosecutor v. Thomas Lubanga Dyilo*, Prosecution's Observations Concerning the Status of Applicants VPRS 1 to 6 and their Participation on the Case of The Prosecutor v. Thomas Lubanga Dyilo, ICC Pre-Trial Chamber I, 7 April 2006, ICC-01/04-01/06, paras. 14, 17 with reference to national laws.

411 Chapter 5 B. I.2). The relevant human rights jurisprudence on the required causal link between the crime and the harm in order for the harm to be compensable will be discussed in Chapter 5 D. II 2. b) ("Compensation and Causation"). For a general discussion on causality in international human rights jurisprudence e.g. D. Shelton: Remedies in International Human Rights Law. 2nd ed. Oxford, 2005, pp. 316 et seq.; E. H. Riedel: "Damages". In: Encyclopedia of Public International Law. Ed. R. Bernhardt. Vol. 1. Amsterdam, 1992, p. 929. at pp. 931 et seq.

412 V. Dervieux; M. Benillouche; O. Bachelet: "The French System". In: European Criminal Procedures. Eds. M. Delmas-Marty; J. R. Spencer. Cambridge, 2002, pp. 218 et seq. at p.p. 227; M. E. I. Brienen; E. H. Hoegen: Victims of Crimes in 22 European Criminal Justice Systems – The Implementation of Recommendation (85) 11 of the Council of Europe on the Position of the Victims in the Framework of Criminal Law and Procedure. Nijmegen, 2000, p. 320.

413 Art. 78. Instituto Iberoamericano de Derecho Procesal, Código Procesal Penal modelo para Iberoamérica, 1989, pp. 69-70; quoted in Situation in the Democratic Republic of The Congo in the Case of *The Prosecutor v. Thomas Lubanga Dyilo*, Prosecution's Observations Concerning the Status of Applicants VPRS 1 to 6 and their Participation on the

sufficient causal link: the nature of the loss, the gravity of the respective faults and policy arguments, based on reasonableness and justice, and the protective purpose principle.[414]

It can be assessed that requirements for causation between a crime or violation of law and the harm suffered vary considerably.[415] However, in national criminal justice systems that allow for compensation claims in criminal proceedings, establishing the causal link generally does not pose great difficulties. As national criminal proceedings regularly deal with crimes committed by one individual against the other, the question as to who qualifies as a victim only arises in exceptional cases, if at all. In the context of state responsibility for international crimes or gross human rights violations it seems less critical to apply relaxed standards for causation. This is because under international human rights law, the state is not only responsible to award reparations for the harm caused by its state actors, but also carries complementary responsibility to pay compensation if the person that caused the harm is unable of unwilling to make reparations.[416]

When determining whether a person is a victim under Rule 85 (a) for the purpose of receiving reparations from a convicted person, both sides are individuals. In this case, with regard to causation between the crime and the harm and its proof it is particularly crucial to reconcile the divergent interests and rights of victims and the convicted person.[417]

Due to the potentially large number of persons applying to be recognized as "victims", the standards for causation in the context of the victim definition should be kept simple, and thus practicable. It seems unlikely that the Court will have the capacity to determine the causal link between the crime and the harm according to complex causation theories.

The success of reparation claims before the ICC depends on the conviction of the person responsible for the harm and is thus subject to the criminal law standards as well as to any defenses and to the general limitations under criminal law. Thus, once this conviction has been achieved, requirements for the reparation claim, especially

Case of The Prosecutor v. Thomas Lubanga Dyilo, 7 April 2006, ICC-01/04-01/06, para. 15.

414 J. Spier; O. H. Haazen: "Comparative Conclusions on Causation". In: Unification of Tort Law – Causation. Ed. J. Spier. The Hague, 2000, pp. 127 et seq. at p. 132 et seq. The protective purpose principle could be described as that if a protective statute forbids a certain behavior in order to protect certain assets, the wrongdoer who violates such a law must indemnify even remote losses (p. 139); in the Anglo-American System this falls into the category of remoteness of damage or proximate cause.

415 D. Shelton: "Righting Wrongs – Reparations in the Articles on State Responsibility". In: American Journal of International Law 96 (2002), pp. 833 et seq. at p. 846, remarks that the ILC Draft Articles do not deal with the complexities of causation and leave it for courts and practioners to deal with it.

416 See Principles 15, 16 of the 2005 Victims Principles, Art. 11 of the 1985 Victims Declaration.

417 See also Rule 97 (3): "[i]n all cases, the Court shall respect the rights of victims and the convicted person."

the establishment of causation, could be lowered.[418] However, this is only justifiable once it has been confirmed that a person was sufficiently affected by the crime in order to qualify as a victim under Rule 85 (a). In fact, requiring direct causation between the harm of a person to the crime for the purpose of exercising rights as an individual victim seems to be the most objective criterion available to select between masses of victims of the conflict in general and those of the crime in question.

2. Organizations and Institutions

In the ICC's legal framework, victims "may include organisations or institutions that have sustained direct harm to any of their property, which is dedicated to religion, education, art or science or charitable purposes, and to their historic monuments, hospitals and other places and objects for humanitarian purposes" (Rule 85 (b)). Compared to the broad and in many aspects unclear victim definition concerning natural persons, the victim status of legal persons is defined in a straightforward manner.

Legal persons in possession of the listed objects might be considered as "victims" if they were harmed directly. Their inclusion in the definition of "victims" corresponds to the specific interests protected through the qualification of certain acts as war crimes under Art. 8 ICC Statute. The victims of some of the acts that constitute crimes contained in Art. 8 are most often and typically legal persons.[419]

Thus, what is encompassed by "harm" in order for organizations or institutions to be categorized as "victims" corresponds to the damage to objects that, if targeted in the course of military operations, constitutes a crime under Art. 8. The crime of intentionally directing attacks against buildings dedicated to religion, education, art, science or charitable purposes, and historic monuments (Art. 8 (2) b ix) has particular significance during religious and ethnic conflicts.[420] This crime might lead to applications from municipalities, foundations, religious institutions and museums.[421]

Furthermore, legal persons that own "hospitals and places where the sick and wounded are collected" (Art. 8 (2) b ix and e iv) might be considered as victims when directly harmed. The protection of "other objects for humanitarian purposes" in Rule 85 (b) corresponds to the protection of "installations, material, units or vehicles involved in a humanitarian assistance or peacekeeping mission in accordance with the Charter of the United Nations" (Art. 8 (2) b iii and e iii) and "buildings, material, medical units and transport using the distinctive emblem of the Geneva Convention" (Art. 8 (2) b xxiv and e ii).

418 See Chapter 5 C. II. 2. b. ("Compensation and Causation") and Chapter 6 C. ("Standard and Burden of Proof").

419 D. Shelton: "Reparations for Victims of International Crimes". In: International Crimes, Peace, and Human Rights – The Role of the International Court. Ed. D. Shelton. Ardsley, New York, 2000, pp. 137 et seq. at p. 142.

420 Ibid., p. 141.

421 Ibid., p. 142.

Which entities are to be considered as victims under Rule 85 (b) is yet to be precisely determined.[422] The Standard Application Form for Organizations lists, in a non-exclusive manner, non-governmental organizations, charitable or non-profit organizations, statutory bodies (such governmental bodies, public schools, hospitals), educational (private) bodies (such as a primary or secondary school or training college), companies (limited, unlimited or limited by guarantee), communication bodies (such as electronic media, the press), institutions for the benefit of members of the community (such as cooperative societies, building societies or micro finance institutions) or partnerships as possible bodies qualifying as victims.[423]

Forms of harm organizations or institutions might have suffered in order to be recognized as a victim under Rule 85 (b) are damage to land, buildings, movable property, religious properties, monuments, community or cultural property, the environment or human resources.[424]

Applications for reparations are to be filed by the duly authorized legal representative of the organization or institution claimed to have been victimized.[425] It is therefore reasonable to conclude that the owners of the objects protected in Art. 8 can potentially be considered as victims of these crimes, and that they have the same rights before the ICC as natural persons.[426] Consequently, even though the definition in Rule 85 (b) does not specify so, it has been suggested to consider legal persons as "victims" primarily for the purpose of requesting reparations.[427] Whether it is appro-

422 During the negotiations of the Preparatory Commission, doubts expressed by delegations referred primarily to the qualification of "powerful commercial corporations" as "victims", see B. Timm: "The Legal Position of Victims in the Rule of Procedure and Evidence". In: International and National Prosecution of Crimes under International Law. Eds. H. Fischer, C. Kreß; S. R. Lüder. (Bochumer Schriften zur Friedenssicherung und zum Humanitären Völkerrecht). Berlin, 2001, pp. 289 et seq. at p. 291; S. A. Fernandez de Gurmendi: "Definition of Victims and General Principle". In: The International Criminal Court – Elements of Crimes and Rules of Procedure and Evidence. Ed. R. S. Lee. Ardsley, New York, 2001, pp. 427 et seq. at p. 433.

423 Part A question 5 Standard Application Form for Organizations.

424 Part F question 2 Standard Application Form for Organizations.

425 Standard Application Form for Organizations, p. 1.

426 S. A. Fernandez de Gurmendi: "Definition of Victims and General Principle". In: The International Criminal Court – Elements of Crimes and Rules of Procedure and Evidence. Ed. R. S. Lee. Ardsley, New York, 2001, pp. 427 et seq. at p. 433. See also C. J. M. Safferling: "Das Opfer Völkerrechtlicher Verbrechen – Die Stellung der Verbrechensopfer vor dem Internationalen Strafgerichtshof". In: Zeitschrift für die Gesamte Strafrechtswissenschaft 115 (2003), pp. 352 et seq. at p. 368 who suggests that the recognition of a victim status for legal persons shall be limited to reparations.

427 C. J. M. Safferling: "Das Opfer Völkerrechtlicher Verbrechen – Die Stellung der Verbrechensopfer vor dem Internationalen Strafgerichtshof". In: Zeitschrift für die Gesamte Strafrechtswissenschaft 115 (2003), pp. 352 et seq. at p. 368.

priate to consider them as victims in the context of participation in proceedings does not have to be decided in the current context.[428]

Organizations and institutions do not automatically qualify as victims when they have been harmed directly as a result of a crime under Art. 8. The wording of Rule 85 (b) ("may") leaves it to the discretion of the Court to decide whether they should in a certain case be recognized as victims and, if yes, for what purpose.

Compared to other victim definitions in national and international legal documents and recognized in practice, the inclusion of organizations and institutions in the ICC victim definition is both precise and progressive.[429]

II. *Collective Beneficiaries of Reparations*

While the ICC's legal framework leaves open whether collectives can qualify as "victims" under the definition of Rule 85 and have the right to apply for reparations[430], it is clear that reparation awards can be directed to a collective of victims (Rule 97 (1)). In order to qualify as a beneficiary of reparations the collective of victims must have suffered harm as a result of a crime under the ICC's jurisdiction. Whether or not this

---

428 C. J. M. Safferling: "Das Opfer Völkerrechtlicher Verbrechen – Die Stellung der Verbrechensopfer vor dem Internationalen Strafgerichtshof". In: Zeitschrift für die Gesamte Strafrechtswissenschaft 115 (2003), pp. 352 et seq. at p. 368 suggests that the recognition of a victim status for legal persons shall be limited to reparations; more circumspect S. A. Fernandez de Gurmendi: "Definition of Victims and General Principle". In: The International Criminal Court – Elements of Crimes and Rules of Procedure and Evidence. Ed. R. S. Lee. Ardsley, New York, 2001, pp. 427 et seq. at p. 433. For a detailed discussion see M. Burkhardt, Victim Participation before the ICC, forthcoming.

429 While legal persons could not qualify as victims under the definition in Rule 2 ICTY and ICTR Rules, in international human rights context no clarity exists as to whether legal persons can generally, or for specific purposes, be recognized as victims. The definition included in para. 1 1985 Victims Declaration leaves open whether legal person can qualify as "victims". While in earlier drafts, judicial persons such as non-governmental and international organizations were expressly included in the victim definition, the adopted 2005 Victims Principles define victims as "persons who individually or collectively suffered harm". The Inter-American System and the European Court of Human rights restrict access of legal persons to "non-government organizations". In national jurisdictions, legal persons harmed by crimes can, under certain circumstances, claim compensation in criminal procedure, see V. Dervieux; M. Benillouche; O. Bachelet: "The French System". In: European Criminal Procedures. Eds. M. Delmas-Marty; J. R. Spencer. Cambridge, 2002, pp. 218 et seq. at p. 226; B. Stephens: "Translating Filártiga – A Comparative and International Law Analysis of Domestic Remedies for International Human Rights Violations". In: Yale Journal of International Law 27 (2002), pp. 1 et seq. at p. 19: in France a legal person may bring a claim for personal, direct harm caused by the offense, and under certain circumstances also when the harm is indirect and concerns collective interests. In Germany, corporate bodies or collective victims can claim through their legal representative, see R. Juy-Birmann: "The German System". In: European Criminal Procedures. Eds. M. Delmas-Marty; J. R. Spencer. Cambridge, 2002, pp. 292 et seq. at p. 303.

430 See Chapter 6 A. I. c) below.

is the result of the recognition of the collective as a victim pursuant to Rule 85 (a) or from the principles of the ICC's reparation system is irrelevant for the determination of the collective benefiting from an ICC reparation order.

Victims of mass and systematic crimes often do not constitute a homogenous group.[431] As collective awards aim at a positive effect on the societal level, the careful selection of the collective beneficiary of reparations is important in order for the ICC to promote, and not negatively impact a process of reconciliation. In contrast to individual awards, those determined by the ICC to be the beneficiaries of collective awards cannot reject it (Rule 95 (2) (b)).

In view of the explicit distinction that Rule 85 makes between individual and legal persons, it seems that the collective benefiting from ICC reparations cannot be a legal person.[432] Harm caused to legal persons as such is dealt with exclusively in Rule 85 (b).

It is crucial who may determine whether a number of individuals form a collective for the purpose of both legal representation and receiving reparations, and according to which criteria. While the ICC's legal instruments do not contain provisions for the determination of the collective beneficiary of reparations, the Rules on common legal representation may provide appropriate guidelines for collective rights of victims in general, including reparations.

The Rules envision that ideally, individuals will group themselves for the purposes of common legal representation (Rule 90 (2)). The group that is commonly represented during the proceedings might then request collective reparations. Even if a request for collective reparation does not follow a group's participation in the proceedings through a common legal representative, it can be concluded that generally the self-constitution of the group or collective has priority. However, the Standard Application Form only allows individuals to request reparations and thus suggests that the collective exercise of victims' rights derives from the exercise of individual rights only. Therefore, victims are in fact not invited to group themselves for the purpose of claiming reparations. However, common legal representation of victim groups in the reparations proceedings might lead to different results.

The Rules provide that when victims do not succeed in agreeing on common legal representatives within a certain time limit, the Chamber may request the Registry to do so (Rule 90 (3)). When the Court orders which group or collective of victims shall benefit from a collective reparations award, the criteria that are to be considered by the Registry provide guidance. Rule 90 (4) demands that the Registry ensures that the

431 See for further implications H. Rombouts; P. Sardaro; S. Vandeginste: "The Right to Reparation for Victims of Gross and Systematic Violations of Human Rights". In: Out of the Ashes – Reparation for Victims of Gross and Systematic Human Rights Violations. Eds. K. de Feyter; S. Parmentier; M. Bossuyt (et al.). Antwerp, 2005, pp. 345 et seq. at p. 472.

432 Agreeing D. Shelton: Remedies in International Human Rights Law. 2nd ed. Oxford, 2005, p. 237. See also the Court's reasoning in *Situation in the Democratic Republic of The Congo*, Decision on the Applications for Participation in the Proceedings of VPRS 1, VPRS 2, VPRS 3, VPRS 4, VPRS 5 and VPRS 6, ICC Pre-Trial Chamber I, 17 January 2006, ICC-01/04-101, para. 104.

"distinct interests of the victims [...] are represented and that any conflict of interest is avoided." "Distinct interests" include "age, gender as defined in article 7, paragraph 3, and health, and the nature of the crime, in particular, but not limited to, where the crime involves sexual or gender violence or violence against children".[433] In the Standard Application Form for Individuals, applicants are asked "[w]hat is your tribe/ethnic group?", thus providing an additional criterion for group determination.[434]

Individuals may have been singled out for persecution because of characteristics they share and that establish common bonds among them. By virtue of the common traits, these individuals may regard themselves as a collective, due to their nature as some form of coherent, identifiable group with an identity that endures over time.[435] Special bonds of groups of individuals might be created by common race, religion or nationality.[436] The crime of genocide typically targets groups that already exist prior to the commission of the crime. In addition to these pre-existing groups, collectives that did not exist prior to the victimization can be created through crime, e.g. similar experiences during, or even after being victimized by a crime under the ICC's jurisdiction. The common identity of the collective of victims tends to be strongest where shared characteristics as a group existed before the victimization and the experiences during the commission of crimes were similar.

However, the subjective perspective is also, or perhaps even more important. When considering whether a number of individuals constitutes a "group" or "collective", it seems to be a necessary precondition that they perceive themselves as such. In fact, those victimized by crimes committed in a particular conflict under the jurisdiction of the ICC might not regard themselves as a victimized collective, or several victimized collectives. The crimes under the ICC's jurisdiction might harm a variety of persons, who become victims of crime for different reasons and in different ways.[437] The reasons for the victimization and the fate of the victims can be so different that

433 Rule 90 (4) read in conjunction with Art. 68 (1).

434 Standard Application Form for Individuals, p. 3.

435 P. R. Dubinsky: "Justice for the Collective – The Current Limits of the Human Rights Class Action". In: Michigan Law Review 102 (2004), pp. 1152 et seq. at p. 1181.

436 C. M. Bassiouni: "The Protection of 'Collective Victims' in International Law". In: International Protection of Victims. Ed. C. M. Bassiouni. Eres, 1988, pp. 181 et seq. at pp. 183 et seq. listing further possible criteria. See also H. Rombouts; P. Sardaro; S. Vandeginste: "The Right to Reparation for Victims of Gross and Systematic Violations of Human Rights". In: Out of the Ashes – Reparation for Victims of Gross and Systematic Human Rights Violations. Eds. K. de Feyter; S. Parmentier; M. Bossuyt (et al.). Antwerp, 2005, pp. 345 et seq. at pp. 467 et seq.

437 The variety of groups that were victims of the Nazi injustices serves as an example that demonstrates that the "interests and views" (Art. 68) of various victims might not coincide as they may have differing concerns and interests: diverse groups of victims were treated differently by the Nazi regime: Jews and Gypsies were targeted for extermination, slaves for slave labor, homosexuals for "cure", political opponents to be deprived of their liberty and then killed when they did not completely renounce their views etc. S. Garkawe: "Victims and the International Criminal Court – Three Major Issues". In: International Criminal Law Review 3 (2003), pp. 345 et seq. at p. 361.

harm caused by a certain crime might not be sufficient to create a common ground that enables victims to form a "collective victim".[438] Thus, depending on the circumstances, crimes under the ICC jurisdiction might or might not create a collective of victims.[439] In addition, the possibility to recognize several collectives of victims being harmed by the same crime also exists under the Rules.[440]

Symbolic reparations are often made in the form of collective awards. Generally, the more dominant the symbolic nature of an award is, the more the willingness of the convicted person to make a certain form of reparations to a particular group of victims becomes relevant. Symbolic reparations such as a public apology or acknowledgment of wrongdoing usually do not fulfill their purpose when they are not authentic. Therefore, in this case the convicted person might also influence the determination of the collective beneficiary of reparation.

Collective reparations, perhaps more than individual awards, have the potential to aggravate conflicts and rifts in already shattered societies. Thus, their grouping both for the purposes of participation and reparations shall be flexibly and carefully adjusted to the different situation the ICC deals with. Consequently, the Rules take the right approach in that they establish that ideally, victims group themselves for the purposes of participation, and then might communicate to the Court their preferred form of collective reparations. If they do not succeed in grouping themselves for the purposes of receiving collective reparations, then the Court shall determine

438 For instance, in the course of reparations awarded by the Federal Republic of Germany to victims of Nazi crimes, the representative body of the Jews, the Jewish Claims Conference ("JCC"), refused to provide representation and enforcement for all those who had become victims of the persecution and genocide of the Jews by the Nazi regime. This was so because while for the Nazis, the fact of belonging to the Jewish confession was irrelevant, persons had been categorized as Jews by means of descent. Consequently, after the war there were persons who, due to their descent, had been persecuted as Jews without being of Jewish confession. The JCC refused to represent all those who were not of Jewish confession. Thus, in 1952 the German government established a Hardship Fund for those non-Jewish victims that had been persecuted for racial reasons (HNG-Fonds), see Richtlinien des Bundesministeriums der Finanzen zur Vergabe von Mitteln für Individuelle Betreuungsmaßnahmen aus dem Härtefonds für Rassisch Verfolgte Nicht Jüdischen Glaubens (HNG-Fonds) sowie zur Vergabe von Mitteln für Globale Betreuungsmaßnahmen aus diesem Fonds, 15 September 1966, Bundesanzeiger of 22 September 1966 No. 178. See for further discussion of the problem of grouping victims in the context of reparations to victims of Nazi crimes H.-J. Brodesser; B. J. Fehn; T. Franosch (et al.): Wiedergutmachung und Kriegsfolgenliquidation – Geschichte, Regelungen, Zahlungen. München, 2000, pp. 126 et seq.; H. Küpper: Kollektive Rechte in der Wiedergutmachung von Systemunrecht. Vol. 2. Frankfurt a. Main, 2004, p. 903.

439 C. M. Bassiouni: "The Protection of 'Collective Victims' in International Law". In: International Protection of Victims. Ed. C. M. Bassiouni. Eres, 1988, pp. 181 et seq. at p. 186 suggests that international criminal law protects categories of victims, and thus the commission of crimes creates identifiable groups of victims.

440 Rule 90 (2) refers to "groups of victims" and allows for several common legal representatives.

the collective beneficiary, guided by the criteria the Rules set forth for common legal representation.

III. Other Eligibility Criteria

The ICC's legal instruments do not provide those qualifying as "victim" under Rule 85 with a "classic claim" for reparations with legally defined conditions that determine the entitlement for reparations.[441] Thus, criteria in addition to the qualification as a "victim" under Rule 85 might have to be met in order for persons to be eligible for reparations.

Reparation mechanisms often set forth additional requirements that a "victim", or person negatively affected by a crime or gross and systematic violations termed otherwise, has to meet in order to determine eligibility. There are practical reasons for the introduction of additional requirements. The aim to process claims efficiently and expeditiously, a lack of resources to compensate all victims, and the desire to avoid awarding reparations to persons considered undeserving are all reasons for introducing additional eligibility criteria. Additional requirements for eligibility could lead to a situation where a person who qualifies as a "victim" is not entitled to reparations.

The ICC's legal instruments will be examined for implicit additional requirements for eligibility to reparations, and, where appropriate, a look will be taken at national and international human rights systems for eligibility criteria possibly applicable in the ICC context. Whether the unavailablility of reparations in other fora and the participation in the Court proceedings are additional requirements for a successful reparations claim is discussed in Chapter 6 below.[442]

1. Neediness

Rule 86 determines that, as a "general principle", the relevant Chamber shall, in its decisions or orders, take into account the needs of victims in accordance with Art. 68, "in particular, children, elderly persons, persons with disabilities and victims of sexual or gender violence".[443] As a consequence of this principle, it could be considered that victims be required to be "needy" in order to be eligible for reparations, in particular where there is a lack of resources. An assumption could be imposed that members of the listed groups are "needy".

Also the 1985 Victims Declaration stresses that when granting reparations, "attention should be given to those who have special needs because of the nature of the harm inflicted" or because of factors "such as race, colour, sex, age, language, religion,

441 See introduction to this Chapter.

442 See Chapter 6 A. 5. ("Other Procedural Requirements").

443 Rule 86 ("general principles") reads: "A Chamber in making any direction or order, and other organs of the Court in performing their functions under the Statute or the Rules, shall take into account the needs of all victims and witnesses in accordance with article 68, in particular, children, elderly persons, persons with disabilities and victims of sexual or gender violence."

nationality, political or other opinion, cultural beliefs or practices, property, birth or family status, ethnic or social origin, and disability."[444]

In reparations mechanisms for victims of gross and systematic crimes, the individual neediness of victims has been a requirement for eligibility to reparations.[445] It is recognized that members of specific groups may emerge as being particularly vulnerable or damaged, e.g. children and women. Apart from direct violations inflicted upon them (e.g. torture, murder and mutilation), they often face severe social and psychological consequences.[446]

However, it seems doubtful that it would be appropriate to impose "need" as an additional criterion to determine eligibility to reparations before the ICC, even where there is a lack of resources for reparations. Firstly, in context of the situations of under investigation of the ICC, many victims are poor and thus this criterion hardly seems to lead to a justifiable restriction of the group of eligible persons. Secondly, it seems difficult to define "neediness" in a fair and objective manner. To determine it on the basis of purely economic criteria might lead to the discrimination of those who are better off in financial terms, but are as directly harmed by the crime as others and might be in need of acknowledgment through an individual reparation award. Determining need only with regard to the groups listed in Rule 86 without regard to other factors might lead to discrimination. It thus seems that imposing "need" as additional qualifying criteria for reparations might lead to potential conflict and competition between survivors.[447]

Thus, whereas the application of this criterion might be justified when a state grants reparations as a part of a social welfare system, and for the distribution of resources for the purposes of awarding Trust Fund assistance, it does not seem appropriate for use when the ICC determines the eligibility of applicants for reparations.[448]

444 Para. 17.

445 See Art. 2 Agreement between the Jewish Claims Conference and the Government of the Federal Republic of Germany of October 1992, which provides that Jewish victims that until then have only received limited compensation per capita and are economically in need can be granted reparations in form of pensions.

446 See H. Rombouts; P. Sardaro; S. Vandeginste: "The Right to Reparation for Victims of Gross and Systematic Violations of Human Rights". In: Out of the Ashes – Reparation for Victims of Gross and Systematic Human Rights Violations. Eds. K. de Feyter; S. Parmentier; M. Bossuyt (et al.). Antwerp, 2005, pp. 345 et seq. at p. 468.

447 See N. Roht-Arriaza: "Reparations, Decisions and Dilemmas". In: Hastings International and Comparative Law Review 27 (2004), pp. 157 et seq. at pp. 177 et seq. for further discussions of the potential problems when restricting eligibility on the grounds of specific requirements for "harm".

448 However, neediness might be relevant in the context of implementation of reparation orders see Chapter 6 F. ("Implementation of Reparation Awards") below.

2. Exclusion of Eligibility

It is worth considering whether it is appropriate to set up certain criteria that exclude persons for specific reasons from eligibility even though they qualify as victims under Rule 85.

Reparations mechanisms for victims of gross or systematic injustices have, for example, imposed the restriction that only harmed persons who meet certain personal requirements can be eligible to receive reparations. The "center piece" of the German reparations scheme to victims of Nazi injustice, the Federal Compensation Law of 1953, required a person to be present in the territory of Germany at specific dates or having been in possession of German citizenship.[449] Under the Statute of the Iraqi High Court, in order to be a potential beneficiary under one of two possible categories, a person must be Iraqi citizens.[450] The United Nations Compensation Commission (UNCC) excluded victims who were Iraqi citizens from eligibility to reparations.[451]

Exclusion from eligibility might be particularly relevant when persons were involved in the commission of crimes, and are at the same time victims under Rule 85. The relevance of this issue is particularly evident in the context of child soldiers, who may be victims of war crimes under the ICC Statute and at the same time be involved in the commission of crimes themselves, and could therefore be considered perpetrators.[452]

Some national schemes that compensate victims of gross and systematic crimes exclude eligibility of persons who were involved in their commission. In the context of reparations to victims of Nazi crimes, compensation awards were only granted to persons that qualified as "honourable".[453] Persons were seen as not "honourable"

449 "Territoriality principle", see §§ 4, 5 Federal German Compensation Law of 1953 ("BEG"); according to the so-called "Diplomat clause", victims of Nazi crimes were excluded from eligibility from compensation if, at the time of the decision on their application, they had permanent residency in a state with which the Federal German Republic did not maintain diplomatic relations at the time the compensation law became effective, see § 238a BEG, Art. II BEG "Schlußgesetz".

450 Art. 22 Statute of the Iraqi High Criminal Court, Law No. 10/2005, Official Gazette of the Government of Iraq No. 4006, 18 October 2005: "Victims' families and Iraqi persons harmed can file a civil suit before the Court "for the harm suffered from the actions that constitute crimes according to the provisions of th[e] Statute".

451 Pursuant to para. 17 Criteria for the Expedited Processing of Urgent Claims, S/AC.26/1991/1. Exceptions were made for applicants that had bona fide citizenship of another state.

452 E.g. the ICC's Prosecutor has charged Thomas Lubanga Dyilo with the war crimes of enlisting and conscripting children under the age of fifteen and using children under the age of fifteen to actively participate in the hostilities (Art. 8 ICC Statute). See for further discussion regarding the difficulties to deal with child soldiers in the context of the Special Court of Sierra Leone V. B. Pinero: The Challenges of Reconstruction and Reconciliation Following an Armed Conflict. The Implementations for Child-Soldiers as Perpetrators". In: Eyes on the ICC 1 (2004), pp. 33 et seq.

453 § 6.

to benefit from compensation when they had contributed, at least indirectly, to the harm the victims of the Nazi regime had suffered.[454] Furthermore, also the applicant's post-war behavior was relevant for the determination whether he or she was honorable to benefit from reparations. Persons that qualified as victims were not eligible when they had fought against the "free democratic order" ("freiheitliche demokratische Grundordnung") since the establishment of the West German state. Also, persons that had been object to sanctions as a result of criminally activity were categorized as not honourable.[455]

In the context of regular crimes, the US Crime Reparation Board restricts eligibility when there is evidence that the victim contributed to the crime.[456] Also, in jurisdictions that allow victims to file reparations claims in criminal procedure, at least some systems impose a moral judgment by excluding those applicants that have committed a crime themselves.[457] In contrast, compensation claims in civil procedure do not impose personal criteria in order to secure that the victim of a tort is "honourable" or "deserving" of reparations.

Eligibility could be denied when applicants used unfair means to obtain reparations. Under the German Compensation Scheme for Nazi victims, applicants could be denied eligibility when they either deliberately or through gross negligence made, or permitted to be made, false or misleading statements affecting the basis for or the amount of compensation.[458] They could also be excluded for using false evidence,

454 See Bericht der Bundesregierung, 31 October 1986, BT-Drucks. 10/687, p. 13. This was, e.g. the case when they had been members of the National Socialist German Workers Party (NSDAP), § 6 I No.1 BEG. Also membership in one of the party's bodies or others who had supported the establishment of the Nazi regime was sufficient. Exceptions were made for those who had merely been formal members of the NSDAP and who had fought against the Nazi regime and by this endangered their freedom, bodily integrity or life.

455 § 6 (1) No. 2, 3, 4 BEG. The first criteria was primarily directed against active communists, see e.g. C. Goschler: Wiedergutmachung – Westdeutschland und die Verfolgten des Nationalsozialismus (1945-1954). München, 1992, pp. 300 et seq.; As a result, many communists were excluded on the grounds of their membership in the German communist Party (KPD).

456 M. K. Browne: "International Victims' Rights Law – What Can Be Gleaned from the Victims' Empowerment Procedures in Germany as the United States Prepares to Consider the Adoption of a 'Victim's Rights Amendment' to its Constitution?". In: Hamline Law Review 27 (2004), pp. 15 et seq. at p. 23.

457 See M. Kaiser; M. Kilchling: "Germany". In: Compensating Crime Victims – A European Survey. Ed. D. Greer. Freiburg i. Br., 1996, pp. 257 et seq. at p. 276.

458 § 7 BEG, see for comments H. Giessler: "Grundsatzbestimmungen des Entschädigungsrechts". In: Die Wiedergutmachung Nationalsozialistischen Unrechts in der Bundesrepublik Deutschland – Das Bundesentschädigungsgesetz. Eds. Bundesminister der Finanzen; W. Schwarz. Vol. 4. München, 1981, pp. 1 et seq. at p. 107. The possibility to exclude claims for false or misleading statements was made use of a great number of times, see K. van Bebber: Wiedergutgemacht? Die Entschädigung für Opfer der Nationalsozialistischen Verfolgung nach dem Bundesergänzungsgesetz durch die Entschädigungsgerichte im OLG-Bezirk Hamm. Berlin, 2001, p. 332 listing further authorities.

even when it was intended to serve the purpose of proving true facts.[459]

The ICC's legal instruments set forth principles that restrict the potential application of the mentioned exclusion criteria. Art. 21 (3) ICC establishes that the interpretation and application of law must be consistent with internationally recognized human rights and be without any adverse distinction founded on grounds such as gender, age, race, color, language, religion or belief, political or other opinion, national, ethnic or social origin, wealth, birth or other status. Therefore, entitlement for reparations ordered by the ICC could clearly not be conditioned on the possession of a certain nationality or speaking a certain language, as required by some existing reparations mechanisms.[460] The same is true for the exclusion of persons due to their political activity. This is not only demanded by Art. 21 (3), but also necessary in order to comply with international standards and "internationally recognized human rights".[461]

459 H. Giessler: "Grundsatzbestimmungen des Entschädigungsrechts". In: Die Wiedergutmachung Nationalsozialistischen Unrechts in der Bundesrepublik Deutschland – Das Bundesentschädigungsgesetz. Eds. Bundesminister der Finanzen; W. Schwarz. Vol. 4. München, 1981, pp. 1 et seq. at p. 107. The claim could furthermore be denied on the grounds of § 7 when the victim did not provide the authorities with information of circumstances which could possibly influence the basis or the scope of the claim, see BGH RzW 1975, 71, 72. The same was true when the victim brought forth contradictory information of which was not clear which was true or false, BGH RzW 1967, 546. Also, the applicant had to stand in for the false behavior of his or her legal or factual representatives, see BGH RzW 1970, 350, 351; also, the victim could be deprived of the award after it had already been determined because of dishonorable behavior after compensation had been awarded. When compensation had been paid already, the refund of payments could be demanded, H.-J. Brodesser; B. J. Fehn; T. Franosch (et al.): Wiedergutmachung und Kriegsfolgenliquidation – Geschichte, Regelungen, Zahlungen. München, 2000, p. 112. The denial of the claim was within the discretion of the authorities. Decisive criterion was the severeness of the applicant's fault, see H. G. Menzel: "Zum Substantiierungs- und Wahrheitsgebot bei der Geltendmachung von Verfolgungsleiden". In: Koblenzer Handbuch des Entschädigungsrechts. Eds. K. P. Kisker; H. H. Bischof. Baden-Baden, 1996, pp. 69 et seq. BGH RzW 1981, 9, 10.

460 In the context of the requirement of a certain nationality for victims, M. Henzelin; V. Heiskanen; G. Mettraux: "Reparations to Victims before the International Criminal Court – Lessons from International Mass Claims Processes". In: Criminal Law Forum 17 (2006), pp. 317 et seq. at p. 323 point out that the principles governing the law of state responsibility and diplomatic protection are not applicable in the ICC proceedings.

461 Para. 3 1985 Victims Declaration states that "[t]he provisions contained herein shall be applicable to all, without distinction of any kind, such as race, colour, sex, age, language, religion, nationality, political or other opinion, cultural beliefs or practices, property, birth or family status, ethnic or social origin, and disability." In a more abstract manner, also Principle 25 2005 Victims Principles sets forth that "[t]he application and interpretation of these Principles and Guidelines must (be consistent with international human rights law and international humanitarian law and) be without any discrimination of any kind or ground, without exception."

However, these provisions do not seem to exclude the application of exclusion criteria based on the applicant's own criminal or willfully improper behavior. In fact, it could lead to outrage or at least to disapproval among victims if persons that were involved in the commission of international crimes will benefit from the ICC reparations regime.[462] Furthermore, in one of its early decisions on victims' participation the relevant ICC Chamber stated that it "reserves the right to reject applications for participation that it deems to be unfounded or incomplete."[463]

Simple solutions in this matter seem inappropriate. As mentioned, the often complex circumstances of the situation concerned have to be considered, e.g. in the context of committing the war crime of conscripting or enlisting children under the age of fifteen years into the national armed forces or using them to participate actively in hostilities.[464] While the children might have committed war crimes themselves, they undoubtedly qualify as victims of crimes under the ICC jurisdiction pursuant to Rule 85.[465] In the context of the Special Court of Sierra Leone, the Secretary General has stated that "although the children of Sierra Leone may be among those who have committed the worst war crimes, they are to be regarded first and foremost as victims."[466] Other problems might arise when persons accused by the ICC of committing crimes under its jurisdiction apply for participation or reparations as victims in other cases.

3. Time Limits

While limitation periods often play an important role in the distribution of reparations, the ICC's legal framework does not provide specific time limitations for the filing of reparations applications. Yet, under Rule 101, the Court can set "time limits regarding the conduct of any proceedings" and in doing that "shall have regard to the need to facilitate fair and expeditious proceedings, bearing in mind in particular the rights of the defence and victims".[467] Given its position in section IV of the

462 See N. Roht-Arriaza: "Reparations, Decisions and Dilemmas". In: Hastings International and Comparative Law Review 27 (2004), pp. 157 et seq. at p. 177 for the discussion of similar dilemmas in Guatemala and Nicaragua where combatants involved in the commission of gross crimes received.

463 *Situation in the Democratic Republic of The Congo*, Decision on the Applications for Participation in the Proceedings of VPRS 1, VPRS 2, VPRS 3, VPRS 4, VPRS 5 and VPRS 6, ICC Pre-Trial Chamber I, 17 January 2006, ICC-01/04-101, para. 95.

464 Art. 8 (2) b) (xxvi).

465 ICC does not have jurisdiction over persons under the age of 18, see Art. 26.

466 UN Security Council: Report of the Secretary-General on the Establishment of a Special Court for Sierra Leone, 4 October 2000, UN Doc. S/2000/915, para.7.

467 Rule 101 (1). Rule 101 (2) reads: "Taking into account the rights of the accused, in particular under article 67, paragraph (1) (c), all those participating in the proceedings to whom any order is directed shall endeavour to act as expeditiously as possible, within the time limit ordered by the Court." See general on time limits Reg. 33-35 Court Regulations. See also Reg. 107 (3) Registry Regulations, which sets forth that in seeking further information on applications for reparations, the Registry shall take into account, i.e. "any time limits for the filing of documents with the Court".

Rules termed "miscellaneous provisions", and its reference to "any proceedings", the Rule is also applicable to the reparations proceedings.[468] Yet, the wording "conduct of any proceedings" seems to refer to the Court's inner functions only, with the consequence that time limitations for applications of victims can only be set connected to a specific case.

In addition to the facilitation of expeditious proceedings, another reason for the introduction of limitation periods is to make the victims file their claims as soon as possible and to, from a certain point of time, have an overview of the means necessary to compensate victims.[469] In the context of criminal proceedings, filing claims within a certain time limit enables the Court to consider all claims for reparations before making a reparation order against the convicted person. Since the Statute envisions that a hearing on reparations may be held in connection with the sentencing, it would make sense to require that the claims be submitted a reasonable time before that.[470] In fact, the Rules encourage that applications for reparations be presented at the earliest opportunity, and oblige the Court to take an active approach by notifying victims and publicizing the reparations proceedings.[471] An early submission of claims may also help the Court in the collection and preservation of evidence and in ordering appropriate measures to prevent the dissipation of assets.[472] Thus, the Court is to engage in raising awareness among victims of the possibility to request reparations. In order to be considered as a potential beneficiary of direct reparation orders (Art. 75 (2) s. 1, Rule 98 (2), it is clear that applications for reparations have to be filed before the reparations hearing. Also, requests for reparations that require the convicted person's cooperation, i.e. measures of a primarily symbolic character, must be filed a reasonable time before the Court makes the final decision on reparations.

468 See for a general analysis of the term "proceedings" *Situation in the Democratic Republic of The Congo*, Prosecution's Application for Leave to Appeal Pre-Trial Chamber I's Decision on the Application for Participation in the Proceedings of VPRS 1, VPRS 2, VPRS 3, VPRS 4, VPRS 5 and VPRS 6, ICC, Office of the Prosecutor, 23 January 2006, ICC - 01/04-103, paras. 28 et seq., relevant due to general examination even though conducted with the purpose of elaborating the questions as to whether "proceedings" exist at the investigative stage.

469 Similarly, in regard to national tort law, D. K. Allen; J. T. Hartshorne; R. M. Martin: Damages in Tort. London, 2000, p. 67 elaborates that the purpose of limitation periods is "to prevent potential claims from hanging over the defendant indefinitely, inhibiting financial decision-making. In addition, old claims are harder to prove, evidence is lost and witnesses can give less accurate accounts, prolonging litigation and making judgments on the facts more difficult".

470 Art. 76 (3). See D. Shelton: "Reparations for Victims of International Crimes". In: International Crimes, Peace, and Human Rights – The Role of the International Court. Ed. D. Shelton. Ardsley, New York, 2000, pp. 137 et seq. at p. 146.

471 Rules 94 (2), 95 (1), 96. See detailed discussion in Chapter 6 B.I. ("Notification and Publication of Reparations Proceedings") below.

472 International Federation for Human Rights: Victims' Rights Before the ICC, 2007. Available at http://www.fidh.org/article.php3?id_article=4208, last accessed 16 April 2009, Chapter IV: Reparations and the Trust Fund for Victims, p. 12.

The Court Regulations set forth that victims' applications for participation are required to be filed before the relevant hearing.[473] The Victims Participation Booklet states that applications shall be filed "in sufficient time for the judges to consider whether they may participate at a particular stage".[474] In contrast, nothing similar has been determined for reparations applications, so the question arises as to what will happen with reparations applications that are not filed a sufficient time before the reparations hearing, or even filed after the hearing.

The Court's authority to proceed with reparations claims on its own motion indicates that time limits for reparations applications might not play a key role in the ICC reparations regime. In fact, in cases where there are large numbers of victims, it is imaginable that the Court could proceed with reparations claims on its own motion on behalf of all those victims of the crime of the convicted person who have not identified themselves to the Court. The task of identifying beneficiaries of reparations may then be delegated to the Trust Fund.[475]

In fact, such proceedings seem to be envisioned by the relevant Trust Fund Regulations. These discuss the situation when the Court orders the reparation award to be made through the Trust Fund and has not identified the beneficiaries of the reparation award. When the number of victims makes it impossible or impracticable for the Trust Fund Secretariat to determine these with precision, there are several options to proceed.[476] Among others, targeted outreach to the beneficiary group can be conducted to invite potential beneficiaries who have not been identified through the reparations phase to identify themselves to the Trust Fund. Following outreach, "reasonable deadlines for the receipt of communications" shall be put into place, "taking into account the situation and location of victims."[477] Thus, when there are large numbers of victims, the Court may order reparations to be made through the Trust Fund. Deadlines for reparations applications might then be installed by the Trust Fund, rather than by the Court itself.

In addition to the difficulty of identifying all potential victims, new victims may arise if injuries continue after the completion of the trial. However, after the conviction, it is not only unreasonable and unmanageable for the Court to continue to reopen cases, but it is a legal requirement that victims can only receive reparations for harm caused by the specific crimes a person was convicted for.[478] The convicted

473 Reg. 86 (3) Court Regulations.

474 Victims Participation Booklet, p. 27.

475 Rule 98 (2) regarding individual awards and Rule 98 (3) regarding collective awards. It is a different question according to which criteria the Court shall, in these cases, determine the scope of a monetary reparation order against the convicted person. See below Chapter 5 D. ("Scope of the Compensation Order").

476 Reg. 60 Trust Fund Regulations.

477 Reg. 61 Trust Fund Regulations. From Rule 102 it is clear that requests, applications for reparations and observations qualify as "communications".

478 See D. Shelton: "Reparations for Victims of International Crimes". In: International Crimes, Peace, and Human Rights – The Role of the International Court. Ed. D. Shelton. Ardsley, New York, 2000, pp. 137 et seq. at p. 147.

person cannot be held responsible for the consequences of crimes under the ICC's jurisdiction that were committed after his or her conviction.[479]

The 2005 Victims Principles take an unambiguous position on the issue of time limits: they provide that "statutes of limitations shall not apply to gross violations of international human rights law and serious violations of international humanitarian law which constitute crimes under international law."[480] In contrast, both in national and in international law, victims are often granted a specific period of time to file their applications.[481] When time limits were applied for reparations claims in the context of mass crimes, this has often proven to be problematic: as victims of mass crimes often take refuge in other countries and are involved in overcoming trauma and in re-building their lives, they might often not be immediately aware of the possibility to claim reparations.[482]

It seems that in view of the Court's power to act *ex proprio motu* and to delegate identification of beneficiaries to the Trust Fund, time limits are not relevant in order to ensure the functioning of the ICC reparations mechanisms. The Court is already responsible for informing victims of the possibility to file reparations and encourage them to file applications for reparations during the trial proceedings. It seems that

479 Thus, the suggestion made ibid. to allow claims to be presented to the Trust Fund could apply for assistance measures only, and not reparations.

480 Principle 6, see also Principle 7.

481 E.g. the Rules of the European Court require that a claim for "just satisfaction" must be made no later than two months after the admissibility decision. The time limit may also be specified in the judgment, Rule 60 (1), 75 (3) Rules of Court of the European Court of Human Rights, July 2006. Argentinian law established time limitations for reparations applications by victims of the former dictatorship of five years, see D. Shelton: Remedies in International Human Rights Law. 1st ed. Oxford, 1999, p. 346. For time limits applicable to claims filed with the Ethiopia Eritrea Claims Commission, see Art. 5 para. 8 Agreement between the Government of the Federal Democratic Republic of Ethiopia and the Government of the State of Eritrea, signed 12 December 2000.

482 With regard to reparations for Nazi injustice, until the 1980s, all compensation laws and regulations required the victims to file their claim within certain limitation periods, which were usually between one and two years. Since victims were spread all over the world, many could not file claims within the deadlines due to factual or legal reasons. As a result, limitation periods were constantly expanded, and the imposition of a final limitation period created pressure on the authorities to develop loopholes in the limitation periods in order to reach reasonable results. See regarding the relevance of limitation periods in the BEG O. Gnirs: "Das Verfahren bei der Entschädigungsbehörde". In: Die Wiedergutmachung Nationalsozialistischen Unrechts durch die Bundesrepublik Deutschland – Entschädigungsverfahren und Sondergesetzliche Entschädigungsregeln. Eds. Bundesminister der Finanzen; W. Schwarz. Vol. 6. München, 1987, pp. 19 et seq. at pp. 41-54. Thus, the imposition of short limitation periods had, in the long run, the opposite of the intended effect, in that it led to the extension of the compensation period for decades. Eventually, in the 1980s, 1990s and in 2000 hardship provisions were established that granted lump sum compensation awards to, among others, all those that had not been able to meet the limitation periods in the 1950s and 1960s; see e.g. § 11 I No. 3 German Foundation Law of 2000.

only once the proceedings have entered the sentencing and reparations stage that it could be purposeful to set specific time limits for requests for particular forms of reparations. However, as the ICC's legal instruments do not require the applicant to identify the person that reparations are claimed from, it seems the ICC has to accept and review all applications even after the completion of the reparations stage. However, in order to benefit from direct reparations, it appears that applications for reparations have to be filed before the reparations hearing. In cases where reparations are awarded to victims indirectly, time limits may be imposed by the Trust Fund.

Considerations of practicability and effectiveness of dealing with reparations issues demand that time limits be imposed. These limits shall take into account, as the Trust Fund Regulations state, the situation of the victims in order to at some point be able to determine the precise scope of reparations. On the other hand, the fact that ICC reparation claims are not designed as legal entitlements seem to make any strict handling of time limits inappropriate. Additionally, it also seems necessary that relief shall be available after expiry of the limitation period. However, these would be measures of assistance financed from general resources of the Trust Fund received under Rule 98 (5), rather than reparations pursuant to the ICC Statute.

IV. Reparations "in Respect of, Victims"

According to Art. 75 (2), the Court may order reparations not only to, but also "in respect of, victims". This makes clear that persons other than those qualifying as victims under Rule 85 can also benefit from reparation awards. It is to be examined who might potentially benefit from reparations other than those qualifying as "victims".

The wording of the French version of Art. 75 (2) differs from the English version in this respect, and is more precise and thus indicative. Instead of using the term "in respect of, victims", it specifically includes "ayant-droit", i.e. dependants or relatives of the direct victim, as beneficiaries of reparations.[483]

A contextual interpretation of Art. 75 (2) provides principally for two possibilities regarding potential beneficiaries of reparations other than "victims". Art. 75 (2) s. 2 clarifies that the Court can order reparation awards through the Trust Fund, "where appropriate". The Statute determines that the Trust Fund's purpose is to serve "the benefit of victims of crimes within the jurisdiction of the Court, and of the families of such victims" (Art. 79 (1)). From this, it can be concluded that family members of victims might benefit, through the Trust Fund, from reparation awards while not being considered as victims themselves. However, corresponding Rule 98 (2) on implementing the Court's individual reparation awards only speaks of "victims" as potential beneficiaries of reparation orders. The Trust Fund Regulations pick up the wording of the Statute and provide that reparation awards may only benefit a "victim as defined in Rule 85 [...] and, where natural persons are concerned, their families,

483 See G. Bitti; G. González Rivas: "The Reparations Provisions for Victims under the Rome Statute of the International Criminal Court". In: Redressing Injustices through Mass Claims Processes – Innovative Responses to Unique Challenges. Ed. The International Bureau of the Permanent Court of Arbitration. Oxford, 2006, pp. 299 et seq. at p. 311.

affected directly or indirectly by the crimes committed by the convicted person".[484] Thus, if individuals do not themselves qualify as "victims", reparations may be ordered "in respect of" family members of victims. Rule 94 only allows "victims" to file reparations claims. However, the Standard Application Form for Individuals clarifies that persons who do not qualify as victims have standing to file applications for reparations on behalf of victims.[485] Particularly in cases where the direct victim is deceased, the person filing the application may be awarded reparations not only on his or her own behalf, but also "in respect of" the deceased victim."[486]

The second possible interpretation is that reparations awarded "in respect of victims" encompass collective reparations. The Court's power to award collective reparations is specified in Rules 97 (1) and 98 (3).

The object and purpose of ordering reparations "in respect of" victims seems to be to enable the Court to award reparations to the benefit of as many of those affected by the crimes under the Court's jurisdiction as possible, in order to contribute to restoration and reconciliation in a broader sense.[487] An examination of the preparatory works leads to the conclusion that the wording "in respect of" victims was chosen to extend the scope of application to persons who are indirectly affected by the crime, such as indirect victims as defined in the 1985 Victims Declaration.[488] However, the drafters of the Statute were not familiar with the future content of the Rules. Thus, as examined above, families and others indirectly harmed, as well as collectives of victims, could be covered by a broad construction of the victim definition in Rule 85.

---

484 Reg. 46 Trust Fund Regulations. See also Reg. 42-45.

485 See Standard Application Form for Individuals, p. 1: "Where a victim is a child, or has a disability that prevents the victims from acting on her or his own behalf, someone else may make an application on their behalf. Where a victim is deceased, someone else may also make the application".

486 In *Situation in the Democratic Republic of The Congo*, Decision on the Applications for Participation in the Proceedings of VPRS 1, VPRS 2, VPRS 3, VPRS 4, VPRS 5 and VPRS 6, Pre-Trial Chamber I, 17 January 2006, ICC-01/04-101, paras. 113 et seq. persons who had lost close relatives allegedly as a result of crimes under the ICC Statute were considered "victims" without even discussing it.

487 See Chapter 3 ("Purposes of Reparations in International Criminal Law") above.

488 D. Donat-Cattin: "Article 75 – Reparations to Victims". In: Commentary on the Rome Statute of the International Criminal Court – Observers' Notes, Article by Article. Ed. O. Triffterer. Baden-Baden, 1999, pp. 965 et seq. at p. 969 referring to the preparatory works and a footnote inserted in the Report of the Working Group on Procedural Matters of the Rome Conference, A/CONF.183/C.1/WGPM/L.2/Add.7 (1998)) designed at orienting the interpretation of the Statutory language "in respect of victims". The footnote states that in order to interpret "victims" and "reparations" reference shall be taken to the 1985 Victims Declaration and the then Draft Basic Principles and Guidelines on the Right to a Remedy and Reparations for Victims of Violations of Human Rights and International Humanitarian Law, now adopted (2005 Victims Principles).

The question of how to determine who shall benefit from reparations "in respect of" victims, whether they be family members, other indirectly harmed persons, or collectives of victims, has been discussed above.[489]

1. International and National Law and Human Rights

As examined previously, it is often recognized in the national and international human rights context that "indirect victims" such as families of direct victims and groups or collectives of victims, can benefit from reparations.[490] There are two more categories of persons that international documents and human rights jurisprudence recognize as additional beneficiaries of reparations. The 1985 Victims Declaration and the 2005 Victims Principles recognize as potential recipients of reparations "persons who have suffered harm in intervening to assist victims in distress or to prevent victimization".[491]

International human rights jurisprudence also recognizes that awards of reparations can be recovered by heirs or successors if the applicant dies during the proceedings.[492]

Before the Inter-American Court of Human Rights, both pecuniary and non-pecuniary claims survive and automatically pass to the victim's heirs or successors.[493] The European Court of Human Rights has recognized that heirs and successors can recover pecuniary damages owed to the direct victim if the applicant dies during the proceedings, though until recently awards for non-pecuniary damages only survived if the court considered it necessary to advance the cause of justice.[494]

489 Chapter 5 B. I. 2) and II ("Direct and Indirect Harm" and "Collective Beneficiaries of Reparations").

490 Ibid.

491 Principle 8 2005 Victims Principles; para. 2 1985 Victims Declaration.

492 See for detailed discussion of relevant international human rights jurisprudence D. Shelton: Remedies in International Human Rights Law. 2nd ed. Oxford, 2005, pp. 242-243. Generally see also H. Rombouts; P. Sardaro; S. Vandeginste: "The Right to Reparation for Victims of Gross and Systematic Violations of Human Rights". In: Out of the Ashes – Reparation for Victims of Gross and Systematic Human Rights Violations. Eds. K. de Feyter; S. Parmentier; M. Bossuyt (et al.). Antwerp, 2005, pp. 345 et seq. at pp. 467 et seq.

493 E.g. *Velásquez Rodríguez v. Honduras*, Inter-American Court of Human Rights, Compensatory Damages, 21 July 1989, Ser. C, No. 7; *Garrido and Baigorria v. Argentina*, Reparations, Inter-American Court of Human Rights, 27 August 1998, Ser. C, No. 39, para. 43; *Godínez Cruz v. Honduras*, Compensatory Damages, Inter-American Court of Human Rights, 21 July 1989, Ser. C, No. 5 for the determination of who can rightfully claim to be a "heir" or "successor".

494 E.g. *X v. United Kingdom*, European Court of Human Rights, 8 October 1982, Application No. 9054/80, paras. 18-19; *Colozza and Rubinat v. Italy*, European Court of Human Rights, 12 February 1985, Application No. 9317/81; *Aksoy v. Turkey*, Judgment, European Court of Human Rights, 18 December 1996, Application No. 21987/93, para 113.

2. Assessment

The wording of the French version of the Statute, a contextual interpretation and the drafting history of the Court's power to order reparations not only to, but also "in respect of" victims clarifies that family members of direct victims shall also be able to benefit from reparations. The inclusion of indirectly harmed persons such as family members as potential beneficiaries of reparations is also consistent with "internationally recognized human rights". Constructed in context and in accordance with international human rights law, collectives of victims could also benefit from reparation orders pursuant to Art. 75 (2). Thus, in cases where indirectly harmed family members and harmed collectives are not already recognized as "victims" under the definition of Rule 85, they can benefit from reparations ordered "in respect of" victims.

V. *Discretionary Decision of the Court to Order Reparations to Victims*

Art. 75 (2) states that the Court "may make an order [...] specifying appropriate reparations to, or in respect of, victims". Thus, while it is mandatory for the Court to establish reparation principles, ordering reparations is entirely within the discretion of the Chamber. Little guidance has been provided as to the factors that shall be relevant in the exercise of this discretion. Art. 75 (2) authorizes the Court to order "appropriate reparations". From this, it could be concluded that the word "appropriate" does not only set a standard for the content of a reparation order, but also for the decision as to whether to order reparations. If the discretion of the Court will be guided by the criterion of "appropriateness" to order reparations, it seems that under the ICC system the criteria will always be fulfilled once the perpetrator's liability is established. It seems appropriate that victims of the grave crimes under the ICC's jurisdiction, committed by a person convicted by the ICC, will receive reparations for their harm suffered. When victims whose rights have been violated by the crimes prosecuted by the ICC receive appropriate reparations for the harm they suffered from the competent national authorities, the principle of complementarity might prevent the ICC from ordering reparations.[495] In all other situations, it is for the ICC to address the issue of reparations. Moreover, it seems appropriate that a perpetrator of the grave crimes under the ICC's jurisdiction will not only be held criminally responsible, but also liable to repair the harm caused. Furthermore, it seems appropriate for the Court to claim reparations on behalf of those victims of the case that have not filed applications for reparations when it must be assumed this is not due to a conscious decision.[496] Thus, unless the convicted person is completely unwilling to cooperate in awarding reparations, it is submitted that it is always appropriate for the Court to order reparations once the liability of the convicted person is established.[497]

495 C. Jorda; J. de Hemptinne: "The Status and Role of the Victim". In: The Rome Statute of the International Criminal Court – A Commentary. Eds. A. Cassese; P. Gaeta; J. R. W. D. Jones. Vol. 2. Oxford, 2002, pp. 1387 et seq. at p. 1398.

496 See Chapter 6 A. II. ("Court-initiated Reparations Procedure") below.

497 When the convicted person is unwilling to cooperate in awarding reparations, the Court could consider to order a fine, given that the preconditions for such an order are met, see

It could be argued that the incorporation of Art. 75 and Art. 79 into the ICC Statute implies the acknowledgment that those who qualifiy as victims of a crime a person was convicted for by the Court shall be able to obtain reparations. In a decision on victims' participation in the investigative stage of the proceedings, the Court stated that Art. 68 (3) on victim participation imposes an obligation on the Court vis-à-vis victims.[498] This argument might likewise be applied to Art. 75 on reparations to victims. In the mentioned decision, the Chamber argued that "the victims' guaranteed right of access to the Court entails a positive obligation for the Court to enable them to exercise that right concretely and effectively".[499] Transferring this statement to ICC's reparation system would mean that as the Statute establishes victims' right to apply for reparations and equips the Court with the power to order reparations to victims, the Court is obliged to give effect to this right granted to victims. In practice, that means, inter alia, that applications for reparations filed by victims have to be seriously considered by the Court and that it shall make use of its power to award reparations to victims.

Apart from this abstract consideration, it is realistic to expect that practically the Court will face pressure to make use of the reparations function. Exercising its discretion to order reparations upon fair, comprehensive, transparent and even-handed criteria in all matters concerning reparations could prove critical for the Court's credibility in general and specifically among victims. It would therefore be recommendable for the Court to set forth criteria as a part of the reparations principles established under Art. 75 (1) so that victims, or persons that consider filing a claim on their behalf, can estimate the chances of a successful claim prior to making an application for reparations. The insecurity that currently derives from the unpredictable nature both of the right to reparations and the reparation order should be, as far as possible, diminished by establishing and consistently applying clear reparation principles.

As to the effect of decisions on reparation claims before the ICC, it is emphasized that nothing in Art. 75 on reparations, and by extension the Courts' decisions based on it, shall not prejudice the rights of victims under national and international law (Art. 75 (6)). This provision is consistent with other provisions in the ICC Statute that aim to prevent the interpretation of ICC jurisprudence as reflecting existing rules in international criminal law and procedure.[500] Consequently, even when a victim's

---

Chapter 6 D. I. 2. ("Reparations and the Imposition of Fines and Forfeiture Orders").

498 *Situation in the Democratic Republic of The Congo*, Decision on the Applications for Participation in the Proceedings of VPRS 1, VPRS 2, VPRS 3, VPRS 4, VPRS 5 and VPRS 6, ICC Pre-Trial Chamber I, 17 January 2006, ICC-01/04-101, p. 18 referring to victims' participation in the proceedings. However, as Art. 68 (3) grants victims the same potential right as Art. 75 (3), the statement may be conversely applied to Art. 75 (2).

499 Ibid, p. 19.

500 See also D. Donat-Cattin: "Article 75 – Reparations to Victims". In: Commentary on the Rome Statute of the International Criminal Court – Observers' Notes, Article by Article. Ed. O. Triffterer. Baden-Baden, 1999, pp. 965 et seq. at p. 976-977, confirming that the formula contained in Art. 75 (6) is a commonly used in international human rights instruments.

claim for reparations filed with the Court is turned down, this shall not be interpreted as implying a general statement on the victim's right to reparations under national and international law or have any impact on the victim's rights in other fora. Its seems essential to clarify this principle particularly when victims that have claimed reparations are not found to be eligible for reparation by the ICC.

VI. Assessment

The crimes under the Court's jurisdiction typically affect large numbers of natural and legal persons. For the purposes of the ICC reparations mechanism, selection of persons or collectives that shall benefit from ICC reparation awards from all those that have also suffered in the course of the conflict is inevitable.

The "victim" definition set forth in the ICC Rules plays a central role in this determination. However, the ICC victim definition is broad and as such offers limited help to determine beneficiaries of reparation orders. In order to develop a realistic system that provides reparations for those who suffered harm as a result of crimes under the ICC's jurisdiction with the inevitably limited resources and capacities of the Court that will be available, interpretation and possibly the imposition of additional criteria are necessary. The selection of beneficiaries should be fair and conducted in a manner that promotes reconciliation among the individuals and groups affected by a conflict instead of aggravating injuries and conflicts.

Victimized collectives and family members of direct victims, as well as other "indirect victims", can benefit from reparations either under a broad interpretation of the term "victim" in Rule 85, or on the grounds of the Court's power to order reparations "in respect of" victims, pursuant to Art. 75 (2).

The determination of who shall be eligible to receive reparations might be justifiably influenced by a number of outside factors like the historic and cultural context and nature of the crime, the number of victims in search of reparations, the form of reparations being requested, the resources available and the willingness of the convicted person to cooperate. Thus, it seems that the criteria for selecting beneficiaries of ICC reparations will have to be adjusted in every case. However, in order to meet the standard of equality and predictability, interpretations and selection criteria that are too flexible and change in every case on the basis of unknown factors are problematic. In order for reparations to achieve its purposes, and for the ICC to not lose its credibility in the eyes of victims and the general public, choices should always be objective.

The first objective criterion according to which beneficiaries of ICC reparation awards are selected from all those affected in a situation under the ICC investigation is the requirement of being harmed by a crime for which the perpetrator was convicted by the Court. Thus, a decisive selection is made through the Prosecutor's decision of whom to prosecute. It is first in the Prosecutor's hands to avoid causing discrimination between victims groups by, for example,. proceeding only against perpetrators representing a particular side of a conflict. The second step in the selection process of determining beneficiaries of reparations is made by the Trial Chamber's conviction of the accused.

Thus, at the point at which the reparations proceedings begin, core choices have been already been made that are principally the result of the combination of reparations with criminal proceedings. Only at the stage of the reparations proceedings are the choices upon the relevant Chamber to decide who of all those harmed by the convicted person's crime shall benefit from reparations.

It is suggested that the approaches to the determination of eligibility should vary according to whether individuals or a collective of victims shall benefit from reparation.[501]

To a certain extent, the selection of beneficiaries of reparations from all those qualifying as victims under the ICC definition is avoided when collective reparations awards are ordered. However, often victims cannot be categorized into homogenous groups. In these cases, when collective reparations are ordered the victimized group or collective that shall benefit from reparations must be selected. This selection shall be conducted on the basis of flexible and understandable criteria, e.g. whether a specific group was particularly targeted or harmed through the crime. Guidelines are provided by the criteria set forth in the ICC's legal instruments for common legal representation of groups of victims, in particular age, gender, health and the nature of crime. The challenge is to ensure that the award of reparations to a specific group does not deepen existing rifts in society instead of contributing to reconciliation. A means to achieve this aim is to consult with representatives of the victimized collectives. If the award is of symbolic nature, the willingness of the convicted person to perform certain necessary acts, e.g. to apologize to a certain ethnic group of victims, is another decisive factor. Ideally, the perpetrator and representatives of victimized collectives agree not only on the precise form of the award, but also on its recipient. Thus, within the rough guidelines set forth in the ICC's legal instruments, the group benefiting from a collective award must be determined with flexibility in each case.

In contrast, when individual victims are the beneficiaries of reparations, a different approach is necessary to secure fairness, equality and predictability. Selection of beneficiaries shall be conducted on the basis of clear and objective criteria that are to be applied consistently in every case. In particular in cases of high-ranking perpetrators, there might be a great number of persons having suffered harm as a result of the crime. It is consistent with internationally recognized human rights to recognize a wide range of forms of "harm", including mental and moral damage. Thus, "harm" as criterion for eligibility for reparations hardly serves as a restrictive principle.[502] The most objective and fair criterion to select individual beneficiaries of ICC reparations from a possibly large number of victims seems to be to require a direct link between the crime and the harm suffered. In case there is a lack of resources, only those individuals that are more directly or personally harmed by the convicted person's crime than others affected shall be eligible for individual awards. However, it might also be justified to take the severity of harm a person suffered as a result of the crime under the ICC's jurisdiction a criterion to select individual beneficiaries of the reparation

501 See Chapter 5. C. I. ("Type of Reparations: Individual and Collective Awards").

502 See also R. G. Teitel: Transitional Justice. Oxford, 2000, p. 134 regarding state reparations.

order, even though it may sometimes be more difficult to determine in an objective manner. In cases where the determination of collective or individual beneficiaries of reparations is complicated and time-consuming, this task may be delegated to the Trust Fund.

It can be assumed that when entering the reparations stage, a number of choices regarding the determination of victims has already made through their participation in the trial proceedings. However, as participation in the trial proceedings is not a pre-condition for eligibility to obtain reparations, and a victim's participation does not automatically lead his or her eligibility to obtain reparations, all final decisions regarding who will receive reparations will remain to be resolved in the reparations stage.

C. Content of ICC Reparation Orders

In this subchapter, the possible content of ICC reparation orders pursuant to Art. 75 (2) will be examined. The content of each order will only be determined after the liability of the convicted person to make reparations to victims has been established, as discussed in the previous subchapters.

ICC reparation orders may take various forms. Principally, reparations can be of an individual or collective nature, and can take monetary or symbolic form. When financial awards are made, a number of factors may have an impact on the scope of the order.

A reparation order specifying that the convicted person shall make reparations to victims necessarily includes the assessment that the rights of the victims were violated and that the convicted person is liable for the violations.[503] The choice of its content depends on the purposes it shall serve.

The quantity and quality of the crimes under the ICC jurisdiction affect the scope and nature of remedies that can and should be afforded. At the same time the determination of the content and scope of the reparation order is, probably more than any other aspect of the ICC reparations regime, characterized by the fact that it is an individual rather than a state or corporation that the order is made against. This is in spite of the collective nature of the crimes under the ICC's jurisdiction.

Art. 75 (2) of the ICC Statute states that reparations should be "appropriate" and expressly mentions, in a non-exclusive manner, three forms of reparations: restitution, compensation and rehabilitation. These are the classic types of reparations for personal loss or damages.[504] The Rules again mention these three kinds of awards and

503 B. Stephens: "Conceptualizing Violence – Present and Future Developments in International Law – Panel I – Human Rights and Civil Wrongs at Home and Abroad – Old Problems and New Paradigms – Conceptualizing Violence under International Law – Do Tort Remedies Fit the Crime?" In: Alabama Law Review 60 (1997), pp. 579 et seq. at pp. 604-605.

504 C. Jorda; J. de Hemptinne: "The Status and Role of the Victim". In: The Rome Statute of the International Criminal Court – A Commentary. Eds. A. Cassese; P. Gaeta; J. R. W. D. Jones. Vol. 2. Oxford, 2002, pp. 1387 et seq. at p. 1409.

give different options as to whom they may be addressed to, i.e. their possible collective or individual nature.[505]

Therefore, as the ICC's legal instruments do not provide details on the potential content of reparation orders, the following examination will again refer to national and international law and human rights for possible clarification.

I. Type of Reparations: Individual and Collective Awards

Except for mentioning restitution, compensation and rehabilitation as possible forms of reparations and providing that they can be ordered "in respect of, victims", the Statute does not provide guidelines as to the type of reparations that can be awarded. The explicit possibility to award both individual and collective reparations has, however, been introduced in the Rules, particularly in Rule 97 (1).[506]

Individual and collective reparations may coexist in the same award (Rule 97 (1)). This seems appropriate in view of the different purposes that individual and collective reparations often serve. A person may therefore be the recipient of an individual award and also benefit from an award made to a collective that he or she is a member of. The possibility to award both collective and individual reparations is also important in situations where individuals belonging to the victimized group cannot benefit from a collective reparations award.[507]

The ICC's legal instruments do no limit the forms of reparations that can be awarded to collective or individual victims. Thus, all forms of reparations, including restitution, compensation, rehabilitation and other forms of reparations can be awarded individually or collectively. As collective awards aim at a broader societal effect, the same form of reparations will look very different when made to the collective, as opposed to individual beneficiaries.

Rule 97 (1) provides that, when determining whether an award should be made to individual or collective recipients, or to both, "the scope and extent of any damage, loss or injury" shall be taken into account. However, no direction is given as to how and for what purpose this should be done. While "damage, loss and injury" are categories of harm that typically refer to the consequences of a crime committed against an individual, this might also just refer to the wording of Art. 75 (1). Rule 98 (3) on implementation through the Trust Fund is more instructive in that it implies

505 Rule 94 (restitution, compensation, rehabilitation), Rule 97 (1), Rule 98 (1)-(3) (collective and individual reparations).

506 Rule 97 (1) states: "Taking into account the scope and extent of any damage, loss or injury, the Court may award reparations on an individualized basis or, where it deems it appropriate, on a collective basis or both."

507 This might be i.e. when children orphaned by an international crime have left their national State to live abroad with adopted parents, the collective award of reparations available to other victims staying behind in their home state would not be available to these children. Reparations on an individualized basis may then be awarded to the children in this situation, K. Kittichaisaree: International Criminal Law. Oxford, 2001, p. 324.

that collective awards shall be made when the "number of victims and scope, forms and modalities or reparations" makes it more appropriate.

When deciding whether to award individual or collective reparations, or both, the Court may consult with experts (Rule 97 (2)). While it is for the Court to determine whether a reparations award shall be directed to individuals or a collective of victims, the determination of the precise content of awards can be delegated to the Trust Fund.

1. Individual Reparations

While the ICC Statute allows for all types and forms of reparations that are "appropriate", the Rules suggest that reparations should, as a rule, be awarded on an individualized basis.[508]

Individual reparations might be similar to awards made to an individual victim as a result of a civil claim for damages in domestic proceedings. At least theoretically, individual awards aim at providing an equivalent to the specific damage, loss or injury suffered by the victim of crime. Individual awards seem to be of a monetary rather than of a non-monetary nature, typically the specific damage caused to a person is compensated in the form of money, as "money is the common measure of valuable things".[509] However, individual victims can request in their applications not only restitution, compensation or rehabilitation, but also "other forms of remedy".[510] These could consist of monetary awards granted to be used for a specific purpose, such as a scholarship or educational expenses, or non-monetary measures aimed at restoring the dignity of the individual, such as an apology or acknowledgment of wrongdoing. However, in view of the collective character of the crimes for which the convicted person was held responsible, it hardly seems justifiable to order symbolic acts, such as an apology, to be made for the exclusive benefit of an individual victim.

Since individual awards regularly aim at redressing a specific harm, in principle the harm must be assessed and the causal link to the crimes of the convicted person must be established in each individual case.[511] However, various methods of determining individual awards are imaginable, ranging from individualized to standardized and uniform awards.[512] When the ICC orders reparations directly to victims, awards might possibly be more individualized than when individual awards are made through the Trust Fund.[513] In fact, the Trust Fund Regulations provide for the applica-

508 Art. 75 (2); Rule 97 (1); Rule 98 (1) and (3).

509 H. Grotius: De Jure Belli Ac Pacis Libri Tres. Transl. by F. W. Kelsey. Vol. 2. Oxford (et al.), 1925, Ch.XVII, 430-431.

510 Rule 94 (1) (f); Part F Question 1 Standard Application Form for Individuals.

511 The Court is competent to delegate this task to experts, the Trust Fund, or an approved organization, see Rule 97 (2), 98 (2)-(4).

512 See Chapter 5 C. IV. ("Scope of the Compensation Order").

513 See Chapter 6 F. ("Implementation of Reparation Awards").

tion of mass claims processing according to standardized criteria, which may result in individual yet uniform awards.[514]

2. Collective Reparations

A collective award of reparations will be made to the victimized "group", rather than an individual victim.[515]

The Rules envision that collective awards are usually made through the Trust Fund (Rule 98 (3)). The Trust Fund is to "set out the precise nature of the collective award(s), where not already specified by the Court, as well as the methods for its/their implementation".[516] Collective awards can be dedicated to exclusively communal or collective purposes. Alternatively, they may be distributed, on the basis of an internal agreement, to the individual members that are part of the collective of victims according to criteria set up internally, possibly in agreement with the Court or Trust Fund.

a) Appropriateness of Collective Awards

The Rules set forth that the Court can order individual reparations, and when it deems it appropriate, it can also award collective reparations alongside, or instead of, individual reparations (Rule 97 (1)). Therefore, collective awards are envisioned to be the exception.[517]

Despite this concept, reality might prove that in the context of the ICC reparations mechanism, individual awards might end up being the exceptions. Rule 98 (3) clarifies that the criteria that determine whether collective awards are appropriate are the "number of the victims and the scope, forms and modalities of reparations".

The financial situation of the convicted person or persons may not allow for compensating a large number of individual victims. In fact, the greater the damage the convicted person caused, the less likely it is that individual awards are appropriate to repair the harm caused to victims in a meaningful and sufficient way. Collective awards may be appropriate because they might in certain cases be the only realistic type of reparations, as individual awards could either not be implemented or would exclude a large part of equally harmed individuals from reparations.[518] Furthermore,

514 Rule 98 (2), Reg. 60 et seq. Trust Fund Regulations.

515 See also Chapter 5 B. II. ("Collective Beneficiaries of Reparations").

516 Reg. 69 Trust Fund Regulations. The determinations of the Trust Fund are to be approved by the Court.

517 See P. Lewis; H. Friman: "Reparations to Victims". In: The International Criminal Court – Elements of Crimes and Rules of Procedure and Evidence. Ed. R. S. Lee. Ardsley, New York, 2001, pp. 474 et seq. at p. 484, also for a summary of the drafting history; K. Kittichaisaree: International Criminal Law. Oxford, 2001, p. 324.

518 See for general discussion on the unlikelihood and inadequateness of individual awards in the wake of mass conflict and genocide see N. Roht-Arriaza: "Reparations, Decisions and Dilemmas". In: Hastings International and Comparative Law Review 27 (2004), pp. 157 et seq. at p. 185.

in view of the limited capabilities of the Court, it might be inappropriate for it to deal with large numbers of individual reparations claims.

The ICC might also find that, in addition to practical reasons, it might often consider it "appropriate" to order collective awards in view of their object and purpose.

The purpose of collective awards differs rationally from that of individual awards. A collective award will not be equivalent to a specific damage, as is generally necessary when making a civil claim for reparations.[519] The reasoning behind the concept of collective reparations, which might also be termed the concept of "collective victims", is linked to the specific nature of crimes such as those under the jurisdiction of the ICC. The assumption is that certain crimes are directed against a specific group and the victimization of the individual is therefore a result of the victimization of the entire group.[520] The group of individuals is linked by special bonds, considerations, factors or circumstances which, for these very reasons, made them a target or object of victimization.[521] Thus, the crime is directed against a person not because of his or her personality, but for his or her belonging to a certain group.[522] This is most clearly demonstrated by the crime of genocide: the perpetrator seeks to persecute or exterminate not primarily the individual person, but rather the group or community the victim is a member of, because of their race, religion, nationality or ethnicity.[523] Other groups may be targeted because of the political opinion or ideology of their members.

Particularly in cases of genocide, but also with certain forms of war crimes and crimes against humanity, the crime can cause harm to the collective that is distinct from the injuries suffered by individual members. Members of a particular collective that were not directly affected may suffer indirectly from persecution inflicted on others: "The murder of intellectuals or religious leaders drains the collective of tradition, leadership, and optimism [...]. Destroying sacred sites and exiling large numbers of individuals can render the group vulnerable to assimilation and loss of identity. If the group's numbers fall below a critical mass, its very survival may be in jeopardy. In each of these scenarios, there is a collective harm, one that is different from those inflicted on individual group members."[524]

---

519 B. Timm: "The Legal Position of Victims in the Rule of Procedure and Evidence". In: International and National Prosecution of Crimes under International Law. Eds. H. Fischer, C. Kreß; S. R. Lüder. (Bochumer Schriften zur Friedenssicherung und zum Humanitären Völkerrecht). Berlin, 2001, pp. 289 et seq. at p. 304.

520 C. M. Bassiouni: "The Protection of 'Collective Victims' in International Law". In: International Protection of Victims. Ed. C. M. Bassiouni. Eres, 1988, pp. 181 et seq. at p. 184. See also Chapter 5 C. II. ("A Collective as a Beneficiary of Reparations") above.

521 Ibid., p. 183.

522 See R. Lemkin: "Genocide as a Crime under International Law". In: American Journal of International Law 41 (1947), pp. 145 et seq. at p. 145.

523 Art. 6 ICC Statute.

524 P. R. Dubinsky: "Justice for the Collective – The Current Limits of the Human Rights Class Action". In: Michigan Law Review 102 (2004), pp. 1152 et seq. at p. 1182.

Therefore, there are commonly affected groups whose members have not all been harmed directly. Individual awards do not address the entire harm, as they are only made to those that succeed in establishing that their harm was directly, or under certain circumstances indirectly caused by the crime.[525] They are thus restrictive and exclude members of the group that have also suffered from the crimes. Furthermore, collective reparations can reach unidentified victims who, due to their victimization or social situation do not claim reparations before the Court.[526] In contrast, ideally, the entire harmed collective can benefit from them.[527]

Furthermore, the traditionally individual concepts of restitution, compensation and rehabilitation might not comprehensively take into account of the nature of the crimes within the ICC jurisdiction. Frequently, the nature of the harm suffered by the individual members of a group victimized by crimes under the ICC's jurisdiction is such that it cannot be repaired, especially by monetary payments only. Collective reparations have a wider scope and may serve as "symbolic measure" that intends to provide moral reparation.[528] They might correspond to the need of the victimized group to have public and transparent acknowledgment of the courses, effects and remedies of the international crimes they suffered from.[529] Collective reparations might thus enable the victimized group or community and their values to live on.[530]

525 See Chapter 5 B. I. 2) ("Direct and Indirect Harm").

526 See A.-M. de Brouwer: "Reparation to Victims of Sexual Violence – Possibilities at the International Criminal Court and at the Trust Fund for Victims and Their Families". In: Leiden Journal of International Law 20 (2007), pp. 207 et seq. at p. 233.

527 P. R. Dubinsky: "Justice for the Collective – The Current Limits of the Human Rights Class Action". In: Michigan Law Review 102 (2004), pp. 1152 et seq. at p. 1182 points out that "[t]he Holocaust presents a compelling case of group injury and the need for group relief. The Final Solution was not primarily a plan for persecuting specific individuals. It was a blueprint for destroying an entire people. Hitler sought to destroy not individual Jews, not even merely all Jews, but also all facets of Jewish culture and Jewish contributions to Western civilization". See also C. Tomuschat: "Darfur – Compensation for the Victims". In: Journal of International Criminal Justice 3 (2005), pp. 579 et seq. at p. 587: "In any process of transitional justice, the primary goal must be to re-establish security and respect for human rights as a matter of collective reparations".

528 B. Timm: "The Legal Position of Victims in the Rule of Procedure and Evidence". In: International and National Prosecution of Crimes under International Law. Eds. H. Fischer, C. Kreß; S. R. Lüder. (Bochumer Schriften zur Friedenssicherung und zum Humanitären Völkerrecht). Berlin, 2001, pp. 289 et seq. at p. 304.

529 D. Donat-Cattin: "Article 75 – Reparations to Victims". In: Commentary on the Rome Statute of the International Criminal Court – Observers' Notes, Article by Article. Ed. O. Triffterer. Baden-Baden, 1999, pp. 965 et seq. at p. 971.

530 C. Jorda; J. de Hemptinne: "The Status and Role of the Victim". In: The Rome Statute of the International Criminal Court – A Commentary. Eds. A. Cassese; P. Gaeta; J. R. W. D. Jones. Vol. 2. Oxford, 2002, pp. 1387 et seq. at p. 1410.

Thus, rather than as a means to satisfy civil debts, collective awards may be appropriate in their contribution to psychological, societal or material improvement of the situation of the victimized group.[531]

It can be concluded that both due to their specific object and purpose as well as for practical reasons, collective awards ordered exclusively or alongside individual awards may be appropriate.

b) Content of Collective Awards

Collective reparations can consist of restitution, compensation, rehabilitation or other remedy awarded to a collective. Due to their different purpose, collective awards allow for, and demand, a more flexible approach to redressing past injustices than individual awards, which can reflect the concrete circumstances of the collective victimization.[532] Thus, it is crucial that the collective that shall benefit is involved in defining the priorities and in shaping the content of the collective award.[533] This is envisioned under the ICC's legal framework which allows for the participation of potential beneficiaries of reparations in the decision-making process (Art. 75 (3), Rule 97 (3)).[534]

Collective awards can be of a financial or symbolic nature. Collective awards that are of a financial nature can address harm suffered by the collective on two different levels: They can address the harmed rights and goods of the collective itself, or damage caused to the individual victims that share certain characteristics and therefore constitute an identifiable group or collective.

First, in cases where harm suffered by the individual members of the victimized collective is to be addressed, one possible form that collective reparations can take is the granting of a certain amount of money ("lump sum") to an organization or foundation that represents the interests of the collective of victims.[535] The organiza-

531 Baumgartner, E.: "Aspects of Victims Participation in the Proceedings of the International Criminal Court". In: International Review of the Red Cross 90 (2008), pp. 409 et seq, at p. 439. argues that in order to satisfy the material needs of victims important for their survival, in situations where there are large numbers of victims, the Court has to envisage collective instead of individual reparations.

532 See B. Timm: "The Legal Position of Victims in the Rule of Procedure and Evidence". In: International and National Prosecution of Crimes under International Law. Eds. H. Fischer, C. Kreß; S. R. Lüder. (Bochumer Schriften zur Friedenssicherung und zum Humanitären Völkerrecht). Berlin, 2001, pp. 289 et seq. at p. 304.

533 See e.g. N. Roht-Arriaza: "Reparations, Decisions and Dilemmas". In: Hastings International and Comparative Law Review 27 (2004), pp. 157 et seq. at p. 200.

534 See further discussion Chapter 6 A. III ("Participation in the Reparations Procedure") below.

535 Especially when reparations shall be awarded to existing organizations or projects, it is essential to assess who the project or organization can represent or represents and whose interests they effectively serve. Also the legitimacy of the victims' organization or project could be assessed, and whether victims feel represented by the organization or project. Organizations or projects could also be established in cooperation with or by the Trust Fund. However, collective awards may be distributed by the Trust Fund or by approved

tion is given the task to set up criteria for the distribution of funds not only for the benefit of the collective but also its individual members, and to decide on claims.[536] Even though the final beneficiary of the reparations is the individual victim, since the organization or other body representing victims' interests is given the right to decide on the distribution of the awards, reparations are initially collective in nature.[537] Collective reparations are also linked to individual harm when the rights or legal positions of individuals are transferred to a body representing the collective of victims.[538] In the context of the ICC, this means that a common representative of victims could claim that a collective reparation award will be made through the Trust Fund to an intermediary or partner or organization representing the collective of victims, which could again choose to distribute individual awards to the victims that are members of the group.[539] Such awards could be categorized as collective compensation.

A second form that collective reparations can take occurs when a financial award is granted to community institutions or projects designed to benefit the group of victims as a whole.[540]

The decision as to which projects or community institution should benefit from the award can be made by the Trust Fund, or by national, international or intergov-

national, international, or inter-governmental organizations that do not represent the collective of victims themselves, but function as distributors, Rule 98 (4). See also Reg. 73 Trust Fund Regulations.

536 Examples for this are the administration of German funds by the Jewish Claims Conference whose purpose it is to compensate individual Jewish victims according to directives enacted by the German government, see e.g. the "hardship funds" (Richtlinien für die Vergabe von Mitteln an jüdische Verfolgte zur Abgeltung von Härten in Einzelfällen im Rahmen der Wiedergutmachung, 3 October 1980, Bundesanzeiger No. 192 of 14 October 1980; Article 2 Agreement of October 1992; see also H. Küpper: Kollektive Rechte in der Wiedergutmachung von Systemunrecht. Vol. 2. Frankfurt a. Main, 2004, p. 941.

537 H. Küpper: Kollektive Rechte in der Wiedergutmachung von Systemunrecht. Vol. 2. Frankfurt a. Main, 2004, pp. 862 et seq.: "originäre und derivative Rechte". Reparations awarded to individual victims may allow for simpler procedures or establish lower requirements for proof due to the membership of the individual beneficiaries in a certain group. Even though these procedural privileges derive from the group membership, the group membership itself is not sufficient to establish eligibility for reparations. The collective element is even more dominant when the membership in a certain collective it is required in order to be eligible, while reparations remain individual at their core.

538 An example is the transferral of heirless Jewish Property and assets to Jewish Claims Conference, H. Küpper: Kollektive Rechte in der Wiedergutmachung von Systemunrecht. Vol. 2. Frankfurt a. Main, 2004, p. 940.

539 Rule 98 (3), (4).; see also C. J. M. Safferling: "Das Opfer Völkerrechtlicher Verbrechen – Die Stellung der Verbrechensopfer vor dem Internationalen Strafgerichtshof". In: Zeitschrift für die Gesamte Strafrechtswissenschaft 115 (2003), pp. 352 et seq. at p. 381.

540 This is different from community service as known for certain categories of perpetrators in many national justice systems, see e.g., N. Roht-Arriaza: "Reparations, Decisions and Dilemmas". In: Hastings International and Comparative Law Review 27 (2004), pp. 157 et seq. at pp. 194-195 with further references.

ernmental organizations approved by the Trust Fund.[541] Even though the ICC's legal instruments do not expressly state so, clearly the relevant Chamber is also capable of determining the precise content of the collective award. As the final beneficiary of this form of collective awards is a collective or communal body, the collective element is more dominant than in the first case presented.[542]

When the convicted person's crime caused harm to a community, e.g. its infrastructure, a possible form of reparations could be to use his or her money to contribute to its re-building. This may be done through the contribution to certain projects, like the building of a rehabilitation center for children traumatized in the course of the conflict. Such measures could be categorized as collective rehabilitation or restitution.

A third category of collective awards are symbolic awards dedicated to restore the moral well-being of a community and its members, such as their dignity, culture or tradition. Certain forms of collective reparations can restitute the harm suffered by the collective and of individual members of the collective at the same time. For example, measures aiming to restore the dignity of victims, such as a public apology, may not only serve to restitute the dignity of the victimized group as such, but also that of the individual members that constitute the group. Collective awards of a symbolic nature may be categorized as satisfaction, or "other forms of remedy" under the ICC's legal instruments.[543]

The effectiveness of symbolic reparations depends on the true willingness of the convicted person to repair a part of his or her "fault" through a symbolic act. For example, if an expression of acknowledgment of wrongdoing or regret is not genuine, there is the danger that the symbolic measure will turn out as a meaningless and ineffective act or a mere fulfillment of a legal obligation with the aim to avoid more severe punishment. Another relevant factor is the readiness of the victimized group to accept such acts from the perpetrator. Thus, while symbolic collective awards have great potential, the ICC can merely provide a forum that opens the possibility for acts leading to redress and reconciliation.

In the aftermath of a number of cases of mass atrocities, such forms of collective reparations have been awarded.[544] International human rights jurisprudence, in particular the Inter-American Court, has ordered measures of reparations that have

541 Rule 98 (3), (4), Reg. 69, 73 Trust Fund Regulations.

542 The institutions that are the recipients of monetary collective awards may have social or communal, medical, psychological or research purposes.

543 Art. 75 (2) and particularly Rule 94 (1) (f).

544 E.g. in *Ferida Selimovic and forty-eight others against the Republika Srpska* ("Srebrenica" cases), Human Rights Chamber for Bosnia and Herzegovina, 7 March 2003, Case Nos. CH/01/8365 et al., instead of ordering individual compensation awards, the Chamber ordered the Republika Srpska to pay a lump sum amount to the Foundation of the Srebrenica-Potocari Memorial and Cemetery, where Srebrenica victims are to be inerred in accordance with applicants' traditions and beliefs. Furthermore, the Republika Srpska was ordered to make four additional annual payments to the memorial fund.

benefited communities.[545] Specific examples of collective awards will be examined in the context of the different forms of reparations discussed below.

3. Assessment

Once the Court has decided to make use of its power to order reparations, it must make the principal decision of whether the award shall be of an individual or collective nature. The decision will often have to be made between distributing resources that provide substantial relief for a few and more modest individual awards for many, with the issue of symbolic in the form of collective awards also contributing to the decision.

The ICC's legal instruments seem to suggest that when the harm caused by the convicted person's crime is great, or the number of victims is large, collective awards may be preferable.

To make a material difference, reparations must be substantial. Most likely, if the Court orders the convicted person to make substantial awards to individuals, they must necessarily be confined to a narrowly defined set of victims. As a consequence, certain groups of victims are privileged, which may lead to division, rather than reconciliation.[546] Additionally, individual compensation awards may be pointless in places where facilities to satisfy the very basic needs of victims are missing. When resources are scarce, contributing the convicted person's money to something that the whole community benefits from might serve the interests of the victims better than an attempt to compensate individual losses.[547] Collective awards may also be more appropriate when considering that one of the core aims of reparations is acknowledgment.[548] If the convicted person is willing, collective reparations of a strictly symbolic

545 E.g. *Plan de Sánchez Massacre v. Guatemala*, Reparations, Inter-American Court of Human Rights, 19 November 2004, Ser. C, No. 105; *Mayagna (Sumo) Awas Tingni Indigenous Community v. Nicaragua*, Inter-American Court of Human Rights, 31 August 2001, Ser. C, No. 79.

546 See S. Gloppen: "Review Essay: Reparatory Justice – A Road to Reconciliation? On the Role of Reparations in Transitional Justice Theory". In: Reparations – Redressing Past Wrongs. Eds. G. Ulrich; L. Krabbe Boserup. (Human Rights in Development – Yearbook 2001). The Hague, 2003, pp. 385 et seq. at p. 396.

547 P. Lewis; H. Friman: "Reparations to Victims". In: The International Criminal Court – Elements of Crimes and Rules of Procedure and Evidence. Ed. R. S. Lee. Ardsley, New York, 2001, pp. 474 et seq. at p. 483; see also C. Ferstman: "The Reparation Regime of the ICC – Practical Considerations". In: Leiden Journal of International Law 15 (2002), pp. 667 et seq. at p. 675.

548 S. Gloppen: "Review Essay: Reparatory Justice – A Road to Reconciliation? On the Role of Reparations in Transitional Justice Theory". In: Reparations – Redressing Past Wrongs. Eds. G. Ulrich; L. Krabbe Boserup. (Human Rights in Development – Yearbook 2001). The Hague, 2003, pp. 385 et seq. at p. 400 referring to R. G. Teitel: Transitional Justice. Oxford, 2000, pp. 218-219; similar N. Roht-Arriaza: "Reparations, Decisions and Dilemmas". In: Hastings International and Comparative Law Review 27 (2004), pp. 157 et seq. at p. 189: "Reparation is secondarily about compensation; its symbolic aspects are paramount".

nature like a public apology to a group that was victimized by his or her crime, should always be awarded.

Yet, individual reparation awards are also important. The purpose of acknowledgment may be more effectively achieved in some circumstances when individual awards are granted.[549] Not all victims of a crime or conflict have suffered equally and thus it might be justified to at least award individual awards to those that were directly and severely affected by the convicted person's crime.[550] Also, from a practical standpoint, individuals may be in need of individual compensation when they have lost their breadwinner or their house as a result of the convicted person's crime.

Thus, if appropriate given the specific circumstances of the case, use should be made of the possibility of ordering both individual and collective awards. Both of these awards have a specific purpose in the context of reparations for mass crimes and therefore complement rather than exclude each other. In fact, both international human rights jurisprudence and national reparations schemes have acknowledged that reparations to victims of mass and systematic violations can only be made effectively and comprehensively when both individual and collective reparations are awarded.[551]

Individual victims and groups should, through a common representative, participate in the decision-making on the type and content of reparation awards. A problem that might arise, particularly with regard to collective awards, is competition between different victim groups or collectives regarding participation and influence on the design and distribution of reparation awards.[552] Collective reparation measures should

549 Similar B. Hamber; T. Mofokeng: From Rhetoric to Responsibility – Making Reparations to the Survivors of Past Political Violence – Centre for the Study of Violence and Reconciliation. Johannesburg, 2000, p. 66: "for reparations to be psychologically restorative it has to be personalised [...] individuals experience violence through their own personal universe. Although socio-economic development is necessary, the physical and psychological impact of the violence has to be addressed directly and individually if we are ever to deal with the traumas of the past and prevent cycles of violence from emerging."

550 For individual awards also I. Bottigliero: Redress for Victims of Crimes under International Law. Leiden, 2004, p. 241.

551 See *Aloeboetoe et al. v. Suriname*, Reparations, Inter-American Court of Human Rights, 10 September 1993, Ser. C, No. 15, para. 52; *Plan de Sánchez Massacre v. Guatemala*, Reparations, Inter-American Court of Human Rights, 19 November 2004, Ser. C, No. 105. See for Western German reparations to victims of Nazi crimes a summary e.g., in particular P. R. Dubinsky: "Justice for the Collective – The Current Limits of the Human Rights Class Action". In: Michigan Law Review 102 (2004), pp. 1152 et seq.; H.-J. Brodesser; B. J. Fehn; T. Franosch (et al.): Wiedergutmachung und Kriegsfolgenliquidation – Geschichte, Regelungen, Zahlungen. München, 2000. See for an overview of relevant national reparations schemes for victims of gross and systematic crimes D. Shelton: Remedies in International Human Rights Law. 2nd ed. Oxford, 2005, pp. 389 et seq.

552 In particular when collective awards of financial nature are made via victim organizations, the organizations have great influence on the rights of the group members. E.g. following the collective reparations payments from the Federal Republic of Germany to the Jewish Claims Conference ("JCC") as a result of The Hague agreement 1953, the JCC

be implemented in a way that facilitates reconciliation between victims and perpetrators, without stigmatizing either.[553] Use should be made of the option for the convicted person and/or his or her representative and victims and/or their representative to get involved in the decision-making on reparations and to possibly reach agreement upon the type and form of measures (Art. 75 (3), Rule 97 (2) s. 2). This possibility is essential particularly in the context of collective awards of reparations, as these can and should be flexibly adjusted on a case-by-case basis, corresponding to the characteristics of the group and of the circumstances of the victimization.

II. *Form of Reparations*

Under the ICC's legal framework, reparations can be ordered in the form of restitution, compensation and rehabilitation (Art. 75 (2)).[554] It does not prioritize between the different forms of reparations. The Statute and Rules also envision the possibility of awarding "appropriate reparations" other than restitution, rehabilitation and compensation.[555] The precise definition of reparation was left purposefully open by the drafters of the Statute.[556] It is the Court's duty under Art. 75 (1) to establish principles regarding reparations, including, but not limited to, restitution, compensation and rehabilitation, and thus to specify the content of reparation awards.[557]

It was the express intention of the parties negotiating the Statute, that, for the purpose of interpreting the term "reparations", the Court shall take into its consideration the definitions of the 1985 Victims Declaration and the "Draft Basic Principles", which have now been adopted as the 2005 Victims Principles.[558]

1. Restitution

Restitution can be defined as the "[r]eturn or restoration of some specific thing to its rightful owner or status".[559] The ICC Statute does not indicate which legal goods are

---

was heavily criticized for utilizing the money received exclusively for collective rather than individual purposes. On victim competition, see e.g. H. Rombouts; P. Sardaro; S. Vandeginste: "The Right to Reparation for Victims of Gross and Systematic Violations of Human Rights". In: Out of the Ashes – Reparation for Victims of Gross and Systematic Human Rights Violations. Eds. K. de Feyter; S. Parmentier; M. Bossuyt (et al.). Antwerp, 2005, pp. 345 et seq. at p. 473.

553 N. Roht-Arriaza: "Reparations, Decisions and Dilemmas". In: Hastings International and Comparative Law Review 27 (2004), pp. 157 et seq. at p. 189.

554 See above Chapter 1 C.

555 Art. 75 (2); Rule 94 (1) (f) "other remedy".

556 See for the drafting history on the relevant Rules, P. Lewis; H. Friman: "Reparations to Victims". In: The International Criminal Court – Elements of Crimes and Rules of Procedure and Evidence. Ed. R. S. Lee. Ardsley, New York, 2001, pp. 474 et seq. at pp. 475 et seq.

557 See Chapter 4 A. ("Establishing Principles pursuant to Art. 75 (1) s. 1 ICC Statute").

558 See also Chapter 4 A.III. ("Scope and Content of Reparation Principles").

559 B. A. Garner (ed.): Black's Law Dictionary. 8th ed. St. Paul, Minnesota, 2004, p. 1339.

meant to be restituted or which principles are to be applied. However, the Rules set forth requirements for reparation claims of victims seeking restitution and indicate the goods that can be restituted upon an ICC reparation order: the legal goods that are the intended objects of ICC restitution orders are "assets, property and other tangible items".[560]

In reverse, it could be concluded that restitution of intangible items such as lost rights, i.e. citizenship, public office, freedom, one's dignity or good name, or a particular environment is not envisioned as restitution that can be ordered by the Court.[561] However, the Standard Application Form for Individuals, in the section titled "reparations", lists "legal rights" and "social status" as recognized types of losses.[562] These types of losses, in particular the loss of rights, can only be remedied through restitution. This seems to indicate that intangible goods might also be the objects of ICC restitution orders.

The ICC Statute and Rules contain an important restriction concerning the possible content of an award regarding the restitution of property to victims: Property in the hands of *bona fide* third parties is not subject to restitution for victims. The rights of *bona fide* third parties in possession of property have been protected throughout the Statute and Rules both regarding reparations and forfeiture orders.[563] Third parties have been granted procedural rights before the Court which enable them to safeguard their substantive rights.[564]

a) International and National Law and Human Rights

Restitution is a generally recognized form of remedy. In the international legal context, restitution takes priority over other forms of reparations. In international law, this principle is based on the Chorzow Factory case[565], and further recognized by the 2005 Victims Principles[566], the ILC Draft Articles[567], the Inter-American Court of

560 Rule 94 (1) (d) reads: "Where restitution of assets, property or other tangible items is sought, a description of them".

561 Victims might suffer injury to these rights and intangible items in particular where the perpetrator was a public official of a state.

562 Part F Question 5.

563 Art. 75 (5) read in conjunction with Art. 109. Art. 109 (1) reads that "States Parties shall give effect to fines or forfeitures ordered by the Court […] without prejudice to the rights of bona fide third parties […]", see also Art. 109 (2). For further discussion, see W. A. Schabas: "Article 109 – Enforcement of Fines and Forfeiture Measures". In: Commentary on the Rome Statute of the International Criminal Court – Observers' Notes, Article by Article. Ed. O. Triffterer. Baden-Baden, 1999, pp. 1191 et seq.

564 See Chapter 6 A. ("Communications of the Court") below.

565 *Factory at Chorzow Case* (F.R.G. v. Pol), Permanent Court of International Justice, 12 September 1928, Ser. A, No. 17.

566 Principle 19.

567 Art. 35.

Human Rights,[568] the European Court of Human Rights[569] and the Bosnian Chamber of Human Rights, among others.[570] In national jurisdictions, approaches to the prioritization of restitution differ.[571]

The purpose and scope of restitution is described in the ILC Draft Articles: it should re-establish the situation that existed before the wrongful act.[572] While the ILC Draft Articles' refer to the reestablishment of the *status quo ante*, some decisions in international law have referred to the situation that would have existed if the wrongful act had not been committed.[573]

As to the content of restitution, international documents and human rights jurisprudence recognize that restitution includes judicial review[574] and "legal rehabilitation", meaning measures to eliminate any wrongfully constituted criminal record[575],

568 See for further discussion of the relevant approaches and jurisprudence D. Shelton: Remedies in International Human Rights Law. 2nd ed. Oxford, 2005, pp. 271-272; V. Madrigal-Borloz: "Damage and Redress in the Jurisprudence of the Inter-American Court of Human Rights (1979-2001)". In: Reparations – Redressing Past Wrongs. Eds. G. Ulrich; L. Krabbe Boserup. (Human Rights in Development – Yearbook 2001). The Hague, 2003, pp. 211 et seq. at pp. 253 et seq.

569 See e.g. *Brigandí v. Italy*, European Court of Human Rights, 19 February 1991, Application No. 11460/85, para. 34; *Quaranta v. Switzerland*, European Court of Human Rights, 24 May 1991, Application No. 12744/87, para. 40.

570 See M. Nowak: "Reparation by the Human Rights Chamber for Bosnia and Herzegovina". In: Out of the Ashes – Reparations for Victims of Gross and Systematic Human Rights Violations. Eds. K. de Feyter; S. Parmentier; M. Bossuyt (et al.). Antwerp, 2005, pp. 245 et seq. at pp. 282 et seq. with a summary of relevant jurisprudence.

571 Some jurisdictions adopt the view that reparation is primarily owed in the form of money, whereas others favor restitution as a general principle, see U. Magnus: "Comparative Report on the Law of Damages". In: Unification of Tort Law – Damages. Ed. U. Magnus. The Hague (et al.), 2001, pp. 185 et seq. at p. 189. In favor of compensation as a general principle are, e.g., England, France, Greece, Italy, Netherlands, South Africa; in favor as restitution as primary form of reparation are Germany, Belgium, Austria, Uganda. See also B. A. Koch; H. Koziol: "Comparative Analysis". In: Compensation for Personal Injury in a Comparative Perspective. Eds. B. A. Koch; H. Koziol. Wien, 2003, pp. 407 et seq. at p. 430.

572 Art. 35. See J. Crawford: The International Law Commission's Articles on State Responsibility – Introduction, Text and Commentaries. Cambridge, 2002, p. 213 contrasting different definitions of restitution, including a return to the situation that existed before the injury, and the establishment of the situation that the victim would be in if the injury had never taken place.

573 See D. Shelton: "Righting Wrongs – Reparations in the Articles on State Responsibility". In: American Journal of International Law 96 (2002), pp. 833 et seq. at p. 850 mentioning that the ICJ continues to quote and apply the Chorzow Factory formulation, stating that the aim is to establish the situation that "would have existed" if there had not been a breach.

574 See e.g. *Loayza Tamayo v. Peru*, Reparations, Inter-American Court of Human Rights, 27 November 1998, Ser. C, No. 42, para. 122.

575 Ibid.

as well as the restoration of occupation.[576] Under the 2005 Victims Principles, restitution includes, "as appropriate: restoration of liberty, enjoyment of human rights, identity, family life and citizenship, return to one's place of residence, restoration of employment and return of property".[577] Forms of restitution recognized in the ILC Draft Principles are the release of wrongfully detained persons, the return of unlawfully seized property, and a revocation of an unlawful judicial measure.[578] The European Court has sometimes ordered restitution with regard to land and/or property.[579] The 1985 Victims Declaration uses the term restitution as a generic term instead of reparation, which also includes the restoration of property and rights.[580]

While restitution is traditionally addressed to individual harm, it can also take collective forms. For example, the Bosnian Human Rights Chamber has ordered the removal of business facilities from the sites of destroyed mosques and the ceding of a school building to the Catholic Church.[581]

b) Assessment

In contrast to international documents and human rights, "restitution" does not have priority in relation to other forms of reparations before the ICC and seems to be restricted to the restitution of tangible goods. This may be an acknowledgement that lost rights and freedom can only be restituted by a state. However, the express listing of loss of "legal rights" in the Standard Application Form for Individuals seems to suggest that legal rights could also be restituted through ICC restitution orders. As the Court is not authorized to order states to make reparations, it seems questionable what purpose it would serve to make such an order against an individual.[582] Broader forms of restitution may take place on the collective or community level.[583]

576 Ibid., para. 113.

577 Principle 19.

578 Art. 35 ILC Draft Articles on State Responsibility.

579 See e.g. *Brumarescu v. Romania* (Just Satisfaction), European Court of Human Rights, 23 January 2001, Application No. 28342/95; *Papamichalopoulos and Others v. Greece* (Just Satisfaction), European Court of Human Rights, 31 October 1995, Application No. 14556/89.

580 Para. 8 states that it "should include the return of property or payment for the harm or loss suffered, reimbursement of expenses incurred as a result of the victimization, the provision of services and the restoration of rights".

581 See for a summary of relevant jurisprudence M. Nowak: "Reparation by the Human Rights Chamber for Bosnia and Herzegovina". In: Out of the Ashes – Reparations for Victims of Gross and Systematic Human Rights Violations. Eds. K. de Feyter; S. Parmentier; M. Bossuyt (et al.). Antwerp, 2005, pp. 245 et seq. at pp. 283-284.

582 However, as discussed above, the Court could recommend States to restitute the rights or freedom of victims. see also C. Muttukumaru: "Reparations to Victims". In: Collection of Essays on the Rome Statute of the International Criminal Court. Eds. F. Lattanzi; W. A. Schabas. Ripa di Fagnano Alto, 1999, pp. 301 et seq. at p. 309.

583 The Court might consider a convicted person's payment to identifiable victims which serves a devastated community to rebuild community facilities. These can include the

However, even the restitution of property and other tangible goods may be difficult for the Court. As such measures regularly touch the relevant state's sovereignty, they only seem possible in cooperation with states. Therefore, it appears that even regarding "property, assets and other tangible items", despite the ICC's authority to order their direct restitution, this form of reparation might be of primary relevance in the context of establishing reparation principles.

2. Compensation

The Statute and Rules do not indicate the possible content and scope of compensation that may be ordered. Generally compensation is made in the form of a monetary payment, though it may be sometimes agreed on other forms of value.[584]

The ICC's legal instruments also do not provide the circumstances under which compensation shall be awarded. Specific kinds of harm can only be redressed through certain forms of reparations. A lost life or personal injury are impossible to restitute, so therefore can only be redressed through compensation awards.[585] In certain cases, restitution of property or other tangible goods may be inappropriate, and compensation can be used as a more appropriate alternative.

As a general rule in international law and human rights, compensation will only be awarded if restitution is materially impossible or not proportionate.[586] Situations

(re)building of a school or a place of worship or to meet the expenses of relocation where the dislocation of the community is the direct result of a criminal act, ibid., p. 304.

584 See International Law Commission: Draft Articles on the Responsibility of States for Internationally Wrongful Acts – With Commentaries, 2001. Available at http://untreaty.un.org/ilc/texts/instruments/english/ commentaries/9_6_2001.pdf, last accessed 16 April 2009; United Nations Commission of Crime Prevention and Criminal Justice, UN Commission of Crime Prevention and Criminal Justice: Handbook on Justice for Victims on the Use and Application of the United Nations Declaration of Basic Principles of Justice for Victims of Crime and Abuse of Power, 1998, E/CN.15/1998/CRP.4/Add.1 ("UN Handbook"), p. 44: "Victim compensation and restitution. Goal: To acknowledge and validate the losses of victims through a system of financial reparation [...]". However D. Donat-Cattin: "Article 75 – Reparations to Victims". In: Commentary on the Rome Statute of the International Criminal Court – Observers' Notes, Article by Article. Ed. O. Triffterer. Baden-Baden, 1999, pp. 965 et seq. at p. 671 uses the term "non-pecuniary forms of compensation".

585 And perhaps rehabilitative measures such as psychotherapy, provided to the relatives of killed victims.

586 E.g. Art. 36 (1) ILC Draft Articles; see also D. Shelton: Remedies in International Human Rights Law. 2nd ed. Oxford, 2005, p. 54 quoting further authorities. The formula included in the ILC Draft articles that allows for greater flexibility as it adds to the traditional concept of "impossibility" a proportionality test to the grounds for not awarding restitution, seems more consistent with current state practice, Art. 35, see D. Shelton: "Righting Wrongs – Reparations in the Articles on State Responsibility". In: American Journal of International Law 96 (2002), pp. 833 et seq. at p. 850. Regarding the European Court of Human Rights, see e.g. P. Leach: Taking a Case to the European Court of Human Rights. 2nd ed. Oxford, 2005, pp. 405-406. Yet, C. D. Gray: Judicial Remedies in International Law. 2 ed. Oxford, 1990, pp. 13-14 notes that "[t]here is little, if anything, to support the

where restitution is impossible or inappropriate arise frequently, and in these cases compensation awards can be utilized as a more viable alternative. Restitution is impossible when the property in question has been destroyed, or forms of harm were caused that are *per se* impossible to restitute, such as certain types of bodily harm or loss or life. Restitution is often inappropriate because the benefit to be gained from it by the victim is wholly disproportionate to its cost to the violator.[587] Thus, while theoretically compensation is an alternative form of reparations where restitution is impossible or inappropriate, compensation is actually the most common form of reparation.[588] This is particularly true in the context of the ICC, as the crimes under its jurisdiction typically cause harm that is impossible to restitute, such as personal injury or death.

a) Types of Compensable Harm

The ICC's legal instruments do not set forth which forms of harm are compensable. In the subchapter on eligibility for reparations it was discussed which forms of harm are recognized for the purpose of qualifying as a victim under Rule 85.[589] It could be assumed that the forms of harm recognized for the qualification as a "victim" under Rule 85 are automatically compensable. However, as indicated by the division in the Standard Application Forms between "Information about the injury, loss or harm suffered" (Part E) and "Reparations" (Part F), in which applicants are asked to specify the types of harm and loss they suffered, the question of "harm" for the purpose of qualifying as a victim under Rule 85 and harm or loss that can be addressed in an reparation award are distinct though intersecting. This reflects the approach taken e.g. in the 2005 Victims Principles as well as national laws.[590]

---

primacy of *restitutio in integrum* in international arbitral practice" and that "[t]he disadvantages of *restitutio in integrum* as a remedy in international law are considerable and explain the rarity of its award, its refusal in certain cases and the preference of claimants for the remedy of damages" with further discussion.

587 E.-C. Gillard: "Reparation for Violations of International Humanitarian Law". In: International Review of the Red Cross 851 (2003), pp. 529 et seq. at p. 531.

588 Regarding the international law context see e.g. D. Shelton: Remedies in International Human Rights Law. 2nd ed. Oxford, 2005, p. 54, and J. Crawford: The International Law Commission's Articles on State Responsibility – Introduction, Text and Commentaries. Cambridge, 2002, p. 218 for "modern claims practice", stating that restitution "may be partially or entirely ruled out either on the basis of the exceptions expressed in Article 35, or because the injured State prefers compensation or for other reasons". For domestic jurisdictions see B. A. Koch; H. Koziol: "Comparative Analysis". In: Compensation for Personal Injury in a Comparative Perspective. Eds. B. A. Koch; H. Koziol. Wien, 2003, pp. 407 et seq. at p. 430.

589 See Chapter 5 B.

590 Forms of "harm" recognized for the purposes of the victim definition in Principle 8 and for the purposes of compensation in Principle 20 are not identical under the 2005 Victims Principles, even though they are to a far extent congruent. In the German law of damages, a distinction is made between the question of "infringement of legally pro-

The 2005 Victims Principles require harm to be "economically assessable"[591], and the ILC Draft Principles require harm to be "financially available", in order for the harm to be compensable. Both documents fail to define what forms of harm are "economically assessable" or "financially available". These requirements appear critical in particular with regard to moral or impecuniary harm. However, the commentary to the ILC Draft Principles states that "[n]o less than material injury sustained [...], non-material damage is financially assessable and may be the subject of a claim of compensation."[592] Also the wording of the 2005 Victims Principles confirms that "moral damage" can be economically assessable.[593] The Inter-American Court held that not only material, but also moral reparations are intended to be compensatory.[594]

Accordingly, while the used terminology may vary, it is widely accepted in the national and international legal context, that not only pecuniary or material harm, but also non-pecuniary harm or moral damages are compensable.

1) Pecuniary or Material Damage

i) ICC Reparation System

The ICC has determined that economic loss constitutes harm within the meaning of Rule 85.[595] The Standard Application Form for Individuals lists "loss of or damage to property" as possible types of harm and sets forth examples for such harm: loss or damage to home(s), land, personal property, including household goods, animal(s) or other losses.[596] Further types of material harm listed for the purposes of reparations are "loss of income, unpaid salaries, loss of support and other losses connected to the employment", "loss of savings at banks, stocks or other securities".[597]

---

tected interest" ("Rechtsgutsverletzung") required in order to determine the eligibility for reparations and the question of "compensable damage" ("ersatzfähiger Schaden").

591 Principle 20 2005 Victims Principles, Art. 36 (2) ILC Draft Articles.

592 International Law Commission: Draft Articles on the Responsibility of States for Internationally Wrongful Acts – With Commentaries, 2001. Available at http://untreaty.un.org/ilc/texts/instruments/english/ commentaries/9_6_2001.pdf, last accessed 16 April 2009, p. 101 referring to the Lusitania Case, see *Lusitania* (United States of America v. Germany), Reports of International Arbitral Awards, 21 February 1924, Vol. VII, pp. 256-257, and stating that international tribunals have frequently granted pecuniary compensation for moral injury to private parties. The phrase "financially assessable" is intended to exclude the award of moral damages to states, since satisfaction is considered the more appropriate form of reparation to states for non-material injury, ibid., p. 99.

593 Principle 20.

594 The term "fair compensation" in Art. 61 (1) of the American Convention is interpreted by the Inter-American Court of Human Rights as compensatory damages, see e.g. *Velásquez Rodríguez v. Honduras*, Compensatory Damages, Inter-American Court of Human Rights, 21 July 1989, Ser. C, No. 7, pp. 27-28, 30-31.

595 *Situation in the Democratic Republic of The Congo*, Decision on the Applications for Participation in the Proceedings of VPRS 1, VPRS 2, VPRS 3, VPRS 4, VPRS 5 and VPRS 6, Pre-Trial Chamber I, 17 January 2006, ICC-01/04-101, para. 116.

596 Part F question 4; Part E question 1.

597 Part F question 5.

ii) International and National Law and Human Rights

In international human rights jurisprudence and documents, as well as national jurisdictions, compensable pecuniary losses include material damages and loss of earnings, costs required for legal or expert assistance, medicine and medical services, and psychological and social services.[598]

Loss of earnings includes all income that the victim failed to receive as a result of the violation.[599] In cases of loss of life or disappearance, the family or dependants have been awarded the amounts which the descendant or disappeared would probably have contributed to the claimant.[600] The Inter-American Court does not award compensation for material damages when there is no evidence that the victim ever provided support.[601] National administrative reparations mechanisms show that less individualized approaches are possible. For example, the Chilean Corporation's reparation program included monthly (life-long) pensions, based on the average income of a Chilean family, for spouses, parents and children of those killed or disappeared.

---

598 See e.g. Principle 20 2005 Victims Principles; Art. 36 (2) ILC Draft Articles; *Garrido and Baigorria v. Argentina*, Reparations, Inter-American Court of Human Rights, 27 August 1998, Ser. C, No. 39, para. 48. The European Court of Human Rights orders compensation for non-pecuniary loss and legal costs and expenses as "just satisfaction" pursuant to Art. 41; Art. 4 European Convention on the Compensation of Victims of Violent Crimes, 24 November 1983, ETS No. 116 provides that compensation shall cover at least loss of earnings; medical, hospitalization, and funeral expenses; and for dependents, loss of maintenance.

599 E.g. *Garrido and Baigorria v. Argentina*, Reparations, Inter-American Court of Human Rights, 27 August 1998, Ser. C, No. 39, para. 58; *El Amparo v. Venezuela*, Reparations, Inter-American Court of Human Rights, 14 September 1996, Ser. C, No. 28, para. 28; *Allenet de Ribemont v. France*, European Court of Human Rights, 10 February 1995, Application No. 15175/98.

600 *Lusitania* (United States of America v. Germany), Reports of International Arbitral Awards, 21 February 1924, Vol. VII, pp. 256-257; *Garrido and Baigorria v. Argentina*, Reparations, Inter-American Court of Human Rights, 27 August 1998, Ser. C, No. 39, para. 58; *El Amparo v. Venezuela*, Reparations, Inter-American Court of Human Rights, 14 September 1996, Ser. C, No. 28, para. 28. The pecuniary value to such claimant of the deceased person's personal services is the claimant's care, education, supervision. Quantification requires an estimate of the deceased's life expectancy and adjustments according to a variety of factors.

601 *Garrido and Baigorria v. Argentina*, Reparations, Inter-American Court of Human Rights, 27 August 1998, Ser. C, No. 39, paras. 60-61. Yet, the Inter-American Court has also awarded damages to the family of a deceased guerilla leader who was not earning wages, upon the argument of the Commission that the deceased would have earned a salary after the end of the civil war, see *Bámaca Velásquez v. Guatemala*, Reparations, Inter-American Court of Human Rights, Ser. C, No. 91.

Thus, the awards were of the same scope regardless of the social, economic or cultural background of the victims.[602] Funeral expenses are also often compensated.[603]

As national courts, international human rights courts have also compensated victims for loss of the value of land.[604] Administrative reparations mechanisms have compensated lost housing or personal property[605], or loss of or injury to property.[606]

2) Non-Pecuniary or Moral Damage

i) ICC Reparation System

The ICC has recognized that emotional suffering constitutes "harm" within the meaning of Rule 85.[607] The section in the Standard Application Form for Individuals termed "reparations" describes in detail four types of "mental pain and anguish": emotional problems, mental problems, physical reactions and behavioral changes and pain, complaints and/or concerns related to experiences of sexual violence.[608] Further descriptions of the three first types are provided in the application form.

602 In addition, beneficiaries were granted a lump-sum payment equal to a year's pension i.e. compensation equivalent to 12 times the monthly allowance, see Art. 23 para 1, 2 Law No. 19.123 of 31 January 1992. See for further discussion E. Lira: "The Reparations Policy for Human Rights Violations in Chile". In: The Handbook of Reparations. Ed. P. de Greiff. Oxford, 2006, pp. 55 et seq.; G. Klumpp: Vergangenheitsbewältigung durch Wahrheitskommissionen – Das Beispiel Chile. Berlin, 2001, pp. 228 et seq. For further examples see Chapter 5 C. IV.1. ("Valuation and Calculation of Damage").

603 For national jurisdictions see D. Shelton: Remedies in International Human Rights Law. 2nd ed. Oxford, 2005, p. 35.

604 See e.g. *Gelsomini Sigeri SRL v. Italy*, European Court of Human Rights, 18 December 03, Application No. 63417/00. Also, interest may be claimed as a pecuniary loss (from the date on which the recoverable element of past pecuniary damage accrued.

605 International Law Commission: Draft Articles on the Responsibility of States for Internationally Wrongful Acts – With Commentaries, 2001. Available at http://untreaty.un.org/ilc/texts/instruments/english/ commentaries/9_6_2001.pdf, last accessed 16 April 2009, pp. 254 et seq. For a recent example, see UNCC category C claims. Under category D, individuals could file claims for reparations for claims for damages exceeding $ 100 000. See for details e.g. A. Gattini: "The UN Compensation Commission – Old Rules, New Procedures on War Reparations". In: European Journal of International Law 13 (2002), pp. 161 et seq.

606 For national jurisdictions see D. Shelton: Remedies in International Human Rights Law. 2nd ed. Oxford, 2005, p. 35; however e.g. in Germany, restitution has priority.

607 *Situation in the Democratic Republic of The Congo*, Decision on the Applications for Participation in the Proceedings of VPRS 1, VPRS 2, VPRS 3, VPRS 4, VPRS 5 and VPRS 6, ICC Pre-Trial Chamber I, 17 January 2006, ICC-01/04-101, paras. 116, 147. The Standard Application Form lists "mental pain and anguish" as a possible form of injury, loss or harm suffered as a result of the crime, see Part E question 1 Standard Application Form for Individuals.

608 Part F question 3 Standard Application Form for Individuals.

The ICC has also recognized that physical suffering constitutes "harm" within the meaning of Rule 85.[609] In the Standard Application Form, "physical injury" is listed as a possible result of the crime and described to encompass "dismemberment, disfigurement, loss or limitation of use of a body organ, member, function or system, including sexual/reproductive health problems".[610]

In the context of reparations and under the heading of "other damage" the standard applications form for individuals lists, among others, "social status" and "legal rights".[611]

ii) International and National Law and Human Rights

International human rights jurisprudence and documents widely recognize physical and mental or moral harm as compensable.[612]

Various forms and varying degrees of fear and suffering are recognized as moral damage: anxiety, humiliation, degradation, inculcation of feelings of inferiority, insecurity, frustration, impotence,[613] loss of social position or injury to credit and reputation, affront to sensibilities associated with intrusion on the person, home or private life, trauma, embarrassment, inconvenience, feelings of isolation and helplessness and loss of relationship.[614]

International reparations mechanisms have awarded compensation for non-pecuniary damages. Awards have been granted to individuals who suffered "serious

---

609 Situation in the Democratic Republic of The Congo. Decision on the Application for Participation in the Proceedings if VPRS 1, VPRS 2, VPRS 3, VPRS 4, VPRS 5, VPRS 6, Pre-Trial Chamber I, ICC-01/04 (original); ICC-01/04-101-tEN 23-01-2006, ICC, 17 January 2006, paras. 116, 147. In the Standard Application Form for Individuals "physical injury" is listed as a recognized form of harm suffered as a result of the crime, see Part E question 1, Part F question 2 Standard Application Form for Individuals.

610 Part F question 2 Standard Application Form for Individuals.

611 Part F question 5 Standard Application Form for Individuals.

612 See e.g. Principle 20 2005 Victims Principles.

613 See for jurisprudence of the Inter-American Court e.g. *Blake Case*, Reparations, 22 January 1999, Ser. C, No. 48, para. 20; *Loayza Tamayo v. Peru*, Merits, Inter-American Court of Human Rights, 17 September 1997, Ser. C, No. 33 and regarding the European Court of Human Rights e.g. *KA v. Finland*, European Court of Human Rights, 14 January 2003, Application No. 27751/95, para.151; *Werner v. Poland*, European Court of Human Rights, 15 November 2001, Application No. 26760/95, para. 53 and generally D. Shelton: Remedies in International Human Rights Law. 2nd ed. Oxford, 2005, pp. 306 et seq. On the Bosnian Human Rights Chamber has awarded compensation for moral suffering and pain, see M. Nowak: "Reparation by the Human Rights Chamber for Bosnia and Herzegovina". In: Out of the Ashes – Reparations for Victims of Gross and Systematic Human Rights Violations. Eds. K. de Feyter; S. Parmentier; M. Bossuyt (et al.). Antwerp, 2005, pp. 245 et seq. at pp. 284 et seq.

614 See e.g. *Kutzner v. Germany*, European Court of Human Rights, 26 Febuary 2002, Application No. 46544/99. See P. Leach: Taking a Case to the European Court of Human Rights. 2nd ed. Oxford, 2005, p. 404 for a summary of relevant jurisprudence.

personal injury" in the form of physical or mental injury resulting from sexual assault, torture, aggravated assault, hostage taking or hiding.[615]

Non-pecuniary loss is also compensable in national legal systems.[616] Compensation for non-pecuniary injury such as harm to reputation and dignity, pain and suffering, injury to health (in particular disability or permanent injury) and other "moral" wrongs are recognized in nearly all legal systems.[617] Some states accept additional losses, reflecting cultural particularities.[618] In contrast to civil law jurisdictions, when compensation is ordered as a part of the criminal proceedings, in common law jurisdictions sometimes not all kinds of damages are recoverable.[619]

615 See UNCC "category B claims" i.e., where serious personal injury included dismembership, permanent or temporary significant disfigurement, or loss or limitation of use of bodily organ, member, function or system, or any injury which, left untreated, is unlikely to result in full recovery, see C. Whelton: "The United Nations Compensation Commission and International Law – A Fresh Approach". In: Ottawa Law Review 25 (1993), pp. 607 et seq. at p. 620. Under "category C", individual claims up to 100 000 $ which can be made for 21 different types of losses contained in a list, including personal injury, mental pain and anguish.

616 U. Magnus: "Comparative Report on the Law of Damages". In: Unification of Tort Law – Damages. Ed. U. Magnus. The Hague (et al.), 2001, pp. 185 et seq. at pp. 190-191: e.g. Belgium, England, Germany, Greece, South Africa, United States, Italy. Most national legal systems refrain from legally defining which damage is recoverable. This can be justified by a need for flexibility in order to secure that the rules would fit even to the most uncommon case and adaptability to changing conditions. See generally UN Commision on Human Rights, Sub-Commission on Prevention of Discrimination and Protection of Minorities: Study Concerning the Right to Restitution, Compensation and Rehabilitation for Victims of Gross Violations of Human Rights and Fundamental Freedoms, Final Report Submitted by Mr. Theo van Boven, Special Rapporteur, 2 Juli 1993, E/CN.4/Sub.2/1993/8, pp. 7-8.

617 See e.g. D. Shelton: Remedies in International Human Rights Law. 2nd ed. Oxford, 2005, pp. 35 et seq. For compensation claims e.g. in French criminal procedure, see V. Dervieux; M. Benillouche; O. Bachelet: "The French System". In: European Criminal Procedures. Eds. M. Delmas-Marty; J. R. Spencer. Cambridge, 2002, pp. 218 et seq. at p. 227: the victim of crime may claim compensation for material or non-pecuniary damage directly caused by the offense.

618 D. Shelton: Remedies in International Human Rights Law. 2nd ed. Oxford, 2005, pp. 36 et seq. listing examples and further references.

619 For example, in Canada, upon conviction, it is possible for the prosecutor to apply for a restitution order to compensate the victim, which however does not allow for broader compensation for pain and suffering or counseling expenses, s. 738 Criminal Code. Covered by the order are specific expenses with respect to property damage, pecuniary damages including loss of income in the case of bodily harm to the victim. However, the guidelines for the value of English compensation orders are based on sums which would be awarded in civil courts, see L. Zedner: "England". In: Wiedergutmachung im Kriminalrecht – Internationale Perspektiven – Reparation in Criminal Law – International Perspectives. Eds. A. Eser; S. Walther. Vol. 1. Freiburg i. Br., 1996, pp. 109 et seq. at p. 174; see also N. Nsereko: "Uganda". In: Wiedergutmachung im Kriminalrecht – Internationale Perspektiven – Reparation in Criminal Law – International Perspectives. Eds. A. Eser; S. Walther. Vol. 2. Freiburg i. Br., 1997, pp. 321 et seq. at p. 340. In jurisdictions that provide victims with the right to file a

In cases before international human rights courts where the direct victim has died, heirs, families and dependants have been awarded compensation for mental suffering or shock.[620] The rights of these indirect victims have also been explicitly recognized by international victims' rights documents[621] International reparations mechanisms also compensated persons whose spouse, child, or parent died during a conflict.[622]

Sometimes, lost opportunity costs are compensated.[623] The Inter-American Court has awarded compensation for damage to the victim's life plan (*proyecto de vida*) "understood as an expectation that is both reasonable and attainable in practice, implies the loss or severe diminution [...] of a person's prospects of self-development."[624] In one case, the Court required the responsible state to fund a scholarship to pay for the victim's remaining university tuition.[625] Other forms of compensable harm that have been recognized in international documents and human rights jurisprudence are lost opportunities regarding employment, education and social benefits.[626]

---

civil claim in the criminal proceedings (adhesion procedure), the whole range of pecuniary and non-pecuniary damages is recoverable. See e.g. P. Xavier; F. Lombard: "Frankreich". In: Wiedergutmachung im Kriminalrecht – Internationale Perspektiven – Reparation in Criminal Law – International Perspectives. Eds. A. Eser; S. Walther. Vol. 3. Freiburg i. Br., 2001, pp. 1 et seq. at pp. 93 et seq. In some jurisdictions, victims can settle the civil claim with the offender, see K. Madlener: "Spanien". In: Wiedergutmachung im Kriminalrecht – Internationale Perspektiven – Reparation in Criminal Law – International Perspectives. Eds. A. Eser; S. Walther. Vol. 3. Freiburg i. Br., 2001, pp. 273 et seq. at pp. 314 et seq.

620 E.g. *Velásquez Rodríguez v. Honduras*, Compensatory Damages, Inter-American Court of Human Rights, 21 July 1989, Ser. C, No. 7, para. 50; *Önen v. Turkey*, European Court of Human Rights, 14 May 2002, Application No. 22876/93, para. 112.

621 Para. 12 1985 Victims Declaration; Art. 8 read in conjunction with Art. 15 2005 Victims Principles.

622 Before the UNCC, these persons are entitled to a maximum amount of US $ 15 000, and a maximum of US $ 30 000 per family, see Determination of Ceilings for Compensation for Mental Pain and Anguish, UN Compensation Commission, 4th session, 22nd Meeting, at 2, UN Doc. S/AC.26 (1992).

623 See e.g. *Allenet de Ribemont v. France*, European Court of Human Rights, 10 February 1995, Application No. 15175/98.

624 *Loayza Tamayo v. Peru*, Reparations, Inter-American Court of Human Rights, 27 November 1998, Ser. C, No. 42, paras. 148 and 150: award of reparations taking into account social and cultural context. Critical to this "heading of damages based on abstraction" V. Madrigal-Borloz: "Damage and Redress in the Jurisprudence of the Inter-American Court of Human Rights (1979-2001)". In: Reparations – Redressing Past Wrongs. Eds. G. Ulrich; L. Krabbe Boserup. (Human Rights in Development – Yearbook 2001). The Hague, 2003, pp. 211 et seq. at pp. 234 et seq.

625 *Cantoral Benavides Case*, Reparations, Inter-American Court of Human Rights, 3 December 2001, Ser. C. No. 88, see M. Hagler; F. Rivera: "Bamaca Velasquez v. Guatemala – An Expansion of the Inter-American System's Jurisprudence on Reparations". In: Human Rights Brief 9 (2000), pp. 2 et seq. at p. 4.

626 E.g. Principle 20 Victims Principles; *Loayza Tamayo v. Peru*, Reparations, Inter-American Court of Human Rights, 27 November 1998, Ser. C, No. 42.; *Sadak and others v. Turkey*,

3) Assessment

As restitution will often be inappropriate or impossible, compensation as a form of reparations seems particularly relevant when considering ICC reparation orders.

The variety of types of losses listed for the purposes of reparation in the Standard Application Form for Individuals conform with international human rights, and suggest a broad notion of compensable harm. Experience in the context of mass crimes has shown that compensation for non-pecuniary losses is especially relevant.[627] However, it is doubtful whether the ICC has the capacity to individually assess and compensate a wide range of types of harm. In fact, most mechanisms awarding reparation to victims of massive and systematic crimes have only compensated certain types of harm. It could thus be justified for the ICC to decide not to order the convicted person to compensate property losses, leaving this type of harm for national courts or programs to deal with.[628] However, the broad definition adopted by the Standard Application Form could raise legitimate expectations among victims that the types of losses listed will be compensated.

b) Compensation and Causation

The ICC's legal instruments do not establish requirements for a causal link to the crime in order for the harm to be compensable.[629]

It is possible for crimes under the ICC's jurisdiction to cause immediate and remote harm. The causal link between the crime under the Court's jurisdiction and the harm a person claims to have suffered for the purpose of being recognized as a victim under Rule 85 has already been examined.[630] In this subchapter, the focus will be on what level of causal link is required in order for the harm to be compensable. The issues are interrelated but distinct: a person can qualify as a victim under Rule 85, but might still not be eligible to receive compensation. A certain level of linkage between the victim's harm and the crime is required in order to oblige the convicted person to pay money to a victim of his or her crime. In order to safeguard the convicted person's rights, the existence of a sufficiently close link between the wrongdoing and

European Court of Human Rights, 17 July 2001, Application Nos. 29900/96, 29901/96, 29902/96, 29903/96.

627 The incorporation of the possibility to award collective reparations indicates that non-pecuniary damages will be compensated as well.

628 E.g. the September 11 Funds did not compensate property losses, J. Cooper Alexander; R. A. Fein: "Procedural Design and Terror Victim Compensation". In: De Paul Law Review 53 (2003), pp. 627 et seq. at p. 690.

629 For a summary of discussions during the Preparatory Commission, see P. Lewis; H. Friman: "Reparations to Victims". In: The International Criminal Court – Elements of Crimes and Rules of Procedure and Evidence. Ed. R. S. Lee. Ardsley, New York, 2001, pp. 474 et seq. at pp. 484 et seq.

630 See Chapter 5 B. I. 1. d).

the harm ordered to be compensated is crucial.[631] Many issues regarding causation are practically linked to the applicable standard of proof.[632]

1) International and National Law and Human Rights

The principle that no compensation needs to be paid for damage which is too remote from the wrongful conduct is undisputed both in international and national legal systems. The approaches taken by different jurisdictions to causation reveal many similarities.[633] The concepts of "remoteness of damage" and proximity, "adequate causation", foreseeability and directness of harm are widely considered to be of key relevance.[634] However, both in national and international legal systems, and also within

631 Liability to make reparations can only be established, when the damage that is to be compensated can be attributed to a person or entity responsible, see above Chapter 5 B. ("Liability to Make Reparations"). D. Shelton: Remedies in International Human Rights Law. 2nd ed. Oxford, 2005, p. 317 states that "[i]n general, all damages directly attributed to the wrong done are compensable and causation is a crucial question [...]. Damages must have been caused in fact by the wrongdoer and the wrong must be the proximate cause of the damage suffered", with further elaboration.

632 See Chapter 5 B. I. 1. d ("Causation"); P. Lewis; H. Friman: "Reparations to Victims". In: The International Criminal Court – Elements of Crimes and Rules of Procedure and Evidence. Ed. R. S. Lee. Ardsley, New York, 2001, pp. 474 et seq. at pp. 484 et seq.

633 For national legal systems see J. Spier; O. H. Haazen: "Comparative Conclusions on Causation". In: Unification of Tort Law – Causation. Ed. J. Spier. The Hague, 2000, pp. 127 et seq. The comparative analysis only refers to the jurisdictions of Austria, Belgium, England, France, Germany, Greece, Italy, South Africa, Switzerland, United States. In national legal systems, the requirement of condicio sine qua non, also known as the but for-test, equivalence-theory, cause-in-fact or factual cause as such as a first test to establish causality for the purposes of compensation claim based on tort law. I.e. the act or omission must be mentally eliminated and to be considered whether or not the loss would have still occurred. If this is not the case, the act or omission is a condicio sine qua non for the loss. Almost all jurisdictions then conduct a second test of which there exist a few differing approaches in the various jurisdictions: the theory of proximate cause and remoteness of damage, which is predominant in common law jurisdictions, the theory of adequate causation which is predominant in a number of civil law jurisdictions, and an "openly flexible approach" which several continental law systems are also said to take. Independent of which approach is taken, in particular remoteness/proximity, foreseeability and directness of harm/damage are widely considered to be of key relevance; see also E. H. Riedel: "Damages". In: Encyclopedia of Public International Law. Ed. R. Bernhardt. Vol. 1. Amsterdam, 1992, pp. 929 et seq. at p. 931: "Whereas civil law jurisdictions tend to treat this problem in terms of equivalent or adequate causal connections between the internationally wrongful act and the actual damage caused, in common law jurisdictions remoteness of damage may vary according to the type of tort, the general rule being that only proximate and natural consequences of acts are considered relevant, while a "reasonable foreseeability" test applies to torts involving negligence"; see also D. Shelton: Remedies in International Human Rights Law. 2nd ed. Oxford, 2005, pp. 316 et seq.

634 For overviews of national approaches see J. Spier; O. H. Haazen: "Comparative Conclusions on Causation". In: Unification of Tort Law – Causation. Ed. J. Spier. The Hague, 2000, pp. 127 et seq. at pp. 135 et seq. with further discussion and references; For inter-

the same legal systems, the use of concepts and terms is often inconsistent and there is controversy regarding the exact restricting standards.[635]

The standard and approach set forth by the Lusitania cases is that "[c]ompensatory damages should repair all the proximate direct and indirect consequences of the harm […]."[636] However, "[t]he distinction between "direct" and "indirect" damage has been criticized both in doctrine and in practice because of its alleged ambiguity and scant utility",[637] and for being devoid of meaning.[638]

The recent international documents on reparations, the 2005 Victims Principles and ILC Draft Articles, do not specify requirements for the causal link required between the harm and the violation.[639] Before the Inter-American Court, the responsible party must "make reparation for the immediate effects of such unlawful acts, but only to the degree that has been legally recognized."[640]

Recently, international human rights courts, national and international reparations schemes and national courts have taken different approaches to the require-

national law approaches see D. Shelton: Remedies in International Human Rights Law. 2nd ed. Oxford, 2005, pp. 316 et seq.; E. H. Riedel: "Damages". In: Encyclopedia of Public International Law. Ed. R. Bernhardt. Vol. 1. Amsterdam, 1992, pp. 929 et seq. at p. 931; International Law Commission: Draft Articles on the Responsibility of States for Internationally Wrongful Acts – With Commentaries, 2001. Available at http://untreaty.un.org/ilc/texts/instruments/english/ commentaries/9_6_2001.pdf, last accessed 16 April 2009, pp. 227 et seq.

635 E. H. Riedel: "Damages". In: Encyclopedia of Public International Law. Ed. R. Bernhardt. Vol. 1. Amsterdam, 1992, pp. 929 et seq. at p. 931.

636 D. Shelton: "Reparations in the Inter-American System". In: The Inter-American System of Human Rights. Eds. D. J. Harris; S. Livingstone. Oxford, 1998, pp. 151 et seq. at p. 171 referring to the Lusitania cases. The failure of the injured party to mitigate damages or its contributory fault may also limit the amount of reparations to be made.

637 E.g. M. Frigessi di Rattalma; T. Treves (eds.): The United Nations Compensation Commission – A Handbook. The Hague, 1999, p. 21.

638 A. Gattini: "The UN Compensation Commission – Old Rules, New Procedures on War Reparations". In: European Journal of International Law 13 (2002), pp. 161 et seq. at p. 172.

639 Principle 20 2005 Victims Principles; Art. 31 (2) ILC Draft Articles. The commentary to the ILC Draft Articles notes that causality actually does not suffice to entail reparations, because the injury may be too remote, inconsequential or indirect for legal causation to be attributed. The line drawn demands the determination of foreseeability, directness or proximity. The degree of fault can affect the scope or remoteness of harm that will be encompassed by the duty to make reparation as well as the purpose of the rule that was breached, see International Law Commission: Draft Articles on the Responsibility of States for Internationally Wrongful Acts – With Commentaries, 2001. Available at http://untreaty.un.org/ilc/ texts/instruments/english/commentaries/9_6_2001.pdf, last accessed 16 April 2009.

640 *Aloeboetoe et al. v. Suriname*, Reparations, Inter-American Court of Human Rights, 10 September 1993, Ser. C, No. 15, para. 49.

ments for causation depending on the form of harm sought to be compensated, and the nature of the violation.[641]

Stricter requirements for causation and proof are applied when pecuniary or material harm are sought to be compensated. If a victim is to succeed in claiming pecuniary losses before the European Court, the applicant must establish a "clear causal connection" between the violation and the losses claimed.[642]

In contrast, the European Court has presumed the existence of non-pecuniary harm once it has been established that a person is a victim of the violation.[643] The Inter-American Court has frequently registered moral damage as a necessary consequence of grave violations.[644] It applies the presumption that moral damage necessarily follows certain human rights violations.[645] The Inter-American Court declared that even in the absence of evidence demonstrating moral harm, "it is clear that the victims suffered moral damages, for it is the characteristic of human nature that anybody subjected to the aggression and abuse described [...] will experience moral suffering."[646] Therefore, once responsibility is established or admitted, no evidence of moral suffering is required to establish the damage or the causal link.[647]

641 See A. Gattini: "The UN Compensation Commission – Old Rules, New Procedures on War Reparations". In: European Journal of International Law 13 (2002), pp. 161 et seq. at p. 174 in the context of the UNCC.

642 See *Cakici v. Turkey*, European Court of Human Rights, 8 July 1998, Application No. 23657/94. D. Shelton: Remedies in International Human Rights Law. 2nd ed. Oxford, 2005, p. 319 notes that this is the reason that awards for pecuniary losses are far less common.

643 E.g. *Mori v. Italy*, European Court of Human Rights, 19 February 1991, Application No. 13552/88, para. 20; Wiesinger v. Austria, European Court of Human Rights, 30 October 1991, Application No. 11796/85, para. 85.

644 E.g. *Velásquez Rodríguez v. Honduras*, Compensatory Damages, Inter-American Court of Human Rights, 21 July 1989, Ser. C, No. 7, para. 51; *Godínez Cruz v. Honduras*, Compensatory Damages, Inter-American Court of Human Rights, 21 July 1989, Ser. C, No. 5; para. 49.

645 E.g. *Aloeboetoe et al. v. Suriname*, Reparations, Inter-American Court of Human Rights, 10 September 1993, Ser. C, No. 15, para. 54.

646 Ibid., para. 52. For a critical assessment regarding the practice of applying presumptions, V. Madrigal-Borloz: "Damage and Redress in the Jurisprudence of the Inter-American Court of Human Rights (1979-2001)". In: Reparations – Redressing Past Wrongs. Eds. G. Ulrich; L. Krabbe Boserup. (Human Rights in Development – Yearbook 2001). The Hague, 2003, pp. 211 et seq. at pp. 232-233.

647 See e.g. *Aloeboetoe et al. v. Suriname*, Reparations, Inter-American Court of Human Rights, 10 September 1993, Ser. C, No. 15, paras. 91-93; *Castillo Páez Case*, Reparations, Inter-American Court of Human Rights, 27 November 1998, Ser. C, No. 43, paras. 86, 87-90.

National and international administrative reparations schemes have presumed that certain events or treatment lead to non-pecuniary harm such as pain and suffering, or lowered requirements for causation regarding non-pecuniary losses.[648]

In national jurisdictions, in addition to the concepts mentioned above, other relevant factors that have an impact on the requirements for causality are the nature of the loss, whether the wrongdoer acted intentionally or grossly negligent, the gravity of the respective fault and policy arguments (based on reasonableness and justice).[649]

2) Assessment

The considerations regarding compensation and causation are of critical importance in the context of legal theory. In practice, however, requirements for causation will to a large extend depend on whether individual or collective awards are made, on the degree to which awards will address the actual damage caused, and the model that is chosen for claims assessment.[650]

---

648 See A. Gattini: "The UN Compensation Commission – Old Rules, New Procedures on War Reparations". In: European Journal of International Law 13 (2002), pp. 161 et seq. at p. 174 for analysis of the practice of the UNCC. For presumed harm in the context of the September 11 Fund see J. Cooper Alexander; R. A. Fein: "Procedural Design and Terror Victim Compensation". In: De Paul Law Review 53 (2003), pp. 627 et seq. After encountering major difficulties in implementing the Western German compensation scheme for victims of Nazi crimes, in particular in establishing the causal link between the loss of life and harm to body and health suffered and the Nazi crimes legal presumptions were introduced: the existence of the causal link between the crime and the harm was presumed on the basis of outer factors. E.g. concerning loss of life, there was a legal assumption that, when the death occurred during deportation or stay in a ghetto or concentration camp or within 8 months after the deportation or deprivation of life has ended, that the death was caused by the Nazi crimes (§ 15 (2) Federal German Compensation Law of 1953 ("BEG")). Furthermore, instead of requiring a death certificate in order to prove ones death, it was assumed that someone was dead, when it was known that his last presence had been in territory hit by war and since 8 May 1945 his whereabouts and continued living was unknown (§ 180, § 15 (2) and §§ 28 (2) in conjunction with § 15 (2) BEG). Furthermore, for a claimant who had been in a concentration camp for at least one year and his or her earning capacity has decreased by at least 25 % due to harm to body or health, it was presumed to his or her benefit that the 25 % reduction of earning capacity is caused by the crime of persecution (§ 31 (2) BEG). The presumption could be disproved. For further discussion, see e.g. H.-J. Brodesser; B. J. Fehn; T. Franosch (et al.): Wiedergutmachung und Kriegsfolgenliquidation – Geschichte, Regelungen, Zahlungen. München, 2000, pp. 112 et seq.

649 J. Spier; O. H. Haazen: "Comparative Conclusions on Causation". In: Unification of Tort Law – Causation. Ed. J. Spier. The Hague, 2000, pp. 127 et seq. at pp. 132 et seq., further stating that the protective purpose principle could be described as that if a protective statute forbids a certain behavior in order to protect certain assets, the wrongdoer who violates such a law must indemnify even remote losses, in the Anglo-American System this falls into the category of remoteness of damage or proximate cause.

650 Individualized claims procedures require a more precise assessment of causation than when uniform awards are made. The Trust Fund Regulations indicate that mass claims processing techniques could be drawn upon, replacing difficult assessment of causation

Principally, in view of the expectedly large numbers of victims that might claim compensation, and the fact that often there will be a lack of a concrete relationship between the individual victims of crime and the convicted person, establishing causation may be time-consuming and difficult. Therefore, it seems that it will often be inappropriate for the Court to precisely examine whether there exists a sufficiently close link between the crime and the victim's harm on an individual basis for the purposes of compensation. As discussed in the context of liability, as a principle it could be assumed that the convicted person is liable to compensate the harm caused to those persons that qualify as victims of his or her crime pursuant to Rule 85. As the practice of the Inter-American and European Court and national reparations mechanisms and courts shown, particularly in the context of grave crimes, possibly committed in a systematic pattern, it may be justified to presume that the offense caused certain types of harm. In particular, it could be presumed that non-pecuniary harm such as moral or psychological injury was caused by the crime once it has been established that a person is a victim of the convicted person's crime.

3. Rehabilitation

a) *ICC Reparation System*

The inclusion of rehabilitation as a form of reparation in the ICC Statute is a progressive development in the protection of the rights of victims.[651]

The Statute and Rules do not contain indications regarding the content or scope of rehabilitation, and under what circumstances it should be awarded. The Trust Fund Regulations mention the possibility of "physical or psychological rehabilitation".[652] However, all types of harm listed in the Standard Application Form for Individuals and discussed above under the heading "non-pecuniary" losses can possibly be addressed through rehabilitative measures.

b) *International and National Law and Human Rights*

Rehabilitation has been broadly described as "the process of restoring the individual's full health and reputation after the trauma of a serious attack on their physical or mental integrity, which aims to restore what has been lost".[653]

The 2005 Victims Principles state that rehabilitation should include medical and psychological care as well as legal and social services.[654] Under the 1985 Victims Declaration, victims shall be provided with "necessary material, medical, psychological

with assumptions built upon objective (outer) circumstances, see for detailed discussion Chapter 5 D. IV. ("Scope of Compensation Order") and Chapter 6 F. ("Implementation of Reparation Awards").

651 See L. Mekhemar: "The Status of the Individual in the Statute of the International Criminal Court". In: The Rome Statute of the International Criminal Court – A Challenge to Impunity. Eds. M. Politi; G. Nesi. Aldershot, 2001, pp. 123 et seq. at p. 127.

652 Reg. 50 (a) (i).

653 D. Shelton: Remedies in International Human Rights Law. 2nd ed. Oxford, 2005, p. 275.

654 Art. 21.

and social assistance"[655] and information on the availability of health and social services and other relevant assistance.[656] It seems that these measures could be summarized under the term "rehabilitation".

The Inter-American Court has ordered awards that included the cost for future medical treatment of the victims and the next of kin of deceased persons[657], or free access for life to a range of social and health services focusing on traumatization.[658] Additionally, the Human Rights Committee recognized "providing medical care and treatment" as a remedy for violations of the Covenant's First Optional Protocol.[659] Rehabilitation has been recognized under the term "public insurance" in the UN Handbook.[660] The Bosnian Chamber of Human Rights ordered rehabilitation measures in exceptional cases, primarily in form of legal rehabilitation.[661]

National reparation programs provide victims of massive and systematic crimes with medical and psychological care and preferential access to education and employment for members of groups that the crime was directed against.[662] Rehabilita-

655 Para. 14 states that these assistance measures should be provided through "governmental, voluntary, community-based and indigenous means".

656 Para. 15.

657 *Loayza Tamayo v. Peru*, Reparations, Inter-American Court of Human Rights, 27 November 1998, Ser. C, No. 42, para. 129; *Caracazo Case*, Inter-American Court of Human Rights, 29 August 2002, Ser. C, No. 95, paras. 86-87.

658 *Barrios Altos Case*, Reparations, Inter-American Court of Human Rights, 30 November 2001, Ser. C, No. 87.

659 *Raul Sendic Antonaccio v. Uruguay*, Human Rights Committee, 28 November 1979, Communication No. R.14/63, UN Doc. Supp. No. 40 (A/37/40) at 114 (1982), para. 20.

660 UN Handbook, p. 43: "In many jurisdictions, victims may have access to the basic social, health, mental health, and other public insurance systems for many of their victimisation-related needs [...]".

661 For rehabilitation awarded by the Bosnian Human Rights Chamber see M. Nowak: "Reparation by the Human Rights Chamber for Bosnia and Herzegovina". In: Out of the Ashes – Reparations for Victims of Gross and Systematic Human Rights Violations. Eds. K. de Feyter; S. Parmentier; M. Bossuyt (et al.). Antwerp, 2005, pp. 245 et seq. at p. 284.

662 The Chilean Corporation for Reparation and Reconciliation granted victims and their families rehabilitation in form of medical and psychological support, and education benefits to the children of victims, see E. Lira: "The Reparations Policy for Human Rights Violations in Chile". In: The Handbook of Reparations. Ed. P. de Greiff. Oxford, 2006, pp. 55 et seq. at pp. 67 et seq.; for further examples see D. Shelton: Remedies in International Human Rights Law. 2nd ed. Oxford, 2005, pp. 354-355 listing additional examples. For a discussion of the necessities and difficulties of implementing collective rehabilitation programs in South Africa, see L. Fernandez: "Possibilities and Limitations of Reparations for the Victims of Human Rights Violations in South Africa". In: Confronting Past Injustice – Approaches to Amnesty, Punishment, Reparation and Restitution in South Africa and Germany. Eds. M. R. Rwelamira; G. Werle. Durban, 1996, pp. 65 et seq.; The South African Truth and Reconciliation Commission recommended community reparations, see H. Mkhize: "Introductory Notes to the Presentation of the Truth and Reconciliation Commission's Proposed Reparation and Rehabilitation Policies". In: When Sorry Isn't Enough – The Controversy over Apologies and Reparations for Human Injustices. Ed.

tion is also an essential component of national compensation programs for victims of crime.[663]

Collective awards aiming at rehabilitating victims and victim communities have been made in the context of the Holocaust. The Federal Republic of Germany paid lump sums to the State of Israel and to the Jewish Claims Conference (JCC) for resettlement and support of victims.[664] The JCC was authorized to also invest in collective needs like hospitals, old peoples' homes and other social institutions that served the purpose of counseling and support of the victims of the Nazi crimes.[665]

c) Assessment

In order to achieve the aims of reparations and enable victims to live on, it is crucial that victims of crimes under the ICC's jurisdiction will benefit from rehabilitative measures, both as individuals and as members of collectives.

However, it might be questioned whether this can and should be done solely through reparation orders. As the ICC lacks authority to make reparation orders against states, ordering certain kinds of rehabilitation, such as judicial rehabilitation, might not be effective, as only states can perform the acts necessary.

While medical, social and psychological rehabilitation are non-monetary remedies in the sense that victims are granted services instead of money, substantial sums of money are required to finance them. In order to truly rehabilitate victims of gross crimes, such services might need to be provided over a long period of time, possibly

R. L. Brooks. New York, 1999, pp. 501 et seq.; see also affirmative action laws in South Africa e.g. Employment Equity Act 55 of 1998, White Paper on Affirmative Action in the Public Service.

663 See e.g. in Germany pursuant to the "Gesetz über die Entschädigung für Opfer von Gewalttaten" of 11 May 1976.

664 On the grounds of the Luxemburg Agreement of 10 September 1952, BBBl II, 1953, West-Germany paid 3 billion Marks to the State of Israel (in kind), see e.g. M. Wolffsohn: "Globalentschädigung für Israel und die Juden? Adenauer und die Opposition in der Bundesregierung". In: Wiedergutmachung in der Bundesrepublik Deutschland. Eds. L. Herbst; C. Goschler. München, 1989, pp. 161 et seq. As a result of the Hague Protocol No. 2 West Germany was obliged to pay 450 Mio. German Marks to the Jewish Claims Conference, see e.g. J. Lillteicher: "Die Rückerstattung in Westdeutschland – Ein Kapitel Deutscher Vergangenheitspolitik?". In: Nach der Verfolgung – Wiedergutmachung Nationalsozialistischen Unrechts in Deutschland?. Eds. H. G. Hockerts; C. Kuller. Göttingen, 2003, pp. 61 et seq.

665 The Hague Protocol did not set forth detailed requirements as to the disbursement of funds. Disagreement concerning the spending of this money arouse after the JCC had spent the monies exclusively for the purposes of jewish social institutions. While the JCC denied that the organization should award reparations to individual victims and insisted on payments to assist jewish institutions, the German government disagreed with this position R. Hebenstreit: "Härteausgleich nach § 171 BEG". In: Die Wiedergutmachung Nationalsozialistischen Unrechts in der Bundesrepublik Deutschland – Das Bundesentschädigungsgesetz. Eds. Bundesminister der Finanzen; W. Schwarz. Vol. 5. München, 1983, pp. 469 et seq. at p. 476.

life-long.[666] It does not seem realistic that such programs could be financed by one, or even a few individuals convicted by the Court. Rather it is a remedy that falls within a state's obligations to provide social security or health services to its citizens in need. Particularly in situations where the victims of crimes under the ICC's jurisdiction live in poor areas where large parts of the population are affected by conflict and poverty, the provision of health and social services to the victimized population could be a task better achieved by the state and humanitarian/national and international organizations. It also seems doubtful whether purposes of reparations such as reconciliation and restoration of the lives of victims would be served if rehabilitation would only be granted to those individuals that qualify as victims of the crime a person was convicted for by the Court. Other individuals living in the same area or society might have equally suffered harm in the course of a certain conflict, and thus are in need of health and other services as well. Also, if rehabilitation is only going to be provided as a part of the reparation order made against a person after his conviction, it will not take into account that victims are often in urgent need of immediate access to basic services.

Thus, it might be more appropriate for the Trust Fund to install or sponsor rehabilitation programs that address the needs of "victims of the situation" from early in the proceedings.[667] While such rehabilitative measures would not constitute reparations in the sense of the Statute, the convicted person could be ordered to pay a financial contribution to the rehabilitation of an individual or to a rehabilitative program as a part of a collective reparation award.[668] Furthermore, the Court could recommend that states implement judicial and other rehabilitation as a part of the principles pursuant to Art. 75 (1).

4. Other Forms of Reparations

The Statute and Rules provide for the possibility to order forms of reparations other than restitution, compensation and rehabilitation (Art. 75 (2), Rule 94 (1) f)).[669]

666 See also C. Muttukumaru: "Reparations to Victims". In: Collection of Essays on the Rome Statute of the International Criminal Court. Eds. F. Lattanzi; W. A. Schabas. Ripa di Fagnano Alto, 1999, pp. 301 et seq. at p. 304.

667 See also D. Donat-Cattin: "Article 75 – Reparations to Victims". In: Commentary on the Rome Statute of the International Criminal Court – Observers' Notes, Article by Article. Ed. O. Triffterer. Baden-Baden, 1999, pp. 965 et seq. at p. 971: "Rehabilitation cannot be limited to forms of reparations imposed on the convicted persons, but must be conducted by society at large" and "should be adopted in conjunction with protective measures ex article 68 throughout the entire procedure before the Court, starting with the Pre-Trial stage."

668 C. Muttukumaru: "Reparations to Victims". In: Collection of Essays on the Rome Statute of the International Criminal Court. Eds. F. Lattanzi; W. A. Schabas. Ripa di Fagnano Alto, 1999, pp. 301 et seq. at pp. 306-307 points out that if "rehabilitation" is understood as resettlement of a victim and maybe also his or her immediate dependants, it is almost certain that such measures are outside the power of the convicted person.

669 As indicated in the non-exclusive manner in which Art. 75 (1) lists forms of reparations; Rule 94 (1) (f) expressly provides for the possibility to claim "other forms of remedy".

The possible content of "other forms of remedy" awarded by the Court has not been specified in the Statute and Rules. Relevant questions in the Standard Application Form for Individuals suggest that forms of reparations other than compensation, restitution and rehabilitation should be determined according to the wishes and interests of victims: they are asked to specify which other forms of reparations they desire.[670] Applicants are also asked "[i]f resources are available [...] what would help you and your community the most?"[671] Therefore, pursuant to Art. 75 (2) the Court is has the power to order the convicted person to perform any possible measure that has a reparatory effect, if it considers it appropriate to do so.

Forms of reparations other than restitution, compensation and rehabilitation may be monetary or non-monetary, and either individual or collective, and might serve a wide range of purposes.

a) Symbolic and Non-Monetary Forms of Reparations

While the types of reparations expressly listed in Art. 75 (2) might also have a symbolic effect, this is not their predominant aim. Compensation and restitution particularly are intended to redress specific economically assessable damage that victims have suffered as a result of the convicted person's crime.

However, crimes can cause harm to certain recognized interests that cannot be calculated, nor can they be remedied through monetary awards. Symbolic or "moral" reparations are intended to repair the shame and humiliation previously inflicted on individuals or groups of victims and to restore their reputation and equal status in the public eye.[672] Reparatory measures might be symbolic to differing degrees – they can range from strictly symbolic forms to monetary awards that are also symbolic.

1) ICC Reparation System

While the ICC Statute does not expressly state that the Court may order symbolic measures of reparations, it does seems indicated.

In the Victims Participation Booklet, "symbolic measures such as public apology or commemoration or memorial" are mentioned as possible forms of reparations.[673] Additionally, during the drafting process of the Rome Statute, symbolic forms of reparations such as the possibility of constructing monuments in memory of those who suffered atrocities and apologies were discussed.[674]

670 Part F question 1 Standard Application Form for Individuals.

671 Ibid., Part F question 6.

672 See R. G. Teitel: Transitional Justice. Oxford, 2000, pp. 126 et seq. "Moral reparation transcend redress to the affected individuals and their survivors for injury, reaching the public eye".

673 Part II Box 7 Victims Participation Booklet, p. 14.

674 C. Muttukumaru: "Reparations to Victims". In: Collection of Essays on the Rome Statute of the International Criminal Court. Eds. F. Lattanzi; W. A. Schabas. Ripa di Fagnano Alto, 1999, pp. 301 et seq. at p. 307.

2) International and National Law and Human Rights

In international documents and practice, non-monetary or symbolic measures are often grouped under the headings "satisfaction" and "guarantees of non-repetition". Under the 2005 Victims Principles these forms of reparations are accepted as measures of the same importance as restitution, compensation and rehabilitation. However, pursuant to the ILC Draft Articles, satisfaction may only be ordered when restitution and compensation cannot better the injury.[675]

Remedies of primarily symbolic or "alternative" character also exist in the criminal procedure of national legal systems.[676] In recent years, the criminal procedure of many legal systems has emphasized the notion of restorative justice.[677] Typically the wrongdoer has been ordered or allowed to perform acts of primarily symbolic nature

675 Art. 37 ILC Draft Articles on State Responsibility determines that where restitution and compensation cannot repair the injury, satisfaction shall be awarded in form of an acknowledgment of a breach, an expression of regret, a formal apology or other appropriate modality, including punishment of the perpetrator or a declaration of illegality. Satisfaction shall be proportionate and not humiliating Thus, satisfaction as a remedy is regarded as an exceptional remedy to be awarded only in "certain cases", International Law Commission: Draft Articles on the Responsibility of States for Internationally Wrongful Acts – With Commentaries, 2001. Available at http://untreaty.un.org/ilc/texts/instruments/english/commentaries/ 9_6_2001.pdf, last accessed 16 April 2009, Art. 37 para. 1. However, the Commentary notes that the remedy of satisfaction for nonmaterial injury "is well-established in international law", see ibid., Art. 37, para. 4.

676 In para. 6 of the Preamble of the Basic Principles on the Use of Restorative Justice Programmes in Criminal Matters, ECOSOC Res. 2002/12 of 12 August 2003 define that "restorative justice gives rise to a range of measures that are flexible in their adaptation to established criminal justice systems and that complement those systems, taking into account legal, social and cultural circumstances". See for the German context e.g. C. Roxin: "Strafe und Wiedergutmachung". In: Festschrift für Werner Lorenz zum 80. Geburtstag. Eds. T. Rauscher; H.-P. Mansel. München, 2001, pp. 51 et seq.; D. Frehsee: "Wiedergutmachung und Täter-Opfer-Ausgleich im Deutschen Strafrecht – Entwicklung, Möglichkeiten und Probleme". In: Die Stellung des Opfers im Strafrechtssystem – Neue Entwicklungen in Deutschland und in den USA. Eds. B. Schünemann; M. D. Dubber. Köln, 2000, pp. 117 et seq.; W. Hassemer; J. P. Reemtsma: Verbrechensopfer – Gesetz und Gerechtigkeit. München, 2002, pp. 86 et seq. For Uganda, see N. Nsereko: "Uganda". In: Wiedergutmachung im Kriminalrecht – Internationale Perspektiven – Reparation in Criminal Law – International Perspectives. Eds. A. Eser; S. Walther. Vol. 2. Freiburg i. Br., 1997, pp. 321 et seq. at p. 336; For Poland, see Z. Doda; E. Weigend: "Polen". In: Wiedergutmachung im Kriminalrecht – Internationale Perspektiven – Reparation in Criminal Law – International Perspectives. Eds. A. Eser; S. Walther. Vol. 1. Freiburg i. Br., 1996, pp. 421 et seq. at pp. 476-477; generally J. Dignan: "Restorative Justice and the Law – The Case for an Integrated, Systematic Approach". In: Restorative Justice and the Law. Ed. L. Walgrave. Cullompton, Devon, 2002, pp. 168 et seq.

677 UN Handbook, p. 43, defining "The framework for restorative justice involves the offender, the victim and the entire community in efforts to create a balanced approach that is offender-directed and, at the same time, victim-centred [...]".

to repair the harm caused. The emphasis of such measures is on reconciliation between the perpetrator and its victim or victims.[678]

i) Cessation of Violations, Exposition of Truth, Punishment of Perpetrators

International documents and human rights jurisprudence recognize cessation of continuing violations, full exposure of the truth and the punishment of perpetrators as possible non-monetary remedies.[679] The Inter-American Court has also recognized disclosure as a measure of satisfaction. For example, it has ordered states to publish the operative paragraphs of its ruling in its official newspapers.[680]

678 Such approaches are practiced both in traditional and modern approaches to justice. For a summary of the models discussed in western legal systems, see M. Heikkilä: International Criminal Tribunals and Victims of Crime. Turku, 2004, pp. 36-39. See also 2001 European Framework Decision Art. 10 ("Penal Mediation in the Course of Criminal Proceedings"). For traditional African laws, in particular Uganda, see K. Kinoti: "Justice in the Eye of the Beholder". July 2005. Available at www.awid.org/go.php?stid=1509, last accessed 16 April 2009.

679 According to Principle 22 2005 Victims Principles satisfaction includes "[e]ffective measures aimed at the cessation of continuing violations; [v]erification of the facts and full and public disclosure of the truth to the extent that such disclosure does not cause further harm or threaten the safety and interests of the victim, the victim's relatives, witnesses, or persons who have intervened to assist the victim or prevent the occurrence of further violations; [t]he search for the whereabouts of the disappeared, for the identities of the children abducted, and for the bodies of those killed, and assistance in the recovery, identification and reburial of the bodies in accordance with the expressed or presumed wish of the victims, or the cultural practices of the families and communities [...]; [j]udicial and administrative sanctions against persons liable for the violations; [...] [i]nclusion of an accurate account of the violations that occurred in international human rights law and international humanitarian law training and in educational material at all levels". Art. 30 ILC Draft Articles recognizes the cessation of wrongful acts as an obligation, while not categorizing it as a form of reparation. Cessation of wrongful acts and guarantees of non-repetition are rather treated as inherent obligations of the responsible state. In its jurisprudence, the Inter-American Court has ordered, mostly under the heading of "cessation of continuing violations," various measures in order to redress the violations. An example of the relevant jurisprudence is *Paniagua Morales et. al. Case*, Inter-American Court of Human Rights, 8 March 1998, Ser. C, No. 37, para. 173 (cessation of wrongful acts). For a summary of the relevant jurisprudence of the Bosnian Human Rights Chamber see M. Nowak: "Reparation by the Human Rights Chamber for Bosnia and Herzegovina". In: Out of the Ashes – Reparations for Victims of Gross and Systematic Human Rights Violations. Eds. K. de Feyter; S. Parmentier; M. Bossuyt (et al.). Antwerp, 2005, pp. 245 et seq. at pp. 285-286.

680 *Cantoral Benavides Case*, Reparations, Inter-American Court of Human Rights, 3 December 2001, Ser. C, No. 88, para. 79.

In contrast, in awarding reparations the European Court of Human Rights has focussed on monetary compensation,[681] while its primary remedy is a declaration that there has been a violation of the Convention.[682]

ii) Guarantees of Non-Repetition

Guarantees of non-repetition, as set forth in the 2005 Victims Principles, include ensuring effective civilian control of military and security forces, requiring that all civilian and military proceedings abide by international standards of due process, fairness and impartiality, and strengthening the independence of the judiciary.[683]

Like satisfaction, the ILC Draft Principles recognize the obligation to guarantee non-repetition of violations, though they do not categorize it as a form of reparations.[684]

iii) Acknowledgment of Responsibility

International documents and jurisprudence view an acknowledgment by the responsible party of the wrongfulness of his or her actions as a form of reparations.[685] The Inter-American Court has ordered responsible states to conduct a public ceremony where victims officially receive awards of compensation and the state accepts responsibility for the wrongs.[686] The European Court has often found that the declaration of

681 However, the European Court of Human Rights has also awarded restitution of property and the release of persons unlawfully detained, see e.g. *Assanidze v. Georgia*, European Court of Human Rights, 8 April 2004, Application No. 71503/01.

682 P. Leach: Taking a Case to the European Court of Human Rights. 2nd ed. Oxford, 2005, pp. 397-398. For a criticism on this approach, see the partly dissenting opinion of Judge Bonellon e.g. in *T.W. v. Malta*, European Court of Human Rights, 29 April 1999, Application No. 25644/94.

683 Principle 23.

684 Art. 30 b).

685 Art. 37 (2) ILC Draft Articles; Principle 22 2005 Victims Principles (element of public apology).

686 *Barrios Altos Case*, Reparations, Inter-American Court of Human Rights, 30 November 2001, Ser. C, No. 87, para. 50.5; *Trujillo Oroza Case*, Reparations, Inter-American Court of Human Rights, 27 February 2002, Ser. C, No. 92, paras. 122, 141.6; *Myrna Mack-Chang v. Guatemala*, Judgment, Inter-American Court of Human Rights, 25 November 2003, Ser. C, No. 101, para. 301.8; *Plan de Sánchez Massacre v. Guatemala*, Reparations, Inter-American Court for Human Rights, 19 November 2004, Ser. C, No. 105, paras. 100, 101, 125.2; *Case of Children's Rehabilitation v. Paraguay*, Inter-American Court of Human Rights, 2 September 2004, Ser. C, No. 112, para. 340.11. Before the Inter-American Court, a state can percept the wrongfulness of its actions under three main procedural avenues: it can acknowledge its responsibility before the issuance of the judgment on the merits (Art. 52 (2) Rules), or by immediate compliance with the measures of cessation and production of a prompt and reasonable agreement on reparations after the condemnatory judgment, or, when the state's behavior neither during proceedings not after the

a violation is in itself sufficient satisfaction for the victim.[687]

iv) Apology

An apology for a crime and its consequences goes beyond the acknowledgment of responsibility, as it implies an expression of regret. The 2005 Victims Principles recognize "[a]n official declaration or a judicial decision restoring the dignity, the reputation and the rights of the victim and of persons closely connected with the victim" and a "[p]ublic apology" as forms of satisfaction.[688] Under the ILC Draft Articles, satisfaction may take the form of an "expression of regret, a formal apology or other appropriate modality", which shall be proportionate and not take the form of a humiliation.[689] The UN Handbook describes that "[i]n some cultures, the admission of responsibility and an apology to the victim may help to satisfy the interests of justice and the needs of victims."[690]

There are numerous recent examples of public apologies of government officials addressed to the victims of mass crimes.[691] In recent years the Inter-American Court has ordered states to make public apologies to victims.[692] In contrast, the Bosnian

judgment provides satisfaction to the victim, an order for other measures of satisfaction is a must.

687 *McCallum v. The United Kingdom*, European Court of Human Rights, 30 August 1990, Application No. 9511/81, para. 37; *Lala v. The Netherlands*, European Court of Human Rights, 22 September 1994, Application No. 14861/89, para. 38.

688 Principle 22.

689 Art. 37.

690 UN Handbook, p. 43.

691 E.g. television-broadcasted apologies made by the (then) President of the Republika Srbska of Bosnia and Herzegovina to the Bosnian people for the crimes committed by the Serbian side in the Bosnian conflict of 1991-1995; public apology to Japanese "comfort women"; Chilean President Aylwin, his official acknowledgment of the responsibility of the entire society and an official apology directed towards the victims; France in 1996 formally acknowledged the responsibility of the French Government for committing crimes against humanity during the Vichy-Regime; then Brazilian President Cardozo issued a statement on responsibility for serious and systematic human rights violations committed during the military dictatorship between 1964 and 1985. See e.g. E. Barkan: The Guilt of Nations – Restitution and Negotiating Historical Injustices. New York, 2001, pp. 323 et seq.; N. Roht-Arriaza: "Reparations, Decisions and Dilemmas". In: Hastings International and Comparative Law Review 27 (2004), pp. 157 et seq. at p. 185; G. Klumpp: Vergangenheitsbewältigung durch Wahrheitskommissionen – Das Beispiel Chile. Berlin, 2001, pp. 225 et seq.; I. Bottigliero: Redress for Victims of Crimes under International Law. Leiden, 2004, pp. 96-97 with further examples.

692 *Barrios Altos Case*, Reparations, Inter-American Court of Human Rights, 30 November 2001, Ser. C, No. 87, para. 50.5 (e); *Cantoral Benavides Case*, Reparations, Inter-American Court of Human Rights, 3 December 2001, Ser. C, No. 88, para. 99.7; *Tibi v. Ecuador*, Judgement on Preliminary Objections, Merits and Reparations, Inter-American Court of Human Rights, 7 September 2004, Ser. C, No. 114, para. 280.2. Until recently, the Inter-American Court rejected claims for an apology, see e.g. *Suárez Rosero Case*, Reparations, Inter-American Court of Human Rights, 20 January 1999, Ser. C, No. 44, para. 69.

Chamber of Human Rights has refrained from ordering an apology on the ground that apologies are only meaningful if they are made voluntarily.[693]

v) Commemoration

The 2005 Victims Principles recognize "[c]ommemorations and tributes to the victims" as a form of satisfaction.[694]

The Inter-American Court has ordered responsible states to name streets, schools and plazas in memory of victims, and to build memorials, usually with commemorative plaques.[695] They have been installed as a part of amicable settlements between the state and the victim or the victim's family, accepted by the Court.[696] The Inter-American Court has also acknowledged that acts or works of a public nature or repercussion can have effects such as recovering the memory of the victims, reestablishing their reputation, consoling their next of kin or transmitting a message of official condemnation of the human rights violations in question and a commitment to the efforts to ensure that they will not happen again.[697]

The UN Handbook emphasizes that "commemoration of victims has an important moral significance".[698] In recent decades, a number of responsible states or the victimized communities have installed measures to commemorate the victims of mass or

693 M. Nowak: "Reparation by the Human Rights Chamber for Bosnia and Herzegovina". In: Out of the Ashes – Reparations for Victims of Gross and Systematic Human Rights Violations. Eds. K. de Feyter; S. Parmentier; M. Bossuyt (et al.). Antwerp, 2005, pp. 245 et seq. at p. 285, referring to the Hermas case, *Hermas v. Federation*, Decision on Admissibility and Merits, 18 February 1998, Case No. CH/97/45.

694 Principle 22 2005 Victims Principles. The ILC Draft Articles adopt a non-exclusive wording regarding measures of satisfaction, thus potentially allowing for commemoration, see Art. 37 (2) "or another appropriate modality".

695 *"Street Children" Case*, Reparations, Inter-American Court of Human Rights, 26 May 2001, Ser. C, No. 77, para. 123.7; *Barrios Altos Case*, Reparations, Inter-American Court of Human Rights, 30 November 2001, Ser. C, No. 87, para. 50.5 (f); *Trujillo Oroza Case*, Reparations, Inter-American Court of Human Rights, 27 February 2002, Ser. C, No. 92, paras. 122, 141.6; *Molina-Theissen v. Guatemala*, Reparations, Inter-American Court of Human Rights, 4 July 2004, Ser. C, No. 108, para. 106.6; *Plan de Sánchez Massacre v. Guatemala*, Reparations, Inter-American Court for Human Rights, 19 November 2004, Ser. C, No. 105, para. 125.6. Until 2001, the Inter-American Court consistently refused to order measures of commemoration, see V. Madrigal-Borloz: "Damage and Redress in the Jurisprudence of the Inter-American Court of Human Rights (1979-2001)". In: Reparations – Redressing Past Wrongs. Eds. G. Ulrich; L. Krabbe Boserup. (Human Rights in Development – Yearbook 2001). The Hague, 2003, pp. 211 et seq. at p. 270.

696 *Benavides Cevallos v. Ecuador*, Judgement, Inter-American Court of Human Rights, 19 June 1998, Ser. C, No. 38, para. 148: here the State of Ecuador agreed to instruct "to memorialise the name of Ms. Consuelo Benavides-Cevallos on streets, squares or schools".

697 *"Street Children" Case*, Reparations, Inter-American Court of Human Rights, 26 May 2001, Ser. C, No. 77, para. 84.

698 UN Handbook, p. 43.

systematic crimes. Examples are the commemorative observance of an event such as Holocaust day in Israel, the erection of a monument, or the naming of a park, street or building in commemoration of a victim or victims;[699] sending a truth commission's report to all families of killed or disappeared victims might be a form of commemoration.[700] The work of the South African Truth and Reconciliation Commission has been termed a form of both collective and individual reparation, as its reports aimed both at the restoration of the dignity of individuals and of groups of victims.[701]

vi) Monetary Measures to Benefit the Harmed Community

Monetary reparations directed toward victimized collectives could also be termed community or collective rehabilitation, restitution or compensation. Their objective is to nurture the communities' self-empowerment, to promote the community's cultural transformation, and to improve the conditions under which the victims live.[702] The 1985 Victims Declaration envisions that "[i]n cases of substantial harm to the environment, restitution, if ordered, should include, as far as possible, restoration of the environment, reconstruction of the infrastructure, replacement of community facilities and reimbursement of the expenses of relocation, whenever such harm results in the dislocation of a community".[703]

The Inter-American Court ruled that collective reparation could be awarded to a community if it was damaged by the violation directly. [704] In one case it ordered the responsible state to reopen and staff a school and health dispensary in the area where

699 Ibid. E.g. in Chile, a memorial for killed victims was erected and a piece of land was given to the organization representing victims on which there had formerly been a torture center. Streets, buildings and parks were named after victims of the dictatorship by Supreme Decree 294 of 13 Mach 1991 of the Ministry of Justice, see for details G. Klumpp: Vergangenheitsbewältigung durch Wahrheitskommissionen – Das Beispiel Chile. Berlin, 2001, pp. 227-228.

700 N. Roht-Arriaza: "Reparations, Decisions and Dilemmas". In: Hastings International and Comparative Law Review 27 (2004), pp. 157 et seq. at p. 171.

701 H. Küpper: Kollektive Rechte in der Wiedergutmachung von Systemunrecht. Vol. 2. Frankfurt a. Main, 2004, p. 827. The reports depicted the particular crimes and injustices directed against the victim. Further proposals made in the South Africa context were, among others, the erection of tombstones and cenotaphs, exhumation and reburial, visits to graves of victims, culturally appropriate ceremonies for the unknown dead and disappeared; restoration of the good name of individuals; museums, see D. Shelton: Remedies in International Human Rights Law. 2nd ed. Oxford, 2005, p. 426. See ibid., pp. 424 et seq. for further examples.

702 R. L. Brooks: "Reflections on Reparations". In: Politics and the Past. Ed. J. Torpey. Oxford, 2003, pp. 103 et seq. at p. 108.

703 Para. 10.

704 *Aloeboetoe et al. v. Suriname*, Reparations, Inter-American Court of Human Rights, 10 September 1993, Ser. C, No. 15, para. 52, while finding that even though the State of Suriname was responsible for killing seven members of the Maroon tribe, regarding the compensation claim for collective reparations to the tribe, it argued that all persons, in addition to being members of their own families and citizens of a state, also generally

the families of a number of killed lived.[705] In the case of a massacre of inhabitants of a Mayan village, the Court ordered the responsible state to provide free medicines and a health clinic, education in Mayan Culture, bilingual teachers, housing assistance and infrastructure investments in roads, sewers and drinking water.[706]

National reparations mechanisms have also awarded monetary collective reparations for the benefit of victim communities.[707]

3) Assessment

In the national and international human rights and legal context, a broad range of predominantly symbolic measures to repair the harm caused to victims are recognized. These measures can have a wider scope than individual restitution or compensation because they are better suited to correspond to the need to acknowledge publicly and transparently the causes, effects and remedies of international crimes. Therefore symbolic measures, addressed to the collective of victims, are particularly relevant to the ICC reparations mechanism. At the same time, these forms of remedies might also have restorative effects for the individual victim. Since the ICC Statute gives the Court the power to order the convicted person to make reparations, it is clear that the conviction and punishment of the perpetrator will not *per se* be sufficient to qualify as "appropriate reparations".

belong to intermediate communities, and the payment of moral compensation does not extend to this community.

705 *Aloeboetoe et al. v. Suriname*, Reparations, Inter-American Court of Human Rights, 10 September 1993, Ser. C, No. 15, paras. 9 , 20. Furthermore, the state was obliged to inform the families on the whereabouts of the bodies of the victims.

706 *Plan de Sánchez Massacre v. Guatemala*, Reparations, Inter-American Court for Human Rights, 19 November 2004, Ser. C, No. 105, paras. 125.7, 125.8, 125.9. In *Juan Chanay Pablo v. Guatemala (Colotenango Case)*, Friendly Settlement, Inter-American Court of Human Rights, 13 March 1997, Case 11.212 OEA/Ser.L/V/II.95, doc.7 rev.447, a settlement was reached between the responsible state and the Commission which included that "the State of Guatemala should provide communal assistance to the affected community of Colotenango, in accordance with a program of projects agreed upon by the parties".

707 E.g. in the context of Western German Compensation to victims of the Nazi crimes, directives of the Federal Ministry of Finance (Richtlinien des Bundesministeriums der Finanzen zur Vergabe von Mitteln für Individuelle Betreuungsmaßnahmen aus dem Härtefonds für Rassisch Verfolgte Nicht Jüdischen Glaubens (HNG-Fonds) sowie zur Vergabe von Mitteln für Globale Betreuungsmaßnahmen aus diesem Fonds, 15 September 1966, Bundesanzeiger of 22 September 1966 No. 178) granted compensation awards only to the individuals in need, but also to institutions like old peoples homes, as long as they provided services to a certain number of victims eligible to compensation from the HNG-fund, or other victims' organizations, see H.-J. Brodesser; B. J. Fehn; T. Franosch (et al.): Wiedergutmachung und Kriegsfolgenliquidation – Geschichte, Regelungen, Zahlungen. München, 2000, p. 127. The German foundation "Remembrance, Responsibility, Future" has granted financial contributions to projects of humanitarian character benefiting Jewish Holocaust survivors, victims of the Nazi crimes that are Sinti and Roma, see http://www.stiftung-evz.de/fonds_erinnerung_und_zukunft/humanitaere_zusammenarbeit/betreuungsprogramm/, last accessed 16 April 2009.

However, numerous forms of symbolic reparations recognized in the context of international law and human rights cannot be applied in the context of individual responsibility. Only states can introduce a national memorial day, name streets and build memorials. The duty to prevent, investigate and punish violations and to amend domestic legislation is not relevant in the context of individual responsibility.[708] It is also not purposeful to order a measure of cessation of wrongful acts against the convicted person, who might face a long period of imprisonment. However, while such orders could not, be their very nature, be implemented against an individual, they could be considered when it appears possible that might be effectively implemented with the co-operation of the state concerned.[709]

Certain symbolic forms of reparations can be performed by an individual. Examples are the acknowledgment of responsibility or a public apology[710]. Additionally, the convicted person can make monetary contributions to the building of a hospital or communal services. The Court could be challenged to develop new forms of reparations. These would be able to take into account that it is an individual that makes reparations in the ICC system, and, if relevant, at the same time acknowledge that his or her crime was predominately directed against the collective the victim was a member of, because of the victim's race, religion or political opinion or ideology.[711] In order to effectively address the particular situation of the victims of the crime, symbolic measures ordered should be adjusted to the circumstances that particular case and the political, cultural and economic setting of the crime.[712]

It could be considered that ICC reparations proceedings might be able to trigger a discourse between the victims and the perpetrators of the crimes prosecuted by the ICC that could result in symbolic forms of reparations that both sides agree on and thus promote reconciliation. However, the pre-condition for this to happen is the willingness of both sides to communicate with each other. Considering the severeness of the crimes under the ICC's jurisdiction, in contrast to restorative justice measures on the national level, this willingness will often not exist. Furthermore, the aim of symbolic reparations in international criminal justice is to achieve reconciliation

708 However these measures might be addressed in the context of the reparation principles pursuant to Art. 75 (1).

709 See D. Donat-Cattin: "Article 75 – Reparations to Victims". In: Commentary on the Rome Statute of the International Criminal Court – Observers' Notes, Article by Article. Ed. O. Triffterer. Baden-Baden, 1999, pp. 965 et seq. at p. 974.

710 R. B. Bilder: "The Role of Apology in International Law and Diplomacy". In: Virginia Journal of International Law 46 (2006), pp. 433 et seq. at pp. 461-462 discusses the question as to whether state-to-state apologies are different from other kinds of apologies.

711 C. Jorda; J. de Hemptinne: "The Status and Role of the Victim". In: The Rome Statute of the International Criminal Court – A Commentary. Eds. A. Cassese; P. Gaeta; J. R. W. D. Jones. Vol. 2. Oxford, 2002, pp. 1387 et seq. at p. 1410.

712 See generally C. Tomuschat: "Darfur – Compensation for the Victims". In: Journal of International Criminal Justice 3 (2005), pp. 579 et seq.; M. Sassoli: "The Victim-Oriented Approach of International Humanitarian Law and of the International Committee of the Red Cross (ICRC)". In: International Protection of Victims. Ed. C. M. Bassiouni. Eres, 1988, pp. 147 et seq.

on the collective rather than individual level, and victims will mostly be involved in the proceedings through a legal representative rather than in person. Thus, it seems that the likelihood for a direct discourse to occur between victims and perpetrators before the ICC which promotes societal reconciliation is rather low. However, this does not change the fact that it is appropriate to involve both sides, possibly through their legal representatives, in the process of determining appropriate forms of symbolic reparations.

Symbolic forms of reparations might also be developed in cooperation with the Trust Fund, approved organizations or appointed experts.

b) Punitive Damages

The ICC's legal instruments neither expressly mention nor exclude the possibility of ordering punitive damages.

Due to the severity of the crimes under the ICC's jurisdiction and the great harm they regularly cause, it could be considered that it would serve the object and purpose of ICC reparations to order the convicted person to pay punitive damages.

Black's Law Dictionary defines punitive damages as damages that "can be awarded in addition to actual damage when the defendant acted with recklessness, malice, or deceit; specif., damages assessed by way of penalizing the wrongdoer or making an example to others."[713] Punitive damages might be considered particularly appropriate in cases of personal injury, "with a view on emphasizing the wrongfulness of the act in question."[714] Their scope is determined "entirely without reference to proven actual loss" suffered by the claimant.[715]

The drafting process of the ICC Statute suggests the exclusion of punitive damages as a form of reparations. The inclusion of the possibility to order punitive damages was not agreed upon, as many delegation thought that punitive damages would confuse compensation with punishment.[716] Furthermore, the proposal submitted at the Rome Conference that would have added reparations on the list of penalties was not adopted.[717]

713 B. A. Garner (ed.): Black's Law Dictionary. 8th ed. St. Paul, Minnesota, 2004, pp. 418-419 further explaining that punitive damages are also termed exemplary damages, vindicative damages, punitory damages, presumptive damages, added damages, aggravated damages, speculative damages, imaginary damages, smart money, punies.

714 E. H. Riedel: "Damages". In: Encyclopedia of Public International Law. Ed. R. Bernhardt. Vol. 1. Amsterdam, 1992, pp. 929 et seq. at p. 932. Punitive or exemplary damages may be awarded in cases of grave wrongdoing and have deterrence or punishment in mind.

715 D. Shelton: Remedies in International Human Rights Law. 2nd ed. Oxford, 2005, p. 41.

716 C. Muttukumaru: "Reparation to Victims". In: The International Criminal Court – The Making of the Rome Statute – Issues, Negotiations, Results. Ed. R. S. Lee. The Hague, 1999, pp. 262 et seq. at p. 266.

717 F. McKay: "Are Reparations Appropriately Addressed in the ICC Statute?". In: International Crimes, Peace and Human Rights – The Role of the International Criminal Court. Ed. D. Shelton. Ardsley, New York, 2000, pp. 163 et seq. at p. 173.

International law requires that the injured party must be compensated for all actual losses. Punitive or exemplary damages are generally unavailable.[718] The language chosen in the 2005 Victims Principles and the ILC Draft Articles also makes clear that the obligation to provide full reparations does not extend beyond the actual harm suffered and therefore exclude exemplary or punitive damages.[719] The Inter-American Court has not ordered punitive damages.[720] It found that awards of amounts meant to deter or to serve as an example are "not applicable in international law at this time".[721] However, it should be noted that while the European Court of Human Rights principally rejects awards for punitive damages, it has awarded high moral damages, that apparently focussed on the wrongdoing of the government.[722]

In the national context punitive damages are found in the United States and a handful of other systems.[723] In the US human rights case of Filartiga v. Pena-Irala,

718 See e.g. E. H. Riedel: "Damages". In: Encyclopedia of Public International Law. Ed. R. Bernhardt. Vol. 1. Amsterdam, 1992, pp. 929 et seq. at p. 932 states that "this category of damages, if ever recognized, today no longer musters support in international law"; S. Wittich: "Awe of the Gods and Fear of the Priests – Punitive Damages in the Law of State Responsibility". In: Austrian Review of International and European Law 3 (1998), pp. 31 et seq.

719 See Principle 20 2005 Victims Principles; Art. 31, 36 (2) ILC Draft Articles: Compensation shall be provided for any "economically assessable damage". See also International Law Commission: Draft Articles on the Responsibility of States for Internationally Wrongful Acts – With Commentaries, 2001. Available at http://untreaty.un.org/ilc/texts/instruments/english/commentaries/9_6_2001.pdf, last accessed 16 April 2009, Art. 36 paras. 4 et seq.

720 It has ruled that punitive damages are not part of the expression "fair compensation" as established by Art. 63 (1) American Convention; see *Velásquez Rodríguez v. Honduras*, Compensatory Damages, Inter-American Court of Human Rights, 21 July 1989, Ser. C, No. 7, para. 38. However, see more recently *Myrna Mack-Chang v. Guatemala*, Judgement, Inter-American Court of Human Rights, 25 November 2003, Ser. C, No. 101 on the notion of punitive damages.

721 *Velásquez Rodríguez v. Honduras*, Compensatory Damages, Inter-American Court of Human Rights, 21 July 1989, Ser. C, No. 7, para. 27.

722 Rejecting punitive damages e.g. in *Hood v. United Kingdom*, European Court of Human Rights, 18 February 1999, Application No. 27267/95; considering the authorities' conduct as an aggravating factor e.g. in *Cicek v. Turkey*, European Court of Human Rights, 27 February 2001, Application No. 25704/94, para. 205, see P. Leach: Taking a Case to the European Court of Human Rights. 2nd ed. Oxford, 2005, p. 400.

723 B. Stephens: "Translating Filártiga – A Comparative and International Law Analysis of Domestic Remedies for International Human Rights Violations". In: Yale Journal of International Law 27 (2002), pp. 1 et seq. at p. 26; The Rt. Hon. the Lord Scott of Foscote; J. R. J. Holland; C. D. Varner: "The Role of 'Extra-Compensatory' Damages for Violations of Fundamental Human Rights in the United Kingdom and the United States". In: Virginia Journal of International Law 46 (2006), pp. 475 et seq.; D. Shelton: Remedies in International Human Rights Law. 2nd ed. Oxford, 2005, p. 41 emphasizes that "punitive damages [...] are neither new nor limited to a few counties, but instead are found in legal systems throughout the world".

while acknowledging the rarity of punitive damages in international law, the Court found that in cases involving individual defendants "it was essential and proper to grant the remedy of punitive damages in order to give effect to the manifest objectives of the international prohibition against torture."[724] In most civil law systems, courts do not order punitive damages. Instead, the focus is on criminal prosecution rather than civil judgments in order to punish and express a moral statement.[725]

It can be concluded that neither the drafting history of the ICC Statute, nor international law or human rights, supports the possibility of ordering punitive damages. As in traditional civil law jurisdictions, reparations are ordered by the ICC at the end of a criminal proceedings. Thus, the purposes punitive damages serve have already been achieved through the criminal conviction, making an additional punishment through reparations unnecessary and perhaps inappropriate.[726]

5. Assessment

Art. 75 (2) equips the Court with the power to order any form of redress it considers appropriate to repair the harm the convicted person caused to victims.

No single form of reparations is likely to be satisfactory to victims of crimes under the ICC jurisdiction. Instead, combinations of reparation measures will be required in order to repair the harm suffered by the victims on multiple levels. Art. 75 provides the framework for the ICC to not only practice retributive, but also restorative forms of justice, within the framework of a international criminal process. This enables the ICC not only to award different forms reparations- monetary and symbolic as well as individual and collective – but also to adjust these different forms to the particular societal context and needs and wishes of victims of the case. Thus, the emphasis might be on symbolic or monetary reparation, depending on the circumstances of each case.[727]

In principle, the Court has full discretion to decide whether to make a reparation order against a convicted person and to determine the kind of reparation to award in each specific case. However, five factors can be summarized to limit the discretion of the Court. First, while flexibility is important in order to take account the factual

724 *Filártiga v. Pena-Irala*, 630 F.2d 876 (2nd Cir. 1980), p. 865.

725 J. H. Merryman; D. S. Clark; J. O. Haley: The Civil Law Tradition – Europe, Latin America, and East Asia. 2nd ed. Charlottesville, Michigan, 1994, p. 1022; I. Bottigliero: Redress for Victims of Crimes under International Law. Leiden, 2004, p. 225, pointing out that while civil law systems are not familiar with the concept of "punitive damages", the award of "moral damages" in civil law systems also can have punitive purposes.

726 See also Chapter 3. C. ("Purposes of Reparations").

727 Thus in fact, very different approaches to ICC reparation awards have been suggested by scholars:. See e.g. C. M. Bassiouni: Introduction to International Criminal Law. Ardsley, New York, 2003, pp. 722 et seq.; I. Bottigliero: Redress for Victims of Crimes under International Law. Leiden, 2004, p. 241 suggests an emphasis on monetary reparations: "In practice, however it is likely that a large proportion of claims will involve monetary compensation, thus requiring the Court to assess the amount of reparation commensurate with the level of damages, injuries and losses suffered". Others have assumed or promoted that ICC reparations will be of primarily symbolic character.

and cultural context of the cases,[728] the ICC as an permanent organ is also obliged to treat victims equally and fairly. Consistency and a certain degree of legal certainty are particularly relevant with regard to individual monetary awards. Second, the options regarding possible forms of reparations are narrowed down by the fact that ICC reparation orders can only be made against individuals.[729] Third, reparations must be sufficiently workable, clear and precise so they are capable of being enforced by the courts or other relevant national authorities of the states parties.[730] Fourth, the discretion of the Court regarding monetary reparation orders is limited by the availability of sufficient resources. Last, in exercising its discretion, the Court should be guided by the views of the persons involved in the case. That means that, to the extent possible, the wishes of victims should be taken into account when determining the form of reparations. Furthermore, the more dominant the symbolic nature of an award is, the more such awards depend on the willingness of the convicted person to cooperate in awarding them.

III. Standard of Reparations

Art. 75 (2) requires reparations ordered by the ICC to be "appropriate". The Statute and Rules suggest that before the ICC orders reparations, it is to assess the scope and

728 See C. Tomuschat: "Darfur – Compensation for the Victims". In: Journal of International Criminal Justice 3 (2005), pp. 579 et seq. at pp. 585-586: "Reparation and, in particular, compensation must always be synchronized with the societal context of the relevant occurrence [...]. In fact, the factual context in which compensation needs to be considered can vary enormously. If, in an otherwise stable and economically viable society, a group of persons has been gravely harmed due to a serious political misorientation of policies, full reparation is not only desirable, but also feasible. After a devastating international or civil war, on the other hand, the national community in whose name the crimes were committed generally finds itself economically ruined. Even those who were not targeted or persecuted have endured huge material losses. The national economy is simply unable to restore the situation existing ex ante". See also C. M. Bassiouni: "The Philosophy and Policy of International Criminal Justice". In: Man's Inhumanity to Man – Essays on International Law in Honour of Antonio Cassese. Eds. L. C. Vorah; F. Pocar; Y. Featherstone (et al.). The Hague, 2003, pp. 65 et seq. at p. 123. For example, researcher have concluded that the impact of monetary reparations awarded to the Mapuche Communities under the Chilean Reparations Programme have distorted family relations of solidarity and negatively affected family and community networks, as their cultural conception of reparations and its ways of mourning, had been disregarded, see E. Lira: "The Reparations Policy for Human Rights Violations in Chile". In: The Handbook of Reparations. Ed. P. de Greiff. Oxford, 2006, pp. 55 et seq. at p. 63.

729 See above Chapter 5 D. II. 4.) ("Symbolic and Non-Monetary Forms of Reparations: Assessment").

730 See also C. Muttukumaru: "Reparations to Victims". In: Collection of Essays on the Rome Statute of the International Criminal Court. Eds. F. Lattanzi; W. A. Schabas. Ripa di Fagnano Alto, 1999, pp. 301 et seq. at p. 307.

extent of the damage, loss or injury resulting from the crime.[731] In determining individual or collective reparations awards, the extent of loss, damage and injury shall be "taken into account" (Rule 97 (1)).[732] It thus seems that the appropriateness of reparations is to be determined in relation to the harm caused.

In the law of state responsibility, the applicable standard for reparations has classically been that of full reparations.[733] However, the standard of "appropriateness" of reparations has been used in recent international documents and jurisprudence in the context of massive crimes and violations of international law and human rights. The 1985 Victims Declaration states that "fair restitution" shall be made to victims, their families or dependants, "where appropriate".[734] The 2005 Victims Principles set forth that reparations should be "[a]dequate [and] proportional to the gravity of the violations and the harm suffered".[735] Furthermore, "[i]n accordance with domestic law and international law, and taking account of individual circumstances, victims of gross violations of international human rights law and serious violations of international humanitarian law should, as appropriate and proportional to the gravity of the

731 See Art. 75 (1) s. 2 and (2), Rule 97: neither from wording nor structure the Court needs to order reparation as a consequence of the assessment of damage, harm and injury. The Court might want to only assess damages and establish within it's principles that a responsible state has to grant reparations to victims in its national jurisdiction. Yet, conversely, when the Court makes a reparation order, it is necessary to before assess the scope and extent of victims' damage. See Chapter 4 B. ("Determination of Damage, Loss and Injury").

732 It has already been discussed that a contextual interpretation of Art. 75 and Rules 85 and 97 leads to the result that, for the purpose of determining the scope of a reparation order, only include such damage, loss and injury caused to victims that is attributable to the convicted person and that he or she was convicted for, see Chapter 5 A. ("Liability to Make Reparations").

733 It has been considered "a general concept of law", that every violation of an international obligation which results in harm creates a duty to make adequate reparation. *Factory at Chorzow Case* (F.R.G. v. Pol), Jurisdiction, Judgment No.8, Permanent Court of International Justice, 12 September 1928, Ser. A, No. 17, p. 29; Reparation for Injuries Suffered in the Services of the United Nations, Advisory Opinion. In: ICJ Reports (1949), pp. 174 et seq. at p. 184. In the Chorzow Factory judgment, the Permanent Court of International Justice set forth that "The essential principle contained in the actual notion of an illegal act [...] is that reparation must, as far as possible, wipe-out all the consequences of the illegal act and re-establish the situation which would, in all probability, have existed if that act had not been committed", *Factory at Chorzow Case* (F.R.G. v. Pol), Jurisdiction, Judgment No.8, Permanent Court of International Justice, 12 September 1928, Ser. A, No. 17, p. 47. Thus, the general principle is that "full reparation" is to be provided by the responsible party, which is – in the context of international law – a state. Accordingly, Art. 34 ILC Draft Articles require "[f]ull Reparation for the injury caused by the internationally wrongful act."

734 Art. 8 1985 Victims Declaration. The term "restitution" is in this document used as generic term, unlike in the ICC Statute, the 2005 Victims Principles and the ILC Draft Articles which use the term "reparation".

735 Principle 15.

violation and the circumstances of each case, be provided with full and effective reparation."[736] Thus, while the standard of full reparations is not abandoned, it only applies under certain conditions and where it is appropriate. Likewise, while the Inter-American Court acknowledges that the standard for violations in international law is full restitution *(restitutio in integrum)*, it recognizes that this is impossible to achieve when the damage suffered is irreversible.[737] In such cases "fair compensation" must be awarded to compensate, to the extent possible, the loss suffered[738], which "must be proportionate to the violations".[739] Similarly, in the European system the respondent state is obliged to restore as far as possible the situation existing before the breach.[740] The African Charter provides that reparation orders shall be appropriate and fair.[741] The Human Rights Committee has recently ordered states to pay "adequate" or "appropriate" compensation for violations of fundamental rights.[742]

736 Principle 18.

737 *Velásquez Rodríguez v. Honduras*, Reparations, Inter-American Court of Human Rights, 21 July 1989, Ser. C, No. 7, para. 26; *Godínez Cruz*, Reparation, para. 26. Art. 63 (1) of the American Convention, determines that the Court shall "rule, if appropriate, that the consequences of the measure or situation that constituted the breach of such right or freedom be remedied and that fair compensation be paid to the injured party". Art. 41 of the ECHR establishes that "[i]f the Court finds that there has been a violation of the Convention or the protocols thereto, and if the internal laws of the High Contracting Party concerned allows only partial reparation to be made, the Court shall, if necessary, afford just satisfaction to the injured party."

738 *Velásquez Rodríguez v. Honduras*, Reparations, Inter-American Court of Human Rights, 21 July 1989, Ser. C, No. 7, paras. 26-27; *Godínez Cruz*, Reparation, para. 26-27. Art. 63 (1) of the American Convention, in determining that the Court shall "rule, if appropriate, that the consequences of the measure or situation that constituted the breach of such right or freedom be remedied and that fair compensation be paid to the injured party".

739 *Castillo Páez Case*, Reparations, Inter-American Court of Human Rights, 27 November 1998, Ser. C, No. 43, para. 51. Furthermore, "[r]eparations are not meant to enrich or impoverish the victim or its heirs", see also *Garrido and Baigorria v. Argentina*, Reparations, Inter-American Court of Human Rights, 27 August 1998, Ser. C, No. 39, para. 43.

740 Art. 41 ECHR establishes that "[i]f the Court finds that there has been a violation of the Convention or the protocols thereto, and if the internal laws of the High Contracting Party concerned allows only partial reparation to be made, the Court shall, if necessary, afford just satisfaction to the injured party", see for a summary of the Court's relevant jurisprudence P. Leach: Taking a Case to the European Court of Human Rights. 2nd ed. Oxford, 2005, p. 398.

741 Art. 27 Protocol to the African Charter on Human and Peoples' Rights on the Establishment of an African Court on Human and Peoples' Rights, 9 June 1998, O.A.U. Doc. OAU/LEG/EXP/AFCHPR/PROT (III).

742 *Smirnova v. Russia*, Human Rights Committee, Views of 5 July 2004, No. 712/1996, CCPR/C/81/D/712/1996, § 12; *Perterer v. Austria*, Human Rights Committee, Views of 20 July 2004, No. 1015/2001, CCPR/C/81/D/1015/2001, § 12; *Kankanamge v. Sri Lanka*, Human Rights Committee, Views of 27 July 2004, No. 909/2000, CCPR/81/D/909/2000, § 11; *Bautista de Arellana v. Colombia*, Human Rights Committee; Views of 27 October 1995, No. 563/1993.

In the national context, full compensation for the victim of a tort remains the primary goal, or at least the starting point when considering reparations.[743] However, regarding non-pecuniary losses there is some controversy as to what function they aim to achieve and whether they should be subject to "caps".[744] In many areas of national laws, limitations (or "caps and thresholds") to liability exist.[745]

Experience of national reparations schemes proves that particularly in the context of gross and systematic violations, full reparation is a standard unlikely to achieve.[746]

Thus, while the general standard of reparations recognized in national and international law and human rights is full restitution, the standard commonly applied to compensation is more flexible, particularly in the context of massive and systematic violations. The standard of "appropriateness" of reparations set forth in the ICC Statute thus complies with standards and recent practice applied in international and national legal systems. The determination of "appropriateness" is to be undertaken in relation to the extent of harm caused, as suggested in the ICC Statute and Rules. An interpretation in light of internationally recognized human rights lead would suggest to additionally take into consideration the gravity of the violation and the circumstances of each case.

743 B. A. Koch; H. Koziol: "Comparative Analysis". In: Compensation for Personal Injury in a Comparative Perspective. Eds. B. A. Koch; H. Koziol. Wien, 2003, pp. 407 et seq. at p. 430; U. Magnus: "Comparative Report on the Law of Damages". In: Unification of Tort Law – Damages. Ed. U. Magnus. The Hague (et al.), 2001, pp. 185 et seq. at p. 188, referring in particular to European jurisdictions

744 S. Deakin; A. Johnston; B. Markesinis: Markesinis and Deakin's Tort Law. 5th ed. Oxford (et al.), 2003, p. 827, noting that "caps", i.e. upper limits exist in some US states.

745 B. A. Koch; H. Koziol: "Comparative Analysis". In: Compensation for Personal Injury in a Comparative Perspective. Eds. B. A. Koch; H. Koziol. Wien, 2003, pp. 407 et seq. at p. 431; see also U. Magnus: "Comparative Report on the Law of Damages". In: Unification of Tort Law – Damages. Ed. U. Magnus. The Hague (et al.), 2001, pp. 185 et seq. at p. 188. When compensation is awarded in common law criminal procedure, often, victims do not receive full compensation, e.g. s. 738 Canadian Criminal Code.

746 E.g. in the Western German compensation scheme for victims of Nazi injustices, while in principle full reparation was aspired to, with the exception of compensation for harm to property and assets, instead of fully compensating harm, the actual pecuniary loss of victims served in principal as grounds for assessing a more generalized sum of compensation. This did, however, often lead to extensive awards. Consequently, the principle of adequate compensation generally ruled the awards granted by the German compensation scheme; H. Giessler: "Grundsatzbestimmungen des Entschädigungsrechts". In: Die Wiedergutmachung Nationalsozialistischen Unrechts in der Bundesrepublik Deutschland – Das Bundesentschädigungsgesetz. Eds. Bundesminister der Finanzen; W. Schwarz. Vol. 4. München, 1981, pp. 1 et seq. at p. 2; B. Heß: "Kriegsentschädigungen aus kollisionsrechtlicher und rechtsvergleichender Sicht". In: Entschädigung nach bewaffneten Konflikten – Die Konstitutionalisierung der Welthandelsordnung. Eds. W. Heintschel von Heinegg; S. Kadelbach; B. Heß (et al.). Heidelberg, 2003, pp. 107 et seq. at pp. 124-125; C. Tomuschat: "Darfur – Compensation for the Victims". In: Journal of International Criminal Justice 3 (2005), pp. 579 et seq. at p. 586.

IV. *Scope of the Compensation Order*

The ICC Statute and Rules do not explicitly provide applicable criteria according to which the scope of compensation awards should be determined. In contrast to symbolic reparations which should be determined flexibly according to the circumstances of the specific case, material awards ought to follow consistent principles in order to be fair and to serve justice.[747]

While the Court alone is competent to determine the scope of the compensation order against the convicted person, if it orders reparations to be made indirectly, the Trust Fund or organizations may be involved in determining the precise nature of awards to victims.[748]

Independent of whether collective or individual compensation awards are ordered, several factors are relevant when determining the scope of the compensation order.

First, it has been held that the primary object of monetary ICC reparation orders is to compensate or repair, rather than to punish or deter, and that the Statute requires compensation to be appropriate, which is to be determined in view of the harm caused.[749] However, compensating the harm caused by crimes which come under the ICC's jurisdiction may often be difficult. There might be a lack of resources to repair the damage suffered by victims appropriately. Furthermore, when massive and systematic crimes have been committed, monetary awards often seem inappropriate, as money is not equivalent to the harm often suffered on a number of layers.[750] Compensation therefore presents arguably the most difficulties as a form of reparation for crimes under international law, and is often the most controversial form of reparation.[751] This must be taken into account when damages are to be assessed and calculated in order to determine the scope of compensation.

747 See Lord Donaldson of Lymington to the First Edition of Judicial Studies Board: Guidelines for the Assessment of General Damages in Personal Injury Cases. 5th ed. London, 1992, p. ix, who has stated, that while "no two cases are ever precisely the same, justice requires that there be consistency between awards".

748 Rule 93 (2)-(4); in particular Reg. 69 et seq. Trust Fund Regulations.

749 See in particular Chapter 3 ("Purposes of Reparation" and Assessment), Chapter 5 D. II. 4. b) ("Forms of Reparation"- Punitive Damages), where it has been concluded, inter alia, that the goal of punishment has been dealt with in the trial proceedings and achieved through the conviction; therefore exemplatory and punitive damages are not appropriate when determining the ICC reparations order.

750 M. du Plessis: "Reparations and International Law – How Are Reparations to Be Determined (Past Wrong or Current Effects), against Whom, and What Form Should they Take?". In: Windsor Yearbook of Access to Justice 22 (2004), pp. 41 et seq. at p. 62. The difficulty of financial damage assessment in the international sphere was already recognized in the *Lusitania* (United States of America v. Germany), Reports of International Arbitral Awards, 21 February 1924, Vol. VII, p. 40.

751 M. du Plessis: "Reparations and International Law – How Are Reparations to Be Determined (Past Wrong or Current Effects), against Whom, and What Form Should they Take?". In: Windsor Yearbook of Access to Justice 22 (2004), pp. 41 et seq. at p. 62; see similarly UN Security Council: Report of the Secretary-General on The Rule of Law and

Second, given the collective nature of the crimes under the ICC's jurisdiction, it is possible that several persons may have caused the victims' harm. It is questionable whether this should be reflected in the scope of compensation orders. It is also possible that the various responsible persons may have different degrees of responsibility for the commission of the crime.

The third basic decision that must be made is whether other factors within the sphere of the convicted person, such as his or her financial capacity, should be taken into account when the scope of a compensation order is determined.

1. Valuation and Calculation of Damages

Valuation and calculation of damages is already complex in the context of individual violations. While material damages can in principle be calculated following an objective standard, there is no such standard for impecuniary harm.[752] Damages for pain, suffering or loss of amenities of life, dignity or cultural damage, the kinds of harm which almost necessarily result from massive and systematic crimes, cannot be assessed by a simple mathematical calculation."[753] Additional difficulties arise with gross and systematic crimes, as they cause often irreparable harm to large numbers of victims and result in a number of practical problems.[754]

a) ICC Reparation System

In the context of the ICC, valuation and calculation of damages seems particularly challenging due to the asymmetry inherent in the ICC reparations mechanism. While the ICC may often be challenged to repair the substantial and multifaceted harm caused by the massive and systematic crimes under its jurisdiction, only individuals can be ordered to make reparations. It is necessary to examined how damages are to be valued and calculated in a way that is realistic and at the same time ensures that compensation awards meet the standard of "appropriateness" as required by Art. 75 (2). What is "appropriate" is to be determined in relation to the harm caused in each

Transitional Justice in Conflict and Post-Conflict Societies, 23 August 2004, UN Doc. S/2004/616, paras. 54-55.

752 In the context of international crimes, another important category is that of personal injury, which can be divided into two distinct kinds of damages which are always discussed under two headings. The first includes such items as are capable of direct translation into money terms: for example, loss of earnings, medical expenses, and other out-of-pocket expenses. It is the nature of non-pecuniary losses that it cannot be translated directly into money, but nevertheless the only form of compensation available is an award of monetary damage, and an assessment of damages has to be made", see W. V. H. Rogers: Winfield and Jolowicz on Tort. 16th ed. London, 2002, pp. 767 et seq.

753 Lord Donaldson of Lymington to the First Edition of Judicial Studies Board: Guidelines for the Assessment of General Damages in Personal Injury Cases. 5th ed. London, 1992, p. ix.

754 See D. Shelton: "Reparations for Victims of International Crimes". In: International Crimes, Peace, and Human Rights – The Role of the International Court. Ed. D. Shelton. Ardsley, New York, 2000, pp. 137 et seq. at p. 141.

case.[755] When the Court orders awards to be made through the Trust Fund, the Trust Fund Regulations envision that the Trust Fund shall take into account the particular injuries to the victims and the nature of evidence to support them.[756]

b) International and National Law and Human Rights

As mentioned above, in international law and human rights, compensation shall be provided for "economically assessable damage" "as appropriate and proportional to the gravity of the violation and the circumstances of each case".[757] There is no unified approach to the calculation of damages in national and international jurisdictions.[758] Rather, the common feature of most legal systems is that most lack clear rules on how to assess damages.[759]

1) Calculating Non-Pecuniary and Pecuniary Harm

In all jurisdictions, approaches to the valuation and calculation of harm tend to differ depending on whether pecuniary or non-pecuniary losses are awarded.

i) *Pecuniary Harm (Material Damage)*

The European Court has stated how difficult it can be to quantify pecuniary damages due to the "uncertain character of the damage flowing from the violation".[760] As with moral damages, in most cases it awarded lump sums, making it difficult or impossible to determine the basis of the award.[761] The Inter-American Court mostly relies on documents or testimony allowing for precise calculation of pecuniary damages.[762]

---

755 See Chapter 5 C. III. ("Standard of Reparations").

756 Reg. 55 Trust Fund Regulations states: "Subject to the order of the Court, the Trust Fund shall take into account the following factors in determining the nature/size of awards, inter alia: the nature of the crimes, the particular injuries to the victims and the nature of the evidence to support such injuries, as well as the size and location of the beneficiary group".

757 Principle 20 2005 Victims Principles.

758 See for a overview D. Shelton: Remedies in International Human Rights Law. 2nd ed. Oxford, 2005, pp. 328-348.

759 E.g. U. Magnus: "Comparative Report on the Law of Damages". In: Unification of Tort Law – Damages. Ed. U. Magnus. The Hague (et al.), 2001, pp. 185 et seq. at p. 190, who points out the exception of the New Dutch Civil Code.

760 *James and Webster v. United Kingdom*, European Court of Human Rights, 18 October 1981, Application Nos. 7601/76 and 7807/77, para. 11; for a case dealing with lost opportunity costs, see *Allenet de Ribemont v. France*, European Court of Human Rights, 10 February 1995, Application No. 15175/98; for further discussion see P. Leach: Taking a Case to the European Court of Human Rights. 2nd ed. Oxford, 2005, pp. 399 et seq.

761 P. Leach: Taking a Case to the European Court of Human Rights. 2nd ed. Oxford, 2005, p. 398.

762 However, the Inter-American Commission has argued that under particular living conditions it is difficult for victims or their families to gather documentary evidence, see *El Amparo v. Venezuela*, Reparations, Inter-American Court of Human Rights, 14 September 1996, Ser. C, No. 28, para. 19. Loss of earnings is calculated on the basis of vic-

As in national jurisdictions, the principal standard for pecuniary damages is full compensation, the general starting point is to compare the two different states of the injured party's pecuniary situation before and after the violation in order to assess whether there is a discrepancy between the two and hence recoverable damage.[763] However, there are exceptions to this approach and a general tendency to allow for abstract, objective calculation.[764] Furthermore, depending on the particular circumstances of the case, damages may be adjusted as the court considers reasonable.[765]

ii) Non-Pecuniary Damage (Moral Damage)

Both the European Court of Human Rights and the Inter-American Court have emphasized in their judgments that moral damage cannot be precisely determined.[766]

tim's income and age at the time of the violation, see also e.g. *El Amparo v. Venezuela*, Reparations, Inter-American Court of Human Rights, 14 September 1996, Ser. C, No. 28, para. 28. In the event of death, the Court has determined the quantum of compensation according to the factors applied in the Lusitania arbitration: estimating the net present value of the amounts (a) which the descendant, had he not been killed, would probably have contributed to the claimant, plus (b) the pecuniary value to such claimant of the deceased's personal services in claimant's care, education and supervision, and (c) reasonable compensation for mental suffering or shock (the latter calculated as moral damages). Adjusted by a number of additional factors, the net present value requires calculating: (i) age at death of each victim and annual earnings at that time, (ii) life expectancy of each victim , (iii) annual earnings taking into account inflation rates, see D. Shelton: "Reparations in the Inter-American System". In: The Inter-American System of Human Rights. Eds. D. J. Harris; S. Livingstone. Oxford, 1998, pp. 151 et seq. at p. 159. The determination of "special damages" (Damnum emergens) or "expenses" for investigation of the violation, medical expenses before the ruling are usually supported by substantial documentation, however the Court has determined these rather on the basis of equity. Regarding costs of accessing domestic and regional courts, there has not been a uniform approach, leading to precise calculation in some cases and determination on the basis of equity on the other, see The Temptation of Christ, Merits, para. 5 on the one and *Garrido and Baigorria v. Argentina*, Reparations, Inter-American Court of Human Rights, 27 August 1998, Ser. C, No. 39, para. 82 on the other hand. For further discussion see V. Madrigal-Borloz: "Damage and Redress in the Jurisprudence of the Inter-American Court of Human Rights (1979-2001)". In: Reparations – Redressing Past Wrongs. Eds. G. Ulrich; L. Krabbe Boserup. (Human Rights in Development – Yearbook 2001). The Hague, 2003, pp. 211 et seq. at p. 262.

763 U. Magnus: "Comparative Report on the Law of Damages". In: Unification of Tort Law – Damages. Ed. U. Magnus. The Hague (et al.), 2001, pp. 185 et seq. at p. 195 ("Differenzmethode") referring to Austria, Belgium, France, Germany, the Netherlands, South Africa, Italy, Greece and pointing out that generally, every position is recognized which is measurable in money.

764 Ibid., p. 196.

765 E.g. T. Lappi-Seppälä: "Finland". In: Wiedergutmachung im Kriminalrecht – Internationale Perspektiven – Reparation in Criminal Law – International Perspectives. Eds. A. Eser; S. Walter. Vol. 1. Freiburg i. Br., 1996, pp. 317 et seq. at p. 377.

766 For the European Court, see *Wiesinger v. Austria*, European Court of Human Rights, 30 October 1991, Application No. 11796/85, para. 85. For the Inter-American Court see e.g.

Instead of applying general principles, both Courts have used equity when determining awards for moral damage on a case-by-case basis, making it often difficult or impossible to determine how the Courts calculated a particular sum.[767]

The awards of compensation for impecuniary losses granted by the Inter-American Court are very diverse, and are tending to become more generous, in particular regarding pain and suffering.[768] Generally, whenever a ruling was made on a presumptive basis, awards have been low and when the Court received medical reports, the awards have been much higher.[769] Next to the factor of severity of injury and existence of proof, the Inter-American Court seems to suggest that the egregiousness of the conduct of the responsible party acts as an additional factor in assessing moral damages.[770] Other factors taken into account were whether the victims were

---

Velásquez Rodríguez v. Honduras, Reparations, Inter-American Court of Human Rights, 21 July 1989, Ser. C, No. 7, para. 34.

767 For the European Court of Human Rights see *Kenmache v. France*, (No. 3), (45/1993/440/519), 24 November 1994, para. 11; *Ferraro v. Italy*, Application No. 13440/87, 19 February 1991, para. 21. For the Inter-American Court of Human Rights, see *Velásquez Rodríguez v. Honduras*, Reparations, Inter-American Court of Human Rights, 21 July 1989, Ser. C, No. 7, para. 27; *Godínez Cruz*, Reparation, para. 25. P. Leach: Taking a Case to the European Court of Human Rights. 2nd ed. Oxford, 2005, pp. 397-398 notes that rather than following specific means to calculate damages, the European Court applies general principles in assessing just satisfaction, therefore it is in many cases difficult or impossible to discern how the European Court has arrived at the sum awarded.

768 Recently, the Inter-American Court found the State of Guatemala responsible for the massacre of 188 persons in the village Plan de Sánchez and ordered uniform compensation awards of US $ 25 000 for each surviving family, *Plan de Sánchez Massacre v. Guatemala*, Reparations, Inter-American Court of Human Rights, 19 November 2004, Ser. C, No. 105. Similarly, the scope of awards have differed for violations that did not result in the death of victims, but where it was foreseeable these will result in "ruinous consequences" for the victims' lives, see for further analysis D. Cassel: "The Expanding Scope and Impact of Reparations Awarded by the Inter-American Court of Human Rights". In: Out of the Ashes – Reparation for Victims of Gross and Systematic Human Rights Violations. Eds. K. de Feyter; S. Parmentier; M. Bossuyt (et al.). Antwerp, 2005, pp. 191 et seq. at pp. 198 et seq. Generally, the Inter-American Court has ruled that it must strictly adhere to the methods ordinarily used in case law to calculate appropriate compensation, see *Aloeboetoe et al. v. Suriname*, Reparations, Inter-American Court of Human Rights, 10 September 1993, Ser. C, No. 15, para. 87.

769 E.g. in *Paniagua Morales et. al. Case*, Judgment, Inter-American Court of Human Rights, 8 March 1998, Ser. C, No. 37, on a presumptive basis US $ 1000 were awarded to the siblings of some of the victims, whereas in *Castillo Páez Case*, Reparations, 27 November 1998, Ser. C, No. 43, the Court received medical reports regarding the mother of the direct victim and was awarded US $ 50 000.

770 D. Shelton: "Reparations in the Inter-American System". In: The Inter-American System of Human Rights. Eds. D. J. Harris; S. Livingstone. Oxford, 1998, pp. 151 et seq. at p. 156.

minors[771] and whether the state acknowledged the facts and accepted responsibility, thus lowering the scope of the award.[772]

The European Court of Human Rights has not awarded damages for non-pecuniary losses on a regular basis.[773] When it did, the factors taken into account in determining the awards were the nature and duration of the wrong, as well as the conduct and apparently the social status of the applicant.[774] In a few decisions, the Court has awarded high amounts for impecuniary losses which seemed to be motivated by the degree of wrongdoing by the government.[775] Also the applicant's behavior might be a factor in the assessment of awards.[776]

In national jurisdictions, the estimation of non-pecuniary harm follows various methods, with some large differences from one state to the other both in theory and in practice, particularly with regard to compensation for pain and suffering.[777]

771 In this case moral damages may be higher in order to recognize that the victims were deprived of the special measures of protection the state owes to children. See e.g. the *"Street Children" Case*, Reparations, Inter-American Court of Human Rights, 26 May 2001, Ser. C, No. 77, paras. 89-91.

772 *El Amparo v. Venezuela*, Reparations, Inter-American Court of Human Rights, 14 September 1996, Ser. C, No. 28, paras. 32-34 (acknowledging responsibility).

773 Also the European Court of Justice has ordered compensation for non-material harm (préjudice moral) for shock, disturbance, uneasiness caused , uncertainty, mental and physical suffering, see above Chapter 5 D. II. 2) a) ("Types of Compensable Harm").

774 D. Shelton: Remedies in International Human Rights Law. 2nd ed. Oxford, 2005, pp. 345 et seq. criticizing the approach to take into account the applicant's social status, see e.g. *De Wilde, Ooms and Versyp*, European Court of Human Rights, 10 March 1972, Series A No. 14, p. 10.

775 E.g. *Bonanzo v. France*, European Court of Human Rights, 1987, Ser. A 124-E; *Cicek v. Turkey*, European Court of Human Rights, 27 February 2001, Application No. 25704/94, para. 205; see P. Leach: Taking a Case to the European Court of Human Rights. 2nd ed. Oxford, 2005, p. 400.

776 E.g. *McCann and others v. United Kingdom*, European Court of Human Rights, 27 September 1995, Application No. 18984/91; D. Shelton: Remedies in International Human Rights Law. 2nd ed. Oxford, 2005, p. 345 criticizes that there are cases in which the Court took into account the "moral worth" of the victim and the wrongdoer.

777 See for summaries G. Comandé: "Non-Pecuniary Damages for Personal Injury in Europe and the US – A Proposal for Judicial Scheduling Models". In: Duke Journal of Comparative & International Law 15 (2005); B. A. Koch; H. Koziol: "Comparative Analysis". In: Compensation for Personal Injury in a Comparative Perspective. Eds. B. A. Koch; H. Koziol. Wien, 2003, pp. 407 et seq. at pp. 425, 432-433. points out that while compensation for personal injury does not vary greatly concerning personal injury in general, damages for pain and suffering, amounts of compensation vary considerably already in Western European jurisdictions. This is a consequence of the fact already mentioned, namely that immaterial loss by its nature cannot be valued in money so that several other factors and valuations are taken into account when calculating the compensations, such as costs and standards of living, and the notion of prevention and the notion that liability should be kept within reasonable limits; see also D. Shelton: Remedies in International Human Rights Law. 2nd ed. Oxford, 2005, pp. 36 et seq., and noting with regard to inter-

In some systems, the valuation of impecuniary damage depends on the amount of pecuniary damages while in others it is an independent claim.[778] When calculating damages for non-pecuniary harm, some courts seek to assess the amount that will enable the injured party to acquire benefits to substitute for those lost. Other courts take a personal approach based on injury to the subjective feelings of the injured person. A third approach practiced is to consider that the victim has been deprived of an asset with has objective value in case of loss or damage.[779] Often, non-pecuniary harm is determined by statutory scales which differentiate between certain types of harm.[780]

Where the calculation of non-pecuniary harm is within the discretion of the Court, even where the same factors are considered relevant, due to the subjective means of assessment, amounts for the same kinds of non-pecuniary harm often differ between states, courts and cases.[781]

2) Standardization and Estimation of Damage

While the ICC Statute and Rules do not contain guidance on the issue, the Trust Fund Regulations include the possibility of standardizing and applying techniques to process mass claims, which may be applied when individual awards are ordered through the Trust Fund: "[T]he Secretariat shall set out all relevant demographic/statistical data about the group of victims", and options for determining any missing details about the beneficiaries of individual awards may include the "use of demographic data to determine the members of the beneficiary group".[782]

International and national courts and reparations schemes have acknowledged that in certain cases precise damage assessment or proof is impossible, and even where it is possible, it might under certain circumstances be inappropriate. A general tendency towards standardized or lump awards can be assessed, which are based on tables or guidelines in cases of typical categories of harm, instead of individual assess-

national human rights jurisprudence at p. 343 that there are "few developed principles for calculating awards of non-monetary injuries like pain and suffering."

778 A number of states also take into account the degree of fault, see Chapter 5 C. IV. 2 a) ("Degree of Fault").

779 D. Shelton: Remedies in International Human Rights Law. 2nd ed. Oxford, 2005, p. 343.

780 See Chapter 5 C. IV 1 a) 2) ("Standardization and Estimation of Damage") below. In the event of impecuniary harm for bodily harm, some legal systems split the assessment into different heads of damage and require that each head be evaluated separately. They are added together and then constitute damages for non-pecuniary harm. In other jurisdictions, no distinction is made between different categories of non-pecuniary damages and only one single sum for all immaterial damage is awarded, see U. Magnus: "Comparative Report on the Law of Damages". In: Unification of Tort Law – Damages. Ed. U. Magnus. The Hague (et al.), 2001, pp. 185 et seq. at pp. 194-195.

781 See D. Shelton: Remedies in International Human Rights Law. 2nd ed. Oxford, 2005, p. 36.

782 Rule 98 (2); Reg. 60, 61 Trust Fund Regulations.

ment of damage.[783] This is particularly true of impecuniary harm and instances where harm has been caused to a number of persons.[784]

In recent years, the Inter-American Court awarded identical amounts of compensation to victims instead of individualizing the awards for moral damages.[785]

In the context of individual liability the wrongdoer is principally responsible for putting victims back in the position they would have been if the wrongful act had not occurred.[786] Consequently, national tort law is based on the determination of individual damage and proof of causation in every case.[787] However, where it is certain that damage occurred but where the precise scope of that damage is too difficult or costly to prove, national courts are regularly allowed to estimate the amount of damage. Alternatively, they may consider it sufficient that the general loss suffered is "well established".[788] Guidelines for determining the amounts for impecuniary harm such as pain and suffering and disability or permanent injury have been used. Categories of amounts are, for example, based on types of harm according to their seriousness, the type and duration of medical care, the number of dependents or severity of

783 H. Lange; G. Schiemann: Schadensersatz. 3rd ed. Tübingen, 2003, p. 18 et seq.; see for a general discussion M. du Plessis: "Reparations and International Law – How Are Reparations to Be Determined (Past Wrong or Current Effects), against Whom, and What Form Should they Take?". In: Windsor Yearbook of Access to Justice 22 (2004), pp. 41 et seq. at p. 63.

784 See e.g. contributions in The International Bureau of the Permanent Court of Arbitration (ed.): Redressing Injustices through Mass Claims Processes – Innovative Responses to Unique Challenges. Oxford, 2006.

785 *El Amparo v. Venezuela*, Reparations, 14 September 1996, Ser. C, No. 28, paras. 28-29, 41 et seq.; *Neira Alegría et al. v. Peru*, Reparations, 19 September 1996, Ser. C, No. 29, paras. 53, 61. Also, the Inter-American Court found the State of Guatemala responsible for the massacre of 188 persons in the village Plan de Sanchez and ordered uniform compensation awards of US $ 25 000 for each surviving family, see *Plan de Sánchez Massacre v. Guatemala*, Reparations, 19 November 2004, Ser. C, No. 105. Individuals injured were ordered to benefit from equal amounts of moral damages in *Moiwana Village v. Suriname*, Judgment, 15 June 2005, Ser. C, No. 124, para. 196.

786 J. Cooper Alexander; R. A. Fein: "Procedural Design and Terror Victim Compensation". In: De Paul Law Review 53 (2003), pp. 627 et seq. at p. 651.

787 "The tort system's legitimacy is based on the fact that damages determinations are individualized". Individual awards must be based on individualized evidence and on the exercise of judgment in some form of individualized adjudication, see ibid., pp. 642, 651.

788 E.g. L. Zedner: "England". In: Wiedergutmachung im Kriminalrecht – Internationale Perspektiven – Reparation in Criminal Law – International Perspectives. Eds. A. Eser; S. Walther. Vol. 1. Freiburg i. Br., 1996, pp. 109 et seq. at p. 175 points out that where there is more than one victim, the total sum should normally be apportioned on a pro rata basis, citing further references; when the ground and extent of the damage cannot be exactly assessed, or not with proportionate efforts, it may be determined according to the estimation of the judge, e.g. pursuant to 287 German Code of Civil Procedure (ZPO); see H. Lange; G. Schiemann: Schadensersatz. 3rd ed. Tübingen, 2003, pp. 177 et seq.; U. Magnus: "Causation in German Tort Law". In: Unification of Tort Law – Causation. Ed. J. M. Spier. The Hague, 2000, pp. 63 et seq. at p. 64.

any continuing injury.[789] Violations of individuals' rights can often be compensated through nominal or symbolic awards.[790] There have also been attempts to standardize monetary awards for pecuniary loss in the field of personal injury.[791] In particular, in state compensation schemes for victims of crime, standard amounts ("heads") of compensation are awarded according to the nature of the injury suffered.[792]

Victims of massive and systematic human rights violations or international crimes have claimed compensation from the individual perpetrator in national courts. In this context, courts have also granted standardized awards for certain categories of harm, often based on the gravity of the violations or harm.[793] In a number of cases in US courts, once the courts had established the liability of perpetrators of large scale human rights violations, they limited individualized decision-making by utilizing statistical sampling methods to determine compensation awards in the damages

789 See for a national administration scheme designed for mass victimization J. Cooper Alexander; R. A. Fein: "Procedural Design and Terror Victim Compensation". In: De Paul Law Review 53 (2003), pp. 627 et seq. at p. 643; for other national compensation schemes T. Lappi-Seppälä: "Finland". In: Wiedergutmachung im Kriminalrecht – Internationale Perspektiven – Reparation in Criminal Law – International Perspectives. Eds. A. Eser; S. Walter. Vol. 1. Freiburg i. Br., 1996, pp. 317 et seq. at p. 377, noting that these guidelines were originally established for traffic accidents, but are in practice used for instances other than traffic offenses; J. Zila: "Schweden". In: Wiedergutmachung im Kriminalrecht – Internationale Perspektiven – Reparation in Criminal Law – International Perspectives. Eds. A. Eser, S. Walther. Vol. 1. Freiburg i. Br., 1996, pp. 231 et seq. at p. 287 pointing out that e.g. in Sweden, damages are calculated according to civil law provisions; the scope of impecuniary damages are determined according to tables; see generally pp. 18 et seq.

790 See U. Magnus: "Comparative Report on the Law of Damages". In: Unification of Tort Law – Damages. Ed. U. Magnus. The Hague (et al.), 2001, pp. 185 et seq. at p. 187 noting that this is done in order to state that a right has been violated irrespective of whether a respective actual loss can be accrued or proved.

791 Ibid., pp. 196-197 describes that in a number of national jurisdictions calculation of future economic loss from personal injuries are standardized by using tables or other methods, leading to abstract rather than concrete calculation of loss.

792 See e.g. UK Criminal Compensation Scheme of 12 December 1995.

793 Victims have filed claims mainly in the US under the Alien Torts Claim Act and similar statutes and have receive compensation under the "tort settlement model". A recent European example is the Riggs Bank settlement in a Spanish Court, leading to a payment of Riggs Bank to a foundation benefiting victims of the Pinochet Regime, see e.g. T. O'Hara, T.: "Allbrittons, Riggs to Pay Victims of Pinochet". In: Washington Post (Saturday, 26 February 2005, p. A01). Available at www.washingtonpost.com/wp-dyn/articles/A53805-2005Feb25.html, last accessed 21 April 2009. Human rights tort litigation has been criticized for, in their vast majority, resulting in a settlement, and the "settlement class" has been described as "one of the last steps along this path toward the lawsuit as a business deal", see S. P. Baumgartner: "Human Rights and Civil Litigation in United States Courts – The Holocaust-Era Cases." In: Washington University Law Quarterly 80 (2002), pp. 835 et seq. at pp. 842 et seq.

stage.[794] In the Marcos case, the expert calculated the amounts for torture victims by ranking the claims on a scale from 1 to 5, according to the severity of abuse and suffering or injury.[795] Other factors included the age of victims and actual losses including medical bills. Loss of earnings was also considered, using a formula that took into account the age of the victim and their annual income.[796] The court argued "that there were sufficient similarities within a rating category to recommend a standard amount to each victim within that grouping".[797] On appeal, the methodology used to determine compensation was challenged, claiming it was inappropriate to lump claims together. In response, the Court stated that the methodology was justified because the time and resources that would have been required when trying all of the nearly 10 000 claims would have made resolution of the claims impossible.[798] In

794 Generally in US human rights cases, "the courts [...] sought to award damages according to their sense of the gravity of the underlying facts. The courts seem to feel free to award damages as they see fit [...] to give effect to the purpose of a statute and in the absence of statutory directives", M. Swan: "International Human Rights Tort Claims and the Experience of United States Courts – An Introduction to the US Case Law, Key Statutes and Doctrines". In: Torture as a Tort- Comparative Perspectives on the Development of Transnational Human Right Litigation. Ed. C. Scott. Oxford, 2001, pp. 65 et seq. at p. 107, with numerous examples of sums awarded. In the Filártiga decision, *Filártiga v. Pena-Irala*, 630 F.2d 876 (2nd Cir. 1980), the competent court awarded a roughly calculated amount of compensation for emotional pain and suffering, loss of companionship, funeral and medical expenses and lost income; as well as punitive damages in an amount many times higher that the compensatory damages, see R. G. Steinhardt: "Fulfilling the Promise of Filártiga – Litigating Human Rights Claims against the Estate of Ferdinand Marcos". In: Yale Journal of International Law 20 (1995), pp. 65 et seq. at p. 94 relating to Filartiga II, 577 F Supp at 577.

795 In *Hilao v. Marcos*, 103 F.3d 767, 782 (9th Cir. 1996): Instead of holding separate hearings on each of the claims, statistical sampling methods were utilized to assist in the determination of compensation in the 10 059 claims in the class action suit against former Philippine president Marcos. After an initial review 518 claims were ruled facially invalid, leaving a pool of 9.541 of which 137 were randomly selected by computer. The number 137 was chosen on the basis of testimony of a statistical expert who stated that a random sample of this number would achieve a 95 % statistical probability that the same percentage determined to be valid among the examined claims could be applicable to the totality of claims filed In the 137 sample claims, which included victims of different kinds of violations, e.g. torture victims, families of those summarily executed and disappeared, were deposed and an expert reviewed the depositions to determine the claims. 5 % of the claims were determined to be invalid, see D. Shelton: Remedies in International Human Rights Law. 2nd ed. Oxford, 2005, pp. 422-423.

796 Where there was no evidence of earnings, the average income for the occupation was utilized. Also, a cap was placed on the amount for lost earnings.

797 The amounts ranged from US $ 20 000 for category 1 and US $ 100 000 for category 5 claims. A jury reviewed the sample claims and testimony of their claimants and followed the expert recommendations in most cases. See the summary in D. Shelton: Remedies in International Human Rights Law. 2nd ed. Oxford, 2005, pp. 422-423.

798 In *Hilao v. Marcos*, 103 F.3d 767, 786 (9th Cir. 1996), and the summary ibid. Though the Court admitted that some individualization was lost and the methods used were unor-

Rwanda, under the legal framework of the gacaca system, gacaca tribunals can make reparation orders against individual perpetrators. The tribunals are to determine the amount of compensation according to fixed scales. These scales for compensation for material losses and bodily harm are envisioned under the law regarding the creation of the Rwandan compensation fund.[799]

In the past decades, national and international reparations mechanisms established to award reparations to victims of mass atrocities have started to abandon individual assessments and valuations of damages. Instead, damages have been quantified and categorized, applying different degrees of standardization.

The Western German mechanism established to compensate victims of Nazi injustice was the first to assess and valuate damages caused to individuals in the context of mass crimes. It pursued a highly individualized approach to calculating compensation.[800] As a consequence of the difficulties and lengthiness of individual damage assessment and calculation, there was a gradual trend towards standardization according to the kind of harm suffered.[801] The UNCC has granted both individual and

thodox, it found their application legitimate in view of the unusual nature of the case.

799 See for detailed discussion of the Rwandan compensation law H. Rombouts; S. Vandeginste: "Reparation for Victims in Rwanda – Caught between Theory and Practice". In: Out of the Ashes – Reparation for Victims of Gross and Systematic Human Rights Violations. Eds. K. de Feyter; S. Parmentier; M. Bossuyt (et al.). Antwerp, 2005, pp. 309 et seq. at pp. 320-321.

800 K. van Bebber: Wiedergutgemacht? Die Entschädigung für Opfer der Nationalsozialistischen Verfolgung nach dem Bundesergänzungsgesetz durch die Entschädigungsgerichte im OLG-Bezirk Hamm. Berlin, 2001, pp. 22 et seq., pp. 33 et seq. With a few exceptions, compensation awards pursuant to the German Federal Compensation Law of 1953 were based on traditional tortious criteria, requiring a complicated procedure of individual claims assessment. See e.g. H. Giessler: "Grundsatzbestimmungen des Entschädigungsrechts". In: Die Wiedergutmachung Nationalsozialistischen Unrechts in der Bundesrepublik Deutschland – Das Bundesentschädigungsgesetz. Eds. Bundesminister der Finanzen; W. Schwarz. Vol. 4. München, 1981, pp. 1 et seq. at p. 107. C. Goschler: "Zwei Wege der Wiedergutmachung". In: Nach der Verfolgung – Wiedergutmachung Nationalsozialistischen Unrechts in Deutschland?. Eds. H. G. Hockerts; C. Kuller. Göttingen, 2003, pp. 115 et seq. at p. 123 notes that this reparations scheme did not follow the principle of "equal compensation for equal suffering", but rather, by applying the classic principles of tort law, compensation was generally awarded only after the pecuniary losses of the victims had been assessed. As a result, compensation aimed at restoring the social status of the victim before the victimization. The only true exception was compensation awarded for deprivation of freedom, were the scope of compensation was calculated in accordance with the length of the deprivation of freedom. See for a critical assessment C. Pross: Paying for the Past – The Struggle over Reparations for Surviving Victims of the Nazi Terror. Baltimore, 1998, p. 51.

801 See for the Hardship Regulations 1981, 1992 H. Pelke: "Bürokratie auf dem Prüfstand – Die Fonds- und Härteregelungen des Bundes und der Länder – Stand Oktober 1995". In: Koblenzer Handbuch des Entschädigungsrecht. Eds. K. P. Kisker; H. H. Bischof. Baden-Baden, 1996, pp. 90 et seq. Pursuant to the Foundation Law of 2000, allocation out of the Foundation "Remembrance Responsibility Future", are divided into four categories

standardized awards according to different categories of harm (according to the gravity of the violation) and proof of harm.[802] In Argentina, the scope of awards for detainees of the military regime was determined on the based on the length detention and additional sums were awarded if the victim died in prison or was seriously wounded.[803] Awards from the 9/11 Compensation Fund were to be determined according to "the extent of the harm to the claimant, including any economic and non-economic losses" and the amount of compensation was to be "based on the harm to the claimant, the facts of the claim, and the individual circumstances of the claimant."[804] Awards for non-pecuniary loss were standardized, based on the number of the victim's dependents.[805]

In contrast to these reparations mechanisms, victims of the South African Apartheid regime only received uniform awards, consisting of the same amount irrespective of the kind or severity of harm suffered.[806] This approach was justified with the

based upon the type of injury suffered under the Nazi regime. Compensation is generally awarded in lump sums in order to accelerate payments and avoid long-lasting assessment procedures. See for detailed discussion E. Kristjánsdóttir; B. Simerova: "Processing Claims for 'Other Personal Injury' under the German Forced Labour Compensation Programme". In: Redressing Injustices through Mass Claims Processes – Innovative Responses to Unique Challenges. Ed. The International Bureau of the Permanent Court of Arbitration. Oxford, 2006, pp. 109 et seq.

802 Under category A, claims of individuals who were forced to leave the country could be filed; category B contained claims of persons who suffered serious personal injuries or whose spouse, parent or child died. Under category C those who suffered personal losses up to $ 100 000 for death or personal injury; losses of income, support, housing or personal property, medical expenses or costs of departure could file claims for compensation. Under category D, individuals could file claims for reparations for claims for damages exceeding $ 100 000, see K. Oellers-Frahm; A. Zimmermann (eds.): Dispute Settlement in Public International Law – Texts and Materials. Vol. 2. 2nd revised ed. Berlin, 2001, p. 1749. Lower requirements for causation for personal injury claims resulted in "(T)he decision of the UNCC Governing Council to establish fixed (and modest) amounts for compensation for mental pain and anguish appears to be "virtually unprecedented in both municipal and international law", see A. Gattini: "The UN Compensation Commission – Old Rules, New Procedures on War Reparations". In: European Journal of International Law 13 (2002), pp. 161 et seq. at p. 174; R. Singh: "Raising the Stakes – Evidentiary Issues in Individual Claims before the United Nations Compensation Commission". In: Redressing Injustices through Mass Claims Processes – Innovative Responses to Unique Challenges. Ed. The International Bureau of the Permanent Court of Arbitration. Oxford, 2006, pp. 61 et seq.

803 Law No. 24 043 (of 11 May 1994). The payments could not exceed $ 220 000.

804 J. Cooper Alexander; R. A. Fein: "Procedural Design and Terror Victim Compensation". In: De Paul Law Review 53 (2003), pp. 627 et seq. at p. 642 quoting further authorities.

805 Ibid.

806 In South Africa, the Regulations Regarding Reparations to Victims of November 2003 determine that each victim identified by the Truth and Reconciliation Commission is entitled to a one-time payment of 30 000 Rand (ca. 6000 €) as individual reparation award. The Chilean and Argentine reparations programs also awarded non-individualized pay-

impossibility to rate degrees of suffering.[807]

Thus, while mixed approaches to valuation and calculation of damages have been taken, it can be assessed that often rather individualized awards for pecuniary losses (requiring adequate proof) and standardized awards for non-pecuniary losses are awarded.

c) *Assessment*

The above analysis has shown that various approaches might be chosen to value and calculate damages in order to determine the scope of compensation awards.

With regard to individual awards, the Court may make uniform, standardized or individualized awards of reparations. While the concrete individual damage can be assessed and calculated in each case, compensation can be awarded according to schedules of damages for different types of harm (standardized awards), or they might not be individualized at all (uniform awards).

---

ments, albeit of a regularly much larger scope. The Chilean reparations program included a monthly (life-long) pension based on the average income of a Chilean family, for spouses, parents and children of those killed or disappeared. Thus, the awards are of the same scope regardless of the social, economic or cultural background of the victims, Art. 23 para 1, 2 Law No. 19.123 of 31 January 1992. In addition, beneficiaries were granted a lump-sum payment equal to a year's pension. In 2004, the reparations program was extended to include torture victims. In Argentina, under Law No. 24411 of 7 December 1994, lump-sum compensation was provided for families of the disappeared and those killed by the security forces, awarded in pensions and bonds. See for further analysis M. J. Guembe: "Economic Reparations for Grave Human Rights Violations – The Argentinean Experience". In: The Handbook of Reparations. Ed. P. de Greiff. Oxford, 2006, pp. 21 et seq.

807 Truth and Reconciliation Commission: Final Report on Reparation and Rehabilitation Policy. In: RRFinpolicy005 (1997), at p. 6, providing that each victim "will receive the same quantum of final reparations regardless the number of occasions that they have suffered a gross violation of human rights, the severity and nature of each violation and the consequences of the violations. This is because it is impossible to devise a set of criteria which provide for varying amounts of reparation to be paid to victims according to their degree of suffering without producing unfair and arbitrary results. For example, one may wish to provide more reparation in instances, where a violation has resulted in death. However, such a policy may prejudice the family of a breadwinner who has been so severely tortured that he/she is unable to work. Those who are debilitated by human rights violation/s, but nevertheless survive, may place a greater burden on those required to care for them than those who die. Furthermore, how does one assess degrees of suffering in order to provide for different awards of reparation? Certain individuals can withstand horrendous long term torture and remain relatively healthy and functional, while other individuals may be permanently as a result of a single act of violence. One cannot devise a set of objective criteria which will allow for different forms of abuse to be differentiated according to severity because the response to different forms and intensities of abuse is so subjective. If one awards more reparation to those who show ill effect after, for example, torture, one might effectively penalize those who cope. It is for this reason that each victim should receive the same award of reparation."

The disadvantages of individualized awards are that they require complex proceedings that may be costly and time-consuming and may exclude victims from compensation because they do not succeed in proving their claim. The higher the degree of individualization, the more evidence that will be required and the longer processing claims will take.[808] Individualization tends to discriminate against the less well-educated and literate victims and thus to privilege wealthier victims.[809] Furthermore, the process of having to establish individual harm and causation can lead to re-traumatization.[810] In the context of impecuniary harm, this leads to the situation of having to value the suffering of one victim differently from another. Furthermore, impecuniary harm such as pain and suffering, by its very nature, cannot be calculated precisely in monetary terms. Also, as it seem unlikely that there are enough resources available to award full compensation to victims, there is no practical reason for precisely assessing and calculating the concrete damage caused to each individual. Thus, in most cases before the ICC individualized awards seem both inappropriate and inefficient.

On the other hand, uniform awards could be criticized as unjust as they do not recognize that some people suffered and continued to suffer more than others.[811] Even more importantly in the current context, uniform awards do not seem to be consistent with the ICC Statute and Rules. These require that in determining reparations, the scope and extent of damage, loss and injury caused to victims is to be "taken into account".

Thus, it seems appropriate that compensation ordered by the ICC be made in the form of uniformized awards. These could differentiate between the kind and severity of injury, as the Statute demands that the extent and scope of harm is taken into account in determining reparations. Furthermore, in line with international practice, the scope of awards could vary in accordance with the degree of evidence provided.[812] The applicability of standardized awards in the context of individual responsibility

808 N. Roht-Arriaza: "Reparations, Decisions and Dilemmas". In: Hastings International and Comparative Law Review 27 (2004), pp. 157 et seq. at pp. 179-180 referring to, inter alia, C. Pross: Paying for the Past – The Struggle over Reparations for Surviving Victims of the Nazi Terror. Baltimore, 1998: the risk of retraumatization of victims forced to justify their "victimhood" in claims proceedings before uncaring or hostile courts or bureaucrats in order to obtain reparations is borne out by studies of Holocaust victims and others.

809 C. Pross: Paying for the Past – The Struggle over Reparations for Surviving Victims of the Nazi Terror. Baltimore, 1998 this may cause detriment of the less well-of victims, creating resentments both within the victims class and generally.

810 Ibid. See generally on the danger of 'secondary victimization' through victim participation in the ICC proceedings Bock, S.: "Das Opfer vor dem Internationalen Strafgerichtshof". In: Zeitschrift für die gesamte Strafrechtswissenschaft 119 (2007), pp. 664 et seq. at pp. 670-672.

811 See e.g. D. Shelton: Remedies in International Human Rights Law. 1st ed. Oxford, 1999, p. 351: "To treat all victims the same seems unjust, and surely it is possible to distinguish long-term disability resulting from severe torture from less severe violations."

812 This would mean offering a relatively low standard, immediate awards to all those that only provide simple proof and higher awards for those who manage to proof their claim.

could be questioned because most precedents regarding uniform and standardized awards deal with state responsibility.[813] However, it has been demonstrated that recent approaches that deal with mass violations in national legal systems prove that standardization of damage can also be applied in the context of individual responsibility.[814] Furthermore, for non-pecuniary damage in particular, even national courts dealing with conflicts between individuals often do not engage in detailed individual damage assessment, but rely on guidelines, scales and estimate to assess the harm caused and scope of awards.[815] Thus, it seems that with regard to non-pecuniary loss and instances where the harm caused cannot be proved with precision, standardized compensation awards would comply with the standard applicable before the ICC, i.e. that of the appropriateness of reparations.

When the convicted person is ordered to make a collective compensation award, determining the scope of the award is less complicated. Since the extent of harm caused to the group or collective is regularly impossible to assess and calculate precisely due to its rather structural nature, the scope of the award may be the result of an estimation of what is thought to be appropriate as a contribution to repairing the harm. With regard to collective awards, the extent of harm caused to victims shall, in line with the Statute and Rules, also be "taken into account". Furthermore, the scope of the award shall be determined in accordance with its envisioned purpose, e.g. it is made to a specific fund, project or organization established for the benefit of the collective of victims. However, collective awards made into a fund might also result in awards made to the benefit of the individual members of the collective.

Therefore, if the Court considers it too complicated or incompatible with the expediency of proceedings to engage in the valuation and calculation of individual harm, it is open to it to order collective awards.[816] The Court can also relieve itself of

813 When a state awards compensation, it seems legitimate if compensation is not restricted to actual losses, e.g. the compensation program could have characteristics of a social welfare or insurance program, which would not be appropriate in the context of the individual responsibility.

814 See e.g. the recent Rwandan compensation model and the programs installed as a result of human rights class actions.

815 In accordance with national laws, fixed awards for impecuniary damages could be awarded and individual, full compensation (even if estimated by the judges) for property and other pecuniary damage.

816 G. Bitti; G. González Rivas: "The Reparations Provisions for Victims under the Rome Statute of the International Criminal Court". In: Redressing Injustices through Mass Claims Processes – Innovative Responses to Unique Challenges. Ed. The International Bureau of the Permanent Court of Arbitration. Oxford, 2006, pp. 299 et seq. at p. 321, point out that unless the Court receives substantial assistance from within the Court, for which they assume an increase of budget is required, and from outside the Court, through commissions or panels of experts which will act at the request of the Court and report to it, "it is likely that the Court will only be in a position to award reparations on a collective basis, leaving the implementation of those awards to the Trust Fund either directly or through an international or national organization."

its burden and delegate the task of assessing and calculating damages.[817]

"Appropriate" compensation should help enable victims to rebuild their lives again and restore their dignity.[818] While claims standardization potentially maximizes the recovery of all victims of the convicted person's crime, it should be imposed along with other remedies, as "[i]n the absence of full compensation, alternative relief becomes even more important".[819]

2. Other Factors Potentially Impacting the Compensation Order

Certain circumstances in the sphere of the convicted person may have to be taken into account when determining the scope of the compensation award.

a) Degree of Fault of the Convicted Person

As the preventive or punitive function of reparations cannot be clearly excluded as additional aims when compensating the harm caused to victims, it may be asked whether the degree of the perpetrator's fault be taken into account when determining the scope of compensation.[820]

However, from the wording of Art. 75 and its relevant Rules, it is the "damage, loss and injury" that is to be taken into account when determining reparations.[821] The object and purpose of reparation, as well as the drafting history of the Statute and Rules indicate that the compensatory function which is directed at the harm caused to victims, is the focus of monetary reparation orders. From these considerations it seems, although the Statute and Rules do not provide further guidance on this point, that the degree of the convicted person's fault or wrongdoing shall not be taken into account when determining the scope of a compensation order.

817 C. Jorda; J. de Hemptinne: "The Status and Role of the Victim". In: The Rome Statute of the International Criminal Court – A Commentary. Eds. A. Cassese; P. Gaeta; J. R. W. D. Jones. Vol. 2. Oxford, 2002, pp. 1387 et seq. at p. 1399 note that "assessing the quantum of damages to be awarded [...] is bound to complicate [the judges] work, and is likely to jeopardize the expeditious administration of justice" and suggest that expert commission also heading the trust fund shall deal with assessment and calculation of damages, p. 1412.

818 Archbishop Tutu stated that "(t)he law alone cannot repair the scars of war, and survivors need financial support to rebuild their lives", Archbishop Desmond Tutu: Statement by His Eminence Archbishop Desmond Tutu on behalf of the Board of Directors of the Trust Fund for Victim, Video Statement at the Ceremony Marking their First Meeting, The Hague, 22 April 2004. Available at http://www.icc-cpi.int/press/video.html, last accessed 21 April 2009.

819 N. J. Kritz: "Coming to Terms with Atrocities – A Review of Accountability Mechanisms for Mass Violations of Human Rights". In: Law & Contemporary Problems 59 (1996), pp. 127 et seq. at p. 353.

820 See above Chapter 3 ("Purpose of Reparations in International Criminal Law") and Chapter 5 C.II.4.b) ("Punitive Damages").

821 See Art. 75 (1), Rule 97 (1).

In general, the Inter-American Court has found that awards of amounts meant to deter or to serve as an example are "not applicable in international law at this time."[822] However, some decisions perhaps indicate that the egregiousness of the conduct of governmental authorities could at as an additional factor in assessing moral damages.[823] Similarly, in a few of its decisions, the European Court of Human Rights has awarded high amounts for impecuniary losses which seem to be motivated by the degree of wrongdoing on the part of the government.[824]

In those national jurisdictions where the deterrent function of redress is prominent, the degree of fault is taken into account when damages are assessed, in particular regarding impecuniary harm.[825] In other jurisdictions, where compensation or restoration is the primary purpose of such orders, the conduct of the person at fault is

---

822 *Velásquez Rodríguez v. Honduras*, Reparations, Inter-American Court of Human Rights, 21 July 1989, Ser. C, No. 7, para. 27.

823 See discussion in D. Shelton: Remedies in International Human Rights Law. 2nd ed. Oxford, 2005, pp. 344 et seq. referring to *Velásquez Rodríguez v. Honduras*, Reparations, Inter-American Court of Human Rights, 21 July 1989, Ser. C, No. 7, para. 27 and *El Amparo v. Venezuela*, Reparations, Inter-American Court of Human Rights, 14 September 1996, Ser. C, No. 28, para. 37. In both cases, the Court assessed that the disappearances were part of a systematic government practice. See more recently *Myrna Mack-Chang v. Guatemala*, Judgement, Inter-American Court of Human Rights, 25 November 2003, Ser. C, No. 101 on the notion of punitive damages.

824 Rejecting punitive damages e.g. in *Hood v. United Kingdom*, European Court of Human Rights, 18 February 1999, Application No. 27267/95; considering the authorities' conduct as an aggravating factor e.g. in *Cicek v. Turkey*, European Court of Human Rights, 27 February 2001, Application No. 25704/94, para. 205; see P. Leach: Taking a Case to the European Court of Human Rights. 2nd ed. Oxford, 2005, pp. 400-401; *Bonanzo v. France*, European Court of Human Rights, 1987, Ser. A 124-E.

825 D. Shelton: Remedies in International Human Rights Law. 2nd ed. Oxford, 2005, pp. 37-38 listing examples. U. Magnus: "Comparative Report on the Law of Damages". In: Unification of Tort Law – Damages. Ed. U. Magnus. The Hague (et al.), 2001, pp. 185 et seq. at p. 187 describes that the degree of fault is generally not considered decisive for the assessment of pecuniary loss, referring to the jurisdictions, Belgium, England, France, Germany, Greece, United States, the Netherlands, Italy, South Africa. However, e.g. Austrian law is an exception to the rule in most jurisdictions that the measure of full compensation generally depends on nothing beyond the loss of the injured party. Under Austrian law, the extent of compensation generally depends on the degree of fault: e.g. lost profits and immaterial losses are only compensated in case of gross negligence or intent, see § 1324 ABGB. However, there are statutory and judge-made exceptions to this rule (at pp. 195 et seq., listing further references,); also e.g. in Poland. When determining reparation for impecuniary losses, in Polish adhesion procedure, the degree of fault and the offenders motivation to commit the crime (as well as his and the victims financial capacities) are taken into account. See Z. Doda; E. Weigend: "Polen". In: Wiedergutmachung im Kriminalrecht – Internationale Perspektiven – Reparation in Criminal Law – International Perspectives. Eds. A. Eser; S. Walther. Vol. 1. Freiburg i. Br., 1996, pp. 421 et seq. at p. 490.

not referred to when compensation is determined, regardless of whether compensation is awarded for pecuniary or non-pecuniary losses.[826]

However, even where the purpose of compensation is purely compensatory, it has been pointed out that it is difficult for the judges not to have regard to the severity of the crime in cases where the damage is incalculable, i.e. in cases of impecuniary loss.[827]

The primary purpose of reparations awarded by the ICC is to address the needs and interests of victims, with regard to the harm they suffered from the crime for which the perpetrator was convicted. Its primarily compensatory purpose is also in line with internationally recognized human rights and other similar mechanisms already in place in national jurisdictions. Yet, international human rights and national jurisdictions show in practice that the degree of fault or wrongdoing of the offender may still be taken into account expressly or implicitly when determining compensation, in particular for non-pecuniary harm. However, in the previous subchapter, the advantages of a consistent application of individual uniformized awards in the context of impecuniary harm have been demonstrated.[828] The degree of fault might be considered when determining the scope of collective awards. However, in general at the ICC, the consideration of the degree of fault is left primarily for the determination of the criminal sentence rather than reparations.

b) Financial Capacity of the Convicted Person

The question of whether, and with which consequences, the financial capacity of the convicted person is to be taken into account when determining the scope of the compensation order is linked to the underlying purpose of the order itself. Assuming that the legal nature of the compensation order is predominantly civil, i.e. that it first and foremost aims at compensating the harm caused, the financial situation of the offender would be irrelevant. A related issue is whether the monetary award ordered against the convicted person has to be made out of its own pocket, or whether it does not matter where the money comes from, as long as the requirements of the reparation order fulfilled. In fact, it is only when the order is assumed to be of a punitive nature, it must be paid from of the convicted person's own resources.[829]

826 E.g. regarding Sweden J. J. Zila: "Schweden". In: Wiedergutmachung im Kriminalrecht – Internationale Perspektiven – Reparation in Criminal Law – International Perspectives. Eds. A. Eser, S. Walther. Vol. 1. Freiburg i. Br., 1996, pp. 231 et seq. at p. 288.

827 See e.g. P. Xavier; F. Lombard: "Frankreich". In: Wiedergutmachung im Kriminalrecht – Internationale Perspektiven – Reparation in Criminal Law – International Perspectives. Eds. A. Eser; S. Walther. Vol. 3. Freiburg i. Br., 2001, pp. 1 et seq. at p. 90.

828 Chapter 5 D. IV. 1. ("Valuation and Calculation of Damages").

829 See B. Timm: "The Legal Position of Victims in the Rule of Procedure and Evidence". In: International and National Prosecution of Crimes under International Law. Eds. H. Fischer, C. Kreß; S. R. Lüder. (Bochumer Schriften zur Friedenssicherung und zum Humanitären Völkerrecht). Berlin, 2001, pp. 289 et seq. at p. 308.

1) ICC Reparation System

The ICC's legal instruments do not specify whether, and if so, to what extent the financial means of the convicted person shall be taken into account when deciding whether to order compensation and in determining the scope of the order.[830] It has been argued above that the object and purpose of ICC reparations is to repair the damage caused rather than to punish the convicted person.[831] This serves as an argument against the consideration of the financial means of the convicted person when determining the scope of the compensation order.

Rule 146 provides that in determining whether and to what extent a fine could be ordered against the convicted person under Art. 77 (2), his or her financial situation must be considered.[832] The limits to the scope of the fine could possibly apply to compensation analogously. Reasons in favor of an analogous application of the criteria contained in Rule 146 to the reparation order are the similarity of the purpose, nature and enforcement procedure for orders of fines and reparations.[833]

However, Rule 146 refers exclusively to fines. Furthermore, a number of other Rules refer expressly to their applicability in the context of fines and forfeiture as well as reparations. It is therefore reasonable to assume that if Rule 146 was meant to be applicable to reparations, it would contain an express reference to reparations. Conceptually and systematically, fines are distinct from reparations. In the ICC Statute, fines are categorized as a penalty whereas reparations are not.[834] Consequently, the primary purpose of fines is to make an example of the perpetrator and strip him or her of any financial gain deriving from the crime. In contrast, the purpose of reparation is to redress the damage caused to the victims of the crime. Thus, an analogous application of Rule 146 to reparations should be rejected.

However, a realistic appraisal of the situation cast doubts on the practice of disregarding the convicted person's financial means. In case the Court decides to order the convicted person to directly compensate victims (Art. 75 (2), Rule 98 (1)), the Trust

830 Ibid.

831 See Chapter 3 ("Purposes of Reparations in International Criminal Law") and previous subchapter ("Degree of Fault").

832 Rule 146 (1) states that "[t]he Court shall give due consideration to the financial capacity of the convicted person, including any orders for forfeiture in accordance with article 77, paragraph 2 (b), and, as appropriate, any orders for reparation in accordance with article 75." Rule 146 (2) states that "[a] fine imposed under article 77, paragraph 2 (a), shall be set at an appropriate level. To this end, the Court shall, in addition to the factors referred to above, in particular take into consideration the damage and injuries caused as well as the proportionate gains derived from the crime by the perpetrator. Under no circumstances may the total amount exceed 75 per cent of the value of the convicted person's identifiable assets, liquid or realizable, and property, after deduction of an appropriate amount that would satisfy the financial needs of the convicted person and his or her dependants". See also examination in Chapter 6 D. 2. ("Reparations and the Imposition of Fines and Forfeiture Orders").

833 See Chapter 6 D. ("Reparations and Penalties").

834 See e.g. Art. 77 on applicable penalties only lists fines and forfeiture.

Fund will not supplement his or her resources.[835] Thus, if the Court has not succeeded in getting hold of his or her assets by the time the reparation order is made, the awards may well fail to be enforced. Even when reparations are ordered through the Trust Fund, it may have insufficient resources to complement ICC reparation orders or decide to invests its "other resources" for assistance measures. Thus, it might in practice be reasonable for the Court consider the financial situation of the convicted person, at least when it decides to order direct awards.

2) International and National Law and Human Rights

International law and human rights jurisprudence does not suggest that the responsible party's ability to pay should be taken into account when determining the scope of compensation.[836]

With regard to claims in tort in national civil proceedings, the financial capacity of the offender is often taken into account when determining the award for impecuniary losses,[837] whereas in most jurisdictions, the financial situation of the persons involved is generally not considered decisive for the assessment of pecuniary loss.[838]

In certain legal systems with common law and civil law background, when compensation is ordered in the course of criminal proceedings, courts will take into account the financial means of the offender to determine whether and to what extent reparations shall be ordered.[839] Where the financial situation is taken into account,

835 See Chapter 6 F. 3 ("Complementing Reparation Awards with "Other Resources of the Trust Fund").

836 In the context of state responsibility, reparations are compensatory and not punitive and therefore, the financial capacity of the violating state is not a factor to be considered. However, when reparations are paid by states, political considerations might let the relevant parties take account of the financial situation of a state.

837 U. Magnus: "Comparative Report on the Law of Damages". In: Unification of Tort Law – Damages. Ed. U. Magnus. The Hague (et al.), 2001, pp. 185 et seq. at pp. 194-195 with further references.

838 Ibid., p. 198 referring to French, German, English, Greek, Dutch, South African law.

839 E.g. in England, the court must take into account the offender's ability to pay both in deciding whether or not to make a compensation order and in setting the amount to be paid, see L. Zedner: "England". In: Wiedergutmachung im Kriminalrecht – Internationale Perspektiven – Reparation in Criminal Law – International Perspectives. Eds. A. Eser; S. Walther. Vol. 1. Freiburg i. Br., 1996, pp. 109 et seq. at pp. 175-176 cites Powers of the Criminal Courts Act 1973 s. 35 (4). However, this is not for the Court, but the offender to establish. For civil law jurisdictions see e.g. Z. Doda; E. Weigend: "Polen". In: Wiedergutmachung im Kriminalrecht – Internationale Perspektiven – Reparation in Criminal Law – International Perspectives. Eds. A. Eser; S. Walther. Vol. 1. Freiburg i. Br., 1996, pp. 421 et seq. at p. 486, noting that, inter alia, the wrongdoer's financial means, as well as his or her personal and professional situation are to be taken into account. In other systems the financial circumstances of the offender might regularly only be taken into account when determining the scope of compensation when the offender acted negligently, see T. Lappi-Seppälä: "Finland". In: Wiedergutmachung im Kriminalrecht – Internationale Perspektiven – Reparation in Criminal Law – International Perspectives. Eds. A. Eser; S. Walter. Vol. 1. Freiburg i. Br., 1996, pp. 317 et seq. at p. 376.

courts may impose differing sums to co-defendants reflecting their respective means. In other national legal systems, the actual and potential financial capacity of the offender is not taken into account.[840] However, in the latter systems, there are safeguards to secure the defendant's minimum subsistence level exist at enforcement stages.[841]

3) Assessment

International law and human rights largely deal with states' responsibility to make reparations. There may therefore be grounds upon which to distinguish the expectation that a state should be financially capable of compensating whatever scope of harm it caused in contrast to harm caused by individuals.

No uniform approach exists in national legal systems as to whether the financial situation of the offender is to be taken into account. The primarily compensatory purpose of compensation ordered by the ICC suggests that the financial capacities of the convicted person are not considered when deciding whether, and to what scope, reparations shall be ordered.

However, as noted above, direct compensation awards can, in practical terms, only be implemented when the Court manages to get hold of a sufficiently large proportion of the convicted person's assets to implement the order, given that he or she is not impecunious. If it fails to do so by the time the Court orders reparations, the order could be enforced once the convicted person is more affluent or when hidden assets are discovered subsequently. However, waiting until a convicted person is more affluent can be an unsatisfactory solution as he or she usually awaits many years in prison. When the convicted person's financial resources are insufficient to pay meaningful compensation to victims, it remains open to the Court to order indirect compensation awards, or symbolic measures of reparations.

If the convicted person's financial means had to be taken into account generally when determining the reparation order, a convicted person's claim to be insolvent would automatically lead to the situation where the Court will not order compensa-

840 In civil law jurisdictions, the view is predominant that the ability of the part of the tortfeasor to pay the judgment debt is a separate issue that ought not to be confused with his or her legal liability, see e.g. N. Nsereko: "Uganda". In: Wiedergutmachung im Kriminalrecht – Internationale Perspektiven – Reparation in Criminal Law – International Perspectives. Eds. A. Eser; S. Walther. Vol. 2. Freiburg i. Br., 1997, pp. 321 et seq. at p. 342; L. Zedner: "England". In: Wiedergutmachung im Kriminalrecht – Internationale Perspektiven – Reparation in Criminal Law – International Perspectives. Eds. A. Eser; S. Walther. Vol. 1. Freiburg i. Br., 1996, pp. 109 et seq. at pp. 175-176, 181 et seq.: restitution ordered by English Courts does not take regard to the financial means of the offender.

841 There exists a similar system in jurisdictions where compensation for victims of crime is usually paid by the state directly to the victim, and then the state takes regress from the offender: only on the level of enforcement the financial capacities of the offender become relevant, as the state will not enforce its claim against the person in case he does not have sufficient means, see J. Zila: "Schweden". In: Wiedergutmachung im Kriminalrecht – Internationale Perspektiven – Reparation in Criminal Law – International Perspectives. Eds. A. Eser, S. Walther. Vol. 1. Freiburg i. Br., 1996, pp. 231 et seq. at p. 302.

tion. In this case, it would become advantageous for perpetrators to hide their assets in order to avoid being held liable to compensate victims for the harm they caused. Furthermore, such a course would rule out the possibility of collecting funds from the perpetrator and using them to implement reparation orders at a later stage.[842]

Thus, it is submitted here that the financial capacity of the convicted person must only be taken into account when determining the scope of compensation in the event that direct reparation awards are ordered (Art. 75 (2) s. 1, Rule 98 (1)), in order to avoid a proliferation of unenforceable reparation orders.[843] Consequently, reparation orders conditional on the convicted person having sufficient assets at the time the orders are made can be avoided when reparations are ordered to the beneficiaries via the Trust Fund, given that it is equipped with sufficient resources.[844]

It remains to be considered whether reparations in monetary forms must be paid from the convicted person's own pocket. It is submitted that due to the predominantly civil nature of financial reparation awards, it should not matter if another person or entity pays on behalf of the offender as this still achieves the goal of redressing the harm caused to victims in financial terms.[845]

c) *Impact on the Scope of the Reparation Order When Several Persons Caused the Harm*

The gross or systematic and thus collective nature of the crimes under the jurisdiction of the Court means that the harm caused to victims is often not only be attributable to one individual, but to several perpetrators. They might be prosecuted and convicted by the Court for committing the same crime, at the same trial or concurrently and be jointly responsible for the damage to be compensated. Their wrongdoing might fulfill different forms of individual criminal responsibility ranging from commission,

842 See Reg. 117 Court Regulations.

843 However, C. Muttukumaru: "Reparations to Victims". In: Collection of Essays on the Rome Statute of the International Criminal Court. Eds. F. Lattanzi; W. A. Schabas. Ripa di Fagnano Alto, 1999, pp. 301 et seq. at p. 307 concludes that reparations "must also take account of the offender's means. In many cases, reparations may be symbolic. That, in itself, is capable of being a significant contribution to justice."

844 See for details Chapter 6 F. ("Implementation of the Reparations Order"). In case the Trust Fund implements awards with its own resources, the awards to victims could be uniform and of a smaller scope than the original awards that the convicted person would have to make. This is similar in state compensation schemes: the measure of compensation from the state is not necessarily as large as that which (theoretically at least) may the offender be ordered to pay. In case the Court manages to get hold of assets of the convicted or sentenced person, the original award ordered could be distributed, after the debts owed to the Trust Fund have been balanced.

845 See also B. Timm: "The Legal Position of Victims in the Rule of Procedure and Evidence". In: International and National Prosecution of Crimes under International Law. Eds. H. Fischer, C. Kreß; S. R. Lüder. (Bochumer Schriften zur Friedenssicherung und zum Humanitären Völkerrecht). Berlin, 2001, pp. 289 et seq. at p. 308.

encouragement and assistance to superior responsibility.[846] Some convicted persons might not have assets, but are truly willing to make symbolic reparations and contribute to reconciliation with the victims. Others might have assets which the Court succeeded in obtaining, but might not be willing to cooperate and provide symbolic reparations. As the ICC intends to concentrate on prosecuting those who bear the greatest responsibility for the crimes under its jurisdiction, it is likely that there are also persons responsible for harm to victims who are not prosecuted by the ICC.[847]

It seems therefore inevitable to decide whether, and if so how, the responsibility of several perpetrators should impact upon the scope of the reparations award the ICC orders against a convicted person.[848] The ICC Statute and Rules do not provide guidance on either of the questions. The provision that the sentence must reflect the culpability of the person refers only to penalties and is therefore not applicable to reparation orders.[849]

In dealing with state responsibility for reparations, international law and human rights jurisprudence have hardly any principles which may be transferred and applied to the issue in the context of international criminal law. However, national laws provide some solutions which are possibly applicable to the ICC reparations mechanism.

---

846 C. Jorda; J. de Hemptinne: "The Status and Role of the Victim". In: The Rome Statute of the International Criminal Court – A Commentary. Eds. A. Cassese; P. Gaeta; J. R. W. D. Jones. Vol. 2. Oxford, 2002, pp. 1387 et seq. at p. 1411 point out that as a consequence it is not clear against whom the victim or his representative shall file a claim for reparations. However, as victims are not required to inform the Court of the identity of person thought responsible for their harm (see Rule 94 (1) (c)) it can be assumed that it is often the duty of the Court to link the applications for reparation with an accused or convicted person or perhaps several persons accused or convicted by the Court.

847 The Office of the Prosecutor has declared its intention to focus on those who bear the greatest responsibility of the crime: "The global nature of the ICC, its statutory provisions and logical constrains support a preliminary recommendation that, as a general rule, the Office of the Prosecutor should focus its investigative and prosecutorial efforts and resources on those who bear the greatest responsibility, such as the leaders of the State or organisation allegedly responsible for those crimes", see Paper on Some Policy Issues before the Office of the Prosecutor, ICC-OTP, September 2003. Available at http://ww.icc-cpi.int/library/organs/otp/03/09/ 05_Policy_Paper.pdf, last accessed 21 April 2009, p. 7.

848 A possible scenario is that first a person is found criminally responsible for personally committing e.g. war crimes, and later, possibly years after the first conviction, this person's superior is found responsible for the same crime.

849 Rule 145 (1) (a) states that "any sentence of imprisonment and fine [...] imposed under article 77 must reflect the culpability of the convicted person" and therefore does not relate to Art. 75 on reparations. However, regarding the determination of the criminal sentence, parallel questions arise: "[t]he task of individualizing a sentence is as difficult as that of determining the gravity of an offence. In war crime trials the most commonly raised mitigating individual circumstance is that the defendant was following superior orders", see F. P. King; A.-M. La Rosa: "Penalties under the ICC Statute". In: Collection of Essays on the Rome Statute of the International Criminal Court. Eds. F. Lattanzi; W. A. Schabas. Ripa di Fagnano Alto, 1999, pp. 311 et seq. at p. 335.

Many national systems of tort[850] are familiar with a concept that can be termed joint (and several) liability or solidarity liability.[851] Joint and several or solidarity liability arises under three constellations. In the first scenario, the action of several independent persons leads to an actual, direct contribution and coincidentally combines to cause indivisible harm ("several concurrent tortfeasors").[852] In a second scenario, indivisible harm is caused by participating in a concerted action with other persons, including through procurement, incitement or encouragement. Finally, in the third

850 Since civil law is applied in national adhesion procedures, these principles also apply when compensation is awarded in national criminal procedures. See, e.g. in the Dutch adhesion procedure when several persons liable: When the criminal deed was committed by several persons, each person is liable for the full damage. The perpetrator that has compensated the damage can claim regression (damages) from the other persons responsible for the crime. M. S. Groenhuijsen; D. van der Landen: "Niederlande". In: Wiedergutmachung im Kriminalrecht – Internationale Perspektiven – Reparation in Criminal Law – International Perspectives. Eds. A. Eser, S. Walther. Vol. 1. Freiburg i. Br., 1996, pp. 1 et seq. at p. 63 elaborates that "The Hog Raad (supreme Court) does not consider the liability of the individual inappropriate, as those liable to compensate the victims' harm can claim regress from each other".

851 In tort law, where several tortfeasors cause different damage to one plaintiff, the torts are independent and each person is liable for the damage he inflicts. Where tortfeasors cause the same damage they may either be joint tortfeasors or several concurrent tortfeasors. In joint liability each tortfeasor is liable for the full amount of the plaintiff's loss, but there is only one tort and so the cause of action against each one is the same and supported by the same evidence, and the plaintiff (victim) is paid only once, see S. Deakin; A. Johnston; B. Markesinis: Markesinis and Deakin's Tort Law. 5th ed. Oxford (et al.), 2003, pp. 850-851; W. V. H. Rogers: "Comparative Report on Multiple Tortfeasors". In: Unification of Tort Law – Multiple Tortfeasors. Ed. W. V. H. Rogers. The Hague, 2004, pp. 271 et seq. at p. 272, pointing out that in common law countries, the term "joint and several liability" is used; in countries with a civil law tradition, the common term is "solidarity liability" or liability in solidum. In the German system, joint offenders of a concerted action with other persons are joint and severally liable, when their participation is established but not the causality of the concrete wrongdoing of a person. When several offenders that acted independently contributed to the harm, each offender is liable for the entire harm if his or her deed was sufficient to cause the entire damage, even though it remains unclear whether his or her actual contribution caused the damages (alternative causality). Likewise, each offender is liable for the entire harm when not his or her specific contribution, but only the cumulation of the contributions caused the harm ("cumulative causality"), see U. Magnus: "Schadensersatz für Körperverletzung in Deutschland". In: Compensation for Personal Injury in a Comparative Perspective. Eds. B. A. Koch; H. Koziol. Wien, 2003, pp. 148 et seq. at p. 167.

852 Several concurrent tortfeasors are those who, acting independently of each other, combine in their actions to cause damage to the plaintiff, see S. Deakin; A. Johnston; B. Markesinis: Markesinis and Deakin's Tort Law. 5th ed. Oxford (et al.), 2003, p. 850.; U. Magnus: "Schadensersatz für Körperverletzung in Deutschland". In: Compensation for Personal Injury in a Comparative Perspective. Eds. B. A. Koch; H. Koziol. Wien, 2003, pp. 148 et seq. at p. 167.

type of situation, one of the offenders is liable for the acts of another person.[853] The second and third constellations are cases of joint liability.[854] Joint liability only applies where the harm caused cannot be apportioned into parts which can be said to have been caused separately by the different persons.[855]

Under this concept, when harm is caused by several wrongdoers, each wrongdoer is individually liable for the whole harm, rather than a proportion thereof.[856] The same is true when several offenders contributed to the damage independently of each other and each act would have been sufficient to cause the entire damage, even if it remains uncertain whose action caused it (alternative causality).[857]

A few jurisdictions have adopted the concept of proportionate liability.[858] How-

---

853 W. V. H. Rogers: "Comparative Report on Multiple Tortfeasors". In: Unification of Tort Law – Multiple Tortfeasors. Ed. W. V. H. Rogers. The Hague, 2004, pp. 271 et seq. at 275-276. The third type of situation is a case of what can be termed vicarious liability. In the majority of jurisdictions, these basic principles are adhered to, even though there are a few constellations where its justification may be disputed, in particular where one of the tortfeasors is subject to strict liability or where the victim is himself or herself at fault; two scenarios of lesser relevance in the ICC context.

854 See for these two constellations J. Spier; O. H. Haazen: "Comparative Conclusions on Causation". In: Unification of Tort Law – Causation. Ed. J. Spier. The Hague, 2000, pp. 127 et seq. at p. 147. W. V. H. Rogers: "Comparative Report on Multiple Tortfeasors". In: Unification of Tort Law – Multiple Tortfeasors. Ed. W. V. H. Rogers. The Hague, 2004, pp. 271 et seq. at pp. 276 et seq. describes that in cases where each tortfeasor's act or omission is insufficient to cause any harm, and only due to the contribution of another tortfeasor the harm is caused, the majority of jurisdictions would hold each tortfeasor jointly and severally liable. While this may be harsh for the tortfeasor the victim decides to sue, in weighing the interests of victims and a tortfeasor acting negligent or even intentionally, it is acceptable that the interest of the victim should prevail. However, in specific situations, such as in mass tort litigation or when the causal contribution of one of the tortfeasors is only minimal, a strict application of this principle may lead to unsatisfactory results, in particular when the other defendants are insolvent. Under such circumstances, imputation may be restricted on the grounds of policy considerations based on reasonableness, fairness and justice. In the second constellation, just as in criminal law, a person that procures or participates in the planning of intentional wrongdoing is (indirectly) liable like a person that is directly involved in the inflicting of harm and thus directly liable.

855 Ibid., p. 279, listing further constellations.

856 Ibid, pp. 272-273. With the exception of the US, national systems display uniform solutions in this basic approach. The countries surveyed were Austria, Belgium, Czech Republic, England, Germany, Israel, Italy, the Netherlands, Poland, Portugal, South Africa, Spain, Sweden, Switzerland and the USA; see also W. V. H. Rogers: Winfield and Jolowicz on Tort. 16th ed. London, 2002, pp. 735 et seq.

857 See e.g. for Germany U. Magnus: "Schadensersatz für Körperverletzung in Deutschland". In: Compensation for Personal Injury in a Comparative Perspective. Eds. B. A. Koch; H. Koziol. Wien, 2003, pp. 148 et seq. at p. 167.

858 According to this approach, every tortfeasor is liable in proportion to his comparative share of responsibility for the harm; see W. V. H. Rogers: "Comparative Report on Multiple Tortfeasors". In: Unification of Tort Law – Multiple Tortfeasors. Ed. W. V. H. Rogers.

ever, even in these jurisdictions solidarity liability continues to apply for harm caused by an intentional, unlawful concerted action.[859]

When joint or concurrent tortfeasors are sued at the same time there will usually be a judgment for a single sum, which they will share between them.

The concept of joint and several or solidarity liability is advantageous when the liability of an individual cannot be determined with sufficient certainty, and because identifying and suing all of the persons responsible imposes a heavy burden upon the victim when one or more of the tortfeasors may be absent or indigent.[860]

When one of the persons responsible for the harm compensated the entire harm, national jurisdictions generally allow contribution between the parties liable in solidum.[861]

A suggested solution to the difficulties arising when several persons are responsible for the victims' harm is that the Court could postpone its assessment of how the financial burden should be coped with after all potentially responsible individuals have been tried in relation to the same crime.[862] From the experiences of the ICTY and ICTR, it is to be expected that it will generally take a long time for suspects to appear before the ICC and be convicted. As it is unlikely that all persons responsible for the crimes under the ICC's jurisdiction will be tried and convicted at the same time, this could lead to an unjustified delay of the reparation payments.

Instead, it is submitted that the ICC should apply solutions developed in national contexts for cases in which harm is caused by several perpetrators. Thus, when the Court decides to order monetary reparations to victims, the first of the persons convicted for the crime shall be held responsible to pay appropriate compensation for the entire harm caused by several persons.[863] This shall be the case when they commit-

The Hague, 2004, pp. 271 et seq. at 279; see e.g. in detail for the Polish system Z. Doda; E. Weigend: "Polen". In: Wiedergutmachung im Kriminalrecht – Internationale Perspektiven – Reparation in Criminal Law – International Perspectives. Eds. A. Eser; S. Walther. Vol. 1. Freiburg i. Br., 1996, pp. 421 et seq. at p. 491.

859 W. V. H. Rogers: "Comparative Report on Multiple Tortfeasors". In: Unification of Tort Law – Multiple Tortfeasors. Ed. W. V. H. Rogers. The Hague, 2004, pp. 271 et seq. at p. 279 listing further references and depicting the variations that exist in the different US states.

860 Ibid., pp. 271 et seq. at pp. 273-274. with further discussion.

861 Ibid., p. 292 again refers to the jurisdictions mentioned above (Austria, Belgium, Czech Republic, England, Germany, Israel, Italy, the Netherlands, Poland, Portugal, South Africa, Spain, Sweden, Switzerland and the USA), and notes that in some legal systems, contribution is restricted or excluded in specific cases.

862 C. Jorda; J. de Hemptinne: "The Status and Role of the Victim". In: The Rome Statute of the International Criminal Court – A Commentary. Eds. A. Cassese; P. Gaeta; J. R. W. D. Jones. Vol. 2. Oxford, 2002, pp. 1387 et seq. at p. 1411; see also M. Henzelin; V. Heiskanen; G. Mettraux: "Reparations to Victims before the International Criminal Court – Lessons from International Mass Claims Processes". In: Criminal Law Forum 17 (2006), pp. 317 et seq. at p. 326.

863 Similarly M. Heikkilä: International Criminal Tribunals and Victims of Crime. Turku, 2004, p. 189. However, it might be that several persons that are tried in a joint trial, as e.g.

ted the crime intentionally and as a result of a common plan or action and when the harm was caused by several wrongdoers who acted independently.[864]

This model has the advantage that when there are several persons responsible for the victims' harm and the funds obtainable from the convicted person are insufficient to implement the reparation order, indirect awards can be ordered and the Trust Fund could provisionally – with its own resources received under Rule 98 (5) – enable implementation.[865] Then, all persons the ICC convicts for the same crime could be ordered to make awards to the Trust Fund, until the sum it invested is recovered.

Of course, when the assets of the person that the ICC first ordered to pay compensation were sufficient to implement the entire award, he or she can seek contribution from others responsible for the harm.[866] It is only at this stage, in which the ICC has no role to play, that the offenders' differing degrees of responsibility might be reflected in their financial obligations.

3. Assessment

It can be concluded that in principle, factors within the personal sphere of the convicted person shall not have an impact on the scope of monetary reparations ordered by the ICC. As the primary aims of monetary ICC reparation orders are compensatory, in determining the scope of compensation, the "scope and extent of any damage, loss or injury" caused to victims shall be taken into account. Compensation awards are appropriate if they serve their aims, i.e. to provide practical improvement of the victims' life with regard to their physical, psychological and material well-being and as a symbolic means of acknowledging their victimization. Awards that are "appropriate" also consider what is realistic and fair, taking into account the number of persons or communities that suffered harm, and the resources available. In fact, the factors set forth by the Trust Fund Regulations for the determination of the nature

practiced by the ICTY in the Srebrenica case, where 9 indictees are tried.

864 As described, this rule does not apply when the victim suffered several, separable kinds of harm at the hands of several offenders, e.g. when, through the act or omission of A, a victim has lost his father, and through the act of omission of B his arm. A and B are only responsible to repair the particular damage that he or she caused. It seems that the exceptions to the concept of joint and several or solidarity liability do not apply regularly in the context of crimes under the jurisdiction of the ICC, where most defendants committed crimes under the ICC's jurisdiction with intention and where most victims are undoubtedly more in need of protection than the person that has been found guilty for committing a crime under international law. In accordance with the national law principles depicted above, that the victim could file a second application, or the victim's application for reparation would be considered another time when a reparation order against a second of several offenders that caused its harm is determined, in case the victim has not been able to obtain full compensation for the damage from the wrongdoer first tried. However, it seems that the standard of reparations before the ICC is "appropriate" rather than "full" reparations, see above Chapter 5 D. III. ("Standard of Reparations").

865 See Chapter 6 F. ("Implementation of Reparation Awards").

866 Another question is under which jurisdiction the convicted person could seek and enforce contribution from the other wrongdoers.

and scope of reparations awards may provide guidance: "the nature of the crimes, the particular injuries of the victims and the nature of the evidence to support such injuries, as well as the size and location of the beneficiary group."[867]

As envisioned in the Trust Fund Regulations, compensation awards to individuals may be uniformized awards, according to a scale applicable for all cases before the Court, particularly those stemming from the same situation, regarding non-pecuniary losses and where there is a lack of evidence. The availability of sufficient assets of the convicted person may not be decisive when awards are made through the Trust Fund, given that it is equipped with sufficient resources.[868] However, in practice it is decisive in the event of direct compensation awards.

When determining the scope of compensation awards, transparency and consistency are important. Otherwise, victims of crimes committed by persons convicted by the ICC might feel that they are subjects of arbitrariness and that their victimization is acknowledged to a lesser degree than the victimization of others. This would contribute neither to the restoration of dignity of victims and reconciliation, nor to the credibility of the ICC and for those reasons is undesirable.

867 Reg. 55 Trust Fund Regulations.

868 When the Trust Fund helps implementing the reparation awards with its own resources, the convicted person may become the debtor of the Trust Fund. There are serious disadvantages when (individual) financial awards shall depend on the financial capacities of the perpetrator: then perhaps such small amounts of money will be distributed among the victims, that do not fulfill the criteria of "appropriateness". Then, in case the Court or Trust Fund later gets hold of the convicted person's assets, they cannot be seized for the purposes of reparations anymore. Also it is administratively onerous to award several time small amounts of money to victims. See below Chapter 6 F. I. 3 "Complementing Reparation Awards with "Other Resources of the Trust Fund"".

Chapter 6 ICC Reparations Proceedings

Reparations proceedings are not a mandatory part of the ICC proceedings.[869] Proceedings that possibly result in a reparation order against the convicted person are conducted only upon initiation by either victims or the Court (Art. 75 (1) s. 2, Rules 94, 95). In case the Court decides that reparations proceedings shall be conducted, they only take place after the Court has found an individual guilty of committing a crime under its jurisdiction.

Before the Court makes a decision on reparations, reparations are discussed at an additional hearing or hearings.[870] Victims cannot initiate such reparations hearings, and the legal representatives of victims that have applied for reparations only have the power to postpone such a hearing.[871]

However, the issue of reparations may be raised by victims or victims' representatives participating in the proceedings already in the investigative or trial stage.[872] As victims can only obtain reparations from a person who caused their harm, it is in their

869 Under relevant Art. 75 (2), the Court's power to order reparations is potential, see also above introduction to Chapter 5.

870 Art. 75 (3), Art. 76 (3), Rule 94 (2), Rule 143, and of organizations Rule 98 (4).

871 Art. 76 (3) and Rule 143. Rule 143 also clarifies that victims who participated in the trial proceedings can apply for postponement of the reparations hearing. Furthermore, the Trial Chamber, the Prosecutor and the defense can initiate the additional hearing on reparations. For the drafting history of Rule 143 see P. Lewis: "Trial Procedure". In: The International Criminal Court – Elements of Crimes and Rules of Procedure and Evidence. Ed. R. S. Lee. Ardsley, New York, 2001, pp. 539 et seq. at p. 552.

872 Victims are entitled to participate in the Court proceedings pursuant to Art. 68 (3), 19 (3), 15 (3); Rules 89-93; Reg. 86, 87 Court Regulations. The drafting history of the Rules also confirms the relevance of pursuing reparations through victims' participation in the trial proceedings: the right to participate through questioning under Rule 91 (3) was finally agreed on after delegates generally accepted that certain evidence presented during the criminal proceeding would be relevant in determining subsequent reparations, see G. Bitti; H. Friman: "Participation of Victims in the Proceedings". In: The International Criminal Court – Elements of Crimes and Rules of Procedure and Evidence. Ed. R. S. Lee. Ardsley, New York, 2001, pp. 456 et seq. at p. 467.

personal interest to already be able to influence the Court's decision against whom it will initiate proceedings, which is made in the end of the investigative stage.[873]

A. Procedural Requirements for a Reparation Order (Art. 75 (1), (2) ICC Statute)

I. Initiation of the Reparations Proceedings by, or on Behalf of, Victims

The ICC's legal instruments envision that regularly, the reparations proceedings are triggered by requests for reparations filed with the Court by, or on behalf of, victims.[874]

1. Victims' Requests for Reparations

Art. 75 (1) s. 2 ICC Statute grants victims the right to file a claim for reparations with the Court. The conditions on how to exercise this right are set out in more detail in Rule 94 (1). The standard forms for reparations which have been approved by the Court's Presidency, lay down further requirements.[875]

a) Claim to be a Victim

Those who qualify as "victims" are granted rights before the ICC, and this recognition as a victim under the ICC's legal framework has a number of procedural consequences. The term "victim" is the only one referred to in order to equip those affected by the crimes under the ICC's jurisdiction with rights. The right to claim and be awarded reparations is determined with reference to "victims".[876]

873 In *Situation in the Democratic Republic of The Congo*, Decision on the Applications for Participation in the Proceedings of VPRS 1, VPRS 2, VPRS 3, VPRS 4, VPRS 5 and VPRS 6, ICC Pre-Trial Chamber I, 17 January 2006, ICC-01/04-101, para. 63 the competent Chamber therefore allowed for victims' participation, although the Prosecutor did not approve of it at this early procedural stage. G. J. Mekjian; M. C. Varughese: "Hearing the Victim's Voice – Analysis of the Victims' Advocate Participation in the Trial Proceeding of the International Criminal Court". In: Pace International Law Review 17 (2005), pp. 1 et seq. at pp. 16-17 state that "[t]he rights afforded to victims in criminal proceedings under the Rules are derived in part from Civilist legal systems, which allow a victim to act as partie civile. Under the doctrine of partie civile, a victim is granted the capacity directly through their counsels, or indirectly, through the prosecution, to present evidence in a criminal proceeding which the victim deems necessary for the subsequent pursuit of damages in civil proceedings". See generally on the purposes of victims' participation before the ICC M. Burkhardt,Victim Participation before the ICC, forthcoming.

874 The Court can initiate this reparation procedure on its own motion only under exceptional circumstances, see Chapter 6 A. II. ("Court-Initiated Reparations Procedure").

875 Reg. 104 Registry Regulations, Reg. 23, 86 Court Regulations.

876 Art. 75 (2). The same is true for the right to receive protection and to participate in the proceedings, see Art. 15 (3), Art. 19 (3), Art. 43 (6), Art. 68 (3), Art. 68 (1), (4). Also in determining the beneficiaries of the Trust Fund, reference is made to "victims", Art. 79 (1). Reg. 42 Trust Fund Regulations reads: "The resources of the Trust Fund shall be for the

In fact, Rule 94 sets forth that only "victims" have the right to claim reparations. However, the Standard Application Form for Individuals extends this right, under certain conditions, to persons "acting on behalf of a victim".[877] A person may act on behalf of a victim in the event that the victim is a child, disabled or deceased, or the victim has consented to the same.[878]

However, the question as to whether the claimant qualifies as a victim before the ICC is a substantive issue.[879] Thus, for the purposes of filing an admissible application for reparations, it is sufficient that a person claims to be a victim, or acts on behalf of a person claimed to be a victim.

b) *Who can Claim to be a Victim?*

Under Rule 85 "[f]or the purposes of the Statute and the Rules of Procedure and Evidence: (a) "Victims" means natural persons who have suffered harm as a result of the commission of any crime within the jurisdiction of the Court; (b) Victims may include organizations or institutions that have sustained direct harm to any of their property which is dedicated to religion, education, art or science or charitable purposes, and to their historic monuments, hospitals and other places and objects for humanitarian purposes."

Rule 85 provides one single definition setting forth the criteria that are to be satisfied in order to be categorized as a victim "for the purposes of the Statute and the Rules of Procedure and Evidence". It is applicable in all instances in the ICC Statute and Rules where "victims" are mentioned, and the Trust Fund Regulations have expanded the scope of application to Trust Fund measures.

The content of the definition is very broad and general and of substantive rather than procedural character.[880] However, it clarifies that both a natural person, i.e. "any person who is not a legal person"[881] and legal persons may file applications for repara-

benefit of victims within the jurisdiction of the Court, as defined in rule 85 of the Rules of Procedure and Evidence, and, where natural persons are concerned, their families".

877 Standard Application Form for Individuals, p. 1.

878 Standard Application Form for Individuals, p. 1.

879 The notion of "victim" is exceptionally used in national criminal laws or codes of procedure. Legal terminology instead includes procedural terms as "the complainant", "the injured party", the "complaining witness" or the "applicant". See M. Joutsen: The Role of the Victim of Crime in European Criminal Justice Systems – A Crossnational Study of the Role of the Victim. Helsinki, 1987, p. 19.

880 See on the drafting history of the victim definition e.g. B. Timm: "The Legal Position of Victims in the Rule of Procedure and Evidence". In: International and National Prosecution of Crimes under International Law. Eds. H. Fischer, C. Kreß; S. R. Lüder. (Bochumer Schriften zur Friedenssicherung und zum Humanitären Völkerrecht). Berlin, 2001, pp. 289 et seq.; P. Lewis; H. Friman: "Reparations to Victims". In: The International Criminal Court – Elements of Crimes and Rules of Procedure and Evidence. Ed. R. S. Lee. Ardsley, New York, 2001, pp. 474 et seq.

881 *Situation in the Democratic Republic of The Congo*, Decision on the Applications for Participation in the Proceedings of VPRS 1, VPRS 2, VPRS 3, VPRS 4, VPRS 5 and VPRS 6, Pre-Trial Chamber I, 17 January 2006, ICC-01/04-101, para.80.

tions when they claim to have suffered harm as a result of a crime under the ICC's jurisdiction.

c) *Do Collectives Have the Right to Claim Reparations?*

In this context, the question whether the victim definition encompasses collectives is relevant in order to examine whether collectives as such have the right to claim reparations.

Rule 85 (a) provides that "natural persons" shall qualify as victims. The entire definition is formulated in the plural form. Thus the wording does neither exclude nor include collectives as victims. In contrast, earlier drafts of the definition of "victim" had expressly described victims as "persons who, individually or collectively, have suffered harm [...]".[882] However, as some delegations expressed the need to clarify the term "collectively", and no consensus could be reached on a definition, the inclusion of the term was dropped.[883]

The Rules clarify that collective forms of reparations to victims are envisioned. Rule 97 (1) provides that the Court can award reparations on a collective basis where it considers it appropriate.[884] Under Rule 90 (2) the Chamber can request "victims or particular groups of victims" applying to participate in the proceedings to choose a common legal representative where the number of victims make this necessary to ensure the effectiveness of proceedings.

It could be considered that the Court's interpretation of the possibility to make collective awards of reparations is a way of allowing certain forms of reparations and does not imply the recognition of a certain victim type.[885] Yet, the consequence of collective forms of reparations that are meant to serve the benefit of a certain community or a number of victims sharing certain characteristics might also be that implicitly, collective beneficiaries are recognized as victims.[886]

The name of the ICC Standard Application Form for reparations that addresses "individuals and persons acting on their behalf" indicates that collectives as such are

882 S. A. Fernandez de Gurmendi: "Definition of Victims and General Principle". In: The International Criminal Court – Elements of Crimes and Rules of Procedure and Evidence. Ed. R. S. Lee. Ardsley, New York, 2001, pp. 427 et seq. at p. 431, referring to a proposal that was later reproduced as Rule Q in the Mont Tremblant Document, at 74.

883 S. A. Fernandez de Gurmendi: "Definition of Victims and General Principle". In: The International Criminal Court – Elements of Crimes and Rules of Procedure and Evidence. Ed. R. S. Lee. Ardsley, New York, 2001, p. 432.

884 See above Chapter 5 B. II. ("Collective Beneficiaries of Reparations").

885 M. Heikkilä: International Criminal Tribunals and Victims of Crime. Turku, 2004, p. 18. Also the wording of Rule 94 does seem to aim at individual victims to file claims for reparations ("A victim's request"; "identity and address of the claimant").

886 B. Timm: "The Legal Position of Victims in the Rule of Procedure and Evidence". In: International and National Prosecution of Crimes under International Law. Eds. H. Fischer, C. Kreß; S. R. Lüder. (Bochumer Schriften zur Friedenssicherung und zum Humanitären Völkerrecht). Berlin, 2001, pp. 289 et seq. at pp. 303 et seq.

not meant to claim reparations.[887] In the form, the applicant is asked "[i]f resources are available (from a person convicted by the ICC or from the ICC's Trust Fund for Victims), what would help you and your community the most?"[888] This wording provides additional support for the argument that only individuals are to apply for, and can impact the shape of, collective reparations.

The object and purpose of recognizing an individual or entity as a victim under the ICC Statute and Rules is to determine who should benefit from the rights granted to those affected by the crimes the Court is prosecuting. Thus, it is to be examined why it could be useful to consider collectives of harmed individuals as a "victim" and therefore equip them with rights before the Court.

The value of recognizing "collective victims" could be that in the context of certain crimes it might be more appropriate to also regard to groups as victims, rather than only to individuals.[889] The category of "collective victims" is intended to include those individual victims that are targeted because they belong to a particular group or collective. The criminal conduct, goals, and outcomes are in this case predicated on the fact that the victim belongs to an identifiable group or collectivity.[890] The groups or groupings of individuals are linked by special considerations, factors or circumstances and are targeted or victimized for these very reasons.[891] International criminal law protects victims as individuals or as a part of a group when either is subjected to international crimes.[892] The intended protected subjects of most of these international crimes are individuals who are part of an identifiable group, while the

887 Standard Application Form for Individuals, in accordance with Reg. 88 Court Regulations developed by the Registrar and approved by the Presidency pursuant to Reg. 23 Court Regulations, p. 1. The only other Standard Application Form available is that for organizations and institutions under Rule 85 (b).

888 Standard Application Form for Individuals, p. 14.

889 "What is intended by 'collective victims' is that category in which the individual victims are targeted because they belong to a certain group or collectivity", C. M. Bassiouni: "The Protection of 'Collective Victims' in International Law". In: International Protection of Victims. Ed. C. M. Bassiouni. Eres, 1988, pp. 181 et seq. at p. 183.

890 Ibid.

891 Ibid, pp. 183 et seq., differentiating between two categories of collective victims in the international context: groups of victims of international crimes and groups of victims of international human rights law.

892 Listing, for instance the crime of aggression, war crimes, crimes against humanity, genocide (apartheid, slavery and slave-related practices, torture, unlawful human experimentation, piracy, aircraft hijacking, kidnapping of diplomats and other internationally protected persons, civilian hostages, unlawful use of the mails, illicit trade and distribution of narcotic drugs and other recognized international crimes), C. M. Bassiouni: "The Protection of 'Collective Victims' in International Law". In: International Protection of Victims. Ed. C. M. Bassiouni. Eres, 1988, pp. 181 et seq. at p. 186, quoting further references. See G. Werle: Principles of International Criminal Law. The Hague, 2005, p. 26, concluding that the crimes relevant in international criminal law are "crimes under international law" rather than "international crimes".

degree of collectivization of victims in each of the crimes as well as the reasons for the victimization might differ.[893]

Thus, a group of individual persons is more than the sum of individuals and groups have their own characteristics that are not identical with the characteristics of the individuals composing the group.[894] Consequently, it could be argued that before the ICC, the right to claim collective reparations should not only derive from individuals' right to claim reparations, but be directly equipped with the right to claim reparations in their own capacity.

It is also increasingly recognized in international and national systems and in international human rights law that collectives can be victims of crimes and human rights violations and can as such claim reparations.[895] Both the 2005 Victims Principles and the 1985 Victims Declaration include collectives in their victims definitions with the result that collectives can also claim reparations.[896] Before the European Court of Human Rights, "groups of individuals" can claim to be the victim of a violation of the Convention, and thus are able to receive "just satisfaction".[897] E.g., also villages have qualified as groups that can receive reparations.[898] Under the Inter-American Convention, "[a]ny person or group of persons, or any nongovernmental

893 C. M. Bassiouni: "The Protection of 'Collective Victims' in International Law". In: International Protection of Victims. Ed. C. M. Bassiouni. Eres, 1988, pp. 181 et seq. at p. 187.

894 H. Rombouts; S. Vandeginste: "Reparation for Victims of Gross and Systematic Human Rights Violations – The Notion of Victim". In: Third World Legal Studies (2000-2003), pp. 89 et seq. at p. 99.

895 See generally D. Shelton: Remedies in International Human Rights Law. 2nd ed. Oxford, 2005, p. 246. For summary on the controversial discussions during the drafting process of the 2005 Victims Principles, see G. Echeverria: "Codifying the Rights of Victims in International Law – Remedies and Reparation". In: Redressing Injustices through Mass Claims Processes – Innovative Responses to Unique Challenges. Ed. The International Bureau of the Permanent Court of Arbitration. Oxford, 2006, pp. 279 et seq. at p. 295.

896 Principle 8 2005 Victims Principles defines that "victims are persons who individually or collectively suffered harm [...]", see also Principle 13 and Preamble: "[...] contemporary forms of victimization, while essentially directed against persons, may nevertheless also be directed against groups of persons who are targeted collectively." Para. 1 1985 Victims Declaration reads: "Victims" means persons who, individually or collectively, have suffered harm [...]."

897 Art. 34 and 41 ECHR. Villages, companies and shareholders, trade unions, religious bodies have been granted access as groups, see P. Leach: Taking a Case to the European Court of Human Rights. 2nd ed. Oxford, 2005, pp. 115 et seq. with references to relevant jurisprudence. For criteria regarding the requirements to qualify as a group, the Commission has defined that this "must be groups which have been established in a regular way according to the law of one of the Contracting States. If that is not the case, the application must have been signed by all of the persons belonging to the group", P. van Dijk; F. van Hoof: Theory and Practice of the ECHR. 3rd ed. The Hague (et al.), 1998, p. 46 with further reference.

898 An example for a claim of a village is *Muonio Saami Village v. Sweden*, 9 January 2001, Application No. 28222/9, concerning the failure to secure a determination of their claim for reindeer herding rights.

entity legally recognized in one or more member states of the Organization, may lodge petitions with the Commission containing denunciations or complaints of violation of this Convention by a State Party."[899] At this point, it is for the Commission to decide whether to refer the case to the Court. The Inter-American Court has recognized "family groups", village communities and tribal groups in past rulings.[900] Before the Human Rights Chamber for Bosnia and Herzegovina, both NGOs and groups of individuals, can file applications.[901] Traditionally in national legal systems the focus has been on individual victims.[902] However, it is widely recognized that the victim of a crime might also be a group, and as such has the right to claim reparations.[903] Collective reparations to groups of victims were first awarded by Germany to Jews for the

---

899 Art. 44.

900 *Castillo Páez Case*, Reparations, Inter-American Court of Human Rights, 27 November 1998, Ser. C, No. 43, para 76; *Aloeboetoe et al. v. Suriname*, Reparations, Inter-American Court of Human Rights, 10 September 1993, Ser. C, No. 15, § 20 (symbolic reparations), paras. 19, 81-84. In 2001, it established a new parameter for the concept of collective victimization by recognizing that the State of Nicaragua had failed to establish an effective proceeding for the delimitation of, and issuance of property titles for, the communal indigenous land, and had violated the right to an effective remedy of the community, see *Mayagna (Sumo) Awas Tingni Indigenous Community v. Nicaragua*, 31 August 2001, Ser. C, No. 79, paras. 127, 134.

901 Art. VIII Annex 6 Peace Agreement for Bosnia and Herzegovina, Concluded in Dayton on 21 November 1995 and Signed in Paris on 14 December 1995, General Framework Agreement. In: International Legal Material 18 (1996), pp. 89 et seq.

902 Generally C. M. Bassiouni: "The Protection of 'Collective Victims' in International Law". In: International Protection of Victims. Ed. C. M. Bassiouni. Eres, 1988, pp. 181 et seq. at p. 183.

903 For the human rights context see D. Shelton: Remedies in International Human Rights Law. 2nd ed. Oxford, 2005, p. 182 citing further authorities. Regarding e.g. the German legal system, see R. Juy-Birmann: "The German System". In: European Criminal Procedures. Eds. M. Delmas-Marty; J. R. Spencer. Cambridge, 2002, pp. 292 et seq. at p. 303 who points out that corporate bodies or collective victims can claim through their legal representative. For the possibility for collective claims in civil procedure see U. Magnus: "Comparative Report on the Law of Damages". In: Unification of Tort Law – Damages. Ed. U. Magnus. The Hague (et al.), 2001, pp. 185 et seq. at p. 202, noting that in national systems damages are considered as collective when either minimal damage was done to a great number of people or where a collective (entity)- an unspecified group of persons- is damaged. Yet, this type of damage is explicitly provided for so far only in French Law, and possible in the US. W. B. Fisch: "European Analogues to the Class Action – Group Action in France and Germany". In: The American Journal of Comparative Law 27 (1979), pp. 51 et seq. at p. 78 states that "[t]he class action, American style, is in the strictest sense unknown in France and Germany, because neither recognizes the right of one member of a group of persons to sue for all without the prior consent of each", while pointing out that there are some group mechanisms available, p. 71.

crimes committed by Nazi Germany, "setting important precedent for other groups to lay claim to a similar status".[904]

Before the ICC, collectives or groups of victims that share common characteristics and interests may organize themselves for the purposes of group participation in the Court's proceedings. Groups that have been commonly represented throughout the proceedings might request collective reparations, possibly through their common representative, without using the standard form. [905] Another possibility is that a person acting on behalf of individual victims could be a representative of a certain collective of victims, provided that each victim gives his or her consent.[906] Thus, for example, a mayor representing inhabitants of village harmed by a certain crime might claim reparations on behalf of a number of individual inhabitants who have given their consent.

Thus, it seems that is it also on the legal representatives of victims to prepare victims' reparations claims accordingly, i.e. by grouping individual claims together, such as by village of by district, and to utilize the procedural opportunities provided in the ICC system.[907]

As this brief examination has depicted, for the purposes of the current examination the question as to whether collectives qualify as victims under Rule 85 (a) can remain open. While the ICC's legal framework suggests an approach to reparations that considers individual victims as a starting point, it leaves procedural opportunities for reparations claims made on behalf of collectives of victims, if so desired.

2. Form of the Request for Reparations

Pursuant to Rule 94 (1) the request for reparations must be made in a written form. The use of the Standard Application Form is encouraged,[908] which should be avail-

904 J. Torpey: "Introduction – Politics and the Past". In: Politics and the Past – On Repairing Historical Injustices. Ed. J. Torpey. Lanham, Maryland, 2003, pp. 1 et seq. at p. 5 notes that "in addition to making war on other countries, the Nazis also made a separate, undeclared war on the defenseless Jews as well as on other groups (e.g. the handicapped, homosexuals, Gypsies). As a result, and despite long-standing debate about whether Jews constitute a "nation", the assault on the Jews eventually gave them a kind of legal standing in international law […]". See also H. Küpper: Kollektive Rechte in der Wiedergutmachung von Systemunrecht. Vol. 2. Frankfurt a. Main, 2004, p. 1082.

905 According to Reg. 88 (1) Court Regulations, the standard reparation forms should be used "to the extent possible".

906 See Standard Application Form for Individuals, pp. 1, 8, 18.

907 See also M. Henzelin; V. Heiskanen; G. Mettraux: "Reparations to Victims before the International Criminal Court – Lessons from International Mass Claims Processes". In: Criminal Law Forum 17 (2006), pp. 317 et seq. at p. 328.

908 Reg. 86, 88 Court Regulations; under Reg. 105 Registry Regulations the ICC Registry shall encourage the use of the Standard Application Form.

able, to the extent possible, in the languages spoken by the victims.[909] So far, standard application forms are available in French and English only.[910]

When victims are unable to make a written request, communications to the Court can be made in audio, video, or other electronic form. This inability may be the result of a disability or illiteracy.[911]

3. Content of the Request for Reparations

a) Information about the Claimant, the Damage and Kind of Reparations Requested

Rule 94 (1) further requires that the application for reparations includes information about the identity and address of the victim and applicant, and a description of the injury, loss or harm suffered.[912] Details of the incident that caused the victim's injury, loss or harm must also be provided.[913] Furthermore, the applicant must specify what form or forms of reparations are requested. While any remedy can be requested, forms expressly listed are restitution, compensation and rehabilitation.[914]

The standard application forms implement these legal requirements in a broad manner. Applicants are asked "[w]hich of the following forms of reparations would you like to claim? [...] You may tick more than one box" and can then choose to tick compensation, restitution, rehabilitation or other form of reparations, which shall be specified.[915] The types of harm listed for the purposes of reparations are likewise very broad, and include, e.g. "legal rights" or "social status".[916] It seems difficult to imagine that the ICC could order the convicted person to effect such forms of damage. While the front pages of the standard application forms state explicitly that the "[c]ompletion of this form will not automatically lead to reparation awards by the ICC",[917] it seems likely that they give rise to victims' expectations towards ICC reparation orders that can hardly be fulfilled.

b) Identification of the Person Believed to be Responsible for the Damage

In the request for reparations, the person believed to be responsible for the injury, harm or damage shall be identified "to the extent possible."[918]

909 Reg. 104 Registry Regulations.

910 See the ICC's homepage at http://www.icccpi.int/Menus/ICC/Structure+of+the+Court/Victims/Reparation/ Forms.htm, last accessed 13 March 2009.

911 Rule 102.

912 Rule 94 (1) (a), (b); Parts A, B, E Standard Application Forms.

913 Rule 94 (1) (d); Part D Standard Application Forms.

914 Rule 94 (1) (d), (e), (f); Part F Standard Application Forms.

915 Part F question 1 Standard Application Form for Individuals.

916 Part F questions 2-5 Standard Application Form for Individuals; Part F question 2 Standard Application Form for Organizations.

917 Standard Application Form for Individuals, p. 1.

918 Rule 94 (1) (c); Part D question 2 Standard Application Forms.

This is an essential and at the same time delicate requirement that relates to principles fundamental to the ICC system. The Court's jurisdiction to order reparation awards is conditional on the conviction of the person responsible for the victim's harm.[919]

Thus the Court needs to link a claim for reparations to the accused person prosecuted before the Court. This can be difficult when the victim does not provide the identity of the person thought responsible.[920] However, requiring applicants to provide the identity of the person responsible for the crime in question acknowledges that on many occasions victims would not know his or her identity.[921] It can also be assumed that in many instances victims are not able to identify the specific defendant as the perpetrator.[922] This can be the case particularly due to the large scale nature of the crimes. Victims cannot be expected to be familiar with legal concepts of responsibility such as superior responsibility. The formula "to the extent possible" avoids the initial exclusion of victims who do not know the perpetrator's identity from potentially benefiting from ICC-ordered reparations. Thus, particularly in cases where the application form does not identify any person thought responsible for the harm is provided in the application, it is for the Court to link the application to specific cases.[923]

4. Documentation of the Data Contained in the Request

The victim should annex to the request "any relevant supporting documentation, including names and addresses of witnesses" (Rule 94 (1) (g)).[924] The purpose of this requirement is to gather documentation in order to help validate the claim. However, documentation has to be provided only "to the extent possible". This means that the request will also be valid when no documentation at all is provided to confirm the

919 Art. 75 (2). See above Chapter 5 A. ("Liability to Make Reparations").

920 P. Lewis; H. Friman: "Reparations to Victims". In: The International Criminal Court – Elements of Crimes and Rules of Procedure and Evidence. Ed. R. S. Lee. Ardsley, New York, 2001, pp. 474 et seq. at p. 479. The draft version of Rule did contain the requirement to identify the person responsible for the injury, loss and or harm.

921 See Chapter 6 C. ("Standard and Burden of Proof").

922 P. Lewis; H. Friman: "Reparations to Victims". In: The International Criminal Court – Elements of Crimes and Rules of Procedure and Evidence. Ed. R. S. Lee. Ardsley, New York, 2001, pp. 474 et seq. at p. 480.

923 The issue is linked to requirements for causation and proof, see Chapter 5 B. ("Eligibility to Reparations" and Chapter 6 C. ("Standard and Burden of Proof"); Reg. 21, 105, 106 Registry Regulations.

924 Rule 94 (1) (g). This is applicable to all data the victim is required to provide pursuant to Rule 94 (1) (a)-(f). However, expectedly in order for an individual damage to be compensated, it is most important to provide the Court with documentation of the loss, injury or damage suffered (Rule 94 (b)), see Chapter 6 C. ("Standard and Burden of Proof").

particulars put forward by the victim and thus avoids automatic disqualification of those without documentation for their claims.[925]

5. Other Procedural Requirements

While the ICC's legal framework does not explicitly provide for procedural requirements other than those already depicted, there might be additional requirements implicitly resulting from other principles governing the ICC.

a) Unavailability of Reparations in Other Fora (Complementarity)

The Preamble and Art. 1 of the Statute provide that the ICC "shall be complementary to national jurisdictions".[926] Complementarity implies that the Court only has jurisdiction over a case when a state that has jurisdiction over it is unwilling or unable to investigate or prosecute.[927]

The complementarity principle could also be applicable in the context of reparations. In this case, as a result of the principle of complementarity, there could be an added requirement that reparations claims filed against the defendant in the domestic jurisdiction were unsuccessful, or that such efforts will obviously be unsuccessful.[928] Reparations claims would be inadmissible if victims could receive reparations from the national authorities originally responsible.

However, no such requirement is explicitly provided for in the Statute or the Rules. The wording of Art. 17 ("investigate", "prosecute") seems to determine restrictions if the Court wants to make use of its power to criminally prosecute. To assume that an unwritten requirement exists that results from an expanded notion of the principle of complementarity would lead to a restriction of victims' rights. The object and purpose of reparations are not restricted to financial compensation and restitution, but include, i.e., the restoration of dignity of victims and the acknowledgement of the harm suffered. Therefore, forms of reparations that require the convicted person to perform acts of primarily symbolic character, such as a public apology or other acts with a broader societal impact may be awarded even if financial reparations have been obtained from national authorities. Such symbolic acts might have a reparatory

925 P. Lewis; H. Friman: "Reparations to Victims". In: The International Criminal Court – Elements of Crimes and Rules of Procedure and Evidence. Ed. R. S. Lee. Ardsley, New York, 2001, pp. 474 et seq. at p. 480. This restriction acknowledges the difficult situation in which some of the victims might find themselves. For many victims, in particular refugees, it might be difficult or even impossible to present documentation of their loss, injury or damage, see Chapter 6 C. ("Standard and Burden of Proof"). For the drafting history of this provision, see ibid., p. 480.

926 Preamble ICC Statute para. 10; Art. 1 ICC Statute. See for discussion of complementarity in the context of the reparations principles, Chapter 4 A. ("Establishing Principles pursuant to Art. 75 (1) s. 1 ICC Statute").

927 Art. 17 and Art. 15, 18, 19; in particular Art. 17 (1) (a).

928 D. Shelton: "Reparations for Victims of International Crimes". In: International Crimes, Peace, and Human Rights – The Role of the International Court. Ed. D. Shelton. Ardsley, New York, 2000, pp. 137 et seq. at p. 147.

effect precisely because they are conducted by the particular person convicted before the Court. Additionally, as in the aftermath of mass crimes, it is rare for any reparations program to grant full reparations, so another reparations award paid from the convicted person's assets would often be justified.

However, reparations can only be awarded for crimes over which the ICC exercises jurisdiction, which is complementary. In practice, it seems that in most cases, if the competent national authorities do not investigate or prosecute the crimes they would also be unwilling or unable to ensure that victims of crimes under the ICC jurisdiction receive reparations.

Internationally recognized human rights do not deal specifically with complementarity issues. However, it might be relevant that the 2005 Victims Principles and 1985 Victims Declaration provide that reparations shall usually be obtained from the person directly responsible, and that there is only a secondary responsibility upon the state to provide compensation.[929] If the crime is attributable to the state, then the state carries primary responsibility to award reparations.[930]

Accordingly, in cases where national authorities have compensated the victims, the Court could order the convicted person to, in accordance with the 2005 Victims Principles, compensate the state "in respect of, victims" for its payments to the victims.[931]

Before the European Court of Human Rights, the applicant can also lose his or her victim status. This is the situation when the state responsible for the violation has acknowledged that there had been a breach of the Convention, the applicant has already been provided with redress and has been treated in a way that there were sufficient indications to allow an assessment of the extent to which the violation was taken into account.[932] Similarly, in some national reparations mechanisms for victims of international crimes, if a person had already been compensated for the harm claimed, he or she is not entitled to again receive compensation.[933]

Furthermore, both in the European and in the Inter-American human rights systems, applicants are required to have exhausted local remedies in order for their application to be admissible.[934] The Bosnian Human Rights Chamber also required the exhaustion of local remedies "where such exist".[935]

929 Principle 16 2005 Victims Principles; para. 12 1985 Victims Declaration provide that the state shall compensate in case the person primarily responsible does not do so.

930 Principle 15 2005 Victims Principles; para. 11 1985 Victims Declaration.

931 Principle 15.

932 See e.g. *Eckle v. Germany*, European Court of Human Rights, 17 July 1982, Application No. 8130/78; *Beck v. Norway*, European Court of Human Rights, 29 June 2001, Application No. 26390/95.

933 See §§ 5, 8 German Federal Compensation Law of 1953 (BEG).

934 Art. 35 ECHR; Art. 46 (1) a) American Convention.

935 Art. VIII Annex 6 (2) Peace Agreement for Bosnia and Herzegovina, concluded in Dayton on 21 November 1995 and Signed in Paris on 14 December 1995, General Framework Agreement. In: International Legal Material 18 (1996), pp. 89 et seq.

Thus, even though it seems appropriate to consider complementarity when ordering reparations, if national reparations programs have established, this is unlikely to lead to the automatic inadmissibility of claims. When the Court has determined to prosecute in a certain situation and has exercised jurisdiction over a person, there will be an assumption that it is also competent to order the convicted person to make reparation to the victims of his or her crimes. It has been demonstrated that reparations made by a person convicted by the ICC can in fact complement national reparations programs. However, as a result of the principle of complementarity, when reparations have been granted to a victim at the national level, the ICC will have to take them into account.[936]

b) Participation in the Court Proceedings

The Court has confirmed that the participation of victims in the proceedings as early as the investigative stage "can serve to clarify the facts, to punish the perpetrators of crimes and to request reparations for the harm suffered."[937] Similarly, obtaining reparations might be seen as one of the main goals of victim participation in the trial.[938] For the current issue it is not necessary to discuss whether the "final purpose of the participation of victims in the criminal proceedings is justified by the idea that they can thus obtain reparation at the outcome of the trial"[939] or whether participation serves other key goals.

While one purpose of participation in the proceedings might be to pursue reparations claims, the issues of reparations and participation are completely separate before the ICC. Consequently, victims may participate in the proceedings and yet request that the Court does not make an order for reparations.[940] Neither the Statute nor the Rules require victims to participate in the proceedings in order to be eligible

936 See also D. Donat-Cattin: "Article 75 – Reparations to Victims". In: Commentary on the Rome Statute of the International Criminal Court – Observers' Notes, Article by Article. Ed. O. Triffterer. Baden-Baden, 1999, pp. 965 et seq. at p. 976.

937 *Situation in the Democratic Republic of The Congo*, Decision on the Applications for Participation in the Proceedings of VPRS 1, VPRS 2, VPRS 3, VPRS 4, VPRS 5 and VPRS 6, Pre-Trial Chamber I, 17 January 2006, ICC-01/04-101, para.63.

938 E.g. it is the concept of partie civile or adhesion procedure that victims are allowed to take part in criminal proceedings in order to present their claim for compensation or restitution. See generally M. Burkhardt, Victim Participation before the ICC, forthcoming; G. Bitti; H. Friman: "Participation of Victims in the Proceedings". In: The International Criminal Court – Elements of Crimes and Rules of Procedure and Evidence. Ed. R. S. Lee. Ardsley, New York, 2001, pp. 456 et seq.; E. Haslam: "Victim Participation at the International Criminal Court – A Triumph of Hope over Experience?". In: The Permanent International Criminal Court – Legal and Policy Issues. Eds. D. Rowe; P. McGoldrick; E. Donnelly. Oxford, 2004, pp. 315 et seq.

939 S. Zappalà: Human Rights in International Criminal Proceedings. Oxford, 2003, p. 225.

940 Rule 95.

for reparations.[941] Thus, victims have the right not to be involved or represented in the proceedings, but can still choose to file an application for reparations.

II. *Court-Initiated Reparations Proceedings*

The Court has the power to initiate, under "exceptional circumstances", the reparations proceedings.[942] In this case, victims may be granted reparations without having made a request before the ICC.[943] The term "Court" means the Chamber competent to deal with the case.[944]

It is not clarified in the ICC's legal framework when the circumstances are sufficiently exceptional to empower the Court to act *ex proprio motu*. The purpose of this exceptional power is that the judges should be able to make up for the absence of victims and thus to safeguard their rights.[945] Victims may be prevented from filing a reparations claim because of their geographical and cultural remoteness from the Court.[946] Other reasons can include the lack information or funds to file an application for reparations.[947] Victims might also be exposed to pressure that might derive from continued offences, in particular where there is evidence that the state in which the victim resides is involved in the crimes.[948] In fact, it can be assumed that the in-

941 Art. 75 and Rule 94 on victims' rights to claim reparation to not contain such requirement.

942 Art. 75 (1), Rule 95 (1). While the wording of Art. 75 (1) is restricted to expressly mention the initiation of the determination of harm, and does not explicitly mention the Court's power to order reparations pursuant to Art. 75 (2), the reference to Art. 75 (3) on representations on reparation orders, as contained in Rule 95 (1), clarifies that this competence also includes reparation orders under Art. 75 (2).

943 If reparations are ordered through the Trust Fund, the Trust Fund Regulations provide for the scenario that the Court orders reparations to beneficiaries it has not identified will be determined through statistical and demographic data analysis that will be used to locate and determine the beneficiaries of the reparations order, Reg. 60, 61 Trust Fund Regulations, including the competence of the Trust Fund to conduct targeted outreach to the beneficiary group.

944 For further discussion see Chapter 4 ("Reparations Principles").

945 See C. Jorda; J. de Hemptinne: "The Status and Role of the Victim". In: The Rome Statute of the International Criminal Court – A Commentary. Eds. A. Cassese; P. Gaeta; J. R. W. D. Jones. Vol. 2. Oxford, 2002, pp. 1387 et seq. at p. 1408; C. Muttukumaru: "Reparation to Victims". In: The International Criminal Court – The Making of the Rome Statute – Issues, Negotiations, Results. Ed. R. S. Lee. The Hague, 1999, pp. 262 et seq.

946 See Interview with Fiona McKay – Head of the Victims Participation and Reparation Section of the International Criminal Court, Conducted by C. Olivier. Published in: Victims' Rights Working Group Bulletin No. 5, Febuary 2006. Available at http://www.vrwg.org/Publications/04/ENG05.pdf, last accessed 14 May 2008, p. 4.

947 This might be the case even though the application for reparations is free of charge, see note on p. 1 of both Standard Application Forms.

948 D. Donat-Cattin: "Article 75 – Reparations to Victims". In: Commentary on the Rome Statute of the International Criminal Court – Observers' Notes, Article by Article. Ed. O.

dividuals or groups most severely victimized are often precisely those who are not in the physical, material or mental condition to apply for reparations.

When victims submit a claim after the Court has already acted on its own motion, pursuant to Rule 95 (2) (a) these late claims will be treated like those of victims that claim reparations in the usual way, i.e. as claims filed under Rule 94. Victims who do not wish for a reparations application to be made on their behalf can notify the Court (Rule 95 (2) (b)). Only in this instance will the Court not proceed with the claim on behalf of that victim.[949] However, the individual victim cannot prevent the Court from ordering collective awards.[950] For example, if the Court decides to order the convicted person to contribute to a memorial in remembrance of a group victimized by his or her crime, an individual group member is not in the position to reject such an order.

The Statute and Rules take into account the concern that the Court's power to initiate reparations proceedings on its own motion conflicts with its duty to ensure the protection of the accused person's right to a fair trial.[951] The accused's rights are safeguarded by the notification requirements of the Court.[952]

Thus, before the ICC, as in several national jurisdictions, the authorities involved in the proceedings are to look after the victims' right to file a claim in criminal proceedings. In some national jurisdictions victims may be assisted by the prosecutor in filing their claims, or the prosecutor will file a claim on behalf of the victim if he or she did not do so herself.[953] In other national jurisdictions, a restitution or compen-

Triffterer. Baden-Baden, 1999, pp. 965 et seq. at p. 972.

949 This takes into account that there might be victims who refuse to benefit from the perpetrator as a matter of conscience and therefore consciously decided not to file a claim for reparations, see C. Muttukumaru: "Reparations to Victims". In: Collection of Essays on the Rome Statute of the International Criminal Court. Eds. F. Lattanzi; W. A. Schabas. Ripa di Fagnano Alto, 1999, pp. 301 et seq. at p. 309.

950 It has been assumed that it might be particularly regarding collective awards that the Court makes use of this power, see B. Timm: "The Legal Position of Victims in the Rule of Procedure and Evidence". In: International and National Prosecution of Crimes under International Law. Eds. H. Fischer, C. Kreß; S. R. Lüder. (Bochumer Schriften zur Friedenssicherung und zum Humanitären Völkerrecht). Berlin, 2001, pp. 289 et seq. at p. 302.

951 A number of delegations were hostile to provide for the possibility for the Court to act "ex propio motu", see ibid., p. 309.

952 See Rule 95 (1) and the detailed discussion in Chapter 6 B. I. ("Notification and Publication of Reparations Proceedings") below.

953 T. Lappi-Seppälä: "Finland". In: Wiedergutmachung im Kriminalrecht – Internationale Perspektiven – Reparation in Criminal Law – International Perspectives. Eds. A. Eser; S. Walter. Vol. 1. Freiburg i. Br., 1996, pp. 317 et seq. at p. 370. In some jurisdictions, the prosecutor or police have the duty to assist victims with their civil claims, e.g. in Sweden, Denmark and Norway. Yet in Finland, it is upon the criminal court to ensure that the complainant is aware of his possibilities regarding compensation under the law, ibid. at p. 371. Also in Spain, compensation to the victim is automatically part of the criminal prosecution, see B. van Schaack: "In Defense of Civil Redress – The Domestic Enforcement of Human Rights Norms in the Context of the Proposed Hague Judgments Convention".

sation order can only be initiated by the Court or the Prosecutor.[954] This stands in contrast to most international and national reparations mechanisms, where usually a victim's application for reparations is a pre-condition for the success of the claim.[955]

Thus, it could be argued that the Court's power to proceed with reparations on behalf of victims under exceptional circumstances, might become an obligation to do so when the Court has reason to assume that victims are not able to safeguard their rights by applying for reparations.

III. Assessment

A reading of the relevant provisions in the legal framework of the ICC might lead one to expect that an application for reparations by, or on behalf of, victims would always trigger reparations proceedings. However, the application for reparations is not required to be directed against a specific person and the reparations procedure only takes place after a conviction. Once a person has been convicted, it is up to the Court to examine applications for reparations which it receives for a possible link

In: Harvard International Law Journal 42.1 (2001), pp. 141 et seq. K. Madlener: "Spanien". In: Wiedergutmachung im Kriminalrecht – Internationale Perspektiven – Reparation in Criminal Law – International Perspectives. Eds. A. Eser; S. Walther. Vol. 3. Freiburg i. Br., 2001, pp. 273 et seq. at p. 314 pointing out that victims can file civil claims, through a representative, in criminal proceedings, otherwise the state prosecutor is also obliged to file the claim on behalf of the victim on its own initiative; in practice, the state prosecutor often files a civil claim on behalf of the victim. In Poland, the reparation order in criminal proceedings is not dependent on the victim's claim, the prosecutor can not only initiate the adhesion procedure, but also assist the victim in pursuing its claim, Z. Doda; E. Weigend: "Polen". In: Wiedergutmachung im Kriminalrecht – Internationale Perspektiven – Reparation in Criminal Law – International Perspectives. Eds. A. Eser; S. Walther. Vol. 1. Freiburg i. Br., 1996, pp. 421 et seq. at pp. 487, 497. J. Zila: "Schweden". In: Wiedergutmachung im Kriminalrecht – Internationale Perspektiven – Reparation in Criminal Law – International Perspectives. Eds. A. Eser, S. Walther. Vol. 1. Freiburg i. Br., 1996, pp. 231 et seq. at p. 282, however, the authorities are not obliged to provide assistance when the victim's claim has obviously no chance to succeed or when is imposes too great difficulties.

954 This is particularly true for traditional common law jurisdictions where victims do not have the right to claims compensation in criminal procedure. For the US, see P. M. Tobolowsky: Crime Victim Rights and Remedies. Durham, North Carolina, 2001, pp. 123 et seq. and 151 et seq.; E. Silverman: "United States of America". In: Wiedergutmachung im Kriminalrecht – Internationale Perspektiven – Reparation in Criminal Law – International Perspectives. Eds. A. Eser; S. Walther. Vol. 2. Freiburg i. Br., 1997 pp. 1 et seq. at p. 106 points out that judges in federal and state courts are now routinely ordering convicted offenders to make restitution to victims who have suffered quantifiable harm as a part of the criminal sanction.

955 E.g. the European Court of Human Rights only awards compensation upon application, see *Moore and Gordon v. The United Kingdom*, European Court of Human Rights, 29 September 1999, Application No. 36529/97, para. 28; *Birutis and Others v. Lithuania*, 28 March 2002, Application No. 47698/99 and 48115/99, paras. 36-38.

between the harm alleged and the convicted person.[956] Only when there appears to be such a link, might the victim's application for reparation indeed trigger the reparations procedure. In practice, it is likely that persons will apply for reparations who have been recognized as "victims of a case" in the trial procedure prior to conviction. In this case it seems that their application would regularly trigger the reparations proceedings.

Compared to the substantive aspects of the ICC reparations regime, the provisions concerning the procedural requirements of an reparation order provide relatively clear guidelines. However, gaps remain in particular regarding sensitive issues such as the Court's power to initiate reparations on behalf of the victims. Clear criteria should be developed, possibly as a part of the reparations principles pursuant to Art. 75 (1), which are to be applied in a consistent manner and guide the Court's decision-making. It is submitted here that the Court's power to act *ex proprio motu* does not only constitute an additional power, but also an obligation to the Court to make use of it in exceptional circumstances. Such circumstances might be exceptional when there is a strong indication that persons or groups severely harmed by the crime have not applied and there is reason to believe that this was not due to a conscious decision, but due to ignorance or to the gravity of their situation.

B. Communications of the Court in the Reparations Proceedings (Art. 75 (3), Art. 76 (3) ICC Statute)

I. Notification and Publication of Reparations Proceedings

1. Notification

There might be little knowledge about the existence of the ICC among those involved in or affected by crimes under the Court's jurisdiction. Social practices, economic restraints, geographic conditions, illiteracy and a number of other factors can all impede access to the ICC and its reparations mechanism.[957]

For victims, the accessibility of the ICC reparations regime is a precondition to the ability to use it.[958] Ensuring that victims know about the ICC reparations mechanism

956 See Reg. 21 (2) (j) Registry Regulations: the situation or case accord shall contain a list of the victims asking for reparations which is maintained by the Registry; under Reg. 110 Registry Regulations the Registry shall present all applications for reparation to the Chamber, together with a report thereon if requested.

957 So far, "[i]n each of the situations before the Court, many victims live in locations that are not easy to access and in insecure conditions" where there exists "little awareness about the ICC and, in particular, the potential role of victims", Interview with Fiona McKay – Head of the Victims Participation and Reparation Section of the International Criminal Court, Conducted by C. Olivier. Published in: Victims' Rights Working Group Bulletin No. 5, Febuary 2006. Available at http://www.vrwg.org/Publications/04/ENG05.pdf, last accessed 14 May 2008, p. 4.

958 See generally e.g. L. Krabbe Boserup; M. Mohammed Cissé: "Accessibility – A Precondition for Reparation? The Case of the Nigerian Commission on Human Rights and Fundamental Freedoms". In: Reparations – Redressing Past Wrongs. Eds. G. Ulrich; L. Krabbe

and thus providing the opportunity to use it is essential to its fair and effective functioning and is required by documents containing relevant international standards.[959] Otherwise, the main beneficiaries of the ICC reparations mechanism would be those best informed, which might not be the persons who suffered the greatest harm.

Furthermore, in order to safeguard the rights of the accused and others possibly affected, such as *bona fide* possessors of property, efforts have to be made in order to inform them about the ICC reparations proceedings.

Art. 75 (3) ICC Statute provides that prior to making a reparation order, the Court "may" invite the convicted person, victims, other interested persons or states to make representations and thus does not oblige the Court to invite those potentially affected by reparation orders.[960]

However, the Rules impose extensive responsibilities of notification and publication on the Registrar.[961] Generally, they oblige the Registrar to notify victims and their legal representatives, those against whom the Court is considering making a reparation order, interested persons and interested states.[962] As the wording of the Statute

Boserup. (Human Rights in Development – Yearbook 2001). The Hague, 2003, pp. 137 et seq. at p. 145.

959 Paras. 4, 5 1985 Victims Declaration; Principles 12, 24 2005 Victims Principles, and Art. 4 2001 EU Framework Decision set forth that victims should be granted access to redress mechanisms, and be informed of their rights to seek redress. E.g. para. 5 1985 Victims Declaration states that "[j]udicial and administrative mechanisms should be established and strengthened where necessary to enable victims to obtain redress through formal or informal procedures that are expeditious, fair, inexpensive and accessible. Victims should be informed of their rights in seeking redress through such mechanisms."

960 Art. 75 (3) states that "[b]efore making an order under this article, the Court may invite and shall take account of representations from or on behalf of the convicted person, victims, other interested persons or interested States."

961 Thus, after the establishment of the Rules, there are no more "serious doubts of interpretation" of the wording in Art. 75 (3) that "the Court may invite" victims and others potentially involved before making a reparations order, see D. Donat-Cattin: "Article 75 – Reparations to Victims". In: Commentary on the Rome Statute of the International Criminal Court – Observers' Notes, Article by Article. Ed. O. Triffterer. Baden-Baden, 1999, pp. 965 et seq. at p. 974. In the drafting of the Rules, there was debate about the cost, practicability and wisdom of widespread notification, see P. Lewis; H. Friman: "Reparations to Victims". In: The International Criminal Court – Elements of Crimes and Rules of Procedure and Evidence. Ed. R. S. Lee. Ardsley, New York, 2001, pp. 474 et seq. at p. 482. See generally on notification Reg. 31-32 Court Regulations.

962 Rules 94 (2), 95 (1) and 96 (1) s. 1. Rule 94 (2) demands that "[a]t commencement of the trial and subject to any protective measures, the Court shall ask the Registrar to provide notification of the request to the person or persons named in the request or identified in the charges and, to the extent possible, to any interested persons or any interested States." According to Rule 95 (1), "[I]n cases where the Court intends to proceed on its own motion pursuant to article 75, paragraph 1, it shall ask the Registrar to provide notification of its intention to the person or persons against whom the Court is considering making a determination, and, to the extent possible, to victims, interested persons and interested States." Rule 96 (1) states "[w]ithout prejudice to any other rules on notification of pro-

lacks clarity on this matter, it seems that the explicit requirements in the Rules are elaborations on the Statute, rather than contradictions thereto.

Under Rule 94 (2), when victims have filed requests for reparations "the person or persons named in the request or identified in the charges" are to be notified about the claims at the commencement of the trial, and "to the extent possible", interested persons and states.[963] While the wording refers primarily to the accused, applicants could also be included, i.e. victims and persons acting on their behalf in accordance with Art. 75 (3). In any case, Rule 96 generally requires the Court to notify those who have requested reparations. Third parties in possession of the property in question might be persons who are potentially "interested" within the meaning of the provisions.[964]

The obligations to notify the accused are even more extensive when the Court considers initiating reparations proceedings on its own motion. Under Rule 95 (1), the person against whom the Court is considering making a reparation order "shall" be notified by the Registry, upon request of the "Court" even when the Court has just formed the intention of initiating proceedings. As in most provisions in this context, "the Court" means the Chamber dealing with the case and victims, interested persons and states shall be notified "to the extent possible".

Rule 95 does not specify which victims should be notified. However, by reading Rule 95 (2) in conjunction with Rule 94, one could conclude that it will be those on whose behalf the Court intends to initiate reparations proceedings, in the event that their identity is known to the Court.

ceedings, the Registrar shall, insofar as practicable, notify the victims or their legal representatives and the person or persons concerned." The requirement to notify "the person or person concerned" in Rule 96 (1) seems to refer to the person that might be ordered to make reparation awards as a result of the proceedings. See also Rule 16 on the Registry's duty to notify victims, as well as witnesses. B. A. Garner (ed.): Black's Law Dictionary. 8th ed. St. Paul, Minnesota, 2004, p. 1091, defines that notification is "[a] formal announcement of a legally relevant fact, action, or intent". In the general context, to notify means to "inform (a person or group) in writing or by any method that is understood". This is also indicated by the wording that Rule 96 shall be applicable "[w]ithout prejudice to any other rules on notification of proceedings".

963 Notifying the accused at an earlier point would link the notification of the claims made to unconfirmed charges and thus create a number of uncertainties, see P. Lewis; H. Friman: "Reparations to Victims". In: The International Criminal Court – Elements of Crimes and Rules of Procedure and Evidence. Ed. R. S. Lee. Ardsley, New York, 2001, pp. 474 et seq. at p. 480. See also Rule 147 that requires the relevant Chamber to notify bona fide third parties with an interests in the proceeds or property subject to potential forfeiture orders. As reparations request can be filed at any stage and without specific reference to a case of accused, the onus is put upon the Court to determine whether a claim can be linked to a person prosecuted before the Court.

964 When no notification was given earlier, affected persons have to be informed on protective measures, Rule 99 (3); and enforcement, Art. 75 (4), Art. 57 (3) e) and Rule 217.

Rule 92 titled "notification to victims and their legal representatives" states that it "shall apply to all proceedings before the Court".[965] It deals primarily with notification in the context of victim participation in the trial and pre-trial proceedings, pursuant to Rule 89-93.[966] It thus seems that Rules 94 and 95, located in the subsection of the Rules entitled "Reparations to victims", are *lex specialis* with regard to notification in the context of reparations and are therefore the primarily applicable rules. However, the general requirements of Rule 92 that concern issues not regulated in Rules 94 and 95, such as formal requirements, are also applicable in the reparations proceedings.[967]

2. Publication

The reparations proceedings shall be publicized: "all the necessary measures" have to be taken in order to give "adequate" publicity of the reparations proceedings to "other victims" and interested states and persons.[968] The wording "other victims" seems to refer to those who have not yet been notified.

The Registry may publish and distribute "guidance booklets and other material, or provide education or training, in order to guide those assisting victims in completing the Standard Application Form".[969] In order to inform as many people as possible of the reparations proceedings, the Court may seek assistance from states parties and intergovernmental organizations.[970] The Court Regulations mention the option that non-governmental organizations (NGOs) can also be relied on for the dissemination

965 Rule 92 (1) further provides that it shall not be applicable "in proceedings provided for in Part 2" ICC Statute, which deals with dealing with "jurisdiction, admissibility and applicable law".

966 Furthermore, Rule 16 sets forth general obligations for the Registry to notify victims and witnesses.

967 Of relevance also in the context of the reparations proceedings is that notifications shall be in writing and "where written notification is not possible, in any other form as appropriate" (Rule 92 (7)). Regarding Rule 96 on notification, this is also indicated by the formula that it shall be applicable "[w]ithout prejudice to any other rules on notification of proceedings" (Rule 96 (1)).

968 Rule 96 (1) s. 2.

969 Reg. 105 (1) Registry Regulations. So far, a booklet that assists in filling in the standard forms for participation has been published.

970 Rule 96 (2). State assistance is to be sought under Part 9 of the Statute. In this provision, it was recognized that it may not be within the Court's capacity to meet the notification and publication requirements itself. In particular in the aftermath of the commission of massive and large scale crimes, the only effective way to spread information will often be through humanitarian organizations. During the making of the Rules, it was debated how these agencies should be defined. By choosing the term "inter-governmental organizations" instead of "non-governmental organizations" the concern that non-governmental organizations could be encouraged to interfere in a states' domestic affair was reconciled, see P. Lewis; H. Friman: "Reparations to Victims". In: The International Criminal Court – Elements of Crimes and Rules of Procedure and Evidence. Ed. R. S. Lee. Ardsley, New York, 2001, pp. 474 et seq. at p. 480.

of application forms for reparations and thus facilitate victims' access to the reparations mechanism.[971] It would seem that reparations proceedings could also made public through the media. In contrast, relying on the internet or other electronic media to publicize proceedings and disseminate information, seems hardly sufficient.[972] Many victims of crimes under the Court's jurisdiction do not have access to the internet.

In contrast to notification aiming to inform a specific person or persons known to have a particular interest in the reparations proceedings, publication aims to create general awareness among the public that might potentially be interested in the reparations proceedings.[973] Ideally, this ensures that all persons affected by the proceedings have the opportunity to invoke their rights before the Court. Thus, it seems that chronologically, publication of proceedings may often be necessary to conduct even prior to notification, in order to provide victims that do not know yet about the possibility to file a reparations claim with the opportunity to properly exercise their rights.

The Court's obligations to notify and publicize the reparations proceedings are restricted as they oblige the Registrar to effect notification and publication with regard to victims only "to the extent possible" and "so far as practicable" respectively.[974]

However, once the Court has ordered reparations to be implemented through the Trust Fund, the Trust Fund may conduct "targeted outreach to the beneficiary group [of individual reparations awards] to invite any potential members of the group [...] to identify themselves to the Trust Fund".[975]

NGOs have so far had a central role in providing information to the Court. The Victims Participation and Reparation Section of the Registry (VPRS) has relied "upon partnerships with civil society institutions that already have relationships with victim populations, drawing upon their prior experience and strong understanding of local customs and norms".[976]

971 Reg. 86 (1) Court Regulations.

972 See M. Henzelin; V. Heiskanen; G. Mettraux: "Reparations to Victims before the International Criminal Court – Lessons from International Mass Claims Processes". In: Criminal Law Forum 17 (2006), pp. 317 et seq. at p. 327 note that international courts and tribunals, including claims commissions, often rely on the internet or other electronic media for information campaigns.

973 Publication is defined as "the act of declaring or announcing to the public", in B. A. Garner (ed.): Black's Law Dictionary. 8th ed. St. Paul, Minnesota, 2004, p. 1264.

974 Rule 94 (2), Rule 95 (1), Rule 96 (1). In contrast, no such restriction clause exists regarding notification of the person named in the reparations request, respectively the person the Court intends to make a reparations order against (Rule 94, 95).

975 Reg. 61 (b) Trust Fund Regulations.

976 Interview with Fiona McKay – Head of the Victims Participation and Reparation Section of the International Criminal Court, conducted by C. Olivier. Published in: Victims' Rights Working Group Bulletin No. 5, Febuary 2006. Available at http://www.vrwg.org/Publications/04/ENG05.pdf, last accessed 14 May 2008, p. 4 with regard to facilitating victims' participation before the Court; similarly Interview with Claudia Perdomo – Head of the Public Information Unit, International Criminal Court, conducted by C.

The ICC has set up field offices in Uganda, the DRC, and also in Sudan and Chad, in order to inform, inter alia, about reparations for victims before the ICC.[977] However, regarding all four situations before the Court, its organs have encountered logistical difficulties in accessing victim populations. The reasons given for this by the organs of the Court are the traumatic events victims have experienced, difficulties gaining the trust of people, widespread unawareness of the existence of the ICC and concepts of international justice, high levels of illiteracy and cultural specificities that include diverse languages, beliefs, traditions and social structures.[978] NGOs and the Outreach Unit of the ICC have identified a number of outreach and communication deficits. Since the ICC's Strategic Plan for Outreach is being implemented, the Court's outreach activities seem to be progressing.[979]

II. Expert Consultation

The Court may receive assistance from experts when assessing harm and deciding on the types and modalities of the reparation awards (Rule 97 (2)).[980] Experts can be ap-

Olivier. Published in: Victims' Rights Working Group Bulletin No. 5, Febuary 2006. Available at http://www.vrwg.org/Publications/04/ENG0 5.pdf, last accessed 14 May 2008, pp. 6 et seq.

977 Outreach activities also take place in Central African Republic, see Outreach Report 2008, Public Information and Documentation Section of the International Criminal Court–Outreach Unit. Available at www.icc-cpi.int/NR/rdonlyres/1109882E-E8FF-4AFE-978E-A7466AEBC947/279522/Outreach_report2008en LR.pdf, p. 61, last accessed 16 April 2009.

978 See statements of the Head of the Public Information Unit C. Perdomo in: Interview with Claudia Perdomo – Head of the Public Information Unit, International Criminal Court, conducted by C. Olivier. Published in: Victims' Rights Working Group Bulletin No. 5, Febuary 2006. Available at http://www.vrwg.org/Publications/04/ENG05.pdf, last accessed 14 May 2008, pp. 6 et seq. at p. 7 regarding the situation in the Democratic Republic of Congo, Uganda, Sudan. Other points she raises are that women and children constitute the majority of the victim population and are most vulnerable and the need to manage pre-existing expectations of the ICC. Similar points are raised by F. McKay in Interview with Fiona McKay – Head of the Victims Participation and Reparation Section of the International Criminal Court, conducted by C. Olivier. Published in: Victims' Rights Working Group Bulletin No. 5, Febuary 2006. Available at http://www.vrwg.org/Publications/04/ENG05.pdf, last accessed 14 May 2008, p. 4.

979 Strategic Plan for Outreach of the Court, ICC-ASP/5/12 (2006); Proposed Programme Budget for 2007 of the International Criminal Court, ICC-ASP/5/9 (2006). Available at www.icc-cpi.int/library/asp/ICC-ASP-5-9_English, last accessed 22 April 2009; Outreach Report 2008, Public Information and Documentation Section of the International Criminal Court– Outreach Unit. Available at www.icc-cpi.int/NR/rdonlyres/1109882E-E8FF-4AFE-978E-A7466AEBC947/279522/Outreach_report2008enLR.pdf, p. 7, last accessed 16 April 2009.

980 F. Terrier: "The Procedure before the Trial Chamber". In: The Rome Statute of the International Criminal Court – A Commentary. Eds. A. Cassese; P. Gaeta; J. R. W. D. Jones. Vol. 2. Oxford, 2002, pp. 1277 et seq. at p. 1307 states that "[t]he Statute does not mention

pointed at the request of victims or their legal representatives, the convicted person or on the Court's own motion.[981] Once the experts have submitted their suggestions regarding the determination of harm and appropriate reparations, Rule 97 (2) provides that the Court "shall invite, as appropriate, victims or their legal representatives, the convicted person and other interested persons and interested States to make observations on the reports of the experts".

As the possible scope of expert consultation has been left open, it may involve everything from assessing the losses of individual victims to suggesting schemes for the benefit of a whole community.[982] The Court may also consult experts regarding the financial situation of a person against whom it has ordered reparations.[983] If the Court requires that all delegated decisions are to be reviewed and approved of by the Court, it is arguable that the delegation of damage assessment and claims processing is not contrary to the Statute.[984]

Delegating preparatory tasks to experts allows the Court to focus on its main duty of prosecuting perpetrators expediently while ensuring effective reparations proceedings.

While it is for the Trust Fund to implement reparation orders, it may also consult with "any competent expert, or expert organizations" regarding the determination of eligible persons and the nature and shape of awards.[985]

III. Participation in the Reparations Proceedings

1. Victims

The ICC's legal instruments provide for the possibility of victims' participation in the reparations proceedings. Under Art. 75 (3) the Court "may invite and shall take ac-

the contribution of experts, who are playing an increasingly major part in all modern justice."

981 Rule 97 (2). The Court shall create and maintain a list of experts, pursuant to Reg. 44 Court Regulations. The Registry can provide information and recommendations regarding appropriate experts, Reg. 110 (1) Registry Regulations.

982 P. Lewis; H. Friman: "Reparations to Victims". In: The International Criminal Court – Elements of Crimes and Rules of Procedure and Evidence. Ed. R. S. Lee. Ardsley, New York, 2001, pp. 474 et seq. at p. 484. It has been pointed out that the possibility to draw upon the expertise of experts not only to verify facts, but also determine appropriate reparations and their distribution through the Trust Fund that resembles a claims facility known from US mass claims proceedings, see B. Heß: "Kriegsentschädigungen aus kollisionsrechtlicher und rechtsvergleichender Sicht". In: Entschädigung nach bewaffneten Konflikten – Die Konstitutionalisierung der Welthandelsordnung. Eds. W. Heintschel von Heinegg; S. Kadelbach; B. Heß (et al.). Heidelberg, 2003, pp. 107 et seq. at pp. 167-168; further similarities with US mass claims mentioned are publication requirements.

983 Reg. 117 (2) Court Regulations.

984 M. Henzelin; V. Heiskanen; G. Mettraux: "Reparations to Victims before the International Criminal Court – Lessons from International Mass Claims Processes". In: Criminal Law Forum 17 (2006), pp. 317 et seq. at p. 333.

985 Reg. 61, 70 Trust Fund Regulations.

count of representations" by victims and therefore seems to be provided with discretion to decide to what extent victims shall be involved.[986] However, the official French and Spanish versions of Art. 75 (3) are clearer in that they simply state that "the Court shall take account of representations".[987]

The Rules clarify that the Court "shall" ask the Registrar to notify victims and is therefore obliged to involve victims (Rules 94 (2), 95 (3)). The Court "shall" also invite victims or their legal representatives to make "observations" on the reports of experts on reparations, "as appropriate" (97 (2)).[988]

Those invited or notified "shall" make "any representation made under article 75, paragraph 3" to the Court.[989] Once representations have been made, the Court is obliged to take them into account (Art. 75 (3)). Victims and other parties potentially affected by a reparation order are therefore to be encouraged to participate in the Court's decision-making process on reparations.

"Representations" in which victims can present their view to the Court can be both in written and oral form. Art. 76 (2) and (3) requires that they "shall be heard" in the reparations hearing or hearings, while the Court Regulations refer to representations under Art. 75 (3) as being in written form.[990]

It may also be the case that victims may be granted a right to participate in the reparations procedure pursuant to Art. 68 (3). Art. 68 (3) grants victims a general right to be "potential parties" in the proceedings: The Court "shall" permit victims' views and concerns to be presented where their personal interests are concerned.[991] Victims or their legal representatives can already inform the Court of their views and

986 "The Court may invite [...] victims" (Art. 75 (3)); "the Court shall invite, as appropriate, victims" (Rule 97 (2)). S. Zappalà: Human Rights in International Criminal Proceedings. Oxford, 2003, p. 229 states that "[t]he wording of paragraph 3 is [...] very obscure. [...] It would have been more correct explicitly to recognize the right of both the convicted person and the victim to be heard and present observations, and submit to the discretionaly evaluation of the Chamber the admission of submissions by other subjects."

987 The French version of Art. 75 (3) states: "Avant de render une ordonnance en vertu du présent article, la Cour tient compte de toutes observations formulées par la personne condamnée, les victimes, les autres personnes intéressés ou au nom de ces personnes ou de ces Etats." The Spanish text states: "La Corte, antes de tomar una decisión con arreglo a este artículo, tendrà en cuenta las obervaciones formuladas por el condenado, las víctimas, otras personas o Estados que tengan un interés, o las que se formulen en su nombre".

988 As stated in the context of notification, it seems that the Rules specify the unclear wording of Art. 75 (3). Those victims shall be notified which have filed applications for reparations, and on whose behalf the Court intends to initiate reparations.

989 Rules 94 (2) s. 2, 95 (1) s. 2.

990 Pursuant to Reg. 38 Court Regulations, representations under Art. 75 shall not exceed the page limit of 100 pages, unless otherwise ordered by the Court.

991 See also relevant Rules 89-93.

concerns related to, *inter alia*, reparations, at the pre-trial stage and during the trial prior to the conviction.[992]

The right to be heard prior to decisions on reparations under Art. 75 (3) could be categorized as a specification of the general right of participation envisioned by Art. 68 (3).[993] It is arguable therefore, that the applicability of Art. 68 (3) is excluded and that victims can only participate in the reparations proceedings when they have been invited to do so by the Court.[994] Also, some Rules explicitly differentiate between victims' participation in the proceedings and victims' involvement in the reparations proceedings.[995] It has been suggested that "victims have – first of all – a general right to be "potential parties" in the proceedings, but they merely have the right to make representations, upon the invitation of the Court, in the post-conviction stages. It is at this point that the need to protect the interests of the convicted person should prevail over the legitimate quest for punishment from victims".[996]

992 Thus, it seems recommendable for victims interested in influencing the potential reparations order to apply for participation in the trial or even pre-trial proceedings and thus be granted the right to express and have considered their views on reparations already before the conviction of a perpetrator. For a critical assessment on the Court's general handling of victims' participation see Chung, C. H.: "Victims' Participation at the International Criminal Court: Are Concessions of the Court Clouding the Promise?". In: Northwestern Journal of International Human Rights 6 (2008), pp. 459 et seq.

993 D. Donat-Cattin: "Article 68 – Protection of Victims and Witnesses and their Participation in the Proceedings". In: Commentary on the Rome Statute of the International Criminal Court – Observers' Notes, Article by Article. Ed. O. Triffterer. Baden-Baden, 1999, pp. 869 et seq. at p. 880; G. J. Mekjian; M. C. Varughese: "Hearing the Victim's Voice – Analysis of the Victims' Advocate Participation in the Trial Proceeding of the International Criminal Court". In: Pace International Law Review 17 (2005), pp. 1 et seq. at p. 18 name as other specifications of the general right to participation under Art. 68 (3) victims' "absolute right to attend within trial proceedings under Rule 91(2) and discretionary right to participate under Rule 91(3)(a), [...] the faculty to make representations before the Court even in the Pre-Trial procedure, as stipulated within Article 15.3, [...] the right to be right to intervene on appeals concerning reparation orders under Article 82.4".

994 Art 75 (3) and Rule 94 (2). Those who have been notified of the reparation proceedings and that are interested in making representations regarding reparations are generally required to file them with the Registrar.

995 E.g. Rule 143 states that "[p]ursuant to article 76, paragraphs 2 and 3, for the purpose of holding a further hearing on matters related to sentence and, if applicable, reparations, the Presiding Judge shall set the date of the further hearing. This hearing can be postponed [...] by the Trial Chamber [...] or at the request of the Prosecutor, the defence or the legal representatives of the victims participating in the proceedings pursuant to rules 89 to 91 and, in respect of reparations hearings, those victims who have made a request under rule 94".

996 D. Donat-Cattin: "Article 75 – Reparations to Victims". In: Commentary on the Rome Statute of the International Criminal Court – Observers' Notes, Article by Article. Ed. O. Triffterer. Baden-Baden, 1999, pp. 965 et seq. at p. 974, referring to the wording of Art. 68

However, it seems doubtful that the perpetrator's interests will be more worthy of protection after the Court has established his or her criminal responsibility than before conviction when the presumption of innocence would still apply. Moreover, victims participating in the ICC reparations proceedings might be interested in becoming actively involved in achieving aims other than retribution, e.g. in the shaping of reparation orders that aim primarily to compensate or reconcile.[997]

Excluding the right to participate pursuant to Art. 68 (3) would contradict the clear wording of the article that states that it is applicable at "all stages of the proceedings determined to be appropriate by the Court". The Standard Application Form for participation clarifies that victim participation is possible from the preliminary examination stage to the appeals stage of the proceedings.[998] According to official documents of the ICC, reparations proceedings, conducted after conviction, are part of the trial stage.[999]

Furthermore, the relevant Rules in the subsection titled "Participation of victims in the proceedings" also refer to victims' participation in "a hearing limited to reparations under article 75".[1000]

Excluding the applicability of Art. 68 (3) would lead to a drastic reduction of victims' participatory rights in the reparations procedure. This seems neither consistent with the broad wording of Art. 68 (3), nor with the purposes of victims' rights to participate and claim reparations. The special provisions for victims' participation in the reparations proceedings seem to deal only with persons or entities who have been invited by the Court to make representations. It seems that the purpose of Art. 75 (3) is to provide the Court with the authority to invite those persons or entities to participate who might not have applied to participate on their own initiative, but the Court is interested to hear their views on reparations.[1001]

---

(3) ("the Court shall permit [victims'] views and concerns to be presented and considered [...]") and Art. 75 (3) "the Court may invite [...] victims [...]".

997 See e.g. Chapter 3 ("Purposes of Reparations in International Criminal Justice")

998 Part C question 1 Standard Application Form for Individuals.

999 See Victims Participation Booklet, p. 11. In contrast, M. Henzelin; V. Heiskanen; G. Mettraux: "Reparations to Victims before the International Criminal Court – Lessons from International Mass Claims Processes". In: Criminal Law Forum 17 (2006), pp. 317 et seq. at p. 330 take the view that the reparations proceedings "need not and should not form part of the trial. They may, and should, be conducted only after conclusion of trial proceedings". See *Situation in the Democratic Republic of The Congo*, Decision on the Applications for Participation in the Proceedings of VPRS 1, VPRS 2, VPRS 3, VPRS 4, VPRS 5 and VPRS 6, ICC Pre-Trial Chamber I, 17 January 2006, ICC-01/04-101, paras. 25 et seq. for a thorough analysis of the term "proceedings".

1000 Rule 91 (4).

1001 Similar to the Court's power provided in Rule 93, which states that "[a] Chamber may seek the views of victims or their legal representatives participating pursuant to rules 89 to 91 on any issue, *inter alia,* in relation to issues referred to in rules 107, 109, 125, 128, 136, 139 and 191. In addition, a Chamber may seek the views of other victims, as appropriate".

Thus, it is submitted that victims can participate in reparations proceedings not only through "representations" upon notification pursuant to Art. 75 (3) and Rule 94 or Rule 95. They can also be allowed to participate upon application pursuant to Art. 68 (3) and Rules 89-93 as long as they qualify as victims under Rule 85, their personal interests are affected, and the Court finds it appropriate to allow them to participate.[1002] This might include victims who have already participated in the entire trial proceedings, or new applicants.

The criterion of "personal interest" is obviously complied when victims filed an application for reparations pursuant to Rule 94. However, it must be asked whether victims who did not to apply for reparations, for example because they oppose that the convicted person will make reparations, also have a "personal interest" to participate in the reparations proceedings. This question is delicate, as a right of these victims to participate could only be based on Art. 68 (3), because Art. 75 (3) and the relevant rules only provide for participation of victims that have applied for reparations. In principle, it seems justified to consider in such case whether the applicant has the required personal interest to participate in the reparations proceedings that might stem from the intention to prevent a reparation order against the convicted person.

It seems that in practice, when victims have applied for reparations, both legal constructions lead to the same conclusions. All those victims who requested reparations under Rule 94 can directly, or indirectly through their legal representative, present their views in the reparations hearings, which the Court is obliged to consider. The challenge of dealing with large numbers of victims, as well as differing victims' interests and different victim groups is likely to persist in the reparations proceedings.[1003]

Victims or their legal representatives also have the right to participate when the Trial Chamber announces its decision on reparations.[1004]

With regard to the modalities of participation, when there is only a limited number of victims applying for reparations, the Court may allow them to participate in person in hearings on reparations (Art. 75 (3), 76 (3)). Victims can also participate through their legal representative and may be obliged to do so where the Court con-

1002 See for further analysis of the requirements *Situation in the Democratic Republic of The Congo*, Decision on the Applications for Participation in the Proceedings of VPRS 1, VPRS 2, VPRS 3, VPRS 4, VPRS 5 and VPRS 6, ICC Pre-Trial Chamber I, 17 January 2006, ICC-01/04-101, paras. 25 et seq.

1003 It can be expected that the Court will be challenged to deal with large numbers of victims applying for participation already in the trial proceedings.

1004 Rule 144. The Rule only refers expressly to victims and their legal representatives "participating in the proceedings pursuant to Rules 89 to 91". Even though this does not seem likely in practice, there might be victims and their legal representatives that only participate in the reparations proceedings. It would make sense to expand the Rule in these cases to also include these victims and legal representatives. Like other decisions of the Trial Chamber, the decision of reparations shall be pronounces in public.

siders it appropriate.[1005] This might be the case when there are large numbers of victims.

In the reparations hearings victims' legal representatives may question witnesses, experts and the convicted person. In contrast to all other stages of the proceedings, during reparations hearings the Court cannot restrict the legal representative to making only written submissions or observations (Rule 91 (2), (4)).[1006] Furthermore, victims or their legal representatives have the right to request that the Court appoints experts to assist in determining the scope and extent of harm and develop concepts for reparations (Rule 97 (2)).

Thus, the role of victims in the ICC reparations proceedings is potentially much stronger than the wording of Art. 75 (3) suggests.

When reparations are awarded through the Trust Fund, the Trust Fund Regulations determine the modalities of victims' involvement in shaping and implementing reparation awards. Where the Court orders that individual awards are to be made through the Trust Fund and has not determined the beneficiaries of individual awards, the Trust Fund's Secretariat may consult, among others, victims or their legal representatives and families of individual victims in developing options for the determination of beneficiaries and processing of claims.[1007] Furthermore, in determining the nature and implementation of collective awards, the Board of Directors may consult the aforementioned persons.[1008]

The provisions on participation of victims in the ICC reparations proceedings comply with international standards. For example, the 1985 Victims Declaration states that in the relevant procedures victims' views shall be heard and considered where their personal interests are concerned.[1009]

2. Parties other than Victims

In addition to victims, "other interested persons", "interested states" and the convicted person are also entitled to make representations concerning reparations.[1010]

Other interested persons can include those who might be affected by the award, such as the offender's family or bona fide third parties in possession of property that is to be restored, or others who are subject to any protective measures.[1011]

1005 See Art. 75 (3): "representations from or on behalf of [...] victims" and Rule 91 (4) that provides for the possibility that victims' views might be represented by legal representatives in the reparation hearings.

1006 Rule 91 (4) states that "[i]n that case, the legal representative may, with the permission of the Chamber concerned, question witnesses, experts and the person concerned."

1007 Reg. 61 Trust Fund Regulations.

1008 Reg. 70 Trust Fund Regulations. In contrast to the reparations proceedings before the Court, states are not mentioned as party potentially to be consulted.

1009 Para. 6 b).

1010 Art. 75 (3) read in conjunction with Art. 76 (3), Rule 94 (2), Rule 95 (1).

1011 See C. M. Bassiouni: Introduction to International Criminal Law. Ardsley, New York, 2003, p. 527. Only Rule 94 (2) contains the requirement "subject to any protection measures". However, B. Timm: "The Legal Position of Victims in the Rule of Procedure and

Interested states are those with an interest in the matter before the Court.[1012] These might be states whose territory was the locus of the crimes in question, or whose nationals were victims of the perpetrators, or those states with custody over particular perpetrators.[1013] As the Statute does not include the possibility of ordering states to make reparations, reparation orders may not have a direct impact on states.[1014] They may therefore often not fulfill the requirement of being "interested".[1015] However, "interested" with regard to reparations might especially be those states on whose territory victims entitled to reparations are located, or whose state officials, or former state officials, are ordered to award reparations. Also where the state is a bona fide third party the state might be reasonably entitled to intervene. When the convicted perpetrator was a public official of a state, forms of reparations may include the restoration of rights or the public acknowledgment of the crimes. Furthermore, certain forms of collective reparations, e.g. the building of a memorial or a hospital, cannot simply be enforced against the convicted person. Even though such measures can be addressed to the convicted person, they can only be effectively implemented with the co-operation of the state.[1016]

Like victims, interested persons and the convicted person can request the Court to appoint experts and make observations on the reports of experts dealing with damage assessment and suggestions for reparations.[1017] Interested persons and interested states can also be consulted by the Trust Fund regarding the implementation of reparation orders.[1018]

In national and international documents and practice there is an emerging consensus that communication and mutual agreements between victim and perpetra-

Evidence". In: International and National Prosecution of Crimes under International Law. Eds. H. Fischer, C. Kreß; S. R. Lüder. (Bochumer Schriften zur Friedenssicherung und zum Humanitären Völkerrecht). Berlin, 2001, pp. 289 et seq. at p. 302 suggests that "it would be sensible to make this restriction generally applicable".

1012 P. Kirsch QC; D. Robinson: "Referral by State Parties". In: The Rome Statute of the International Criminal Court – A Commentary. Eds. A. Cassese; P. Gaeta; J. R. W. D. Jones. Vol. 1. Oxford, 2002, pp. 619 et seq. at p. 622.

1013 Ibid.

1014 See Art. 73 (2) (b) of the ICC Draft Statute and further discussion in Chapter 4 A. IV. ("Who can the Reparations Principles be Addressed to?").

1015 D. Donat-Cattin: "Article 75 – Reparations to Victims". In: Commentary on the Rome Statute of the International Criminal Court – Observers' Notes, Article by Article. Ed. O. Triffterer. Baden-Baden, 1999, pp. 965 et seq. at 974 points out that this is especially so because "States have a role *strictu sensu* in the penal process only when there is an issue of admissibility of a case before the ICC".

1016 See Chapter 5 C. II. 4 above.

1017 See Rule 97 (2): e.g. also states can make observations on the expert reports.

1018 Reg. 61, Reg. 70 Trust Fund Regulations. Concerning collective awards, the option to consult with states is not mentioned.

tor shall be fostered in both criminal and civil proceedings.[1019] This can be done by utilizing informal mechanisms for the resolution of disputes, including mediation, arbitration, customary justice or indigenous practices where appropriate to facilitate reconciliation and redress for victims.[1020] The participation of both victims and the convicted person in the ICC reparations proceedings might trigger such broader processes among those affected by and involved in the crimes.

IV. Assessment

The ICC's legal instruments give specific and far-reaching responsibilities to the Court regarding the conduct of its reparations procedure. With regard to victims' rights, the ICC's legal instruments do not restricted the role of the Court to that of a simple remedy enforcement forum. The Court's function goes beyond that as it is also responsible for actively safeguarding the interests and rights of the persons affected by its mandate. Victims are the weakest and most vulnerable of those affected by the crimes. Thus, in order to fulfill this task the Court will often be obliged to approach victims or act on their behalf in order to ensure that its proceedings result in justice that integrates the victims in the whole process. It seems the Court will face a constant challenge to fulfill the expectations laid down by the ICC's legal instruments in that regard.

The provisions on publication and notification and their implementation are important in order to ensure the accessibility of the ICC and to comply with international standards. The Court is only required to notify victims and publicize reparations proceedings "to the extent possible". It thus has wide discretion as to the extent of outreach activities it engages in. Informing victims of crimes under its jurisdiction of the possibility of claiming reparations before the ICC is, and will remain, difficult. In spite of this, it should be considered a priority to make the reparations regime accessible to victims through notification and publication. The involvement of the persons affected by the crimes prosecuted by the ICC is a basic pre-condition for the ICC reparations regime functioning in a fair and effective manner. Therefore, it still remains for standard applications forms and guidance booklets on ICC reparations to be made available in the languages of the victim populations, as required by the ICC's legal instruments.

Thus, if the Court does not succeed in making itself assessable through extensive outreach work, it seems that responsibility shall rest with the Court to proceed on

1019 See e.g. para. 7 1985 Victims Declaration; Art. 10 EU Framework Decision ("Penal mediation in the course of criminal proceedings"). Art. 3 of the Decision generally requires Member States to safeguard victims' right to be heard during proceedings and to supply evidence; see for the practice of the Inter-American Court to foster agreements between the responsible state and the commission acting on behalf of the victim see e.g. *El Amparo v. Venezuela*, Reparations, Inter-American Court of Human Rights, 14 September 1996, Ser. C, No. 28. For the national context, see e.g. for German law, see § 46 German Criminal Code (StGB) and § 278 German Code of Civil Procedure (ZPO).

1020 E.g. para. 7 1985 Victims Declaration.

behalf of victims to ensure that the results of the reparations proceedings are just and fair.[1021]

The ICC's legal instruments envision that the views and interests of victims will be considered when determining the reparation order. The reparations proceedings are intended to be a communicative process in which the Court consults with a number of persons and parties affected by the order. At the same time, Rule 97 (3) emphasizes that the Court is urged to respect the rights of victims and the convicted person when awarding reparations. This also incorporates the procedural aspect of restorative justice by providing for the possibility of bringing together perpetrators and those affected by their wrongdoing.[1022]

While it is important to involve victims in the decision-making process on reparations, at the same time it is not realistic to consider all of the individual interests and opinions of large numbers of victims in the process. However, it has been noted that "genuine consultation may be difficult to achieve given that victims may be internally or externally displaced, severely traumatized or otherwise distanced from the process".[1023] In addition, victimized individuals and groups may have very different needs and ideas regarding appropriate reparations. One of the key arguments against victim participation in the proceedings that also applies to the reparations stage is that it will lead to delays and additional expenses.[1024]

1021 See also above Chapter 6 A.II. ("Court-Initiated Reparations Proceedings").

1022 See D. Shelton: Remedies in International Human Rights Law. 2nd ed. Oxford, 2005, p. 15.; G. Ulrich: "The Moral Case for Reparations – Three Theses about Reparations for Past Wrongs". In: Reparations – Redressing Past Wrongs. Eds. G. Ulrich; L. Krabbe Boserup. (Human Rights in Development – Yearbook 2001). The Hague, 2003, pp. 369 et seq. at p. 381 states that "[b]ecause they are fundamentally ambiguous and therefore subject to debate, reparation claims related to past wrongs inscribe their protagonists involved in a communicative relationship that is governed by an ethics of recognition and reciprocity".

1023 C. Ferstman: "The International Criminal Court's Trust Fund for Victims – Challenges and Opportunities". In: Yearbook of International Humanitarian Law 2003. Ed. A. McDonald. Vol. 6. The Hague, 2006, pp. 424 et seq. at pp. 431-432.

1024 F. N. M. Mumba: "Topics within the Sphere of Sentencing in International Criminal Law". In: Man's Inhumanity to Man – Essays in Honour of Antonio Cassese. Eds. L. C. Vorah; F. Pocar; Y. Featherstone (et al.). The Hague, 2003, pp. 567 et seq. at p. 586 with further references; also C. Jorda; J. de Hemptinne: "The Status and Role of the Victim". In: The Rome Statute of the International Criminal Court – A Commentary. Eds. A. Cassese; P. Gaeta; J. R. W. D. Jones. Vol. 2. Oxford, 2002, pp. 1387 et seq. at p. 1389. There have been concerns that taking into consideration the victims' view in practice causes a number of problems, most of which, however, refer to the pre-conviction stage and are therefore not (less) relevant in the context of the reparations proceedings, see e.g. the danger that defendants would challenge the content of victims' statements by subjecting victims to unpleasant cross-examination on their statements and that victims' input might produce pressure on the court in high profile cases; see M.-B. Dembour; E. Haslam: "Silence Hearings? Victim-Witnesses at War Crimes Trials". In: European Journal of International Law 15 (2004), pp. 151 et seq.; for further examination see M. Burkhardt, Victim Participation before the ICC, forthcoming.

The Rules suggest solutions to these possible difficulties: the delegation of tasks to experts or the Trust Fund, and indirect participation of victims through their legal representatives. However, it remains at the Court's discretion as to whether and to what extent victims and others are allowed to participate, and whether the expressed interests of applicants will be taken into account.[1025]

In order to avoid disappointing victims, they should not only be informed of the existence of the ICC reparations regime, but also what can be reasonably expected from it. It is doubtful that what the Court has done in this regard so far is sufficient.[1026]

C. Standard and Burden of Proof

Since the ICC deals with crimes perpetrated during war or other situations of widespread conflict, it is natural to expect that it will be confronted with situations where evidence of the victimization might be difficult to access, scarce or even non-existing.[1027] In particular, in cases of mass crimes victims are often left without means to document their losses and harm suffered in order to prove their eligibility for reparations. Witnesses and evidence are likely to be scattered throughout the world. The

1025 It has been suggested to establish a commission of independent experts to deal with all technical matters concerning the compensation of victims, C. Jorda; J. de Hemptinne: "The Status and Role of the Victim". In: The Rome Statute of the International Criminal Court – A Commentary. Eds. A. Cassese; P. Gaeta; J. R. W. D. Jones. Vol. 2. Oxford, 2002, pp. 1387 et seq. at p. 1415.

1026 On the front page of the Standard Application Forms for reparations, applicants are told that "[t]he information provided in the Application Form will be presented to a Chamber of Judges in the ICC which will consider your request. Please be advised that criminal proceedings take time and it may be some time before the Court makes a decision on reparations". However, e.g. in Part F. question 1 applicants are asked "[w]hich of the following forms of reparations would you like to claim? [....] You may tick more than one box", followed by a list with various forms of reparations and the option to request other forms of reparations that are not listed. Without further explanation, this question may create the expectation among victims that they will receive whatever they ask for from the Court, and that they will obtain material forms of reparation. Only question 6 of Part F is clear in its wording: "If resources are available (from a person convicted by the ICC or from the ICC's Trust Fund for Victims), what would help you and your community the most?", see also concurrent question 6 of Part F on the Standard Application Form for Organizations. S. Garkawe: "The Victim-Related Provisions of the Statute of the International Criminal Court – A Victimological Analysis". In: International Review of Victimology 8 (2001), pp. 269 et seq. at p. 287 emphasizes that "there will be a need to explain to victims in a patient and sensitive manner the complexity of the procedures and the length of time they and the trial may take to be completed".

1027 See generally on evidence and ICC e.g. C. M. Bassiouni: Introduction to International Criminal Law. Ardsley, New York, 2003; R. May; M. Wierda: International Criminal Evidence. Ardsley, New York, 2002; K. R. Gray: "Evidence before the ICC". In: The Permanent International Criminal Court – Legal and Policy Issues. Eds. D. McGoldrick, P. Rowe; E. Donnelly. Oxford, 2004, pp. 287 et seq.

task of attributing a victim's damage to a certain deed may prove challenging, in particular in view of the numbers of victims and perpetrators involved. Here, the reality of victims confronts with the necessity to safeguard the rights of the convicted person. Also, reparations claims must meet certain requirements in order to guarantee a sufficient degree of fairness and equality.

The issue of claims verification is connected in a practical manner to a number of other questions discussed in this work, in particular the valuation and calculation of harm and issues of causation.[1028]

I. *ICC Reparation System*

In order to determine whether a person or entity is entitled to reparations, the Court has to be convinced to some degree that the eligibility criteria for reparations are fulfilled. When reparations are awarded upon application, this requires that it is established that the applicant, or person on whose behalf the application is made, as a minimum, qualifies as a victim under Rule 85 and meets all other requirements set forth in Rule 94.[1029] However, the Statute and Rules do not set forth explicitly which standard of proof is to be required for reparations, or who is to state the facts of the claim or who carries the burden of proof.

There are three different procedures in which relevant evidence for reparations claims may be obtained. First, evidence and the Court's findings in respect to reparations might be accepted in the trial proceedings. Second, additional evidence might be introduced in the Court's reparations proceedings.[1030] Third, the Trust Fund may engage in claims processing and thus deal with claims verification.[1031] In these different stages of proceedings, different standards of evidence and assessment (verification) procedures might apply.

1. Standard of Proof

In the reparations procedure, the Court may rely on its findings on damage, losses and injury to victims proven in the trial proceedings for the purpose of the criminal conviction. Pursuant to the Court Regulations, the Trial Chamber "may hear the witnesses and examine the evidence for the purposes of a decision on reparations in accordance with article 75, paragraph 2, at the same time as for the purposes of trial".[1032]

1028 See Chapter 5 C. II. 2. b) ("Compensation and Causation") and Chapter 5 C. IV. 1. ("Valuation and Calculation of Damages").

1029 See Chapter 5 B. ("Eligibility to Reparations before the ICC").

1030 On these two procedures of obtaining evidence and other proposals on evidence see the examination of drafting history of the Rules in P. Lewis; H. Friman: "Reparations to Victims". In: The International Criminal Court – Elements of Crimes and Rules of Procedure and Evidence. Ed. R. S. Lee. Ardsley, New York, 2001, pp. 474 et seq. at pp. 484 et seq.

1031 Reg. 62 et seq. Trust Fund Regulations. Also, the task of processing claims may be assigned to experts, see Rule 97.

1032 Reg. 56 Court Regulations. In this way, it can be avoided that witnesses have to appear before the Court several times in the same trial in order to give evidence concerning the

Since these findings serve the criminal conviction, the applicable standard is "proof beyond reasonable doubt" (Art. 66 (3)).

The standard of proof is unclear with regard to additional evidence introduced for the first time in the reparations proceedings (Art. 76 (2) and (3)). One option might be to apply the provisions in the Statute and Rules dealing with evidence and related issues, in particular the standard of proof as set forth in Art. 66 (3) to the reparations procedure.[1033] In that case, the requisite standard of proof in the reparations procedure would also be proof beyond reasonable doubt. The explicit wording of the provision, which refers to the criminal conviction of the accused, does not speak in favor of its applicability to reparation claims. However, from a contextual point of view, Art. 66 is located in Part 6 of the Statute titled "the Trial", and therefore in the same chapter of the Statute as Art. 75 on reparations. From this, it could be assumed that Art. 66 (3) also applies to the establishment of the convicted person's liability to make reparations. As reparations can only be obtained upon conviction, and the Statute only provides for a standard of proof for convictions, it could be assumed that the same standard will have to be applied to reparations.[1034] However, it could be argued that the claim for reparations is essentially a civil claim heard in a court of criminal jurisdiction.[1035] The standard of proof is usually lower in procedures governing civil claims than in criminal procedure.[1036]

In particular, it is doubtful when considering the object and purpose of reparations, whether the standard of "proof beyond reasonable doubt" should also apply in the Court's reparations procedure.[1037] First of all, the criminal conviction of a person is the precondition for an award of reparations. The guilt of the offender has already been established when reparations are ordered, and thus, the presumption of innocence no longer applies. Thus, victims not only do not need to prove the responsibility of a certain person for a particular deed, but it may not even be necessary to require such a high standard of proof in the reparations proceedings following the

criminal conviction and reparations. See also F. McKay: "Victim Participation in Proceedings before the International Criminal Court". In: Human Rights Brief 15/3 (2008), pp. 1 et seq at p.4, describing the Court's application of this provision.

1033 Art. 64 -69, Rules 63-89.

1034 P. Lewis; H. Friman: "Reparations to Victims". In: The International Criminal Court – Elements of Crimes and Rules of Procedure and Evidence. Ed. R. S. Lee. Ardsley, New York, 2001, pp. 474 et seq. at p. 482. Ibid., p. 484.

1035 See Chapter 3 ("Purposes of Reparations in International Criminal Law"); D. Shelton: "Reparations for Victims of International Crimes". In: International Crimes, Peace, and Human Rights – The Role of the International Court. Ed. D. Shelton. Ardsley, New York, 2000, pp. 137 et seq. at p. 146.

1036 See Chapter 6 C. II. ("International and National Law and Human Rights") below; M. Heikkilä: International Criminal Tribunals and Victims of Crime. Turku, 2004, p. 182.

1037 The same is true regarding the Rules on evidence. Even though the provisions on evidence are contained in Chapter 4 of the Rules, which is titled "Provisions applicable in various stages of the proceedings", most of them refer to proceedings dealing with evidence in regard to the conviction of a person.

conviction.[1038] Moreover, taking into account the victims' perspective requires consideration of the fact that victims will often be unable to gather the written or oral evidence needed to prove their victimization. This might be due to the hostilities, possibly their refugee status, homelessness and lack of medical care where certificates or evidence of injury can be obtained.[1039]

This situation of victims was also acknowledged by the drafters of the Rules. In general, all proposals for provisions on evidence regarding reparations required a standard lower than "proof beyond reasonable doubt".[1040] For example, the Paris draft rules contained a provision titled "evidence". In the commentary attached thereto, it was noted that "the working group suggested adding at the end of the paragraph: 'on the balance of probabilities'. The aim was to provide a lower standard of proof for the purposes of [...] reparations than the standard of proof required to established criminal responsibility [...], having regard to the difficulty likely to be experienced by victims in gathering evidence".[1041] As a result of a lack of consensus on this and other related questions, no provision on evidence in the reparations proceedings was incorporated.[1042]

Essentially, the Statute and Rules leave open the questions of whether the harm suffered and whether the causal link between that harm and the crimes perpetrated has to be proven beyond reasonable doubt, or whether a less onerous burden of proof is sufficient.[1043]

This is confirmed by the finding of ICC's Pre-Trial Chamber I, in its decision on victims' participation of 17 January 2006, that with regard to the burden of proof to be applied in assessing whether applicants may be accorded the status of victims

---

1038 See D. Shelton: "Reparations for Victims of International Crimes". In: International Crimes, Peace, and Human Rights – The Role of the International Court. Ed. D. Shelton. Ardsley, New York, 2000, pp. 137 et seq. at p. 147.

1039 Ibid., p. 146; P. Lewis; H. Friman: "Reparations to Victims". In: The International Criminal Court – Elements of Crimes and Rules of Procedure and Evidence. Ed. R. S. Lee. Ardsley, New York, 2001, pp. 474 et seq. at p. 484.

1040 P. Lewis; H. Friman: "Reparations to Victims". In: The International Criminal Court – Elements of Crimes and Rules of Procedure and Evidence. Ed. R. S. Lee. Ardsley, New York, 2001, pp. 474 et seq. at pp. 484 et seq.

1041 UN Doc. PCNICC/1999/WGRPE/INF/2, pp. 7 and 9.

1042 P. Lewis; H. Friman: "Reparations to Victims". In: The International Criminal Court – Elements of Crimes and Rules of Procedure and Evidence. Ed. R. S. Lee. Ardsley, New York, 2001, pp. 474 et seq. at pp. 485 et seq. The concept "balance of probabilities" did not find the consensus as considered unclear by many delegations. A related controversial aspect were the requirements for causality.

1043 C. Jorda; J. de Hemptinne: "The Status and Role of the Victim". In: The Rome Statute of the International Criminal Court – A Commentary. Eds. A. Cassese; P. Gaeta; J. R. W. D. Jones. Vol. 2. Oxford, 2002, pp. 1387 et seq. at p. 1411; D. Shelton: "Reparations for Victims of International Crimes". In: International Crimes, Peace, and Human Rights – The Role of the International Court. Ed. D. Shelton. Ardsley, New York, 2000, pp. 137 et seq. at p. 146.

"no criterion for making such an assessment is to be found in the Statute or in the Rules".[1044]

Therefore, it "borrows the criterion that exists at the same stage of the proceedings [...] which is applicable to the procedural rights of a person other than the victims."[1045] Accordingly, the standard of proof required to establish victim status at the investigative stage is that there are "grounds to believe" that the criteria of Rule 85 are fulfilled.[1046] After the issue of an arrest warrant, the examination criterion is that of "reasonable grounds to believe"[1047] and at the stage of confirmation of charges, the criterion is "substantial grounds to believe" that Rule 85 is complied with.[1048] The Pre-Trial Chamber assessed whether the victims' applications for participation in the investigative stage meet the criteria set forth by examining "whether the victim's account of the events is consistent with official reports (particularly United Nations reports)."[1049]

Pre-Trial Chamber I did not refer to the standard of proof applicable to establishing the status in the reparations proceedings. However, at the reparations stage the relevant standard of proof for the procedural rights of "the person other than the victims" is "proof beyond reasonable doubt", in accordance with Art. 66 (3). Following the approach taken by the Court, the status of a person as a victim for the purposes of reparations would also have to be established "beyond reasonable doubt".

It seems that in view of the often difficult situation of victims, once it has been established that a person is the victim of a crime for which the convicted person is responsible, the standard of proof for the harm suffered by the victim could, and should, be lower.

The precise standard of proof applicable to reparations could be determined by the Court as part of the reparations principles to be established under Art. 75 (1). In any case, the Court seems to have discretion in whether it regards claims to be sufficiently well founded.[1050]

The standard of proof to be applied by the Court when deciding on the eligibility of applicants to reparations is not necessarily identical to the standard of proof the Trust Fund may apply when it determines the beneficiaries of indirect awards. In contrast to the Court's legal foundations, the Trust Fund Regulations contain provisions on the verification of individual awards.[1051] The relevant provisions state that the "Secretariat shall verify that any persons who identify themselves to the Trust Fund

1044 *Situation in the Democratic Republic of The Congo*, Decision on the Applications for Participation in the Proceedings of VPRS 1, VPRS 2, VPRS 3, VPRS 4, VPRS 5 and VPRS 6, Pre-Trial Chamber I, 17 January 2006, ICC-01/04-101, para. 97.

1045 Ibid., para. 98.

1046 Art. 55 (2); see ibid., para. 98.

1047 Art. 58 (1) a); see ibid.

1048 Art. 61 (7); see ibid.

1049 Ibid., para. 101.

1050 E.g. under Rule 97 (1) the Court is to "take into account" damage, loss and injury to victim when determining reparations.

1051 Reg. 62-65.

are in fact members of the beneficiary group",[1052] and that "the Board of Directors shall determine the standard of proof for the verification exercise, having regard to the prevailing circumstances of the beneficiary group and the available evidence."[1053] Thus, the Trust Fund Regulations provide that the applicable standard of proof shall be determined flexibly and on a case-by-case basis. It was argued that this would enable the necessary sensitive and flexible approach, which takes into account that the circumstances and information that victims can provide to the Trust Fund will vary greatly in different situations.[1054] Thus, the Trust Fund can certainly depart significantly from the high standard of "proof beyond reasonable doubt".

2. Burden of Proof and Demonstration of Facts

The only provision in the ICC Statute regarding the burden of proof refers to proving the guilt of the accused (Art. 66 (2)). The burden of proof applicable to reparations claims before the ICC is not explicitly regulated.

It is a general principle that a claimant is responsible for submitting evidence to prove that a particular claim is eligible for compensation.[1055]

Before the ICC, the burden of proof upon claimants is simplified because they do not have to establish the responsibility of the convicted person under international criminal law – this has already been done by the competent Trial Chamber.

While there is no explicit provision regarding the documentation and assessment of claims and the burden of proof in the ICC's legal instruments, there are some indications at to the applicable standard. Rule 94 on victims' requests for reparations require that applicants add to the claim "any relevant supporting documentation, including names and addresses of witnesses". In particular, it is relevant that the victim establishes that the harm for which he or she seeks reparations was a consequence of the acts of conduct for which the accused was found guilty.

However, victims are only required to do so "[t]o the extent possible" (Rule 94 (1) g)). Thus, while in principal it is for applicants to prove their claim, if this is impossible, it seems that the Court, or certain organs of the Court, are also responsible for engaging in information gathering to substantiate claims. Victims are also not required to have filed their claim against the person convicted by the Court in order

1052 Reg. 62. This shall be done "in accordance with any principles set out in the order of the Court".

1053 Reg. 63. This shall be done "[s]ubject to any stipulations set out in the order of the Court".

1054 Victims' Rights Working Group: Comments on the Draft Regulations of the ICC Trust Fund for Victims, February 2005. Available at www.vrwg.org/Publications/01/VRWG_Feb2005.pdf, last accessed 22 April 2009.

1055 See e.g. M. Kazazi: Burden of Proof and Related Issues – A Study of Evidence before International Tribunals. The Hague (et al.), 1996, pp. 369: "[...] the party who makes the allegations regarding a disputed fat or issue bears the burden of providing such oat or issue.[...] This is a principle which is generally recognized and accepted in different legal systems and in international law", noting that there are differences between international law and the municipal laws of every country.

for their claim for reparation to be successful.[1056] The application for reparation that victims may file requires them to identify the person responsible for the crime that caused their harm "to the extent possible" (Rule 94 (1) (c)). This not only takes into account the difficult situation that victims of mass crimes might often be in when it is for them to file applications to reparations. It also recognizes that victims cannot be expected to be familiar with legal concepts such as superior responsibility and thus might simply not know or be aware of who is legally responsible for the crime perpetrated against them. Consequently, victims can also receive reparation from a convicted person whom they did not suggest to be responsible for the harm for which reparations are sought.[1057] The practical consequence of this is that it might often be up to the Court to link a victim's claim to a person convicted.

It might be assumed the Chambers themselves will not be directly involved in the establishment of claims. In principle, the judges of both Pre-Trial and Trial Chambers are also not supposed to involve themselves in the gathering of evidence during the criminal part of the proceedings.[1058]

It seems that rejecting applications will not be easy when the applicants explicitly claim that their harm is linked to the crime of the accused or convicted person, even when it is not documented. When the Court makes use of its power to initiate reparations proceedings on behalf of victims who have not applied for reparations (Art. 75 (1), Rule 95), it seems that the Court's responsibility to prove their eligibility to reparations is even more important.

The Court Regulations support the finding that the victim does not carry alone the responsibility to submit evidence or document his or her claim. They provide that "the Registrar shall seek all necessary additional information from a victim in order to complete his or her request in accordance with rule 94, sub-rule 1, and shall assist victims in completing such a request".[1059] The Registry Regulations describe in

1056 Rules 94; Part D question 2 Standard Application Form for Individuals. Furthermore, the Court can initiate reparations proceedings on behalf of victims, see Rule 95.

1057 This concept departs remarkably from the general concept of civil claims for damages, where it is constitutive for the claim that there is a defendant.

1058 Thus, unlike in traditional civil law jurisdictions where an investigating judge collects items of evidence in order to contribute to establishing the truth, before the ICC the whole body of evidence will be produced by the parties, see C. Jorda; J. de Hemptinne: "The Status and Role of the Victim". In: The Rome Statute of the International Criminal Court – A Commentary. Eds. A. Cassese; P. Gaeta; J. R. W. D. Jones. Vol. 2. Oxford, 2002, pp. 1387 et seq. at p. 1412.

1059 Reg. 88 (2) Court Regulations. It seems that the Victims Participation and Reparations Section, established pursuant to Reg. 86 (9) Court Regulations, is responsible. Also, the Victims and Witnesses Unit of the Registry has the general task that is put upon the Registry with regard to victims (and witnesses) in Rule 16: Assisting them in obtaining legal advice and organizing their legal representation, and providing their legal representatives with adequate support, assistance and information, including such facilities as may be necessary for the direct performance of their duty, for the purpose of protecting their rights during all stages of the proceedings in accordance with Rules 89 to 91. It would seem that regarding applications for reparations, as with victims' applications for partici-

further detail the Registry's duty to assist victims in gathering information. In assisting victims, the Registry is to take into account whether the victim is represented, the victim's security and any time limits for filing documents. It is also to inform them that their application may be accepted or rejected on the basis of the information they provide.[1060] The information can be obtained by the Registry from the victim in writing or via the phone.[1061] Thus, the Court's Registry's obligation to assist and help victims in filing reparations applications may make filing and documenting the claim much easier for victims, without going so far as to reverse the onus of proof.

Furthermore, experts may be appointed to assist the Court in assessing reparations pursuant to Rule 97 (2) and to determine the extent and scope of damage, loss and injury to and in respect of victims. This might also include an active approach that encompasses claims assessment. The Trust Fund may also be active in the process of identifying beneficiaries of reparation orders and in the substantiation of claims. In the event that the Court proceeds on its own motion regarding reparations and orders individual reparations to be made through the Trust Fund without having identified all of its beneficiaries, its "Secretariat shall set out all relevant demographic/statistical data about the group of victims, as defined in the order of the Court".[1062]

In order to collect missing details, the Secretariat may use "demographic data to determine the members of the beneficiary group", engage in "[t]argeted outreach to the beneficiary group to invite any potential members of the group who have not already been identified [...] to identify themselves to the Trust Fund."[1063] Thus, it is also possible for the Trust Fund's organs to support victims actively in filing claims and establishing their eligibility.

The relevant provisions in the Rules, and in the Regulations of the Trust Fund, Court and Registry show that it is the duty of certain organs of the Court and the Trust Fund to assist potential beneficiaries of reparations in filing and documenting their claims. Court-appointed experts can also provide documentation. However, the obligation to state the facts and the burden of proof remains principally with the claimants.

II. International and National Law and Human Rights

A variety of approaches have been and continue to be taken in national and international legal systems in order to verify reparations claims, including rules on the stan-

pation, the Registry might assist victims by seeking information, inter alia, from states, the Prosecutor and inter-governmental or non-governmental organizations (Reg. 86 (4) Court Regulations).

1060 Reg. 107 (3) Registry Regulations. The Registrar shall also inform applicants on the right to file a new application in case the one filed is rejected.

1061 Reg. 107 (4) Registry Regulations. However, information via the phone may only be obtained under particular circumstances.

1062 Reg. 60 Trust Fund Regulations.

1063 Reg. 61 Trust Fund Regulations. Pursuant to Reg. 60 Trust Fund Regulations, these options are to be approved by the Board of Directors.

dard and burden of proof, respectively documentation of claims.[1064] There is a general tendency, that requirements for moral damages and fixed amounts of reparations are lower than for economic and actual damages. Further factors that influence the rules on claims are the kinds of violations for which reparations are sought, and whether harm was inflicted as a part of a systematic pattern leading to mass victimization.

The Inter-American Court of Human Rights has repeatedly held that its proceedings are not subject to the same formalities as a domestic court and that in applying rules of evidence, particular attention shall be paid to the circumstances of each case, respect for legal certainty and the equality of the parties.[1065]

Generally, both the European and the Inter-American Human Rights Court tend to apply a higher standard of proof for economic damages than for moral damages.[1066] It has become a practice of the Inter-American Court to presume different types of damages.[1067] In particular, it has applied the presumption that moral damage is a necessary consequence of grave human rights violations.[1068] It has argued that even in the

1064 Most international documents on victims and reparations, e.g. the 2005 Victims Principles, the 1985 Victims Declaration and the ILC Draft Articles do not address issues related to evidence.

1065 See *Velásquez Rodríguez v. Honduras*, Compensatory Damages, Inter-American Court of Human Rights, 21 July 1989, Ser. C, No.7, para. 127; generally on the Inter-American Court and issues of proof and causation D. Shelton: Remedies in International Human Rights Law. 2nd ed. Oxford, 2005, pp. 249 et seq.

1066 Among the first rulings were the Inter-American Court of Human Rights applied legal presumptions for existence of moral damage, as the responsible state did not disprove them, are *Aloeboetoe et al. v. Suriname*, Reparations, Inter-American Court of Human Rights, 10 September 1993, Ser. C, No. 15 and *Godínez Cruz v. Honduras*, Compensatory Damages, Inter-American Court of Human Rights, 21 July 1989, Ser. C, No. 5. Before the European Court of Human Rights, a failure to back up claims for pecuniary damages with reliable documentary evidence may lead to no award, or a reduced award, see, e.g. *Bilgin v. Turkey*, European Court of Human Rights, 16 November 2000, Application No. 23819/94, para. 140. In order for costs and expenses, constituting forms of pecuniary damages, to be compensated before the European Court, detailed documentation has to be filed with the Court. However, where applicants are unable to provide evidence due to circumstances beyond their control, the Court may take this into account when deciding any claim for non-pecuniary damages, see, e.g. *Hasan and Chaush v. Bulgaria*, European Court of Human Rights, 26 October 2000, Application No.30985/96, para. 118. See for further analysis of the jurisprudence of the European Court of Human Rights e.g. P. Leach: Taking a Case to the European Court of Human Rights. 2nd ed. Oxford, 2005, pp. 400, 407 et seq.

1067 For a detailed list see D. Shelton: Remedies in International Human Rights Law. 2nd ed. Oxford, 2005, p. 251.

1068 E.g. *Loayza Tamayo v. Peru*, Reparations, Inter-American Court of Human Rights, 27 November 1998, Ser. C, No. 42; *Aloeboetoe et al. v. Suriname*, Reparations, Inter-American Court of Human Rights, 10 September 1993, Ser. C, No. 15, para. 54; *Suárez Rosero Case*, Reparations, Inter-American Court of Human Rights, 20 January 1999, Ser. C, No. 44, also specifying that grave cases may include killings, forced disappearances, incommunicado detention and torture, among others, paras. 63, 65, 67; for legal presumptions

absence of evidence demonstrating moral harm, "it is clear that the victims suffered moral damages, for it is the characteristic of human nature that anybody subjected to the aggression and abuse described [...] will experience moral suffering."[1069] This is not only presumed for the direct victims of the violation, but also for their parents, spouse or permanent companion and children.[1070] Therefore, once responsibility is established or admitted, no evidence of moral suffering is required from the victims of that act.[1071] The burden of proof is on the responsible party to show that the injury for which the victims claim to be compensated does not exist.[1072] In case of loss of life, this presumption is restricted to actual and moral damages successors are presumed to have suffered.[1073]

In domestic legal systems, the requirements of proof regarding reparations ordered against a convicted person are usually lower than for a criminal conviction.[1074] However, the general starting point in tort law, at least in most traditionally civil law systems, seems to be that strict proof is required of the existence and extent of

regarding the existence of moral damage, before the European Court of Human Rights, see e.g. *Mori v. Italy*, European Court of Human Rights, 19 February 1991, Application No. 13552/88, para. 20; *Wiesinger v. Austria*, European Court of Human Rights, 30 October 1991, Application No. 11796/85.

1069 *Aloeboetoe et al. v. Suriname*, Reparations, Inter-American Court of Human Rights, 10 September 1993, Ser. C, No. 15, para. 52; for a critical assessment on the application of presumptions V. Madrigal-Borloz: "Damage and Redress in the Jurisprudence of the Inter-American Court of Human Rights (1979-2001)". In: Reparations – Redressing Past Wrongs. Eds. G. Ulrich; L. Krabbe Boserup. (Human Rights in Development – Yearbook 2001). The Hague, 2003, pp. 211 et seq. at pp. 232-233.

1070 See for summaries of relevant jurisprudence D. Shelton: Remedies in International Human Rights Law. 2nd ed. Oxford, 2005, p. 251.

1071 See e.g. *Aloeboetoe et al. v. Suriname*, Reparations, Inter-American Court of Human Rights, 10 September 1993, Ser. C, No. 15, paras. 91-93; *Castillo Páez Case*, Reparations, Inter-American Court of Human Rights, 27 November 1998, Ser. C, No. 43, paras. 86, 87-90.

1072 *Aloeboetoe et al. v. Suriname*, Reparations, Inter-American Court of Human Rights, 10 September 1993, Ser. C, No. 15, para. 54.

1073 While claimants who are not successors must provide specific proof of their damage, ibid., para. 75. Similarly, claimants must plead and prove expenses connected with the human rights violations in order for them to be compensable. *Velásquez Rodríguez v. Honduras*, Reparations, Inter-American Court of Human Rights, 21 July 1989, Ser. C, No. 7, para. 42. However, in some cases the Court has awarded compensation for expenses even though the families of the victims failed to present any proof of expenses, see *El Amparo v. Venezuela*, Reparations, Inter-American Court of Human Rights, 14 September 1996, Ser. C, No. 28, para. 21; *"Street Children" Case*, Reparations, Inter-American Court of Human Rights, 26 May 2001, Ser. C, No. 77, para. 107.

1074 Generally M. Heikkilä: International Criminal Tribunals and Victims of Crime. Turku, 2004, p. 182.

damage. Strict proof means that the judge verifies a fact so that no reasonable doubt remains although the degree of probability required varies.[1075]

However, in national jurisdictions there are a number of exceptions to and variations of this principle.[1076] As mentioned above, lower standards of proof are often required once the responsibility or guilt of the offender has been established. In particular, when compensation is claimed in criminal procedure, courts are allowed to estimate the extent and scope of harm when comprehensive evidence cannot be provided or can only be provided after disproportionately great efforts.[1077] Similarly, civil courts are allowed to estimate the amount of damage where it is certain that some damage occurred but where the precise amount is too difficult or too costly to prove.[1078]

While the burden of proof is regularly on the claimant, there are variations of this principle in a number of national jurisdictions when compensation is claimed

1075 While under English law probability of the kind "more likely than not" suffices, e.g. in German and Belgian law in general demand probability next to certainty, see U. Magnus: "Comparative Report on the Law of Damages". In: Unification of Tort Law – Damages. Ed. U. Magnus. The Hague (et al.), 2001, pp. 185 et seq. at p. 204 (referring to numerous jurisdictions). See also Ugandan law N. Nsereko: "Uganda". In: Wiedergutmachung im Kriminalrecht – Internationale Perspektiven – Reparation in Criminal Law – International Perspectives. Eds. A. Eser; S. Walther. Vol. 2. Freiburg i. Br., 1997, pp. 321 et seq. at p. 348. See also K. M. Clermont; E. Sherwin: "A Comparative View of Standards of Proof". In: American Journal of Comparative Law 50 (2002), pp. 243 et seq.

1076 U. Magnus: "Comparative Report on the Law of Damages". In: Unification of Tort Law – Damages. Ed. U. Magnus. The Hague (et al.), 2001, pp. 185 et seq. at p. 204.

1077 This is the case e.g. in Sweden, see J. Zila: "Schweden". In: Wiedergutmachung im Kriminalrecht – Internationale Perspektiven – Reparation in Criminal Law – International Perspectives. Eds. A. Eser, S. Walther. Vol. 1. Freiburg i. Br., 1996, pp. 231 et seq. at p. 283. However, the condition is that the scope of damage does not exceed a certain amount. The maximum amount for this provision was in 1996 about 18 000 sk, i.e. about € 2 800. For England see L. Zedner: "England". In: Wiedergutmachung im Kriminalrecht – Internationale Perspektiven – Reparation in Criminal Law – International Perspectives. Eds. A. Eser; S. Walther. Vol. 1. Freiburg i. Br., 1996, pp. 109 et seq. at p. 171; U. Magnus: "Comparative Report on the Law of Damages". In: Unification of Tort Law – Damages. Ed. U. Magnus. The Hague (et al.), 2001, pp. 185 et seq. at p. 204 points out that the lower standard is already reflected by the multiplier (standardization method) adopted in personal injury cases, referring in particular to the English legal system, furthermore stating at p. 193 with reference to several legal systems that actual and future damage (damnum emergens and lucrum cessans) are mainly distinguished for purposes of evidence: Since future losses are less certain, the standard of proof is usually reduced. For future loss, mere probability is sufficient.

1078 U. Magnus: "Comparative Report on the Law of Damages". In: Unification of Tort Law – Damages. Ed. U. Magnus. The Hague (et al.), 2001, pp. 185 et seq. at p. 204. In German civil procedure courts are allowed to estimate not only the damage, but also whether the damage resulted from the infringement of some right (§ 287 German Code of Civil Procedure (ZPO) whereas the fact and causation of the primary infringement normally requires full proof (§ 286 ZPO). In Dutch law, the damage must be "plausible".

in criminal proceedings. In some jurisdictions, it is the sole task of the police and organs of justice organs to assess the facts necessary while the victim is only obliged to cooperate; therefore the full investigative facilities of the state can be employed in the interest of the victim.[1079] In other jurisdictions, the burden of proof is on the victim but the police and prosecutor's office are obliged to help them in preparing and pursuing the claim.[1080]

While national systems are generally designed to repair harm deriving from individual violations, a number of specific mechanisms and procedures have been established both nationally and internationally to deal with reparations for mass victimization. A number of these mechanisms and procedures incorporate practical principles regarding proof and claims assessment that take into account the special circumstances of reparations claims arising out of mass crimes.[1081] Many victims of mass violations do not have access to evidence to support their claims, or do not have the necessary knowledge to present their claims properly. However, reviewing the pieces of evidence attached to the claim forms or engaging in efforts to obtain some kind of evidence is perhaps the most time-consuming aspect of claims processing.[1082] The distinctive feature of what has been termed "mass claims processing" is that large numbers of claims are involved and that the legal and factual issues the claims deal

1079 E.g. M. S. Groenhuijsen; D. van der Landen: "Niederlande". In: Wiedergutmachung im Kriminalrecht – Internationale Perspektiven – Reparation in Criminal Law – International Perspectives. Eds. A. Eser, S. Walther. Vol. 1. Freiburg i. Br., 1996, pp. 1 et seq. at p. 63: only when the victim willfully refuses cooperation it endangers its access to reparations; B. van Schaack: "In Defense of Civil Redress – The Domestic Enforcement of Human Rights Norms in the Context of the Proposed Hague Judgments Convention". In: Harvard International Law Journal 42.1 (2001), pp. 141 et seq. at p. 146 with particular reference to the French action civile.

1080 E.g. regarding Sweden, Spain and Finland J. Zila: "Schweden". In: Wiedergutmachung im Kriminalrecht – Internationale Perspektiven – Reparation in Criminal Law – International Perspectives. Eds. A. Eser, S. Walther. Vol. 1. Freiburg i. Br., 1996, pp. 231 et seq. at p. 283; yet the police and prosecutor's office are not obliged to assist the victim when its claim has no chance to succeed or is to cause great difficulties; K. Madlener: "Spanien". In: Wiedergutmachung im Kriminalrecht – Internationale Perspektiven – Reparation in Criminal Law – International Perspectives. Eds. A. Eser; S. Walther. Vol. 3. Freiburg i. Br., 2001, pp. 273 et seq. at p. 314; T. Lappi-Seppälä: "Finland". In: Wiedergutmachung im Kriminalrecht – Internationale Perspektiven – Reparation in Criminal Law – International Perspectives. Eds. A. Eser; S. Walter. Vol. 1. Freiburg i. Br., 1996, pp. 317 et seq. at p. 373.

1081 See for more detailed discussion e.g. H. Das: "The Concept of Mass Claims and the Specificity of Mass Claims Resolution". In: Redressing Injustices through Mass Claims Processes – Innovative Responses to Unique Challenges. Ed. The International Bureau of the Permanent Court of Arbitration. Oxford, 2006, pp. 5 et seq.

1082 C. Gibson: "Mass Claims Processing – Using Computers to Evaluate Arbitral Claims – The Experience of the United Nations Compensation Commission". In: Arbitration International – Journal of the London Court of International Arbitration 13 (1997), pp. 167 et seq. at p. 175 points out, generally, that applying a specific evidentiary standard in the context of mass claims is, for a number of reasons, difficult.

with are sufficiently similar.[1083] Several techniques employed seem relevant to the ICC reparations mechanism, as both are likely to be confronted with similar challenges which the mass claims procedure attempts to solve. This includes the need for efficiency and speed in dealing with large numbers of claims on the one hand, and for individualized justice on the other. Mass claims techniques attempt to process large numbers of claims in a manner that avoids individually proving and assessing claims, or allows for comparatively relaxed standards of proof. The techniques that have been applied are, among others, precedent-setting and common issue determination, computerized data matching, statistical sampling and regression analysis.[1084]

In the context of individual responsibility for grave and systematic human rights violations, US national courts have applied mass claims processing techniques, including claims sampling and relieved the victims of burden of proof on the victims by using expert testimony.[1085]

In the context of state responsibility, at the UNCC claimants were "responsible for submitting documents and other evidence which demonstrates satisfactorily that a particular claim or group of claims is eligible for compensation" and were thus not required to prove the facts relied upon.[1086] It was acknowledged that "considering the difficult circumstances of the invasion and occupation [...] many claimants cannot, and cannot be expected to, document all aspects of the claim [...]."[1087] The Court

1083 H. Das: "The Concept of Mass Claims and the Specificity of Mass Claims Resolution". In: Redressing Injustices through Mass Claims Processes – Innovative Responses to Unique Challenges. Ed. The International Bureau of the Permanent Court of Arbitration. Oxford, 2006, pp. 5 et seq. at pp. 6-7.

1084 H. M. Holtzmann: "Mass Claims Processes". In: American Review of International Arbitration 13 (2002), pp. 69 et seq. at pp. 73-74; F. E. McGovern: "The Intellectual Heritage of Claims Processing at the United Nations Compensation Commission". In: The United Nations Compensation Commission – Thirteenth Sokol Colloquium. Ed. R. Lillich. Irvington, 1995, pp. 187 et seq. at pp. 191-195.

1085 In particular for the sampling techniques applied in the Marcos case see above Chapter 5 D. IV. 1. ("Valuation and Calculation of Damages") and R. G. Steinhardt: "Fulfilling the Promise of Filártiga – Litigating Human Rights Claims against the Estate of Ferdinand Marcos". In: Yale Journal of International Law 20 (1995), pp. 65 et seq. at pp. 96 et seq.

1086 Art. 35 (1) UN Compensation Commission: Provisional Rules for Claims Procedure, adopted by the Governing Council on 26 June 1992, UN Doc. S/AC.26/1992/10; see for further discussion e.g. J. J. van Haersolte-van Hof: "Innovations to Speed Mass Claims – New Standards of Proof". In: Redressing Injustices through Mass Claims Processes – Innovative Responses to Unique Challenges. Ed. The International Bureau of the Permanent Court of Arbitration. Oxford, 2006, pp. 13 et seq. at p. 15. H. M. Holtzmann: "Mass Claims Processes". In: American Review of International Arbitration 13 (2002), pp. 69 et seq. at p. 72 points out that the phrase "demonstrate satisfactorily" was intended to establish a lesser standard of proof than the stricter requirement that "each party shall have the burden of proving the facts relied on to support his claim of defence", usually applicable in international (arbitral) tribunals Art. 24 UNCITRAL Rules.

1087 First Report by the category "D" panel of Commissioners, UN Doc.S/AC.26/1998/1 further elaborates that "[a]ccordingly, the level of proof [...] is close to what has been called "the balance of probability" as distinguished from the concept of "beyond reasonable

therefore applied the principle that the standard of proof depended on the category in which the claim was filed, and the scope of the claim, thus allowing for precedent-setting procedures.[1088] For claims for small and fixed amounts of compensation, lenient standards of proof were set and documentation of the actual amount of loss was not required.[1089] When compensation for actual losses was claimed, the rule was that, the higher the amount claimed, the higher were the requirements for proof.[1090]

It was up to the UNCC to match the individual claims received as far as possible against the information in its computerized database.[1091] It was provided that the

---

doubt" required in some jurisdictions to prove guilt in a criminal trial. Moreover, the test of "balance of probability" has to be applied having regard to the circumstances existing at the time of the invasion and loss".

1088 See also Rules 35, 37 UN Compensation Commission: Provisional Rules for Claims Procedure, adopted by the Governing Council on 26 June 1992, UN Doc. S/AC.26/1992/10. See also J. J. van Haersolte-van Hof: "Innovations to Speed Mass Claims – New Standards of Proof". In: Redressing Injustices through Mass Claims Processes – Innovative Responses to Unique Challenges. Ed. The International Bureau of the Permanent Court of Arbitration. Oxford, 2006, pp. 13 et seq. at p. 17. According to H. M. Holtzmann: "Mass Claims Processes". In: American Review of International Arbitration 13 (2002), pp. 69 et seq. at p. 72, "[t]he UNCC pioneered the concept that the standard of proof can be less demanding than the customary standard applied in traditional arbitration". For criticism towards this approach, see C. Gibson: "Mass Claims Processing – Using Computers to Evaluate Arbitral Claims – The Experience of the United Nations Compensation Commission". In: Arbitration International – Journal of the London Court of International Arbitration 13 (1997), pp. 167 et seq. at p. 175 questioning the fairness of the approach of different evidentiary requirements in relation to the amount of loss claimed.

1089 E.g. for small claims for departure of Iraq or Kuwait, serious injury or death, simple documentation is sufficient: for departure claims the date and the fact of departure, and in case of death, simple documentation of the death and family relationship (Art.35 (2)) One reason for this relaxed standard is the humanitarian nature of these claims, see M. Kazazi: Burden of Proof and Related Issues – A Study of Evidence before International Tribunals. The Hague (et al.), 1996, p. 221.

1090 For individual claims up to US $ 100 000 claimants should provide "appropriate evidence of the circumstances and amount of the claimed loss [...] Documents and other evidence required will be the reasonable minimum that is appropriate under the particular circumstances of the case". A lesser degree of documentary evidence ordinarily was set to be sufficient for smaller claims, such as those below US $ 20 000, see Art. 35 (2). Regarding even larger claims of individuals, claims of corporations, governments or international organizations it was required that they are "supported by documentary and other appropriate evidence sufficient to demonstrate the circumstances and amount of the claimed loss", Art. 35 (3). The interpretation by the panels is limited by the restriction that they cannot apply higher standards of proof than those spread out in the Rules, M. Kazazi: Burden of Proof and Related Issues – A Study of Evidence before International Tribunals. The Hague (et al.), 1996, pp. 222 et seq. citing further authorities.

1091 Art. 37 (2) UN Compensation Commission: Provisional Rules for Claims Procedure, adopted by the Governing Council on 26 June 1992, UN Doc. S/AC.26/1992/10 provides that the Commission shall "proceed to check individual claims by matching them, as far as possible, against the information of a computerized database. The results may be

claims that could not be verified in this way may be checked by applying sampling techniques.[1092] Thus, claims were determined with reference to a range of evidence and information submitted by claimants, rather than by taking into account only the information provided by the individual claimant.[1093] In contrast, personal injury and death claims were largely resolved in a claim-by-claim review.[1094] In personal injury claims, a claim-by-claim review was necessary as the requirement of a causal relation to the invasion had to be closely evaluated. However, claims filed for compensation for mental pain and anguish were resolved using the sampling method.[1095]

---

cross-checked by the Panel". The approximately one million "departure claims" (category A claims) that had been filed were verified to a large extent by means of the computerized matching of data: Data provided on the claimants' claim forms was matched against a vast volume of information and records gathered by the Secretariat on departures from Iraq or Kuwait, e.g. lists of residents in Kuwait and Iraq as of 2 August 1990, flight manifests, border post records, list of evacuees by international organizations etc., see M. Kazazi: Burden of Proof and Related Issues – A Study of Evidence before International Tribunals. The Hague (et al.), 1996, p. 223 referring to UN Doc. S/AC.26/1994/2, section IV, p. 39-42.

1092 Art. 37 (2) provides that "individuals' claims [may be checked] on the basis of sampling with further verification only as the circumstances warrant". The claims that could not be "matched" were reviewed using sampling techniques with the assistance of statistician, see M. Kazazi: Burden of Proof and Related Issues – A Study of Evidence before International Tribunals. The Hague (et al.), 1996, p. 223 referring to UN Doc. S/AC.26/1995/4, paras. 45-88. Thus, over 420 000 claims for losses up to US $ 100 000 were verified using mainly sampling and various averaging techniques, providing recommended award amounts conditioned by the information provided by (i) all of the claimants who filed claims in a particular sub-category; (ii) all of the claimants with the same nationality as the claimant and (iii) the characteristics of the claimants (e.g. age, profession, sex etc.).

1093 M. Kazazi: Burden of Proof and Related Issues – A Study of Evidence before International Tribunals. The Hague (et al.), 1996, p. 223 referring to UN Doc. S/AC.26/1994/3; 1996/1; 1996/2; 1996/4; 1999/11.

1094 C. Gibson: "Mass Claims Processing – Using Computers to Evaluate Arbitral Claims – The Experience of the United Nations Compensation Commission". In: Arbitration International – Journal of the London Court of International Arbitration 13 (1997), pp. 167 et seq. at p. 176.

1095 Category C claims. Under Decision 8 of the UNCC's Governing Council [S/AC.26/1992/8; 27 January 1992], lump-sum amounts were fixed for losses from suffering mental pain and anguish for being forced to hide of having been held hostage: for persons having been hostages, or illegally detained US $ 1500 per claimant for at least 3 days, plus $ 100 for each day detained beyond this, up to a cap of US $ 5000. The computers could thus determine an individual sum for each claimant. The basic objective was to determine how many claimants, on the basis of the sample claims reviewed, met the criteria that had been adopted for this specific kind of damages. One the commission had evaluated the sampling results and decided to award compensation, the computer was used to identify the claims matching the samples' characteristics. The computer was programmed to calculate compensation by multiplying the number of days an individual was forced to hide or held as a hostage or both by a specific formula adopted by the Governing Council.

Relaxed standards of proof and legal presumptions regarding both harm and its causation were also applied by a number of other reparations mechanisms for victims of grave and systematic crimes.[1096]

For example, in implementing the German compensation scheme for victims of Nazi crimes, legal assumptions were introduced that acknowledged that certain groups of persons had suffered collective persecution that had typically resulted in certain types of harm. This thereby removed the requirement of proof of individual victimization.[1097] The Second Claims Resolution Tribunal for Dormant Accounts in

1096 See e.g. German Federal Compensation Law of 1953 for Nazi victims, International Organization for migration claims programs; the International Commission on Holocaust Era Insurance claims, Claims Resolution Tribunals for Dormant Accounts in Switzerland, for more details see J. J. van Haersolte-van Hof: "Innovations to Speed Mass Claims – New Standards of Proof". In: Redressing Injustices through Mass Claims Processes – Innovative Responses to Unique Challenges. Ed. The International Bureau of the Permanent Court of Arbitration. Oxford, 2006, pp. 13 et seq. at p. 15.

1097 In implementing the German Federal Compensation Law of 1953, in principle the competent authorities were obliged to investigate victims' applications ex officio, §§ 179, 209 BEG while applicants were required to cooperate and to substantiate their claim, as far as necessary and reasonable, see BGH RzW 1972, 31, 32; H. G. Menzel: "Zum Substantiierungs- und Wahrheitsgebot bei der Geltendmachung von Verfolgungsleiden". In: Koblenzer Handbuch des Entschädigungsrechts. Eds. K. P. Kisker; H. H. Bischof. Baden-Baden, 1996, pp. 69 et seq. at p. 70; BGH Rzw 1975, 276, 277; RzW 1976, 153; RzW 1981, 126. After practice had shown that the establishment of the causal link between the Nazi criminal measures and the harm was very difficult, legal presumptions in favor of the applicant were introduced. §§ 15 (2) (harm to life); 28 (2), 31 (2) (harm to body and health), 51 (4) (harm to property) 56 (4) (harm to assets); 63 (harm through payment of fines, additional taxes); 64 (2) (harm in professional and economic development); another legal assumption that dealt with requirements other than causality was § 47 (2) (harm to freedom). Yet, the legal assumptions could only substitute the proof of causality between criminal act and the harm; they neither substituted the proof that harm had occurred nor that a Nazi criminal measure was directed against the claimant. Concerning loss of life (§ 15 (2) BEG), there was a legal assumption that, when the death occurred during deportation or deprivation of freedom pursuant to the BEG or within 8 months after the deportation or deprivation of life has ended, the death was caused by the Nazi crimes. Also, regarding harm to body and health, when the applicant got ill during or within 8 months after the deportation or deprivation of freedom, it was assumed that the harm to body and health or life was caused by the Nazi persecution, § 28 (2) BEG read in conjunction with § 15 (2) BEG; furthermore, for a claimant who had been in a concentration camp for at least one year and his earning capacity decreased by at least 25 %, it was assumed to his or her benefit that the 25 % reduction of earning capacity is caused by the crime of persecution, § 31 (2) BEG. This presumption was confutable. Regarding proof of harm to professional and economic development, it was not required to prove that the harm had been caused by an individual measure. For this category of harm in cases the person was a member of a group that had been collectively persecuted, the person had only to prove his membership and the harm suffered. Then it was assumed, that a nazi criminal measure had been directed against the applicant and this had caused the harm, H. G. van Dam; H. Loos: Das Bundesentschädigungsgesetz – Kommentar. Berlin, 1967, pp. 88-89,

Switzerland work with a large number of fairly specific presumptions, which apply in the absence of evidence to the contrary.[1098] Recently, most existing international claims programs following mass atrocity use mass claims processing tools such as information technology, which allows for an entirely different approach to claims verification than individual assessment.[1099] It may be assessed that *ex officio* or *proprio motu* verification of claims has become a standard feature of international mass claims processing.[1100]

As the experience of the National Compensation Tribunal (NCT) in Malawi demonstrates, whether applicants will be required to prove their claims depends not only on the relevant legislation, but also on whether sufficient resources are available to the decision-making authority. While the NCT had all powers of investigation necessary to establish the facts of any case before it, it rarely had the resources to actually conduct independent investigations.[1101]

III. Assessment

Both national and international courts and administrative bodies have taken approaches to verification of claims that depart from the general principle that the burden of proof rests on the claimant and the standard of proof is proof beyond reasonable doubt. It has been acknowledged that under certain circumstances it is inappropriate to put such burdens on victims of crime. In particular, when dealing with the consequences of mass crimes, techniques that avoid individual claims assessment have been applied and considered more efficient.

---

§2. Despite the relaxed requirements for proof and the introduction of legal assumptions, it was often difficult for applicants to substantiate their claims. However, this was also linked to the difficult eligibility criteria and not (only) high requirements for proof. Thus, in principle, in the course of history of reparations to Nazi victims, requirements for burden and standard of proof were constantly lowered. The lowering of requirements went together with the simplification of eligibility criteria and uniformization of awards.

1098 E.g. Art. 28 CRT-II Rules; see for further discussion J. J. van Haersolte-van Hof: "Innovations to Speed Mass Claims – New Standards of Proof". In: Redressing Injustices through Mass Claims Processes – Innovative Responses to Unique Challenges. Ed. The International Bureau of the Permanent Court of Arbitration. Oxford, 2006, pp. 13 et seq. at p. 19. Also the Property Claims Commission of the German Foundation "Remembrance, Responsibility, Future" applied a relaxed standard of proof in assessing claims.

1099 V. Heiskanen: "Virtue Out of Necessity – International Mass Claims and New Uses of Information Technology". In: Redressing Injustices through Mass Claims Processes – Innovative Responses to Unique Challenges. Ed. The International Bureau of the Permanent Court of Arbitration. Oxford, 2006, pp. 25 et seq. at p. 26, pointing out that the methods used are borrowed from US class action suits.

1100 M. Henzelin; V. Heiskanen; G. Mettraux: "Reparations to Victims before the International Criminal Court – Lessons from International Mass Claims Processes". In: Criminal Law Forum 17 (2006), pp. 317 et seq. at p. 329.

1101 D. Cammack: "Reparations in Malawi". In: The Handbook of Reparations. Ed. P. de Greiff. Oxford, 2006, pp. 215 et seq. at pp. 232, 252.

In international and national practice, requirements for the standard and burden of proof have varied according to the kind of damage that the applicant seeks to have redressed. It is also widespreadly practiced to apply comparatively lower requirements for moral (impecuniary) damages and fixed awards than for economic and individually assessed damages.

The appropriateness of transferring these practices to the ICC may be questionable, as the ICC is a court and not an administrative mechanism and deals with individual and not state responsibility.

In the context of individual responsibility, basing reparation awards on presumptions or otherwise lowering legal requirements could violate the rights of the convicted person with regard to a reparation order, as specifically safeguarded in Rule 97 (3). The ICC decides on the fate of an individual, which differs qualitatively from entities such as a state or international organization that may also order measures that are of a humanitarian or social welfare character. At the same time, is seems appropriate that the particularly difficult situation of victims of genocide, war crimes and crimes against humanity is taken into account when determining whether the harm is attributable to a convicted person.

When the proceedings enter the reparations phase, the criminal responsibility of the individual has already been established. Thus, the principle of presumption of innocence, safeguarded in Art. 66 (1) ICC Statute, and other obligations to safeguard the rights of an accused are no longer relevant. Courts in national legal systems also apply lower standards of proof or estimate harm once the liability of a person has been established, in particular when compensation is awarded for moral damages. The approaches of US Courts demonstrate that sampling and other mass claims processing techniques that ease the burden on applicants and make claims assessment more efficient can be applied in the context of individual responsibility.

It therefore appears that it would be in line with international and national practice for the Court and Trust Fund to apply a standard of proof lower than "beyond reasonable doubt", once the person has been convicted.

Thus, once the perpetrator has been convicted and it has been established that the applicant is a victim of the crime for which the person was convicted, a relaxed standard of proof can be applied by the Court and Trust Fund regarding reparations. It can be assumed that he or she suffered moral damages (e.g. pain and suffering) without requiring further proof of harm and its causal link to the crime. In line with national and international practice, this rule would not apply to economic losses. Furthermore, it seems that the larger and more individualized claims are, the higher the standard of proof that should apply, while standardized claims of a modest scope require a lower standard of proof. As collective and symbolic awards do regularly not address a actual damage occurred to a certain person, questions regarding standard and burden of proof of the harm sought to be compensated are not as relevant compared with individual material awards.

The Court is obliged to find solutions that both respect the rights of the victims and those of the convicted person.[1102] In cases that this seems difficult to achieve be-

1102 As emphasized in Rule 97 (3).

fore the Court, the competent chamber could delegate the implementation of awards or order the convicted person to make collective (monetary) reparations and thus avoid having to deal with individual claims.[1103]

There are international and national precedents for shifting the burden of proof to the wrongdoer, or making it for the prosecutor or court to establish a compensation claim or assist the victim in so doing. When the Court initiates reparations proceedings on behalf of victims (Art. 75 (1) s. 2, Rule 95) in certain cases it might be appropriate for the Court to also engage in efforts to establish their eligibility for reparations.

While the Rules do not make it a condition for applicants to document their claims, regularly each individual applicant will regularly have to demonstrate the facts and to establish his or her claim, in particular that the convicted person caused his or her harm through the conduct that forms the factual basis upon which conviction was entered.[1104] However, the often difficult situation of victims of crimes under the ICC's jurisdiction to prove their claims might be balanced by the obligations of the Court's Registry,[1105] Court-appointed experts[1106] or, in case of indirect awards, the Trust Fund, to actively assist applicants in establishing their claims.[1107] Compared to those national jurisdictions where the prosecutor is directly obliged to support that victims in claiming reparations, the support victims might receive from the ICC seems modest. However, if the ICC Registry, Trust Fund and experts are competent and well equipped with resources, they might be in the position to provide active and efficient support to victims.

Thus, we may conclude that the requirements for the standard and burden of proof applicable to the ICC reparations mechanism may vary according to the stage of proceedings at which evidential material is introduced and the way in which the reparations proceedings are triggered. They might differ with regard to the establishment of victim status and the harm suffered, between monetary and symbolic awards and individual or collective awards and according to the type of harm to be compensated. However, while flexibility is important, so is consistency, in particular when there are large numbers of individual claims for monetary reparations.

In fact, while the Court might deal with individual cases of claims verification, it seems that mass claims processing techniques would not be practiced by the Court itself. More appropriate organs for this task might be the Trust Fund, which is com-

1103 See Rule 98 (2), (3), (4). It might then be for the organization or institution that benefited from the award to decide to distribute it to individuals whose eligibility is based on legal assumptions or otherwise relaxed standard of proof.

1104 See M. Henzelin; V. Heiskanen; G. Mettraux: "Reparations to Victims before the International Criminal Court – Lessons from International Mass Claims Processes". In: Criminal Law Forum 17 (2006), pp. 317 et seq. at p. 328.

1105 Reg. 88 (2) Court Regulations, in particular the Victims Participation and Reparations Section (Reg. 86 (9) Court Regulations). For example, liaison offices established by the Court ay assist claimants in filling out application forms and collecting evidence.

1106 Rule 97 (2).

1107 See Reg. 61 (a) and (b), Reg. 66-68 Trust Fund Regulations.

petent to apply these techniques to verify claims pursuant to its Regulations, as well as national and intergovernmental organizations or appointed experts.[1108]

D. Reparations and Penalties (77 (2), 78 (1) ICC Statute)

The reparations mechanism of the ICC is connected to its penalty system.

The penalties the Court may impose on a person it convicted are life imprisonment, imprisonment for a specified number of years, and, in addition to imprisonment, fines and forfeiture of proceeds, property and assets deriving from the crime (Art. 77).[1109] In accordance with the principle of *nulla poena sine lege*, the list of applicable penalties is exhaustive.[1110] The possibility of ordering reparations is located in

1108 See Rule 98 (4). Reg. 61 Trust Fund Regulations set forth to use relevant demographic/statistical data about the group of victims, as well as matching or standardization techniques. For a possible role of experts, see Reg. 61 (a) Trust Fund Regulations.

1109 The order is listed among the "applicable penalties" listed in Art. 77 (2). However, questions remain at to whether a forfeiture order qualifies as a penalty, see J. Peglau: "Penalties and the Determination of the Sentence in the Rules of Procedure and Evidence". In: International and National Prosecution of Crimes under International Law. Ed. H. Fischer; C. Kreß; S. R. Lüder. (Bochumer Schriften zur Friedenssicherung und zum Humanitären Völkerrecht). Berlin, 2001, pp. 141 et seq. at p. 149 mainly referring to a number of European jurisdictions, where forfeiture orders are rather a "measure" than a penalty (e.g. § 11 para. 2 No. 8 German Criminal Code; Art. 20 Austrian Penal Code; Art. 127, 128 Spanish Codigo Penal). In the drafting process of the Statute opinions were divided as to whether forfeiture should be included as a penalty, rather than a mechanism to be used by the court to execute an order for reparations, see W. A. Schabas: "Penalties". In: The Rome Statute of the International Criminal Court – A Commentary. Ed. A. Cassese; P. Gaeta; J. R. W. D. Jones. Vol. 2. Oxford, 2002, pp. 1497 et seq. at p. 1516; C. Kreß; G. Sluiter: "Fines and Forfeiture Orders". In: The Rome Statute of the International Criminal Court – A Commentary. Eds. A. Cassese; P. Gaeta; J. R. W. D. Jones. Vol. 2. Oxford, 2002, pp. 1823 et seq. at p. 1826, also referring to fines. Eventually it was agreed that forfeiture should be included in the Statute as an additional and optional penalty, see R. E. Fife: "Article 77 – Applicable Penalties". In: Commentary on the Rome Statute of the International Criminal Court – Observers' Notes, Article by Article. Ed. O. Triffterer. Baden-Baden, 1999, pp. 985 et seq. at p. 993.

1110 Reflected in Art. 23. Other penalties proposed during the drafting of the Statute included the loss or suspension of rights, disqualification and disfranchisement, i.e. loss of the right to vote or to seek public office. However, it was eventually decided that this should be left for national law and courts to deal with, see R. E. Fife: "Penalties". In: The International Criminal Court – The Making of the Rome Statute – Issues, Negotiations, Results. Ed. R. S. Lee. The Hague, 1999, pp. 319 et seq. at p. 330 referring to Art. 75 c) (i) of the Prep Com Draft Statute. For the discussion of criminal responsibility for legal persons and possibly applicable penalties see Chapter 4 A. IV. ("Who can the Reparations Principles be addressed to?").

Chapter 6 of the Statute, which is titled "The Trial" and which does not deal with penalties.[1111] Therefore, reparations are not categorized as a penalty in the ICC Statute.

This subchapter analyses the two-fold interrelation between penalties and reparations before the ICC. First, making reparations and the impact of the offender's behavior on victims are circumstances which are generally relevant to the determination and reduction of the sentence (Art. 78 (1) and Art. 110).[1112] Second, money and property collected through the penalties of fines and forfeiture orders may be used for the same purposes as reparations (Art. 77 (2) and 79 (2)).[1113] Furthermore, there are procedural links. The enforcement regime for reparations, as well as relevant protective measures, is to a large extent parallel to that of fines and forfeiture orders (Art. 75 (4) and Art. 93, Art. 75 (5) and Art. 109).[1114] Due to their interdependence in the ICC system, reparations and penalties may be discussed in the same hearing.[1115]

While criminal sanctions and reparation of the harm caused by a crime are traditionally linked in the context of national mechanisms, their interrelation is without precedent in the international context.[1116]

1111 On the legal nature of ICC reparations, see also Chapter 3 ("Purpose of Reparations"). The practical relevance of the legal nature of the orders for the enforcement by state Parties has been emphasized, see B. Timm: "The Legal Position of Victims in the Rule of Procedure and Evidence". In: International and National Prosecution of Crimes under International Law. Eds. H. Fischer, C. Kreß; S. R. Lüder. (Bochumer Schriften zur Friedenssicherung und zum Humanitären Völkerrecht). Berlin, 2001, pp. 289 et seq. at pp. 306 et seq. However, states are competent to decide through which procedure under their national laws they will enforce orders. See also R. E. Fife: "Penalties". In: The International Criminal Court – The Making of the Rome Statute – Issues, Negotiations, Results. Ed. R. S. Lee. The Hague, 1999, pp. 319 et seq. at p. 340 who remarks that Art. 80 ICC Statute clarifies that the penalties system of the Statute only applies to the ICC and does not effect national criminal justice systems, noting that this is also relevant to the inclusion of forfeiture in the Statute as a penalty rather than a civil remedy.

1112 See also Rule 145 (determination of sentence), Rules 223, 224 (review of sentence).

1113 See also Rules 146-148; Rule 221.

1114 See also Rules 217-222; Reg. 116, 117 Court Regulations; for more details regarding the enforcement of reparation orders see Chapter 6 G. ("Protective Measures and Enforcement") for details regarding reparation orders.

1115 Art. 76 (2), (3), Rule 143.

1116 The interrelation of fines and forfeiture and reparations before the ICC goes back to the ILC Draft Statute of 1993. Art. 47 provided for the possibility to transfer fines to be paid by the convict to the state of nationality of the victim of the crime or to a trust fund established by the Security Council – the "traditional" concept of reparations in international law was drawn upon where victims are not provided with possibility to be awarded reparations directly and cannot claim individually. However, under this proposal, victims were to benefit from the fines ordered, even though indirectly, D. Donat-Cattin: "Article 75 – Reparations to Victims". In: Commentary on the Rome Statute of the International Criminal Court – Observers' Notes, Article by Article. Ed. O. Triffterer. Baden-Baden, 1999, pp. 965 et seq. at p. 967; the Nuremberg Charter contained an extremely wide discretion for applicable penalties, and thus the Tribunal could have ordered fines. See also F. Terrier: "The Procedure before the Trial Chamber". In: The Rome Statute of the

I. Reparations and the Determination of Sentence

1. Impact of the Offender's Behavior towards Victims on the Sentence

The Statute itself does not provide elaborate criteria for the determination of sentences.[1117] In order to limit the apparently broad discretion given to the Court and to avoid violating the *nulla poena sine lege* principle, Rule 145 contains further specifications: next to general factors that are to be considered in determining the sentence, specific references are made to victims and reparations.[1118]

In the group of listed sentencing factors which characterize the commission of the crime without determining whether they are aggravating or mitigating, contained in Rule 145 (1), the Court has to "give consideration, *inter alia,* to the extent of the damage caused, in particular the harm caused to the victims and their families [...]."[1119]

One aggravating circumstance which the Court must take into account, among others listed in Rule 145 (2) (b), includes the manner in which the offender committed the crime, namely the commission "where the victim is particularly defenceless" and

---

International Criminal Court – A Commentary. Eds. A. Cassese; P. Gaeta; J. R. W. D. Jones. Vol. 2. Oxford, 2002, pp. 1277 et seq. at p. 1317: "In the system of the ICC, through manifest borrowings from the procedural system in the Latin tradition, civil reparations are associated with the penal sanction."

1117 Rule 78 (1) states: "In determining the sentence, the Court shall, in accordance with the Rules of Procedure and Evidence, take into account such factors as the gravity of the crime and the individual circumstances of the convicted person". See for further examination e.g. W. A. Schabas: "The Penalty Provisions of the ICC Statute". In: International Crimes, Peace and Human Rights – The Role of the International Criminal Court. Ed. D. Shelton. Ardsley, New York, 2000, pp. 105 et seq.; J. C. Nemitz: Strafzumessung im Völkerstrafrecht – Ein Beitrag zur Strafzwecklehre und zur Strafzumessungsmethode unter Besonderer Berücksichtigung des Römischen Statuts. Freiburg i. Br., 2002, p. 24; W. A. Schabas: "Penalties". In: The Rome Statute of the International Criminal Court – A Commentary. Ed. A. Cassese; P. Gaeta; J. R. W. D. Jones. Vol. 2. Oxford, 2002, pp. 1497 et seq.; R. E. Fife: "Penalties". In: The International Criminal Court – Elements of Crimes and Rules of Procedure and Evidence. Ed. R. S. Lee. Ardsley, New York, 2001, pp. 555 et seq.

1118 Relevant factors to be applied when determining the sentence pursuant to Art. 78 (1) are listed in Rule 145. Rule 145 (1) (a) embodies the principle of culpability; the degree of culpability sets the upper limit for the penalty even if specific sentencing purposes could suggest a different penalty, see J. Peglau: "Penalties and the Determination of the Sentence in the Rules of Procedure and Evidence". In: International and National Prosecution of Crimes under International Law. Ed. H. Fischer; C. Kreß; S. R. Lüder. (Bochumer Schriften zur Friedenssicherung und zum Humanitären Völkerrecht). Berlin, 2001, pp. 141 et seq. at p. 147 pointing out that here the principle was acknowledged that "sanction must fit the crime's perpetrator and not merely the crime itself", with reference to the jurisprudence of the ICTY.

1119 Rule 145 (1) (c). Other factors listed in Rule 145 are the nature of the unlawful behavior and the means employed to execute the crime; the degree of participation of the convicted person; the degree of intent; the circumstances of manner, time and location; and the age, education, social and economic condition of the convicted person.

where the crime was committed "with particular cruelty", when it deems appropriate to do so.[1120] An additional aggravating factor is the scope of the crime's consequences, namely "where there were multiple victims".[1121]

Of particular relevance in the context of reparations are the aforementioned mitigating factors, contained in Rule 145 (2) (a). Pursuant to this provision, the convicted person's conduct after the commission of the crime, "including efforts to compensate the victims and any cooperation with the Court", shall be taken into account as a mitigating circumstance when determining the sentence, where the Court considers it appropriate.

The convicted person's conduct must have taken place between the commission of the crime and before the conviction in order to be relevant for the determination of sentence. Thus, compensating victims pursuant to Rule 145 (a) (ii), does not include payments made as a consequence of Court's reparation order, which are only made after conviction. However, reparations made by the accused in the course of the trial proceedings, even when made at a late stage of the trial and he or she might already expect the conviction, shall be taken into account.

"[E]fforts to compensate the victims" might include voluntary direct payments by the offender to the victims of his or her crime, or payments from which victims benefit indirectly, e.g. to the ICC's Trust Fund or other institutions engaged in activities beneficial to victims.

The wording "compensate the victims" seems to refer to monetary forms of reparations only.[1122] "Cooperation with the Court" might include providing the Court with information which enables the enforcement of Court orders such as arrest warrants. It could also be informing the Court of the location of assets of other accused persons enabling the imposition of protective measures to enforce reparations, fines or forfeiture orders at a later point.[1123] However, the list of acts that have a mitigating effect is open, as the non-exhaustive list in Rule 145 (2) (a) (ii) clarifies ("including"). Thus, in determining the sentence the Court has discretion to reward the convicted person for other efforts to repair the harm caused by the crime. These might include genuine non-monetary efforts to contribute to reparation and reconciliation which go beyond "compensation" in the narrow sense.

While the Court is to take the aforementioned factors into account when considering the sentence, Rule 145 (2) makes clear that it is only to mitigate the sentence

1120 Rule 145 (2) (b) (iii), (iv).

1121 Rule 145 (2) (b) (iv). In the ICTY and ICTR sentencing practice, aggravating circumstances included terrorizing the victims and the number of victims. See *Prosecutor v. Tadić*, Judgment in Sentencing Appeals, International Tribunal for the Former Yugoslavia, Appeals Chamber, 26 January 2000, Case No. IT-94-1-AS, paras. 16, 20, 32, 44, 47, 55, 56, 59.

1122 See Chapter 5 C. II. 2. ("Compensation").

1123 See Rule 101 (B) (iii) ICTY Rules contains that mitigating circumstances include "the substantial cooperation with the Prosecutor by the convicted person before or after conviction"; see e.g. *The Prosecutor v. Erdemović*, Sentencing Judgement, Trial Chamber I, 29 November 1996, Case No. IT 96-22-T, para. 16.

if it finds it "appropriate" to do so. In order to determine when it is appropriate to mitigate the sentence, one should be aware that mitigation of sentence as a reward for the offender's behavior after the commission of the crime is a sensitive and often controversial issue. Generally, it is in line with international guidelines and national and international practice that a criminal court has the power to "encourage the offender to provide reparation to victims by rewarding him or her through mitigation of sentence."[1124]

However, there are two key concerns in this regard. First, it might often be impossible to know whether reparative action by the defendant represents genuine remorse and desire to make good a wrong, or simply a calculating tactic to secure leniency in court. Paying compensation might seem to permit defendants to "buy off victims or to buy their way out of jail".[1125] Second, there is a concern that it privileges a rich offender over a poor offender and thus potentially contravenes the principle of equality before the law.[1126]

With regard to the first concern, it has been suggested that it is appropriate to consider (financial) reparation as mitigation only if it is effected before a defendant is indicted or even under investigation.[1127] However, it is in line with international guidelines and many national jurisdictions that serious efforts to repair or compensate the harm caused to the victims of crime can qualify as mitigating circumstances for sentencing purposes even if they take place at a later stage.

1124 Art. 9 (2) 2001 EU Framework Decision. However, Art. 10 states that member states shall promote mediation in criminal cases for "offences which it considers appropriate for this sort of measure".

1125 See e.g. S. Glickman: "Victims' Justice – Legitimizing the Sentencing Regime of the International Criminal Court". In: Columbia Journal of Transnational Law 43 (2005), pp. 229 et seq. at p. 262; L. Zedner: "England". In: Wiedergutmachung im Kriminalrecht – Internationale Perspektiven – Reparation in Criminal Law – International Perspectives. Eds. A. Eser; S. Walther. Vol. 1. Freiburg i. Br., 1996, pp. 109 et seq. at. p. 169; D. Frehsee: "Wiedergutmachung und Täter-Opfer-Ausgleich im Deutschen Strafrecht – Entwicklung, Möglichkeiten und Probleme". In: Die Stellung des Opfers im Strafrechtssystem – Neue Entwicklungen in Deutschland und in den USA. Eds. B. Schünemann; M. D. Dubber. Köln, 2000, pp. 117 et seq. at p. 132 expresses doubts that the offender engages voluntarily, as he or she is under constant force of the criminal justice system.

1126 E.g. D. Frehsee: "Wiedergutmachung und Täter-Opfer-Ausgleich im Deutschen Strafrecht – Entwicklung, Möglichkeiten und Probleme". In: Die Stellung des Opfers im Strafrechtssystem – Neue Entwicklungen in Deutschland und in den USA. Eds. B. Schünemann; M. D. Dubber. Köln, 2000, pp. 117 et seq. at pp. 132 et seq. quoting further authorities; L. Zedner: "England". In: Wiedergutmachung im Kriminalrecht – Internationale Perspektiven – Reparation in Criminal Law – International Perspectives. Eds. A. Eser; S. Walther. Vol. 1. Freiburg i. Br., 1996, pp. 109 et seq. at. p. 168; T. Lappi-Seppälä: "Finland". In: Wiedergutmachung im Kriminalrecht – Internationale Perspektiven – Reparation in Criminal Law – International Perspectives. Eds. A. Eser; S. Walter. Vol. 1. Freiburg i. Br., 1996, pp. 317 et seq. at pp. 362 et seq.

1127 S. Glickman: "Victims' Justice – Legitimizing the Sentencing Regime of the International Criminal Court". In: Columbia Journal of Transnational Law 43 (2005), pp. 229 et seq. at p. 262.

The ICTY and ICTR Rules oblige the Tribunals to take into account the convicted person's cooperation with the Prosecutor as a mitigating circumstance, even if it takes place after the conviction.[1128] However, the Tribunals' jurisprudence also considered an expression of remorse, given that it was "real and sincere", as mitigating factor.[1129] The acceptance of responsibility and benevolent actions towards some of the victims have also been rewarded through mitigation.[1130]

In national jurisdictions, voluntary pre-conviction efforts are generally taken as a mitigating factor, while in some jurisdictions the sentence is also mitigated upon the payment of a civil compensation order.[1131]

1128 Rule 101 (B) (ii).

1129 See for the ICTY e.g. *The Prosecutor v. Todorović*, Sentencing Judgement, Trial Chamber I, 31 July 2001, Case No. IT-95-9/1, paras. 89-92; *Sikirica et al.*, Sentencing Judgement, Trial Chamber III, 13 November 2001, Case No. IT-95, paras. 152, 194, 230; *The Prosecutor v. Simić*, Sentencing Judgement, Trial Chamber II, 17 October 2002, Case No. IT-95-9/2-S, paras. 90 et seq.; *The Prosecutor v. Erdemović*, Appeals Sentencing Judgement, Appeals Chamber, 5 March 1998, Case No. IT-96-22, para. 16 (iii); *The Prosecutor v. Jelisić*, Judgement, Trial Chamber I, 14 December 1999, Case No. IT-95-10-T, para. 127; *The Prosecutor v. M. Nikolić*, Sentencing Judgement, Trial Chamber II, 2 December 2003, Case No. IT-02-60/1-S, para 161.

1130 See e.g. *The Prosecutor v. Blaskić*, Judgement, Trial Chamber I, 3 March 2000, Case No. IT-95-14, paras. 775 et seq.; *Sikirica et al.*, Sentencing Judgement, Trial Chamber III, 13 November 2001, Case No. IT-95, paras. 195, 229; *The Prosecutor v. Serushago*, Judgement, Trial Chamber I, 5 February 1999, ICTR-98-39-S, para. 38; *The Prosecutor v. Rutaganda*, Judgement and Sentence, Trial Chamber I, 6 December 1999, ICTR-96-3-T, para. 471; *The Prosecutor v. Niyitegeka*, Judgement, Trial Chamber I, 16 May 2003, ICTR-96-14- T, para. 494; see also W. A. Schabas: An Introduction to the International Criminal Court. 2nd ed. Cambridge, 2004, p. 168.

1131 In Sweden, the offender is required to have engaged in efforts to repair on his or her own initiative and before the revelation of the crime, J. Zila: "Schweden". In: Wiedergutmachung im Kriminalrecht – Internationale Perspektiven – Reparation in Criminal Law – International Perspectives. Eds. A. Eser, S. Walther. Vol. 1. Freiburg i. Br., 1996, pp. 231 et seq. at p. 272; in the German system, mitigation of sentence is not excluded *per se* when the wrongdoer only engages in efforts to repair the harm caused after his or her conviction, when the other requirements are fulfilled, i.e. voluntariness and seriousness of efforts, see A. Schönke; H. Schröder (et al.): Strafgesetzbuch. 27th ed. München, 2006, § 46a para. 6. Also in Poland and Finland, e.g. voluntariness by the offender (to prevent and) remove the effects of the offense or to further the clearing up of the offense is required in order for it to have a mitigating effect on the sentence, see Z. Doda; E. Weigend: "Polen". In: Wiedergutmachung im Kriminalrecht – Internationale Perspektiven – Reparation in Criminal Law – International Perspectives. Eds. A. Eser; S. Walther. Vol. 1. Freiburg i. Br., 1996, pp. 421 et seq. at pp. 481 et seq., T. Lappi-Seppälä: "Finland". In: Wiedergutmachung im Kriminalrecht – Internationale Perspektiven – Reparation in Criminal Law – International Perspectives. Eds. A. Eser; S. Walter. Vol. 1. Freiburg i. Br., 1996, pp. 317 et seq. at pp. 361 and 378, further noting that Finish courts are allowed to also take compensation orders into account as a mitigating factor, however this has mainly been practiced regarding economic or property crimes.

Furthermore, the relevance of the perpetrator's mental state is questionable regarding financial reparations. When victims have received compensation or otherwise benefited from the offender's reparative conduct, reparation may be deemed to have been achieved, irrespective of the offender's motives. In contrast, when the offender engages in symbolic (non-monetary) forms of reparations, his or her mental state has to be taken into account and it is only appropriate to mitigate the sentence when the remorse is "real and sincere".

With regard to the second concern that mitigation privileges rich offenders over poor offenders, it is crucial that symbolic forms of reparations as well as compensation, are recognized as potential mitigating factor under ICC system. Otherwise, there will be unjustifiable discrimination against defendants on the basis of their financial means.

However, offenders without financial resources can "only" engage in efforts to repair the consequences of their crime through symbolic acts if he or she wants to benefit from mitigation. Thus, he or she is required to demonstrate genuine remorse. A wealthy offender has the option of simply paying compensation without showing personal regret and the Court might still take this into account as a mitigating factor (if payment is made prior to conviction). However, the fact that the options for an offender with little or no resources to achieve mitigation are more limited than those of wealthy offenders does not violate the requirement of equality before the law. It merely constitutes the single reduction of the many factors that that might lead to the mitigation of a sentence.

Therefore, the Court should not hesitate to use the possibility to mitigate the sentence as an incentive for pre-conviction reparations, as long as the behavior of the offender makes this "appropriate".

2. Reparations and the Imposition of Fines and Forfeiture Orders

Before the ICC, orders of fines and forfeiture and reparations are linked and may have the identical effect with regard to both their nature and their underlying purpose.

a) Fines

Before the ICC, a fine can be imposed in addition to a sentence of imprisonment and is thus a penalty that is both optional and subsidiary (Art. 77 (2) a)).[1132] A fine can be

1132 Art. 77 (2), Rules 146, 148. Art. 77 (2) states that "In addition to imprisonment, the Court may order (a) A fine under the criteria provided for in the Rules of Procedure and Evidence". While at the Rome Conference there was a general agreement to include the option of fines as an ordinary penalty in the Statute, views varied widely as to the modalities of their imposition. Fines as a separate penalty were eventually considered inappropriate in view of the seriousness of the crimes under the Court's jurisdiction, see R. E. Fife: "Penalties". In: The International Criminal Court – The Making of the Rome Statute – Issues, Negotiations, Results. Ed. R. S. Lee. The Hague, 1999, pp. 319 et seq. at p. 330; generally see C. Kreß; G. Sluiter: "Fines and Forfeiture Orders". In: The Rome Statute of the International Criminal Court – A Commentary. Eds. A. Cassese; P. Gaeta; J. R. W. D. Jones. Vol. 2. Oxford, 2002, pp. 1823 et seq.

defined as a "pecuniary criminal punishment".[1133] In the history of international criminal justice, it is the first time that fines are open as a penalty option.[1134]

In deciding whether to impose a fine, the Court "shall determine whether imprisonment is a sufficient penalty" (Rule 146 (1)). Other relevant factors are whether forfeiture or reparations will be ordered, the financial capacity of the convicted person and whether and to what degree the crime was motivated by personal financial gain.[1135] Particularly where convicted persons are still benefiting financially from the crime, the Court might consider ordering a fine to ensure that they no longer profit from their criminal conduct.[1136] This is in accordance with the purpose of fines to provide an additional element of deterrence by penalizing the convict through his or her own pocket.[1137]

The amount of the fine shall be "appropriate" and be determined by taking into consideration the aforementioned factors and, in particular, the damage and injuries caused as well as the proportionate gains derived from the crime by the perpetrator (Rule 146 (2)).[1138] The Court must also take into account the general sentencing factors, such as the convicted person's conduct after the commission of crime, including

---

1133 It has furthermore been defined as a "civil penalty payable to the public treasury", B. A. Garner (ed.): Black's Law Dictionary. 8th ed. St. Paul, Minnesota, 2004, p. 664.

1134 The Nuremberg and Tokyo Tribunals could impose "death or such other punishment as shall be determined to be just" (Art. 27 Nuremberg Charter) and thus could have ordered all kinds of penalties, including fines – an option they did not make use of. The ICTY Statute and the ICTR Statute only provide for the imposition of fines for procedural crimes such as contempt of court and not as a penalty for crimes committed under the tribunals' jurisdiction, Rules 77 (b) and 91 (e).

1135 Rule 146 (1). In particular Rule 146 (1) s. 2 states that in "determining whether to order a fine under article 77 paragraph 2 (a), and in fixing the amount of the fine (…) [t]he Court shall give due consideration to […], as appropriate, any orders for reparation in accordance with article 75". Also, the general criteria contained in Rule 145, which mainly deal with the nature and impact of the crime, as well as the perpetrator's conduct after the crime, shall be considered (Rule 145 (1) last sentence).

1136 See also J. Peglau: "Penalties and the Determination of the Sentence in the Rules of Procedure and Evidence". In: International and National Prosecution of Crimes under International Law. Ed. H. Fischer; C. Kreß; S. R. Lüder. (Bochumer Schriften zur Friedenssicherung und zum Humanitären Völkerrecht). Berlin, 2001, pp. 141 et seq. at p. 147, pointing out that Rule 146 on fines is based on the idea that perpetrators who are driven by a profit motivation in committing the crime, are to be hit financially.

1137 R. E. Fife: "Penalties". In: The International Criminal Court – The Making of the Rome Statute – Issues, Negotiations, Results. Ed. R. S. Lee. The Hague, 1999, pp. 319 et seq. at p. 328 referring to discussions at the Rome Conference.

1138 In this context J. Peglau: "Penalties and the Determination of the Sentence in the Rules of Procedure and Evidence". In: International and National Prosecution of Crimes under International Law. Ed. H. Fischer; C. Kreß; S. R. Lüder. (Bochumer Schriften zur Friedenssicherung und zum Humanitären Völkerrecht). Berlin, 2001, pp. 141 et seq. at p. 152 remarks that the idea of "crime-tailored" retaliation is central to the understanding of Rule 146.

"any efforts of the person to compensate the victims and any cooperation with the Court".[1139]

In order for a fine not to have confiscatory effect, its total amount is limited to 75 % of the value of the convicted person's identifiable assets and property.[1140]

In contrast to both forfeiture orders and reparations, where a fine goes unpaid, the Court may impose sanctions, as laid down in Rule 146 (5). As a first step, it must adopt the regular cooperation and enforcement measures provided for in the Statute and Rules which also apply to reparations and forfeiture orders.[1141] These are not special sanctions. In the event of continued willful non-payment, the term of imprisonment can be extended as a last resort and with certain limitations. It is for the Presidency to determine the additional term of imprisonment, on the condition that other measures have proven unsuccessful and the convicted person has been warned and heard.[1142] Concerns have been raised that extending the term of imprisonment might "arguably [be] a violation of the *non bis in idem* principle".[1143] The ability to impose sanctions for non-payment might obviously increase the effectiveness of fines. The victims of crimes under the ICC's jurisdictions might benefit from the fines through the Trust Fund.[1144]

1139 Rule 146 (1) s. 3 read in conjunction with Rule 145 (2) (a) (ii).

1140 Following the idea that the perpetrator should be deprived of the benefits obtained as result of the crime, no maximum amount was needed to be fixed in the Rules. Yet, in opposite to the procedure applying to forfeiture orders, there was no need seen to prove the exact amount of the benefits. The underlying idea is especially directed towards perpetrators at the highest level of hierarchy, who have generally plenty of opportunities to hide the benefits from the crime, ibid. The modes of payment of the fine the Court may choose are elaborated in Art. 146 (3) and (4).

1141 Rule 146 (5) s. 1 refers to Rules 217 to 222 (located in the section termed "Enforcement of fines, forfeiture measures and reparation orders") and to Art. 109 ("Enforcement of fines and forfeiture measures").

1142 Rule 146 (5) s. 2.

1143 W. A. Schabas: "Penalties". In: The Rome Statute of the International Criminal Court – A Commentary. Ed. A. Cassese; P. Gaeta; J. R. W. D. Jones. Vol. 2. Oxford, 2002, pp. 1497 et seq. at p. 1513; see also F. P. King; A.-M. La Rosa: "Penalties under the ICC Statute". In: Collection of Essays on the Rome Statute of the International Criminal Court. Eds. F. Lattanzi; W. A. Schabas. Ripa di Fagnano Alto, 1999, pp. 311 et seq. at p. 327 who suggest that that extending the term of imprisonment would present a case of "re-sentencing". See also discussions in the Preparatory Commission on whether to provide for imprisonment as a sanction for willful non-payment, J. Peglau: "Penalties and the Determination of the Sentence in the Rules of Procedure and Evidence". In: International and National Prosecution of Crimes under International Law. Ed. H. Fischer; C. Kreß; S. R. Lüder. (Bochumer Schriften zur Friedenssicherung und zum Humanitären Völkerrecht). Berlin, 2001, pp. 141 et seq. at p. 152 summarizing the concerns of the French and Dutch Delegations in the drafting process of the Rules.

1144 Art. 79 (2) states that "[t]he Court may order money and other property collected through fines or forfeiture to be transferred, by order of the Court, to the Trust Fund."

While fines transferred to the Trust Fund, and monetary reparations may be used for the same purpose, i.e. for the benefit of victims, they are also essentially distinct. Fines emphasize that the payment is a punishment, whereas reparations aim primarily to repair the damage caused to victims.[1145] The amount of the fine is limited in accordance with the scope of the assets owned by the convicted person, while the key factor that determines the scope of the reparation order is the scope and extent of the damage caused.[1146] In the event that the sentenced person does not pay the fine, sanctions can be imposed in order to ensure its enforcement, while no such measures are available with regard to reparations.

The ICC's legal foundations only require that a decision to order reparations, or the intention to do so, shall be taken into account before ordering fines, and not that the orders are mutually exclusive.[1147] However, the restrictions contained in Rule 146 (2) concerning the maximum scope of the fine would be undermined if monetary reparations were ordered at the same time. When the assets of the defendant are only sufficient to finance either a fine or monetary reparations, in accordance with Rule 221 (2) and similar concepts in national jurisdictions, reparations shall have priority.[1148] International documents safeguarding victims' rights also provide that the enforcement and payment of reparations should take priority over fines.[1149]

However, when it can be assumed from the convicted person's behavior that he or she is unwilling to make financial reparations although in possession of assets that seem to be difficult to access, the benefit of victims might be better served by the Court ordering a fine rather than reparations. As the amount of a fine cannot be determined in accordance to the harm caused, the consequences of choosing one order over the other should be carefully weighed, in communication with participating victims or their legal representatives.

1145 See also Chapter 3 ("Purposes of Reparations").

1146 See also Chapter 5 C. IV.2.b) ("Financial Capacity of the Convicted Person").

1147 J. J. M. van Dijk: "The United Nations Declaration on Crime Victims – Priorities for Policy Makers". In: International Protection of Victims. Ed. C. M. Bassiouni. Eres, 1988, pp. 117 et seq. at p. 120 points out that in national jurisdictions, "[t]he claims of the so-called *partie civile* can often be sustained by means of a partially suspended fine with the condition that full restitution be paid to the victim".

1148 See Rule 221 (2); P. Xavier; F. Lombard: "Frankreich". In: Wiedergutmachung im Kriminalrecht – Internationale Perspektiven – Reparation in Criminal Law – International Perspectives. Eds. A. Eser; S. Walther. Vol. 3. Freiburg i. Br., 2001, pp. 1 et seq. at pp. 93 et seq.; L. Zedner: "England". In: Wiedergutmachung im Kriminalrecht – Internationale Perspektiven – Reparation in Criminal Law – International Perspectives. Eds. A. Eser; S. Walther. Vol. 1. Freiburg i. Br., 1996, pp. 109 et seq. at. p. 178; A. Ashworth: "Victims' Rights, Defendants' Rights and Criminal Procedure". In: Integrating a Victim Perspective within Criminal Justice – International Debates. Eds. J. Crawford; J. Goodey. Aldershot, 2000, pp. 185 et seq. at p. 195.

1149 See Art. 38 2005 Guidelines on Child Victims.

b) *Forfeiture Orders*

The Court is empowered to order the forfeiture of proceeds, property and assets that derived from the crime as an optional penalty in addition to a sentence of imprisonment (Art. 77 (2) b)).[1150]

The Statute or Rules do not define the terms "forfeiture", "proceeds", "property" or "assets". Black's Law Dictionary defines forfeiture as the "divestiture of property without compensation".[1151] Even though the International Military Tribunal of Nuremberg, the ICTY and the ICTR had the power to order the forfeiture of stolen property and the restitution of property, there is no jurisprudence from the tribunals that could potentially provide applicable definitions and principles.[1152]

In contrast to fines, the Rules do not provide guidance regarding the circumstances in which forfeiture shall be ordered. A key purpose of forfeiture is to prevent the offender from benefiting any further from the crime. Due to its direct connection to the crime, it would seem that in principle, property, proceeds and assets obtained by

1150 See also Rules 147 and 148. For a discussion on the drafting history of the provision of forfeiture in the Statute see e.g. R. E. Fife: "Penalties". In: The International Criminal Court – The Making of the Rome Statute – Issues, Negotiations, Results. Ed. R. S. Lee. The Hague, 1999, pp. 319 et seq. at pp. 328, 332; W. A. Schabas: "Penalties". In: The Rome Statute of the International Criminal Court – A Commentary. Ed. A. Cassese; P. Gaeta; J. R. W. D. Jones. Vol. 2. Oxford, 2002, pp. 1497 et seq. at pp. 1515 et seq. On ICC forfeiture orders in general, see C. Kreß; G. Sluiter: "Fines and Forfeiture Orders". In: The Rome Statute of the International Criminal Court – A Commentary. Eds. A. Cassese; P. Gaeta; J. R. W. D. Jones. Vol. 2. Oxford, 2002, pp. 1823 et seq. at p. 1823.

1151 B. A. Garner (ed.): Black's Law Dictionary. 8th ed. St. Paul, Minnesota, 2004, p. 676.

1152 The International Military Tribunal in Nuremberg could also "deprive the convicted person of any stolen property and order its delivery to the Control Council for Germany", Art. 28 Nuremberg Charter. In one of the so-called Nuremberg follow-up trials, the Tribunal ordered the forfeiture of the entire assets of Alfried Krupp von Bohlen Halbach with regard to the complicity of the Krupp company in the planning and waging a war of aggression. However, the forfeiture orders was nullified by an act of pardon of McCloy on 31 January 1951, see W. Maser: Nürnberg – Tribunal der Sieger. Düsseldorf, 1977, p. 619. Similarly, the ICTY and ICTR have so far not applied Art. 23 (3) ICTR Statute or Art. 24 (3) ICTY Statute that enables the restitution of property. It has been suggested by R. E. Fife: "Article 77 – Applicable Penalties". In: Commentary on the Rome Statute of the International Criminal Court – Observers' Notes, Article by Article. Ed. O. Triffterer. Baden-Baden, 1999, pp. 985 et seq. at p. 997 that guidance for definitions and principles relevant to forfeiture could be drawn from the 1990 European Convention on laundering, search, seizure and confiscation of the proceeds from crime: Under Art. 1 a)"proceeds" are any economic advantage from criminal offences. It may consist of any "property". "Property" is defined in Art. 1 b) as property of any description, whether corporeal or incorporeal, movable or immovable and legal documents or instruments evidencing title to, or interest in such a property. "Assets" creates possible overlap with the category of property and underlines the broad scope of the forfeiture provision. According to B. A. Garner (ed.): Black's Law Dictionary. 8th ed. St. Paul, Minnesota, 2004, p. 1252 "Property" may include "[a]ny external thing over which the rights of possession, use and enjoyment are exercised." An "asset" is "[a]n item that is owned and has value", ibid., p. 125.

the offender as a result of a crime should always be forfeited.[1153] The preconditions for this are that the property, proceeds and assets are in the possession of the convicted person and that he or she must have obtained them as a direct or indirect result of the crime. It is yet to be defined how "indirect" the benefits from the crime can be in order to still be considered a "proceed from crime". In any case, the wording" directly or indirectly" is very broad and lessens the evidentiary burden.[1154]

The Statute provides that the only effect of forfeiture orders is to deprive the perpetrators of proceeds, property and assets deriving from the crime.[1155] Thus, in contrast to both fines and reparations, the Court has little discretion in determining the scope of forfeiture.

Art. 77 (2) b) of the Statute provides that the forfeiture of proceeds, property and assets shall be "without prejudice to the rights of bona fide third parties" and thus protects the rights of those in good faith.[1156] However, in situations of armed conflict or other situations where gross violations of humanitarian law occur or have occurred, it may be difficult for the third parties in possession of the property to meet the standards of a bona fide possessory title. This can be particularly true where the property in question is cultural or real property. It can be expected that the origin of movable goods and other issues will in many instances be more difficult to determine.[1157]

1153 However, while taking account of the rights of bona fide third parties.

1154 R. E. Fife: "Article 77 – Applicable Penalties". In: Commentary on the Rome Statute of the International Criminal Court – Observers' Notes, Article by Article. Ed. O. Triffterer. Baden-Baden, 1999, pp. 985 et seq. at p. 997, suggesting that guidance might be drawn from Art. 5 UN Convention Against Illicit Traffic in Narcotic Drugs and Psychotropic Substances, 20 December 1988.

1155 J. Peglau: "Penalties and the Determination of the Sentence in the Rules of Procedure and Evidence". In: International and National Prosecution of Crimes under International Law. Ed. H. Fischer; C. Kreß; S. R. Lüder. (Bochumer Schriften zur Friedenssicherung und zum Humanitären Völkerrecht). Berlin, 2001, pp. 141 et seq. at p. 149.

1156 See also Rule 147, which provides that when a Chamber considers an order of forfeiture it shall hear the evidence concerning the identification of property and assets, as well as identify interests of bona fide third parties. The purely procedural content of this Rule contrasts with Rule 145 which is of general application and Rule 146 dealing with fines which contain conditions referring to, inter alia, the gravity of the crime and the culpability. R. E. Fife: "Article 77 – Applicable Penalties". In: Commentary on the Rome Statute of the International Criminal Court – Observers' Notes, Article by Article. Ed. O. Triffterer. Baden-Baden, 1999, pp. 985 et seq. at pp. 997-998 points out that the wording in the ICC Statute is similar to the UN Convention Against Illicit Traffic in Narcotic Drugs and Psychotropic Substances, 20 December 1988 and a general principle applicable in national legal systems.

1157 E.g. issues of choice of law in determining the ownership arise in particular where victim, property and third parties are located in different jurisdictions, see R. E. Fife: "Article 77 – Applicable Penalties". In: Commentary on the Rome Statute of the International Criminal Court – Observers' Notes, Article by Article. Ed. O. Triffterer. Baden-Baden, 1999, pp. 985 et seq. at pp. 997-998.

In contrast to the Statutes of the ICTY and ICTR, which only permitted the tribunals in question to order the return of any property and proceeds acquired by criminal conduct to their rightful owners, forfeiture orders under the ICC Statute can be made in respect of any property related to the crimes regardless of whether the ICC can identify the property's "rightful owner."[1158]

3. Review Concerning the Reduction of Sentence and the Impact of the Offender's Post-Conviction Behavior Towards Victims

Art. 110 ICC Statute authorizes the Court to reduce the sentence after fixed periods of time, providing that certain conditions are met.[1159] One of the conditions that may lead to the Court reducing the sentence are efforts of the sentenced person to repair, or assist in repairing, the harm caused by crimes under the Court's jurisdiction.

Among the factors listed in the Statute is the person's provision of voluntary assistance which enables the enforcement of judgments and orders of the Court in other cases and "in particular providing assistance in locating assets subject to orders of fine, forfeiture or reparation which may be used for the benefit of victims [...]" (Art. 110 (4) b)).

However, Rule 223 (d) provides that in reviewing the sentence, the judges appointed by the Appeals Chamber shall take into account "any significant action taken by the sentenced person for the benefit of the victims". This wording is broad and allows the Court to reward a wide range of activities. It might include the sentenced person's cooperation with the Court which facilitated the smooth enforcement of orders of forfeiture, fines or reparations made against him- or herself. Activities to repair the harm he or she caused to victims in a way that is unconnected to the ICC might also be rewarded. The requirement that the action must be "significant" clarifies that not any effort will suffice. Rather, in line with the standard required by the Statute, the action of the sentenced person must benefit victims in a way that constitutes "a clear and significant change of circumstances" (Art. 110 (4) c)). This might be achieved on various levels, e.g. the sentenced person's active or leading role in the transition of a state or payments that help to rebuild victimized communities.

Rule 223 (d) also requires the Court to take into account "any impact on the victims and their families as a result of early release" in deciding whether to reduce the sentence.

Victims or their legal representatives who participated in the proceedings are to be invited to participate in the hearings at which the reduction of sentence is discussed or to submit written representations (Rule 224 (1)).[1160] In this way, the Court can assess the views of victims on the perpetrator's an early release.

The notion that cooperation with the Court and efforts which enable the enforcement of orders of reparations, fines and forfeiture and other activities beneficiary to

1158 As neither Art. 77 (2) nor the Rules on forfeiture contain any relevant restriction.

1159 See also Rules 223, 224.

1160 However, in contrast to the Prosecutor, the state of enforcement of the penalty and, if applicable, the reparation order, victims or their legal representatives shall only be invited "to the extent possible".

victims may be rewarded with a reduction of sentence might increase the convicted person's motivation to engage in such activities. It seems that in most cases it would serve the interests of victims if the Court utilized these instruments to provide incentives for the sentenced person to cooperate.

II. Use of Money or Property Collected through Orders of Reparations, Fines and Forfeiture and the Role of the Victims Trust Fund

The ICC's legal instruments do not determine a specific purpose for which money and property collected through the enforcement of fines and forfeiture orders must or should be used. The only option for which the Statute explicitly provides is that the Court "may" transfer money and property deriving from fines and forfeiture to the Trust Fund (Art. 79 (2)).[1161] Thus, it is within the discretion of the Court to decide on the allocation of money and property collected through fines and forfeiture orders.

However, the ICC's legal framework does suggest that the money and property obtained by the Court should be used solely for the benefit of victims. Funds deriving from fines and forfeiture are not intended to be a source of the Court's general funding. The transfer of fines and forfeited goods to the Trust Fund, whose mandate is to serve the benefit of victims and their families, is the only purpose listed in the Statute (Art. 79 (2)). Furthermore, Rule 221 (2) determines that the Presidency, in its decision "on the disposition or allocation of property or assets belonging to the sentenced person, shall give priority to the enforcement of measures concerning reparations to victims". It serves the purposes of penalties before the ICC to use the money and property obtained for the benefit of victims.[1162] Fines and forfeiture are to be ordered in particular where the convicted person derived personal financial gain from the crime.[1163] Depriving the offender of the gain not only punishes him or her, but also contributes to the redress of the harm caused.

1161 Art. 79 (2) reads: "The Court may order money and other property collected through fines or forfeiture to be transferred, by order of the Court, to the Trust Fund."

1162 Collective reconciliation and reparation to crime victims are often listed as a purpose of penalties in particular in the context of international criminal law, see R. E. Fife: "Article 77 – Applicable Penalties". In: Commentary on the Rome Statute of the International Criminal Court – Observers' Notes, Article by Article. Ed. O. Triffterer. Baden-Baden, 1999, pp. 985 et seq. at p. 986, listing further authorities and further discussing the purposes of fines and forfeiture, see ibid., pp. 991-992: "A common rationale behind the possibility for both orders is to penalize the convicted person through his or her pocket, and such orders should be regarded as an integral part of the total penalty. With regard to forfeiture orders, there is in addition the traditional criminal law rationale that the offender should not profit from his wrongdoing. Depriving persons engaged in international crimes under article 5 of the proceeds of their criminal activities may remove an incentive for so doing. It is reasonable to believe that such crimes may in certain cases lead to substantial unlawful profits, for example seizure of real property or valuable assets in cases of "ethnic cleansing". On-going work in tracing Jewish gold seized by the Nazis before and during the Second World War provides another illustration."

1163 See Art. 77 (2) b) on forfeiture and Rule 146 (1) regarding fines.

The drafting debates regarding Art. 79 on the Trust Fund show that it was the intention of the Statute's drafters that funds acquired through fines and forfeiture should be used primarily for the benefit of victims.[1164]

The Court may involve the Trust Fund in the decision on the use of money and property obtained through the enforcement of fines and forfeiture orders. Before allocating money or property deriving from fines or forfeiture to the Trust Fund or otherwise, the competent Chamber or the Presidency, may ask Trust Fund representatives to comment on the intended order (Rules 148, 221 (1)).[1165]

The ICC Statute and Rules do not stipulate whether the Court or the Trust Fund should decide on the allocation of funds which have been obtained through fines and forfeiture orders and which the Court has ordered to be transferred to the Trust Fund. However, given the hierarchical relation between the Court and the Trust Fund, it is clear that it is up to the Court to determine how funds shall be allocated, while the Trust Fund's role is to implement the award in accordance with the Court's stipulations. This is also confirmed in the Trust Fund Regulations.[1166] Thus, the roles of the Court and the Trust Fund regarding the allocation of assets and property obtained through fines and forfeiture orders is identical to that on reparations ordered to be made through the Trust Fund.

The Trust Fund Regulations provide that the use of money and property obtained through fines and forfeiture is to be determined in accordance with the relevant Rules and Court decisions on reparations, in case the Court has not ordered a specific use of the funds.[1167]

1164 Other ways to utilize the assets that were proposed in the drafting process of the Statute included defraying the costs of the trial and compensating the state of the nationality of the victims, see Art. 79 Prep Com Draft Statute, which intended the establishment of a Trust Fund.

1165 Rule 148 reads "Before making an order pursuant to article 79, paragraph 2, a Chamber may request the representatives of the Fund to submit written or oral observations to it." This wording seems to encompass both the question as to whether to order the transferral at all, as well as the content of the order. This does not, of course, prevent the Court from requesting information from any other additional institution. Reg. 31, 32 Trust Fund Regulations provide that at the request of the Chamber pursuant to Rule 148, the Trust Fund's Board of Directors shall make written observations on the transfer of fines of forfeiture to the Trust Fund and the allocation of property and assets pursuant to Rule 221. In contrast, the Statute and Rules do not require that the Court regularly consult the Trust Fund before ordering reparations to be made through it. Explicitly, the Rules only provide that the Court shall consult the Trust Fund before ordering to award reparation to an organization, Rule 98 (4) and regarding the allocation of property and assets obtained through enforced Court orders, including fines and forfeiture, but also reparation orders pursuant to Rule 221 (1).

1166 Reg. 31-33, 43-46 Trust Fund Regulations.

1167 Reg. 44 Trust Fund Regulations. Particular reference is made to Art. 75 (1) and Rules 97, 98.

Thus, the intended use of money and property transferred to the Trust Fund is almost identical to that of reparation orders.[1168] The important difference as set out in the Trust Fund Regulations concerns the potential beneficiaries of resources obtained through fines and forfeiture: while beneficiaries have to qualify as victims pursuant to Rule 85 or families of an individual victim, they are not required to be affected by crimes committed by the convicted person.[1169] Thus, a potentially broader group of victims can benefit from money and property obtained through fines and forfeiture than from reparation orders. The convicted person's assets collected through fines and forfeiture are not earmarked for the benefit of victims of the case. They might therefore also be used for the benefit of victims of other cases in which a convicted person has insufficient resources to effect reparations or pay a fine, for the benefit of victims of the situation or perhaps even victims of cases in a different situation.

While money and property deriving from fines and forfeiture should therefore be used for the benefit of victims, this does not necessarily have to be done through the Trust Fund. The money and property obtained can also be used to benefit victims directly. In particular forfeited property might be restored directly to victims who are its rightful owners and thus be utilized to implement direct reparation orders.[1170]

While fines and forfeiture deal with the side of the offender, reparations are primarily concerned with repairing the harm caused to victims. Money and property collected through fines and forfeiture orders may be used to enforce reparations awards, directly or through the Trust Fund. Fines and forfeiture and monetary reparations are therefore often two sides of the same token.

III. Assessment

The interdependence of reparations and penalties in the ICC system is not coincidental. Reparations and certain kinds of penalties not only serve similar or often identical purposes, but they also take shapes that are often identical.

Equipping the Court with the power to reward behavior of the offender that is beneficial to victims through the mitigation or reduction of the sentence potentially provides an incentive for the offender to do so. It increases the chances that victims will receive reparations, as it increases the chance that these orders will actually be enforced.

1168 See Reg. 43-45 Trust Fund Regulations. On the determination and implementation of reparations through the Trust Fund, see Chapter 6 F. ("Implementation of Reparation Awards").

1169 *Argumentum e contrario* in view of Reg. 42, 46 Trust Fund Regulations.

1170 Thus, problems of determining the ownership that have been discussed in the context of the ICTY and ICTR system may also arise in the ICC context, see C. M. Bassiouni; P. Manikas: The Law of the International Criminal Tribunal for the Former Yugoslavia. Irvington-on-Hudson, New York, 1996, pp. 703-704; V. Morris; M. P. Scharf: The International Criminal Tribunal for Rwanda. Vol. 1. Irvington-on-Hudson, New York, 1998, pp. 594 et seq.

Fines, forfeiture and reparation orders could be ordered parallel to each other. However, due to the additional sanctions available with regard to fines in particular, in certain circumstances victims may be more likely to benefit from fines and forfeiture than from reparation orders.[1171] Money and property obtained through fines and forfeiture should be exclusively used for the benefit of victims. Where the Court transfers assets collected through fines or forfeiture to the Trust Fund but does not stipulate how they should be used, their allocation should be guided by the provisions and decisions on reparations, although they do not have to be used for the victims of the case. However, in line with Rule 221 (2) and principles applied in national legal systems, using the funds for reparations shall always take priority. Thus, the penalties of fines and forfeiture might, in practical terms, serve to secure the enforcement of monetary reparation orders. Prior to ordering fines, forfeiture or reparations, all alternatives and the impact of the order on other possible orders should be considered.[1172] As a principle, orders should be made that best serve the interests of victims.

The ICC's penalty system provides several tools that the Court may utilize in order to increase the likelihood that victims of crimes under its jurisdiction will actually benefit from reparations. The interrelation between reparations and penalties before the ICC may be central to the effective functioning of the ICC reparations regime.

However, it seems questionable whether high-profile perpetrators of crimes under the ICC's jurisdiction are likely to engage voluntarily in activities that are of meaningful benefit to victims in order to perhaps be rewarded by the ICC. The successful enforcement both of fines and forfeiture and monetary reparation orders, will to a large extent depend on the willingness of states rather than the accused or sentenced person to cooperate. Despite this, the Court should not hesitate to use the tools provided in its penalty system to provide incentives for the offender to engage in activities for the benefit of victims, and, if necessary, to exercise pressure.

E. Appeal against a Reparation Order (Art. 82 (4) ICC Statute)

Art. 82 (4) grants victims the right to appeal against reparation orders. This is the only means for victims to challenge decisions made by the Court on reparations. At the same time, the Statute and Rules grant victims explicit rights of appeal only with regard to the reparation order.[1173]

1171 See also Chapter 6 G. ("Protective Measures and Enforcement of Reparation Orders").

1172 This is procedurally possible pursuant to Art. 76 (2) and (3), Rule 143: the issues can be discussed in the same hearing.

1173 Victims participating in the proceedings pursuant to Rules 89-91 do not have the right to appeal. However, it has been discussed whether victims (and witnesses) have appeal rights concerning protective measures or special measures pursuant to Art. 81 (1) (d), Rule 87, 88, see H. Brady: "Appeal". In: The International Criminal Court – Elements of Crimes and Rules of Procedure and Evidence. Ed. R. S. Lee. Ardsley, New York, 2001, pp. 575 et seq. at pp. 595-596. However, victims may have the right to participate in the appeals proceedings pursuant to Art. 68 (3); see also Situation of the Democratic Republic of The Congo in the Case of *The Prosecutor v. Thomas Lubanga Dyilo*, Decision of the Ap-

Victims can only exercise their right to appeal against a reparation order through their legal representatives.[1174] Other persons with a right of appeal against the reparation order include the convicted person or bona fide owners of property adversely affected by the reparations decision (Art. 82 (4)).

It is unclear whether victims' right to appeal against a reparation order encompasses an appeal against the Court's decision not to order reparations. Art. 82 (4) states that a "legal representative of the victims [...] may appeal against the order for reparations". The wording therefore suggests that victims do not have a right of appeal against the Trial Chamber's decision not to order reparations. Rule 153 (1) describes the Appeals Chamber's power to "confirm, reverse or amend a reparation order made under article 75". It therefore also presupposes the existence of a reparation order. Likewise, the Court Regulations dealing with appeals refer exclusively to an existing reparation order.[1175]

Commentators have presumed that it would also be possible for a legal representative of the victims to appeal against a decision which refused to make an order for reparations.[1176] It could be argued that it would be in line with the object and purpose of granting victims a right of appeal against the Court's decisions on reparations and that the right also encompasses cases in which a reparation order has not been made. It could even be argued that the right to appeal is equally, or even particularly important in order to safeguard victims' rights when no reparation order has been made.

However, the provisions in the Statute and Rules dealing with appeals regulate precisely which persons or institutions can appeal against which decisions of the Court, and seem to do so in an exhaustive manner. Furthermore, the drafting debates on Rule 153 support the argument that victims' right to appeal is conditional on the

peals Chamber, 12 December 2006, ICC-01/04-01/06 on the applications regarding the request of the Defence for the early release of Lubanga, holding that "victims a/0001/06, a/0002/06 and a/0003/06 are granted the right to participate in this appeal for the purpose of presenting their views and concerns respecting their personal interests in the issues raised on appeal".

1174 Art. 82 (4). The appeal must be filed with the Registrar within 30 days after notification of the reparation order unless the Appeals chamber extends that period, upon application of the victims representative, for a good cause, see Rule 150; Reg. 57, 58 Court Regulations set forth formal requirements for filing an appeal. R. Roth; M. Henzelin: "The Appeal Procedure of the ICC". In: The Rome Statute of an International Criminal Court – A Commentary. Eds. A. Cassese; P. Gaeta; J. R. W. D. Jones. Vol. 2. Oxford, 2002, pp. 1535 et seq. at p. 1551 point out that "The expression 'legal representatives of the victims' is confusing, since it normally refers to the person(s) considered in law to represent another person, e.g. parents representing children who are minors. Article 82 (4) probably envisages [...] any person or organization duly admitted to represent a victim before the ICC"; furthermore raising the question as to whether a state could represent itself as the legal representative of victims.

1175 Reg. 57 b) Court Regulations.

1176 C. Staker: "Article 82 – Appeal against Other Decisions". In: Commentary on the Rome Statute of the International Criminal Court – Observers' Notes, Article by Article. Ed. O. Triffterer. Baden-Baden, 1999, pp. 1029 et seq. at p. 1032.

existence of a reparation order as a proposal for a broader wording allowing the Appeals Chamber to "order a new hearing" on reparations was rejected.[1177]

Thus, the wording, context and drafting history of the Court's legal foundations suggest that the right to file an appeal depends on the existence of a reparation order. Accordingly, when the Trial Chamber decides not to make use of its power to order reparations under Art. 75, it seems that the Appeals Chamber cannot revise the Trial Chamber's decision in that respect, so there is no right to appeal.

Injured persons have the right to complain or to appeal against the decision of a criminal court not to order compensation, or against the modalities of an order in a number of national jurisdictions where such persons have the right to file compensation claims in criminal proceedings.[1178] In international human rights the right of appeal in criminal proceedings is reserved to the convicted person.[1179] The Human Rights Committee has indicated that the ICCPR does not guarantee a right of appeal in civil proceedings.[1180]

The appeal might be directed against the decision not to include a certain individual applicant or applicants in the group of beneficiaries of the reparation order. The form, scope and extent of the reparation order might also be challenged.

While Art. 82 (4) only requires that the persons represented by legal counsel qualify as "victims", according to Rule 150 (1) they also must be "parties" that have been notified of the Court's reparation order. Only victims who have claimed reparations

1177 See H. Brady: "Appeal". In: The International Criminal Court – Elements of Crimes and Rules of Procedure and Evidence. Ed. R. S. Lee. Ardsley, New York, 2001, pp. 575 et seq. at pp. 587-588.

1178 However, in civil procedure often the right to appeal only exists with regard to specific grounds; in the German adhesion procedure, the person claiming reparations in criminal procedure only has a right to complain when the Court declares its intention not to decide on the claim, otherwise he or she does not have a right to appeal, see § 406 a) German Code of Criminal Procedure (StPO); in Austria, the civil claimant may appeal when, even though there was sufficient evidence to produced in the criminal trial, the court refers the claim, see M. E. I. Brienen; E. H. Hoegen: Victims of Crimes in 22 European Criminal Justice Systems – The Implementation of Recommendation (85) 11 of the Council of Europe on the Position of the Victims in the Framework of Criminal Law and Procedure. Nijmegen, 2000, p. 78. In France, civil claimants in criminal procedure have the right to appeal decisions of the court that affect their civil rights, see V. Dervieux; M. Benillouche; O. Bachelet: "The French System". In: European Criminal Procedures. Eds. M. Delmas-Marty; J. R. Spencer. Cambridge, 2002, pp. 218 et seq. at pp. 227; M. E. I. Brienen; E. H. Hoegen: Victims of Crimes in 22 European Criminal Justice Systems – The Implementation of Recommendation (85) 11 of the Council of Europe on the Position of the Victims in the Framework of Criminal Law and Procedure. Nijmegen, 2000, p. 321.

1179 Art. 14 (5) ICCPR.

1180 The only potential protection for a right of appeal in civil trials derives from Art. 14 (1). However, the Human Rights Committee has not yet been called upon to decide whether civil appeals are required by Art. 14 (1) ICCPR; see S. Joseph; J. Schultz; M. Castan: The International Covenant on Civil and Political Rights – Cases, Materials, and Commentary. 2nd ed. New York, 2004, pp. 402 et seq., 452 et seq.

pursuant to Rule 94 are notified.[1181] However, problems might arise when victims have requested reparations pursuant to Rule 94, but the Court decided not to link the request to the case before it and therefore did not notify a victim. In this case, the victim is prevented from bringing an appeal and might therefore try to challenge the Court's decision on notification.

It seems that the requirements that victims have been notified before and are represented by legal counsel, are designed to prevent a situation where large numbers of victims file different appeals.[1182] In order to ensure the effectiveness of the appeals proceedings, the Court might require victims, or groups of victims, to choose a common legal representative, in the event that they do not already have one from the trial stage.[1183]

Due to the great number of victims potentially eligible for reparations ordered by the ICC, as well as the low likelihood of full reparations, it is probable that it will be impossible for the ICC to satisfy the needs and wishes of all victims who apply for reparations. It can therefore be expected that in most cases victims will make use of the right to file an appeal. If challenged, the Appeals Chamber has the final say on all issues regarding reparations, with the possible exception of the decision on whether to make a reparation order under Art. 75. A reparation order only becomes final when no appeal against the reparation order is filed within 30 days after notification of the parties, or upon the decision of the Appeals Chamber on the appeal.[1184]

1181 According to Rule 92, those victims or their legal representatives are to be notified of the Court's decisions in the stage of proceedings they have participated in, i.e. here the reparations proceedings, see also Rules 143, 144 (1) and H. Brady: "Appeal". In: The International Criminal Court – Elements of Crimes and Rules of Procedure and Evidence. Ed. R. S. Lee. Ardsley, New York, 2001, pp. 575 et seq. at pp. 587-588. at p. 596.

1182 This would be in line with the intention of the drafters of the Statute: a footnote was inserted to Art. 73 on reparations to victims in Report of the Working Group on Procedural Matters of the Rome Conference, A/CONF.183/C.1/WGPM/L.2/Add.7 (1998) which provided that "where there are more than a few victims, this provision [now Art. 75, commented by the author] will not authorize their separate appeals to the Appeals Chamber. It is anticipated that the Rules will limit the number of victims who can appeal and will require that if there are large numbers of victims, their appeals will be jointly presented by a single representative", see P. Lewis; H. Friman: "Reparations to Victims". In: The International Criminal Court – Elements of Crimes and Rules of Procedure and Evidence. Ed. R. S. Lee. Ardsley, New York, 2001, pp. 474 et seq. at p. 478.

1183 Rule 90 (2). It is possible that several common legal representatives represent victims or groups of victims. In case victims are unable to agree on a legal representative, the Court might ask the Registry to do so (Rule 90 (3)).

1184 See Rule 150 (4), Art. 83. Pursuant to Rule 150 (4), the Appeals Chamber may, on application of one of the parties, extend the time limit. No other party but the convicted person has a right to initiate, under certain conditions, revision proceedings, Art. 84.

F. Implementation of ICC Reparation Awards (Art. 75 (2), Art. 79 ICC Statute)

The ICC reparations mechanism allows for direct distribution of awards to victims, or indirect distribution through the Trust Fund (Art. 75 (2), Rule 98).

I. ICC Reparation System

1. Role of the ICC and the Trust Fund for Victims

The ICC Statute and Rules envision that redress is to be achieved through individual reparation awards that are paid directly by the convicted person to a victim or to victims upon an order of the Court (Art. 75 (2) s. 1, Rule 98 (1)). Only in exceptional cases, are reparation awards to be distributed through the Trust Fund (Art. 75 (2) s. 2, Rule 98 (2), (3)).

However, ordering reparations to be made directly to victims creates a number of difficulties for the Court. It may not have the capacity to deal with often technical and complicated issues concerning reparations, as it must focus on its core task to prosecute crimes within its jurisdiction. Another problem is that it seems doubtful that the harm caused to victims of crimes under the ICC jurisdiction can be redressed appropriately from the assets of one – or even several – individuals whom the ICC orders to make reparations.

In consequence, the Trust Fund may play a crucial role in the effective functioning of the ICC reparations mechanism.[1185] The ICC Statute and Rules envision that the Trust Fund should constitute an integral part of the reparative function of the Court.[1186]

The Trust Fund was established in April 2004 as a complementary organ of the Court "for the benefit of victims of crimes within the jurisdiction of the Court, and of the families of such victims".[1187] A Board of Directors presides over the Fund.[1188]

1185 The first proposal suggesting the establishment of a Trust Fund was made by the International Law Commission and provided that fines and forfeiture orders are to be made to a state whose nationals were victims of the crime or to a Trust Fund, while the possibility of reparation orders was not mentioned, Art. 47 (3) ILC Draft Statute, ch. II.

1186 See e.g. Art. 75 (2), 79 (2), Rule 98.

1187 The main provisions on the Trust Fund appear in Art. 79 and Rule 98; additional references are made in Art. 75 (reparations to victims), Rule 218 (Orders for fines and forfeiture) and Rule 221 (Decision on disposition or allocation of property or assets). Its activities are not restricted to the complementation of the Court's reparative function, see Chapter 7 ("Assistance for Victims and Their Families through the Trust Fund").

1188 However, at its first meeting in September 2002, the ASP already accepted the Resolution on the Establishment of a Fund for the Benefit of Victims of Crimes within the Jurisdiction of the Court, and the Families of such Victims, ICC-ASP/1/Res.6 (2002) establishing a Board of Directors and which addressed issues such as funding sources and the relationship between the Board of Directors, the Registry of the ICC, and the ASP. The resolution determines that the Board shall have five sitting members, each from a different region of world, nominated and elected through the Bureau of the Directors for a term

The Trust Fund was created to be independent from the Court; as a result, its decisions are not the decisions of the Court.[1189] Part 12 of the ICC Statute, which deals with financing, only refers to the Court. Thus, the Trust Fund's and the Court's budgetary regimes are entirely separate. Consequently, the Trust Fund can neither profit from voluntary contributions made under Art. 116 nor from budgetary allotments made to other organs of the ICC.

The ICC Statute and Rules leave open fundamental questions as to the functioning of the relationship between the Trust Fund for Victims and the Court. The Assembly of State Parties has made use of its power to further determine the relation of the Trust Fund to the Court and established Trust Fund Regulations.[1190] The Regulations also contain provisions clarifying the division of competence regarding the implementation of ICC reparation orders.[1191]

2. Reparations

There is a distinct hierarchy which characterizes the relationship between the Court and the Trust Fund with regard to reparations. It is entirely within the discretion of the Court to decide whether to order reparations and, if so, how awards are to be distributed. The Trust Fund cannot object a decision of a Court to award direct instead of indirect reparations.[1192] It is also for the Court to decide whether to order

of three years with the option being re-elected once. In September 2003, the Members of the Board of Directors were elected by the ASP. The Resolution on the Procedure for the Nomination and Election of Members of the Board of Directors of the Trust Fund for the Benefit of Victims, ICC-ASP/1/Res.7 (2002) of 9 September 2002. The first Board of Directors was composed of Her Majesty Queen Rania Al-Abdullah of Jordan, His Excellency Dr. Oscar Arias Sánchez from Costa Rica, His Excellency Mr. Tadeuz Mazowiecki from Poland, Madam Minister from France (Chairperson) and His Eminence Archbishop Emeritus Desmond Tutu from South Africa. They met for the first time in April 2004.

1189 Resolution on the Establishment of the Secretariat of the Trust Fund for Victims, ICC-ASP/3/Res.7 (2004); the ICC Statute and RPE leave open whether the Fund is to be administered by the Court or other entities (among the suggestions were, next to the Court, the UN Secretariat, the UNDP, the ASP, see T. Ingadottir: "The Trust Fund for Victims (Art. 79 of the Rome Statute)". In: The International Criminal Court – Recommendations on Policy and Practice – Financing, Victims, Judges, and Immunities. Ed. T. Ingadottir. Ardsley, New York, 2003, pp. 111 et seq. at pp. 134 et seq.

1190 Pursuant to Art. 79 (3), which requires the "adoption of management criteria", the Trust Fund Regulations were adopted at the 4th plenary meeting on 3 December 2005 with the Resolution: Trust Fund Regulations, Resolution, ICC-ASP/4/Res.3 (2005).

1191 For an examination of the Trust Fund's activities other than implementing ICC reparation orders, and their required connection to the Court, see below Chapter 7 ("Assistance to Victims and their Families by the Trust Fund").

1192 The Statute foresees that in exceptional situations, reparations shall be awarded through the Trust Fund to victims, in the Rules these situations are further specified. However, the Trust Fund cannot demand from the Court to order awards through it on the grounds that one of the "exceptional" situations described in Rule 98 (2) und (3) applies to a certain case. "The Court may order that an award for reparations [...] be deposited with

individual or collective reparations awards or both, and whether they should be made through an international, national or intergovernmental organization.[1193]

a) *Direct Awards (Art. 75 (2) 1. Alt., Rule 98 (1))*

According to the ICC Statute and Rules, reparations awards are regularly made directly from the convicted person to victims. While Art. 75 (2) governs this process in a general manner, Rule 98 primarily refers to individual awards. In the case of direct reparations, the Trust Fund is not involved in the process of distributing reparations.[1194]

The Court's power to order direct reparations is the core innovation of the ICC's reparations regime. At the same time, direct reparations were one of the controversial issues in the drafting of the Rome Statute.[1195] Delegations expressed concern that a direct reparation system would not be compatible with the Court's main activities of prosecution and punishment of the offender.[1196]

b) *Awards through the Trust Fund (Art. 75 (2) 2. Alt., Rule 98 (2) and (3))*

The Court may order the convicted person to make reparations to victims indirectly through the Trust Fund. Reparations are to be made through the Trust Fund where direct awards are impossible or impracticable, or where appropriate.[1197]

The wording that reparations can be awarded through the Trust Fund (rather than "into" the Fund) makes clear that it does not acquire proprietary rights but merely acts as an intermediary between the Court and the beneficiaries of reparations.[1198]

---

the Trust Fund" respectively "The Court may order that an award for reparations [...] be made through the Trust Fund".

1193 Art. 75 (2), Rules 97 (1) and 98 (1)-(4).

1194 Art. 75 (2) states that "[t]he Court may make an order directly against a convicted person specifying [...] reparations to [...] victims. Where appropriate, the Court may order that the award for reparations be made through the Trust Fund". Rule 98 (1) provides that "[i]ndividual awards for reparations shall be made directly against a convicted person".

1195 UN Doc. A/AC.249/1997/WG.4/DP.3.

1196 I. Bottigliero: Redress for Victims of Crimes under International Law. Leiden, 2004, pp. 222-223 citing further authorities.

1197 According to Art. 75 (2), s. 2 this can be done "[w]here appropriate". This is confirmed both in the wording and the structure of Rule 98: Subrule 1 describes the rule ("shall be made directly", while from the wording of Subrules 2 and 3, awarding reparations indirectly through the Trust Fund shall be only ordered in situations that are envisioned to be exceptional. Rule 98 (2) determines that reparations shall be awarded through the Trust Fund when it is "impossible or impracticable to make individual awards directly to each victim"; Rule 98 (3) contains that awards "should be made through the Trust Fund where the number of the victims and the scope, forms and modalities of reparations makes a collective award more appropriate".

1198 T. Ingadottir: "The Trust Fund for Victims (Art. 79 of the Rome Statute)". In: The International Criminal Court – Recommendations on Policy and Practice – Financing, Victims, Judges, and Immunities. Ed. T. Ingadottir. Ardsley, New York, 2003, pp. 111 et seq. at pp.

When the Court decides to award reparations through the Trust Fund, "the Board of Directors shall determine the uses of such resources in accordance with any stipulations or instructions contained in such orders".[1199] Only when no further stipulations or instructions accompany the orders, may the Board of Directors determine the uses of the resources "in accordance with Rule 98 [...] taking into account any relevant decisions issued by the Court."[1200] It also "may seek further instructions from the relevant Chamber on the implementation of its orders."[1201] Thus, the Court maintains control of reparations even when it orders awards through the Trust Fund. The extent of the Trust Fund's discretion regarding the distribution of funds collected through orders for reparations, as well as fines and forfeiture, is largely determined by the Court in its transfer orders to the Trust Fund.[1202]

1) Individual Awards

Rule 98 (2) provides that the Trust Fund can be involved in the distribution of individual awards where it is impossible or impracticable for the Court to make reparations directly. The award is then deposited with the Trust Fund until it is possible to forward it to the victim or victims.[1203] The Rules do not specify in any more detail when it is impossible or impractical to make a direct award. The Trust Fund Regulations indicate that it might be impossible or impractical to directly award reparations to individuals in two different scenarios. First, when the Court has identified each beneficiary but their names or locations or other necessary information are

122 et seq.; this task within the ICC reparations regime can be termed "transfer function" or "intermediary function".

1199 Reg. 43 Trust Fund Regulations further reads "in particular on the scope of beneficiaries and the nature and amount of the award(s)", the same is true for orders of fines and forfeiture. This indicates that the Court may in particular determine the scope of beneficiaries of reparations and the nature and size of awards. In addition to the requirement to comply with the Court's orders, the Board of Directors shall consult, as far as possible, victims and their families or their legal representatives in conducting the activities and projects of the Trust Fund, see Reg. 49.

1200 Reg. 44 Trust Fund Regulations reads: "Where no further stipulations or instructions accompany the order, the Board of Director may determine the uses of such resources in accordance with Rule 98 of the Rules of Procedure and Evidence, taking into account any relevant decisions issued by the Court on the case at issue and, in particular, decisions issued pursuant to article 75, paragraph 1, of the Statute and rule 97 of the Rules of Procedure and Evidence".

1201 Reg. 45 Trust Fund Regulations.

1202 Regarding funds collected through fines and forfeiture orders pursuant to Art. 77 (2), see Chapter 6 D. ("Reparations and Penalties").

1203 See Rule 98 (2) "The Court may order that an award for reparations against a convicted person be deposited with the Trust Fund where at the time of making the order it is impossible or impracticable to make individual awards directly to each victim. The award for reparations thus deposited in the Trust Fund shall be separated from other resources of the Trust Fund and shall be forwarded to each victim as soon as possible."

unknown.[1204] Second, where the Court has not identified each beneficiary of awards, and names and/or locations of the victims are not known, or where there are great numbers of potential beneficiaries that make it burdensome to identify them individually.[1205] Furthermore, individual awards may be made through the Trust Fund where it is burdensome for the Court to deal with the verification of claims and the disbursement of awards.[1206]

When the Rules were drafted, the types of cases that the delegations had in mind when they spoke of impracticability or impossibility of direct awards were: young age or mental incapacity of the individual victim, where the whereabouts of the victims were not known or it would be extremely difficult to contact the victim in a remote area.[1207]

From the wording of Rule 98 (2) it remains unclear which body decides when the appropriate time has come to forward the awards to the beneficiaries. The Fund's purpose of relieving the Court of organizational questions regarding the identification of beneficiaries and their whereabouts suggests that this decision should regularly be made by the Trust Fund. However, due to the hierarchy between the Court and the Trust Fund, the Court is competent to determine the appropriate point in time to pass the award on to the victims, if it wishes to do so.

The Trust Fund Regulations introduce a new feature regarding the implementation of individual awards: "phased or priority verification and disbursement procedures".[1208] The Board of Directors may decide that a certain sub-group of victims is in particularly urgent need and thus should be prioritized.[1209] Rule 86 provides generally that particularly vulnerable groups of victims are children, elderly persons, persons with disabilities and victims of sexual and gender violence, in compliance with Art. 68.[1210] While it only obliges the organs of the Court to consider their particular needs in performing their functions, it might also be justified for the Trust Fund to prioritize one or several of these sub-groups.

1204 Reg. 59. Identification of beneficiaries and the collection of the missing details and disbursement of awards is then delegated to the Trust Fund.

1205 Reg. 60 Trust Fund Regulations.

1206 Reg. 62-65, 66 Trust Fund Regulations.

1207 B. Timm: "The Legal Position of Victims in the Rule of Procedure and Evidence". In: International and National Prosecution of Crimes under International Law. Eds. H. Fischer, C. Kreß; S. R. Lüder. (Bochumer Schriften zur Friedenssicherung und zum Humanitären Völkerrecht). Berlin, 2001, pp. 289 et seq. at p. 305.

1208 Reg. 65 Trust Fund Regulations.

1209 Ibid.

1210 Rule 86 (termed "general principle") states that a "Chamber in making any direction or order, and other organs of the Court in performing their functions under the Statute or the Rules, shall take into account the needs of all victims and witnesses in accordance with article 68, in particular, children, elderly persons, persons with disabilities and victims of sexual or gender violence."

2) Collective Awards

In contrast to individual reparations that can be awarded to beneficiaries directly or via the Trust Fund, the Rules envision that the competent organ to administer collective awards ordered by the Court is the Trust Fund (Rule 98 (3)).[1211] However, the Statute is open on this matter in that it only determines that the Court may make orders through the Trust Fund if it considers it appropriate (Art. 75 (2) s. 2).

Furthermore, the object and purpose of collective reparation do not, in principle, require that collective awards shall be made to victims through the Trust Fund. In fact, certain forms of collective reparations are difficult to imagine as an indirect award, i.e. strictly symbolic gestures by the convicted person, such as his or her public apology. Thus, despite what might be suggested by the wording and systematic interpretation of Rule 98, if the Court considers it appropriate to order direct awards of collective reparations, it may do so.[1212]

As with individual awards, the Trust Fund's tasks may be limited to implementing the collective award ordered by the Court. However, a comparison of the wording of Rule 98 (3) on collective awards with that of Rule 98 (2) on individual awards seems to indicate a greater influence of the Trust Fund in determining the nature and recipients of collective awards.[1213] However, the hierarchy between the Court and Trust Fund dictates that, again, it is exclusive role of the Court to decide how precisely it wants to determine the nature and beneficiaries of the collective reparations award.[1214] Consequently, the Trust Fund Regulations acknowledge that the Trust Fund's "draft implementation plan shall set out the precise nature of the collective award(s), where not already specified by the Court".[1215] They further envision that it will usually be for the Trust Fund to develop methods of implementation of the award.[1216] The determinations are to be approved by the Court.[1217] Thus, despite the different wording of

1211 Rule 98 (3) states that "[t]he Court may order that an award for reparations against a convicted person be made through the Trust Fund where the number of the victims and the scope, forms and modalities of reparations makes a collective award more appropriate". This can also be concluded from Rule 98 (1).

1212 See also B. Timm: "The Legal Position of Victims in the Rule of Procedure and Evidence". In: International and National Prosecution of Crimes under International Law. Eds. H. Fischer, C. Kreß; S. R. Lüder. (Bochumer Schriften zur Friedenssicherung und zum Humanitären Völkerrecht). Berlin, 2001, pp. 289 et seq. at p. 305.

1213 Rule 98 (2) expressly states that individual awards shall be deposited separate from other awards, and passed on as soon as possible while regarding collective awards, Rule 98 (3) contains no such guidelines.

1214 According to Reg. 57, 59, 69, 73 Trust Fund Regulations , the regular procedure intended seems to be that the Trust Fund (its Board) creates – in consultation with victims – a implementation plan for the collective reparation award, which is to be approved of by the Court.

1215 Reg. 69.

1216 Reg. 69 further reads: "as well as the methods for its/their implementation".

1217 Ibid.

the Rule 98 concerning collective awards, the allocation of competences between the Court and Trust Fund is identical with regard to individual awards.[1218]

c) Distribution through Organizations (Rule 98 (4))

In some cases neither the Court nor the Trust Fund may be in a position to distribute reparations in the area where the beneficiaries are situated. The Court may decide that reparations awards made through the Trust Fund shall be made to a national, international or intergovernmental organization which has been approved by the Trust Fund and which is in a more appropriate position to deal with distribution.[1219] Before making such a referral, the Court must consult the Trust Fund and interested states.[1220] If the Court has not determined a specific use for the award to the intergovernmental, international or national organization, the Trust Fund may determine how to use the award, in accordance with the relevant Regulations.[1221] It is for the Trust Fund's Secretariat to monitor the implementation of the Court's order, while a power of general oversight remains with the Court.[1222] However, the Regulations also grant the Trust Fund the power to decide on using intermediaries or partners to facilitate the disbursement of reparations awards.[1223]

1218 E.g. Reg. 43 and 44 Trust Fund Regulations do not differentiate between individual and collective awards.

1219 Rule 98 (4); Reg. 73 Trust Fund Regulations sets forth that the Trust Fund shall establish a draft implementation plan which "shall set out, where not already specified by the Court: (a) The concerned organization(s) and a summary of their relevant expertise; (b) A list of the specific functions that the concerned organization(s) is/are to undertake in fulfillment of the Court's order; (c) a memorandum of understanding and/or other contractual terms between the Board of Directors and the concerned organization(s) setting out roles and responsibilities, monitoring and oversight". The organization might be one representing a collective of victims which is the recipient of the collective award and or involved in humanitarian work or projects in areas where the victim group is present.

1220 Rule 98 (4). Cooperation with the state concerned might be necessary to carry out the task given to the Trust Fund and delegated to another institution. Thus, the purpose of the consultation procedure is to ensure the approvement and support of the state regarding the agencies' activities to implement the reparation order which are carried out on its territory. Otherwise, the involvement of the agencies in the internal affairs of a state could be regarded as an infringement of sovereignty of the state.

1221 Reg. 73 and 75 Trust Fund Regulations.

1222 Reg. 74 Trust Fund Regulations.

1223 Regarding individual awards, Reg. 67 determines that "[t]he Trust Fund may decide to use intermediaries to facilitate the disbursement of reparations awards, as necessary, where to do so would provide greater access to the beneficiary group and would not create any conflict of interest. Intermediaries may include interested States, intergovernmental organizations, as well as national or international non-governmental organizations in close proximity with the beneficiary groups." Regarding collective awards, Reg. 71 specifies that "[t]he Trust Fund may identify intermediaries or partners, or invite proposals for the implementation of awards."

3. Complementing Reparation Awards with "Other Resources of the Trust Fund"

In some cases resources collected through orders for reparations, fines and forfeiture may not be sufficient to implement reparation awards. In the event that the Court orders reparations to be made through the Trust Fund, the Trust Fund may decide to complement funds for reparation awards with its "other resources".[1224] These resources may consist of funds received through voluntary contributions[1225] or be financed by the Assembly of State Parties (ASP).[1226] It has been suggested that also, competent international bodies, such as the Security Council might confiscate or otherwise set aside state assets and place them in the custody of the Trust Fund for the purpose of satisfying reparations claims.[1227] As resources obtained through orders of reparations, fines and forfeiture can often be limited or not immediately available, the option to complement the available resources with voluntary contributions is crucial for the functioning and the success of the ICC reparations regime.

From its Regulations it seems unclear whether the Trust Fund has the power to complement all awards the Court ordered, or only collective awards. Under Reg. 50 (b), the Trust Fund can be seized when "the Court makes an order for reparations [...] in accordance with rule 98, sub-rules 2 to 4, of the Rules [...]". In contrast, under Reg. 56, "[t]he Board of Director's shall determine whether to complement [...] payments for awards under rule 98, sub-rules 3 and 4 [...]", thus excluding indirect individual awards pursuant to Rule 98 (2). However, the more generous reading of the Regulations, which allows for the complementation of all awards seems preferable, as the Trust Fund uses its own resources, and there are options for the Assembly of State Parties to intervene if it disagrees with the Trust Fund's use of the funds in question.[1228]

The resources that can be utilized to complement reparation awards are funds the Trust Fund received through voluntary contributions pursuant to Rule 98 (5). However, it is the sole decision of the Trust Fund whether the resources transferred to it by the Court shall be supplemented by money received through voluntary con-

1224 Reg. 50 (b), Reg. 56 Trust Fund Regulations. While this option is not mentioned in the Statute, Rule 98 (5) provides for the possibility for the Trust Fund to receive funds through voluntary donations of individuals, states, organizations, corporations and other entities in addition to Court-ordered reparations and money and other property collected through fines and forfeiture orders.

1225 Reg. 22-30 Trust Fund Regulations. Yet, one-third of voluntary contributions made by other sources than governments may be ear-marked and consequently have to be used by the Trust Fund in accordance with the request of the donor (Reg. 27).

1226 Reg. 35-36 Trust Fund Regulations. However, the ASP may stipulate how the resources allocated by it are to be used.

1227 M. Henzelin; V. Heiskanen; G. Mettraux: "Reparations to Victims before the International Criminal Court – Lessons from International Mass Claims Processes". In: Criminal Law Forum 17 (2006), pp. 317 et seq. at p. 330.

1228 E.g. by amending the Trust Fund Regulations pursuant to Reg. 76.

tributions in accordance with Rule 98 (5).[1229] It is significant that during the drafting of the Rules, delegates rejected the option of granting the Court the power to order the Trust Fund to complement awards with its own resources.[1230]

Thus, while the Trust Fund is obliged to implement awards according to the Court's orders, the Trust Fund also has a powerful position vis-à-vis the Court. It is within the discretion of the Trust Fund to decide whether to complement reparations awards and thus to secure the functioning of the ICC reparations regime. If the Court does not succeed in obtaining funds from the convicted person to implement reparation awards, the Trust Fund's organs might in fact be in a better position to effect the nature and scope of reparation awards, as well as its beneficiaries.

When the Trust Fund decides to allocate its own resources to implement the reparation award ordered by the Court, the convicted person becomes the debtor of the Trust Fund.[1231] It might then become necessary for the Court to "monitor the financial situation of the sentenced person on an ongoing basis, even following completion of a sentence of imprisonment", as provided for in the Court Regulations.[1232] Once the Court takes control of his or her assets, the convicted person shall be required to reimburse the sums due to the Trust Fund.[1233]

Both the 2005 Victims Principles and the 1985 Victim Declaration establish that states should establish national programs for reparation and other assistance to victims in the event that the party liable for the harm suffered is unable or unwilling to pay adequate reparations.[1234] In many national legal systems, state compensation programs ensure that victims of (serious) crime do not remain uncompensated in

1229 The Trust Fund has the power to use these resources according to its own discretion, as long as they are used in accordance with its mandate, i.e. for the benefit of victims of crimes under the jurisdiction of the Court and their families, Art. 79 (1), Rule 98 (1).

1230 The reason for the rejection was that the Trust Fund was considered an organ independent of the Court, see P. Lewis; H. Friman: "Reparations to Victims". In: The International Criminal Court – Elements of Crimes and Rules of Procedure and Evidence. Ed. R. S. Lee. Ardsley, New York, 2001, pp. 474 et seq. at p. 486.

1231 This must be so even though the convicted person is likely to spend many years in prison, making it unlikely that the debt will be paid back quickly. However, the Court, through the State parties, might get hold of assets belonging to the convicted person at an earlier point in time.

1232 Reg. 117 Court Regulations. The same is true with regard to the enforcement of fines and forfeiture orders. The obligations are on the Presidency and the Registry.

1233 C. Jorda; J. de Hemptinne: "The Status and Role of the Victim". In: The Rome Statute of the International Criminal Court – A Commentary. Eds. A. Cassese; P. Gaeta; J. R. W. D. Jones. Vol. 2. Oxford, 2002, pp. 1387 et seq. at p. 1416 with reference to national legal systems and their incorporation of the principle of "collective solidarity" in similar cases.

1234 Principle 16. They further contain that in "cases where a person, a legal person, or other entity is found liable for reparation to a victim, such party should provide reparation to the victim or compensate the State if the State has already provided reparation to the victim", see also Art. 15 2005 Victims Principles; Art. 37 2005 Guidelines on Child Victims; Art. 12-13 1985 Victim Declaration.

case where the offender is, for example, unknown or insolvent.[1235] Also, often social security or insurance companies pay for the victim's losses and may then be able to claim from the wrongdoer the amount paid to the victim.[1236]

The ICC reparations regime is based on principles incorporated in recent international legal documents and many national legal systems with regard to the rights of victims of crime: the guilty party is primarily responsible for making reparations. If he or she cannot or does not pay, the public will assume this responsibility. With regard to the ICC, this complementary function can be fulfilled by the international community, through the Trust Fund.

Even though the ICC's legal instruments see the involvement of the Trust Fund in the implementation of reparations as the exception to the rule, in practice, direct monetary awards only make sense under two conditions. First, when at the time the Court's reparation order is made, it has succeeded in taking control of the perpetrator's assets, or there is sufficient reason to assume that the perpetrator owns assets and the Court will take control of them within a reasonable time. Second, when the identities and whereabouts of those harmed by the convicted person's crime are

1235 See for a overview on state compensation for victims in the US M. Heikkilä: International Criminal Tribunals and Victims of Crime. Turku, 2004, pp. 49-50; for France, pp. 53-54; for Finland, p. 55. In the context of mass crimes, the Rwandan law that established the gacaca system links reparations made by the individual perpetrator with a compensation fund, see H. Rombouts; S. Vandeginste: "Reparation for Victims in Rwanda – Caught between Theory and Practice". In: Out of the Ashes – Reparation for Victims of Gross and Systematic Human Rights Violations. Eds. K. de Feyter; S. Parmentier; M. Bossuyt (et al.). Antwerp, 2005, pp. 309 et seq. at pp. 316, 320.

1236 M. Heikkilä: International Criminal Tribunals and Victims of Crime. Turku, 2004, p. 54 regarding France. However, often compensation is restricted in that it is only awarded for specific kinds of damages caused as a result of the crime, or to a limited extent. Para. 12 1985 Victims Declaration states "a) Victims who have sustained significant bodily injury or impairment of physical or mental health as a result of serious crimes; b) The family, in particular dependants of persons who have died or become physically or mentally incapacitated as a result of such victimization." Para. 13 provides that "[t]he establishment, strengthening and expansion of national funds for compensation to victims should be encouraged. Where appropriate, other funds may also be established for this purpose, including those cases where the State of which the victim is a national is not in a position to compensate the victim for the harm." Pursuant to paras. 19-21, victims of abuse of power are to be provided with appropriate rights, restitution, compensation and assistance including material, medical and psychological support. R. S. Clark: "The 1985 United Nations Declaration of Basic Principles of Justice for Victims of Crime and Abuse of Power". In: The Living Law of Nations – Essays on Refugees, Minorities, Indigenous People and the Human Rights of other Vulnerable Groups in Memory of Atle Grahl-Madsen. Eds. G. Alfredsson; P. Macalister-Smith. Kehl am Rhein (et al.), 1996, pp. 355 et seq. at p. 363 points out that the amount granted by the state compensation schemes is not necessarily as large as reparations ordered against the offender by a court; confirming M. Heikkilä: International Criminal Tribunals and Victims of Crime. Turku, 2004, p. 55 with regard to Finland. Also, it might be that not all damages will be compensated and only those will benefit who have become victims of certain crimes.

known, and claims have been substantiated, and thus distribution of reparations does not complicate the Court's task to any significant degree.[1237] In all other circumstances, it seems more appropriate to implement reparations through the Trust Fund.

Thus, while it falls to the Court alone to decide on the scope of the reparation order against the convicted person,[1238] depending on which mode of implementation the Court selects, the Trust Fund or an organization may also decide on the scope of awards and determine beneficiaries.[1239]

First, when the Court orders compensation awards to be made directly to individual victims pursuant to Rule 98 (1), the scope of the reparation order against the convicted person will be determined by the sum of individual reparation awards made to victims. The second option is to order the convicted person to pay reparations to victims through the Trust Fund. For individual awards pursuant to Rule 98 (2), the scope is the estimated amount required to compensate all victims eligible, since the exact number of beneficiaries might not be clear. In this case, it might be for the Trust Fund to determine the individual recipients of the awards and perhaps also their scope. Third, the Court might determine that the convicted person makes a collective award through the Trust Fund to the community of victims, e.g. to certain projects (Rule 98 (3)), or both individual and collective awards via organizations (Rule 98 (4)). Fourth, all of these possibilities might be combined, in that individual awards are made to a few victims that are more directly or severely affected by the crime than others and at the same time, a collective award is ordered for the benefit of a broader spectrum of victim in the particular case. The fourth option may be best suited to ensuring that reparations are made to all those victimized by the convicted person's crime, while acknowledging that some may have been harmed more severely or directly than others.

With regard to reparations, the Trust Fund has two key functions. The first is to ensure that victims will actually benefit from the Court's reparation orders within reasonable time. The second is to relieve some of the burden on the Court to deal

1237 The Court might decide to order direct individual awards or indirect individual awards where it has already determined all beneficiaries. In this case, when monetary awards are made, it is for the Court to determine all individual awards by calculating pecuniary damage, harm and injury and the amount of impecuniary damage for injuries attributable to the convicted person. It is for the Court to determine individual or collective compensation awards that take into account damage, loss and injury caused by the crime and fulfill the criterion of appropriateness. These amounts have to be calculated by adding the amounts ordered to those eligible together. In contrast, when the Court decides to order indirect individual awards and leaves it for the Trust Fund to determine every beneficiary, it can only determine the award to be made by the convicted person based on estimations as to the scope of awards and number of beneficiaries.

1238 While it can appoint experts to assess damages and suggest appropriate types and modalities of reparations (Rule 97 (2)).

1239 See Reg. 55 Trust Fund Regulations: "the Trust Fund shall take into account the following factors in determining the nature and/or size of awards, inter alia: the nature of the crimes, the particular injuries to the victims and the nature of the evidence to support such injuries, as well as the size and location of the beneficiary group".

with reparations and thus enable it to focus on its main function of prosecuting the perpetrators of crimes under its jurisdiction.

It may be questionable whether reparations made through and complemented by the Trust Fund are indeed best suited to achieve the purposes of reparation. It could be argued that in this case, the element of acknowledgment of responsibility and the direct link to the perpetrator and its victims is absent, or at least less evident. However, the link to the perpetrator is not entirely missing, as he or she either provided some, albeit insufficient, funds or becomes the debtor of the Trust Fund. Furthermore, victims might have the practical need to receive certain financial means to ease the damage caused by the crime, regardless of the identity of the person or entity paying. Awards funded by the international public also represent a recognition of the victimization and an affirmation of the victims' rights.[1240]

When the Trust Fund complements awards with its own resources, considerations as to their distribution could differ compared to situations in which reparations are financed entirely from the perpetrator's own funds. Awards funded by the Trust Fund could prioritize those who are particularly needy, such as those referred to in Rule 86, or compensate only certain types of harm, such as bodily harm or pain and suffering rather than damage to property, as suggested in the 1985 Victims Declaration and as practiced in many national jurisdictions. Furthermore, it seems appropriate to ensure that as many victims as possible benefit from awards. As mentioned above, the Trust Fund Regulations seem to suggest that collective awards in particular will be supplemented.

The clear hierarchy between the Court and the Trust Fund with regard to the implementation of reparation awards seems to break down once convicted persons' funds obtained by the Court are insufficient to implement reparation awards. As it is only for the Trust Fund to decide on the allocation of its resources received through voluntary contributions, it might in practice be in a better position to influence the decision on the nature and scope of awards, and its beneficiaries.

One of the most serious challenges that stands to endanger the entire functioning of the ICC's reparations regime is a shortfall in the convicted persons' assets or

1240 S. Gloppen: "Review Essay: Reparatory Justice – A Road to Reconciliation? On the Role of Reparations in Transitional Justice Theory". In: Reparations – Redressing Past Wrongs. Eds. G. Ulrich; L. Krabbe Boserup. (Human Rights in Development – Yearbook 2001). The Hague, 2003, pp. 385 et seq. at p. 390: "When those who caused the harm provide redress to their victims [...] there is a convincing argument that this will contribute to reconciliation between perpetrator(s) and victim(s).This is particularly true where the process is voluntary. However, this is rarely the case [...]. The absence of a direct link between the perpetrator, and the lack of a dimension of contrition, weakens the psychological argument [that reparations should be made in order to achieve] [...] reconciliation. Nevertheless, redress provided through alternative measures [that are provided by some other entity than the direct perpetrator] does represent acknowledgment, an affirmation of the victim's rights in the eyes of society. The importance of the practical remedies [to restore the physical, psychological, social and economic damage caused by past abuses] should also not be underestimated." See also S. Zappalà: Human Rights in International Criminal Proceedings. Oxford, 2003, p. 228 referring particularly to compensation.

assets of which the Court can take control.[1241] The Trust Fund can play a crucial role in securing the functioning of the ICC reparations mechanism by supplementing reparation awards. Thus, the precondition for an effective and reliable functioning of the ICC reparations mechanism is that the Trust Fund is equipped with sufficient resources.

In the event that the ICC orders reparations at a time when there are insufficient funds available or the precise number of beneficiaries of the award is yet unknown, it seems reasonable to utilize methods developed in the context of state responsibility: priority disbursement of reparations awards, or the immediate payment only of a basic amount, leaving the difference to an appropriate reparations award potentially to be paid at a later stage.

G. Protective Measures and Enforcement of Reparation Orders (Art. 75 (4) and (5) ICC Statute)

I. Protective Measures

It is crucial to secure the perpetrator's assets as early as possible in the proceedings in order to ensure the implementation of ICC reparation orders. Otherwise, the accused will have the opportunity to conceal or destroy his or her means and profits of his or her alleged crime, or any other assets he or she owns.

From the time a warrant of arrest or summons has been issued, the Pre-Trial Chamber can order a state to take "protective measures for the purpose of forfeiture, in particular for the ultimate benefit of victims" (Art. 57 (3) e)).[1242] Relevant protective measures may consist of the "identification, tracing and freezing or seizure of proceeds, property and assets and instrumentalities of crimes"(Art. 93 (1) k)).

The Trial Chamber has the same power after the conviction of the offender (Art. 75 (4), Art. 93 (1)).[1243] Victims or their legal representatives can trigger this power of the Pre-Trial Chamber or the Trial Chamber.[1244]

1241 Also, whether fines and forfeiture orders can be successfully enforced depends, to a large extent, on the cooperation of states. According to The Redress Trust: Enforcement of Awards for Victims of Torture and Other International Crimes, London, 2006, p. 61 "[t]o date, there have been few human rights cases under the ATCA or TVPA in which assets have been successfully collected. In a class action suit brought by survivors against former Philippine president Ferdinand Marcos, a award of more than $ 1 billion was made against the Marcos' estate. Only a very small portion of that judgment has been collected due to numerous logistical and political roadblocks."

1242 In making this decision, the Pre-Trial Chamber has to give regard to the strength of evidence and the rights of the parties concerned, Art. 93 (1) (k), Rule 99. See also the competences of the Prosecutor pursuant Rule 54.

1243 See also Rule 99.

1244 Rule 99 read in conjunction with Art. 57 (3) (e) and Art. 75 (4). Also the Prosecutor may apply to the Court to impose protective measures.

Art. 75 (4) gives the Court the power to order protective measures for the purpose of giving effect to orders under Art. 75 only "after a person is convicted of a crime within the jurisdiction of the Court".[1245] It could be considered that the explicit wording of the provision rules out ordering protective measures to secure funds for potential reparation awards at any stage of proceedings before conviction. The consequence would be that the Pre-Trial Chamber's competence to order protective measures would not encompass measures for the purposes of reparations.[1246] The drafting debates surrounding Art. 75 support this view. A proposal to adopt protective measures in the field of reparations in the pre-trial stage (Art. 57 (3) e)) was rejected.[1247]

However, Pre-Trial Chamber I has taken the view that "cooperation requests pursuant to Art. 57 (3) e) and 93 (1) k) of the Statute for the taking of protective measures to secure the enforcement of reparation awards should be transmitted simultaneously with cooperation requests for arrest and surrender if the warrants of arrest are not issued under seal"[1248] The Chamber has expressed the view that "existing technology makes it possible for a person to place most of his assets and moveable property beyond the Court's reach in only a few days. Therefore, if assets and property are not seized or frozen at the time of the execution of a cooperation request for arrest and surrender, or very soon thereafter, it is likely that the subsequent efforts of the Pre-Trial Chamber, Prosecution or the victims participating in the case will be fruitless."[1249]

Moreover, at the time of ordering a warrant of arrest or summons, it is impossible for the Pre-Trial Chamber to know whether the Trial Chamber will order a fine, for-

1245 See Art. 75 (4):" In exercising its power under this article, the Court may, after a person is convicted of a crime within the jurisdiction of the Court, determine whether, in order to give effect to an order which it may make under this article, it is necessary to seek measures under article 93, paragraph 1".

1246 See, e.g. D. Donat-Cattin: "Article 75 – Reparations to Victims". In: Commentary on the Rome Statute of the International Criminal Court – Observers' Notes, Article by Article. Ed. O. Triffterer. Baden-Baden, 1999, pp. 965 et seq. at p. 975.

1247 C. Kreß; G. Sluiter: "Fines and Forfeiture Orders". In: The Rome Statute of the International Criminal Court – A Commentary. Eds. A. Cassese; P. Gaeta; J. R. W. D. Jones. Vol. 2. Oxford, 2002, pp. 1823 et seq. at p. 1834; D. Donat-Cattin: "Article 75 – Reparations to Victims". In: Commentary on the Rome Statute of the International Criminal Court – Observers' Notes, Article by Article. Ed. O. Triffterer. Baden-Baden, 1999, pp. 965 et seq. at p. 975: states feared that early protective measures might violate the presumption of innocence and that "non-crime related property" could be subject to such measures.

1248 Situation in the Democratic Republic of the Congo in the Case of *The Prosecutor v. Thomas Lubanga Dyilo*, Decision on the Prosecutor's Application for a Warrant of Arrest, Article 58, ICC Pre-Trial Chamber I, 10 February 2006, ICC-01/04-01/06 (annexed to ICC-01/04-01/06, 24 February 2006), para. 139. In this case, the Chamber did so *proprio motu* pursuant to Rule 99 (1). However, it noted that regarding future applications for a warrant of arrest or a summons to appear, "the effectiveness of the reparation system would greatly benefit from the Prosecution's due consideration of this matter during the investigation stage" (para. 141).

1249 Ibid., para. 137.

feiture or reparations in the event that the proceedings result in a conviction. Thus, the Pre-Trial Chamber could provisionally order states to seize property and assets "for the ultimate benefit of victims".[1250] After conviction, the seized goods could, inter alia, be used for the purposes of reparations to victims.[1251] However, as protective measures can only be imposed for the purposes of eventual forfeiture, in accordance with Art. 77 (2) b) only proceeds, property and assets that derived from the crime can be secured in this way.

II. *Enforcement*

The ICC Statute provides that the enforcement regime for fines and forfeiture order shall apply to its reparation orders (Art. 75 (5), Art. 109 (1)).[1252]

States are obliged to fully enforce ICC reparation orders like orders of fines and forfeiture, in accordance with their national laws.[1253] National authorities are not allowed to modify reparations specified by the Court, the scope or extent of any damage, loss or injury determined by the Court or the principles stated in the order.[1254] It seems that the enforcement procedure differs depending on whether an individual or collective reparation award is enforced, and whether it concerns monetary or non-monetary forms of reparations.[1255]

1250 Art. 57 (3) e) and 93 (1) k).

1251 This view is supported by Rule 221 (2). D. Donat-Cattin: "Article 75 – Reparations to Victims". In: Commentary on the Rome Statute of the International Criminal Court – Observers' Notes, Article by Article. Ed. O. Triffterer. Baden-Baden, 1999, pp. 965 et seq. at p. 975 also suggests that Art. 57 (3) e) could make possible to take protective measures before conviction for the purposes of reparations.

1252 See also Rules 217-222; Reg. 116, 117 Court Regulations.

1253 Art. 75 (5) read in conjunction with Art. 109 (1); see also Rules 217-222; Reg. 116 Court Reg. for formal requirements and modalities of enforcement. See C. Ferstman: "The Reparation Regime of the ICC – Practical Considerations". In: Leiden Journal of International Law 15 (2002), pp. 667 et seq.; for a discussion of the developing of the Rules on enforcement of reparation orders see R. E. Fife: "Penalties". In: The International Criminal Court – Elements of Crimes and Rules of Procedure and Evidence. Ed. R. S. Lee. Ardsley, New York, 2001, pp. 555 et seq. at pp. 692 et seq. Generally see C. Kreß; G. Sluiter: "Fines and Forfeiture Orders". In: The Rome Statute of the International Criminal Court – A Commentary. Eds. A. Cassese; P. Gaeta; J. R. W. D. Jones. Vol. 2. Oxford, 2002, pp. 1823 et seq.

1254 Rule 219. Rule 219 (3) contains requirements for the content of the reparation order; see similarly the well-established jurisprudence of the Inter-American Court, e.g. *Garrido and Baigorria v. Argentina*, Reparations, Inter-American Court of Human Rights, 27 August 1998, Ser. C, No. 39, para. 46.

1255 C. Kreß; G. Sluiter: "Fines and Forfeiture Orders". In: The Rome Statute of the International Criminal Court – A Commentary. Eds. A. Cassese; P. Gaeta; J. R. W. D. Jones. Vol. 2. Oxford, 2002, pp. 1823 et seq. at pp. 1835-1836. E.g., it is unclear whether the national enforcement procedure of individual awards must be triggered by the individual itself; or

When states are unable to give effect to a reparation order, they may "take measures to recover the value of the proceeds, property or assets ordered by the Court to be forfeited" (Art. 109 (2)).[1256] In either case, effect shall be given to the reparation order "without prejudice to the rights of bona fide third parties".[1257] It seems that national authorities are to determine who qualifies as a "bona fide third party", as the ICC Statute and Rules do not define the concept.[1258]

The property or proceeds of sold property obtained as a result of the enforcement of a decision of the Court, such as a reparation order, shall be transferred to the Court (Art. 109 (3)).

Thus, whether ICC reparation orders will be implemented effectively depends, at the end of the day, on the interaction and cooperation of ICC member states and possibly states that are not parties to the ICC.[1259]

The Presidency must decide "on all matters related to the disposition or allocation of property or assets realized through enforcement of an order of the Court" (Rule 221 (1)). The Presidency is also to monitor the financial situation of the sentenced person in order to enforce fines, forfeiture and reparation orders, if necessary after completion of the sentence of imprisonment. It must also request information and make inquiries regarding the sentenced person's financial situation.[1260] Thus, "[t]he Presidency of the Court is effectively the body for enforcement of reparations to vic-

whether the request for cooperation by the Presidency triggers the obligation of the state party to give effect to the reparation order.

1256 See also Rule 218 (1) (c). Thus, it is clear that monetary reparations do not need to be made from the property, assets and instrumentalities of crimes, as could be interpreted from Art. 75 (4) and Art. 93 (1) k), and has been questioned by I. Bantekas; S. Nash: International Criminal Law. 2nd ed. London, 2003, p. 137.

1257 Art. 75 (5) read in conjunction with Art. 109 (1), (2).

1258 C. Kreß; G. Sluiter: "Fines and Forfeiture Orders". In: The Rome Statute of the International Criminal Court – A Commentary. Eds. A. Cassese; P. Gaeta; J. R. W. D. Jones. Vol. 2. Oxford, 2002, pp. 1823 et seq. at p. 1830, who point out that the Presidency should be competent to determine when this concept has in a specific case been used in an abusive manner. Bona fide third parties may – just as victims through their legal representatives and the convicted person – appeal reparation orders in case they are adversely affected, see Art. 82 (4).

1259 See for a more detailed discussion of protective measures and enforcement of ICC reparation orders and challenges in this context, as well as national implementation on cooperation with the ICC C. Ferstman: "The Reparation Regime of the ICC – Practical Considerations". In: Leiden Journal of International Law 15 (2002), pp. 667 et seq. at p. 677; see also I. Bottigliero: Redress for Victims of Crimes under International Law. Leiden, 2004, pp. 243 et seq. for examination of national implementing legislation on matters relating reparations.

1260 Reg. 117 Court Regulations. The Registry might be required to assist, if necessary.

tims".[1261] Finally, the enforcement of reparations measures to victims has priority over all other orders.[1262]

III. Assessment

The success of the ICC reparations mechanism depends largely on the willingness of the member states to cooperate with the Court in its search for assets and property. Most forms of reparations, including monetary forms such as restitution or rehabilitation, and symbolic forms such as the construction of a memorial, can only be enforced with the support of the relevant states. Moreover, without the support of states, it is almost impossible for reparations ordered by the ICC to contribute in a meaningful way to societal reconciliation.

International experiences on recovering money from individual perpetrators for the purposes of reparations is rather discouraging. Thus far, most defendants prosecuted succeeded in claiming insolvency before the ICTY and ICTR, with the consequence that the tribunals are paying their attorney fees.[1263] It has been noted that the irony is that these are the very people who are widely believed to have looted the countries where they once ruled.[1264] Reparation orders obtained by victims of international crimes in national forums against individual perpetrators have often

1261 G. Bitti; G. González Rivas: "The Reparations Provisions for Victims under the Rome Statute of the International Criminal Court". In: Redressing Injustices through Mass Claims Processes – Innovative Responses to Unique Challenges. Ed. The International Bureau of the Permanent Court of Arbitration. Oxford, 2006, pp. 299 et seq. at p. 317.

1262 Rule 221 (2). See also Chapter 6 D. ("Reparations and Penalties").

1263 See C. Ferstman: "The International Criminal Court's Trust Fund for Victims – Challenges and Opportunities". In: Yearbook of International Humanitarian Law 2003. Ed. A. McDonald. Vol. 6. The Hague, 2006, pp. 424 et seq. at p. 430; concerning reparations in *The Prosecutor v. Théoneste Bagosora*, Decision on the Amicus Curiae Application by the Government of the Kingdom of Belgium, International Criminal Tribunal for Rwanda, Trial Chamber II, 6 June 1998, ICTR-96-7-T, the competent Chamber of the ICTR did not grant leave to file an amicus curiae brief concerning the authorization of Belgian victims and their rightful claimants to appear before the Chamber as plaintiffs in accordance with Art. 23 (3) ICTR Statute and Rules 105, 106 of the ICTR Rules on restitution and compensation.

1264 W. A. Schabas: An Introduction to the International Criminal Court. 2nd ed. Cambridge, 2004, p. 150. Similar concerns are raised by R. E. Fife: "Penalties". In: The International Criminal Court – Elements of Crimes and Rules of Procedure and Evidence. Ed. R. S. Lee. Ardsley, New York, 2001, pp. 555 et seq. at p. 567; F. P. King; A.-M. La Rosa: "Penalties under the ICC Statute". In: Collection of Essays on the Rome Statute of the International Criminal Court. Eds. F. Lattanzi; W. A. Schabas. Ripa di Fagnano Alto, 1999, pp. 311 et seq. at p. 327; skeptical with regard to the possibilities of the ICC's reparations mechanism M. Arsanjani; M. W. Reisman: "Developments at the International Criminal Court – The Law-in-Action of the International Criminal Court". In: American Journal of International Law 99 (2005), pp. 385 at pp. 401-402.

remained unenforced.[1265] Before the ICC, even where offenders have assets, they may use them for attorney fees or their dependants may make representations as "interested persons" (Art. 75 (3)), or there might be other potential creditors competing with the potential beneficiaries of ICC reparation orders.[1266]

States parties have a general obligation to cooperate with the ICC (Art. 86) and thus to give effect to both protective measures and reparation orders. In order to implement protective measures or reparation orders, the ICC might also depend on the voluntary cooperation of states that are not members (Art. 87 (5)). States with which the ICC seeks to cooperate might not be interested in such cooperation. There might be a number of reasons for this, e.g. they themselves were involved in the crimes or other political considerations. When member states fail to cooperate in enforcing the Court's orders, the ICC may refer the matter to the Assembly of State Parties or the Security Council where it has referred the case (Art. 87 (7)).[1267] However, it is not clear what these institutions can do in response to the non-cooperation of a state party and it seems there is little the ICC can do to bring its member states to cooperate.

As non-cooperation can often be assumed to be politically-motivated, reactions at a political level might be particularly effective in bringing a reluctant state to cooperate. Thus, in practice, the ICC might also have to rely on the support of its member states to exercise political pressure in order to ensure state cooperation.

There are also encouraging developments in the context of the implementation of reparations for international crimes. For instance, a fund was created to benefit victims of the Pinochet regime as a result of a settlement reached with Riggs Bank in the context of proceedings against General Pinochet in a Spanish Court. Moreover, Taylor's assets were frozen upon initiation of the Special Court of Sierra Leone, and

1265 See e.g. for non-enforcement of reparation orders against individual perpetrators in Rwanda H. Rombouts; S. Vandeginste: "Reparation for Victims in Rwanda – Caught between Theory and Practice". In: Out of the Ashes – Reparation for Victims of Gross and Systematic Human Rights Violations. Eds. K. de Feyter; S. Parmentier; M. Bossuyt (et al.). Antwerp, 2005, pp. 309 et seq. at pp. 316, 320, 340. Most of the awards ordered by US Courts against individuals in human rights cases on the basis of ATCA or Torture Victim Protection Act (TVPA) have not been enforced, see generally The Redress Trust: Enforcement of Awards for Victims of Torture and Other International Crimes, London, 2006, pp. 60 et seq.

1266 C. Ferstman: "The International Criminal Court's Trust Fund for Victims – Challenges and Opportunities". In: Yearbook of International Humanitarian Law 2003. Ed. A. McDonald. Vol. 6. The Hague, 2006, pp. 424 et seq. at p. 430 notes that "[i]t plausible or even likely that in the trial of government leaders, the state of the territory where the crime occurred will have a competing claim against the perpetrator for corruption or misappropriation of state funds or other economic crimes", with reference to the government of the Philippines that continues to compete against victims for assets of the Marcos regime.

1267 This also applies to non-state parties which have entered an agreement with the Court, Art. 87 (5).

the EU froze the assets of all persons charged before the ICTY.[1268] In a few human rights cases in US courts, assets of individual perpetrators have been obtained.[1269]

However, given the aforementioned difficulties, securing the assets of a perpetrator at an early stage is crucial to securing the eventual enforcement of the reparation order. Pre-Trial Chamber I's broad interpretation of its competences in its early jurisprudence proves willingness to take a pro-active approach to protective measures also with regard to securing the enforcement of reparation orders.

The Court has the power to reward personally a convicted or sentenced person for his or her efforts to repair the consequences of the crime due to the connection of the ICC reparations function to its penalty system. This power might give offenders a greater incentive to facilitate the enforcement of reparations to victims. Indeed, additional incentives for cooperation may come from the Court's express obligation to monitor the financial situation of the offender in order to enforce fines, forfeiture or reparation orders even after completion of a prison sentence and the fact that seizable assets are not restricted to the proceeds of the crime.[1270]

1268 Furthermore, C. Ferstman: "The International Criminal Court's Trust Fund for Victims – Challenges and Opportunities". In: Yearbook of International Humanitarian Law 2003. Ed. A. McDonald. Vol. 6. The Hague, 2006, pp. 424 et seq. at p. 430 points out that "it is feasible that some of the individuals that the Office of the Prosecutor may bring to trial in mineral rich Democratic Republic of Congo, for example, will have assets worth locating".

1269 Of the judgment of more than $ 1 billion against the Estate of former Philippine Dictator Marcos, only a small portion has been collected. US authorities succeeded in collecting assets of the scope of $ 270,00 from General Carlos Eugeio Vides Casanova in order to enforce compensation awarded to three Salvadoran torture survivors who won a verdict of $ 54.6 million, see generally The Redress Trust: Enforcement of Awards for Victims of Torture and Other International Crimes, London, 2006, pp. 60 et seq.

1270 See above, Reg. 117 Court Regulations; Art. 109 (2).

Chapter 7 Assistance to Victims and their Families by the Trust Fund (Art. 79 ICC Statute, Rule 98 (5))

This final chapter does deal not with the ICC reparations function in the narrow sense, but with the potential complementary mechanism thereto provided by the Trust Fund.

The Trust Fund for Victims was set up "for the benefit of victims of crimes within the jurisdiction of the Court, and of the families of such victims" (Art. 79 (1)). Its role is not limited to acting as a complementary organ of the Court by implementing the Court's reparation orders.[1271] It has a broader role and can, with its own resources received under Rule 98 (5), finance measures other than reparations which are beneficial to victims and their families.[1272]

Whether victims of crimes under the ICC's jurisdiction will benefit from ICC reparation orders depends on a variety of conditions. These conditions derive from the peculiar features of a reparations mechanism which is linked with an international criminal trial. These include the decision of the ICC Prosecutor to prosecute the person responsible for a victim's harm and the fact that the proceedings result in a conviction. Furthermore, the convicted person must be ready to provide non-monetary reparations, or the Court must succeed in getting hold of assets belonging to the convicted person in case of financial reparations.

Even if it is possible to establish a sufficiently close link between the harm to be repaired and the convicted person's crime, it will usually take years until victims are awarded reparations. Furthermore, while victims of gross and systematic crimes such as those under the ICC's jurisdiction regularly have a variety of needs,[1273] reparations from the offender primarily address the harm caused to persons rather than their

1271 See for further examination Chapter 6 F. ("Implementation of Reparation Awards").

1272 This is not only suggested in Art. 79 (1) and Rule 98 (5), but clearly the approach taken in the Trust Fund Regulations.

1273 The report of International Centre for Comparative Criminology, Research Group Victimology and Restorative Justice, University of Montreal: Reparation and the International Criminal Court – Meeting the Needs of Victims, Report of the Workshop Held January 28th 2006. Available at www.cicc.umontreal.ca/activities_publiques.conferences/joanne_wemmers/ rapport_reparation, last accessed 22 April 2009, pp. 6 et seq. names as primary needs of victims: information, medical and emotional support, practical support, reparation, protection and inclusion in the criminal justice system's processes.

current needs. Reparations ordered by the ICC may also be strictly symbolic even when victims need material support. Most of these factors are beyond the control of victims.

The broader mandate of the Trust Fund allows it potentially to balance, first, injustices that might flow from the possibly narrow scope of beneficiaries of ICC reparation orders. Secondly, it might be in a position to address urgent needs of victims that predate the conviction of an offender.

The Trust Fund's own activities undertaken for the benefit of victims of crimes under the ICC's jurisdiction, in particular those committed in situations investigated by the ICC, or victims of a case prior to the conviction of the offender, do not constitute reparations under the ICC Statute. Art. 75 (2) is clear in stating that only the Court can order reparations, and only it can make a reparation order against a person it convicts. The Trust Fund is an organ independent of the Court and therefore, in implementing measures to benefit victims, does not act on the Court's behalf. Furthermore, the Trust Fund finances the measures with its own resources and does not have to link them to the person or entity responsible for the suffering or the need addressed by its measures. The presence of a certain element of responsibility for, or recognition of, past wrongdoing can be seen as a qualifying element for reparations.[1274] Consequently, the Trust Fund Regulations describe the measures which the Trust Fund may finance from its own resources as "activities and projects".

Nevertheless, these "activities and projects" dedicated to assist victims and their families might contribute to repairing the harm suffered as a result of the crimes under the ICC's jurisdiction. On behalf of the Board of Directors of the Trust Fund, Archbishop Tutu has described the meaning of assistance to victims like this: "[W]hen a country, a nation, the international community says, symbolically 'we cannot compensate you but we want to show that we care, we want to show you that we hope that this small thing that we do for you will somehow pour balm on your wounds and help those wounds to heal [...].'" [1275]

While not qualifying as reparations under the ICC Statute, in practice, Trust Fund assistance might also have reparatory effects on victims.

A. Funding

The Trust Fund has a variety of possible funding sources. Resources collected through fines, forfeiture and for the purpose of reparation awards that are transferred to the

1274 See P. Greiff; M. Wierda: "The Trust Fund for Victims of the International Criminal Court – Between Possibilities and Constraints". In: Out of the Ashes – Reparation for Victims of Gross and Systematic Human Rights Violations. Eds. K. de Feyter; S. Parmentier; M. Bossuyt (et al.). Antwerp, 2005, pp. 225 et seq. at p. 236.

1275 Archbishop Desmond Tutu: Statement by His Eminence Archbishop Desmond Tutu on behalf of the Board of Directors of the Trust Fund for Victim, Video Statement at the Ceremony Marking their First Meeting, The Hague, 22 April 2004. Available at http://www.icc-cpi.int/press/video.html, last accessed 21 April 2009.

Trust Fund are to be used in accordance with the Court orders.[1276] Furthermore, the Assembly of State Parties (ASP) can decide to allocate contributions to the Trust Fund, and may determine how they are to be used.[1277]

Beyond that, the Trust Fund may receive voluntary contributions from governments, international organizations, individuals, corporations and other entities, in accordance with Rule 98 (5) and relevant criteria set forth in the Trust Fund Regulations and criteria to be adopted by the ASP.[1278] The Trust Fund's Board of Directors, possibly with the assistance of the Court's Registry, can conduct campaigns where it considers it useful for the purpose of collecting voluntary contributions.[1279]

All contributors other than states are allowed to earmark a maximum of one third of the amount of their contribution.[1280] Earmarking is allowed under the condition that it does not result in discrimination on the grounds of race, color, sex, language, religion, political or other opinion, ethnic or other origin, property, birth or other status, unless the group enjoys special protection under international law.[1281]

The voluntary contributions it receives, and possibly also contributions from the ASP, constitute "[o]ther resources" of the Trust Fund under Rule 98 (5).

In 2008, the total amount of available Trust Fund resources were € 3,050,000.[1282]

B. Measures for the Benefit of Victims and their Families other than Reparations

The Trust Fund's Board can decide to use the resources it obtains through voluntary contributions and through allocations by the ASP to provide "psychological rehabilitation or material support for the benefit of victims and their families".[1283] The Trust Fund thus has the power to implement activities and projects which can address the needs of a broader range of victims in a more flexible manner than reparations. As-

1276 See Art. 75 (2), Art. 79 (2), Rule 98 and discussion above Chapter 5 ("Implementation of Reparation orders").

1277 Reg. 35, 36 Trust Fund Regulations; Resolution on the Establishment of a Fund for the Benefit of Victims of Crimes Within the Jurisdiction of the Court, and the Families of such Victims, adopted 9 September 2002, ICC-ASP/1/Res.6 (2002), para.2.

1278 Rule 98 (5); Reg. 21 (a) Trust Fund Regulations; Resolution on the Establishment of a Fund for the Benefit of Victims of Crimes Within the Jurisdiction of the Court, and the Families of such Victims, adopted 9 September 2002, ICC-ASP/1/Res.6 (2002), para.2. Reg. 22-30 Trust Fund Regulations set forth criteria for e.g. the reception of voluntary contributions, earmarking of funds.

1279 Reg. 53 Trust Fund Regulations.

1280 Reg. 27 Trust Fund Regulations.

1281 Reg. 27 b) Trust Fund Regulations.

1282 http://www2.icc-cpi.int/Menus/ICC/Structure+of+the+Court/Victims/Trust+Fund+for+Victims/Current+Projects/, last accessed 23 March 2009.

1283 Reg. 50 (a) (i) Trust Fund Regulations. The ASP may also decide their allocations be used for a specific purpose, Reg. 35, 36 Trust Fund Regulations.

sistance measures may include setting up centers that provide medical and psychological treatment, or schools, in victimized communities.

It can grant assistance to victims and their families before the commencement of, or during the trial proceedings or even independently of the Court proceedings. As the Court cannot grant awards prior to a person's conviction, it may be for the Trust Fund to provide interim relief or other measures to support victims before that.[1284]

As for the beneficiaries of the Trust Fund's activities, the Trust Fund Regulations provides that assistance can be provided to "victims of crimes under the jurisdiction of the court as defined in rule 85 of the Rules of Procedure and Evidence, and, where natural persons are concerned, their families, who have suffered physical, psychological and/or material harm as a result of these crimes".[1285] Thus, in contrast to ICC reparations, Trust Fund assistance in the form of "activities and projects" can be granted to persons other than victims of a case prosecuted by the ICC and their families.[1286] Beneficiaries can fall within a broader class of victims, in particular "victims of the situation" under investigation by the ICC and the families of those victims.[1287]

1284 Additionally, those victims participating in the Court's proceedings may receive assistance as a part of protection measures pursuant to Art. 68 (1). D. Donat-Cattin: "Article 75 – Reparations to Victims". In: Commentary on the Rome Statute of the International Criminal Court – Observers' Notes, Article by Article. Ed. O. Triffterer. Baden-Baden, 1999, pp. 965 et seq. at p. 971 suggests that interim relief should be adopted in conjunction with protective measures from the Pre-Trial Stage and be granted throughout the entire procedure before the Court. However, it seems questionable whether measures provided in accordance with Art. 68 can be granted to all victims of the crimes potentially committed by the accused and not only these victims who appear as witnesses before the Court, as this could be "prejudicial to or inconsistent with the rights of the accused" protected in Art. 68 (1) last sentence. Furthermore, victims that are not interested in participation before the trial but only in claiming reparations could thus not receive interim relief.

1285 Reg. 42, 48 Trust Fund Regulations. For a discussion of term "family" see Chapter 5 B. ("Eligibility to Reparations").

1286 During the drafting of the Trust Fund Regulations, suggestions as to the scope of victims ranged from interpreting Art. 79 (1) very literal, by regarding all victims of genocide, war crimes and crimes against humanity as potential beneficiaries, regardless of the activities of the Court, to a restrictive interpretation that only considers victims of crimes that are prosecuted by the Court as beneficiaries. See e.g. Victims' Rights Working Group: Comments on the Draft Regulations of the ICC Trust Fund for Victims, February 2005. Available at www.vrwg.org/Publications/01/VRWG_Feb2005.pdf, last accessed 22 April 2009. This complies with para. 2 1985 Victims Declaration that states: "[a] person may be considered a victim [...] regardless of whether the perpetrator is identified, apprehended, prosecuted or convicted [...]".

1287 Reg. 50 Trust Fund Regulations. However, the Trust Fund's Secretariat has to first notify the Court, which may object the imposition of assistance measures. On victims of the situation, see Victims Participation Booklet, p. 19 "What is the difference between a victim of the situation and a victim of the case?"

The Board of Directors of the Trust Fund has announced that it will "place emphasis on projects aimed at the most marginalized and vulnerable victims."[1288]

Requests for assistance can be submitted to the Trust Fund, which the Board of Directors intends to review against the criteria of credibility, necessity and effectiveness of the proposed projects.[1289]

C. Relation between the Court and the Trust Fund for Victims

The degree of the Trust Fund's independence from the Court regarding the allocation of its resources other than those collected through fines, forfeiture and reparation orders has not been specified in the ICC Statute or Rules.[1290] The drafters of the Statute considered that the criteria governing the Trust Fund would be complex and may need adjustment over time, which would be difficult under the stringent requirements for the Statute and delegated the task of establishing the criteria to the Assembly of State Parties (Art. 79 (3)).[1291] The Trust Fund Regulations are therefore decisive in determining the precise relation of the Trust Fund to the Court regarding activities other than its implementation of reparation orders.

The Regulations provide that the Trust Fund is responsible for using the money received through voluntary contributions to implement projects and activities for the benefit of victims and their families on its own initiative.[1292]

When the Trust Fund's Board decides to implement certain projects or activities to benefit victims, it must notify the relevant Chamber. The Chamber can then inform the Board that the suggested activity would "pre-determine any issue to be determined by the Court, including the determination of jurisdiction pursuant to article 19, admissibility pursuant to articles 17 and 18, or violate the presumption of

1288 Simone Veil, Statement, Fifth Session of the Assembly of States Parties – Statement, The Hague, 23 November 2006. Available at www.icc-cpi.int/library/vtf/SV_20061123_en.pdf, last accessed 22 April 2009.

1289 The Trust Fund Regulations do not mention such a possibility explicitly, however the existence of such a possibility becomes clear in the statement of Simone Veil, Statement, Fifth Session of the Assembly of States Parties – Statement, The Hague, 23 November 2006. Available at www.icc-cpi.int/library/vtf/SV_20061123_en.pdf, last accessed 22 April 2009.

1290 See Art. 79, Rule 98.

1291 Art. 79 (3) reads "The Trust Fund shall be managed according to criteria to be determined by the Assembly of States Parties", even though "manages" seems to refer only to the organizational structure, see M. Jennings: "Article 79 – Trust Fund". In: Commentary on the Rome Statute of the International Criminal Court – Observers' Notes, Article by Article. Ed. O. Triffterer. Baden-Baden, 1999, pp. 1005 et seq. at pp. 1006-1007. On the issues debated at the lengthy discussions prior to the adoption of the Trust Fund Regulations see, e.g. P. Greiff; M. Wierda: "The Trust Fund for Victims of the International Criminal Court – Between Possibilities and Constraints". In: Out of the Ashes – Reparation for Victims of Gross and Systematic Human Rights Violations. Eds. K. de Feyter; S. Parmentier; M. Bossuyt (et al.). Antwerp, 2005, pp. 225 et seq. at pp. 237 et seq.

1292 Reg. 50 Trust Fund Regulations.

innocence pursuant to article 66, or be prejudicial to or inconsistent with the rights of the accused and a fair and impartial trial".[1293]

If the Chamber does not respond within 45 days, it must consult with the Board to extend the time limit. The Board and the Chamber may enter an agreement regarding the extension of the time limit; otherwise the extension is 30 days.[1294] Thus, the Court can veto activities proposed by the Trust Fund's Board with reference to the argument that they predetermine issues that are to be determined by the Court, albeit only on a limited number of grounds.[1295] However, if the competent Chamber has not consulted the Trust Fund's Board within 75 days, the Board may implement the proposed activities without the explicit approval of the Chamber.[1296]

From the Regulation's reference to the "relevant Chamber" and the grounds on with the Court can veto the suggested activity, it seems that Trust Fund may initiate projects or activities from the time of Court's initial announcement of the opening of a formal investigation into a particular situation.[1297] However, the Regulations do not explicitly restrict the potential beneficiaries of Trust Fund assistance to victims of a situation under investigation by the Court.

1293 Reg. 50 (a) (ii). Yet it might be less problematic when the Trust Fund as a non-judicial organ is acting, as opposed to the Court.

1294 Reg. 50 (a) (iii) Trust Fund Regulations.

1295 For a summary of the various views in the drafting process of the Regulations on the degree of independence the Trust Fund was to be provided with in relation to the Court see A.-M. de Brouwer: "Reparation to Victims of Sexual Violence – Possibilities at the International Criminal Court and at the Trust Fund for Victims and Their Families". In: Leiden Journal of International Law 20 (2007), pp. 207 et seq. at pp. 232-233 on the various view on the degree of independence the Trust Fund shall be provided with in relation to the Court in the drafting process of the Regulations.

1296 There are a number of reporting requirements for the Trust Fund to the ASP and the Committee for Budget and Finance. These encompass the Board's determinations on the use and disbursement of voluntary contributions received under Rule 98 (5), see Reg. 76; and Resolution on the Establishment of a Fund for the Benefit of Victims of Crimes Within the Jurisdiction of the Court, and the Families of such Victims, adopted 9 September 2002, ICC-ASP/1/Res.6 (2002), Annex, para. 11: "The Board shall report annually to the Assembly of States Parties on the activities and projects of the Trust Fund and on all voluntary contributions, regardless of whether they are accepted or refused." These different responsibilities suggest that it is appropriate to arrange the Board of the Trust Fund outside the structure of the Court, even though the Trust Fund's administrative structure is temporarily located within the Registry of the Trust Fund, C. Ferstman: "The International Criminal Court's Trust Fund for Victims – Challenges and Opportunities". In: Yearbook of International Humanitarian Law 2003. Ed. A. McDonald. Vol. 6. The Hague, 2006, pp. 424 et seq. at pp. 428-429.

1297 Art. 79 (3), Rule 98 (5), Reg. 50 Trust Fund Regulations. Prior to the adoption of the Trust Fund Regulations, the option was also discussed to only allow the Trust Fund's intervention at a much later stage, namely after the criminal prosecution has ended. See for a summary of the key arguments made I. Bottigliero: Redress for Victims of Crimes under International Law. Leiden, 2004, pp. 230-233.

D. Assessment

The Court does not have the power to address the often urgent medical, emotional or material needs of the victims of crimes under its jurisdiction through its reparation orders or otherwise. In particular it cannot do so in an immediate or comprehensive manner. Thus, the role of the Trust Fund is crucial in ensuring that victims of crimes under its jurisdiction, especially needy victims of the crimes committed in a situation under investigation of the Court, can receive assistance from the ICC system.[1298] The Trust Fund can provide assistance to victims of crimes within the jurisdiction of the Court who are not involved in the few cases that will be prosecuted by the Court. It should also be in a position to grant psychological assistance and material support to victims involved in cases before the Court prior to the offender's conviction.

Similarly to the function of a national state compensation program, the Trust Fund should counterbalance the hardships on victims of crime and injustices, that might be the result of the strict requirements that necessarily apply when reparations are ordered in the context of criminal proceedings.[1299] The existence of such a complementary organ that ensures that victims of crime can receive practical assistance and material support is in line with national practices and international standards.[1300] It may, to a certain degree, countervail competition between victims for available reparations.[1301] Requiring that there be a connection between the beneficiaries of Trust Fund assistance and situations investigated by the ICC, as indicated in the Trust Fund

1298 A.-M. de Brouwer: "Reparation to Victims of Sexual Violence – Possibilities at the International Criminal Court and at the Trust Fund for Victims and Their Families". In: Leiden Journal of International Law 20 (2007), pp. 207 et seq. at p. 231 stresses that if rehabilitation and support are to have a meaningful effect on victims' lives, it is imperative that when a situation is referred to the Court, the Prosecutor starts investigations as soon as possible and the Trust Fund takes immediate action.

1299 See also International Centre for Comparative Criminology, Research Group Victimology and Restorative Justice, University of Montreal: Reparation and the International Criminal Court – Meeting the Needs of Victims, Report of the Workshop Held January 28th 2006. Available at www.cicc.umontreal.ca/ activities_publiques.conferences/ joanne_wemmers/rapport_reparation, last accessed 22 April 2009, p. 24.

1300 E.g., according to the 1985 Victims Declaration, assistance should be provided to enable victims to recover, by providing specific support needed in such areas as health, social service and justice. Victims should receive this assistance through "governmental, voluntary, community-based and indigenous means", whose existence the victims shall be informed of, paras. 14-17. The 2005 Victims Principles contain that "[s]tates should endeavour to establish national programmes for reparation and other assistance to victims in the event that the party liable for the harm suffered is unable or unwilling to meet their obligations", see Art. 16; Art. 13 2001 EU Framework Decision.

1301 See for further discussion on victim competition H. Rombouts; P. Sardaro; S. Vandeginste: "The Right to Reparation for Victims of Gross and Systematic Violations of Human Rights". In: Out of the Ashes – Reparation for Victims of Gross and Systematic Human Rights Violations. Eds. K. de Feyter; S. Parmentier; M. Bossuyt (et al.). Antwerp, 2005, pp. 345 et seq. at pp. 473 et seq.

Regulations, would prevent assistance measures becoming akin to development aid, entirely unconnected to the proceedings before the Court.

The Trust Fund Regulations distribute competences between the Court and the Trust Fund in a manner that enables a balanced decision-making process regarding the use of the Trust Fund's own resources for assistance to victims. However, several issues which are decisive for the relationship between the Court and the Trust Fund remain unresolved. First, it is unclear which organ has the final say on the length of the extension requested by the Chamber, in the event that no agreement can be reached in the course of the consultations. Second, it is not obvious what happens if the Trust Fund's Board disagrees with the view of the Chamber that the activity it suggested contradicts the issues or is inconsistent with rights of accused mentioned in Reg. 50 (a) (ii). Due to the broad or vague character of the admissible grounds to veto activities proposed by the Trust Fund, there is a risk that one of them could always be drawn upon to justify a rejection of the proposed activities. It is as yet unresolved whether the Trust Fund's organs can appeal against a veto of the Court regarding the suggested activity, and if so, which organ is competent to decide on an appeal.

Thus, in theory, the Trust Fund has a sufficient degree of independence from the Court concerning the use of its own funds. However, it seems that under the current Regulations, the Court has the power to block the Trust Fund's intended activities. Therefore, it is necessary to determine an organ that has the authority to decide on disagreements between the Trust Fund and the relevant Chamber.

While the Trust Fund's power to assist victims is of central importance in the ICC system, it would also be inappropriate if all resources obtained through voluntary contributions would be used for assistance, with the result that resources necessary to complement the ICC reparations function would not be available.[1302] One can expect that the Trust Fund is unlikely to have resources such that it could provide sufficient support and assistance to all victims of crimes under investigation by the ICC. This responsibility can and should be shared with other institutions and organizations. In contrast, the Trust Fund is the only institution that can secure the provisional implementation of ICC reparation orders. Thus, despite the necessity of a certain degree of independence from the Court, the fact that the Trust Fund's existence is essentially linked to the proceedings before the ICC should be reflected in its actions.

However, the effectiveness of the Trust Fund in complementing the role of the Court in respect of victims depends on the extent of available funding more than any other factors. Thus far, it seems difficult to imagine that the Trust Fund will, in the foreseeable future, possess sufficient resources to fulfill satisfactorily its vast tasks. These include addressing the needs of victims of situations under investigation by the ICC and balancing the narrow scope and imponderabilities of the ICC reparations mechanism. It is therefore necessary that the Trust Fund's organs engage in large-scale fundraising campaigns. Active support in securing funds should also

---

1302 P. Greiff; M. Wierda: "The Trust Fund for Victims of the International Criminal Court – Between Possibilities and Constraints". In: Out of the Ashes – Reparation for Victims of Gross and Systematic Human Rights Violations. Eds. K. de Feyter; S. Parmentier; M. Bossuyt (et al.). Antwerp, 2005, pp. 225 et seq. at pp. 242-243 take a similar view.

be afforded by the Court, the ASP and state parties. All of the ICC's organs have an interest in the effective functioning of the Trust Fund's complementary tasks. If the Trust Fund succeeds in actively assisting victims and their families, it may also relieve the Court of some pressure and allow it to concentrate fully on its core function of prosecuting perpetrators of the crimes under its jurisdiction. It is the Trust Fund that can potentially be the first to show victims of crimes in question that the international criminal justice system acknowledges their victimization and is actively addressing the harm they suffered, thus going beyond rhetoric and promises. In that sense, the success of the Trust Fund's assistance of victims and their families also has an impact on the general credibility of the Court.

Chapter 8 Summary and Conclusion

A. Towards the Implementation of the ICC Reparation System (Summary)

This study has undertaken an analysis of the ICC reparation system, and a clarification of its potential functioning. While the ICC's legal instruments are fragmentary, particularly regarding the substantive issues of reparations, this study has shown that principles for the implementation of ICC reparations mechanism result from the peculiarities of international criminal justice. In international criminal justice, an individual is held responsible for a crime whose nature and consequences are collective. Thus, when reparations are awarded in the ICC system, the symmetry that exists both in national and international systems is missing. National civil or criminal procedures regularly order an individual to make reparations as a result of violations of the rights or goods of another individual.[1303] International law regularly attributes liability to repair the harm resulting from gross and systematic crimes of a collective nature to an identified state or other collective entity, rather than to an individual. Consequently, this study has consistently confirmed the assumption that neither national nor international systems provide principles that are directly and comprehensively applicable to the ICC reparation system.

Several related factors can be summarized as formative for the potential design of a reparations mechanism within the ICC system that is effective and fair. The first parameter is set by the distinct asymmetry between the individual perpetrator's responsibility to make reparations and the often extensive and grave harm caused to victims by collective crimes, as assumed in the beginning of the study. The second decisive factor is the need to avoid actual or apparent arbitrariness in the selection

1303 In the national contexts some examples exist for the concept of individual liability to make reparations to victims of crimes under international law. E.g. in Rwanda, tribunals can order the individual perpetrators to pay compensation to victims under the 1996 and 2010 Organic law, also as a part of the gacaca system, and compensation awarded by US courts against the perpetrators of human rights crimes as a result of class actions. However, US class actions can only be filed in civil procedure, and the gacaca system differs from the ICC reparations mechanism in a number of aspects. The judgments victims have obtained in both systems have often remained unenforced.

of the beneficiaries of the ICC reparations mechanism, which might result from the uncertainties that determine the outcome of international criminal trials, while simultaneously safeguarding the rights of the convicted persons.[1304] A third factor is the necessity to secure fair and expeditious trial proceedings while tackling the complex issues that inevitably arise when making reparations to the victims of large scale crimes, especially when an individual is ordered to do so. Lastly, there is a need to balance flexibility in determining the beneficiaries and nature of reparations awards with consistency, predictability and legal certainty, which are also essential to securing the credibility and legitimacy of the Court.

The unique nature of the ICC reparations mechanism does not rule out the application of principles derived from national and international legal systems, where appropriate. In accordance with the ICC Statute, the implementation of the reparations provisions has to be consistent with internationally recognized human rights.[1305] It has been shown in this study that in many respects, international legal documents dealing with victims' rights and reparations are too general to provide answers to most of the complex issues that arise in the context of reparations awarded in international criminal trials. Similarly, a number of principles recognized in international human rights law are not applicable to the ICC reparations mechanism, as they only make sense in the context of state responsibility. However, the 2005 Victims Principles and the 1985 Victims Declaration in particular, and the jurisprudence of the regional human rights courts, do provide important guidelines for key aspects of the ICC reparations regime.

After this summary of factors generally relevant to the ICC reparation system, some of the thoughts presented throughout this study as to its possible implementation shall be briefly summarized. In this context, it is reemphasized that Art. 75 (1) ICC Statute leaves it up to the Court alone to establish reparation principles and thus to determine the exact form and functioning of the ICC reparations mechanism.

1. The ICC's legal instruments leave it to the discretion of the Court whether to order the convicted person to make reparations to, or in respect of, victims. It has been argued in this study that in principal, the Court can and should always make use of this power. Art. 75 ICC Statute on reparations to victims and Art. 79 ICC Statute on the Victims' Trust Fund imply the acknowledgment that victims shall be able to obtain reparations. The automatic consequence of the Court's finding a perpetrator to be guilty should be his or her liability to make reparations for the harm caused by the crime for which he or she was convicted. However, the effectiveness of certain forms of reparations depends on the convicted person's true willingness to make them, or the potential availability of resources, which need to be considered before making a specific reparation order.

1304 Among the uncertain factors that decide whether victims will be successful in obtaining reparations are whether the Prosecutor decides to proceed against a certain perpetrator, whether the Court succeeds in getting hold of him or her, finds enough evidence to convict him or her, gets hold of his or her assets.

1305 See Art. 21 (3).

2. Regarding the question of who may benefit from its reparations mechanism, the ICC's Statute and Rules allow for the inclusion not only of direct victims of crimes under the ICC's jurisdiction, but also of persons indirectly harmed, such as family members, as well as legal persons and collectives. It seems that it may not always be possible to make financial reparations to a large number of individuals in a satisfactory manner. Under these circumstances reparations could be made to collectives of victims rather than to individuals, in order to avoid unfair or arbitrary results by attempting to distinguish and select those deserving from those undeserving of reparations from all who qualify as victims under the ICC system. When reparations are ordered to the benefit of individuals, the beneficiaries should be determined according to consistent criteria. Individual beneficiaries might be those victims whose harm is directly linked to the crime of the convicted person. Direct causation seems to be the most objective criterion to select individuals eligible for reparation awards ordered by the ICC from others also qualifying as victims under the ICC's legal framework.

3. The ICC's legal instruments equip the Court with unlimited discretion as to the determination of damage and the form and nature of its reparation orders. The asymmetry resulting from the circumstance that an individual is ordered to make reparations to the potentially large group of victims of his or her crime can be balanced by awarding collective reparations. Thus, it seems that, contrary to what the ICC's legal instruments suggest, individual awards might be the exception rather than the rule. Collective reparations can be of both symbolic and monetary in nature. Most strictly symbolic forms of reparations are only meaningful if the convicted person is willing to perform them. Collective and symbolic reparations should be determined flexibly, with regard to the historical, cultural and political context and in accordance with the wishes of victims.

As the various possible forms of reparations serve different aims, it may be appropriate also to order individual reparations. The determination of compensation and other monetary forms of reparations should follow consistent criteria to ensure a sufficient degree of predictability and evenhandedness in the Court's decision making. Particularly in situations where compensation is awarded for non-pecuniary harm such as pain and suffering, and where the harm suffered is not precisely proven, it might be appropriate to order standardized awards, and possibly differentiate only according to the severity of harm suffered.

4. The ICC Statute and Rules provide the Court with the option of delegating the task of assessing damages, developing concepts for appropriate reparations and implementing awards to experts, the Trust Fund and organizations. The delegation of tasks seems crucial in order for the Court to succeed in efficiently implementing its reparations function without the expedient and expeditious conduct of the trial proceedings being compromised.

It seems that it will be for the Trust Fund in particular to secure the implementation of all reparations awards except for those that have been ordered directly. It also appears that direct reparations only make sense when there is a small number of identified individual beneficiaries, or the convicted person is ordered to perform a symbolic act, such as an apology. In order to prevent the implementation failure of monetary awards due to a successful claim of indigence by the convicted person, the Court should utilize all its tools both to provide incentives for and put pressure on the convicted person, and possibly member states. In the event that the Court is unsuccessful in its efforts to obtaining the convicted person's resources by the time that reparations must be ordered, the reparation order can only be implemented provisionally if the Trust Fund allocates some of its own resources. Under these circumstances, the convicted person would become the debtor of the Trust Fund.

Under the ICC Statute and Rules, priority implementation of awards to certain classes of victims could be justified for the benefit of children, elderly persons, persons with disabilities, and victims of sexual or gender violence in need.

5. Concerning the verification of applications for reparations, the standard and burden of proof applicable to the ICC reparations mechanism may vary according to the stage of proceedings in which evidential material is introduced, and the way in which the reparations proceedings are initiated. They might also differ between monetary and symbolic awards, individual and collective awards, and according to the type of harm to be compensated. However, while flexibility is important, so is consistency, particularly when there are large numbers of individual claims for monetary reparations. Generally it is submitted that modern mass claims processing techniques should be utilized by the Trust Fund or other organizations or institutions when individual awards are to be made. The existence of moral damages, such as those for pain and suffering, could be presumed once it is established that the applicant is a victim of a crime for which the offender was convicted by the Court.

6. Under its legal framework, the ICC carries specific and far reaching responsibilities regarding the conduct of its reparations procedure. It is envisioned that the Court's function is not restricted to providing a forum for victims to enforce their rights. The Court's role goes beyond this in that it also carries the responsibility of safeguarding the interests and rights of the persons affected by its mandate. As victims are the weakest and most vulnerable of those affected, it seems that the Court will need to place particular emphasis on identifying victims through outreach and notification, or to act on their behalf, in order to ensure that its proceedings integrates victims and achieve justice.

In order to implement most of these suggestions, it appears crucial that the reparation principles the Court is obliged to establish under Art. 75 (1) be clear and fair, and that they be applied in a consistent manner. Furthermore, the role of the Trust Fund is of key importance, both regarding the implementation of ICC reparation orders, and in order to assist a wider range of victims of crimes under the ICC's jurisdiction who are in need, and their families.[1306]

1306 The fund may not only consist of the reparation award made by the convicted person and assets obtained through fines and forfeiture orders. As there is regularly collective responsibility for crimes under international law, it is justified to share the financing of reparation awards to victims.

B. Potential of the ICC Reparation System

Finally, a core question that must be answered is whether the reparation system of the ICC is appropriate to redress the harm caused to victims of crimes under its jurisdiction.

Justice demands that the wrongdoer must not only be held accountable for his or her crimes, but also repairs the harm he or she caused. Accordingly, it is increasingly accepted that criminal courts should not only hold the perpetrator criminally responsible for his or her actions, but also have the task to safeguard that the harm caused to the victims of the crime is repaired. In view of the changed position of the individual in international law, it is furthermore appropriate to recognize that the person whose individual criminal responsibility has been established in an international forum is required to repair the harm caused by the crime, moving reparations based on international law beyond the law of state responsibility. The ICC reparations mechanism also contributes to the recognition of the right of individual and collective victims of gross and systematic crimes to reparations. Thus, both from theory and concept, the incorporation of the reparations mechanisms into the ICC's legal framework is in line with contemporary developments in national and international law and human rights.

However, when considering the actual potential of the ICC reparations mechanism to redress the harm caused by crimes under the ICC's jurisdiction, a rather cautious preliminary estimation seems indicated, at least for the near future. The potential of the ICC to, through its reparations function, redress harm caused, reconcile individuals and collectives and restore the dignity and lives of victims of crimes under its jurisdiction is restricted by several factors. Some of them are inherent in the concept of reparations in international criminal justice in general, while others are linked to the particularities of the current structure of the ICC reparations mechanism. At this point the key factors shall only be summarized.

Key factors that generally restrict the potential of a reparations mechanism established in the context of international criminal law to sufficiently and comprehensively repair the harm suffered by victims of crimes under its jurisdiction concern both potential beneficiaries and the content of reparations. In contrast to administrative reparations programs, whether and to whom a national or international criminal court can order reparations depends on the criminal prosecutions before it. Thus, only those victims before the ICC whose harm was caused by a person convicted by the Court can hope to directly benefit from reparations. At the same time, the ICC, like any other international criminal tribunal, only prosecutes against selected individuals for certain acts that constitute crimes under international law. It does not have comprehensive prosecutorial obligations. Furthermore, while victims of crimes under international law have a variety of needs, the power of a criminal court, whether national or international, is restricted to ordering a convicted person to repair the harm caused by his or her crime. Thus, its underlying principles mean that the reparations function of an international criminal court necessarily leaves victims of crimes under its jurisdiction uncompensated, and fails to address certain needs of those who do benefit from its reparation orders. In addition, there is a chance that, in practice, even those that are meant to benefit from reparation orders in fact do not. This might be due to insufficient resources of the convicted person to repair the harm he or she caused to the often multiple victims of his or her crime.

Moreover, there are two aspects of critical importance to the potential of the specific reparations provisions in the ICC's instruments to redress the harm caused to victims and possibly to contribute to reconciliation, although it is only possible to reach preliminary conclusions at this stage, as the Court is still to establish reparation principles.

Firstly, the ICC's reparations provisions, the Standard Application Form for reparations, and perhaps also the Court's early jurisprudence on victims' participation[1307] give rise to the concern that expectations are created among victims that are likely to be disappointed. Under its legal framework, the ICC's power to order reparations is discretionary, and whether victims will indeed receive reparations depends on imponderabilities. However the broad and almost unspecific wordings of key provisions in the ICC's legal instruments, in particular Art. 75 and Rule 85, do not communicate the narrow nature of the ICC's reparations mechanism in a sufficiently clear manner. Art. 75 seems to promise that the Court will order reparations that are "appropriate" and Rules 97 and 98 are likely to give the impression that individual awards are the rule rather than the exception. The standard application forms, in their current version, might also contribute to the creation of expectations that cannot be fulfilled. On the forms' front pages it is noted that "[c]ompletion of this form will not automatically lead to reparation awards by the ICC". However, given the questions applicants are asked in the forms' following pages this does not seem sufficient to make it clear to applicants that filing an application might not result in reparations, nor does it prevent and the impression that applicants will receive from the Court whatever they apply for, without having to prove damage nor causality.

In order to avoid false expectations of the ICC reparations function, it seems essential that the Court not just relies on legal representatives and NGOs to inform victims. The Court should formulate clear reparations principles. These should enable victims to understand the conditions under which they might benefit from reparations, and which forms of reparations they can reasonably expect. This should also be clarified in the standard application forms, as most victims or persons acting on their behalf are more likely to read the forms than the relevant provisions in the ICC's legal framework. It is crucial to prevent false expectations in order to avoid, as far as

1307 For a critical assessment of the ICC's decisionmaking on victims' participation so far see Chung, C. H.: "Victims' Participation at the International Criminal Court: Are Concessions of the Court Clouding the Promise?". In: Northwestern Journal of International Human Rights 6 (2008), pp. 459 et seq. However, see the Court's latest narrower approach in Situation of the Democratic Republic of The Congo in the Case of *The Prosecutor v. Thomas Lubanga Dyilo,* Judgment on the appeals of the Prosecutor and the Defence against Trial Chamber I's Decision on Victims' Participation of 18 January 2008, Appeals Chamber, 11 July 2008, ICC-01/04-01/06-1432 and Situation of the Democratic Republic of The Congo in the Case of *The Prosecutor v. Thomas Lubanga Dyilo,* Redacted version of "Decision on 'indirect victims'", Trial Chamber I, 8 April 2009, ICC-01/04-01/06-1813.

possible, disappointment and the feeling of not being acknowledged as victims, as this might be counterproductive in the recovery process from victimization.

In one of its first decisions on victims' rights, the ICC has held that "the victims' guaranteed right of access to the Court entails a positive obligation on the Court to enable them to exercise that right concretely and effectively".[1308] It has taken the view that "the success of the Court is, to some extent, linked to the success to its reparation system".[1309] This shows the general awareness and willingness of the Court to give effect to victims' rights as guaranteed in the ICC system, including reparations to victims. However, due to the inevitable restrictions of its reparations mechanism, it still seems indicated for the Court to take a pro-active approach to managing victims' expectations.

The establishment of clear reparation principles and their consistent application are also essential in order to achieve a certain degree of predictability and legal certainty. The Court's reparation orders may effect a potentially large number of people personally. Thus, it is crucial for the moral and legal legitimacy of the Court that the ICC's decisions on reparations are perceived as fair.

A second critical aspect is that the success of the ICC reparation system depends, to a large extent, on the cooperation of states. From the perspective of international legal development, the establishment of a direct international law relationship between the individual perpetrator of an international crime and the individual crime victim is the true novelty of the ICC reparations regime. However, the role of states in the implementation of reparations to victims of large-scale and systematic crimes is crucial. Typically, states also bear responsibility for the type of crimes under the ICC's jurisdiction. In view of the scope, gravity and complexity of crimes under the ICC's jurisdiction, it seems impossible to comprehensively or effectively compensate the harm caused through reparations solely made by individual offenders. Whether or not the ICC's lack of power to order responsible states to provide reparations is considered to be the only model consistent with the principles of international criminal law, it weakens its potential to adequately redress victims' harm and facilitate reconciliation between individuals, groups and societies.

Furthermore, without the cooperation of states, the Court will have great difficulty in obtaining control of the perpetrators' assets, and its reparation orders will therefore be hardly enforceable. This is true of both monetary reparations, such as restitution of property or rehabilitation programs, and symbolic reparations such as building memorials or naming streets. Thus, a state's unwillingness to cooperate could prevent the effective implementation of ICC reparation orders. The ICC reparations mechanism might also be used by states and other responsible entities to the

1308 *Situation in the Democratic Republic of The Congo*, Decision on the Applications for Participation in the Proceedings of VPRS 1, VPRS 2, VPRS 3, VPRS 4, VPRS 5 and VPRS 6, ICC Pre-Trial Chamber I, 17 January 2006, ICC-01/04-101, para. 71.

1309 Situation in the Democratic Republic of the Congo in the Case of *The Prosecutor v. Thomas Lubanga Dyilo*, Decision on the Prosecutor's Application for a Warrant of Arrest, Article 58, ICC Pre-Trial Chamber I, 10 February 2006, ICC-01/04-01/06 (annexed to ICC-01/04-01/06, 24 February 2006), para. 136.

disadvantage of victims. A state might declare that victims have been compensated through the ICC and that it therefore no longer has any responsibility to do so, despite the fact that some of the victims might not have received reparations at all or might not have received full reparation. Such a position might be politically justifiable, irrespective of what the ICC Statute states.[1310]

Constitutional structures, truth-finding processes, and securing peace and reconciliation at a societal level are necessary to repair the consequences of the types of crimes under the ICC's jurisdiction, as far as possible. The Court should therefore not hesitate to remind states, corporations and other entities of their responsibilities under national and international law, and appeal to the solidarity of the international community. The ICC has the authority to do so in its reparation principles pursuant to Art. 75 (1), despite their non-binding nature. Furthermore, the Court should secure the implementation of its reparation orders by supervising the implementing state or other entity.

C. Conclusion

As the Court is yet to establish reparations principles which will be decisive for the precise form of its reparation system, any conclusion at this stage can only be preliminarily. However, it seems unrealistic to expect the ICC to have the sole responsibility of ensuring that victims of crimes under its jurisdictions receive appropriate reparations. In fact, it appears that through the ICC's reparation system the harm caused by crimes under its jurisdiction can at best be partially repaired.

In spite of the insufficiencies of the ICC reparations function, from the perspective of contemporary legal development, there is no alternative to the concept of combining international criminal proceedings with reparations proceedings as such.

The primary task of the ICC reparation system is to complement the ICC's core function of prosecuting crimes under international law by obliging convicted persons to repair the consequences of their crime. Ideally, the ICC would also succeed in triggering or supporting comprehensive transitions at the national level where needed, which also encompass the implementation of the right to reparations from the responsible state. This could be achieved both by making use of the power to order reparations pursuant to Art. 75 (2), by seeking cooperation with states and possibly addressing states, corporations and the international community in the reparations principles to be established under Art. 75 (1). An effective ICC reparations mechanism, complemented by the Trust Fund, could serve as a role model for national jurisdictions to give effect to victims' right to reparations.

The ICC reparations mechanism does not substitute for the reparatory efforts of other actors. Rather, the success of redressing harm caused to victims of crimes under the ICC's jurisdiction, restoring their lives and their dignity, and achieving broader reconciliation depends on the combined efforts of the ICC with states, public and private entities, and the international community.

1310 According to Art. 75 (6) "[n]othing in this article shall be interpreted as prejudicing the rights of victims under national and international law".

Appendix

A. Bibliography

Addo, M. K. (ed.): Human Rights Standards and the Responsibility of Transnational Corporations. The Hague, 1999.

Alfredsson, G.; P. Macalister-Smith (eds.): The Living Law of Nations – Essays on Refugees, Minorities, Indigenous People and the Human Rights of other Vulnerable Groups in Memory of Atle Grahl-Madsen. Kehl am Rhein (et al.), 1996.

Allen, D. K.; J. T. Hartshorne; R. M. Martin: Damages in Tort. London, 2000.

Ambos, K.: Der Allgemeine Teil des Völkerstrafrechts – Ansätze einer Dogmatisierung. Berlin, 2002.

An-Naim, A. A.: "Toward a Universal Doctrine of Reparation for Violations on International Human Rights and Humanitarian Law". In: International Law Forum 5 (2003), pp. 27 et seq.

Arsanjani, M.; M. W. Reisman: "Developments at the International Criminal Court – The Law-in-Action of the International Criminal Court". In: American Journal of International Law 99 (2005), pp. 385 et seq.

Ashworth, A.: "Some Doubts About Restorative Justice". In: Criminal Law Forum 4 (1993), pp. 277 et seq.

---: "Victims' Rights, Defendants' Rights and Criminal Procedure". In: Integrating a Victim Perspective within Criminal Justice – International Debates. Eds. A. Crawford; J. Goodey. Aldershot, 2000, pp. 185 et seq.

Bachrach, M.: "The Protection and Rights of Victims under International Criminal Law". In: The International Lawyer 34 (2000), pp. 7 et seq.

Bank, R.: "The New Programs for Payments to Victims of National Socialist Injustice". In: German Yearbook of International Law (Jahrbuch für Internationales Recht) 44 (2001), pp. 307 et seq.

Bantekas, I.; S. Nash: International Criminal Law. 2nd ed. London, 2003.

Barkan, E.: The Guilt of Nations – Restitution and Negotiating Historical Injustices. New York, 2001.

Bassiouni, C. M. (ed.): International Protection of Victims. Eres, 1988.

---: "The Protection of 'Collective Victims' in International Law". In: International Protection of Victims. Ed. C. M. Bassiouni. Eres, 1988, pp. 181 et seq.

---: Introduction to International Criminal Law. Ardsley, New York, 2003.

---: "The Philosophy and Policy of International Criminal Justice". In: Man's Inhumanity to Man – Essays on International Law in Honour of Antonio Cassese. Eds. L. C. Vorah; F. Pocar; Y. Featherstone (et al.). The Hague, 2003, pp. 65 et seq.

---: The Legislative History of the International Criminal Court. Vol. 3. Ardsley, New York, 2005.

---: "International Recognition of Victims' Rights". In: Human Rights Law Review 6 (2006), pp. 203 et seq.

Bassiouni, C. M.; P. Manikas: The Law of the International Criminal Tribunal for the Former Yugoslavia. Irvington-on-Hudson, New York, 1996.

Baumgartner, E.: "Aspects of Victims Participation in the Proceedings of the International Criminal Court". In: International Review of the Red Cross 90 (2008), pp. 409 et seq.

Baumgartner, S. P.: "Human Rights and Civil Litigation in United States Courts – The Holocaust-Era Cases." In: Washington University Law Quarterly 80 (2002), pp. 835 et seq.

Bebber, K. van: Wiedergutgemacht? Die Entschädigung für Opfer der Nationalsozialistischen Verfolgung nach dem Bundesergänzungsgesetz durch die Entschädigungsgerichte im OLG-Bezirk Hamm. Berlin, 2001.

Bederman, D. J.: "The United Nations Compensation Commission and the Tradition of International Claims Settlement". In: New York Journal of International Law and Politics 27 (1994), pp. 1 et seq.

---: "Eligible Claimants before the Iran-United States Claims Tribunal". In: The Iran-United States Claims Tribunal – Its Contribution to the Law of State Responsibility. Eds. R. Lillich; D. B. Magraw. New York, 1998, pp. 47 et seq.

Bergsmo, M.; O. Triffterer: "Preamble". In: Commentary on the Rome Statute of the International Criminal Court – Observers' Notes, Article by Article. Ed. O. Triffterer. Baden-Baden, 1999, pp. 1 et seq.

Bernhardt, R. (ed.): Encyclopedia of Public International Law. Vol. 1-3. Amsterdam, 1991-1997.

Bilder, R. B.: "The Role of Apology in International Law and Diplomacy". In: Virginia Journal of International Law 46 (2006), pp. 433 et seq.

Bitti, G.; H. Friman: "Participation of Victims in the Proceedings". In: The International Criminal Court – Elements of Crimes and Rules of Procedure and Evidence. Ed. R. S. Lee. Ardsley, New York, 2001, pp. 456 et seq.

Bitti, G.; G. González Rivas: "The Reparations Provisions for Victims under the Rome Statute of the International Criminal Court". In: Redressing Injustices through Mass Claims Processes – Innovative Responses to Unique Challenges. Ed. The International Bureau of the Permanent Court of Arbitration. Oxford, 2006, pp. 299 et seq.

Bock, S.: "Das Opfer vor dem Internationalen Strafgerichtshof". In: Zeitschrift für die gesamte Strafrechtswissenschaft 119 (2007), pp. 664 et seq.

Bottigliero, I.: Redress for Victims of Crimes under International Law. Leiden, 2004.

Boven, T. van: "The Right to Restitution, Compensation and Rehabilitation for Victims of Gross Violation of Human Rights and Fundamental Freedoms". In: The Living Law of Nations – Essays on Refugees, Minorities, Indigenous People and the Human Rights of other Vulnerable Groups in Memory of Atle Grahl-Madsen. Eds. G. Alfredsson; P. Macalister-Smith. Kehl am Rhein (et al.), 1996, pp. 339 et seq.

---: "The Position of the Victims in the Statute of the International Criminal Court". In: Reflections on the International Criminal Court – Essays in Honour of Adriaan Bos. Eds. H. von Hebel; J. G. Lammers; J. Schukking. The Hague, 1999, pp. 77 et seq.

Boyle, D.: "The Rights of Victims – Participation, Representation, Protection, Reparation". In: Journal of International Criminal Justice 4 (2006), pp. 307 et seq.

Brady, H.: "Appeal". In: The International Criminal Court – Elements of Crimes and Rules of Procedure and Evidence. Ed. R. S. Lee. Ardsley, New York, 2001, pp. 575 et seq.

Bridgeford, T. A.: "Imputing Human Rights Obligations on Multinational Corporations – The Ninth Circuit Strikes Again in Judicial Activism". In: American University International Law Review 18 (2003), pp. 1009 et seq.

Brienen, M. E. I.; E. H. Hoegen: Victims of Crimes in 22 European Criminal Justice Systems – The Implementation of Recommendation (85) 11 of the Council of Europe on the Position of the Victims in the Framework of Criminal Law and Procedure. Nijmegen, 2000.

Brodesser, H.-J.; B. J. Fehn; T. Franosch (et al.): Wiedergutmachung und Kriegsfolgenliquidation – Geschichte, Regelungen, Zahlungen. München, 2000.

Brooks, R. L. (ed.): When Sorry Isn't Enough – The Controversy over Apologies and Reparations for Human Injustice. New York, 1999.

---: "Reflections on Reparations". In: Politics and the Past. Ed. J. Torpey. Oxford, 2003, pp. 103 et seq.

Brouwer, A.-M. de: "Reparation to Victims of Sexual Violence – Possibilities at the International Criminal Court and at the Trust Fund for Victims and Their Families". In: Leiden Journal of International Law 20 (2007), pp. 207 et seq.

Browne, M. K.: "International Victims' Rights Law – What Can Be Gleaned from the Victims' Empowerment Procedures in Germany as the United States Prepares to Consider the Adoption of a 'Victim's Rights Amendment' to its Constitution?". In: Hamline Law Review 27 (2004), pp. 15 et seq.

Bundesminister der Finanzen; W. Schwarz (eds.): Die Wiedergutmachung Nationalsozialistischen Unrechts in der Bundesrepublik Deutschland – Das Bundesentschädigungsgesetz. Vol. 4 & 5. München, 1981-83.

--- (eds.): Die Wiedergutmachung Nationalsozialistischen Unrechts in der Bundesrepublik Deutschland – Entschädigungsverfahren und Sondergesetzliche Entschädigungsregeln. Vol. 6. München, 1987.

Burkhardt, M.: Victim Participation before the ICC, (forthcoming).

Cammack, D.: "Reparations in Malawi". In: The Handbook of Reparations. Ed. P. de Greiff. Oxford, 2006, pp. 215 et seq.

Cárdenas, C.: Die Zulässigkeitsprüfung vor dem Internationalen Strafgerichtshof – Zur Auslegung des Art. 17 IStGH-Statut unter besonderer Berücksichtigung von Amnestien und Wahrheitskommissionen. Berlin, 2005.

Cassel, D.: "The Expanding Scope and Impact of Reparations Awarded by the Inter-American Court of Human Rights". In: Out of the Ashes – Reparation for Victims of Gross and Systematic Human Rights Violations. Eds. K. de Feyter; S. Parmentier; M. Bossuyt (et al.). Antwerp, 2005, pp. 191 et seq.

Cassese, A.: International Criminal Law. Oxford, 2003.

---: "The Statute of the International Criminal Court – Some Preliminary Reflections". In: European Journal of Crime, Criminal Law and Criminal Justice 10 (1999), pp. 144 et seq.

Cassese, A.; P. Gaeta; J. R. W. D. Jones (eds.): The Rome Statute of the International Criminal Court – A Commentary. Vol. 1 & 2. Oxford, 2002.

Chiavario, M.: "Private Parties – The Rights of the Defendant and the Victims". In: European Criminal Procedures. Eds. M. Delmas-Marty; J. R. Spencer. Cambridge, 2002.

Chifflet, P.: "The Role and Status of the Victim". In: International Criminal Law – Developments in the Case Law of the ICTY. Eds. W. A. Schabas; G. Boas. Leiden, 2003, pp. 75 et seq.

Chung, C. H.: "Victims' Participation at the International Criminal Court: Are Concessions of the Court Clouding the Promise?". In: Northwestern Journal of International Human Rights 6 (2008), pp. 459 et seq.

Clapham, A.: "The Question of Jurisdiction under International Criminal Law over Legal Persons – Lessons from the Rome Conference on an International Criminal Court". In: Liability of Multinational Corporations under International Law. Eds. M. T. Kamminga; S. Zia-Zarifi. The Hague, 2000, pp. 139 et seq.

Clark, R. S.: "The 1985 United Nations Declaration of Basic Principles of Justice for Victims of Crime and Abuse of Power".In: The Living Law of Nations – Essays on Refugees, Minorities, Indigenous People and the Human Rights of other Vulnerable Groups in Memory of Atle Grahl-Madsen. Eds. G. Alfredsson; P. Macalister-Smith. Kehl am Rhein (et al.), 1996, pp. 355 et seq.

Clermont, K. M.; E. Sherwin: "A Comparative View of Standards of Proof". In: American Journal of Comparative Law 50 (2002), pp. 243 et seq.

Comandé, G.: "Non-Pecuniary Damages for Personal Injury in Europe and the US – A Proposal for Judicial Scheduling Models". In: Duke Journal of Comparative & International Law 15 (2005).

Condé, H. V.: A Handbook of International Human Rights Terminology. 2nd ed. Lincoln (et al.), 2004.

Coomans, F.; F. Grünfeld; I. Westendorf; J. Willems (eds.): Rendering Justice to the Vulnerable – Liber Amicorum in Honour of Theo van Boven. The Hague (et al.), 2000.

Cooper Alexander, J.; R. A. Fein: "Procedural Design and Terror Victim Compensation". In: De Paul Law Review 53 (2003), pp. 627 et seq.

Cornu, G.: Vocabulaire Juridique. Paris, 2003.

Crawford, J.: The International Law Commission's Articles on State Responsibility – Introduction, Text and Commentaries. Cambridge, 2002.

Crawford, A.; J. Goodey (eds.): Integrating a Victim Perspective within Criminal Justice – International Debates. Aldershot, 2000.

Dam, H. G. van; H. Loos: Das Bundesentschädigungsgesetz – Kommentar. Berlin, 1967.

Das, H.: "The Concept of Mass Claims and the Specificity of Mass Claims Resolution". In: Redressing Injustices through Mass Claims Processes – Innovative Responses to Unique Challenges. Ed. The International Bureau of the Permanent Court of Arbitration. Oxford, 2006, pp. 5 et seq.

Deakin, S.; A. Johnston; B. Markesinis: Markesinis and Deakin's Tort Law. 5th ed. Oxford (et al.), 2003.

Delmas-Marty, M.: "The ICC and the Interaction of International and National Legal Systems". In: The Rome Statute of the International Criminal Court – A Commentary. Eds. Cassese, A.; P. Gaeta; J. R. W. D. Jones [eds.]: The Rome Statute of the International Criminal Court – A Commentary. Vol. 2. Oxford, 2002.

---: "The Contribution of Comparative Law to a Pluralist Conception of International Criminal Law". In: Journal of International Criminal Law 1 (2003), pp. 13 et seq.

Delmas-Marty, M.; J. R. Spencer (eds.): European Criminal Procedures. Cambridge, 2002.

Dembour, M.-B.; E. Haslam: "Silence Hearings? Victim-Witnesses at War Crimes Trials". In: European Journal of International Law 15 (2004), pp. 151 et seq.

Dervieux, V.; M. Benillouche; O. Bachelet: "The French System". In: European Criminal Procedures. Eds. M. Delmas-Marty; J. R. Spencer. Cambridge, 2002, pp. 218 et seq.

Deutsch, A.: "Prosecutors will Investigate Businesses for Links to Congo War Crimes". Associated Press Newswires. 23 September 2003. Available at www.encyclopedia.com/doc/1P1-81326245.html, last accessed 14 May 2008.

Dignan, J.: "Restorative Justice and the Law – The Case for an Integrated, Systematic Approach". In: Restorative Justice and the Law. Ed. L. Walgrave. Cullompton, Devon, 2002, pp. 168 et seq.

Dijk, J. J. M. van: "The United Nations Declaration on Crime Victims – Priorities for Policy Makers". In: International Protection of Victims. Ed. C. M. Bassiouni. Eres, 1988, pp. 117 et seq.

Dijk, P. van; F. van Hoof: Theory and Practice of the European Convention on Human Rights. 3rd ed. The Hague (et al.), 1998.

Doda, Z.; E. Weigend: "Polen". In: Wiedergutmachung im Kriminalrecht – Internationale Perspektiven – Reparation in Criminal Law – International Perspectives. Eds. A. Eser; S. Walther. Vol. 1. Freiburg i. Br., 1996, pp. 421 et seq.

Donat-Cattin, D.: "Article 68 – Protection of Victims and Witnesses and their Participation in the Proceedings". In: Commentary on the Rome Statute of the International Criminal Court – Observers' Notes, Article by Article. Ed. O. Triffterer. Baden-Baden, 1999, pp. 869 et seq.

---: "Article 75 – Reparations to Victims". In: Commentary on the Rome Statute of the International Criminal Court – Observers' Notes, Article by Article. Ed. O. Triffterer. Baden-Baden, 1999, pp. 965 et seq.

Dubinsky, P. R.: "Justice for the Collective – The Current Limits of the Human Rights Class Action". In: Michigan Law Review 102 (2004), pp. 1152 et seq.

---: "Human Rights Law Meets Private Law Harmonization – The Coming Conflict". In: Yale Journal of International Law 30 (2005), pp. 211 et seq.

Dupuy, P.-M.: "International Criminal Responsibility of the Individual and International Responsibility of the State". In: The Rome Statute of the International Criminal Court – A Commentary. Eds. A. Cassese; P. Gaeta; J. R. W. D. Jones. Vol. 2. Oxford, 2002, pp. 1085 et seq.

Dupuy, P.-M.; B. Fassbender; M. N. Shaw; K.-P. Sommermann (eds.): Völkerrecht als Wertordnung – Common Values in International Law – Festschrift für Christian Tomuschat – Essays in Honour of Christian Tomuschat. Kehl am Rhein (et al.), 2006.

Echeverria, G.: "Codifying the Rights of Victims in International Law – Remedies and Reparation". In: Redressing Injustices through Mass Claims Processes – Innovative Responses to Unique Challenges. Ed. The International Bureau of the Permanent Court of Arbitration. Oxford, 2006, pp. 279 et seq.

Eser, A.: "Individual Criminal Responsibility". In: The Rome Statute of the International Criminal Court – A Commentary. Eds. A. Cassese; P. Gaeta; J. R. W. D. Jones. Vol. 2. Oxford, 2002, pp. 767 et seq.

Eser, A.; S. Walther (eds.): Wiedergutmachung im Kriminalrecht – Internationale Perspektiven – Reparation in Criminal Law – International Perspectives. Vol. 1-3. Freiburg i. Br., 1996-2001.

Ferencz, B.: "The Experience of Nuremberg". In: International Crimes, Peace and Human Rights – The Role of the International Criminal Court. Ed. D. Shelton. Ardsley, New York, 2000, pp. 1 et seq.

Fernandez, L.: "Possibilities and Limitations of Reparations for the Victims of Human Rights Violations in South Africa". In: Confronting Past Injustice – Approaches to Amnesty, Punishment, Reparation and Restitution in South Africa and Germany. Eds. M. R. Rwelamira; G. Werle. Durban, 1996, pp. 65 et seq.

Fernandez de Gurmendi, S. A.: "Definition of Victims and General Principle". In: The International Criminal Court – Elements of Crimes and Rules of Procedure and Evidence. Ed. R. S. Lee. Ardsley, New York, 2001, pp. 427 et seq.

Fernandez de Gurmendi, S. A.; H. Friman: "The Rules of Procedure and Evidence of the International Criminal Court". In: Yearbook of International Humanitarian Law. Ed. A. McDonald. Vol. 3. The Hague, 2000, pp. 289 et seq.

Ferstman, C.: "The Reparation Regime of the ICC – Practical Considerations". In: Leiden Journal of International Law 15 (2002), pp. 667 et seq.

---: "The International Criminal Court's Trust Fund for Victims – Challenges and Opportunities". In: Yearbook of International Humanitarian Law 2003. Ed. A. McDonald. Vol. 6. The Hague, 2006, pp. 424 et seq.

Feyter, K. de; S. Parmentier; M. Bossuyt (et al.) (eds.): Out of the Ashes – Reparation for Victims of Gross and Systematic Human Rights Violations. Antwerp, 2005.

Fife, R. E.: "Article 77 – Applicable Penalties". In: Commentary on the Rome Statute of the International Criminal Court – Observers' Notes, Article by Article. Ed. O. Triffterer. Baden-Baden, 1999, pp. 985 et seq.

---: "Penalties". In: The International Criminal Court – The Making of the Rome Statute – Issues, Negotiations, Results. Ed. R. S. Lee. The Hague, 1999, pp. 319 et seq.

---: "Penalties". In: The International Criminal Court – Elements of Crimes and Rules of Procedure and Evidence. Ed. R. S. Lee. Ardsley, New York, 2001, pp. 555 et seq.

Fisch, W. B.: "European Analogues to the Class Action – Group Action in France and Germany". In: The American Journal of Comparative Law 27 (1979), pp. 51 et seq.

Fischer, P. G.: "The Victim's Trust Fund of the International Criminal Court – Formation of a Functional Reparations Scheme". In: Emory International Law Review 17 (2003), pp. 187 et seq.

Fischer, H.; C. Kreß; S. R. Lüder (eds.): International and National Prosecution of Crimes under International Law. (Bochumer Schriften zur Friedenssicherung und zum Humanitären Völkerrecht). Berlin, 2001.

Foscote, The Rt. Hon. the Lord Scott of; J. R. J. Holland; C. D. Varner: "The Role of 'Extra-Compensatory' Damages for Violations of Fundamental Human Rights in the United Kingdom and the United States". In: Virginia Journal of International Law 46 (2006), pp. 475 et seq.

Frehsee, D.: "Wiedergutmachung und Täter-Opfer-Ausgleich im deutschen Strafrecht – Entwicklung, Möglichkeiten und Probleme". In: Die Stellung des Opfers im Strafrechtssystem – Neue Entwicklungen in Deutschland und in den USA. Eds. B. Schünemann; M. D. Dubber. Köln, 2000, pp. 117 et seq.

Frigessi di Rattalma, M.; T. Treves (eds.): The United Nations Compensation Commission – A Handbook. The Hague, 1999.

Friman, H.: "The Rules of Procedure and Evidence in the Investigative Stage". In: International and National Prosecution of Crimes under International Law. Eds. H. Fischer; C. Kreß; S. R. Lüder. (Bochumer Schriften zur Friedenssicherung und zum Humanitären Völkerrecht). Berlin, 2001, pp. 191 et seq.

Frulli, M.: "Jurisdiction Ratione Personae". In: The Rome Statute of the International Criminal Court – A Commentary. Eds. A. Cassese, P. Gaeta; J. R. W. D. Jones. Vol. 1. Oxford, 2002, pp. 527 et seq.

Garkawe, S.: "The Victim-Related Provisions of the Statute of the International Criminal Court – A Victimological Analysis". In: International Review of Victimology 8 (2001), pp. 269 et seq.

---: "Victims and the International Criminal Court – Three Major Issues". In: International Criminal Law Review 3 (2003), pp. 345 et seq.

Garner, B. A. (ed.): Black's Law Dictionary. 8th ed. St. Paul, Minnesota, 2004.

Gattini, A.: "The UN Compensation Commission – Old Rules, New Procedures on War Reparations". In: European Journal of International Law 13 (2002), pp. 161 et seq.

Gibson, C.: "Mass Claims Processing – Using Computers to Evaluate Arbitral Claims – The Experience of the United Nations Compensation Commission". In: Arbitration International – Journal of the London Court of International Arbitration 13 (1997), pp. 167 et seq.

Giessler, H.: "Grundsatzbestimmungen des Entschädigungsrechts". In: Die Wiedergutmachung Nationalsozialistischen Unrechts in der Bundesrepublik Deutschland – Das Bundesentschädigungsgesetz. Eds. Bundesminister der Finanzen; W. Schwarz. Vol. 4. München, 1981, pp. 1 et seq.

Gillard, E.-C.: "Reparation for Violations of International Humanitarian Law". In: International Review of the Red Cross 851 (2003), pp. 529 et seq.

Glickman, S.: "Victims' Justice – Legitimizing the Sentencing Regime of the International Criminal Court". In: Columbia Journal of Transnational Law 43 (2005), pp. 229 et seq.

Gloppen, S.: "Review Essay: Reparatory Justice – A Road to Reconciliation? On the Role of Reparations in Transitional Justice Theory". In: Reparations – Redressing Past Wrongs. Eds. G. Ulrich; L. Krabbe Boserup. (Human Rights in Development – Yearbook 2001). The Hague, 2003, pp. 385 et seq.

Gnirs, O.: "Das Verfahren bei der Entschädigungsbehörde". In: Die Wiedergutmachung Nationalsozialistischen Unrechts durch die Bundesrepublik Deutschland – Entschädigungsverfahren und Sondergesetzliche Entschädigungsregeln. Eds. Bundesminister der Finanzen; W. Schwarz. Vol. 6. München, 1987, pp. 19 et seq.

Goldmann, N.: "Über die Bedeutung der Wiedergutmachung des Nationalsozialistischen Unrechts". In: Die Freiheit des Anderen – Festschrift für Martin Hirsch. Eds. H. J. Vogel; H. Simon; A. Podlech. Vol. 5. München, 1981, pp. 215 et seq.

Goschler, C.: Wiedergutmachung – Westdeutschland und die Verfolgten des Nationalsozialismus (1945- 1954). München, 1992.

---: "Zwei Wege der Wiedergutmachung". In: Nach der Verfolgung – Wiedergutmachung Nationalsozialistischen Unrechts in Deutschland?. Eds. H. G. Hockerts; C. Kuller. Göttingen, 2003, pp. 115 et seq.

Grassi, S.: "Italien". In: Wiedergutmachung im Kriminalrecht – Internationale Perspektiven – Reparation in Criminal Law – International Perspectives. Eds. A. Eser; S. Walther. Vol. 3. Freiburg i. Br., 2001, pp. 130 et seq.

Gray, C. D.: Judicial Remedies in International Law. 2 ed. Oxford, 1990.

Gray, K. R.: "Evidence before the ICC". In: The Permanent International Criminal Court – Legal and Policy Issues. Eds. D. McGoldrick, P. Rowe; E. Donnelly. Oxford, 2004, pp. 287 et seq.

Greer, D. (ed.): Compensating Crime Victims – A European Survey. Freiburg i. Br., 1996.

Greiff, P. de (ed.): The Handbook of Reparations. Oxford, 2006.

Greiff, P. de; M. Wierda: "Reparations and the International Criminal Court – A Prospective Role for the Trust Fund for Victims". April 2004. Available at http://www.ictj.org/downloads/TrustFundPaperFinal.pdf, last accessed 2 April 2007.

---: "The Trust Fund for Victims of the International Criminal Court – Between Possibilities and Constraints". In: Out of the Ashes – Reparation for Victims of Gross and Systematic Human Rights Violations. Eds. K. de Feyter; S. Parmentier; M. Bossuyt (et al.). Antwerp, 2005, pp. 225 et seq.

Groenhuijsen, M. S.; D. van der Landen: "Niederlandc". In: Wiedergutmachung im Kriminalrecht – Internationale Perspektiven – Reparation in Criminal Law – International Perspectives. Eds. A. Eser, S. Walther. Vol. 1. Freiburg i. Br., 1996, pp. 1 et seq.

Grotius, H.: De Jure Belli Ac Pacis Libri Tres. Transl. by F. W. Kelsey. Vol. 2. Oxford (et al.), 1925.

Guembe, M. J.: "Economic Reparations for Grave Human Rights Violations – The Argentinean Experience". In: The Handbook of Reparations. Ed. P. de Greiff. Oxford, 2006, pp. 21 et seq.

Haersolte-van Hof, J. J. van: "Innovations to Speed Mass Claims – New Standards of Proof". In: Redressing Injustices through Mass Claims Processes – Innovative Responses to Unique Challenges. Ed. The International Bureau of the Permanent Court of Arbitration. Oxford, 2006, pp. 13 et seq.

Hagler, M.; F. Rivera: "Bamaca Velasquez v. Guatemala – An Expansion of the Inter-American System's Jurisprudence on Reparations". In: Human Rights Brief 9 (2000), pp. 2 et seq.

Hall, C. K.: "The First Proposal for a Permanent International Criminal Court". In: International Review of the Red Cross 322 (1998), pp. 57 et seq.

Hamber, B.; T. Mofokeng: From Rhetoric to Responsibility – Making Reparations to the Survivors of Past Political Violence – Centre for the Study of Violence and Reconciliation. Johannesburg, 2000.

Harris, D. J.; S. Livingstone (eds.): The Inter-American System of Human Rights. Oxford, 1998.

Haslam, E.: "Victim Participation at the International Criminal Court – A Triumph of Hope over Experience?". In: The Permanent International Criminal Court – Legal and Policy Issues. Eds. D. Rowe; P. McGoldrick; E. Donnelly. Oxford, 2004, pp. 315 et seq.

Hassemer, W.; J. P. Reemtsma: Verbrechensopfer – Gesetz und Gerechtigkeit. München, 2002.

Hawkins, J. M.; R. Allen (eds.): Oxford Encyclopedic English Dictionary. Oxford, 1991.

Hayner, P.: Unspeakable Truths – Confronting State Terror and Atrocity – How Truth Commissions around the World Are Challenging the Past and Shaping the Future. New York (et al.), 2001.

Hebenstreit, R.: "Härteausgleich nach § 171 BEG". In: Die Wiedergutmachung Nationalsozialistischen Unrechts in der Bundesrepublik Deutschland – Das Bundesentschädigungsgesetz. Eds. Bundesminister der Finanzen; W. Schwarz. Vol. 5. München, 1983, pp. 469 et seq.

Heikkilä, M.: International Criminal Tribunals and Victims of Crime. Turku, 2004.

Heintschel von Heinegg, W.: "Kriegsentschädigung, Reparation oder Schadensersatz". In: Zeitschrift für vergleichende Rechtswissenschaft 90 (1991), pp. 113 et seq.

---: "Entschädigung für Verletzungen des Humanitären Völkerrechts". In: Entschädigung nach bewaffneten Konflikten – Die Konstitutionalisierung der Welthandelsordnung. Eds. W. Heintschel von Heinegg; S. Kadelbach; B. Heß (et al.). Heidelberg, 2003, pp. 1 et seq.

Heintschel von Heinegg, W.; S. Kadelbach; B. Heß (et al.) (eds.): Entschädigung nach bewaffneten Konflikten – Die Konstitutionalisierung der Welthandelsordnung. Heidelberg, 2003.

Heiskanen, V.: "Virtue Out of Necessity – International Mass Claims and New Uses of Information Technology". In: Redressing Injustices through Mass Claims Processes – Innovative Responses to Unique Challenges. Ed. The International Bureau of the Permanent Court of Arbitration. Oxford, 2006, pp. 25 et seq.

Henzelin, M.; V. Heiskanen; G. Mettraux: "Reparations to Victims before the International Criminal Court – Lessons from International Mass Claims Processes". In: Criminal Law Forum 17 (2006), pp. 317 et seq.

Herbst, L.; C. Goschler (eds.): Wiedergutmachung in der Bundesrepublik Deutschland. München, 1989.

Heß, B: "Kriegsentschädigungen aus Kollisionsrechtlicher und rechtsvergleichender Sicht". In: Entschädigung nach bewaffneten Konflikten – Die Konstitutionalisierung der Welthandelsordnung. Eds. W. Heintschel von Heinegg; S. Kadelbach; B. Heß (et al.). Heidelberg, 2003, pp. 107 et seq.

Hirsch, A. v.; A. Ashworth; C. Shearing: "Specifying Aims and Limits for Restorative Justice – A 'Making Amends' Model?". In: Restorative Justice and Criminal Justice -Competing or Reconcilable Paradigms. Eds. A. v. Hirsch; J. v. Roberts; A. Bottoms (et al.). Oxford, 2003, pp. 21 et seq.

Hirsch, A. v.; J. v. Roberts; A. Bottoms (et al.) (eds.): Restorative Justice and Criminal Justice – Competing or Reconcilable Paradigms. Oxford, 2003.

Hockerts, H. G.; C. Kuller (eds.): Nach der Verfolgung – Wiedergutmachung Nationalsozialistischen Unrechts in Deutschland?. Göttingen, 2003.

Hofmann, R.: "Victims of Violations of International Humanitarian Law – Do They Have an Individual Right to Reparation against States under International Law?". In: Völkerrecht als Wertordnung – Common Values in International Law – Festschrift für Christian Tomuschat – Essays in Honour of Christian Tomuschat. Eds. P.-M. Dupuy; B. Fassbender; M. N. Shaw; K.-P. Sommermann. Kehl am Rhein (et al.), 2006, pp. 341 et seq.

Holmes, J. T.: "The Principle of Complementarity". In: The International Criminal Court – The Making of the Rome Statute – Issues, Negotiations, Results. Ed. R. S. Lee. The Hague, 1999, pp. 41 et seq.

Holtzmann, H. M.: "Mass Claims Processes". In: American Review of International Arbitration 13 (2002), pp. 69 et seq.

Hörnle, T.: "Die Rolle des Opfers in der Straftheorie und im Materiellen Strafrecht". In: Juristenzeitung 61 (2006), pp. 950 et seq.

Ingadottir, T. (ed.): The International Criminal Court – Recommendations on Policy and Practice – Financing, Victims, Judges, and Immunities. Ardsley, New York, 2003.

---: "The Trust Fund for Victims (Art. 79 of the Rome Statute)". In: The International Criminal Court – Recommendations on Policy and Practice – Financing, Victims, Judges, and Immunities. Ed. T. Ingadottir. Ardsley, New York, 2003, pp. 111 et seq.

The International Bureau of the Permanent Court of Arbitration (ed.): Redressing Injustices through Mass Claims Processes – Innovative Responses to Unique Challenges. Oxford, 2006.

Jennings, M.: "Article 79 – Trust Fund". In: Commentary on the Rome Statute of the International Criminal Court – Observers' Notes, Article by Article. Ed. O. Triffterer. Baden-Baden, 1999, pp. 1005 et seq.

Jolowicz, J. A.: "Procedural Questions". In: International Encyclopedia of Comparative Law. Ed. A. Tunc. Vol. 11. Tübingen, 1986, pp. 13-4 et seq.

Jorda, C.; J. de Hemptinne: "The Status and Role of the Victim". In: The Rome Statute of the International Criminal Court – A Commentary. Eds. A. Cassese; P. Gaeta; J. R. W. D. Jones. Vol. 2. Oxford, 2002, pp. 1387 et seq.

Joutsen, M.: The Role of the Victim of Crime in European Criminal Justice Systems – A Cross-national Study of the Role of the Victim. Helsinki, 1987.

Judicial Studies Board: Guidelines for the Assessment of General Damages in Personal Injury Cases. 5th ed. London, 1992.

Jumagers, N.: "The Legal Status of the Multinational Corporation under International Law". In: Human Rights Standards and the Responsibility of Transnational Corporations. Ed. M. K. Addo. The Hague, 1999, pp. 259 et seq.

Joseph, S.; J. Schultz; M. Castan: The International Covenant on Civil and Political Rights – Cases, Materials, and Commentary. 2nd ed. New York, 2004.

Juy-Birmann, R.: "The German System". In: European Criminal Procedures. Eds. M. Delmas-Marty; J. R. Spencer. Cambridge, 2002, pp. 292 et seq.

Kaiser, M.; M. Kilchling: "Germany". In: Compensating Crime Victims – A European Survey. Ed. D. Greer. Freiburg i. Br., 1996, pp. 257 et seq.

Kaleck, W.; M. Ratner; T. Singelnstein; P. Weiss (eds.): International Prosecution of Human Rights Crimes. Berlin, 2007.

Kamminga, M. T.; S. Zia-Zarifi (eds.): Liability of Multinational Corporations under International Law. The Hague, 2000.

Kazazi, M.: Burden of Proof and Related Issues – A Study of Evidence before International Tribunals. The Hague (et al.), 1996.

King, F. P.; A.-M. La Rosa: "Penalties under the ICC Statute". In: Collection of Essays on the Rome Statute of the International Criminal Court. Eds. F. Lattanzi; W. A. Schabas. Ripa di Fagnano Alto, 1999, pp. 311 et seq.

Kinoti, K.: "Justice in the Eye of the Beholder". July 2005. Available at www.awid.org/go.php?stid=1509, last accessed 16 April 2009.

Kirsch QC, P.; D. Robinson: "Referral by State Parties". In: The Rome Statute of the International Criminal Court – A Commentary. Eds. A. Cassese; P. Gaeta; J. R. W. D. Jones. Vol. 1. Oxford, 2002, pp. 619 et seq.

Kisker, K. P.; H. H. Bischof (eds.): Koblenzer Handbuch des Entschädigungsrechts. Baden-Baden, 1996.

Kittichaisaree, K.: International Criminal Law. Oxford, 2001.

Klumpp, G.: Vergangenheitsbewältigung durch Wahrheitskommissionen – Das Beispiel Chile. Berlin, 2001.

Koch, B. A.; H. Koziol: "Comparative Analysis". In: Compensation for Personal Injury in a Comparative Perspective. Eds. B. A. Koch; H. Koziol. Wien, 2003, pp. 407 et seq.

--- (eds.): Compensation for Personal Injury in a Comparative Perspective. Wien, 2003.

Krabbe Boserup, L.; M. Mohammed Cissé: "Accessibility – A Precondition for Reparation? The Case of the Nigerian Commission on Human Rights and Fundamental Freedoms". In: Reparations – Redressing Past Wrongs. Eds. G. Ulrich; L. Krabbe Boserup. (Human Rights in Development – Yearbook 2001). The Hague, 2003, pp. 137 et seq.

Kreß, C.; G. Sluiter: "Fines and Forfeiture Orders". In: The Rome Statute of the International Criminal Court – A Commentary. Eds. A. Cassese; P. Gaeta; J. R. W. D. Jones. Vol. 2. Oxford, 2002, pp. 1823 et seq.

Kristjánsdóttir, E.; B. Simerova: "Processing Claims for 'Other Personal Injury' under the German Forced Labour Compensation Programme". In: Redressing Injustices through Mass Claims Processes – Innovative Responses to Unique Challenges. Ed. The International Bureau of the Permanent Court of Arbitration. Oxford, 2006, pp. 109 et seq.

Kritz, N. J.: "Coming to Terms with Atrocities – A Review of Accountability Mechanisms for Mass Violations of Human Rights". In: Law & Contemporary Problems 59 (1996), pp. 127 et seq.

Küpper, H.: Kollektive Rechte in der Wiedergutmachung von Systemunrecht. Vol. 1 & 2. Frankfurt a. Main, 2004.

Lagodny, O.: "Legitimität und Bedeutung des Ständigen Internationalen Strafgerichtshofs". In: Zeitschrift für die gesamte Strafrechtswissenschaft 113 (2001), pp. 800 et seq.

Lange, H.; G. Schiemann: Schadensersatz. 3rd ed. Tübingen, 2003.

Lappi-Seppälä, T.: "Finland". In: Wiedergutmachung im Kriminalrecht – Internationale Perspektiven – Reparation in Criminal Law – International Perspectives. Eds. A. Eser; S. Walter. Vol. 1. Freiburg i. Br., 1996, pp. 317 et seq.

Lasco, C.: "Repairing the Irreparable – Current and Future Approaches to Reparations". In: Human Rights Brief 10 (2003), pp. 18 et seq.

Lattanzi, F.; W. A. Schabas (eds.): Collection of Essays on the Rome Statute of the International Criminal Court. Vol. 1. Ripa di Fagnano Alto, 1999.

Leach, P.: Taking a Case to the European Court of Human Rights. 2nd ed. Oxford, 2005.

Lee, R. S. (ed.): The International Criminal Court – The Making of the Rome Statute – Issues, Negotiations, Results. The Hague, 1999.

--- (ed.): The International Criminal Court – Elements of Crimes and Rules of Procedure and Evidence. Ardsley, New York, 2001.

Lemkin, R.: "Genocide as a Crime under International Law". In: American Journal of International Law 41 (1947), pp. 145 et seq.

Lewis, P.: "Trial Procedure". In: The International Criminal Court – Elements of Crimes and Rules of Procedure and Evidence. Ed. R. S. Lee. Ardsley, New York, 2001, pp. 539 et seq.

Lewis, P.; H. Friman: "Reparations to Victims". In: The International Criminal Court – Elements of Crimes and Rules of Procedure and Evidence. Ed. R. S. Lee. Ardsley, New York, 2001, pp. 474 et seq.

Lillich, R. B. (ed.): The United National Compensation Commission – Thirteenth Sokol Colloquium. Irvington, New York, 1995.

Lillich, R.; D. B. Magraw (eds.): The Iran-United States Claims Tribunal – Its Contribution to the Law of State Responsibility. Ardsley, New York, 1998.

Lillteicher, J.: "Die Rückerstattung in Westdeutschland – Ein Kapitel deutscher Vergangenheitspolitik?". In: Nach der Verfolgung – Wiedergutmachung Nationalsozialistischen Unrechts in Deutschland?. Eds. H. G. Hockerts; C. Kuller. Göttingen, 2003, pp. 61 et seq.

Lira, E.: "The Reparations Policy for Human Rights Violations in Chile". In: The Handbook of Reparations. Ed. P. de Greiff. Oxford, 2006, pp. 55 et seq.

Madlener, K.: "Spanien". In: Wiedergutmachung im Kriminalrecht – Internationale Perspektiven – Reparation in Criminal Law – International Perspectives. Eds. A. Eser; S. Walther. Vol. 3. Freiburg i. Br., 2001, pp. 273 et seq.

Madrigal-Borloz, V.: "Damage and Redress in the Jurisprudence of the Inter-American Court of Human Rights (1979-2001)". In: Reparations – Redressing Past Wrongs. Eds. G. Ulrich; L. Krabbe Boserup. (Human Rights in Development – Yearbook 2001). The Hague, 2003, pp. 211 et seq.

Magnus, U.: "Causation in German Tort Law". In: Unification of Tort Law – Causation. Ed. J. M. Spier. The Hague, 2000, pp. 63 et seq.

---: "Comparative Report on the Law of Damages". In: Unification of Tort Law – Damages. Ed. U. Magnus. The Hague (et al.), 2001, pp. 185 et seq.

--- (ed.): Unification of Tort Law – Damages. The Hague, 2001.

---: "Schadensersatz für Körperverletzung in Deutschland". In: Compensation for Personal Injury in a Comparative Perspective. Eds. B. A. Koch; H. Koziol. Wien, 2003, pp. 148 et seq.

Malmström, S.: "Restitution of Property and Compensation to Victims". In: Essays on ICTY Procedure and Evidence in Honour of Gabrielle Kirk McDonald. Eds. R. May; D. Tolbert; J. Hocking (et al.). The Hague, 2001, pp. 373 et seq.

Maser, W.: Nürnberg – Tribunal der Sieger. Düsseldorf, 1977.

May, R.; D. Tolbert; J. Hocking (et al.) (eds.): Essays on ICTY Procedure and Evidence in Honour of Gabrielle Kirk McDonald. The Hague, 2001, pp. 373 et seq.

May, R.; M. Wierda: International Criminal Evidence. Ardsley, New York, 2002.

McDonald, A.: "The Role of Victims and Witnesses in International Criminal Trials". In: Treaty Enforcement and International Cooperation in Criminal Matters with Special Reference to the Chemical Weapons Convention. Eds. R. Yepes-Enriques; L. Tabassi. The Hague, 2002, pp. 257 et seq.

--- (ed.): Yearbook of International Humanitarian Law 2003. Vol. 6. The Hague, 2006.

McGoldrick, D., P. Rowe; E. Donnelly: The Permanent International Criminal Court – Legal and Policy Issues. Oxford, 2004.

McGovern, F. E.: "The Intellectual Heritage of Claims Processing at the United Nations Compensation Commission". In: The United Nations Compensation Commission – Thirteenth Sokol Colloquium. Ed. R. Lillich. Irvington, 1995, pp. 187 et seq.

McKay, F.: "Are Reparations Appropriately Addressed in the ICC Statute?" In: International Crimes, Peace and Human Rights – The Role of the International Criminal Court. Ed. D. Shelton. Ardsley, New York, 2000, pp. 163 et seq.

--- : "Victim Participation in Proceedings before the International Criminal Court". In: Human Rights Brief 15/3 (2008), pp. 1 et seq.

Mekhemar, L.: "The Status of the Individual in the Statute of the International Criminal Court". In: The Rome Statute of the International Criminal Court – A Challenge to Impunity. Eds. M. Politi; G. Nesi. Aldershot, 2001, pp. 123 et seq.

Mekjian, G. J.; M. C. Varughese: "Hearing the Victim's Voice – Analysis of the Victims' Advocate Participation in the Trial Proceeding of the International Criminal Court". In: Pace International Law Review 17 (2005), pp. 1 et seq.

Menzel, H. G.: "Zum Substantiierungs- und Wahrheitsgebot bei der Geltendmachung von Verfolgungsleiden". In: Koblenzer Handbuch des Entschädigungsrechts. Eds. K. P. Kisker; H. H. Bischof. Baden-Baden, 1996, pp. 69 et seq.

Merryman, J. H.; D. S. Clark; J. O. Haley: The Civil Law Tradition – Europe, Latin America, and East Asia. 2nd ed. Charlottesville, Michigan, 1994.

Mettraux, G.: International Crimes and the Ad Hoc Tribunals. Oxford, 2005.

Minow, M.: Between Vengeance and Forgiveness – Facing History after Genocide and Mass Violence. Boston, 1998.

Mkhize, H.: "Introductory Notes to the Presentation of the Truth and Reconciliation Commission's Proposed Reparation and Rehabilitation Policies". In: When Sorry Isn't Enough – The Controversy over Apologies and Reparations for Human Injustices. Ed. R. L. Brooks. New York, 1999, pp. 501 et seq.

Möller, C.: Völkerstrafrecht und Internationaler Strafgerichtshof – Kriminologische, Straftheoretische und Rechtspolitische Aspekte. Münster, 2003.

Morris, V.; M. P. Scharf: The International Criminal Tribunal for Rwanda. Vol. 1. Irvington-on-Hudson, New York, 1998.

Mumba, F. N. M.: "Topics within the Sphere of Sentencing in International Criminal Law". In: Man's Inhumanity to Man – Essays in Honour of Antonio Cassese. Eds. L. C. Vorah; F. Pocar; Y. Featherstone (et al.). The Hague, 2003, pp. 567 et seq.

Muttukumaru, C.: "Reparation to Victims". In: The International Criminal Court – The Making of the Rome Statute – Issues, Negotiations, Results. Ed. R. S. Lee. The Hague, 1999, pp. 262 et seq.

---: "Reparations to Victims". In: Collection of Essays on the Rome Statute of the International Criminal Court. Eds. F. Lattanzi; W. A. Schabas. Ripa di Fagnano Alto, 1999, pp. 301 et seq.

Nemitz, J. C.: Strafzumessung im Völkerstrafrecht – Ein Beitrag zur Strafzwecklehre und zur Strafzumessungsmethode unter besonderer Berücksichtigung des Römischen Statuts. Freiburg i. Br., 2002.

Nowak, M.: "The Right of Victims of Gross Human Rights Violations to Reparation". In: Rendering Justice to the Vulnerable – Liber Amicorum in Honour of Theo van Boven. Eds. F. Coomans; F. Grünfeld; I. Westendorf; J. Willems. The Hague, 2000, pp. 203 et seq.

---: "The Right to Reparation of Victims of Gross Human Rights Violations". In: Reparations – Redressing Past Wrongs. Eds. G. Ulrich; L. Krabbe Boserup. (Human Rights in Development – Yearbook 2001). The Hague, 2003, pp. 275 et seq.

---: "Reparation by the Human Rights Chamber for Bosnia and Herzegovina". In: Out of the Ashes – Reparations for Victims of Gross and Systematic Human Rights Violations. Eds. K. de Feyter; S. Parmentier; M. Bossuyt (et al.). Antwerp, 2005, pp. 245 et seq.

Nsereko, N.: "Uganda". In: Wiedergutmachung im Kriminalrecht – Internationale Perspektiven – Reparation in Criminal Law – International Perspectives. Eds. A. Eser; S. Walther. Vol. 2. Freiburg i. Br., 1997, pp. 321 et seq.

Oellers-Frahm, K.; A. Zimmermann (eds.): Dispute Settlement in Public International Law – Texts and Materials. Vol. 2. 2nd revised ed. Berlin, 2001.

O'Hara, T.: "Allbrittons, Riggs to Pay Victims of Pinochet". In: Washington Post (Saturday, 26 February 2005, p. A01). Available at www.washingtonpost.com/wp-dyn/articles/A53805-2005Feb25.html, last accessed 21 April 2009.

Orrego Vicuna, F.: International Dispute Settlement in an Evolving Global Society. Cambridge, 2004.

Peglau, J.: "Penalties and the Determination of the Sentence in the Rules of Procedure and Evidence". In: International and National Prosecution of Crimes under International Law. Ed. H. Fischer; C. Kreß; S. R. Lüder. (Bochumer Schriften zur Friedenssicherung und zum Humanitären Völkerrecht). Berlin, 2001, pp. 141 et seq.

Pelke, H.: "Bürokratie auf dem Prüfstand – Die Fonds- und Härteregelungen des Bundes und der Länder – Stand Oktober 1995". In: Koblenzer Handbuch des Entschädigungsrecht. Eds. K. P. Kisker; H. H. Bischof. Baden-Baden, 1996, pp. 90 et seq.

Pinero, V. B.: The Challenges of Reconstruction and Reconciliation Following an Armed Conflict. The Implementations for Child-Soldiers as Perpetrators". In: Eyes on the ICC 1 (2004), pp. 33 et seq.

Pisillo Mazzeschi, R.: "Reparation Claims by Individuals for State Breaches of Humanitarian Law and Human Rights – An Overview". In: Journal of International Criminal Justice 1 (2003), pp. 339 et seq.

Plessis, M. du: "Reparations and International Law – How Are Reparations to Be Determined (Past Wrong or Current Effects), against Whom, and What Form Should they Take?". In: Windsor Yearbook of Access to Justice 22 (2004), pp. 41 et seq.

Politi, M.; G. Nesi (eds.): The Rome Statute of the International Criminal Court – A Challenge to Impunity. Aldershot, 2001.

Porat, A.; A. Stein: Tort Liability under Uncertainty. Oxford, 2001.

Paust, J. J.: "On Human Rights – The Use of Human Right Precepts in US History and the Right to an Effective Remedy in Domestic Courts". In: Michigan Journal of International Law 10 (1989), pp. 618 et seq.

Pross, C.: Paying for the Past – The Struggle over Reparations for Surviving Victims of the Nazi Terror. Baltimore, 1998.

Randelzhofer, A.; C. Tomuschat (eds.): State Responsibility and the Individual – Reparation in Instance of Grave Violations of Human Rights. The Hague, 1999.

Rauscher, T.; H.-P. Mansel (eds.): Festschrift für Werner Lorenz zum 80. Geburtstag. München, 2001.

Rheingold, P. D.: Mass Tort Litigation. Deerfield, Illinois, 1996.

Riedel, E. H: "Damages". In: Encyclopedia of Public International Law. Ed. R. Bernhardt. Vol. 1. Amsterdam, 1992, pp. 929 et seq.

Roberts, P.: "Restoration and Retribution in International Criminal Justice – An Exploratory Analysis". In: Restorative Justice and Criminal Justice – Competing or Reconcilable Paradigms. Eds. A. v. Hirsch; J. v. Roberts; A. Bottoms (et al.). Oxford, 2003, pp. 117 et seq.
Rock, P.: Constructing Victims' Rights – The Home Office, New Labour, and Victims. Oxford, 2004.
Rogers, W. V. H.: Winfield and Jolowicz on Tort. 16th ed. London, 2002.
---: "Comparative Report on Multiple Tortfeasors". In: Unification of Tort Law – Multiple Tortfeasors. Ed. W. V. H. Rogers. The Hague, 2004, pp. 271 et seq.
--- (ed.): Unification of Tort Law – Multiple Tortfeasors. The Hague, 2004.
Roht-Arriaza, N.: "Reparations, Decisions and Dilemmas". In: Hastings International and Comparative Law Review 27 (2004), pp. 157 et seq.
Romano, C. P. R.; A. Nollkaemper; J. K. Kleffner: International Criminal Courts and Tribunals – Sierra Leone, East Timor, Kosovo and Cambodia. Oxford, 2004.
Rombouts, H.; P. Sardaro; S. Vandeginste: "The Right to Reparation for Victims of Gross and Systematic Violations of Human Rights". In: Out of the Ashes – Reparation for Victims of Gross and Systematic Human Rights Violations. Eds. K. de Feyter; S. Parmentier; M. Bossuyt (et al.). Antwerp, 2005, pp. 345 et seq.
Rombouts, H.; S. Vandeginste: "Reparation for Victims of Gross and Systematic Human Rights Violations – The Notion of Victim". In: Third World Legal Studies (2000-2003), pp. 89 et seq.
---: "Reparation for Victims in Rwanda – Caught between Theory and Practice". In: Out of the Ashes – Reparation for Victims of Gross and Systematic Human Rights Violations. Eds. K. de Feyter; S. Parmentier; M. Bossuyt (et al.). Antwerp, 2005, pp. 309 et seq.
Roth, R.; M. Henzelin: "The Appeal Procedure of the ICC". In: The Rome Statute of an International Criminal Court – A Commentary. Eds. A. Cassese; P. Gaeta; J. R. W. D. Jones. Vol. 2. Oxford, 2002, pp. 1535 et seq.
Roxin, C.: "Strafe und Wiedergutmachung". In: Festschrift für Werner Lorenz zum 80. Geburtstag. Eds. T. Rauscher; H.-P. Mansel. München, 2001, pp. 51 et seq.
Rwelamira, M. R.; G. Werle (eds.): Confronting Past Injustice – Approaches to Amnesty, Punishment, Reparation and Restitution in South Africa and Germany. Durban, 1996.
Saathoff, G.: "Entschädigung für Zwangsarbeiter? Entstehung und Leistungen der Bundesstiftung 'Erinnerung, Verantwortung und Zukunft' im Kontext der Debatte um die 'Vergessenen Opfer'". In: Nach der Verfolgung – Wiedergutmachung Nationalsozialistischen Unrechts in Deutschland?. Eds. H. G. Hockerts; C. Kuller. Göttingen, 2003, pp. 241 et seq.
Safferling, C. J. M.: "Das Opfer völkerrechtlicher Verbrechen – Die Stellung der Verbrechensopfer vor dem Internationalen Strafgerichtshof". In: Zeitschrift für die gesamte Strafrechtswissenschaft 115 (2003), pp. 352 et seq.
Sarkin, J.: "Reparations for Gross Human Rights Violations as an Outcome of Criminal versus Civil Proceedings". In: Out of the Ashes – Reparation for Victims of Gross and Systematic Human Rights Violations. Eds. K. de Feyter; S. Parmentier; M. Bossuyt (et al.). Antwerp, 2005, pp. 151 et seq.
Sassoli, M.: "The Victim-Oriented Approach of International Humanitarian Law and of the International Committee of the Red Cross (ICRC)". In: International Protection of Victims. Ed. C. M. Bassiouni. Eres, 1988, pp. 147 et seq.

Saul, B.: "Compensation for Unlawful Death in International Law – A Focus on the Inter-American Court of Human Rights". In: American University International Law Review 19 (2004), pp. 523 et seq.

Schaack, B. van: "In Defense of Civil Redress – The Domestic Enforcement of Human Rights Norms in the Context of the Proposed Hague Judgments Convention". In: Harvard International Law Journal 42.1 (2001), pp. 141 et seq.

Schabas, W. A.: "Sentencing by International Tribunals – A Human Rights Approach". In: Duke Journal of Comparative and International Law 7 (1997), pp. 461 et seq.

---: "Article 109 – Enforcement of Fines and Forfeiture Measures". In: Commentary on the Rome Statute of the International Criminal Court – Observers' Notes, Article by Article. Ed. O. Triffterer. Baden-Baden, 1999, pp. 1191 et seq.

---: "The Penalty Provisions of the ICC Statute". In: International Crimes, Peace and Human Rights – The Role of the International Criminal Court. Ed. D. Shelton. Ardsley, New York, 2000, pp. 105 et seq.

---: "Penalties". In: The Rome Statute of the International Criminal Court – A Commentary. Ed. A. Cassese; P. Gaeta; J. R. W. D. Jones. Vol. 2. Oxford, 2002, pp. 1497 et seq.

---: "Interpreting the Statutes of the Ad Hoc Tribunals". In: Man's Inhumanity to Man – Essays on International Law in Honour of Antonio Cassese. Eds. L. C. Vorah; F. Pocar; Y. Featherstone (et al.). The Hague, 2003, pp. 846 et seq.

---: An Introduction to the International Criminal Court. 2nd ed. Cambridge, 2004.

---: "Reparation Practices in Sierra Leone and the Truth and Reconciliation Commission". In: Out of the Ashes – Reparation for Victims of Gross and Systematic Human Rights Violations. Eds. S. Parmentier; K. de Feyer; M. Bossuyt; P. Lemmens. Antwerp, 2005, pp. 289 et seq.

Schafer, S. (1977): Victimology – The Victim and His Criminal. Reston, Virginia, 1977.

Schönke, A.; H. Schröder (et al.): Strafgesetzbuch. 27th ed. München, 2006.

Schröder, R.: "Zwangsarbeit – Rechtsgeschichte und Zivilrechtliche Ansprüche". In: Jura 3 (1994), pp. 118 et seq.

Scott, C. (ed.): Torture as a Tort – Comparative Perspectives on the Development of Transnational Human Rights Litigation. Oxford, 2001.

Seidl-Hohenveldern, I.: "Reparations". In: Encyclopedia of Public International Law. Ed. R. Bernhardt. Amsterdam, 1982, pp. 178 et seq.

Shaw, M. N.: International Law. 5th ed. Cambridge, 2003.

Shelton, D.: "Reparations in the Inter-American System". In: The Inter-American System of Human Rights. Eds. D. J. Harris; S. Livingstone. Oxford, 1998, pp. 151 et seq.

---: Remedies in International Human Rights Law. 1st ed. Oxford, 1999.

--- (ed.): International Crimes, Peace, and Human Rights – The Role of the International Criminal Court. Ardsley, New York, 2000.

---: "Reparations for Victims of International Crimes". In: International Crimes, Peace, and Human Rights – The Role of the International Court. Ed. D. Shelton. Ardsley, New York, 2000, pp. 137 et seq.

---: "Righting Wrongs – Reparations in the Articles on State Responsibility". In: American Journal of International Law 96 (2002), pp. 833 et seq.

---: Remedies in International Human Rights Law. 2nd ed. Oxford, 2005.

Silverman, E.: "United States of America". In: Wiedergutmachung im Kriminalrecht – Internationale Perspektiven – Reparation in Criminal Law – International Perspectives. Eds. A. Eser; S. Walther. Vol. 2. Freiburg i. Br., 1997 pp. 1 et seq.

Singh, R.: "Raising the Stakes – Evidentiary Issues in Individual Claims before the United Nations Compensation Commission". In: Redressing Injustices through Mass Claims Processes – Innovative Responses to Unique Challenges. Ed. The International Bureau of the Permanent Court of Arbitration. Oxford, 2006, pp. 61 et seq.

Sliedregt, E. van: The Criminal Responsibility of Individuals for Violations of International Humanitarian Law. The Hague, 2003.

Spier, J. (ed.): Unification of Tort Law – Causation. The Hague, 2000.

Spier, J.; O. H. Haazen: "Comparative Conclusions on Causation". In: Unification of Tort Law – Causation. Ed. J. Spier. The Hague, 2000, pp. 127 et seq.

Staker, C.: "Article 81 – Appeal and Revision". In: Commentary on the Rome Statute of the International Criminal Court – Observers' Notes, Article by Article. Ed. O. Triffterer. Baden-Baden, 1999, pp. 1015 et seq.

---: "Article 82 – Appeal against Other Decisions". In: Commentary on the Rome Statute of the International Criminal Court – Observers' Notes, Article by Article. Ed. O. Triffterer. Baden-Baden, 1999, pp. 1029 et seq.

Steinhardt, R. G: "Fulfilling the Promise of Filártiga – Litigating Human Rights Claims against the Estate of Ferdinand Marcos". In: Yale Journal of International Law 20 (1995), pp. 65 et seq.

Stephens, B.: "Conceptualizing Violence – Present and Future Developments in International Law – Panel I – Human Rights and Civil Wrongs at Home and Abroad – Old Problems and New Paradigms – Conceptualizing Violence under International Law – Do Tort Remedies Fit the Crime? ". In: Alabama Law Review 60 (1997), pp. 579 et seq.

---: "Translating Filártiga – A Comparative and International Law Analysis of Domestic Remedies for International Human Rights Violations". In: Yale Journal of International Law 27 (2002), pp. 1 et seq.

Stolle, P.; T. Singelnstein: "On the Aims and Actual Consequences of International Prosecution". In: International Prosecution of Human Rights Crimes. Eds. W. Kaleck; M. Ratner; T. Singelnstein; P. Weiss. Berlin, 2007, pp. 37 et seq.

Strand, A.: "Bombs and Butter – Compensation Issues in Protracted Conflicts and the Case of Afghanistan". In: Reparations – Redressing Past Wrongs. Eds. G. Ulrich; L. Krabbe Boserup. (Human Rights in Development – Yearbook 2001). The Hague, 2003, pp. 109 et seq.

Swan, M.: "International Human Rights Tort Claims and the Experience of United States Courts – An Introduction to the US Case Law, Key Statutes and Doctrines". In: Torture as a Tort – Comparative Perspectives on the Development of Transnational Human Right Litigation. Ed. C. Scott. Oxford, 2001, pp. 65 et seq.

Teitel, R. G.: Transitional Justice. Oxford, 2000.

Terrier, F.: "The Procedure before the Trial Chamber". In: The Rome Statute of the International Criminal Court – A Commentary. Eds. A. Cassese; P. Gaeta; J. R. W. D. Jones. Vol. 2. Oxford, 2002, pp. 1277 et seq.

Timm, B.: "The Legal Position of Victims in the Rule of Procedure and Evidence". In: International and National Prosecution of Crimes under International Law. Eds. H. Fischer, C.

Kreß; S. R. Lüder. (Bochumer Schriften zur Friedenssicherung und zum Humanitären Völkerrecht). Berlin, 2001, pp. 289 et seq.

Tobolowsky, P. M.: Crime Victim Rights and Remedies. Durham, North Carolina, 2001.

Tomuschat, C.: "Reparation for Victims of Grave Human Rights Violations". In: Tulane Journal of International and Comparative Law 10 (2002), pp. 157 et seq.

---: "The Duty to Prosecute International Crimes Committed by Individuals". In: Tradition und Weltoffenheit des Rechts – Festschrift Für Helmut Steinberger. Eds. H.-J. Cremer; T. Giegerich; D. Richter (et al.). Berlin, 2002, pp. 315 et seq.

---: "Darfur – Compensation for the Victims". In: Journal of International Criminal Justice 3 (2005), pp. 579 et seq.

Torpey, J.: "Introduction – Politics and the Past". In: Politics and the Past – On Repairing Historical Injustices. Ed. J. Torpey. Lanham, Maryland, 2003, pp. 1 et seq.

---: (ed.): Politics and the Past – On Repairing Historical Injustices. Lanham, Maryland, 2003.

Trangsrud, R. H: "Mass Trials in Mass Tort Cases – A Dissent". In: University of Illinois Law Review 89 (1989), pp. 69 et seq.

Trenczek, T.: Restitution – Wiedergutmachung, Schadensersatz und Strafe? – Restitutive Leistungsverpflichtungen im Strafrecht der USA und der Bundesrepublik Deutschland. Baden-Baden, 1996.

Triffterer, O. (ed.): Commentary on the Rome Statute of the International Criminal Court – Observers' Notes, Article by Article. Baden-Baden, 1999.

---: "Preliminary Remarks – The Permanent International Criminal Court – Ideal and Reality". In: Commentary on the Rome Statute of the International Criminal Court – Observers' Notes, Article by Article. Ed. O. Triffterer. Baden-Baden, 1999, pp. 17 et seq.

---: "The Preventive and the Repressive Function of the International Criminal Court". In: The Rome Statute of the International Criminal Court – A Challenge to Impunity. Eds. M. Politi; G. Nesi. Aldershot, 2001, pp. 137 et seq.

Tunc, A. (ed.): International Encyclopedia of Comparative Law – Torts. Vol. 11 Pt. 2. Tübingen, 1986.

Ulrich, G.: "The Moral Case for Reparations – Three Theses about Reparations for Past Wrongs". In: Reparations – Redressing Past Wrongs. Eds. G. Ulrich; L. Krabbe Boserup. (Human Rights in Development – Yearbook 2001). The Hague, 2003, pp. 369 et seq.

Ulrich, G.; L. Krabbe Boserup (eds.): Reparations – Redressing Past Wrongs. (Human Rights in Development – Yearbook 2001). The Hague, 2003.

Vandeginste, S.: "Victims of Genocide, Crimes against Humanity, and War Crimes in Rwanda – The Legal and Institutional Framework of their Right to Reparation". In: Politics and the Past. Ed. J. Torpey. Oxford, 2003, pp. 249 et seq.

Vest, H.: "Humanitätsverbrechen – Herausforderung für das Individualstrafrecht?". In: Zeitschrift für die gesamte Strafrechtswissenschaft 113 (2001), pp. 457 et seq.

Vogel, H. J.; H. Simon; A. Podlech (eds.): Die Freiheit des Anderen – Festschrift für Martin Hirsch. Baden-Baden, 1981.

Walgrave, L. (ed.): Restorative Justice and the Law. Cullompton, Devon, 2002.

Warner, K.: "Australia". In: Wiedergutmachung im Kriminalrecht – Internationale Perspektiven – Reparation in Criminal Law – International Perspectives. Eds. A. Eser. Vol. 2. Freiburg i. Br., 1997, pp. 162 et seq.

Weiss, K.: "Schaden an Körper oder Gesundheit aus rechtlicher Sicht". In: Die Wiedergutmachung Nationalsozialistischen Unrechts in der Bundesrepublik Deutschland – Das Bundesentschädigungsgesetz. Eds. Bundesminister der Finanzen; W. Schwarz. Vol. 4. München, 1981, pp. 185 et seq.

Werle, G.: Principles of International Criminal Law. The Hague, 2005.

Whelton, C.: "The United Nations Compensation Commission and International Law – A Fresh Approach". In: Ottawa Law Review 25 (1993), pp. 607 et seq.

Winstel, T.: "Über die Bedeutung der Wiedergutmachung im Leben der Jüdischen NS-Verfolgten – Erfahrungsgeschichtliche Annährungen". In: Nach der Verfolgung – Wiedergutmachung Nationalsozialistischen Unrechts in Deutschland?. Eds. H. G. Hockerts; C. Kuller. Göttingen, 2003, pp. 199 et seq.

Wittich, S.: "Awe of the Gods and Fear of the Priests – Punitive Damages in the Law of State Responsibility". In: Austrian Review of International and European Law 3 (1998), pp. 31 et seq.

Wolffsohn, M.: "Globalentschädigung für Israel und die Juden? Adenauer und die Opposition in der Bundesregierung". In: Wiedergutmachung in der Bundesrepublik Deutschland. Eds. L. Herbst; C. Goschler. München, 1989, pp. 161 et seq.

Xavier, P.; F. Lombard: "Frankreich". In: Wiedergutmachung im Kriminalrecht – Internationale Perspektiven – Reparation in Criminal Law – International Perspectives. Eds. A. Eser; S. Walther. Vol. 3. Freiburg i. Br., 2001, pp. 1 et seq.

Yeager, J. D.: "The Human Rights Chamber for Bosnia and Herzegovina – A Case Study in Transitional Justice". In: International Legal Perspectives 14.1 (2004), pp. 44 et seq.

Zappalà, S.: Human Rights in International Criminal Proceedings. Oxford, 2003.

Zedner, L.: "England". In: Wiedergutmachung im Kriminalrecht – Internationale Perspektiven – Reparation in Criminal Law – International Perspectives. Eds. A. Eser; S. Walther. Vol. 1. Freiburg i. Br., 1996, pp. 109 et seq.

Zila, J.: "Schweden". In: Wiedergutmachung im Kriminalrecht – Internationale Perspektiven – Reparation in Criminal Law – International Perspectives. Eds. A. Eser, S. Walther. Vol. 1. Freiburg i. Br., 1996, pp. 231 et seq.

B. Table of Cases

International Criminal Court

Situation of the Democratic Republic of The Congo in the Case of *The Prosecutor v. Thomas Lubanga Dyilo,* Redacted version of "Decision on 'indirect victims'", Trial Chamber I, 8 April 2009, ICC-01/04-01/06-1813

Situation of the Democratic Republic of The Congo in the Case of *The Prosecutor v. Thomas Lubanga Dyilo,* Judgment on the appeals of the Prosecutor and the Defence against Trial Chamber I's Decision on Victims' Participation of 18 January 2008, Appeals Chamber, 11 July 2008, ICC-01/04-01/06-1432

Situation of the Democratic Republic of The Congo in the Case of *The Prosecutor v. Thomas Lubanga Dyilo,* Decision of the Appeals Chamber, 12 December 2006, ICC-01/04-01/06

Situation in the Democratic Republic of The Congo in the Case of *The Prosecutor v. Thomas Lubanga Dyilo*, Decision on the Application for Participation in the Proceedings Submitted by VPRS 1 to VPRS 6, Pre-Trial Chamber I, 29 June 2006, ICC-01/04-01/06

Situation in the Democratic Republic of The Congo in the Case of *The Prosecutor v. Thomas Lubanga Dyilo*, Prosecution's Observations on the Applications for Participation of Applicants a/0001/06 to a/0003/06, 6 June 2006, ICC-01/04-01/06

Situation in the Democratic Republic of The Congo in the Case of *The Prosecutor v. Thomas Lubanga Dyilo*, Prosecution's Observations concerning the Status of Applicants VPRS 1 to 6 and their Participation on the Case of The Prosecutor v. Thomas Lubanga Dyilo, 7 April 2006, ICC-01/04-01/06

Situation in the Democratic Republic of the Congo in the Case of *The Prosecutor v. Thomas Lubanga Dyilo*, Decision on the Prosecutor's Application for a Warrant of Arrest, Article 58, Pre-Trial Chamber I, 10 February 2006, ICC-01/04-01/06 (annexed to ICC-01/04-01/06-8-Corr, 24 February 2006)

Situation in the Democratic Republic of The Congo, *Prosecution's Application for Leave to Appeal Pre-Trial Chamber I's Decision on the Application for Participation in the Proceedings of VPRS 1, VPRS 2, VPRS 3, VPRS 4, VPRS 5 and VPRS 6, ICC*, Office of the Prosecutor, 23 January 2006, ICC -01/04-103

Situation in the Democratic Republic of The Congo, Decision on the Applications for Participation in the Proceedings of VPRS 1, VPRS 2, VPRS 3, VPRS 4, VPRS 5 and VPRS 6, Pre-Trial Chamber I, 17 January 2006, ICC-01/04-101

International Criminal Tribunal for the Former Yugoslavia

The Prosecutor v. Blaskić, Judgement, Trial Chamber I, 3 March 2000, Case No. IT-95-14

The Prosecutor v. Blaskić, Judgement on the Request of the Republic of Croatia for Review of the Decision of Trial Chamber II, Appeals Chamber, 18 July 1997, Case No. IT-95-14

The Prosecutor v. Erdemović, Appeals Sentencing Judgement, Appeals Chamber, 5 March 1998, Case No. IT-96-22

The Prosecutor v. Erdemović, Sentencing Judgement, Trial Chamber I, 29 November 1996, Case No. IT 96-22-T

The Prosecutor v. Furundzija, Judgement, Trial _Chamber II, 10 December 1998, Case No. IT-95-17/1-T

The Prosecutor v. Jelisić, Judgement, Trial Chamber I, 14 December 1999, Case No. IT-95-10-T

The Prosecutor v. M. Nikolić, Sentencing Judgement, Trial Chamber II, 2 December 2003, Case No. IT-02-60/1-S

The Prosecutor v. Sikirica et al., Sentencing Judgement, Trial Chamber III, 13 November 2001, Case No. IT-95-8-S

The Prosecutor v. Simić, Sentencing Judgement, Trial Chamber II, 17 October 2002, Case No. IT-95-9/2-S

The Prosecutor v. Tadić, Judgement in Sentencing Appeals, Appeals Chamber, 26 January 2000, Case No. IT-94-1-AS

The Prosecutor v. Tadić, Judgement, Appeals Chamber, 15 July 1999, Case No. IT-94-1-A

The Prosecutor v. Todorović, Sentencing Judgement, Trial Chamber I, 31 July 2001, Case No. IT-95-9/1

International Criminal Tribunal for Rwanda

The Prosecutor v. Niyitegeka, Judgement, Trial Chamber I, 16 May 2003, ICTR-96-14- T
The Prosecutor v. Rutaganda, Judgement and Sentence, Trial Chamber I, 6 December 1999, ICTR-96-3-T
The Prosecutor v. Serushago, Judgement, Trial Chamber I, 5 February 1999, ICTR-98-39-S
The Prosecutor v. Théoneste Bagosora, Decision on the Amicus Curiae Application by the Government of the Kingdom of Belgium, Trial Chamber II, 6 June 1998, ICTR-96-7-T

Inter-American Court of Human Rights

Aloeboetoe et al. v. Suriname, Reparations, 10 September 1993, Ser. C, No. 15
Bámaca Velásquez v. Guatemala, Reparations, 22 February 2002, Ser. C, No. 91
Barrios Altos Case, Reparations, 30 November 2001, Ser. C, No. 87
Benavides Cevallos v. Ecuador , Judgement, 19 June 1998, Ser. C, No. 38
Blake Case, Merits, 24 January 1998, Ser. C, No. 36
Blake Case, Reparations, 22 January 1999, Ser. C, No. 48
Cantoral Benavides Case, Reparations, 3 December 2001, Ser. C, No. 88
Castillo Páez Case, Reparations, 27 November 1998, Ser. C, No. 43
Case of Children's Rehabilitation v. Paraguay, 2 September 2004, Ser. C, No. 112
Caracazo Case, Reparations, Judgement, 29 August 2002, Ser. C, No. 95
El Amparo v. Venezuela, Reparations, Inter-American Court of Human Rights, 14 September 1996, Ser. C, No. 28
Juan Pablo Chanay v. Guatemala (Colotenango Case), Friendly Settlement, 13 March 1997, Case 11.212 OEA/Ser.L/V/II.95, doc.7 rev.447
Gangaram Panday Case, 21 January 1994, Ser. C, No. 16
Garrido and Baigorria v. Argentina, Reparations, 27 August 1998, Ser. C, No. 39
Godínez Cruz v. Honduras, Compensatory Damages, 21 July 1989, Ser. C, No. 5
Loayza Tamayo v. Peru, Merits, 17 September 1997, Ser. C, No. 33
Loayza Tamayo v. Peru, Reparations, 27 November 1998, Ser. C, No. 42
Mayagna (Sumo) Awas Tingni Indigenous Community v. Nicaragua, 31 August 2001, Ser. C, No. 79
Molina-Theissen v. Guatemala, Reparations, 4 July 2004, Ser. C, No. 108
Myrna Mack-Chang v. Guatemala, Judgment 25 November 2003, Ser. C, No. 101
Moiwana Village v. Suriname, Judgment, 15 June 2005, Ser. C, No. 124
Neira Alegría et al. v. Peru, Reparations, 19 September 1996, Ser. C, No. 29
Paniagua Morales et. al. Case, Judgment, 8 March 1998, Ser. C, No. 37
Plan de Sánchez Massacre v. Guatemala, Reparations, 19 November 2004, Ser. C, No. 105
"Street Children" Case, Reparations, 26 May 2001, Ser. C, No. 77
Suárez Rosero Case, Reparations, 20 January 1999, Ser. C, No. 44
Tibi v. Ecuador, Judgement on Preliminary Objections, Merits and Reparations, 7 September 2004, Ser. C, No. 114
Trujillo Oroza Case, Reparations, 27 February 2002, Ser. C, No. 92
Velásquez-Rodríguez v. Honduras, Judgement, 29 July 1988, Ser. C, No. 4
Velásquez Rodríguez v. Honduras, Compensatory Damages, 21 July 1989, Ser. C, No. 7

European Court of Human Rights

Aksoy v. Turkey, 18 December 1996, Application No. 21987/93
Allenet de Ribemont v. France, 10 February 1995, Application No. 15175/98
Assanidze v. Georgia, 8 April 2004, Application No. 71503/01
Ayder and Others v. Turkey, 8 January 2004, Application No. 23656/94
Beck v. Norway, 29 June 2001, Application No. 26390/95
Birutis and Others v. Lithuania, 28 March 2002, Application Nos. 47698/99 and 48115/99
Bilgin v. Turkey, 16 November 2000, Application No. 23819/94
Brigandí v. Italy, 19 February 1991, Application No. 11460/85
Brumarescu v. Romania, 28 October 1999, Application No. 28342/95
Brumarescu v. Romania (Just Satisfaction), 23 January 2001, Application No. 28342/95
Cakici v. Turkey, 8 July 1998, Application No. 23657/94
Cicek v. Turkey, 27 February 2001, Application No. 25704/94
Colozza and Rubinat v. Italy, 12 February 1985, Application No. 9317/81
De Wilde, Ooms and Versyp, 10 March 1972, Series A No. 14, p. 10.
Eckle v. Germany, 17 July 1982, Application No. 8130/78
Ferraro v. Italy, 19 February 1991, Application No. 13440/87
Gelsomini Sigeri SRL v. Italy, 18 December 2003, Application No. 63417/00
Hasan and Chaush v. Bulgaria, 26 October 2000, Application No.30985/96
Hood v. UK, 18 February 1999, Application No. 27267/95
KA v. Finland, 14 January 2003, Application No. 27751/95
Kenaan v. United Kingdom, 3 April 2001, Application No. 27229/25
Kenmache v. France, 24 November 1994, (No. 3), (45/1993/440/519)
Kutzner v. Germany, 26 February 2002, Application No.46544/99
Lala v. The Netherlands, 22 September 1994, Application No. 14861/89
McCallum v. The United Kingdom, 30 August 1990, Application No. 9511/81
McCann and others v. United Kingdom, 27 September 1995, Application No. 18984/91
Moore and Gordon v. The United Kingdom, 29 September 1999, Application No. 36529/97 and 37393/97
Mori v. Italy, 19 February 1991, Application No. 13552/88
Muonio Saami Village v. Sweden, 9 January 2001, Application No. 28222/95
Olsson v. Sweden, 24 March 1988, Application No.10465/83
Papamichalopoulos and Others v. Greece (Just Satisfaction), 31 October 1995, Application No. 14556/89
Önen v. Turkey, 14 May 2002, Application No.22876/93
Quaranta v. Switzerland, 24 May 1991, Application No. 12744/87
Sadak and others v. Turkey, 17 July 2001, Application No. 29900/96; 29901/96; 29902/96; 29903/96
Selmouni v. France, 28 July 1999, Application No. 25803/94
T.W. v. Malta, 29 April 1999, Application No.25644/94
Velikova v. Bulgaria, 18 May 2000, Application No. 41488/98
Werner v. Poland, 15 November 2001, Application No. 26760/95
Wiesinger v. Austria, 30 October 1991, Application No. 11796/85
X v. Federal Republic of Germany, 30 July 1970, Application 4185/69

X v. United Kingdom, 8 October 1982, Application No. 9054/80
X and Y v. the Netherlands, 26 March 1985, Application No. 8978/80
Y.F. v. Turkey, 22 July 2003, Application No. 24209/94
Human Rights Committee
Bautista de Arellana v. Colombia, Views of 27 October 1995, No. 563/1993.
Kankanamge v. Sri Lanka, Views of 27 July 2004, No. 909/2000, CCPR/81/D/909/2000
Perterer v. Austria, Views of 20 July 2004, No. 1015/2001, CCPR/C/81/D/1015/2001
Quinteros v. Uruguay, 17 September 1981, No. 107/1981, UN Doc. Supp. N.40 (A/38/40)
Raul Sendic Antonaccio v. Uruguay, 28 November 1979, Communication No. R.14/63, UN Doc. Supp. No. 40 (A/37/40)
Smirnova v. Russia, Views of 5 July 2004, No.712/1996, CCPR/C/81/D/712/1996

Human Rights Chamber for Bosnia and Herzegovina

Cegar v. Federation, Decision on the Merits, 6 April 1998, Case No. H/96/21
Damjanovic v. Federation, Decision on the Claim for Compensation, 16 March 1998, Case No. CH/96/30
Ferida Selimovic and forty-eight others against the Republika Srpska ("Srebrenica" cases), 7 March 2003, Case No. CH/01/8365 et al.
Hermas v. Federation, Decision on Admissibility and Merits, 18 February 1998, Case No. CH/97/45
Marceta v. Federation, Decision on Admissibility and Merits, 6 April 1998, Case No. CH/97/41
Medan, Bastijanovic and Marcovic v. BH and the Federation, Decision on the Merits, 7 November 1997, Cases No. CH/96/3, 8, and 9
Odobasic v. R.S., Decision on the Admissibility and Merits, 5 November 1999, Case No. CH/98/1786
O.K.K. v. R.S., Decision on the Admissibility and Merits, 9 March 2001, Case No. CH/98/834

International Court of Justice and Permanent Court of International Justice

Avena and Other Mexican Nationals (Mexico v. United States of America), 31 March 2004, International Court of Justice 128
Factory at Chorzow Case (F.R.G. v. Pol), Permanent Court of International Justice, 12 September 1928, Ser. A, No. 17
LaGrand Case (Germany v. United States of America), 27 June 2001, International Court of Justice 466
Legal Consequences of the Construction of a Wall in the Occupied Palestinian Territory, Advisory Opinion, 9 July 2004, International Court of Justice 131
Lusitania (United States of America v. Germany), Reports of International Arbitral Awards, 21 February 1924, Vol. VII, pp. 256-257

German Courts

Bridge of Varvarin case, Federal Supreme Court (Bundesgerichtshof), Decision of 2 November 2006, Case No. III ZR 190/05

Bridge of Varvarin case, Higher Regional Court of Köln (Oberlandesgericht Köln), Decision of 28 July 2005, Case No. 7 U 8/04

Bridge of Varvarin case, Regional Court of Bonn (Landgericht Bonn), Decision of 10 December 2003, Case No. 1 O 361/02

Distomo Massacre case, Federal Constitutional Court (Bundesverfassungsgericht), Decision of 15 February 2006,Case No. 2 BvR 1476/03

Distomo Massacre case, Federal Supreme Court (Bundesgerichtshof) Case No. III ZR 245/98, Decision of 26 June 2003. In: International Legal Materials 42 (2003), pp. 1030 et seq.

Greek Courts

Prefecture of Voiotia v. Federal Republic of Germany, Case No. 137/1997, Court of First Instance of Leivdia, Case No.11/2000, Hellenic Supreme Court, 4 May 2000

US Courts

Abebe-Jira v. Negewo, 72 F.3d 844 (11th Cir 1996)

Doe I v. Unocal Corp., Nos. 00-56603, 00-57197, 00-56628, 00-57195, 2002 WL 31063976 (9th Cir. 2002)

Filártiga v. Pena-Irala, 630 F.2d 876 (2nd Cir. 1980)

Forti v. Suarez-Mason, 672 F.Supp.1531 (1987) and 674 F.Supp.707 (1988) (ND California)

Hilao v. Marcos, 103 F.3d 767, 776 to 778 (9th Cir. 1996)

In Re Estate of Marcos Litigation, 25 F.3d 1467 (9th Cir. 1994)

In Re Estate of Marcos Litigation, 978 F.2d 493 (9th Cir. 1992)

In Re Estate of Marcos Litigation, No. 86-0207 (D. Haw. 19 May 1991)

In Re Estate of Marcos Litigation, 878 F.2d 1438 (9th Cir. 1989)

Kadic v. Karadzic, 70 F.3d 232 (2nd Cir. 1995)

Mehinovic et al. v. Vuckovic, 198 F.Supp.2d 1322 (N.D.GA 2002)

Mushikiwabo v. Barayagwiza, 1996 WL 164496 (S.D.N.Y. 1996)

Tachiona et al. v. Mugabe, 216 F.Supp.2d 262 (S.D.N.Y. 2002)

Xuncax et al. v. Gramajo, 886 F.Supp.162 (D Mass 1995)

C. Other Legal Sources

Statutes of International Courts and Tribunals

Charter of the International Military Tribunal for the Far East. Reprinted in: The Tokyo War Crimes Trial. Ed. J. Pritchard; S. M. Zaide. Vol. 1. New York (et al.), 1981

Charter of the International Military Tribunal, Nuremberg. In: American Journal of International Law 39 (1945). Supp., pp. 257 et seq.

Rome Statute of the International Criminal Court of 17 July 1998, In: International Legal Materials 37 (1998), pp. 999 et seq.
Statute for the International Criminal Tribunal for Rwanda, UN Doc. S/RES/955 (1994)
Statute for the International Criminal Tribunal for the Former Yugoslavia, UN Doc. S/RES/808 (1993)
Statute of the Iraqi High Criminal Court, Law No. 10/2005, Official Gazette of the Government of Iraq No. 4006, 18 October 2005
Statute of the Special Court for Sierra Leone, annexed to the Agreement between the United Nations and the Government of Sierra Leone on the Establishment of a Special Court for Sierra Leone, signed on 16 January 2002

ICC Documents and ICC-related Documents

Draft ICC Statute "Zutphen-Draft", UN Doc. A/AC.249/1998/L.13
Outreach Report 2008, Public Information and Documentation Section of the International Criminal Court– Outreach Unit. Available at www.icc-cpi.int/NR/rdonlyres/1109882E-E8FF-4AFE-978E-A7466AEBC947/279522/Outreach_report2008enLR.pdf, last accessed 16 April 2009.
Paper on Some Policy Issues before the Office of the Prosecutor, ICC-OTP, September 2003. Available at http://ww.icc-cpi.int/library/organs/otp/03/09/ 05_Policy_Paper.pdf, last accessed 21 April 2009
Proposed Programme Budget for 2007 of the International Criminal Court, ICC-ASP/5/9 (2006). Available at www.icc-cpi.int/library/asp/ICC-ASP-5-9_English, last accessed 22 April 2009
Regulations of the Registry, ICC/BD 03-01-06 (2006)
Regulations of the Court, ICC/BD/01-01-04 (2004)
Regulations of the Trust Fund for Victims, ICC-ASP/4/Res.3 (2005)
Report on the Establishment of an International Criminal Court, Draft Statute and Final Act, UN Doc. A/Conf.183/2/Add.1 (1998)
Report of the International Criminal Court, UN Doc. A/60/177 (2005)
Report of the Preparatory Commission's third session, Rule E (C), PCNICC/1999/L.5/Rev.1/Add.1 (1999)
Report of the Working Group on Procedural Matters of the Rome Conference, A/CONF.183/C.1/WGPM/L.2/Add.7 (1998)
Resolution on the Establishment of a Fund for the Benefit of Victims of Crimes Within the Jurisdiction of the Court, and the Families of such Victims, adopted 9 September 2002, ICC-ASP/1/Res.6 (2002)
Resolution on the Establishment of the Secretariat of the Trust Fund for Victims, ICC-ASP/3/Res.7 (2004)
Resolution on the Procedure for the Nomination and Election of Members of the Board of Directors of the Trust Fund for the Benefit of Victims, ICC-ASP/1/Res.7 (2002)
Rules of Procedure and Evidence, ICC-ASP/1/3 (2002)
Strategic Plan for Outreach of the Court, ICC-ASP/5/12 (2006)

International Treaties and Conventions

African (Banjul) Charter on Human Rights and Peoples' Rights, 27 June 1981, O.A.U. Doc. CAB/LEG/3 rev.5. Reprinted in: International Legal Materials 21 (1982), pp. 58 et seq.

American Convention on Human Rights, 22 November 1969, O.A.ST.S. 36 No.36 at 1, O.A.S. Doc. OEA/Ser.L./V/II.50.doc.6 at 27 (1980)

Cairo Declaration on Human Rights in Islam, adopted and issued 5 August 1990

Convention Against Illicit Traffic in Narcotic Drugs and Psychotropic Substances, 20 December 1988

Convention against Torture and Other Cruel, Inhuman or Degrading Treatment or Punishment, 10 December 1984

Convention for the Protection of Minorities, 15 May 1922

Convention on the Prevention and Punishment of the Crime of Genocide, 9 November 1948

Convention on the Rights of the Child, 20 November 1989

Convention Respecting the Laws and Customs of War on Land (Hague Convention IV), 18 October 1907

European Convention on the Compensation of Victims of Violent Crimes, 24 November 1983, ETS No. 116

European Convention for the Protection of Human Rights and Fundamental Freedoms, 4 November 1950, 213 UNTS 222

(Geneva) Convention for the Amelioration of the Condition of the Wounded and Sick in Armed Forces in the Field, 12 August 1949 (Geneva Convention I)

(Geneva) Convention for the Amelioration of the Conditions of the Wounded, Sick and Shipwrecked Members of Armed Forces at Sea, 12 August 1949 (Geneva Convention II)

(Geneva) Convention Relative to the Treatment of Prisoners of War, 12 August 1949 (Geneva Convention III)

(Geneva) Convention Relative to the Protection of Civilian Persons in Time of War, 12 August 1949 (Geneva Convention IV)

International Convention on the Elimination of All Forms of Racial Discrimination, 7 March 1966

International Covenant on Civil and Political Rights, 19 December 1966, 999 UNTS 171

Protocol Additional to the Geneva Conventions of 12 August 1949, and Relating to the Protection of Victims of International Armed Conflicts (Protocol I), 8 June 1977 (Additional Protocol I)

Protocol Additional to the Geneva Conventions of 12 August 1949, and Relating to the Protection of Victims of Non-International Armed Conflicts (Protocol II) of 8 June 1977 (Additional Protocol II)

Protocol to the African Charter on Human and Peoples' Rights on the Establishment of an African Court on Human and Peoples' Rights, 9 June 1998, O.A.U. Doc. OAU/LEG/EXP/AFCHPR/PROT (III)

Treaty of Versailles, 28 June 1919

UN Resolutions

Universal Declaration of Human Rights, G.A. Res. 217 A (III) of 10 December 1948

Declaration of Basic Principles of Justice for Victims of Crime and Abuse of Power, G.A. Res. 40/34 of 29 of November 1985
Principles on the Effective Prevention and Investigation of Extra-legal, Arbitrary and Summary Executions, ECOSOC Res. 1989/65 of 24 May 1989
Declaration for the Protection of All Persons from Enforced Disappearances, G.A. Res. 47/133 of 18 December 1992
Basic Principles on the Use of Restorative Justice Programmes in Criminal Matters, ECOSOC Res. 2002/12 of 12 August 2003
Guidelines on Justice in Matters involving Child Victims and Witnesses of Crime, ECOSOC Res. 2005/20 of 22 July 2005
World Summit Outcome 2005, G.A. Res. 60/1 of 24 October 2005
Basic Principles and Guidelines on the Right to a Remedy and Reparation for Victims of Gross Violations of International Human Rights Law and Serious Violations of International Humanitarian Law, G.A. Res. 60/147 of 16 December 2005

Reports and Other Relevant Materials

Archbishop Desmond Tutu: Statement by His Eminence Archbishop Desmond Tutu on behalf of the Board of Directors of the Trust Fund for Victim, Video Statement at the Ceremony Marking their First Meeting, The Hague, 22 April 2004. Available at http://www.icc-cpi.int/press/video.html, last accessed 22 April 2009
Bericht der Bundesregierung, 31 October 1986, BT-Drucks. 10/687
Council of the European Union: Framework Decision of 15 March 2001 on the Standing of Victims in Criminal Proceedings, Official Journal of the European Communities, 22 March 2001, L.82/1
Determination of Ceilings for Compensation for Mental Pain and Anguish, UN Compensation Commission, 4th session, 22nd Meeting, at 2, UN Doc. S/AC.26 (1992)
International Federation for Human Rights: Victims' Rights Before the ICC, 2007. Available at http://www.fidh.org/article.php3?id_article=4208, last accessed 16 April 2009
International Centre for Comparative Criminology, Research Group Victimology and Restorative Justice, University of Montreal: Reparation and the International Criminal Court – Meeting the Needs of Victims, Report of the Workshop Held January 28th 2006. Available at www.cicc.umontreal.ca/activities_publiques.conferences/joanne_wemmers/ rapport_reparation, last accessed 22 April 2009
International Law Commission: Report of the ILC on the Work of its Forty-sixth Session, 22 July 1994, 49 UN G.A.O.R. Supp. No. 10, UN Doc. A/49/10 (1994)
International Law Commission: Draft Articles on Responsibility of States for Internationally Wrongful Acts, Report on the Work of its Fifty-third Session, Official Records of the General Assembly, Fifty-sixth Session, Supp. No. 10, UN Doc. A/56/10 (2001)
International Law Commission: Draft Articles on the Responsibility of States for Internationally Wrongful Acts – With Commentaries, 2001. Available at http://untreaty.un.org/ilc/texts/instruments/english/commentaries/9_6_2001.pdf, last accessed 16 April 2009
International Commission of Jurists: Iraq – The Trial of Saddam Hussein and the Rights of Victims, October 2005. Available at www.icj.org/IMGpdf/IQTrial_Saddam_R. victims_pdf, last accessed 22 April 2009

ICTR: Letter of the President of the ICTR to the UN Secretary General, Annex to a Letter from the UN Secretary General to the Security Council, UN Doc. S/2000/1198 of 14 December 2000

ICTY: Victims' Compensation and Participation, Report prepared by the ICTY Rules Committee, Appendix to a Letter dated 12 October 2000 from the President of the ICTY addressed to the UN Secretary-General, Annex to UN Doc. S/2001/1063 of 3 November 2000

ICTY: Eighth ICTY Annual Report, UN Doc. A/56/352 of 17 September 2001

Interview with Claudia Perdomo – Head of the Public Information Unit, International Criminal Court, Conducted by C. Olivier. Published in: Victims' Rights Working Group Bulletin No. 5, Febuary 2006. Available at http://www.vrwg.org/Publications/04/ ENG05.pdf, last accessed 14 May 2008, pp. 6 et seq.

Interview with Fiona McKay – Head of the Victims Participation and Reparation Section of the International Criminal Court, Conducted by C. Olivier. Published in: Victims' Rights Working Group Bulletin No. 5, Febuary 2006. Available at http://www.vrwg.org/ Publications/04/ENG05.pdf, last accessed 14 May 2008, p. 4

Peace Agreement for Bosnia and Herzegovina, Concluded in Dayton on 21 November 1995 and Signed in Paris on 14 December 1995, General Framework Agreement. In: International Legal Material 18 (1996), pp. 89 et seq.

Reparation for Injuries Suffered in the Services of the United Nations, Advisory Opinion. In: ICJ Reports (1949), pp. 174 et seq.

The Redress Trust: Enforcement of Awards for Victims of Torture and Other International Crimes, London, May 2006

---: Limited ICC Charges May Trigger Recriminations in Eastern Congo – Press Statement, The Hague, 28 November 2006. Available at http://www.redress.org/news/ Limited%20ICC%20charges%2028-11-2006.pdf, last accessed 29 April 2008

The Redress Trust; FIDH: Legal Remedies for Victims of "International Crimes" – Fostering an EU Approach to Extraterritorial Jurisdiction – Final Report, May 2004. Available at www.redress.org/publications/LegalRemediesFinal.pdf, last accessed 25 April 2007

Richtlinien des Bundesministeriums der Finanzen zur Vergabe von Mitteln für Individuelle Betreuungsmaßnahmen aus dem Härtefonds für Rassisch Verfolgte Nicht Jüdischen Glaubens (HNG-Fonds) sowie zur Vergabe von Mitteln für Globale Betreuungsmaßnahmen aus diesem Fonds, 15 September 1966, Bundesanzeiger of 22 September 1966 No. 178

Richtlinien für die Vergabe von Mitteln an jüdische Verfolgte zur Abgeltung von Härten in Einzelfällen im Rahmen der Wiedergutmachung, 3 October 1980, Bundesanzeiger No. 192 of 14 October 1980; Article 2 Agreement of October 1992

Simone Veil, Statement, Fifth Session of the Assembly of States Parties – Statement, The Hague, 23 November 2006. Available at www.icc-cpi.int/library/vtf/SV_20061123_en.pdf, last accessed 22 April 2009

UN Commission of Crime Prevention and Criminal Justice: Handbook on Justice for Victims on the Use and Application of the United Nations Declaration of Basic Principles of Justice for Victims of Crime and Abuse of Power, 1998, E/CN.15/1998/CRP.4/Add.1

UN Commission of Inquiry on Darfur: UN Report of the International Commission of Inquiry on Darfur, 11 February 2005, UN Doc. S/2005/60

UN Commission on Human Rights: Norms on the Responsibility of Transnational Corporations and Other Business Enterprises with Regard to Human Rights, 13 August 2003, E/CN.4/Sub.2/2003/12/Rev.2

UN Commision on Human Rights, Sub-Commission on Prevention of Discrimination and Protection of Minorities: Study Concerning the Right to Restitution, Compensation and Rehabilitation for Victims of Gross Violations of Human Rights and Fundamental Freedoms, Final Report Submitted by Mr. Theo van Boven, Special Rapporteur, 2 Juli 1993, E/CN.4/Sub.2/1993/8

UN Compensation Commission: Provisional Rules for Claims Procedure, Adopted by the Governing Council on 26 June 1992, UN Doc. S/AC.26/1992/10

UN Economic and Social Council: Revised Final Report Prepared by Mr. Joinet Pursuant to Sub-Commission Decision 1996/119, 2 October 1997, ECOSOC E/CN.4, Sub.2/1997/20/Rev.1

UN Office for Drug Control and Crime Prevention: Guide for Policymakers on the Implementation of the United Nations Declaration of Basic Principles of Justice for Victims of Crime and Abuse of Power. New York, 1999. Available at http://www.uncjin.org/Standards/9857854.pdf, last accessed 16 April 2009

UN Security Council: Report of the Secretary-General on The Rule of Law and Transitional Justice in Conflict and Post-Conflict Societies, 23 August 2004, UN Doc. S/2004/616

UN Security Council: Report of the Secretary-General on the Establishment of a Special Court for Sierra Leone, 4 October 2000, UN Doc. S/2000/915

UN Transitional Administration in East Timor (UNTAET): Regulation No. 2001/10, On the Establishment of a Commission for Reception, Truth and Reconciliation in East Timor, 13 July 2001

UN Transitional Administration in East Timor (UNTAET): Reg. 2000/15, On the Establishment of Panels with Exclusive Jurisdiction over Serious Criminal Offences, 6 June 2000

Victims' Rights Working Group: Comments on the Draft Regulations of the ICC Trust Fund for Victims, February 2005. Available at www.vrwg.org/Publications/ 01VRWG_Feb2005.pdf, last accessed 22 April 2009

D. Materials

I. ICC Statute

Article 75 – Reparations to Victims

1. The Court shall establish principles relating to reparations to, or in respect of, victims, including restitution, compensation and rehabilitation. On this basis, in its decision the Court may, either upon request or on its own motion in exceptional circumstances, determine the scope and extent of any damage, loss and injury to, or in respect of, victims and will state the principles on which it is acting.
2. The Court may make an order directly against a convicted person specifying appropriate reparations to, or in respect of, victims, including restitution, compensation and rehabilitation.

Where appropriate, the Court may order that the award for reparations be made through the Trust Fund provided for in article 79.

3. Before making an order under this article, the Court may invite and shall take account of representations from or on behalf of the convicted person, victims, other interested persons or interested States.
4. In exercising its power under this article, the Court may, after a person is convicted of a crime within the jurisdiction of the Court, determine whether, in order to give effect to an order which it may make under this article, it is necessary to seek measures under article 93, paragraph 1.
5. A State Party shall give effect to a decision under this article as if the provisions of article 109 were applicable to this article.
6. Nothing in this article shall be interpreted as prejudicing the rights of victims under national or international law.

Article 76 – Sentencing

1. In the event of a conviction, the Trial Chamber shall consider the appropriate sentence to be imposed and shall take into account the evidence presented and submissions made during the trial that are relevant to the sentence.
2. Except when article 65 applies and before the completion of the trial, the Trial Chamber may on its own motion and shall, at the request of the Prosecutor or the accused, hold a further hearing or hear any additional evidence or submissions relevant to the sentence, in accordance with the Rules of Procedure and Evidence.
3. Where paragraph 2 applies, any representations under article 75 shall be heard during the further hearing referred to in paragraph 2 and, if necessary, during any additional hearing.
4. The sentence shall be pronounced in public and, wherever possible, in the presence of the accused.

Article 77 – Applicable Penalties

[...]

2. In addition to imprisonment, the Court may order:
   (a) A fine under the criteria provided for in the Rules of Procedure and Evidence;
   (b) A forfeiture of proceeds, property and assets derived directly or indirectly from that crime, without prejudice to the rights of bona fide third parties.

Article 78 – Determination of the Sentence

1. In determining the sentence, the Court shall, in accordance with the Rules of Procedure and Evidence, take into account such factors as the gravity of the crime and the individual circumstances of the convicted person.

[...]

Article 79 – Trust Fund

1. A Trust Fund shall be established by decision of the Assembly of States Parties for the benefit of victims of crimes within the jurisdiction of the Court, and of the families of such victims.
2. The Court may order money and other property collected through fines or forfeiture to be transferred, by order of the Court, to the Trust Fund.
3. The Trust Fund shall be managed according to criteria to be determined by the Assembly of States Parties.

Article 82 – Appeal against other decisions

[...]

4. A legal representative of the victims, the convicted person or a bona fide owner of property affected by an order under Article 75 may appeal against the order for reparations, as provided in the Rules of Procedure and Evidence.

II. ICC Rules of Procedure and Evidence

Rule 85 – Definition of victims

For the purposes of the Statute and the Rules of Procedure and Evidence:

(a) "Victims" means natural persons who have suffered harm as a result of the commission of any crime within the jurisdiction of the Court;

(b) Victims may include organizations or institutions that have sustained direct harm to any of their property which is dedicated to religion, education, art or science or charitable purposes, and to their historic monuments, hospitals and other places and objects for humanitarian purposes.

Rule 94 – Procedure upon request

1. A victim's request for reparations under article 75 shall be made in writing and filed with the Registrar. It shall contain the following particulars:
   (a) The identity and address of the claimant;
   (b) A description of the injury, loss or harm;
   (c) The location and date of the incident and, to the extent possible, the identity of the person or persons the victim believes to be responsible for the injury, loss or harm;
   (d) Where restitution of assets, property or other tangible items is sought, a description of them;
   (e) Claims for compensation;
   (f) Claims for rehabilitation and other forms of remedy;
   (g) To the extent possible, any relevant supporting documentation, including names and addresses of witnesses.
2. At commencement of the trial and subject to any protective measures, the Court shall ask the Registrar to provide notification of the request to the person or persons named in the request or identified in the charges and, to the extent

possible, to any interested persons or any interested States. Those notified shall file with the Registry any representation made under article 75, paragraph 3.

Rule 95 – Procedure on the motion of the Court

1. In cases where the Court intends to proceed on its own motion pursuant to article 75, paragraph 1, it shall ask the Registrar to provide notification of its intention to the person or persons against whom the Court is considering making a determination, and, to the extent possible, to victims, interested persons and interested States. Those notified shall file with the Registry any representation made under article 75, paragraph 3.
2. If, as a result of notification under sub-rule 1:
   (a) A victim makes a request for reparations, that request will be determined as if it had been brought under rule 94;
   (b) A victim requests that the Court does not make an order for reparations, the Court shall not proceed to make an individual order in respect of that victim.

Rule 96 – Publication of reparation proceedings

1. Without prejudice to any other rules on notification of proceedings, the Registrar shall, insofar as practicable, notify the victims or their legal representatives and the person or persons concerned. The Registrar shall also, having regard to any information provided by the Prosecutor, take all the necessary measures to give adequate publicity of the reparation proceedings before the Court, to the extent possible, to other victims, interested persons and interested States.
2. In taking the measures described in sub-rule 1, the Court may seek, in accordance with Part 9, the cooperation of relevant States Parties, and seek the assistance of intergovernmental organizations in order to give publicity, as widely as possible and by all possible means, to the reparation proceedings before the Court.

Rule 97 – Assessment of reparations

1. Taking into account the scope and extent of any damage, loss or injury, the Court may award reparations on an individualized basis or, where it deems it appropriate, on a collective basis or both.
2. At the request of victims or their legal representatives, or at the request of the convicted person, or on its own motion, the Court may appoint appropriate experts to assist it in determining the scope, extent of any damage, loss and injury to, or in respect of victims and to suggest various options concerning the appropriate types and modalities of reparations. The Court shall invite, as appropriate, victims or their legal representatives, the convicted person as well as interested persons and interested States to make observations on the reports of the experts.
3. In all cases, the Court shall respect the rights of victims and the convicted person.

Rule 98 – Trust Fund

1. Individual awards for reparations shall be made directly against a convicted person.
2. The Court may order that an award for reparations against a convicted person be deposited with the Trust Fund where at the time of making the order it is impossible or impracticable to make individual awards directly to each victim. The award for reparations thus deposited in the Trust Fund shall be separated from other resources of the Trust Fund and shall be forwarded to each victim as soon as possible.
3. The Court may order that an award for reparations against a convicted person be made through the Trust Fund where the number of the victims and the scope, forms and modalities of reparations makes a collective award more appropriate.
4. Following consultations with interested States and the Trust Fund, the Court may order that an award for reparations be made through the Trust Fund to an intergovernmental, international or national organization approved by the Trust Fund.
5. Other resources of the Trust Fund may be used for the benefit of victims subject to the provisions of article 79.

Rule 99 – Cooperation and protective measures for the purpose of forfeiture under articles 57, paragraph 3 (e), and 75, paragraph 4

1. The Pre-Trial Chamber, pursuant to article 57, paragraph 3 (e), or the Trial Chamber, pursuant to article 75, paragraph 4, may, on its own motion or on the application of the Prosecutor or at the request of the victims or their legal representatives who have made a request for reparations or who have given a written undertaking to do so, determine whether measures should be requested.
2. Notice is not required unless the Court determines, in the particular circumstances of the case, that notification could not jeopardize the effectiveness of the measures requested. In the latter case, the Registrar shall provide notification of the proceedings to the person against whom a request is made and so far as is possible to any interested persons or interested States.
3. If an order is made without prior notification, the relevant Chamber shall request the Registrar, as soon as is consistent with the effectiveness of the measures requested, to notify those against whom a request is made and, to the extent possible, to any interested persons or any interested States and invite them to make observations as to whether the order should be revoked or otherwise modified.
4. The Court may make orders as to the timing and conduct of any proceedings necessary to determine

Rule 143 – Additional hearings on matters related to sentence of reparations

Pursuant to Article 76, paragraphs 2 and 3, for the purposes of holding a further hearing related to sentence and, if applicable, reparations, the Presiding Judge shall set the date of the further hearing. This hearing can be postponed, in exceptional circumstances, by the Trial Chamber, on its own motion or at the request of the Prosecutor, the defence or legal representatives of the victims participating in the proceedings pursuant to rules 89 to 91 and, in respect of reparations hearings, those victims who have made a request under rule 94.

Rule 148 – Orders to transfer fines or forfeiture to the Trust Fund

Before making an order pursuant to article 79, paragraph 2, a Chamber may request the representative of the Fund to submit written or oral observations to it.

Rule 150 – Appeal

1. Subject to sub-Rule 2, an appeal against a decision of conviction or acquittal under Article 74, a sentence under Article 76 or a reparation order under Article 75 may be filed no later than 30 days from the date on which the party filing the appeal is notified of the decision, the sentence or the reparation order.
2. The Appeals Chamber may extend the time limit set out in sub-Rule 1, for good cause, upon the application of the party seeking to file the appeal.
3. The appeal shall be filed with the Registrar.
4. If an appeal is not filed as set out in sub-Rules 1 to 3, the decision, the sentence or the reparation order of the Trial Chamber shall become final.

Rule 153 – Judgement on appeals against reparation orders

1. The Appeals Chamber may confirm, reverse or amend a reparation order made under Article 75.
2. The judgment of the Appeals Chamber shall be delivered in accordance with Article 83, paragraphs 4 and 5.

Rule 217 – Cooperation and measures of enforcement of fines, forfeiture or reparation orders

For the enforcement of fines, forfeiture or reparation orders, the Presidency shall, as appropriate, seek cooperation and measures for enforcement in accordance with Part 9, as well as transmit copies of relevant orders to any State with which the sentenced person appears to have direct connection by reason of either nationality, domicile or habitual residence or by virtue the location of the sentenced person's assets and property or with which the victim has such a connection. The Presidency shall, as appropriate, inform the State of any third-party claims or of the fact that no claim was presented by a person who received notification of any proceedings conducted pursuant to article 75.

Rule 218 – Orders for forfeiture and reparations

1. In order to enable States to give effect to an order for forfeiture, the order shall specify:
   (a) The identity of the person against whom the order has been issued;
   (b) The proceeds, property and assets that have been ordered by the Court to be forfeited; and

(c) That if the State Party is unable to give effect to the order for forfeiture in relation to the specified proceeds, property or assets, it shall take measures to recover the value of the same.

2. In the request for cooperation and measures for enforcement, the Court shall also provide available information as to the location of the proceeds, property and assets that are covered by the order for forfeiture.
3. In order to enable States to give effect to an order for reparations, the order shall specify:
   (a) the identity of the person against whom the order has been issued;
   (b) In respect of reparations of a financial nature, the identity of the victims to whom individual reparations have been granted, and, where the award for reparations shall be deposited with the Trust Fund, the particulars of the Trust Fund for the deposit of the award; and
   (c) The scope and nature of reparations ordered by the Court, including, where applicable, the property and assets for which restitution has been ordered.
4. Where the Court awards reparations on an individual basis, a copy of the reparation order shall be transmitted to the victim concerned.

Rule 219 – Non-modification of orders for reparation

The Presidency shall, when transmitting copies of orders for reparations to States Parties under rule 217, inform them that, in giving effect to an order for reparations, the national authorities shall not modify the reparations specified by the Court, the scope and extent of any damage, loss or injury determined by the Court or the principles stated in the order, and shall facilitate the enforcement of such order,

Rule 221 – Decision on disposition or allocation of property or assets

The Presidency shall, after having consulted, as appropriate, with the Prosecutor, the sentenced person, the victims or their legal representatives, the national authorities of the State of enforcement or any relevant third party, or representatives of the Trust Fund provided in article 79, decide on all matters related to the disposition or allocation of property or assets realized through enforcement of an order of the Court.

2. In all cases, when the Presidency decides on the disposition or allocation of property or assets belonging to the sentenced person, it shall give priority to the enforcement of measures concerning reparations to victims.

III. Court Regulations

Regulation 88 – Requests for reparations in accordance with Rule 94

1. For the application of rule 94, the Registrar shall develop a standard form for victims to present their requests for reparations and shall make it available to victims, groups of victims, or intergovernmental and non-governmental organizations which may assist in its dissemination, as widely as possible. This standard form shall be approved in accordance with regulation 23, sub-regulation 2, and shall, to the extent possible, be used by victims.

2. The Registrar shall seek all necessary additional information from a victim in order to complete his or her request in accordance with rule 94, sub-rule 1, and shall assist victims in completing such a request. The request shall then be registered and stored electronically in order to be notified by the unit described in regulation 86, sub-regulation 9, in accordance with rule 94, sub-rule 2.

Regulation 117 – Ongoing monitoring of financial situation of the sentenced person

The Presidency shall, if necessary, and with the assistance of the Registrar as appropriate, monitor the financial situation of the sentenced person on an ongoing basis, even following completion of a sentence of imprisonment, in order to enforce fines, forfeiture orders or reparation orders, and may, *inter alia:*

(a) Request relevant information, expert opinions or reports, where necessary by way of a request for cooperation, and, if appropriate, on a periodic basis;
(b) Contact, where appropriate in the manner described in rule 211, paragraph 1 (c), the sentenced person and his or her counsel in order to inquire into the financial situation of the sentenced person;
(c) Ask for observations from the Prosecutor, victims and legal representatives of victims.

IV. Registry Regulations

Regulation 107 – Review of applications

[...]

3. In seeking further information in accordance with regulation 86, sub-regulation 4, or regulation 88, sub-regulation 2, of the Regulations of the Court, the Registry shall consider the interests of the victim and shall take into account, *inter alia,* whether the victim is represented, the security of the victim, and any time limits for the filing of documents with the Court. When contacting victims or their legal representatives to request further information, the Registry shall inform them that their requests may be granted or rejected by the Chamber on the basis, *inter alia,* of information provided by them and that they may submit a new application later in the proceedings if their application is rejected by the Chamber.

[...]

V. Trust Fund Regulations

Chapter II- Implementation of the Activities and Projects of the Trust Fund

[...]

50. For the purposes of these regulations, the Trust Fund shall be considered to be seized when:

(a) (i) the Board of Directors considers it necessary to provide physical or psychological rehabilitation or material support for the benefit of victims and their families;

and

(ii) the Board has formally notified the Court of its conclusion to undertake specific activities under (i) and the relevant Chamber of the Court has responded and has not, within a period of 45 days of receiving such notification, informed the Board in writing that a specific activity or project, pursuant to rule 98, sub-rule 5 of the Rules of Procedure and Evidence, would pre-determine any issue to be determined by the Court, including the determination of jurisdiction pursuant to article 19, admissibility pursuant to articles 17 and 18, or violate the presumption of innocence pursuant to article 66, or be prejudicial to or inconsistent with the rights of the accused and a fair and impartial trial.

(iii) Should there not be a response from the Chamber or should additional time be needed by the Chamber, consultations may be held with the Board to agree on an extension. In the absence of such an agreement, the extension shall be 30 days from the expiry of the period specified in sub-paragraph (a) (ii). After the expiry of the relevant time period, and unless the Chamber has given indication to the contrary based on the criteria in sub-paragraph (a) (ii), the Board may proceed with the specified activities.

(b) When the Court makes an order for reparations against a convicted person and orders that the award be deposited with or made through the Trust Fund in accordance with rule 98, sub-rules 2 to 4 of the Rules of Procedure and Evidence.

Chapter III- Individual Awards to Victims Pursuant to Rule 98 (2)

[...]

Section II – Cases where the Court does not identify the beneficiaries

60. Where the names and/or locations of the victims are not known, or where the number of victims is such that it is impossible or impracticable for the Secretariat to determine these with precision, the Secretariat shall set out all relevant demographic/statistical data about the group of victims, as defined in the order of the Court, and shall list options for determining any missing detail for approval by the Board of Directors.

61. Such options may include:
    (a) the use of demographic data to determine the members of the beneficiary group; and/or:
    (b) Targeted outreach to the beneficiary group to invite potential members of the group who have not already been identified through the reparations process to identify themselves to the Trust Fund, and, where appropriate, these actions may be undertaken in collaboration with interested States, intergovernmental organizations, as well as national and international non-

governmental organizations. The Board of Directors may put in place reasonable deadlines for the receipt of communications, taking into account the situation and location of victims.

(c) The Secretariat may consult victims or their legal representatives and the families of individual victims, as well as interested persons, interested States and any competent expert or expert organization, in developing these options.

[...]

VI. ICC Standard Application Forms

1. Standard Application Form for Individuals

Cour
Pénale
Internationale

International
Criminal
Court

STANDARD APPLICATION FORM FOR REPARATIONS BEFORE THE INTERNATIONAL CRIMINAL COURT FOR INDIVIDUAL VICTIMS AND PERSONS ACTING ON THEIR BEHALF

FORM REPARATIONS-1

Please complete this Application Form if you believe you have suffered harm as a result of a crime under the jurisdiction of the International Criminal Court (ICC) and wish to submit a request for reparations to the ICC, or if you are acting on behalf of such a person.

The purpose of this Application Form is to collect information to help a Chamber of Judges in the ICC decide on matters relating to reparation. Completion of this form will not automatically lead to reparation awards by the ICC.

The information provided in the Application Form will be presented to a Chamber of Judges in the ICC which will consider your request. Please be advised that criminal proceedings take time and it may be some time before the Court makes decisions on reparations.

Please review the accompanying Booklet before completing the Application Form as it will help you fill it in correctly. The Booklet contains explanations regarding:

- What the International Criminal Court is
- The purpose of this Application Form and what will happen to it
- Instructions on how to complete each section of the Application Form. Please note that each Part of this Application Form corresponds to the same Part of the Booklet.

Who should use this Application Form?

A victim who is seeking to submit a request for reparations to the ICC
For the purposes of the ICC, a victim is a person who has suffered harm as a result of the commission of any crime within the jurisdiction of the Court.

☞ Victims that are organizations or institutions should use FORM REPARATIONS-2.

A person acting on behalf of a victim
Where a victim is a child, or has a disability that prevents the victim from acting on her or his own behalf, someone else may make an application on their behalf. Where a victim is deceased, someone else may also make the application. In addition, a person may make the application with the consent of a victim. In any of above circumstances, the person making the application should complete Part B.

A person assisting a victim
Where a victim or a person acting on behalf of a victim is filling in this Application Form, they may be assisted in filling in the Application Form by another person. This would be the case, for example, if either the victim or the person acting on behalf of the victim is unable to read or to write. Where a person assists in filling in this Application Form, she or he should complete Part I.

NOTE

This Application Form and the process of applying are free of charge. The ICC, as a matter of practice, does not charge any fee at any stage of the application process.

2

Instructions:

Please take into account the following instructions when completing this Application Form:

- Please fill in this Application Form to the extent possible.
- Please type or write your answers clearly.
- Please attach answers to the questions on a separate sheet of paper if you need more space.
- You must sign your Application Form, or add your thumbprint or other mark where indicated at the end of Part J.
- Please also put initials of the applicant in the box located at the bottom of each page of this Application Form as well as of any other documents accompanying it. This will help prevent pages of the Application Form from being lost.
- Please provide photocopies of documents requested to the extent possible. If you do not have the documentation requested your application will still be considered. If possible, please staple all the pages of the Application Form and the accompanying documents. Do not send original documents at this time, but please take good care of original documents, which the Court may request at a later stage.

If you seek help in filling in this Application Form, you may contact the ICC or an ICC Field Office which will put you in touch with someone near you to help you fill in this Application Form.

Note regarding disclosure of information:

The information contained in your Application Form may be forwarded to the Defence and other interested persons, including States, at the relevant stage. In addition, part or all of the information may be made available to the general public in the course of proceedings. If you do not wish for part or all of the information in the form to be disclosed or made public for reasons related to your security or well-being, you should tick the relevant boxes in Part H of the Application Form and provide the information requested. The Chamber of Judges will decide on the request, and their decision will be communicated to you.

The Application Form should be sent directly to one of the following addresses:

ICC HEADQUARTERS

International Criminal Court
Victims Participation and Reparations Section (VPRS)
P.O. Box 19519, 2500 CM The Hague
The Netherlands
Fax: + 31 70 515 9100
Email: vprsapplications@icc-cpi.int

ICC FIELD OFFICES

ICC Field Office in Kampala
Victims Participation and Reparations Section (VPRS)
P.O. Box 72735 - Kampala
Telephone: + 256 77 2 706062

ICC Field Office in Kinshasa
Victims Participation and Reparations Section (VPRS)
Telephone: + 243 998011426, + 243 998011403

PART A 3

PERSONAL INFORMATION ABOUT THE VICTIM. *See Part A of the Booklet.*

Have you already submitted an application for participation or reparations to the ICC?

☐ Yes ☐ No

If yes, when?

Day ☐ Month ☐ Year ☐

If you have a registration number, please indicate it:

VPRS- ☐☐/☐☐ - ☐☐/☐☐

1. Surname(s): ______

2. Other name(s): ______

3. Please provide the following information as far as relevant:

   Father's name: ______

   Mother's name: ______

   Name of next of kin or, if you are under 18 years old, guardian: ______

4. Sex: ☐ Female ☐ Male

5. Age or, if not known, approximate age: ☐☐

   or date of birth, or if not known, approximate date of birth:

   Day ☐ Month ☐ Year ☐

6. Place of birth: ______

7. Nationality (ies): ______

8. What is your tribe/ethnic group?

   ______

   ______

9. What is your occupation? 4

- ☐ Agriculture (crops, livestock)
- ☐ Seller (self-employed, trade)
- ☐ State employee
- ☐ Teacher
- ☐ Medical worker
- ☐ Artisan/skilled labor/ casual worker
- ☐ Work for NGO or UN
- ☐ Unemployed
- ☐ Other - Specify:

____

10. What is your marital status?

- ☐ Single
- ☐ Married
- ☐ Divorced
- ☐ Widow/widower
- ☐ Other (such as abandoned spouse, co-habitee)

____

11. How many dependants do you have? *Please write number.*

____

12. If you have a disabilty or disabilities, please specify.

____

____

____

13. Which of the following proof of identity do you have? *Please indicate the number or other reference and attach a photocopy if possible. Please note that one of the following is sufficient. If you have no documentation your application will still be considered.* 5

Type of proof of identity	Number or other reference
☐ Passport	
☐ Driver's licence	
☐ Identity card (such as students, employees)	
☐ Letter from Local Authority	
☐ Camp registration card	
☐ Card from humanitarian agency (such as UNHCR, WFP)	
☐ Tax document	
☐ Voting card	
☐ Other. *Please specify and provide number or other reference:*	
☐ None	

14. Where do you currently live? *Please complete all that apply to you.*

Street: Number/Plot:

Camp/Zone/Sector/Cell:

Village/Parish/Subcounty/Town:

County/District:

P.O. Box: Postal Code:

Country:

If you have been displaced from your home, please indicate your place of origin:

Village/Parish/Subcounty/Town:

County/District:

Country:

6

15. Where would you like to be contacted? *Please tick as appropriate.*

☐ Please use the address mentioned in question 14.

☐ Please contact me through a person acting on my behalf.
If you tick this box, please fill in Part B of this Application Form as appropiate.

☐ Please use the following address. *Please complete all that apply to you:*

C/O: __________

Street: __________ Number/Plot: __________

Camp/Zone/Sector/Cell: __________

Village/Parish/Subcounty/Town: __________

County/District: __________

P.O. Box: __________ Postal Code: __________

Country: __________

☐ Please use the following telephone number (*please give area code*):

____

☐ Please use the following mobile phone number:

____

☐ Please use the following fax number (*please give area code*):

____

☐ Please use the following e-mail address:

____

16. Which languages do you speak?

____

____

17. In which of the following languages are you able to understand written correspondence?

☐ English

☐ French

☐ Other language. *Please specify:* __________

☐ Cannot read

PART B **7**

INFORMATION ABOUT A PERSON ACTING ON BEHALF OF THE VICTIM. *See Part B of the Booklet.*

If this Application Form is being completed by a person acting on behalf of the victim (as outlined on page 1 of the Application Form), that person should provide her or his details below.

1. **Surname(s):** ____________________

2. **Other name(s):** ____________________

3. **Sex:** ☐ Female ☐ Male

4. **Age or, if not known, approximate age:** ____________________

   or date of birth, or if not known, approximate date of birth:

   Day ☐ Month ☐ Year ☐

5. **Which of the following proof of identity do you have?** *Please indicate the number or other reference and attach a photocopy if possible. Please note that one of the following is sufficient. If you have no documentation your application will still be considered.*

Type of proof of identity	Number or other reference
☐ Passport	
☐ Driver's licence	
☐ Identity card (such as students, employees)	
☐ Letter from Local Authority	
☐ Camp registration card	
☐ Card from humanitarian agency (such as UNHCR, WFP)	
☐ Tax document	
☐ Voting card	
☐ Other. *Please specify and provide number or other reference:*	
☐ None	

10. What is your relationship to the victim? ______________________ 9

Do you have proof of the relationship (such as marriage certificate, birth certificate, family registration booklet, will or testament or court document)?

☐ Yes ☐ No

If yes, please provide a photocopy.

PART C

NOT APPLICABLE. *See Part C of the Booklet.*

PART D

INFORMATION ABOUT THE ALLEGED CRIME(S). *See Part D of the Booklet.*

Please attach answers to this section on a separate sheet of paper if necessary.

1. **Please give a detailed description of the alleged crime(s) which form the basis of this application (please explain in detail what happened to you).**

When did the event or events occur? If possible, please specify day(s), month(s) and year(s).

Where did the event or events take place? If necessary you may attach a drawing or a map of the location. 10

2. **Who do you believe is responsible for the event or events and why do you believe this?**
Please answer to the extent possible.

3. **Were there any other victims of the event or events?**

Yes No

If yes (and if you can), please give their names and addresses, unless you know that they wish to remain anonymous, or it would put the applicant or anyone else at risk.

4. **Were there any witnesses?**

Yes No

If yes (and if you can), please give their names and addresses, unless you know that they wish to remain anonymous or it would put the applicant or anyone else at risk.

5. **Do you have any relationship with these witnesses (are they family members, neighbours, friends, etc.)?**

Yes No

If yes, please indicate:

PART E **11**

INFORMATION ABOUT THE INJURY, LOSS OR HARM SUFFERED. *See Part E of the Booklet.*

1. **Please describe the injury, loss or harm you have suffered, and give brief descriptions (such as physical injuries, mental pain and anguish, loss of or damage to property).**

2. **Were you examined by a doctor after the event or events occurred?**

   ☐ Yes ☐ No

3. **Did you receive any medical or psychological treatment?**

   ☐ Yes ☐ No

4. **If yes, do you have (or have access to) any records regarding any medical or phychological treatment?** *If yes, please tick as appropriate and provide a photocopy, if available.*

   ☐ Medical report from doctor, hospital or health center

   ☐ X-rays

   ☐ Prescriptions/Invoices for medicines

   ☐ Other. *Please specify:*

   ☐ None

5. **Does your condition persist today?**

   ☐ Yes ☐ No

   If yes, please give details:

PART F **12**

Reparations. *See Part F of the Booklet.*

1. **Which of the following forms of reparations would you like to claim?** *Please see the accompanying Booklet for descriptions of the terms listed below. You may tick more than one box.*

   ☐ Compensation

   ☐ Restitution

   ☐ Rehabilitation

   ☐ Other form of reparations - Specify:

   ____

   ____

2. **Physical injuries**

   What physical injuries have you suffered as a result of the alleged crime(s) (such as dismemberment, disfigurement, loss or limitation of use of a body organ, member, function or system, including sexual/ reproductive health problems)?

   ____

   ____

   ____

3. **Mental pain and anguish**

   Do you experience any of the following reactions as a result of the alleged crime(s)?
   You may tick more than one box.

Type of harm	Description
☐ Emotional problems (such as anxiety, anguish and guilt, shame, sadness, nightmares, irritability and anger, defeat and apathy, feeling overwhelmed)	
☐ Mental problems (such as intrusive images and thoughts, slowing of thought process, concentration problems, memory dysfunction, confusion)	
☐ Physical reactions and behavioural changes (such as aches and pains, sleep disturbances, excessive sweating, breathing problem, increased heart rate)	
☐ Pain, complaints and/or concerns related to experiences of sexual violence	

4. Loss of or damage to property 13

Have you lost or suffered damage to any of the following as a result of the alleged crime(s)? *You may tick more than one box.*

Type of loss	Description
☐ Home(s)	
☐ Land	
☐ Personal property, including household goods	
☐ Animal(s)	
☐ Other	

5. Other damage

Have you lost any of the following as a result of the alleged crime(s)? *You may tick more than one box.*

Type of loss	Description
☐ Loss of income, unpaid salaries, loss of support and any other losses connected to employment. *Please explain impact of the loss on how you sustain your life.*	
☐ Loss of savings at banks, stocks and other securities	
☐ Social status	
☐ Legal rights	
☐ Other	

6. **If resources are available (from a person convicted by the ICC or from the ICC's Trust Fund for Victims), what would help you and your community the most?** 14

____

____

____

____

____

____

PART G

LEGAL REPRESENTATION. *See Part G of the Booklet.*

A victim may be represented before the ICC by a legal representative. A victim is free to choose her or his legal representative before the ICC, who must be a person with 10 years' relevant experience as a criminal lawyer, judge or prosecutor, and be fluent in one of the Court's working languages (English or French).

1. **Do you have a legal representative?**

   ☐ Yes ☐ No

   If yes, please provide her/his name, and contact details:

   Name: ______________________________

   Address:

   Street: ______________ Number/Plot: ______________

   Camp/Zone/Sector/Cell: ______________________________

   Village/Parish/Subcounty/Town: ______________________________

   County/District: ______________________________

   P.O. Box: ______________________________

   Country: ______________________________

   Telephone number. *Please give area code:* ______________________________

   Mobile phone number: ______________________________

   Fax number. *Please give area code:* ______________________________

   Email address: ______________________________

2. Standard Application Form for Organizations and Institutions (Excerpt)

4

- [ ] Please use the following telephone number (*please give area code*):

- [ ] Please use the following mobile phone number:

- [ ] Please use the following fax number (*please give area code*):

- [ ] Please use the following e-mail address:

4. The property that was harmed is dedicated to *(Please tick one or more boxes as appropriate):*

- [ ] Religion
- [ ] Education
- [ ] Art
- [ ] Science
- [ ] Charitable purposes
- [ ] Historic monument
- [ ] Hospital
- [ ] Humanitarian purposes
- [ ] Other – Specify: ______

5. What was the legal status of the organization/institution on the date that the alleged harm occurred?

Please provide evidence of the incorporation, establishment or registration of the organization or institution, if appropriate, at the date the alleged harm occurred (such as certificate of incorporation or registration), if possible, certified or authenticated copies.

- [ ] Non-governmental organization (organization established to provide voluntary services, including religious, educational, artistic, scientific, social or charitable services to the community or any part of it)
- [ ] Charitable or non-profit organization
- [ ] Statutory body (such as governmental organization, public school, hospital)
- [ ] Education (private) body (such as primary school, secondary school, training college)
- [ ] Company (limited, unlimited or limited by guarantee)
- [ ] Communication body (such as electronic media, the press)
- [ ] Institution for the benefit of members of a community (such as cooporative society, building society or micro-finance institution)
- [ ] Partnership
- [ ] Other – Specify: ______

PART E	**8**

INFORMATION ABOUT THE HARM SUFFERED. *See Part E of the Booklet.*

Please attach answers to this section on a separate sheet of paper if necessary.

1. **What direct harm to the property resulted from the alleged crime(s)?**

____

____

____

____

____

____

____

____

____

____

____

____

____

____

____

____

____

____

____

____

____

PART F

REPARATIONS. *See Part F of the Booklet.*

1. **Which of the following forms of reparations would you like to claim?** *Please see attached the accompanying Booklet for descriptions of the terms listed below. You may tick more than one box.*

☐ Compensation

☐ Restitution

☐ Rehabilitation

☐ Other forms of reparations – *Specify*: _______________________________

2. **Have you lost or suffered damage to any of the following as a result of the alleged crime(s)?** **9**
You may tick more than one box.

Type of loss	Description
☐ Land (such as agricultural land, farming land)	
☐ Buildings (such as schools, hospitals or clinics, offices or homes)	
☐ Movable property (such as education/research materials/ facilities, office equipment/ facilities, medical equipment/ facilities, recreational equipment/facilities)	
☐ Religious properties (such as church/mosque/temple, symbols, books)	
☐ Monuments/community/ cultural property (such as cemeteries, museums, works of art)	
☐ Environmental damage (such as water sources)	
☐ Human Resources (such as teachers, students, leaders, doctors, nurses, patients, social workers)	
☐ Other	

3. **If resources are available (from a person convicted by the ICC or from the ICC's Trust Fund for Victims), what would help the organization/institution and the community the most?**

____

____

____

____

Index

Acquittal 69-70
Adhesion Procedure 14, 41, 72, 140, 182, 189, 196, 207, 210, 254, 263
Alien Tort Claims Act 22, 174, 277, 282
Apology 43, 101, 120, 126, 128, 150-151, **154-155**, 158, 205, 270, 298
Appeal 17, 219, **261-265**, 292
Appeals Chamber 48, 86-87, 248, 250, 257, 262-264, 300
Assembly of States Parties (ASP) 265-266, 272, 287, 289-290, 293
Bosnian Chamber of Human Rights 8, 81, 131, 147,
Child Soldiers 104
Chorzow Factory Case 15, 37, 130-131, 163
Command Responsibility, see *Superior Responsibility*
Commemoration 150, 155-156
Compensation 10, 16, 18, 19, 22, 24, 40, 43, 60, 95, 119, 125, 127, **133-146**, **166-195**, 236, 249, 251, 275, 297
Complementarity 49, 53, 91, 114, **205-207**
Corporations 19, 51, 56-59, 61, 97, 118, 239, 272, 287, 302
Crimes against Humanity 31, 35, 63, 81-83, 90, 122
Damage, see *Harm*
Deterrence 30-31, 40-41, 43, 159, 252
Discretion 45, 48, 64, 67, 76, 98, 114-116, 161-162, 172, 218, 224, 226, 230, 247-248, 256, 258, 266, 268, 273, 296-297, 300
Eligibility to Reparations 61, 68, **75-118**, 226-227, 230, 233, 242, 244
European Court of Human Rights 81-84, 98, 113, 131-133, 136-138, 140-141, 144, 153-154, 160, 168-171, 182, 200, 206, 210, 234-235
Experts, Role of 3, 62, 64, 120, 136, 159, 180-181, 216-218, 222-223, 226, 233, 244-245, 275, 297
Extraordinary Chambers in the Courts of Cambodia 26-27
Fault 95, 126, 143, 145, 181-183
Filártiga Case 40, 72, 98, 160-161, 175, 238
Fine 68, 114, 130, 184, 188, 245-246, 248, 251-261, 265, 268, 272-273, 277-280, 283, 286, 289, 298
Forfeiture 130, 184, 213, 245-246, 248, 251-261, 265, 268, 272, 277, 279-280, 283, 286, 289, 298
Genocide 9, 21, 31, 35, 49, 60, 79, 100, 121-122
Guarantee of Non-Repetition 11, 151, 153
Harm
– Direct/Indirect 79, 84-90, 96, 98, 197
– Environmental 63, 84, 97, 130, 156
– Immaterial (Non-Pecuniary) 80, 84, 135, 167, 172-173, 179, 182-183
– Material (Pecuniary) 80, 82-84, 135, 144, 288
– Psychological (Mental) 82-83, 139
– Valuation and Calculation of 167-181, 227
Inter-American Court of Human Rights 8, 81-83, 88-89, 113, 127-128, 131, 135-136, 138, 140, 143-144, 147, 152-157, 160, 164, 168-171, 182, 201, 224, 234-235, 279
Interim Relief 69, 288
International Community 25-26, 30, 32-34, 36, 40, 46, 51, 59-61, 274, 286, 302
International Criminal Law
– History of Reparations 23-29, 61
– Liability 71, 188
– Protected Interests 32-37, 101, 199
– Purposes 29-45

International Criminal Tribunal for Rwanda (ICTR) 23-25, 31, 59, 86, 98, 191, 248, 250, 255, 257, 260, 281
International Criminal Tribunal for the Former Yugoslavia (ICTY) 23-25, 29, 59, 71, 86, 98, 191-192, 247, 250, 252, 255, 257, 260, 281, 283
Iraqi High Criminal Court 27, 104
Legal Certainty 46, 48, 61, 162, 234, 296, 301
Liability
– Civil 26, 71-74
– Joint and Several 74, 189, 191-192
– Legal Person, see *Corporations*
Lubanga 1, 70-71, 86-87, 94-95, 104, 261-262, 278, 300-301
Lusitania Case 37, 135-136, 143, 166, 169
Marcos Case 73, 175, 238, 277, 282-283
Mass Claims Processing 121, 145, 237-240, 242-244, 298
Non-Governmental Organizations (NGOs) 200-201, 214-216, 271, 300
Nuremberg Tribunal 23, 25, 53, 58, 246, 252, 255
Office of the Prosecutor, see *Prosecutor*
Participation, see *Victims Participation*
Partie Civile, see *Adhesion Procedure*
Penalty, see *Sentencing*
Preparatory Commission for an International Criminal Court 69, 78, 93, 97, 141, 253
Presumption of Innocence 91, 220, 228, 243, 278
Proof
– Burden of 78, 94, 227, 229, 231-238, 242-244, 298
– Legal Presumption 144-145, 234-235, 241-243
– Standard of 50, 142, 227-231, 234, 236, 238-239, 242-244
Prosecutor 4, 25, 41, 46, 55, 57, 62, 70, 75-76, 90-91, 94, 104, 116, 188, 209-210, 219, 233, 237, 244, 250, 257, 277, 285, 291, 296
Protective Measures 52, 149, 212-213, 222, 246, 248, 277-280, 282-283, 288
Punitive Damages 40, 159-161, 175, 182
Rehabilitation 31, 33, 48, 71, 126, 131, **146-149**, 287, 291, 301
Reparation
– Apartheid, see *South Africa*
– Appropriateness, see *Standard*
– Argentina 177-178
– Collective 52, 76, 85, 99, 101, 112, 117, 119-129, 149, 156-157, 163, 199-202, 223, 267, 270, 279, 297
– 9/11 Compensation Fund 177
– Direct and Indirect Awards 185, 192, 230, 244, 267-272,
– Enforcement 19, 41, 57, 64, 184, 186, 246, 248, 253-254, 261, 277-281, 283
– Holocaust, see *Nazi crimes*
– Implementation 46, 55, 64, 119, 180, 192, 222-224, 244, 265-277, 282, 289, 292, 297-298, 301-302
– Individual 36, 41, 99, 101, 103, 111, 117, 119-125, 127-128, 156, 172, 178, 215, 222, 230, 233, 265, 267-272, 275, 279, 297-298, 300
– Nazi crimes 21, 74-75, 100-101, 104-105, 110, 123, 128, 145, 148, 156-157, 165, 176-177, 179, 202, 241-242
– Order, Legal Nature 183, 246
– Principles 45-62, 114-115, 133, 158, 296, 298, 300-302
– Purpose 29-46, 112, 119, 122, 128, 141, 149, 159, 161, 181, 183-184, 205, 228, 270, 276-277
– Right to 4, 17, 19, 26, 86, 115-116, 302
– Rwanda 24-25, 69, 72, 176, 180, 274, 282, 295
– South Africa 147-148, 156, 177
– Standard 162-167, 169, 192
– Status quo ante 37, 131
– Symbolic 101, 126, 158-159, 166, 174, 188, 243-244, 251, 297-298, 301
Reparations Proceedings
– Communications 109, 203, 211-226, 254
– Convicted Person 212, 217, 219, 222, 224, 227-228, 232, 243-244, 247-248, 256, 258, 262, 273, 296, 298
– Initiation 62, 65, 195-211, 213, 218, 232, 244, 298
– Notification 209, 211-215, 221, 224, 264, 298
– Participation, see *Victims Participation*
– Publication 212, 214-216, 224
– States, Role of 205-206, 208, 212-214, 217, 222-223, 246, 257, 259, 261-262, 266, 271-273, 277, 280-282, 301
Restitution 23-24, 48, 54, 126, 129-134, 137, 141, 153, 163-165, 255, 301
Restorative Justice 15, 23, 39, 42, 151, 158, 225
Satisfaction 64, 84, 110, 126, 135, 151-155, 200

Sentencing 29-30, 32, 108, 111, **247-258**, 260-261, 280
Serious Crimes Panels in East Timor 27
Special Court for Sierra Leone 26, 104, 107, 282
Standard Application Form for Reparations 63, 80, 82-83, 97, 99-100, 112, 130, 132, 134-135, 137-138, 141, 146, 150, 197-199, 202-203, 208, 214, 220, 226, 300, **341-356**
States, Role of in the Reparations Proceedings, see *Reparations Proceedings*
State Responsibility 9, 15-22, 40, 51, 53-54, 57, 74, 95, 163, 180, 188, 238, 243, 277, 296, 299
Superior Responsibility 73, 188, 204, 232
Time Limits 19, 99, 107-111, 233, 290
Tokyo International Military Tribunal 23, 53, 252
Trauma 37, 70, 81, 110, 126, 138, 146-147, 179, 216, 225
Trust Fund for Victims
- Assistance 62, 71, 92, 103, **285-295**
- Board of Directors 65, 71, 181, 222, 231, 233, 259, 265-266, 268-269, 271, 286-287, 289
- Complementation of Reparation Awards 265, 271-272, 292
- Funding 258, 265, 286-287, 292
- Regulations 92, 109, 111, 120, 146, 168, 172, 192-193, 197, 222, 230-231, 259-260, 266, 268-272, 276, 286-290, 292
- Relation to the Court 289-291

United Nations 58, 90
United Nation Compensation Commission (UNCC) 9, 64, 74, 104, 137, 139-140, 144-145, 176-177, 238-240
Victims
- Families 36, 71, 85-90, 92-93, 111-114, 116, 247, 257-258, 268, 285-288, 297
- Groups 17-22, 33-36, 38, 43, 79, 84, 87, 89, 99-103, 109, 113, 116-117, 119, 125-129, 147, 150, 156, 162, 172, 175, 180, 193, 199-202, 209, 211, 221, 225, 233, 238, 241, 260, 269, 297
- Legal Persons 56
- Legal Representative/Representation 97, 99, 102, 117, 159, 195, 198, 202, 212, 218, 220-222, 226, 232, 262, 264, 277, 300
- Organizations 89, 96-98, 124-125, 128, 156-157, 197, 244
- Participation 7, 10, 77-79, 89, 91, 115, 207, 214, 220, 225

Victims and Witnesses Unit 71, 232
Victims Participation and Reparation Section 215
War Crimes 34-35, 57, 63, 81, 96, 104, 107, 122
Witnesses 25, 36, 108, 204, 222, 226-227, 231, 286, 288

www.ingramcontent.com/pod-product-compliance
Lightning Source LLC
La Vergne TN
LVHW080846300926
849162LV00003B/348
* 9 7 8 9 0 0 4 1 7 8 1 0 6 *